the s psychology of leisure and recreation

Seppo E. Iso-Ahola
University of Iowa

wcb

Wm. C. Brown Company
Publishers
Dubuque, Iowa

Consulting Editors

Parks and Recreation

David Gray
California State University, Long Beach

Health

Robert Kaplan
The Ohio State University

Physical Education

Aileene Lockhart
Texas Woman's University

contents

Contents   v

preface

This book is a direct outgrowth of two social psychological courses I have been teaching at The University of Iowa since the Fall of 1976. One of these courses is an undergraduate class entitled "Introduction to Social Psychology of Leisure," and the other is a graduate class bearing the title "Advanced Theory and Methods of Social Psychology of Leisure." The content and approach taken in these courses are a result of my strong dissatisfaction with past attempts to explain leisure and recreation behavior by sociological approaches using such variables as occupation, income, and social class. The book is based upon the lectures of both classes and therefore represents a combination of introductory and advanced material.

When starting this project, my goal was to write a book which would be sufficiently simple to be comprehended by students with little or no knowledge of social psychology and research, and sufficiently complex to interest students familiar with the approach and concepts of this area. To the degree that this objective is achieved, the book can serve as a textbook for undergraduate and graduate students taking introductory courses in the psychological and social psychological aspects of leisure and recreation. The book can also be used as a supplement to other textbooks and journal articles for advanced undergraduate and graduate students. While the book was written with students of recreation in mind, I believe that it is also applicable to courses in related fields such as psychology and physical education.

In addition to college and university students, the book is intended for recreation practitioners. While it contains some material irrelevant to the actual delivery of leisure and recreation services, the work presents essential information to practitioners. For example, research reviewed on children's play clearly condemns the present practice of furnishing playgrounds with standard equipment such as swings and slides. Furthermore, based upon theoretical and empirical research, I developed the point that Little League baseball players should be *randomly* divided into teams before the season, and no recruitment should be allowed. Research reviewed in the chapter on leisure needs and motives shows that social interaction is as important as (if not more important than) equipment and physical areas where recreational participation takes place. Yet, attention is typically centered on the physical aspects of recreational activities when delivering leisure services. On the other hand, this is hardly surprising in light of the fact that recreation curricula throughout the country are organized around such courses as parks and recreation facility management. To state it bluntly, it seems to be more important to know where volleyball nets are put after a game than to know how to best facilitate social interaction and feelings of competence during the game! It seems to be more important to first build recreation centers and programs and then worry later about people, rather than vice versa.

To give still another example of relevance of this book to practitioners, consider the finding (discussed in the chapter on therapeutic recreation) that lack of perceived responsibility and control over life has detrimental effects on psychological and physical well-being of the institutionalized aged; it has also been found that these factors increase the mortality rate among the institutionalized elderly. In view of such drastic impact of lack of personal responsibility and control, it is hard for me to see how we can permit our students to work as therapeutic recreation specialists in nursing homes and other settings, without knowledge of these influencing processes. To stretch the point to the extreme, it may be stated that through the provision of leisure services therapeutic recreation specialists are in fact manipulating their patients' perceived responsibility and control and thereby affecting the death rate of patients. In addition to this area, social psychological research was reviewed on such relevant and "applied" topics as drug abuse, vandalism, and littering. In sum, despite its theoretical orientation, the book spells out practical implications. Since practitioners, in most cases, are "social psychologists" who use leisure and recreation services as tools of improving people's quality of life, they should be familiar with a social psychological analysis of leisure and recreation behavior.

Finally, this book is intended to be of heuristic value for researchers. I have not only reviewed past research on each topic as thoroughly as I could but have pointed out weaknesses of previous studies. In doing so I have attempted to be a constructive critic, in that new directions for future research have been identified in many areas. Past research is frequently criticized, not to minimize the work of individual researchers, but to help advance the field. This work presents new ideas, hypotheses and models which should be subjected to rigorous empirical testing. If the book is able to stimulate theoretical and empirical research, it has achieved one of its objectives.

The way in which problems and topics are approached reflects not only my strong belief in social psychology, but also the peculiar blend of my educational training. By relying almost exclusively on past research when explaining given phenomena and by reviewing previous studies as objectively and critically as possible, I stress the importance of empirical research in general. This is a result of my research training in American experimental social psychology. Empirical research, however, should not be an end in itself, but in part a tool of making conceptualizations clearer, more concrete and differentiated. Yet, all too often researchers have become slaves of their work, in that they hesitate to draw conclusions and spell out the implications from their findings. While there is always a need for care in interpreting and generalizing empirical findings, it is also necessary to identify the behavioral and societal implications of the results. As a reader will discover, throughout the text I have not hesitated to state assumptions, conclusions, suggestions and claims. Despite its seemingly objective character, the writing of the book has been influenced by personal ("liberal") values and opinions adopted during my university studies in Finland. This, I believe, is important for a reader to know, especially in light of the fact that many researchers claim their scientific endeavors to be objective and free from subjective value systems. Of course, such assertions are foolish as long as human beings conduct research and write textbooks. Thus, I do not pretend to have written an objective and infallible bible, but a book which hopefully stimulates subjective interpretations of leisure and recreation behavior, and which may help a reader to understand better the social psychological nature of leisure and recreation.

As a final note, it should be made clear that the generic *he* and the masculine pronoun throughout the text are intended to refer to both females and males. *Only* to avoid problems of repetition and inept wording, the *he* form has been used in the text.

Seppo E. Iso-Ahola
Iowa City, Iowa

acknowledgments

While writing the first book on any subject is a great challenge and privilege, it is also a difficult task. This certainly holds true for the present work. When designing the content and topics to be covered and when actually writing, I had no precedent to follow. On the other hand, this was an advantage because of greater creative freedom. I truly enjoyed this liberty when preparing the book, and I wish to acknowledge my deep gratitude for having the opportunity.

Since this study is based upon past research, it is, in part, made possible through the works of countless investigators. Thus, although I am the sole author of the text, the book would not have been possible without other researchers' work, and they should therefore be credited by readers of this work. Although I have developed many new ideas and new ways of looking at old phenomena, it is clear that my thinking has been strongly stimulated by previous research and writing. By stating this I simply want to acknowledge the fact we live in the interdependent world.

Two social environments have contributed to the birth of this book. First, I have been fortunate to be able to work in a helpful, progressive academic setting at The University of Iowa. For their support and encouragement, I want to thank my colleagues and friends, Benjamin Hunnicutt, Richard MacNeil, John Nesbitt and Michael Teague. I am particularly grateful to Pat Hoback who not only typed without errors and at incredible speed various drafts of the manuscript, but also took personal interest in the project, providing encouragement and first-hand criticism. Thanks are expressed also to Nancy Peterson and Donna Simpson for their secretarial help in various phases of the project. My work on this book was sponsored and greatly facilitated by Old Gold Summer Fellowship in 1978 from the University of Iowa. This support is much appreciated.

The second social environment contributing to this book is my family, especially my wife, Leena. We often discussed issues and topics I was writing about; and her ideas and feedback were useful and encouraging. In addition, she took the main burden of family affairs, looking after our sons so that I could spend more time in writing the book. Needless to say, my words are inadequate to thank her for her support.

Last, but not least, I want to thank the reviewers of an earlier draft of the manuscript for their most helpful comments and encouragement. I am deeply indebted to David Gray of California State University, Long Beach, whose detailed comments throughout the manuscript not only improved the quality of the book but provided a continuous inspiration. In addition, Mounir Ragheb, Florida State University, Roger Mannell, Acadia University, and Bo Shelby, Oregon State University, read most of the manuscript and made very helpful, constructive suggestions and comments. Besides improving the quality of the manuscript, their constructive criticism confirmed my belief in the scientific process as a whole. Finally, it has been enjoyable to work with a sincere, helpful and supportive publishing staff of the Wm. C. Brown Company. Many thanks to Louise Barrett-Welp.

Seppo E. Iso-Ahola
Iowa City

Cartoon by Mordillo. Camera Press London, 22901–1X (77). Reprinted from
Suomen Kuvalehti 1979, No. 24 (June), p. 62, by permission of Mordillo.

introduction ^{part} 1

introduction

This book is about human social behavior during a specific time—free-time. The work is based upon the premise that human social behavior has different antecedents and consequences when it takes place during one's free-time as compared to what occurs within working hours. Given these general boundaries, we face the problem of defining free-time. Free from what? By free-time we simply refer to nonwork hours. Depending on subjective perceptions this period may or may not be free from work. Freedom is a relative concept, and therefore is a matter of individual definition. Furthermore, there is no magic about time in relation to human social behavior. Time in itself does not make behavior change. Rather, it is people who perceive, conceive, and think of time in a certain perspective, then alter their behavior accordingly.

Thus, this is a book about human social behavior during nonworking hours. Being loyal to the social psychological approach, we focus on an *individual* whose behavior is influenced on the one hand by other humans and environment, and conversely, an individual who affects other human beings and his environment. The bulk of the book, therefore, is devoted to the examination of the effects of "social factors" on human leisure behavior, that is, the individual (his beliefs, thoughts and behaviors) is analyzed against the background of social factors (cf. Hollander, 1976). A psychologist examines an individual in a vacuum without considering social factors, a sociologist looks at human behavior in larger groups and institutions, and an anthropologist dwells upon the importance of cultures in human behavior, while we, as social psychologists, analyze an individual's behavior as a function of another individual, of several individuals together (group) and of his ethnic background and other cultural factors (culture) (McDavid and Harari, 1968). Since we are interested in the social psychology of *leisure* behavior, we are essentially placing these background variables in a specific setting. We examine the effects of social factors in leisure environments and in so doing, we narrow down or provide specific meaning to the theories of general social psychology.

In very simple terms, general social psychology can be divided into two principal areas: the social psychology of work (Argyle, 1972) and the social psychology of leisure. Although this breakdown may be too simple, it is nevertheless needed at this point in the history of our knowledge. An analysis of human behavior in these two domains is helpful in order to understand how the general concepts of social behavior apply to various leisure and work situations. In a sense, the social psychology of leisure (or work) opens up a new level of analysis in social psychology: an examination of the effects of social factors on human behavior as a function of social settings. When general social psychologists talk about attitudes and behavior, we do not know what the objects of attitudes are and what behavior specifically (leisure, work, both or none) they are referring to. Similarly, when they talk about motivation of human behavior, it is not clear how well their theories explain leisure motives. Thus, the social psychology of leisure seeks to give more specific meaning to the broad theories of general social psychologists.

The social psychology of leisure may be viewed as a replication or extension of general social psychology. This view means that the study of leisure and recreation is used as a tool for advancing the understanding of general social psychology. Another way of looking at the new field is from the standpoint of using general social psychology as a tool of advancing understanding of specific aspects of leisure and recreation behavior. If we are to focus on the former ("replication"), our starting point is general social psychology. But, if our concern is the latter ("application") we begin with the specific features of recreation and leisure and then test the theories of general social psychology in relation to leisure behavior, that is, we put social psychology into leisure and recreation rather than vice versa. If the purpose of this new field is to help us understand people's leisure and recreation behavior in general, we should center on "application" rather than "replication." We need such knowledge for its own sake as well as for helping leisure and recreation practitioners make sound decisions in their important tasks. In sum, since the social psychology of leisure and recreation is an applied field, we should "apply" and exploit general social psychology rather than extend and replicate it. In an effort to achieve this objective, the book pays a special tribute to two important specialties of the entire field of leisure studies: therapeutic and outdoor recreation.

research book

This book does not present a new philosophy and definition of leisure and recreation. It is our contention that speculative books are already plentiful in the field of leisure studies. In fact, most recreation and leisure books are arm-chair speculations presenting the authors' personal views of leisure and recreation behavior. While interesting, such studies do not necessarily enhance our understanding of leisure behavior, since they are based upon one person's (author's) ideas about what leisure and recreation is or *should* be. Consequently, we lack *people's* perceptions of leisure and recreation. If, for example, we want to know what attitudes individuals hold toward leisure, when they are motivated to participate in given leisure activities, and how they experience recreational participation, our analysis should be based upon systematic theorizing and empirical research. Besides being informative about people's actual leisure behavior, such an approach is more realistic than armchair speculations, because it is based upon many individuals' perceptions rather than on one author's speculation. Therefore, this book is research-oriented and draws heavily on past theoretical and empirical studies.

The work does not present a single, simple theory of leisure behavior. Rather, the purpose is first to review theoretical work done in relation to a given topic and then to indicate whether empirical studies have substantiated it. After describing the theoretical and empirical state of affairs relative to a topic, attempts are made to identify new directions for future research. Subsequent chapters will point out some of the areas lacking empirical research as well as possible weaknesses in past research. Since we believe in the usefulness of criticism in general, we will review previous work as critically as possible. Obviously, the intent of the criticism is not to belittle individual researchers, but rather to enhance the field. Consistently, our own research has to be examined in the same way.

In reviewing past research our objective is where possible to integrate various theoretical constructs and different empirical approaches. To reach this overall objective is difficult, however, because little research has been done in some areas. Group dynamics serves as a prime example of this deficiency. It then follows that here and there we have to make big and small leaps to produce coherent chapters. On the other hand, we trust that those assumptions are sufficiently challenging to stimulate rigorous empirical testing of them.

In one sense, our approach can be characterized as that of research. We use past investigation as a tool of explaining human leisure behavior from the social psychological perspective. But more specifically, the approach of this book is an *attributional* one. In pointing out new directions for future research and outlining alternatives to past studies, our suggestions and ideas spring from the attribution theory (Heider, 1958; Jones and Davis, 1965; Kelley, 1967; Jones, Kanouse, Kelley, Nisbett, Valins, and Weiner, 1971; Harvey, Ickes, and Kidd, 1976). Although no rigid attribution theory per se has been presented as yet, there are certain common elements to all attribution research. That is, we are "naive psychologists" whose cognitions (beliefs, thoughts) and behaviors are influenced by our causal analysis of our own and others' performance. We constantly strive to understand *why* something happened. Depending on the causal attributions we make, our cognitions and behaviors will change in the future (Weiner, 1974). For example, when a person plays tennis during his free-time, he has certain reasons for doing so. One day he may play because his boss asked him to play. Another day he may go to the tennis court to be in the fresh air and sunshine. And yet another day he may play tennis to get his daily allotment of physical exercise. Depending on how he perceives the causes of playing tennis, the resultant satisfaction/enjoyment will vary considerably. As an alternative to previous theorizing, we will, where appropriate, use this type of attributional approach throughout the book.

Another way of characterizing this approach is to consider it in part as a *dialectical* analysis of leisure and recreation. The major theme is the changing individual in a changing social environment. Therefore, the social psychology of leisure and recreation has to incorporate developmental and historical aspects of behavior in its approach. People do not simply exist in the time-vacuum, but rather influence and are influenced by others and thus change across the life span. Although this is our way of looking at things, we realize the limitations of the approach at the present time, mainly due to the dearth of dialectical research. Despite the fact that we have to use results of conventional research to support some of our theoretical positions, we will deliberately view past findings in the light of dialectical theorizing wherever possible.

why is this book needed?

Although the above discussion should in part indicate the need for this book, one salient reason justifies this work: the contention that leisure studies is a human service field. Professionals and practitioners continuously emphasize that leisure studies constitute a practical discipline. They are right. However, they often forget that our purpose is to prepare students to deal with other human beings in various leisure and recreation settings. Almost all jobs that the students with either a B.S. or M.S. degree can presently obtain are oriented toward delivering leisure services to other human beings. This is true whether we speak of activity therapists in rehabilitation institutions, outdoor recreation specialists in camping settings, or administrators in park districts and private agencies. Because of this, it is not surprising that employers in this field are looking for graduates who are capable of effectively interacting and communicating with other human beings. This social interaction is a skill which practitioners of leisure delivery systems have to acquire in order to be successful leaders, supervisors and administrators. Every time when we talk about "dealing, communicating or interacting with" other human beings we hit right at the core of the social psychology of leisure behavior.

Since even practitioners stress the importance of social psychology (although they do not use the words) in delivering leisure services, there is a definite need for all recreation departments to offer psychology or social psychology-related courses centering on leisure behavior. This demand becomes even more evident when we look at it from the perspective of subfields of leisure studies such as therapeutic recreation. Activity or recreation therapists strive to improve the quality of life for their patients—whether mentally or physically disabled, emotionally distressed, or otherwise "abnormal." We contend that unless these specialists are familiar with the principles underlying human social behavior, they are ill prepared to deliver their leisure services. Regardless of the level of physical disability, if one's mind is geared to function in an effective fashion, a person can live "normally" and enjoy life. This prerequisite calls for the recreation therapist to move toward solving the client's psychological problems and improving his state of mind through wholesome recreation experiences.

Without underestimating the problems associated with physical disabilities, we contend that such disabilities are technical (functional) matters. The most important factor is a patient's mind and his view of himself in relation to the disability. Thus, activity therapists should be trained to work with both normal and abnormal minds. At the same time, they have to know how to deal technically with the disabled persons. However, the main emphasis should be placed on comprehending the cognitive processes of both normal and disabled persons; and the social psychological analysis of therapeutic recreation should be a central part of this endeavor. Because the task of activity therapists is to exert influence over another person, the patient, they have to know how people—normal and abnormal—view themselves, what the consequences of this self-perception are, how their leisure attitudes are formed and changed, what leisure needs and motives they have, etc.

Unless both general and theoretical knowledge regarding these and other social psychological issues are provided by the universities, therapeutic recreation can hardly be called the most advanced subfield of leisure studies. Many recreation departments currently direct their students to take relevant courses in psychology departments. Our view, however, is that such courses alone are not particularly helpful. First of all, general psychologists and social psychologists do not have the background to understand problems and issues germane to leisure and recreation. Moreover, they are not even interested in leisure and recreation.[1] (Of course, there are always exceptions, but we are referring to the majority of social psychologists.) Therefore, the knowledge that recreation students are acquiring from the general social psychologists is almost void of application to leisure and recreation behavior unless the student can interpret it in terms of the recreation field. As we mentioned earlier and as will be explicitly pointed out later, there is an appreciable difference between general social psychology and the social psychology of leisure behavior.

To summarize, leisure studies are a human service field in which social interaction is the main ingredient. Therefore, the field is implicitly and inherently based upon the social psychological principles of human behavior. Not only must some sub-areas of leisure be interpreted in the light of social psychology, but the whole field has to be subjected to the social psychological analysis. In an effort to contribute to that approach, I undertook the writing of this book.

Any book dealing with free-time, leisure and recreation has to face the challenge of defining leisure. There is no paucity of definitions; indeed the problem stems from too many of them. Despite this fact, leisure can be defined in a simple but yet comprehensive way: either objectively or subjectively (Neulinger, 1974). Objectively, leisure may be defined as time left over after work. The subjective definition denotes a subjective state of mind, or, as it has been stated elsewhere (Iso-Ahola, 1976a): "leisure is a person's own perception and inference of quan-

on the definition of leisure and recreation

---

[1]It should go without saying that this is not to accuse general social psychologists of neglect. Rather, the purpose is to provide another reason why there is a need for the social psychology of leisure and recreation.

tity and quality of activities. Therefore, leisure becomes subjective perception of an actual or imagined activity a person participates in at a given time.''

While we acknowledge Neulinger's distinction, we disagree with his contention that leisure is only a subjective state of mind. In our view, it is misleading and self-defeating not to accept the difference between work and nonwork. The fact that some persons' work and free-time have common elements (e.g., both are intrinsically motivated) does not mean that individuals do not make a distinction in their minds between the job and free-time. Even the *workaholics,* who spend much of their free-time on the job because of the resultant satisfaction, admit the difference between work and free-time. Their motto is: ''My work is my leisure.'' By adhering to this principle they are in essence saying that leisure follows work, but they have chosen to extend their work-hours to ''free-time.'' They do not have to put in ''extra'' hours, but *they* have chosen to do so. At the same time, they know that the great majority of people work ''only'' eight hours a day. Such a national standard regarding the length of work-time sets the stage for social comparison and therefore reminds the *workaholics* that they have extended their work beyond the necessary and required level. As long as these standards of time exist it is impossible for any workers not to acknowledge the difference between work and free-time, regardless of the number of hours they put in every day working. Moreover, there are few, if any, jobs which *require* more than 40 hours of work-time per week. Thus, to be fortunate enough to have a satisfying and rewarding job should by no means invalidate the distinction between work and nonwork.

If a person sees his work and leisure time equally satisfying, there is no reason to assume that the two things have become one and the same. The person cannot earn his living by leisure and he knows that. Leisure and work cannot be substituted for each other. Thus, both objectivity and subjectivity have to be taken into account in any definition of leisure. Without free-time a person cannot have leisure. While it is a necessary condition for leisure, free-time is seldom equated with leisure. These considerations lead to the suggestion that the simplest difference between the two concepts is one in which ''free-time'' is employed to refer to the *quantitative* aspects of time left over after work and ''leisure'' to the *qualitative* aspects of ''free-time'' and activities performed during it (Iso-Ahola, 1977a). Although this distinction comes close to that of Neulinger (1974), there is an important difference between the two. According to Neulinger, leisure can occur in one's work if certain criteria are met. In our view, this cannot occur because free-time is a prerequisite for leisure. We, therefore, contend that a social psychological analysis of leisure has to focus on human behavior during one's nonwork hours.

The above reasoning does not simply represent our theoretical speculation. Recent empirical research lends support to the previous discussion. The first evidence comes from Neulinger (1974) himself. He reported that an overwhelming majority of people (95%) view leisure objectively. This clearly suggests that people make a distinction between work and free-time and that leisure is associated with nonwork hours only. Second, two studies (Iso-Ahola, 1977a; 1978) were recently conducted to demonstrate that subjects' definitions and perceptions of leisure vary considerably as functions of several factors, most notably as a function of perceived freedom and intrinsic-extrinsic motivation. Thus, the quality of leisure experiences during non-working hours can be ameliorated by enhancing a person's perceived freedom and the intrinsic motivation in his leisure activities. Thus, leisure is a "subjective state of mind" experienced to a certain degree while an individual is engaged in activities during free-time or non-working hours. People judge leisure experiences at their best when free-time activities are freely chosen and are intrinsically motivated.

How about the definition of recreation? Gray (1972) has suggested that recreation is not a leisure activity but rather the result of participation in an activity; it is "an emotional condition within an individual human being that flows from a feeling of well-being and self-satisfaction." Unquestionably, this definition assumes a very positive attitude toward recreation, accepting only those leisure experiences as recreational that are highly satisfying. In a way, it expresses the goal of our entire profession. Although we wholeheartedly agree with Gray's view in this sense, we contend that from the psychological standpoint his definition is quite limited. If we were to study recreation and leisure within the confines of this definition, we would probably, though not necessarily, exclude a host of leisure experiences from our scrutiny. In itself and without Gray's definition, "recreation" as a term is psychologically one-sided because it connotes relaxation, re-creation. Yet relaxation is but one aspect of recreation. For these reasons, we simply refer to recreation as a form of individual leisure experience. Whether or not a given leisure experience is recreation, therefore, becomes an empirical question.

The book is divided into eight major parts. Following the introduction, the second part defines the field of social psychology of leisure and recreation. A basic definition, content area and approach to this field are developed. This analysis borrows extensively from general social psychology. Particular attention is paid to similarities and differences between the two fields. Since the book represents the first attempt to delineate the social psychology of leisure and recreation, it is important to show the historical steps that have led to recent advancement of the field. The history of the social psychology of leisure is shown as originating in the early times of humankind in general, and in the early theories of play in particular.

organization of the book

The third part describes the nature of social psychological research. This section examines typical methods of data collection and conventional strategies of data analysis in social psychological research. Despite its wide array of research methods, social psychological research is strongly experiment- and laboratory-oriented. The studies available on social psychology of leisure behavior, however, do not reveal a trend toward the preponderance of one method or technique over another. Studies vary from laboratory experiments to field studies and surveys. This is viewed as a promising sign for the emerging field.

The following part focuses on leisure behavior as a developmental process. This section starts with a discussion of children's unorganized play, first examining how the need for the optimal arousal directs play behavior; it then proceeds to demonstrate the detrimental effects of extrinsic rewards and sanctions on free play and intrinsic motivation, thereby showing how adults often turn children's recreation into children's work. Next, cognitive benefits of play are described. The second chapter of the fourth part examines the importance of children's social play and organized games. In this context, particular emphasis is placed upon a social psychological analysis of Little League baseball, which is one of the most institutionalized forms of children's leisure.

The following two chapters continue the analysis of leisure behavior as a developmental process, emphasizing leisure socialization as a lifetime process. The link between childhood recreation and adult leisure behavior is analyzed in light of recent empirical research. While this relationship has been shown to exist to a reliable extent, most of the total variance remains unaccounted for, suggesting that adults acquire new leisure skills and replace old leisure activities by new ones. This section also discusses the influence of socialization agents (parents, peers and school teachers) on the formation and change of the young's leisure patterns and leisure life style, analyzing the most notable failures (drug abuse and vandalism) of socialization. The unit concludes with an examination of the role of leisure and recreation in the daily life of the aging individual.

The purpose of the fifth part is to set forth some basic social psychological factors in leisure behavior. The unit begins with a discussion of the social psychological determinants of perceptions of leisure. Based upon recent empirical research, the first chapter shows that perceived freedom and intrinsic motivation are the principal ingredients in perception of leisure. It then proceeds to explain how perceived recreational freedom can be enhanced. The part continues with a discussion of the relationship between personality and leisure behavior. It is shown that personality traits such as self-esteem, need for achievement, and locus of control are insufficient to explain leisure behavior. What is needed is the interaction approach, which views leisure behavior as a multiplicative function of personality and environment. In addition, the relationship between personality and leisure is examined from the standpoint of "phenomenal causality," focusing on attributions of leisure behavior to personality. The degree of participation in a given leisure activity depends on the extent to which people make dispositional or situational attributions for their performance in that activity. How interpersonal perceptions and relations are affected by observers' causal analysis of actors' leisure choices and leisure participation is also discussed. In the following chapter, leisure needs and motives are discussed in terms of relevant theories such as Maslow's concept of need hierarchy. Previous empirical research, however, is taken to demonstrate the lack of validity of earlier need theories. The concept of intrinsic motivation is used to account for leisure behavior. Furthermore, recent studies have consistently revealed that, to a major extent, leisure needs and motives are socially determined. The final chapter in the fifth section should provide students with an understanding of how leisure attitudes are formed and how they are changed. Particular attention is devoted to the relationship between leisure attitudes and actual leisure behavior.

The sixth section highlights one of the unique features of the social psychology of leisure and recreation. This part of the book examines the social psychological antecedents and consequences of outdoor recreation. The section begins with a survey of how people perceive and experience outdoor recreation environments. Such perceptions and experiences, in turn, affect people's cognitions, participation in and enjoyment of outdoor recreation. The unit also discusses the social psychological reasons why certain types of outdoor recreation environments attract leisure participants. An integral portion of this analysis is the influence of crowding and the need for privacy as these affect outdoor recreation participation. Solitude, emotional and aesthetic experiences rank as the foremost factors or needs motivating participation among wilderness hikers. Outdoor recreation serves as a means of coping with crowding and environmental stress, and therefore contributes in an important way to people's psychological well-being. These influences are examined in detail in the last chapter of the sixth section.

The seventh part introduces students to another major subfield of leisure studies, namely therapeutic recreation. After considering the content and approaches to therapeutic recreation, the chapter points out a need for social psychological analysis in this field. It then focuses on labeling processes, illustrating some of the implications of the fact that the disabled are frequently labeled as insane in sane places rather than vice versa (Rosenhan, 1973a). The thrust of the section, however, is in a new theoretical framework put forth for therapeutic recreation. This attributional paradigm centers on persons' self-perceptions and causal analyses of leisure skills and performance. Internal and external causal attributions critically affect tendencies to approach and to avoid leisure activities. By knowing what kinds of causal attributions exist, and to what extent these determine the disabled persons' leisure performance, and why, therapeutic recreation specialists should be able to prevent their clients from forming self-destructive causal ascriptions in the future. The task of such therapists is not simply to deliver leisure services, but especially, to prevent their clients from sinking into the state of helplessness because of their disabilities. The section concludes with a discussion of the importance of perceived control for the institutionalized aged. Recent empirical research has dramatically demonstrated that the death rate is much higher among the elderly whose perception of control has been diminished in the institutionalized environment, than it is among those who perceive themselves as having control over their daily lives. Thus, it is not the recreation services per se that are important, but rather the extent to which they can increase the perception of control over the environment. Whether recreation becomes therapeutic depends on feelings and inferences of control brought about by recreation participation.

The concluding part of the book is devoted to a social psychological analysis of the interrelationship between work, leisure, and the quality of life. Surveying the effects of work on leisure and vice versa, this discussion criticizes past attempts to explain the work-leisure relationship by such simple hypotheses as ''compensation'' and ''spill-over.'' Instead, it provides alternative ways of viewing the relationship. The second half of the concluding part first examines the pursuit of happiness. This examination reveals that leisure satisfaction plays an important role in the individual's perceived quality of life. It appears, however, that interpersonal behaviors, which often take place in free-time, are the key to the pursuit and achievement of happiness, as exemplified by the importance of ''family life'' to the married (Haavio-Mannila, 1971) and of ''friends and social life'' to the single (Shaver and Freedman, 1976).

In short, the book demonstrates that it is not simply enough to plan, organize and deliver leisure services. Services in themselves are meaningless. It is the people, service recipients, who attach certain values and purposes to leisure activities. Since their ultimate objective is to improve people's quality of life through leisure services, practitioners must be aware of the reasons for people's engaging in certain leisure activities, what people are likely to derive from participation in these activities, and why. Answers to these and other pertinent questions provide practitioners with basic knowledge about human leisure behavior. It is reasonable to assume that this knowledge can provide the basis for improving the quality of life in a wide variety of communities throughout the country.

defining the field of social psychology of leisure and recreation

what is the social psychology of leisure and recreation? 1

Social psychology represents a systematic analysis of human social behavior. Its mission is to help people recognize causes and effects of social behavior so that they can better understand themselves and others and improve the quality of interpersonal behavior. There are many formal definitions of social psychology in the literature. In spite of variations, all of them seem to center around two distinctive characteristics: (1) an *individual* as a participant in social relationships, and (2) an emphasis on understanding the social influence processes underlying these relationships (Hollander, 1976).

general social psychology

Like Allport (1969), many social psychologists regard their discipline as "an attempt to understand how the thought, feeling, and behavior of individuals are influenced by the actual, imagined, or implied presence of other human beings." Social psychology then becomes "the scientific study of the experience and behavior of individuals in relation to other individuals, groups, and culture" (McDavid and Harari, 1968). It is important to note that social psychologists examine interrelationships: the effects of social environment on an individual and the effects of an individual on the social environment. Social influence, which is the key concept in social psychological analysis, is said to occur whenever one individual responds to the actual, imagined or implied presence of one or more others. In its simplest form, this can be seen in person-to-person relationships. It can also be observed in group-to-person (e.g., conformity), person-to-group (e.g., leadership) and group-to-group relationships (e.g., competition and cooperation).

What have social psychologists investigated? Allport (1969) noted that the distinct characteristic of American social psychological research stems from its overwhelming emphasis on attitudes, that is, how attitudes are formed, changed and related to actual behavior. Even if attitudes have received more attention, other phenomena and areas have been studied as well. On the individual level, for example, social psychologists have focused on interpersonal perception, self-perception, impression formation, liking and friendship, social reinforcement, and psychological reactance. At the group level, they have scrutinized such phenomena as group structure, cohesiveness and composition, communication patterns, leadership, risk taking, competition and cooperation. It is only very recently that social psychologists have become interested in environmental effects on social behavior. In this context, attitudinal and behavioral responses to temperature, noise, pollution, urban stress, population density and crowding have been subjected to both theoretical and empirical testing.

From this brief overview we see that the subject matter of social psychology is quite extensive by our present standards, and it appears that this scope is becoming broader. New areas and topics come under review continually. The recent upsurge of environmental social psychology serves as a useful example of the rapidly expanding scope of social psychological inquiry; and of course, this book is also part of the attempt to widen the spectrum of the field. But regardless of their specific interest areas, all social psychologists start from the same place: an individual as a participant in a social environment. This is exactly the point that distinguishes social psychology from other branches of behavioral science.

While anthropologists also attempt to explain human behavior, they are chiefly concerned with culture and cultural differences. Many anthropologists have spent much time studying primitive cultures and tribes, thereby attempting to acquire a body of knowledge which explains the nature of the individual from a cultural perspective. The basic unit of a sociologist's analysis is the social system. Such groups and institutions as family, school, industrial organizations, and the mass media are examples of the levels of sociological analysis. The psychologist's basic unit is the individual who is considered apart from social relationships and social environment. Some physiological psychologists, for example, seek to explain behavior in terms of human anatomy and in doing so, believe that the explanation of human cognition and behavior (e.g., emotions and motives) can ultimately be traced to brain cells. As another example, personality psychologists begin by explicating the importance and sufficiency of inherited traits as causes of behavior, without recognizing the influence of the social environment on human cognitions and behaviors. In attempting to provide explanations for human behavior, social psychologists acknowledge such determinants of behavior as personality traits, but they stress that these factors become meaningful only when they are investigated in their social (interpersonal and cultural) and historical context. In brief, social psychology may be defined as the "psychology of the individual in society" (Hollander, 1976).

basic assumptions   As in any other field, social psychology is based upon a set of assumptions. Its most fundamental premise is that cognitions (i.e., what goes on in a person's head) are critical determinants of a person's relationship to fellow human beings. Following the gestalt-field theory, the concept of mind is accepted and interpreted as a totality (Lana, 1969). This S-O-R approach[1] is in sharp contrast to

[1]In this conceptualization, S stands for stimulus, R for response, and O for organism (i.e., cognitions) variables.

the behavioristic S-R paradigm, which examines behavior only in terms of stimuli (S) and responses (R) and assumes that human beings are robots "whose behavior is determined by reinforcement histories and contingencies in the present environment" (Deci, 1975b). The S-O-R model, often called cognitive social psychology, assumes that several cognitive mechanisms (e.g., processes of person perception, causal attribution and decision making) mediate all human responses to a varying degree. Thus cognitions, emotions and motives play a central role in energizing and directing behavior. Because social behavior is highly complex and multifaceted and because cognitive mechanisms underlie all (simple and complex) responses, we contend that the S-R model has no place in social psychology.

In contrast to this, someone might argue that certain behaviors frequently tend to reduce to very simple schema, thereby suggesting that the S-R paradigm may adequately account for these behaviors. For example, every Tuesday when it is 6:15 p.m., Bob leaves for the local recreation center to play basketball. A behaviorist would say that the time (6:15 p.m.) serves as a stimulus which elicits Bob's response. He would argue that Bob's conditioned response (playing basketball) to the time is highly predictable. Social psychologists, on the other hand, present their basic assumption that before every Tuesday night Bob goes through cognitive processes, which determine whether or not he will go and play. Each Tuesday provides a new situation, and every time he has to decide separately about going to the recreation center. Many variables may interfere with his schedule, and he then has to take these variables into account in his weekly decisions. Depending on the importance of the intervening factors, Bob may continuously have to reconsider and revise the priority of basketball in his repertoire of leisure activities. The point is: even though some regularity may be observed in Bob's leisure patterns as a function of some arbitrarily selected stimuli (e.g., time), such simple S-R connections do not advance our understanding of his leisure behavior and motives behind it. Only when studying the role of central cognitive mechanisms in leisure choices, decisions, and behaviors can we begin to comprehend social behavior in leisure contexts.

Social psychology owes much to various theoretical systems. Stimulus-response and reinforcement theories, psychoanalytic theory, and role theory have all contributed significantly to the development of social psychology (see Deutch and Krauss, 1965; Shaw and Costanzo, 1970). But by far the greatest impact on modern social psychology stems from the gestalt (cognitive) and field theories. Although these two theroretical frameworks differ from one another in some instances, their approach to analyzing social behavior is basically the same: human behavior is viewed as integrated and goal oriented because the brain, through its central cognitive processes, organizes our thoughts, beliefs, perceptions and sensations (Wrightsman, 1972). In his field theory, Lewin (1951) postulates that human behavior is an interactive function of the person and the environment. Thus, all psychological events can be explained in terms of the properties of the "field" or "life space" composed of the person and environment viewed as interdependent factors. This paradigm, therefore, assumes that any behavioral or cognitive response in any given situation is a result of the characteristics (abilities, motives, feelings, etc.) of the person and features of the environment (the presence of others, group composition, noise, etc.). Obviously, this two-factor account is not intended to be a theory of social behavior as such but rather an underlying paradigm from which more detailed explanations are derived. Whether or not this paradigm is accepted is critical, because it affects the theoretical scope of social psychological inquiry. Many social psychologists accept one component of this basic approach but reject another. For example, social learning theorists (e.g., Bandura, 1969; Mischel, 1968) insist on the importance of the environmental aspect while personality psychologists (e.g., Cattell, 1950) emphasize the person component in this respect. The present book, however, is built upon the fundamental assumption that both personal and situational factors are jointly responsible for human social behavior in changing leisure contexts.

a definition and approach of social psychology of leisure and recreation

There are probably many ways of defining the social psychology of leisure and recreation. But regardless of semantics, any definition of the social psychology of leisure will probably include two key elements: an individual component and social influence component. Given these essential characteristics of social psychological inquiry, variations in the definitions are unimportant. Thus, social psychology of leisure may be regarded *as that branch of scientific leisure studies which examines how the feelings, cognitions (thoughts or beliefs) and behaviors of one individual are influenced by the feelings, cognitions and behaviors of others during a period of time subjectively designated as unobligated, free, or leisure.* The social psychology of leisure then becomes the scientific study of experiences and behaviors of individuals within the social leisure context. Its focus is on the individual in dynamic interactions with other individuals, groups or culture during his subjectively experienced leisure. These interactions should not be regarded as static, but rather as dynamic and changing relationships, in which the individual is at once the cause and consequence of the social environment and society.

Implicit in the above definition is one critical idea: a changing and developing individual. Since a person influences and is influenced by others, he and his environment are continually changing. Hence, for the social psychology of leisure to be scientific, it must rely on the utilization of the scientific method, employing an historical and developmental approach. Social behavior does not exist in a time vacuum and hence cannot be adequately analyzed without considering its past, without its historical context (Gergen, 1973). Our main theme—the changing individual in a changing world—however, does not represent the mainstream of thought among social psychologists. Traditionally, the developmental and historical contexts of social phenomena are practically ignored, on the metatheoretical ground that the laws of social behavior are transhistorical and universal (Schlenker, 1974). This basic approach is reflected in the same psychologists' vehement research interest into stable traits and abilities (Riegel, 1976), with the vain hopes of discovering the all-explaining static characteristics of human behavior.

We object to such a doctrine and submit that the examination of social behavior should be approached from the *dialectical* standpoint, i.e., the premise that human beings are continuously changing—be it slowly or rapidly. This is not to deny the stability of behavior. For example, it has been shown that both infants and adults intentionally seek novelty, complexity, and incongruity (i.e., change), but only to the extent that their mental and physical environment is stable, structured and secure (McCall, 1974). This does not mean, however, that stability is more important than change. When the child continuously seeks and conquers the incongruity or interplays between the new and the old environment, such dynamic interaction changes his concept of "stability," thereby continuously altering stable traits. This may be called a paradox of change and stability in human development. Individuals experience contradictions and conflicts within themselves as well as in their relations to other individuals, groups and societies (Rappoport, 1977). Such contradictory conditions constitute the basis for change and development. Just as individual development seems to be stabilizing, new questions and doubts arise in a person, resulting in never-ending change and development (Riegel, 1976). It is because of this that the social psychology of leisure and recreation cannot ignore the historical context of social behavior. Unfortunately, past research has omitted this point of view, thereby restricting attempts to give dialectical explanations of social behavior in leisure environments. This we regard as a major defect of this book.

Although the above definition is rather general, it nevertheless sets the stage for research in the field. Some studies may be easily classified as social psychological studies of leisure, others not so readily. Instead of imposing strict categories and labels, one should realize that the boundaries of social psychology of leisure remain flexible. We should not forget that our purpose is to provide the best possible explanation of human social behavior within the confines of our present knowledge. If this task calls for stepping over discipline lines, such action should be accepted. For example, when we examine the effects of the properties of the physical environment on human social behavior, strictly speaking, such studies could not be labeled as social psychological because "others" are not the influence source. However, since the definition of social psychology includes "culture" as a social factor and since culture is broadly defined as a product of other human beings, (McDavid and Harari, 1968) it is then evident that the physical environment, or at least some parts of it, is the product of "others." Pollution certainly qualifies as an example of such products. Thus, the examination of the physical environment in relation to human social behavior can be categorized as a social psychological inquiry.[2] It is also conceivable that many "main effects" of the physical environment are superseded by their interactive effects with "others." For example, while it may be true that some environments attract more persons experiencing outdoor recreation than do others, a person's decision to participate in outdoor recreation in certain environments may depend on crowdedness and other social psychological variables. In sum, the definition

[2]The interrelationship between the physical environment and social behavior was perhaps best expressed by Winston Churchill: "We shape our buildings, and afterwards our buildings shape us."

of the social psychology of leisure behavior should be viewed as a general framework and starting point for research rather than as an arbitrary rule constraining investigations.

At first glance, the above definition seems to differ very little from that of general social psychology. The principal distinguishing feature stems from the period of time, leisure, to which the occurrence of social influence is limited. This qualifying aspect in the definition, as insignificant as it may seem, is very important for several reasons. First, it opens up the social psychological inquiry of leisure and recreation and simultaneously outlines the boundaries of this investigation. One might argue that this new subfield is already included in the general and vague definition of general social psychology. True, but if it remains there it will never be subjected to systematic research, and our knowledge of social psychological aspects of leisure behavior will be fragmentary. Piecemeal research does not advance our understanding of leisure and recreation-related problems. If the social psychology of leisure remains as an implied and hidden subfield of general social psychology, we can expect to collect pieces of information twenty years from today, handed to us by general social psychologists as accidental by-products of other research interests. Since most social psychologists are general social psychologists who believe in transhistorical laws of human behavior (Schlenker, 1974), it apparently makes little, if any, difference to them where social influence phenomena take place. Thus, they do not care about tasks, situations or time periods in which these phenomena occur, because the social psychological phenomena are believed to be generalizable across time and space. Since the majority of social psychologists share this basic paradigm, we are very pessimistic about their becoming interested in leisure and recreation-related problems.[3]

There is, however, an optimistic side to the story. Gergen (1973) has convincingly argued that social psychology is an historical inquiry. Accordingly, the time and space limitations of human behavior are acknowledged. As we pointed out, this view does not completely reject the possibility that some aspects of human social behavior are universal and enduring. What it states is that time and space limitations of the laws regarding behavior should be considered and identified. It is clear that Gergen's thesis places a heavy emphasis on applied social psychology and thus indirectly calls for the establishment of the social psychological inquiry of leisure and recreation. Attitudes, for example, have certain objects to which they are directed. From our point of view, these objects are leisure activities. Thus, how a person forms and changes his leisure attitudes is not necessarily related to his attitude formation and change in relation to, say, political parties. To understand the role of attitudes in leisure behavior, we have to study them in their own context.

Besides these philosophical reasons for defining the social psychology of leisure, many of our leisure- and recreation-related social problems cannot be

[3]This, of course, is not to accuse general social psychologists of a failure to investigate leisure and recreation behavior, but merely to suggest the consequences of not aiming systematic research at leisure and recreation.

resolved without social psychologists' perspectives and contributions. For example, to improve people's mental health and psychological well-being, how can and should the quality of leisure experiences be increased? Or, how should we approach and influence disabled persons so that their view of themselves, others, and the whole world will remove barriers to experiencing satisfying leisure? Or, in their constant struggle to obtain money for leisure services, recreation admininstrators have to classify recreation services in the order of importance, and they are therefore faced with the dilemma of where to eliminate and what activities to maintain in the program. In making such decisions, recreation personnel would serve their public much better, if they knew the social psychological basis of leisure needs, motives, satisfactions, and attitudes. Finally, much of juvenile delinquent behavior and vandalism takes place during free-time. Social psychologists can make a major contribution to alleviating this pressing social problem, since such behavior represents an individual's reaction to his social environment. In resolving these and other important problems, social psychologists can make substantial contributions. But these are not likely to result unless we change priorities and place the social psychology of leisure and recreation first. Fortunately, we are not the only ones to demand this priority for social psychological inquiry (see Verhoven and Goldstein, 1976).

The final justification for so defining the field comes from the words "free-time" or "leisure" themselves. Zimbardo (1975) has dramatically shown that prisoners, who are full of "free-time," tend to lose their sense of time. They cannot make a distinction between yesterday, today, and tomorrow. Thus, time, and how we view it, becomes very important to our cognitions and behaviors. Being conscious of free-time sets the stage for our actions. Leisure experiences are linked to the degree of perceived freedom and intrinsic motivation when participating in given activities (Iso-Ahola, 1977a, 1978). Without actually being in prison, we can destroy our concept of free-time and thus, make ourselves prisoners of time and environment. It is therefore of paramount significance to understand the social processes that facilitate and/or hinder the formation of a subjectively meaningful and rewarding sense of free-time and leisure.

It is perhaps fitting to conclude this discussion with a simple notion. Since *individual* choice and freedom constitute the foundations of "free-time" and since the basic unit of social psychology is *individual,* there is hardly a setting or framework for examining human social behavior more justified than leisure. If a need for social psychological analysis of leisure is demonstrated, what is then the content area of this field? What kinds of phenomena will social psychologists investigate in the area of leisure and recreation? Let us illustrate this by some concrete examples:

1. A factory worker has just gotten home. He drinks his beer and turns the TV on. He sits down in his recliner and is ready to spend the evening in front of the television. At the same time, he sees through the window, a fellow worker from the same assembly line, passing by. This prompts him to say to his wife: "There he goes again to his blasted evening classes. Who does he think he is? Smarter than others? Stupid, that's what!!"

2. "Ben!" yells Frances, his wife. "Look at that. Even your boss is jogging. You never do anything for exercise. You could go and play tennis." After a while, Ben says, "Hey, that's not a bad idea." Simultaneously, a neighboring couple had this conversation: "Rich, why don't you ever do anything with me? You play golf four times a week with Mike. Why can't we play together?" "Mary," says Rich, "You are not on my level. Besides I wanna beat that turkey!"

3. Ten-year-old Fred is an avid baseball player and his Dad is an equally avid spectator at Fred's games. After one disappointing game, he says to Fred, "How about if we make a deal? For each home run you hit, I pay you $10." In the following three weeks of intensive playing, Fred astonishes his dad by saying that he is not interested in baseball and does not like to play any more.

4. Bill, a college undergraduate, in New York City, comes home from shopping and finds his friend packing. "What's the matter?" asks Bill. The friend answers, "I'm fed up with this city life and crowds. I'm gonna leave for hiking in the Finger Lakes area for a while. How about you?" Bill replies, "I am going to stay here. The Yankees are playing the Red Sox tomorrow. It's a sell-out. Should be an exciting game."

5. In a midwestern small town, a mother observes five black boys playing basketball. She says to herself: "No wonder the blacks have learning problems in school. They never do anything but play basketball after school is over."

6. Harry gets kicked by an opponent in the midst of a soccer game and feels great pain in his right ankle. He is about to retaliate by kicking back when all of a sudden, he remembers what the team decided before the game: Let's play a fair and sportsman-like game. This is only fun and we are here to have a recreational match. Instead of retaliating, Harry turns to a referee and asks for substitution.

7. A year after her accident, Betty decided to continue her favorite hobby, pottery. Since she is partially paralyzed, she experiences several notable failures in her attempts to make what she was able to make before the accident. At the same time, she observes her old friends making beautiful pottery pieces. She soon gives up and starts to cry, "I have nothing left. I have lost everything. There is nothing for me to do in this world."

Thus, social psychologists examine how people form impressions about others based upon their leisure participation (Case No. 1), how the leisure patterns of others affect our attitudes and prejudices concerning people of a different race (No. 5), how our leisure needs and motives are socially determined (No. 2), how competition, social comparison, need for self-esteem shape the types of leisure activities we choose and types of people we interact with (No. 2), the manner in which crowding and need for privacy may lead to different recreational pursuits (No. 4), the effects of social reinforcement on leisure performance and effects of extrinsic rewards on intrinsic motivation in leisure activities (No. 3), how the nature of leisure activity, the level of competition and social companions influence aggressive tendencies in recréational activities (No. 6), and under what conditions and how recreation becomes therapeutic and how leisure participation can be used to prevent the feelings of helplessness (No. 7).

These are but a few instances of social influence phenomena observed in leisure and recreation settings. These and other social influences will be discussed in detail later in the book. However, it is important to realize that the content area of the field is not by any means fixed. Many social processes will undoubtedly remain to be discovered. At this point we can only examine and emphasize those phenomena that have been noted and subjected to scientific study. Since people evolve continuously so also does the knowledge of them. By definition, social change is at the heart of social psychological inquiry because social influence implies change.

summary

Social psychology emphasizes an individual as a participant in social relationships, and the understanding of social influence processes underlying these relationships. Thus, the social psychology of leisure behavior was defined as that branch of scientific leisure studies which examines how the feelings, cognitions and behaviors of one individual are influenced by those of others during a period of time subjectively designated as unobligated, free, or leisure. While the social and physical environments provide a wide variety of leisure and recreational alternatives, it is the individual who, because of his personality, experiences and social encounters, perceives and determines the range of leisure options available to him. Thus, in its broadest sense social psychology attempts to help us understand how a person influences and is influenced by others' leisure behavior. The main theme is the changing individual in a changing social environment. We asserted that this branch of leisure studies is badly needed (1) for historical and philosophical reasons, (2) for the sake of knowledge, (3) for improving the understanding of the social nature of leisure behavior in order to enhance intrapersonal and interpersonal experiences, and (4) for solving pressing social problems. The chief objective of this new field is the improvement of human psychological well-being and the quality of life.

2 the historical antecedents of the new field

a brief look at the history of general social psychology

The history of social psychology (or perhaps more appropriately, the history of social psychological thinking) is as long as the history of people. But it was not until ca 350 B.C. that this sort of thinking was expressed, for the first time, in Aristotle's writing. Modern social psychologists (e.g., Aronson, 1972) regard Aristotle as their intellectual father and believe that he was the first to enunciate some of the basic principles of social influence and persuasion. But tracing the path from Aristotle to the beginning of modern social psychology is a formidable task, because, for one thing, social psychology as a formal discipline did not exist until 1908. This means, therefore, that the intellectual roots of social psychology are very scattered. Many philosophers (Compte, Hegel, Nietzsche, Plato, Rousseau, Spencer, Spinoza, Voltaire) have tried to explain the nature of people and human social behavior, thereby contributing indirectly to the social psychological analysis of human behavior. Although these philosophers have examined social behavior, they have not written anything under the specific title of social psychology. Due to this unsystematic approach it is difficult to assess exactly the historical significance of such contributors to the development of the field. Persons interested in a detailed description of the background of social psychology are referred to Allport's (1969) excellent chapter and Karpf's (1932) classic book on the topic.

the first half of the 20th century

While the historical roots of social psychology may be traced back to the early times of humankind, the real breakthrough did not come until the 20th century; more specifically, it was 1908 when the first books bearing the title *Social Psychology* appeared. Ross, a sociologist, focused on crowd behavior and other social influence processes, while McDougall, a psychologist, stressed the importance of instinct factors and forces as the determinants of human social behavior. McDougall is also known for his theory of action, in which he posited that ''the motive of all action is the desire to obtain increase of pleasure or diminution of pain." Following these ground-breaking works, the 1920s had at least two historically important developments. First, the scope of the *Journal of Abnormal Psychology* was enlarged to include social psychology in 1922. This new publication, *Journal of Abnormal and Social Psychology,* soon became the main forum for reporting social psychological research. During the decade of the 1920s, empiricism assumed a dominant position in social psychology, with the result that by 1931 Murphy and Murphy were able to list over 800 relevant studies.

Second, in 1924, Floyd H. Allport published an influential textbook entitled *Social Psychology*. This book was historically important for several reasons. First of all, he clearly identified the focus and emphasis of the field. "Social psychology is a part of the psychology of the individual, whose behavior it studies in relation to that sector of his environment comprised by his fellows" (p. 4). In doing so, he expressed his strong opposition to the idea that social psychologists should use "the crowd mind" or "collective mind" of a group as a basic unit of analysis. Allport (1924, p. 4) stated that "there is no psychology of groups which is not essentially and entirely a psychology of individuals." Also, his text was significant because it reported empirical findings relative to many social influence processes, thereby paving the way for the advanced scientific and empirical study of varied aspects of human social behavior. Finally, Allport's text should be recognized for its theoretical richness in such areas as emotions, facial expression, attitudes, and personality.

The 1930s and 1940s witnessed extensive progress in the investigation of social behavior. Social psychology became a clearly established and recognized field, and the carefully controlled studies reflected the strength of experimental orientation in research. Much of the important work was done under the leadership and inspiration of Kurt Lewin and his talented students. For example, Lewin, Lippitt and White's study (1939) on climates of leadership was groundbreaking. Other investigators like Muzafer Sherif also conducted outstanding research during this period. Sherif's study (1936) concerning the effects of social norms on human behavior, and Dollard, Doob, Miller, Mowrer and Sears' (1939) study of frustration and aggression, had far-reaching impact on the development of the body of knowledge in this field. But it is undoubtedly Lewin who influenced most. He not only contributed to theoretical and empirical knowledge through his own research, but above all, developed a paradigm, or school of thought, which now constitutes the foundation of cognitive social psychology. Lewin's impact was so great that his students almost exclusively dominated social psychological research in the 1950s and set the stage for experimental studies by others in the 1960s.

Lewin's field theory emphasized the total situation. His most fundamental concept was "life space" (or psychological field), which consists of the person and the environment. Lewin postulated that since all psychological events and behaviors are a function of life space, they are determined by the person-times-environment interaction, symbolically $B = f(P, E)$, where B = behavior, P = person, E = environment. Lewin also introduced topological psychology and stressed the importance of mathematics in the social psychological analysis. His other contributions included a dynamic theory of personality, the study of level of aspiration and group dynamics (Research Center for Group Dynamics was established in Massachusetts Institute of Technology in 1945), action research, and attempts to resolve social conflicts. Besides Lewin himself, his students conducted pioneering research. Here Lippitt and White's study (1943) on the effects of autocratic and democratic leadership on human behavior, Deutsch's (1949) investigation of competition and cooperation, and Asch's (1946) experiment on the formation of impressions, should be noted.

the last 30 years

In the 1950s, Lewin's impact was reflected by his students' significant contributions to research, perhaps most notably those of Festinger. In addition to his influential studies on level of aspiration, informal social communication and group cohesiveness, Festinger formulated two theories which later in the 1960s served as a basis for much of the social psychological investigation: a theory of social comparison (1954) and a theory of cognitive dissonance (1957). In terms of its impact upon the conduct of empirical research, the latter theory appears to be the most influential in the entire history of the field. If there is any challenge to this honor, it comes from another important work published in the 1950s, namely Heider's (1958) book entitled *The Psychology of Interpersonal Relations*. This volume laid the foundations for the attribution research that has dominated the present decade. Through its balance theory, Heider's book was also very influential in stimulating research on attitude formation and change. The fundamental idea in both Festinger's and Heider's work is cognitive consistency or balance. According to this, people have a tendency to act or react psychologically so as to reach cognitive consistency (or balance).

Another dominant feature of the social psychology in the 1950s was its emphasis on the study of group dynamics (Cartwright and Zander, 1960; Thibaut and Kelley, 1959). This can be seen in extensive work on such topics as "power field," group cohesiveness, communication processes within groups, affiliation, and conformity. In addition, Hovland, Janis and Kelley's work (1953) on persuasive communication, McClelland, Atkinson, Clark, and Lowell's (1953) on achievement motivation, and Atkinson's (1957) extension of Lewin's level of aspiration work into a theory of achievement motivation, have attracted the attention of many social psychologists and have therefore been of historical value to the field.

Inspired by Festinger and Heider's cognitive consistency theories, attitude research became a dominant feature of the 1960s. Other much-researched topics include aggression and violence, attraction and liking, altruism and helping, imitation and modeling, social exchange and person perception (Baron, Byrne and Griffitt, 1974). The decade of the 1960s may be characterized as a period of experimental and basic research. This is reflected by the establishment of a new journal in 1966, *Journal of Experimental Social Psychology,* which, along with the *Journal of Personality and Social Psychology,* rapidly became the leading outlet for the reports of methodologically rigorous activity.

While the experimental trend of the 1960s has continued to the 1970s, a need for new directions has recently begun to shape the field. The almost-exclusive emphasis on experimental investigations in the 1960s has raised some incisive questions about the adequacy and sufficiency of basic research, as so vividly expressed by Allport (1969, p. 68): "Some current investigations seem to end up in elegantly polished triviality—snippets of empiricism, but nothing more. Can the improved objectivity in method be brought to serve broad theory and practical application?" This sort of self-criticism culminated in Gergen's (1973) influential article, in which he posited that social psychology represents an historical inquiry into human social behavior. Accordingly, social psychologists "essentially engage in a systematic account of contemporary affairs" and are therefore "sensitizing" people to social influences rather than building transhistorical laws of human behavior. Since social behavior is limited in time and place, generalizations regarding human social behavior are not possible; prediction and control should therefore be rejected as the aims of social psychology. Gergen, however, points out that social influence phenomena can be placed on a "continuum of historical durability," with these phenomena varying in their degree of susceptibility to historical influences. Some aspects of social behavior are more durable than others.

Following Gergen's (1973) original arguments, Schlenker (1974) quickly responded, strongly defending social psychology as a scientific enterprise. Schlenker argued that in essence social psychologists compile systematic information to construct "high-order theories" to explain the diversity of social phenomena. If the search for constants in social behavior is a difficult task, it "should not be confused with an impossible one," he added. Schlenker also gave several examples to illustrate that there are regularities in social behavior observable over time and cultures. He maintained that whether social influence phenomena are historically bound is an empirical question which should by no means invalidate the search for universal theories and should "in no way distinguish the social sciences from the natural sciences." Thus, social psychology is indeed a science, the objective of which is to understand, explain, predict, and control human social behavior. Although Schlenker (1974) accepts applied research, he does not question that basic research is more important, because it lays the foundations for the comprehensive explanation of social behavior in the future.

Discussion of new directions in social psychology did not stop at the Schlenker rebuttal (e.g., Manis, 1976; Rappoport, 1977; Sampson, 1977; Strickland, Aboud, and Gergen, 1976). The debate is still going on and has already become the leading theme of the 1970s. Although Gergen and Schlenker have their own followers, many scholars seem to fall in between the two, in the middle of the road, as echoed by Greenwald (1976): "Durable laws of social behavior are possible in principle even if they are very difficult to arrive at in practice."

The crisis of the 1970s has, in part, been a crisis in self-confidence of social psychologists (Elms, 1975). The suggestions for coping with the problems seem to call for (1) an increase in theory construction and shift from "mini-theories" to process models, (2) a greater volume of field research, with simultaneous interplay between the laboratory and field research, (3) the inclusion of socially relevant variables in research, (4) the recognition of multivariate nature of social phenomena and thus an increase in multivariate research, (5) and most importantly, the acceptance of the historical context of social behavior. The criticism of social psychology has mainly been directed to the present emphasis on atomistic theories dealing with temporarily isolated and spatially limited social events. The critics (e.g., Taylor, 1976) insist that social psychologists should focus on studying how the individual gathers, interprets, and uses information and how such processes affect behavior. This shift in theoretical scope is intended to bring forth process or schematic models for explaining the individual's responses over a period of time, under a wide range of social situations.

In addition to providing these and other possible solutions for improving the quality of social psychological research, recent discussion concerning the status of the field has cleared the air from the practical point of view. That is, depending on whether social psychology is viewed as "historical inquiry" or "science," federal grant money is allocated predominantly to either applied or basic research. If decision-makers see social psychology as a study of contemporary affairs and problems, applied research is likely to receive the main share of the federal dollars. On the other hand, Schlenker's thesis calls for strong federal commitment to basic research. Another practical implication ensuing from the Gergen-Schlenker debate deals with applied fields of social psychology. Gergen's position encourages the study of social problems. With our own biases but without hesitation, we can claim that leisure is and will be one of the major social concerns of our time. Therefore, Gergen's position is applicable and valued in the field of leisure and recreation, which will enable us to embark on a systematic analysis of leisure and recreation from the social psychological perspective.

the historical antecedents of social psychology of leisure and recreation

The Greeks discovered leisure (de Grazia, 1962). Leisure as a concept played a basic part in the systems of thought of such great philosophers as Plato and Aristotle. Thus, it is interesting to note that both social psychologists (Aronson, 1972) and leisure scientists (de Grazia, 1962) trace the roots of their respective fields back to the same period and civilization in the history of humankind. This speaks strongly for the intellectual uniqueness of the Greek culture and its transhistorical philosophies, most notably for Aristotle. The identical ancient background of these two fields suggests that the convergence of social psychology and leisure studies is an historical inevitability. Since the social psychology of leisure behavior did not exist prior to modern times, the historical antecedents of this field may best be considered from three different points of view: (1) what philosophers have said about leisure and its relation to social behavior; (2) what psychologists/social psychologists have written about leisure and recreation behavior; and (3) how leisure scientists have treated social psychological aspects of leisure and recreation. We begin with the first one.

To Aristotle, leisure was a state of being or mind free from the necessity to labor, a state in which activity was performed for its own sake or as its own end (de Grazia, 1962). This concept followed from his philosophy that life can be divided into action and leisure. While making a distinction between work and leisure, Aristotle, however, did not equate leisure with free-time. In his view, time itself is not enough to create leisure. Whether free-time was used rightly and wisely became the defining criterion of leisure. Aristotle also made it clear that work is a means and leisure is the final goal. A person is extrinsically motivated by his work, for the purpose of attaining leisure. Vigorous work is necessary for defending the state, thereby securing leisure. Work can never become leisure and leisure must not have any relationship to work. Thus, happiness and the quality of life rest on the shoulders of leisure, not work. While Aristotle acknowledged the need for relaxation, this should not be the goal of work. In other words, a person does not work to recuperate to re-create himself for work but rather, he works to attain leisure to achieve happiness (even if play leads to relaxation, it does not represent a state of happiness). Aristotle specifically spelled out two activities which should make up the core of one's leisure life and thus are the basis of happiness: music and contemplation.

Although Aristotle emphasized cultivation of the mind in leisure through music and contemplation, he and other Athenian philosophers believed in the unity of mind and body. The balanced citizen was a combination of soldier, athlete, artist, statesman and philosopher (Kraus, 1971). This meant that leisure was used for intellectual cultivation (mainly through music and philosophical discussions), as well as for sports and gymnastics. Besides participating personally in physical activities, the Greeks were also avid sports spectators, as evidenced by their festivals of which the Olympiad was a part. It is also important to note that play was recognized as a legitimate part of child development. Plato, for example, urged that children should be allowed to play naturally between the ages of three and six. But when they grow older, then music, dance and sports should become their primary activities. Participation was viewed as essential to keeping physically fit and strong, thereby making people capable of defending the state.

As a word of caution we should note that the Aristotelian philosophy, though clearly reflected in people's leisure pursuits, is hardly an accurate description of the Greeks' leisure patterns and motives. Music and contemplation could not have satisfied all people's leisure needs at all times, as is indicated by people's strong interest in active and passive sports. But despite this deficiency we can see the psychological importance of leisure to the Greeks. It was leisure which was supposed to provide the major avenue for the development of a self-concept. Leisure was expected to form the basis for life satisfaction as well as mental and physical well-being. Leisure was to serve as a medium for social interaction and interpersonal behavior. It also had an important socialization function: to teach children life-time leisure skills which laid the foundations of happiness and psychological well-being. All this is in sharp contrast to modern Western societies in which one's self-concept, self-esteem and happiness are determined by money and the social prestige of one's occupation. In a way, leisure is presently used as a tool for increasing the extrinsic value of one's work. In the work-ethic societies people behave as if life satisfaction were a direct result of financial rewards obtained from one's occupation.

other civilizations

Although the Greek philosophers may have discovered leisure and its psychological potential, earlier civilizations also recognized leisure and its importance. Kraus (1971) notes that in primitive cultures playlike activities had many psychological functions, such as increasing solidarity and cohesiveness in tribes, improving communication, enhancing aesthetic pleasure and relaxation. Leisure was also used as a way of socializing the young into sex-role patterns: boys, through their play, learned strenuous warlike activities, while girls were taught household crafts. Another notable characteristic of pre-Christian civilization (e.g., ancient Egypt) was that leisure was mainly used for cultivation of the mind, either in a more serious way (religious rituals and festivals) or in a somewhat lighter manner (social entertainment in clubs and drinking associations). Work catered to physical aspects of human activity. Again, this shows that social interaction was an integral part of leisure, though it took different forms, depending on people's social class background. Social entertainment as a form of leisure reached its peak during the Roman empire. At the early stages of this era, however, leisure was a serious business; people participated actively in games and sports to be able to vigorously fight for the state. Besides these utilitarian reasons, many forms of sports and games were carried on for religious purposes. But with increasing military power Roman citizens began changing their active leisure habits into passive spectator roles, and celebrations. The mentality of social entertainment found its climax in A.D. 354 when the Roman year consisted of 200 public holidays of which 175 days were devoted to various games. Humankind had entered the first "leisure society!" Kraus (1971) concluded that these wild and corrupt "Roman holidays," reflecting inability to deal with leisure, were the chief reason for the downfall of Rome. Since the majority of Roman citizens used their leisure in this way, this is a prime example of the "effects of actual and implied presence of others" (i.e., social psychological forces) on individual leisure choices.

a social psychological account of the downfall of rome

The question then arises as to why the Romans were unable to deal with free-time. The typical historical explanation is that they were not used to such a vast amount of free-time. Although to my knowledge no one has attempted to do it before, we venture to give a social psychological account of the downfall of Rome and of the basis of wisdom of ancient Greece. Our speculation stems from three recently discovered social psychological facts: (1) extrinsic sanctions and rewards are detrimental to intrinsic motivation; (2) individuals have a need to feel competent and self-determined; (3) human behavior is goal-oriented, that is, people are in an ongoing process of seeking and conquering challenges (Deci, 1975a). As discussed earlier, to the Greeks work was a means and leisure an end. They engaged in a variety of physical, mental and social activities for continual self-development. The physical and spiritual strength they pursued was also desirable from the standpoint of defending the state; but such a goal was never established as an explicit/extrinsic reason for leisure behavior. Rather, the Greek philosophers encouraged people to seek and conquer challenges through activities which apparently led to feelings of competence and self-determination. Music and contemplation, as strongly emphasized by Plato and Aristotle, provided excellent vehicles for this psychological undertaking. More important, these types of leisure activities offered an enduring forum for engaging in the process of seeking and conquering challenges. In short, the wisdom of the great Greek philosophers was capable of *intrinsically* motivating people in certain leisure activities considered both physically and psychologically beneficial to citizens. Individuals motivated by intrinsic forces were more capable of securing their state which in turn helped them to attain and maintain leisure. It is important to note the Greeks did not explicitly use their leisure for such external goals as defending the state, nor did they engage in leisure activities because of external sanctions and rewards. Among other things, this was clearly reflected by Plato's proposal that children be provided with opportunities for natural modes of amusement, that is, intrinsically motivated behaviors.

The Romans, in contrast, were *extrinsically* sanctioned and rewarded, as inducements to participate in both physical (e.g., sports) and intellectual (music, theater) activities. They were told that such expenditure of leisure builds strong individuals who are able to vigorously fight for their state. This was the sole purpose of participating in varied leisure activities. Leisure became a medium for the end, work. Although the Greek and Roman leisure patterns were similar, there was one critical difference between the two. The former engaged in them for intrinsic, the latter for extrinsic reasons. Consequently, the Romans were psychologically denied opportunities to seek and conquer challenges; they were hindered from feeling competent and self-determined in their leisure. We suggest that this was the actual cause for the downfall of Rome. As the Romans had finally overcome all their enemies, they decided that people no longer had to participate in those leisure activities that were needed to prepare citizens for defending the state. There was nothing left to conquer. By reaching that conclusion and decision, the Romans removed extrinsic sanctions and rewards from engaging in the "good" leisure activities.

During the last decade or so (i.e., about 2,000 years after the Roman empire) social psychologists (e.g., Deci, 1975a; Lepper, Greene, and Nisbett, 1973) have convincingly demonstrated that once external rewards and sanctions are removed from activities (which were originally intrinsically motivated), people lose interest in them..Thus, it was extrinsic rewards/sanctions that destroyed the Romans' intrinsic interest in "good" leisure activities; once the external sanctions were removed, little or no intrinsic motivation was left. In a way, the Romans destroyed their need to seek and conquer challenges, to feel competent and self-determined. Since intrinsically motivated leisure did not exist any more and because there were no external reasons to participate in beneficial leisure activities, the Romans had only one option left: to turn to "Roman holidays'' and thus to self-destruction. This is why the Roman lesson reminds us of the folly of excess, while the Greek wisdom advises us of the importance of intrinsic motivation. Unfortunately, modern work-ethic societies have exploited leisure for work rather than vice versa. As in Rome, work has again become the end and leisure a medium to that end. History suggests that soon there will be an era characterized by the excesses of the ''American holiday.'' Unfortunately, there are no signs to indicate that we are better prepared to handle this second ''leisure society'' than were the Romans. Before it is too late, we should learn the lesson of the Roman error and of Greek wisdom, as echoed by Bernardt Russel: ''The future of mankind rests on our ability to use leisure wisely.''

post-roman times

From the psychological standpoint, the historical development of leisure and recreation was quite continuous since ancient Greece and Rome. Immediately following the downfall of Rome the new conquerors condemned and forbade the Roman way of living, destroying stadiums, theaters and many other forms of the Roman leisurely life-style. People were expected to be occupied in manual labor almost all the time, leaving little, if any, hours for leisure. According to Kraus (1971), this marked the beginning of the Protestant work ethic. Life was harsh even for people with upper social class backgrounds, but it was especially hard for those who came from the lower socio-economic classes. This countervailing reaction to the Roman life-style continued for centuries and only gradually began to decrease. It follows from the above that the period between the downfall of Rome and the industrial revolution was characterized psychologically by two dominant features.

First, work constituted one's central life-interest, and this for extrinsic reasons. Whatever free-time was available was used for recuperating from work, so that one could continue to labor effectively the next day. Relaxation from and for work was the function of leisure. Although leisure consisted of a wide variety of physical vs. intellectual or active vs. passive activities at times (e.g., during the Renaissance period), it is important to note that these elaborate forms of amusement were aimed at relaxation and diverting one's mind temporarily from work; they served as a means of re-creating or restoring physical and psychological well-being to prepare oneself for work. Regardless of a great number of annual workless days during the Middle Ages, these holidays were not taken as opportunities for leisure. The idea that people's free-time was predominantly extrinsically motivated was reflected by their strong interest in games of chance during the Middle Ages. Roberts and Sutton-Smith (1962) have provided evidence indicating that such games are popular in societies where people's behavior is externally controlled.

The second distinguishing characteristic was the marked social class differences with respect to the amount of free-time and the types of leisure available to people. Despite struggles to equalize these differences, the problem was not solved until the arrival of the industrial revolution, which made it possible even for people from the lower social classes to have some free-time. The industrial revolution, on the other hand, did not eliminate qualitative differences between people's free-time pursuits. Furthermore, it strengthened rather than weakened the Protestant work ethic. This new-born glorification of work and minimizing of leisure has ever since continued to be the fundamental characteristic of Western societies, especially in the United States. Even though countless modes of amusement have been invented for free-time expenditure, in their attitude toward leisure, modern societies remain distinctly different from ancient Greece and conspicuously similar to ancient Rome. Leisure continues to be a means to the end: work.

Plato and Aristotle were not the only philosophers who stressed the importance of play and leisure. During the seventeenth and eighteenth centuries, Locke and Rousseau, among others, emphasized play and games as media of learning (Kraus, 1971). While children's play was seen as of intrinsic value, its utilitarian functions were more attractive to these philosophers. Play, games and sports were regarded as useful and beneficial because of their presumed impact upon building character, preventing idleness and antisocial activities, and providing relaxation. These activities were viewed as instrumental in providing exercise for both mind and body, consistent with the old philosophy of the unity of mind and body. As life became easier and leisure more accessible to the masses of people, many forms of social entertainment (e.g., drinking and dancing clubs) grew in popularity. This general leisure pattern, however, did not escape the negative comments of such philosophers as Voltaire (Kraus, 1971). He opposed "excessive leisure" because of its detrimental effects on workers' performance in industry and thus on the whole economy. It was believed that excessive leisure led to excessive social entertainment and relaxation, with the result that working hours had to be spent in recuperating from leisure.

Like Voltaire, Karl Marx was also concerned about leisure, but for very different reasons. In adapting Hegel's idea of alienation, Marx (1894) argued that class society degrades human beings and leads to "false consciousness," a distorted mental picture of reality. He argued that the capitalistic system is based upon a division of labor which results in a class-divided society and human alienation. Labor becomes external and nonvoluntary to the worker; he works only to be able to live. Labor is his life-activity, a commodity which he sells to the bourgeoisie to secure his living. Being divided against his fellow men and feeling helpless over his work, the worker finds that his working-day impinges upon his leisure. Consequently, his attempts to assure intellectual development, social interaction and growth, and healthy maintenance of the body are hampered. An alienated person does not understand the world he is living in. Although Marx regarded labor as a sacrifice of the worker's life, he acknowledged that leisure is essential to the worker. In the third volume of *Capital,* Marx (1894) claimed that the "realm of freedom" and "the development of human personality for its own sake" can begin only after work. Marx viewed the shortening of the working day as indispensable to securing human freedom and the full development of individuality. By freedom, Marx did not simply mean free-time, but freedom from materialism, which is conducive to the free development of individuality.

karl marx

Thus, we see that Marx's primary concern lay in the individual and the development of his awareness of himself and of the world about him. And it is in this sense that Marx was concerned with political, social and economic systems. He criticized prevailing social orders because he considered them detrimental to the free development of individuality, that is, the intellectual and social growth of the individual. Hence Marx's rejection of the capitalistic society stemmed from his desire to help establish a social system in which the individual would be able to discover his true, fulfilled nature. Due to the manner in which labor was exploited, Marx did not see the search for the ultimate truth as possible in a capitalistic society. We should note, however, that Marx attacked the "capitalistic" system in his own time and did not have models of societies which today call themselves Marxist or Communist. Unquestionably, Marx's contention that societies are exploiting workers (thereby making labor alien to them) is nowhere closer to the truth than in the modern Communist (Soviet Union and China) societies. This derogatory statement, however, should not be taken as endorsement of the American social structure. Somewhat idealistically, we advocate a social order that systematically and vigorously aims at the reduction of the working day and the enrichment of the remaining work-hours for people in all occupations. Potentially such a society provides favorable conditions for an individual to seek to understand human nature and existence, as first advocated by Aristotle over 2,000 years ago.

summary

In sum, our cursory review of the history of leisure reveals that prominent philosophers have attached important functions to leisure. Significantly, these functions seem to be social psychological in nature. Generally it appears that the main concern has been centered on the wise use of leisure, from the standpoint of developing one's mind and body. Some philosophers, most notably Aristotle and Marx, have regarded leisure as providing the only opportunity to search for understanding of man's true nature and existence. This knowledge will free people from external constraints, enabling them to achieve a true state of mind, or psychological well-being. Consequently, proper leisure is intrinsically motivated, and unrelated to one's work.

There are other functions of leisure which are frequently mentioned by philosophers and which clearly have social psychological connotations: (1) socialization of the young into the mainstream of society through play and leisure participation, (2) the enhancement of one's work performance by improving work-related skills during leisure, (3) the development and maintenance of skills for interpersonal behavior and social interaction, (4) social entertainment and relaxation, (5) enhancement of character and personality through wholesome leisure activities, (6) prevention of idleness and antisocial activities, and (7) development of a sense of community. In short, philosophers have viewed leisure as a unique and irreplaceable opportunity for improving both intrapersonal and interpersonal behavior. They argue that if most people succeed in using their leisure to this end, the entire society will ultimately benefit from such leisure orientation. Consequently, the social climate will become conducive to psychologically healthful leisure participation. Hence, individual leisure choices contribute positively to the social psychological leisure environment, which in turn advances "good" leisure choices. On the other hand, this self-fulfilling circle may also turn in a negative direction, as demonstrated by the social excesses of the Roman empire.

To understand better the development of social psychological view of leisure behavior, we next survey what the general psychologists and social psychologists have written about leisure and recreation. At the very outset we note that from the first to the latest, not a single social psychological textbook has included chapters specifically dealing with leisure and recreation. (On the other hand, this is not surprising in view of the focus and mission of general social psychology.) But a closer inspection of these texts reveals that some authors have touched upon leisure-related issues, chiefly play behavior.

social psychologists' considerations of leisure

In the first social psychological text, McDougall (1908) suggested that "the human mind has the tendency to play." Although he talked about "play impulse" he never espoused the idea that play is solely motivated by instincts (p. 91). In fact, he rejected attempts to explain play by heredity and by instinct-oriented concepts such as Groos' (1901) theory that man plays because of his instincts and because of the need to prepare for the serious business of life. In a similar vein, he did not endorse Spencer's (1896) idea of play as motivated by surplus energy. Nor did he accept the recapitulation hypothesis (Hall, 1916; Gulick, 1920), that in play people rehearse and repeat their ancestors' activities stage by stage. McDougall's own account of play, however, did not rule out the effects of innate factors on play. He saw play as influenced both by "the native tendencies of the mind" and by environmentally-induced motives such as the desire to excel and get the better of others, the first component being more important. Hence, modern (e.g., Ellis, 1973) interactional (person-times-environment) views of the causes of play have their roots in McDougall's analysis. McDougall also emphasized positive socialization influences through play, games and sports. He suggested that modern Olympic games and other sporting contests have political significance, bringing nations into more "sympathetic relations."

social psychologists on leisure

Like McDougall, Allport (1924) did not devote any chapters to an analysis of leisure, recreation or even play behavior. However, in referring to industrial conflict, strikes and labor agitation, Allport acknowledged the importance of free-time:

> Psychological causes, other than those resulting from the oppression of the worker, must be sought to explain the prevailing unrest . . . If the worker is thus fated to remain at a modest economic and vocational level, vicarious compensations should be sought in avocational interests, wise employment of leisure and pleasures of home life. Employers must assume their share of the problem by enabling the worker to find outlets in useful and pleasurable channels for the desires which are thwarted by his limited vocational status. . . . so as to satisfy the needs of human life and bring contentment to their workers (Allport, 1924, pp. 411–414).

Therefore, corporations should not only be interested in profit-making but should assume the responsibility for their workers' social adjustment through leisure activities. Similar to Allport, Krech and Crutchfield (1948) stressed the importance of recreational activities in augmenting work satisfaction, in reducing on-the-job tensions, and in solving industrial conflicts. Unfortunately, this was the only domain of leisure behavior to which Allport applied his social psychological thinking.

In a sense, Allport's text (1924) established the pattern for future writing in the field. Since many authors accepted his definition and outline of the field, this meant that they devoted little, if any, attention to such applied perspectives of social psychology as leisure and recreation. Only occasional references to leisure and recreation could be seen in social psychological writing. However, in all cases leisure was regarded as a tool rather than as a target of the systematic study of social influences. LaPiere and Farnsworth (1936), for example, discussed briefly recreational clubs and the recreational functions of a conference and game behavior in the context of personal leadership situations. They suggested that the social prestige value of belonging to recreational clubs often provides the principal source of satisfaction derived from the participation, especially when social relationships are not particularly congenial. In his classic work, Sherif (1936) propounds the thesis that when people interact, social norms develop. These norms, which postulate expected modes of behavior, specify acceptable and expected conduct in given situations, and to a large extent, regulate "the economic and social activities of the individual members in their quest for the satisfaction of their needs" (p. 154). Accordingly, social norms not only influence our leisure choices but also how we behave in a given leisure context.

According to Lewin (1935, p. 39) any psychological behavior can be explained and understood in terms of the momentary structure, the state of the person, and the psychological environment. Lewin's approach, therefore, was to a major extent, "historical." That is, each psychological event has to be examined in terms of its peculiar personal and situational properties; and applied aspects (e.g., leisure context) have to be incorporated in all analyses of human behavior. Lewin (1948) argued that this starting point is not only useful for theory-building but above all, in resolving social conflicts. He (Lewin, 1935, p. 105–106) also discussed play behavior, arguing that the adults cannot determine whether children's behavior is playful or nonplayful. According to Lewin's dynamic theory of play, the basic property of play is its closeness and remoteness to reality, play activity being visible to other persons but less bound by the laws of reality and by external constraints. Play is more likely to offer pleasure than nonplay activities, provided that the "rules of the game" do not become too strict and approach the rigidity of reality. In his later work in this area, Lewin was concerned with constructiveness of play (Barker, Dembo and Lewin, 1941).

Following these earlier works, modern social psychologists have exhibited little, if any, interest in the study of play, leisure and recreation. Recent demand for applied research, however, has extended to include many leisure-related problems: the social psychological analysis of drug use and drinking behavior

(Davis, 1972), TV-watching (Himmelweit, 1975), work (Argyle, 1972) and organizational process (Hollander and Hunt, 1971), imprisonment (Zimbardo, 1975), to name but a few. Systematic examination of leisure behavior nevertheless remains conspicuously absent. Neulinger (1974) has recognized leisure as a social psychological problem in a social psychological context. His approach, however, is more sociological in nature, because he examines leisure and leisure attitudes as a function of such "background" variables as income or occupation, and simultaneously does not consider important social influence processes observed in leisure.

This is not to say that social psychological research of leisure is nonexistent. Some social psychologists have conducted research in this area. In their classic study, Hastorf and Cantril (1954) demonstrated the powerful (distorting) effects of leisure group affiliation (i.e., loyalty to a sports team) on an individual's (spectator's) perception and behavior. Mann (1974) and Cialdini, Borden, Thorne, Walker, Freeman, and Sloan (1976) have provided further evidence on spectators' intense identification with their reference group, sports team. In another line of research, Sherif, Harvey, White, Hood, and Sherif (1961) studied group behavior in a leisure setting (boys' camps), focusing particularly on the antecedents of conflict and cooperation. Other examples include attempts to show the effects of feelings of competence achieved in a leisure activity on the development of self-concept (Koocher, 1971), and efforts to determine the relationship between leisure attitudes and actual leisure behavior (Ajzen and Fishbein, 1969). These are but a few examples of empirical studies on the social psychology of leisure which are available.

While many social psychological leisure studies have been reported, the problem is the lack of studies specifically aimed at increasing our understanding of leisure behavior. For example, when researchers recently determined the effects of extrinsic rewards on children's free play (e.g., Lepper, *et al.*, 1973) their purpose was merely to demonstrate the empirical validity of the "overjustification" hypothesis; play itself clearly was not the central focus of the investigation. That is, this research is not part of systematic attempts to discover the effects of social factors on children's play, though it certainly has implications for such an analysis.

As for other than "pure" social psychologists, many prominent psychologists have examined play behavior at length. Freud's (1946; 1955) and Erikson's (1943; 1950) psychoanalytic formulations, and Piaget's (1951) developmental approach are well known. Since Ellis' (1973) thorough review of the classical, recent, and modern psychological theories of play is available, there is no need to dwell on these theories here. Patrick's classic text on the *Psychology of Relaxation* (1916), however, deserves special attention. Patrick developed the thesis that popular leisure activities ("amusement crazes") are a form of reaction against too serious and tense life styles in modern society. He pointed out that after great tension there must be great relaxation for a person to be able to survive. But because of increasing tension in modern society (mainly due to the

psychologists' views of leisure

work world), natural forms of relaxation (sleep, play, sport, laughter, etc.) are replaced by artificial means of relieving the strain, and thereby temporarily restoring mental balance. He maintained that these artificial methods include drugs, alcohol, recreation "crazes," and perhaps great social upheavals like war. In fact, he suggested that "the psychology of play may throw much light on the psychology of war." He further noted that if children are not allowed to play and relax, they will never grasp the idea of successful and natural forms of relaxation. To him, play was spontaneous, pursued for its own sake, without any external compulsion.

The above points clearly reflect Patrick's social psychological approach toward leisure and recreation. He saw the forms of individual relaxation as affecting on the one hand other individuals and the entire society, and society influencing the choices of individual relaxation on the other. More specifically, Patrick made some excellent observations concerning social influence processes occurring in leisure. For example, he noted (p. 63) that since emotional expression is socially inhibited in modern civilized man, spectator sports provide a substitute avenue for expressing emotions freely. At another point (p. 74), he discussed the importance of social approval or disapproval in relation to the sudden increase or decline of popularity of leisure activities, and how imitation as a social force shapes people's leisure pursuits. Yet at another point (pp. 83–85), he hypothesized that participation in simple games, particularly in outdoor games, harmonizes the family and makes many groups more cohesive. This occurs because "all valuable games and sports are social and the mere mingling with our fellows lowers the mental stress and tension." These insights have a definite place in the development of social psychological thinking of leisure and recreation.

Although play (e.g., Berlyne, 1969; Bruner, 1974; Gilmore, 1966; Klinger, 1969; Millar, 1968; Singer, 1973; Weisler and McCall, 1976) and leisure (e.g., Cutten, 1926; Davis, 1938; Super, 1940) have attracted many psychologists' attention since the early works of the 20th century, relatively little attention has been directed to social aspects of play and leisure behavior. Lehman and Witty (1927) investigated sex and race differences in play behavior but did not find "conspicuous" sex differences; however, black children were more social in their play than white children. Although social participation slightly declined with increasing age, the level of this participation remained quite high in all age groups. Parten (1933) studied preschool children's play and concluded that these children most often play in groups of two, the group size, however, increasing with age. Hartley, Frank, and Goldenson (1952) examined the effects of play on the development of the child's personality, but also discussed such social functions of play as imitation and learning of real life roles. Roberts and Sutton-Smith (1962) studied game training and game involvement of children against their cultural background. They found evidence of a relationship between the types of games (strategy, skill, and luck) played by children and child-rearing patterns (obedience, achievement and responsibility) in various societies and cultures. Sutton-Smith, Roberts and Kozelka (1963) provided evidence indicating that the differences in adult game involvement can be explained, in part, by this association. Eifermann (1971) studied social play and differences of the participation in competitive games between urban and rural children. She argued that competitive activities, especially in urban areas, create excessive tension and strain for children. Finally, Caplan and Caplan (1973) recently discussed the role of play in social development, suggesting that play with other children, more than any other activity, contributes to the child's social competence.

Besides these few examples of psychologists' work in this area, several sociologists' views sociologists have studied social aspects of play and leisure behavior. In his classic text, Veblen (1899) pointed out that leisure behavior was predominantly determined by social class. He argued that leisure had become the hallmark of the upper class who lived on the toil of others. In another classic study, Lundberg, Komarovsky, and McInerney (1934) investigated leisure expenditure of people with various occupational status (e.g., executive, housewives), and found that the groups differed not only in the absolute amounts of leisure available but above all, in the qualitative use of the same activities. Riesman (1950; 1954; 1958) suggested that the general objectives of leisure participation include self-development and creativity on the one hand and recreation and diversion on the other. He maintained that people often pursue these goals through "standard consumer packages" like mass media. Riesman also claimed that work and leisure have become fused in the business and professional world, but work nevertheless maintains its function as a psychological stabilizer. Havighurst (1957; 1961) investigated the meanings of leisure and concluded that personality is a more significant factor in determining the meaning which people find in their favorite leisure activities than age, sex or social class. In a similar vein, Neumeyer and Neumeyer (1949) had earlier suggested that while personality characteristics have an important bearing on recreational choices, leisure pursuits also affect personality. They studied various group aspects of recreation such as the nature of recreation groups, social processes involved in recreation, and the relationship between crowding and leisure behavior. Somewhat consistent with the above findings, Anderson (1961) proposed and Gerstl (1963) reported data indicating that life style associated with certain occupations, rather than the social class itself, is instrumental in affecting leisure behavior.

Other sociologically oriented studies deal with the functions of leisure. Based upon Parsons' theory of action (1951), Gross (1963) hypothesized that leisure had four major functions: pattern-maintenance and tension-management, adaptation, goal-attainment, and integration. Dumazedier (1967), in turn, presented the functions of leisure as follows: (1) relaxation and diversion, (2) social participation and entertainment, (3) personal development and learning. Mead (1958), a cultural anthropologist, emphasized the family environment for leisure activity and suggested that as home life and interpersonal relations become the center of the stage for leisure, work becomes secondary to leisure in its contribution to personal development. Finally, Huizinga (1949) expressed the ultimate necessity and function of leisure by concluding that "real civilization cannot exist in the absence of a certain play-element." This is why play, leisure, and recreation have had (and will have) an irreplaceable role in the history of humankind.

The above citations, though not by any means exhaustive, illustrate a somewhat unexpected sociological perspective of leisure. That is, sociologists have more or less directly acknowledged that many of their standard variables (e.g., social class) are inadequate to explain leisure behavior, that personal and interpersonal factors have to be included in the analysis of leisure and recreation. It is particularly noteworthy that the effects of personality "systems" have been considered against the background of social environments and structures. Through their functional approach, sociologists also seem to offer motivational "systems" to account for leisure choices. This drift toward social psychology is nicely reflected by a recent development in which J. Kelly (1976), a leisure sociologist, decided to incorporate motivation (intrinsic vs. social) in his theoretical model of leisure following his empirical work.

summary

In sum, we examined the development of social psychological thinking of leisure among notable scientists. Surprisingly, only a few social psychologists have exhibited interest in applied aspects of their field. Some of them have touched briefly upon a relationship of industrial conflicts and work satisfaction with leisure or recreation (Allport, 1924; Krech and Crutchfield, 1948). In his important contribution, Patrick (1916) delineated the social origin and nature of relaxation. Sherif's (1936) analysis illustrated how social norms may influence leisure choices on the one hand, and behavior within a given leisure context on the other. Lewin's (1935) approach suggested the importance of studying the effects of personality and situational variables jointly, in a variety of leisure environments. Several authors stressed the significance of cultural and societal differences in leisure behavior (e.g., Roberts and Sutton-Smith, 1962). Psychologists have directed considerable attention to children's play behavior, particularly to the role of play in the child's cognitive development (e.g., Bruner, 1974), but they have to a large extent forgotten social aspects of play. The few sources that are available, however, point to the predominantly social nature of play and the significance of play for social growth. Finally, we took notice of the fact that several sociologists have emphasized individual and interpersonal functions of leisure behavior. In conclusion, this survey of earlier work unquestionably demonstrates the lack of the *systematic* study of leisure behavior from the social psychological perspective, but simultaneously points out the need for such analysis.

social psychological thinking among leisure scientists

In this last section we will briefly examine the extent to which various leisure authors have attempted to explain leisure behavior in social psychological terms. Characteristically, many influential texts have included chapters dealing with the effects of play and leisure on the individual in general and on his personality development in particular. But very little space has been devoted to the discussion of social forces related to leisure participation, or social influence processes observed in various leisure environments.

Curtis (1924) stressed educational values of play and argued that virtues by far outweigh the possible vices in play. Play is basically good for children because, among other things, it develops a sense of justice, honesty, the will, sportsmanship, and team work. It also provides training in judgment and decision-making, and prepares for practical life. In a similar vein, Bowen and Mitchell (1930) contended that the impact of play upon character formation cannot be overestimated, the effects being three-fold: play develops (1) individualistic qualities (courage, ingenuity, initiative, perseverance, self-control, ambition, aggressiveness, etc.), (2) socially desirable qualities such as kindness, friendliness, justice, honesty, sociability, generosity and tolerance, and (3) civic qualities like cooperation, obedience, morality, loyalty and freedom. Bowen and Mitchell discussed briefly differences according to sex in children's interests in various play activities, and concluded these differences to be attributable to both ''instinctive tendencies'' and social influences (e.g., teachers).

Nash (1960), a philosopher, subscribed to the ''hereditary urges and drives'' in explaining the child's playful responses and denounced adult pressures and rewards as methods of enticing the child to take part in an activity. On the other hand, he acknowledged human vulnerability to social influences as reflected by such popular forms of leisure as spectator entertainment. Nash argued that since children's and adolescents' world is mechanized and routinized, their need for exploratory, investigative and manipulative experiences is hampered. As a result, the young may become passive reactors to their environment, being socialized into passive leisure consumers and spectators. He further emphasized the social nature of the individual, positing that people have a need to belong to a group and feel needed, trusted and wanted. Recreational activities can provide such group spirit and feeling of loyalty to some group. He hypothesized that this feeling of belonging is a distinguishing characteristic of ''happy people.''

In 1958, Larrabee and Meyersohn edited a book of readings called *Mass Leisure*. Although their collection contained many philosophical and ideological articles, the volume nevertheless made some social psychological contributions. The papers on the following topics illustrate this: sex as play (Foote, 1958), the motivational pattern of drinking (Riley, Marden, and Lifshitz, 1958), and voluntary association memberships of American adults (Wright and Hyman, 1958). In 1960, two important texts were published. Brightbill's (1960) book was a predominantly philosophical statement of leisure and recreation, but it also discussed briefly the relationship between leisure and personality, particularly the impact of leisure upon personality formation. Kaplan (1960), on the other hand, studied leisure behavior in relation to social and cultural factors from the sociological perspective more systematically. He suggested that a person's leisure-time action originates in one of the three sources, or their combination: (1) the group to which he belongs, (2) the culture into which he is born and (3) his individual limitations and potentials, that is, personality. Regardless of this seemingly social psychological approach, Kaplan emphasized the inseparable nature of personality and the group, thereby stressing the social role and the group as a basic unit in the analysis of leisure behavior.

Sapora and Mitchell (1961) underscored the self-expressive function of play and recreation and contended that the tendency to seek self-expression in leisure is the result of learned responses, "social conditioning." Miller and Robinson (1963) were mainly concerned with the historical analysis of leisure. But they also dealt with the contributions of leisure and recreation to the gratification of basic human needs (biological, psychological, social), noting the importance of social psychology to the field of leisure and recreation in general: "Recreation methodology should be undergirded by the contribution of social psychology, including such concepts as the group needs of the individual, the patterns and dynamics of group interaction" (p. 424). More recently, when proposing that the "new frontier is the exploration of inner space," Gray (1972) made a similar but indirect appeal for the social psychological analysis of recreation. He hypothesized that psychologically rewarding recreational experiences reinforce one's positive self-image.

Despite these encouraging demands for social psychological analysis, little systematic work has materialized. This state of affairs is clearly represented by Kraus' (1971) much-used text on the foundations of recreation and leisure. In his book, he devoted only about 20 of some 500 pages to the discussion of psychological functions and social aspects of play and recreation. This treatment is surprising in the sense that recreation and leisure as a professional field are supposed to be concerned with the enhancement of psychological well-being for various groups of individuals. Instead of the systematic and extensive study of psychological antecedents and consequences of leisure behavior, the recreation curricula throughout the country comprise such courses as parks and recreation facility management. It seems to be more important to know where volleyball nets are put after a game than to know how to best facilitate enjoyable social interaction and feelings of competence during the game! Some seem to think that it is more important to build recreation centers and programs and later worry about people, rather than vice versa. Despite this criticism, however, we should credit earlier writers with at least recognizing the importance of social psychological forces in recreation experiences. But this recognition does not entitle us to a better conclusion than that made by Glasser (1970), a philosopher: "the use of increasing leisure involves growing personal and social perplexity."

Though leisure philosophers and textbook writers have not provided certain answers, leisure researchers have begun recently to improve the situation to some extent. In this respect the establishment of the *Journal of Leisure Research* in 1969 may be considered the turning point. Even though the *Journal* has not been psychologically oriented, it nevertheless has provided an outlet for contributions in this area. The early studies focused on such social psychological concepts as leisure attitudes (Neulinger and Breit, 1969, 1971; Heberlein, 1973), group cohesiveness (West and Merriam, 1970), psychological stability (Bishop, 1970), perception (Mercer, 1971), environmental forces (Witt and Bishop, 1970; Knopp, 1972), recreational need (Mercer, 1973) and socialization (Kelly, 1974). Of course, social psychological leisure research has also been published in other journals, as shown by Bishop and Witt's (1970) now classic study on the joint influence of personality and environment on leisure behavior and Bishop and

Chace's (1971) important investigation on the effects of parental conceptual systems and home play environment on children's potential creativity. Interest and growth of leisure research was recently reinforced by the establishment of the second research journal of the field, *Leisure Sciences*.

In sum, most leisure philosophers and writers have acknowledged the importance of social psychological variables in leisure behavior and vice versa. Systematic theorizing regarding the relationship between social processes and leisure behavior, however, is conspicuously absent. Much emphasis has been placed upon the potentially positive effects of recreation experiences on personality development, but empirical testing of this hypothesis remains to be done. Examples of recent research attempts include such topics as the role of attitudes in leisure behavior, and the relationship between leisure participation and interpersonal relations, group cohesiveness, self-concept and children's creativity. Among other things, the relative contributions of personality and environmental factors to leisure choices have been subjected to vigorous empirical testing.

---

summary

The historical antecedents of the emerging field were first examined in the light of the development of general social psychology. Next, the intellectual roots of the field were looked at from three different points of view: (1) what philosophers have said about leisure and its relation to social behavior, (2) what psychologists and social psychologists have written about leisure and recreation behavior, and (3) how leisure scientists have treated social psychological aspects of leisure and recreation. It appears that many philosophers have viewed leisure as a unique opportunity to improve both intrapersonal and interpersonal behavior. Some of them, especially Aristotle and Marx, have proceeded to suggest that leisure is the only avenue of approach in seeking to understand the individual's true nature and existence. In addition to describing what philosophers have said about leisure, we presented a social psychological account of the use and misuse of leisure in the history of humankind, particularly in relation to the ancient Greeks and Romans. This explanation focused on the consequences of intrinsically and extrinsically motivated leisure behavior.

Not surprisingly, general social psychologists have explicitly paid little attention to leisure and recreation. On the other hand, some authors have briefly and implicitly noted the role of social psychology in explaining leisure behavior. These included Patrick's discussion of the social origin and nature of relaxation, Sherif's analysis of social norms and their possible impact upon leisure choices, and Lewin's personality-times-environment approach to accounting for human behavior. While numerous psychologists have studied children's play, their main interest has centered around the effects of play on child development, particularly on cognitive development. The social aspects of play have received considerably less attention from scholars. Historically, this one-sided approach is expected, for philosophers have frequently speculated about the positive influences of play on the child's personality formation. Sociologically oriented authors have also offered some insights into the social psychological nature of leisure and recreation. Especially, they have stressed the relationships between personality systems and social roles on the one hand, and various groups and social structures on the other.

Finally, we took notice of the interest of leisure scientists in the social and psychological aspects of leisure. Although allusions to social psychological thinking can be found in almost all textbooks of leisure, this recognition has hardly been more than lip service to the emerging field. In the few pages that have been devoted to our approach, the possible positive and negative effects of play and recreation on personality development have become an overwhelming concern among leisure authors. From the social psychological standpoint, however, the situation has significantly improved in recent years, owing to the efforts of several leisure researchers. Such important aspects of leisure behavior as attitudes, needs, interpersonal relations, and group affiliation have finally been subjected to scientific investigation. As a result, our understanding of the antecedents and consequences of leisure behavior has improved.

Although, as expected, the review of the historical antecedents revealed a lack of systematic analysis of leisure and recreation from the social psychological standpoint, it nevertheless indicated that many relevant scientific studies are available. What is needed, therefore, is to combine and integrate in one place, the piecemeal information scattered throughout textbooks and journals. Our attempt to systematically analyze leisure and recreation from this "new" perspective will begin with a review of research methodology in social psychological inquiry.

tools of social psychological inquiry

part 3

nature of social psychological analysis   3

To grasp the character of social psychological research it is perhaps better to first start by answering the question of why research is needed in general. In earlier pages it was suggested that the objective of social psychological analysis of leisure and recreation is to help understand individual leisure behavior in relation to other individuals, groups, and cultures. Such understanding calls for knowledge of social influence phenomena occurring in a wide range of leisure environments. The acquisition of such knowledge in turn requires the use of various methods and techniques.

why should we conduct research?

Hollander (1971) suggested that there have been three distinct stages in obtaining knowledge about social behavior. The first, *social philosophy,* is the oldest and dominated the investigation till the 19th century. Hollander maintained that social philosophy can be characterized by speculation, conjecture, and rationalization on the one hand, and by the absence of systematic collection of factual information on the other. It exclusively "relies on the power of thought apart from testable data." The next stage, *social empiricism,* was the predominant approach in such knowledge seeking in the 19th century. Systematic data-gathering, which is the distinguishing criterion of this state, "goes beyond speculation and conjecture," because it provides factual information of people's behavior patterns. Finding out how many people participate in given leisure activities and for how many hours (Szalai, 1973) is an example of simple polling procedures characteristic of social empiricism. The third stage, *social analysis,* is the product of the 20th century. While social empiricism aims at describing behavior, social analysis looks below the surface, probing why people behave as they do. Social analysis is best represented by the studies that are directed to verification of underlying relationships between variables. In so doing, this type of research strives to test and revise existing theories.

social analysis needed

Where does the study of leisure and recreation stand in terms of these stages? It appears that most discussions of leisure can best be described as "social philosophy," because speculation and conjecture have been the main tools used by scholars in this field. In the 1960s, however, "social empiricism" entered the field of leisure studies through the popular time-budget studies and other simple polling techniques. Nevertheless, social philosophy still seems to dominate the field. This is convincingly illustrated by the accumulated knowledge available in various subfields of leisure studies, with therapeutic recreation as a prime example. Regardless of numerous textbooks published, no single study has been carried out to test the most fundamental assumption of therapeutic recreation: what psychological effect does "therapeutic" recreation have on an individual? Under what conditions and for what type of people are these effects more likely to be positive than negative? Instead of systematic gathering of data, leisure authors working in this area continue to rely on speculation and conjecture when attempting to answer these fundamental questions.

If one agrees that "social philosophy" presently dominates leisure studies, one should then realize that this approach cannot be very helpful in understanding leisure behavior. Social philosophy simply formulates new phrases and new wordings of the same phenomena, with the consequence that leisure writers are only putting new labels on old bottles. Social philosophy not only fails to increase understanding of leisure and recreation but becomes counter-productive, as illustrated by the recent dispute of whether "therapeutic recreation" or "recreation therapy" is the proper wording. It is for this reason that leisure research is needed. While the systematic gathering of data is badly needed, specialists in this field should not settle for descriptive information (social empiricism) alone. The systematic collection of data should be testing the underlying relationship between variables (social analysis). To avoid any misunderstanding, it should be stated that this does not necessitate the exclusion of social philosophy. But it is here asserted that social philosophy has dominated knowledge seeking too long, perhaps at the expense of social empiricism and social analysis, thereby hindering the scientific analysis of leisure behavior. When properly used, social philosophy can stimulate and even guide social empiricism and analysis, but it can never be the primary instrument for explaining leisure behavior. Since the purpose of social psychology is to help *explain* social leisure behavior, researchers cannot attain this objective by the tools of social philosophy nor by those of social empiricism.

common sense is insufficient

The above discussion implies that research is only possible in the stages of social empiricism and social analysis, particularly in the latter. This follows because "scientific research is systematic, controlled, empirical, and critical investigation of hypothetical propositions about the presumed relations among natural phenomena" (Kerlinger, 1973, p. 11). Research is systematic and controlled in the sense that it rules out competing explanations for one and the same phenomenon, thereby increasing other investigators' confidence in the findings. Research is empirical when subjective beliefs, hypotheses and theories are tested "against objective reality." Through systematic and controlled testing, scientific research

Tools of Social Psychological Inquiry

makes explicit its reasons for ruling out the rival explanations. Being critical of itself, research is constantly looking for alternatives and discovering new ones. This is why common sense, and speculation based on it (social philosophy), is insufficient for enhancing understanding of leisure behavior.

The difficulty with common sense is that it "limits us to the familiar" (Selltiz, Wrightsman and Cook, 1976). For example, it is commonly stated that the disapproval of the United States entry into the Viet Nam war came most frequently from the youth because of their general tendency to rebel and by reason of their numerous demonstrations. However, scientific research (see Selltiz, *et al.,* 1976) has shown that this "common sense" is wrong; in fact, the youth supported the war more extensively than other age groups. This is surprising because the public was frequently exposed to antiwar demonstrations via the mass media and perhaps because most friends or acquaintances did not *seem* to support the war. In these and many other cases, common sense is based upon a "unrepresentative minority" which gives a false picture of objective reality. Thus, it is clear that social philosophy as a method of knowing may be not only insufficient but above all, distorting.

Besides the above fundamental need for scientific research, there are other reasons to advocate the "social analysis" approach in leisure studies. One of them, closely related to the above one, is the application of scientific findings to implementing recreation programs. If, for example, the recreational needs of a given population are known, the community is better able to provide satisfying leisure services to them. Similarly, if it is known how leisure activities can replace each other with minimal loss in satisfaction, leaders can plan recreational programs which are sound and substantial. In addition to improving the actual delivery of leisure services, research findings can provide relevant information for policy advice and decision-making for those who are directly responsible for the development of the profession, as well as for those at the top level of the federal government who are concerned with improving the quality of life. other reasons

Other reasons for scientific research include the position in the academic world. To survive as an academic field, scholars must supply evidence to the effect that their methods of investigation are valid and reliable rather than "soft." This becomes increasingly important in obtaining grants from sources inside and outside academic institutions. Improving the quality of investigative methodology also has a positive side-effect, in that it can improve the image and position of our field in the scientific and academic community in general. Social philosophy will not succeed in this task.

Scientific research, if applied to leisure studies, has another important positive concomitant. As the world is becoming more and more scientific, and as people are therefore, to an increasing extent, becoming consumers of research results, they have to be familiar with the research process. It is essential to understand where research findings come from, how reliable they are and how critical one should be about them. If students comprehend this process reasonably well, then, rather than by relying entirely on somebody else's interpretation, they may be able to read research reports and evaluate the reported findings critically. Consequently, they are much better equipped to live in a scientific world.

Understanding the research process is also useful because it provides people with powerful conceptual tools, whether or not they are researchers. Indeed, knowledge of experimental methods and designs (to be discussed later) is very applicable in the course of everyday living and in finding solutions to many daily problems. Scientific research is more than research; it is a way of thinking. As such it is also very appealing intellectually. If nothing else, understanding of research process teaches students to be careful not to make sweeping generalizations about human behavior. This in itself is likely to increase patience and understanding in interpersonal encounters.

nature of social psychological research

causality

Social psychological research can perhaps best be characterized by "social analysis." Its objective is to find out the "whys" of social behavior rather than simply describing it. In doing so, social psychologists strive to present their findings in terms of cause and effect: "A causes B" or "B is the consequence of A." To be able to make these types of statements, a researcher must provide evidence of the following kind:

1. The variables in question must be shown to vary together in some systematic fashion.
2. There must be some basis for inferring that the hypothesized consequence did not precede the hypothesized antecedent.
3. There must be evidence that rules out an interpretation in terms of other determining conditions (Secord and Backman, 1964).

The task of social psychologists is to meet these three criteria as fully as possible, regardless of the type of research methods used. It is obvious that this may be difficult. In fact, it is seldom that all of these requirements are satisfactorily taken into account in one study. The *well-conducted* experiment, strictly speaking, is the only major method to permit unambiguous causal statements about the relationship between variables. For this reason it is easy to understand why social psychological research is predominantly experimental in nature. Levine (1976) reported that about 90% of all social psychological studies are experiments.

scientific method

The prevalence of experiments reflects social psychologists' strong belief in the scientific method. What do they specifically mean by scientific method? First of all, it implies an iteration between theory and practice (Box, 1976). Since the mere theoretical statements on the one hand and the undirected accumulation of practical facts on the other are insufficient alone to advance our knowledge, the scientist is engaged in a continuous process of inductive and deductive reasoning. The process starts with current practices, data, or facts, from which hypotheses and/or theories are derived (induction). Once a hypothesis/theory is built, the researcher has to deduce its consequences (deduction) so that the hypothesis can be tested against objective reality. Following the empirical test, the scientist again has to make an inductive judgment as to whether the original hypothesis

Figure 1   Research process (Reprinted by permission from American Statistical Association and G.E.P. Box, "Science and Statistics." *Journal of the American Statistical Association,* 1976, 71, 791–799).

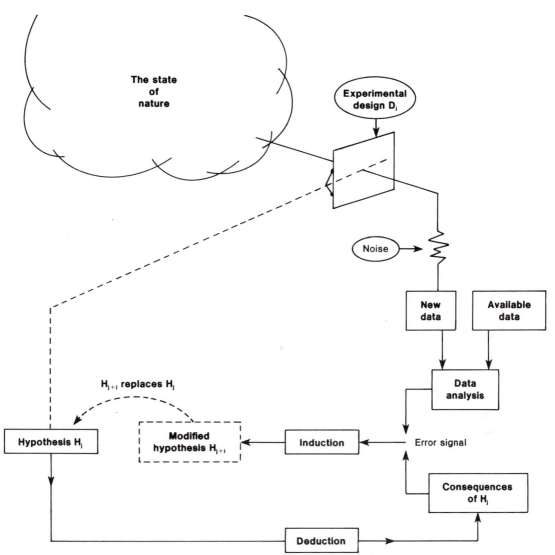

should be retained or modified. If the original hypothesis is modified, the researcher again has to deduce the consequences of this "new" hypothesis and test it empirically. If the data support the original hypothesis fully, the process can then continue by deducing new consequences of the same hypothesis and testing them, or the confirmed hypothesis can be used as a basis for generating totally new hypotheses (and deducing their consequences) about the "true state of nature." This process (Box, 1976) is illustrated in figure 1.

Better to understand this aspect of the scientific method, one may use an example. Based upon our daily observations, a person may hypothesize that women's attitudes toward leisure are more positive than men's. To test this hypothesis, its consequences have to be deduced. In other words, given the truth of the hypothesis, what does it specifically imply? To operationalize the hypothesis, for example, one may propose that women's liking of arts and crafts as well as volleyball is greater than that of men. This could be tested by taking a sample of college students. Even if the hypothesis turned out to be correct, it would not necessarily be the end of research dealing with the differences between women's and men's attitudes toward leisure. This follows because new and different consequences can be deduced from the original hypothesis. In this example, other deduced consequences of the hypothesis could include different leisure activities, different attitude scales, and different populations.

The above illuminates the scientific method at the general level and demonstrates that inductive and deductive reasoning is inexplicably interwoven in the research process. It also highlights some of the main features of the scientific method. These are (Anderson, 1966): (1) operational definitions of constructs and variables; e.g., attitude may be operationalized by subjects' response to a given question, (2) controlled observations and empirical data, that is, the statements of a researcher are exclusively justified by his observations regarding variables in question, (3) generality and repeated observations, meaning that the statements are not limited to a narrow class of things and showing that the statements based upon a sample can be generalized to the entire population in question. These principles help researchers maximize the objectivity of the scientific method and therefore put them in sharp contrast with philosophers and other intellectual colleagues. Total objectivity, of course, will hardly ever be reached as long as human beings conduct behavioral research.

In sum, social psychologists attempt to plan their studies in such a way that the effects of extraneous variables are minimized. If they are successful in this, they can conclude with confidence that the experimental variables or treatments indeed make a difference in the study (Campbell and Stanley, 1966). The *internal validity* will then be high. At the same time, social psychologists also strive to maximize the representative character of their findings and conclusions (i.e., *external validity*). There, however, is a trade-off between internal and external validity. That is, when one is high the other is low. Well-designed studies (experiments) conducted in a laboratory environment generally have a high internal validity but poor external validity, especially because of the frequent use of volunteer college students as subjects. When the social psychologist leaves the laboratory to carry out his studies in the field, internal validity will decrease but external validity will improve. Field studies are usually carried out on more "realistic" subjects in more "realistic" settings, but with loss in control over influencing variables. Since most of the social psychological research uses university students in laboratory settings, it is reasonable to suggest that such research has low external but high internal validity.

Although the scientific method emphasizes the well-designed and carefully controlled collection of data, it does not reject theory in social psychological inquiry. As was noted earlier, theory is as indispensible as empirical data in the research process. To avoid the haphazard accumulation of facts, social psychologists build, test, and modify theories. Theories are sought and needed because they can provide a systematic, integrated, and concise view of interrelationships among variables. Theories are used as instruments for summarizing, describing, and explaining phenomena about social behavior (Marx, 1971).

**theory-building
and theory-testing**

Despite variations in definitions, most scientists (e.g., Kerlinger, 1973; Marx, 1971) agree that a theory consists of a nexus of explanatory statements about observed and inferred relationships among conceptual variables. Besides summarizing and describing, this network of explanatory principles provides an account of the psychological mechanisms presumed to underlie such relationships (Marx, 1971). Festinger's theory of social comparison processes (1954) and that of cognitive dissonance (1957) serve as examples of theory construction in social psychology. Both theories contain a set of several explanatory propositions about how human behavior is motivated by a social need to compare one's abilities and opinions, as well as by a need to reduce cognitive dissonance. In his social comparison theory, for example, Festinger hypothesized that (among other things) a person has a desire to possess correct opinions about the world and to make an accurate evaluation of his abilities. Festinger related this to other propositions, by suggesting that given a range of possible persons for comparison, someone whose ability or opinion is close to one's own will be selected for comparison.

An important function of theory is that it provides a framework for empirical research. Therefore, one way to describe social psychological investigation is to characterize it as theory-testing. Since it is almost impossible to test the whole theory by one study (depending on the scope of the theory), it may then be more appropriate to define social psychological research as hypothesis-testing. A hypothesis represents only a segment of theory and constitutes an explanatory statement which specifies the relationship(s) between variables. Given a theory, the social psychologist begins his research by deriving a hypothesis which has clear implications for empirical testing. For example, if Festinger's social comparison theory is true, a person who plays tennis during his free-time is more likely to compare his tennis skills to those of other individuals who are in his "category" than to Bjorn Borg's (Wimbledon champion) ability. That is, he is likely to choose to play tennis with individuals who are close to his ability level.

The theory-testing is a continuous process. It involves the repeated comparison of the predicted relationships with the results of controlled observations. A theory is like a well from which water is continuously drawn for a crowd of people. The well is better, the longer it can supply water and the more people it can satisfy. Sooner or later, however, the well will run dry. A new well which can satisfy the need for water of a greater number of people for a longer period of time must then be found. The same with the theory. The more the research fails to discredit the hypotheses derived from a theory, the better and the more adequate to explain human social behavior is the theory. Ultimately, however, somebody will succeed in disconfirming certain facets of the theory. As a consequence, the old theory has to be expanded to incorporate all the past findings *and* the otherwise unaccounted phenomena. The new theory will explain a wider range of social behavior with better accuracy. Because human beings and their world have always changed (slowly or rapidly) and continue to change, so also will theories about human social behavior. Thus, social psychologists' task, theory-testing, is never-ending.

How wide then is the scope of social psychological theories? This question has to be answered in the light of the historical record. Crano and Brewer (1973) argued that social psychological theories are quite limited in range, often focusing upon a narrow aspect of social behavior. An example is Zajonc's (1965) popular theory of social facilitation. The basic tenet of this theory posits that the presence of others impairs human performance in the learning stage, but improves it once the task has been learned. Crano and Brewer suggested that such mini-theories reflect the developmental phase of the field. Small-scale theory construction tends to dominate the initial stages of growth of any scientific field; accordingly, social psychology may still be too young a discipline to have produced comprehensive theories. These writers also contended that the progress takes place in cycles. That is, the accumulation of data finally reaches the point where the theory is unable to reconcile all the findings. Research continues, though often no longer guided by the theory, until a breakthrough is achieved and a new theoretical paradigm developed.

This breakthrough yields a new and more complete theory, which then serves as a basis of hypothesis-testing until another breakthrough emerges. There are reasons to believe that social psychology is on the verge of making its first breakthrough. As noted earlier, cognitive consistency and balance theories have had primary acceptance in the field, but they have also become increasingly inadequate to account for the mass of data associated with them. A new theoretical paradigm may be emerging. It can be characterized as one of information processing and attribution. Although it is premature to suggest that the breakthrough has been made, the probabilities have increased. What is badly needed now is more theoretical work and less emphasis on methodological concern, so that wide-ranging agreement on an integrating principle can be reached. The discussion of new directions in social psychology seems to echo this contention (cf. Allport, 1969; Gergen, 1973; McGuire, 1973; Sampson, 1977; Smith, 1972; Strickland, *et al.*, 1976).

basic versus applied research

Finally, the nature of social psychological research in terms of its social relevance is examined. Perhaps the most convenient way of distinguishing basic and applied research from one another is to compare their short-term and long-term gains. Accordingly, a given piece of research can be placed on a continuum (whose extreme poles are "basic" and "applied"), its exact location depending upon the immediate applicability of research outcomes at hand. If the findings

Tools of Social Psychological Inquiry

are relevant to resolving social problems, research may be classified as applied. But in the absence of immediate social relevance of the results, the category of "basic" is indicated. It follows from the above that only short-term gains can be expected if research is directed toward specific problems and phenomena of social behavior. Another consequence of the above principle is that socially relevant research must be utilized before it can be labeled *applied* (cf. Helmreich, 1975). On the other hand, it is not clear whether this position also necessitates the *successful* utilization of knowledge. In other words, research may have been directed to an important social concern but it may have failed to resolve the problem, or practitioners may have failed to apply it successfully.

Many social psychologists, however, agree that the distinction between applied and basic research is artificial and quite meaningless. Notably, one of these is Streufert (1973), the former editor of the *Journal of Applied Social Psychology*. He states that "applied social psychology includes all work which has potential or real relevance to applied problems." Thus, he includes experimentalists who bring real world problems to their laboratories as well as practitioners who utilize experimental methods and theories in solving their problems. Streufert (1973) even accepts the efforts of laboratory research if investigators only see their studies as providing the foundations for resolving some problems one day in the far future. Thus, social psychological research is anything from what is remotely to what is directly applicable. This general definition, however, creates many problems. Among them are the following: What type of research is "potentially relevant" to applied problems? Who is to determine whether or not research has this potential? And perhaps most important, what are the "applied problems" and who defines them? The more vague the definition, the more difficult it is to characterize *bona fide* applied research, and the easier to justify all research as "basic."

social psychologists
are "basic"
researchers

In the light of the primary objective of seeking to explain and understand human social behavior, it is not surprising that social psychologists have been principally concerned with basic research. They seem to contend that research which is directed toward investigating general principles of human social behavior will in the future automatically be applicable to important social issues. This reasoning is based upon a wide-spread assumption that resolving social problems calls for understanding of the fundamental causes of human social behavior. But to determine the underlying cause(s), they argue, is possible only by basic research. If so, basic research will ultimately provide a better explanation of the causes of social behavior than "narrowly" focused applied research. Therefore, basic research, rather than applied, is seen as inherently better qualified to resolve pressing social problems. This seems to follow Lewin's famous statement that nothing is more practical than a good theory, and it appears to justify all research as related to the search for the "good" theory.

That social psychological research is predominantly "basic" is reflected by the copious use of experimental method and by the selection of research topics. As to the former, Helmreich (1975) reported that a majority of studies published in the *Journal of Applied Social Psychology* have used college students in laboratory experiments, and in more theoretically oriented journals such practice is even more common. This is not surprising in the view of the editor's (Streufert) philosophy of applied social psychology, as discussed above. The second aspect, research topics, also reveals social psychologists' overwhelming preference for basic research. Mini-theories have predominantly guided their research efforts. This is reflected by the popularity of such topics as risky-shift. (This "theory" states that people are more willing to take risks when they are in groups than when alone.) Mini-theories are "basic" in the sense that they do not address important social concerns.

why applied research is needed

As noted above, social psychologists justify their quest for basic knowledge by the presumed capability of "pure" research ultimately to reveal the underlying mechanisms of social behavior. Once the fundamental causal relationships are discovered, one is well equipped to suggest changes for the betterment of human social behavior, especially if the laws of social behavior are assumed to be transhistorical (Schlenker, 1974). Thus, no matter how trivial their research may seem, social psychologists can defend their efforts by claiming that any piece of research is a part of the broader line of systematic investigation to discover the transhistorical laws of social behavior. Thus, one study should not be subjected to criticism because it seems lacking in social relevance. If one stone cannot make a pyramid, one study cannot deal with broad social concerns. Consequently, they argue that the bulk of federal grants should be allocated to basic research. This proposition, however, can be challenged on several grounds.

First, many social concerns and problems are so pressing and critical that there is not time to await the formulation of comprehensive (basic) theories. The use of drugs and the spread of crime are certainly examples of a need for applied knowledge. Time is particularly important when it is recalled that social psychologists have been in the business for 70 years, without being able to construct more than mini-theories. At this pace, there is no reason to believe that basic research during the next 100 years will yield comprehensive theories capable of providing adequate answers to the above type of problems. To this should be added the fact that the world and human beings, and theories about human social behavior, are changing at an increasing pace (Proshansky, 1973).

Second, those who insist on the paramount importance of basic research imply that applied research cannot do justice to social concerns. While they may to some extent be right, applied research nevertheless can significantly alleviate social problems. Consider the case of a disease like cancer. Even though basic research has to reveal the underlying cause of this illness, applied researchers have invented numerous ways of alleviating human suffering which it causes. In so doing, they have increased the life expectancy for countless patients by many years. It is therefore not necessary, nor desirable, but rather dangerous, to wait for the outcome of basic research to solve social problems. Unquestionably, this applies to issues associated with social behavior as to those linked with medical problems. It therefore becomes important to direct applied research to the right targets so that researchers can avoid harmful accusations against them. In recent congressional hearings on violent behavior, for example, basic researchers were strongly criticized for "spending so much federal money to learn so little about violent crime." By avoiding basic social issues and pursuing research fads (Ring, 1967), "pure" researchers make it possible for laymen to accuse them of useless contributions to society. But perhaps more critically, the failure of basic research may make the public draw unfavorable conclusions as to the usefulness of research even in the area of applied problems, with the probable consequence of diminished funds.

Third, basic researchers often claim that their studies should not be criticized before completion for lack of social relevance. While this argument is correct to some extent, it is also one which can easily be misused. That is, every study can be justified by claiming that it is part of a larger undertaking which will ultimately provide the comprehensive and accurate explanation of social behavior. In fact, it often looks as if social psychologists are like pyramid builders who do not know why they are collecting their stones—for a pyramid or a trashpile—or what kinds of stones they should gather. Theories and methods of social psychologists frequently appear as awkward as those of the pyramid-builders who began their construction without a careful plan of how to move stones to the building site and how to put one stone on top of another. Basic researchers have a responsibility to show that their "stones" are not part of the process of piling up trash, that instead they constitute significant steps in expanding a theory of human social behavior. If cognitive dissonance, social facilitation, and "risky shift" are important links in such a theory, then it should be easy for basic researchers to show how they contribute to this theory-building. In the absence of such demonstrations, the patience and faith of the public and applied researchers in basic research, will rapidly wear thin.

The "fundamentalists" often criticize this view by pointing to the accidental nature of all great discoveries in physics. That is, researchers accidentally made discoveries which later turned out to be some of the important findings of the century and which greatly benefitted humankind. Basic researchers maintain that such discoveries would not be possible should applied research dominate the scientific community. Others contend that such discoveries have never been accidental, but rather part of systematic and well-planned investigations attempting to test and expand the existing theories. If these research workers had carried on their studies at random (i.e., whatever came to their mind and whatever was most convenient to carry out) and yet had achieved great results, their findings could be labeled accidental. It appears, however, that such scientific research does not exist. Therefore, basic research is, and must be, a systematic, long-term investigative program aimed at attaining certain scientific goals. Even if these goals were "applied" or socially relevant, "great" discoveries would be achieved.

Fourth, the importance of basic research can be challenged on the ground that its scientific studies tend to perpetuate the status quo. Basic research appears to lean on the assumption that human behavior is stable and relatively unchanged, as Leontiev (in Bronfenbrenner, 1977, p. 528) observed: "It seems to me that American researchers are constantly seeking to explain how the child came to be what he is; we in the USSR are striving to discover not how the child came to be what he is, but how he can become what he not yet is." Through its objective of describing and explaining phenomena, basic researchers assume a passive role in studying social behavior. Their interest seems to lie in the "now" and in factors that have led to the formation of the present behavior patterns. This approach is in sharp contrast to scientific endeavor which begins with a value judgment that some aspects of the current social behavior should be changed, and then continues with the investigation planned to determine the factors conducive to such change. For example, traditional "pure" social psychologists are likely to exert considerable effort to explain social cognitions and behaviors of the self-contained individual, whereas a more liberal social psychologist proceeds from the value judgment that self-contained individualism is not desirable in a highly interdependent society. Consequently, the latter directs his research efforts toward identifying variables which will make people condemn self-contained individualism, but value the importance of interdependence. In sum, basic research, for one thing, may be criticized because of its emphasis on the status quo and because of purposefully avoiding value judgments about social behavior.

For all the above and possibly for other reasons, social psychologists should pay more attention to applied aspects of social behavior. Research should be targeted to the priority areas, and basic social issues and problems should constantly be studied by competent investigators. By doing *research of research,* social psychologists should determine what the "basic issues and problems" are. This book proceeds from a fundamental value judgment that leisure is one of the basic social issues of today and tomorrow. It is contended that this is becoming an increasingly important societal concern. Therefore, more social psychologists should join in studying this "narrow" and "applied" aspect of social behavior, so that the quality of leisure experiences could be improved for both "normal" and "abnormal" populations. Leisure also provides important targets for those social psychologists who are concerned about insistent problems such as vandalism, juvenile delinquency, and drug abuse. There is no question whether or not the social psychological research of leisure is applied. It is "applied" because it is directed toward important social issues and concerns, as well as toward specific aspects of social behavior. Its social relevance can immediately be identified and therefore *can be* applied. Of course, who will actually utilize the obtained knowledge and how is another consideration. It is not the researchers' task to ensure that applied knowledge is actually utilized. Applied social psychologists have done their share if they have been able to provide highly relevant information.

summary

Social psychological research can be characterized as "social analysis." Rather than relying on speculation and conjecture (social philosophy) or descriptive data (social empiricism), social psychologists when testing the underlying relationships between variables are engaged in systematic data-gathering. They strive to probe beneath the surface of descriptive information, to determine the "whys" of human social cognitions, feelings and behavior. To reach this objective, researchers most frequently use the experimental method; more than 80 percent of all social psychological studies are experiments. Strictly speaking, a well-conducted experiment is the only method which allows such statements as "A causes B" or "B is the consequence of A." Since the overall goal is to explain the antecedents and consequences of social behavior, it is not surprising that non-experimental, correlational research is unappreciated and even rejected by social psychologists.

Because of its scientific approach, social psychological research emphasizes (1) operational definitions of constructs and variables, (2) controlled observations and empirical data, and (3) generalized and repeated observations. This is a continuous process of inductive and deductive reasoning, and theory-testing. To avoid the undirected or haphazard accumulation of facts, social psychologists build, test, and alter theories. These theories, however, are presently quite limited in scope, often focusing upon a narrow aspect of social behavior. Historically, the small-scale theory construction is typical of the initial stages in any scientific field.

Another reason why social psychologists are preoccupied with "mini-theories" is their unshakeable belief in "basic" research. They often contend that to resolve social problems one has to understand the deep-seated causes of human social behavior. Thus, they are more apt to develop general principles than to address important social concerns. In so doing they seek to justify any mini-theory research as search for a good and practical theory. This approach was criticized on several grounds. Among these are the following: many social problems are so pressing that they cannot wait for the formulation of grand theories; to a great extent applied research can alleviate social concerns without basic knowledge of underlying causes in question; and scientific theories often perpetuate the status quo and ignore social change. For these and other reasons, social psychologists should become more concerned about social relevance of their research.

4 types of methods in social psychological inquiry

phases of research

Conducting a scientifically acceptable study involves more than collecting data. While the method used in gathering information constitutes an inseparable part of the research process, it nevertheless is only one link in the chain of events. Most social psychological studies include all of the following stages:

1. Conceptualization of the research question and problems;
2. Formulation and use of research methods in acquiring data and information;
3. (Statistical) analysis of the collected data;
4. Interpretation of the findings for possible conclusions, generalizations and implications.

While the above sequence of steps may seem obvious, procedures are not always that simple. To give an example, let's consider a friend of mine who walked to my office the other day. I asked how his basketball study was coming along. He said that since the initial run of hundreds of t-tests (often called ''data snooping'') he has not done anything. But, he said he is planning to factor analyze the data in an effort to reduce the number of variables to a workable one! It is clear that this researcher had neglected the first step of the above sequence and consequently he will suffer from it.

Incidents like this are not rare, especially in correlational research. It is relatively easy to construct an instrument and ask people to answer countless questions, then throw the data into the standard computer programs such as factor analysis. Or, some researchers have access to data banks accumulated by survey research institutes. These data can be obtained and later analyzed without preconceived theoretical frameworks. This author contends, however, that research should always start with a clear conceptualization of the idea to be investigated. He even claims that nothing is more critical in the research process than the first stage. Indeed, poor conceptualization cannot be replaced by brilliant methodology or nationwide samples. A good researcher not only formulates his problem and hypotheses concisely on an *a priori* basis, but plans precisely how he will use the methods and statistical techniques for testing his conceptualization. If a study is well conceived before its implementation, the investigator can readily interpret and explain even unexpected findings. Assuming that we have satisfactorily conceptualized the problem to be studied, we next have to construct new methods or borrow old ones to collect data to test our conceptualization. The remaining portion of this chapter deals with the major methods of social psychological inquiry. The basic philosophical contention is that methodology and statistics are a tool rather than the master of a researcher (Signorelli, 1974).

According to the methods used, social psychological research may be divided into two major classes: experimental and non-experimental/correlational. As noted earlier, most studies in social psychology are based upon experiments. Thus, experimental methodology will be examined first.

major methods: experimental

The fundamental assumption of experimental research is that the investigator plays an active role. The researcher does not passively observe the naturally occurring events, but instead actively *creates* new situations, in which subjects' cognitions, feelings and behaviors are measured. The core of this approach is an *experimental design*. It lays out in a systematic way the variables to be manipulated and effects to be observed. The experimental design is a conceptual tool that the researcher can use in distinguishing independent variables from dependent ones, in describing experimental and control groups, and in statistically analyzing the data. An *independent variable* in pure experimental research is one which is manipulated by the researcher. It is a presumed cause, antecedent, the factor from which the effects are predicted. A *dependent variable,* on the other hand, is one which is a presumed effect, consequence, or the variable to which effects are predicted (Kerlinger, 1973). Before discussing the role of independent and dependent variables in the experimental design, it is useful to illustrate the difference between these two types of variables.

independent and dependent variables

Assume that one is interested in determining the effects of recreation experience on the self-concept of the physically disabled in a rehabilitation institution. The questions are: Does recreation participation have therapeutic effects on patients? If so, what kinds of programs are more conducive to the enhancement of patients' self-concepts? In asking these questions, the investigator is implicitly distinguishing between independent and dependent variables. That is, he expects changes in the clients' self-concept as a result of their participation in recreation programs. Recreational participation is therefore presumed to cause something, specifically, improvement in one's self-concept. So, the former is an independent and the latter is a dependent variable. Another example would be the case in which a leisure scientist wants to investigate the influence of toy structure on children's imaginative and creative free-play. The investigator asks: Do highly structured toys impair imagination and creativity in children's free-play, as compared to the effects of nonstructured toys? The independent variable consists of toy structure while creativity/imagination in free-play defines the dependent variable. Toy structure is presumed to cause changes in the degree of creativity of free-play. More specifically, this researcher might anticipate that the highly structured toys are more detrimental to the level of creativity in children's free-play than are nonstructured toys.

The latter example illustrates an important characteristic of the independent variable in experimental research: a number of levels (groups). Thus, the causal effect of the independent variable is determined by comparing the observed means of the dependent variable between the levels of the independent variable. For example, given a reliable and valid measure of creativity, we compare the mean creativity of those children who played with structured toys to that of the individuals who played with unstructured toys. If the difference is "significant," (this has to be determined by statistical tests), one can then conclude that besides being systematically related to children's creativity in free-play, toy structure is a *causal* determinant of creativity in free-play. Specifically, we can say (if these were the actual results) that highly structured toys impede creativity in children's play behavior, as compared to the unstructured ones.

Most experimental research utilizes two or three levels (groups) for each independent variable in a study. Of course, each independent variable could have almost an infinite number of levels in it (varying from extremely high to extremely low toy structure), but for theoretical as well as practical reasons social psychologists most frequently use two extremes (highs and lows) and/or the medium level. If one were to pinpoint, for practical purposes, the exact degree of structural complexity at which toys become detrimental to children's creativity, the observer obviously should employ many more levels than just two or three. But if the chief purpose is to understand how the variable "toy structure" is linked with the dependent variable, then the extremes will suffice.

There are several other things to be noted about the independent variable. First, most social psychological experiments are based upon two to four independent variables. It is very seldom that one encounters more than four of them in one study, but it is common for only two of them to be utilized. The selection of both independent and dependent variables for a given study should be dictated by theoretical considerations. Second, although an experiment is based upon the idea of the manipulated independent variable, many experiments also include so-called "subject" independent variables (e.g., sex, personality trait, and social class). In our earlier example, the effects of both toy structure and sex on children's creativity might have been investigated, that is, the influence of toy structure for boys and girls separately.

The reason social psychologists use so few independent variables as 2 to 4 stems from theoretical and practical considerations. These considerations are theoretical, in the sense that the prevalent theories in social psychology are mini-theories which do not lend themselves to multivariate studies. Also, the "true" experimental designs (Campbell and Stanley, 1966) upon which experiments are built, are directed toward dealing with only a few independent variables. These reasons are practical, in that it becomes very tedious to run an experiment which has more than 15 different treatment conditions (groups) built into it. For one thing, such an experiment becomes difficult in practice, because there should be at least ten subjects in each experimental condition. Where and how do you get 150 factory workers to come to your laboratory for experimentation? If an experimenter is able to lure workers once, he should not expect to carry on another experiment on them in the next five years! So, even though one often criticizes the use of university students as experimental subjects, the researcher should credit their willingness to participate. After all, social psychology, as we know it today, would not exist without university sophomores.

Since social psychologists frequently use three independent variables with two levels in each, one may have a typical experiment based upon a $2 \times 2 \times 2$ factorial design. Thus, there are eight experimental conditions to be observed by the investigator in such a study. Each factorial design in turn is based on an experimental design. Two most commonly used "true" designs (Campbell and Stanley, 1966) are the pretest-post-control-group design and the posttest-only-control-group design. The former can be expressed as follows:

$$R \quad 0_1 \quad X \quad 0_2 \quad \text{where}$$
$$R \quad 0_3 \qquad 0_4 \quad R = \text{random assignment}$$
$$X = \text{treatment}$$
$$0_1 \text{ and } 0_3 = \text{pretest measures}$$
$$0_2 \text{ and } 0_4 = \text{posttest measures}$$

In order to illustrate the use of this design, consider now the earlier example of recreation therapy. The purpose of the study was to determine the effects of recreation participation on the self-concept of the physically disabled. Using a group of subjects in a rehabilitation institution as well as a valid and reliable instrument of self-concept, the research worker can then run the experiment based upon the above design as follows. First, randomly (R) divide all the subjects into two groups: those who will participate in the experimental recreation program (i.e., they will get the "treatment," X) and those who will not (control group). Before beginning the experiment, test the self-concept of both experimental (0_1) and control (0_3) groups. Then, expose experimental subjects to the treatment for a period of about three weeks (i.e., these subjects participate regularly every day in the predetermined recreation program; the control group, on the other hand, does not participate in any recreation program during that time). At the conclusion of the treatment, measure the self-concept of the experimental group (0_2) and control group.(0_4). The effectiveness of the recreation program can subsequently be evaluated by comparing the change in scores of the two groups.

If the recreation program was effective in enhancing the patients' self-concept, there should be a "significant" difference in the measured self-concept between the time of 0_1 and 0_2. Of course, there should not be any differences between 0_3 and 0_4, or if there is one, the *change* score of the experimental group should be "significantly" greater than that of the control group. This is precisely why the control group is essential in this design. That is, if only the experimental group was considered, it would be impossible to determine whether the change from 0_1 to 0_2 was indeed due to the treatment (recreation program), or to some other factors such as "history" and "maturation" (Campbell and Stanley, 1966). The control group will provide a base value from which the rate of the change attributable to these intervening factors can be measured. Thus, if the recreation program does have a "significant" effect on patients' self-concept, the change from 0_1 to 0_2 should be much ("significantly") greater than that from 0_3 to 0_4. Assuming that history, maturation, and other factors did not have any effect on the dependent variable (self-concept, or specifically, the change score in the self-concept), we might have obtained the following results in our study (i.e., means of the four measurements):

$$50.0 \ (0_1) \quad X \quad 60.0 \ (0_2) \quad = \quad +10.0$$
$$50.0 \ (0_3) \quad \quad \quad 50.0 \ (0_4) \quad = \quad \underline{\quad 0.0}$$
$$10.0$$

Thus, the change in the patients' self-concept exclusively attributable to the recreation program was 10 units when using the given instrument. Whether this change is "significant" enough to warrant the conclusion about the effectiveness of our recreation program should be determined by statistical tests (e.g., t-test).

What kind of "factorial" design was the above study based upon? Since we have only one independent variable (recreation program) with two levels (participation vs. no participation), strictly speaking there was none. Of course, one could have extended the design to include another independent variable. If sex had been chosen to be the second variable, we would then have had a 2×2 factorial design. In other words, recreation program (participation vs. no participation) and sex (males vs. females) would be the independent variables and the change score in the self-concept the dependent variable. In sum, it appears that the factorial design is always expressed in terms of independent variables. The expression of the factorial design in journal articles immediately informs a reader how many independent variables the study had and how many levels (groups) each of them contained. For example, a $3 \times 3 \times 3$ design would indicate the presence of three independent variables, each one of them consisting of three levels, thereby yielding a total of 27 experimental conditions. Further study of the article would reveal what those variables specifically were and how they were operationalized in detail.

The second and perhaps the most popular experimental plan is the post-test-only-control-group design. It is depicted (Campbell and Stanley, 1966) as follows:

$$R \quad X \quad 0_1$$
$$R \quad \quad \ 0_2$$

As we can see, the subjects are randomly divided into two groups, one (experimental) having a treatment and another (control) having no treatment. There is no pretest for either group in this design, only the posttest. To avoid possible confusion we should point out that this design does not constitute the entire plan of an experiment. Like the pretest-posttest-control-group design, it constitutes the basis for the design of each manipulated independent variable at a time. For example, consider a 2 × 2 experiment in which the toy structure (structured vs. nonstructured) and the expectation of rewards (expected rewards vs. no expectation of rewards) are the independent variables. The degree of creativity in children's free-play is the dependent variable. The two independent variables either have a "treatment" (structured toys and expected rewards) or they do not (unstructured toys and no expected rewards). Subjects are randomly assigned to all four conditions, and tested only at the end of the experimental session.

The factorial design is conventionally depicted in the form of a diagram. The above design (2 × 2) can be presented as in figure 2. Thus, the subjects (say, 80) would be randomly assigned to one of the above conditions, with 20 subjects placed in each cell. The experimental session for each cell could last 45 minutes, each subject being tested individually. In the first situation, a child would play with structured toys and with the experimentally-induced expectation that he would receive ten candies (extrinsic reward) at the conclusion of 45 minutes. In the second situation, a child would play with the same expectation as the children in the first situation but now with the unstructured toys (playdoh). The third group of children would play with the structured toys without any expectation of rewards. Finally, the fourth group would play without any expectations of rewards, and with unstructured toys.

To measure the degree of creativity, the subjects would be asked to come to the laboratory the next day and play at a playlike task for 15 minutes. The extent of creativity could be determined by observers' ratings of children's preferences for complexity, novelty, and combined use of the playlike task. The effects of

Figure 2   A graphic presentation of the 2 × 2 factorial design.

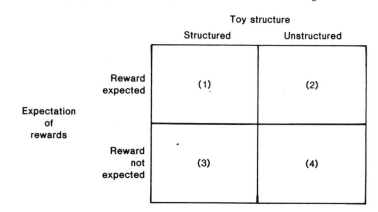

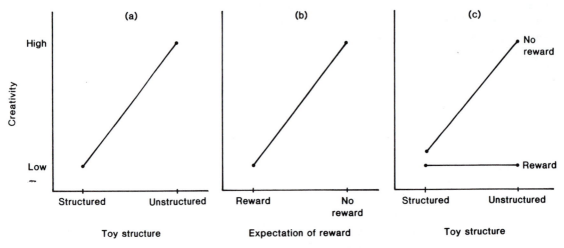

the two independent variables on the dependent variable could then be determined by comparing the means obtained for the groups. Theoretically, the data might reveal that toy structure and expectation of reward contributed either independently or interactively to the manifestation of creativity in the subjects' subsequent play behavior. Figure 3 depicts the hypothetical results. The left-hand panel indicates that creativity is greater in the group who played with unstructured toys during the experimental session, than in the group who played with structured toys, irrespective of rewards. In a similar vein, the middle panel shows the "main" effect of reward expectation, independent of toy structure. The right-hand panel reveals the interaction effects of the two variables. In other words, unstructured toys enhanced creativity relative to structured toys, provided that no rewards were expected for playing with the unstructured toys. Thus, the use of rewards would be detrimental to children's creativity, especially when playing with unstructured toys.

To be sure, the above examples are simplified versions of experimental research. The actual execution of one study is a complicated and tedious endeavor. This discussion practically ignored the important decisions concerning the exact operationalization of the dependent variable, creativity. The purpose, however, was to emphasize the conceptual basis and design of an experiment. Like Kerlinger (1973), this writer believes that experimental thinking in the form of factorial designs is very helpful in clarifying one's conceptualization of almost any type of study. Many *non*experimental studies can and should be presented in terms of the factorial design. Such a study plan is useful not only for the conceptualization of independent and dependent variables, but also for showing how intervening variables have been dealt with in a study. In the earlier example there might have been theoretical or other reasons to be concerned about the confounding effects of social class on children's creativity. To control or to avoid such possibly intervening effects of social class, this variable might have been built into the factorial design (Kerlinger, 1973), thereby extending it to a $2 \times 2 \times 2$ (toy structure $\times$ reward $\times$ social class) design. Alternatively, one could have tested the effects of the two independent variables, using children from either high or low socio-economic background. Of course, the latter mechanism of control represents a more limited approach because the results can be generalized only to the level selected. That is, if children from the low socio-economic class alone are selected, one could subsequently generalize the results to children from this class only.

The earlier examples illuminate another typical feature of experimental research: most studies are conducted in the laboratory. Helmreich (1975) found that 84 percent of all research reports published in the leading journal of social psychology were laboratory experiments. Despite this predominance of the laboratory setting, a few field experiments have also been carried out. One of the best and most famous is the Robbers Cave Experiment (Sherif, *et al.*, 1961). These investigators were concerned with the antecedents and consequences of competitive (conflict) and cooperative behavior during three weeks of summer camp for boys. The experiment was conducted in three stages, in such a way that the first week was aimed at the formation of friendships, the second week at the introduction of intergroup conflict, and the third week at the resolution of this conflict.

field experiments

After the initial, spontaneous development of friendships, boys were divided into two groups and housed in separate cabins so that about two-thirds of one's best friends were placed in the other group. This quickly led to a new pattern of friendships and ingroup cohesiveness. To bring about intergroup conflict, the two groups were required to compete in a series of sport activities (e.g., tug-of-war). Winning was emphasized and prizes were awarded to the winning group. As hypothesized, negative out-group attitudes and stereotypes arose, and in-group solidarity increased. But the consequences were not only attitudinal. The defeated group (''the eagles'') in a tug-of-war context burned the winners' (''the rattlers'') flag, which in turn resulted in retaliation by the rattlers, eventually leading to one ''raid'' after another. These hostile and violent outbursts were a direct and spontaneous outgrowth of frustrations encountered in the intergroup sport competition. In the third stage, the investigators used various techniques and tasks to reduce the friction between the groups. Critical to this process was the introduction of a series of ''superordinate goals'' which could not be achieved by the efforts of one group alone. These goals included the fixing of a water tank, collecting funds to rent an expensive movie, and pulling a broken truck. The groups did cooperate to achieve the common goals. As a consequence, albeit not immediately, negative attitudes and stereotypes toward the out-group weakened and the state of intergroup conflict eventually disappeared —much to the relief of the investigators.

As the above example shows, field and laboratory experiments have the same characteristics, except that the former are carried out in more realistic situations. Like a laboratory experiment, a field experiment is based upon the investigator's creation and manipulation of one or more independent variables; and these variables often turn out to be more powerful than the same ones used in the laboratory. The fact that field experiments usually allow for the random assignment of subjects to the manipulated conditions guarantees relatively good control over the experimental situations. On the other hand, many variables cannot be manipulated, and randomization is not always possible in the field settings. Also, there is a greater chance for contaminating variables to intervene when the experiment is done in the field than when it is carried out in the laboratory. Despite an apparent lack of precision (and control to some extent), Kerlinger (1973) concluded that in studying complex social influence processes field experiments are more appropriate than the laboratory experiments, because of their greater flexibility and applicability to a wide range of social concerns. This conclusion is further justified by recent advances in the methodology of field experimentation (Cook and Campbell, 1976; Tunnell, 1977).

advantages versus disadvantages

To summarize the above discussion, some of the principal advantages and disadvantages of experimental research are considered next. The chief reason for the popularity of this method lies in its ability to provide unambiguous evidence about causation (Aronson and Carlsmith, 1969). Unlike correlation techniques, the experimental method provides the researcher with a unique possibility of complete control over situations and variables. This in turn enables the investigator to say X caused Y, not vice versa. Experimental control is chiefly realized by means of randomization. By randomly assigning subjects into various manipulated conditions, the experimenter can achieve better control over extraneous variables. Even though each subject brings unique characteristics to the experiment, these qualities are evenly distributed among all experimental conditions (cells) if the randomization is utilized correctly. This, however, is not possible if volunteers are used as subjects, because they differ substantially from nonvolunteers (Rosenthal and Rosnow, 1969). As discussed earlier, two other possibilities for exercising control are: (1) building into the design the variable thought to contaminate the results, or (2) selecting one homogeneous level of the confounding variable.

Experimental research is also advantageous because of its "operational strength" (Kerlinger, 1973). There is a high degree of specificity in the operational definition of the conceptual variables. Such precision, of course, permits firmer conclusions about the exact aspect of the variable that causes certain effects. For example, the experimenter interested in the motivational effects of success-failure feedback can systematically and precisely vary the levels of this variable in the laboratory and select any specific outcome ratio (from 0% to 100%) for scrutiny. The nonexperimentalist, on the other hand, has to take what is offered in natural situations and thus combine several individuals (or teams) with different win-loss ratios under the general rubric of success or failure. Operational strength is also desirable due to the possibilities it creates for exact and "constructive replications" (Lykken, 1968) of the original experiment. In sum, the experimental method is useful because it allows the investigator to exercise control over his variables.

But despite these inherent advantages, the experimental method is not without its problems. Perhaps the most frequently cited weakness is the artificiality of the experimental situation. In an effort to maximize control, the investigator often ends up operationally defining the variables in a manner which does not correspond to "real life." Many conceptual variables carry multiple meanings, of which the experimenter's operational definition is only one. The other aspect of this artificiality is what Aronson and Carlsmith (1969) call "mundane realism," that is, the extent to which the laboratory events occur in the "real world." The lower the mundane realism, the higher the artificiality and the less generalizable the results are. By lessening the impact of independent variables on subjects, the artificial nature of the experiment further reduces the representative character of the results. Unfortunately, the experimental control and operational strength (i.e., internal validity) are achieved to a major degree at the expense of external validity (i.e., generalizability and representativeness of the findings).

An experimental situation may create an additional distorting effect due to the "demand characteristics" (Orne, 1962) and experimenter effects (Rosenthal, 1966). Subjects may think that they have to be "good subjects" and may therefore try to do what the experimenter appears to want them to do. Finally, the experimental control is in part achieved at the expense of simplified social experiences. Critics often contend that human social behavior is complex, multi-determined, and cannot therefore adequately and justifiably be analyzed by a method that takes into account two to four variables at a time.

Another set of problems involved in experimental research stems from ethical considerations. To a varying degree every experiment utilizes deception procedures and conveys false information in dealing with subjects. That is, in concealing the actual purpose of the study, the experimenter has to lie. Another type of ethical problem arises when the experimental tasks are potentially harmful to participants psychologically, socially, or even physically. The classical example is a series of studies on obedience conducted by Milgram (1963, 1965). Subjects were asked to increase the intensity of electrical shocks (from "light" to "danger: severe shocks") to a person (confederate) every time his response was "incorrect" in the "learning" task. Despite the recipient's suffering (i.e., severe pain, pounding on the door, and finally becoming silent) the majority of subjects obeyed and increased the intensity even after the recipient had fallen silent. Of course, subjects did not know that nobody actually received those shocks. It is striking that subjects were willing to harm the "learner" even when there was reason to believe that he might have fainted or died due to the shocks given.

These dramatic effects, however, did not occur without psychological penalties; the experiment left scars on subjects—at least temporarily. Milgram reported that there was extreme loss of composure in subjects. As a result, they laughed nervously and uncontrollably, trembled, perspired, and stuttered. Not surprisingly, these effects raised ethical questions about how far the experimenter should go with experimental manipulations. Since the Milgram studies, the American Psychological Association has imposed rather stringent rules upon conducting experiments, and a federal law has been enacted to protect subjects' rights. Many ethical problems can be avoided by carefully debriefing subjects after the experiment, explaining the actual purpose and nature of the study. Evidently, ethical considerations limit the use of the experimental method more than that of nonexperimental or correlational method. For further discussion of this problem, see Aronson and Carlsmith, 1969; Carlsmith, Ellsworth and Aronson, 1976; Crano and Brewer, 1973.

major methods: nonexperimental/ correlational

Experimental and correlational methods differ from each other in one critical aspect: the latter represents ex post facto research while the former does not (Kerlinger, 1973). An investigation can be defined as ex post facto if the researcher is not able to exercise control over the independent variables. It is as though the investigator arrives at the scene after the independent variables have fallen into place, does not manipulate any of them, but makes observations afterwards and subsequently correlates the variables in question. This, of course, is completely opposite to experimental research.

The major weakness of post hoc research is that inferences concerning *causal* relationships between variables are not possible or are at best very limited. Strictly speaking, the nonexperimentalist can only say that X and Y are significantly related, but not whether X is causing Y or vice versa. For example, if we find that women have a more positive attitude toward leisure than do men, we should not immediately conclude that sex is a cause of the difference in leisure attitudes. Many environmental variables such as occupation and employment may be correlated with sex and therefore may be the actual causes of the sex difference in leisure attitudes. On the other hand, there are numerous situations where the causal relationship between two variables can go only one way (e.g., attitudes cannot be a cause of sex). In addition, recent advances in statistical techniques (analysis of covariance, cross-lagged correlations, and path analysis) have increased the validity of causal statements derived from post hoc data. Despite this progress, correlational research still remains handicapped with respect to causal inferences.

correlational designs

Earlier it was noted that the factorial design forms the basis of experimental conceptualization. But it was also noted that this is not restricted to experimental research alone. Many ex post facto studies can be presented in terms of factorial designs. Consider the example of the researcher who is interested in determining the relationship between the home environment and outdoor recreation participation. The investigator hypothesizes that the crowded character of home environment is significantly related to outdoor recreation; specifically, the hypothesis suggests that the number of children in the family is positively related, and the number of rooms is negatively correlated to the participation rate. Let it be assumed, for simplicity, that the researcher divided both independent variables into two levels—families with eight children versus one child, and families with extensive living space (five bedrooms) versus very limited living space (one bedroom), and then proceeds to test this 2×2 design by determining the frequency and pattern of outdoor recreation participation (dependent variable) of the four types of families. Obviously, the study is correlational because the independent variables are not manipulated by the investigator. As for the results, one might find on the one hand, that persons from the families with many children are more likely to participate in outdoor recreation than persons from the families with few or no children, and that persons from the families with little living space are more likely to participate than persons from the families with a lot of living space, on the other. But even if these conditions were real, variables other than those associated with the home environment could have caused outdoor recreation participation. This, however, does not invalidate the use of factorial designs as an approach to conceptualizing correlational research.

Another way of designing nonexperimental research is to use continuous variables and to correlate statistically the variables in question. [A correlation is a statistical index of association between two variables, ranging from the perfect positive $(+1.0)$ to the perfect negative (-1.0).] Although a correlation between two variables is expressed numerically at a time, one study may include many sets of such correlations. In this approach, the distinction between the independent and dependent variable becomes hazy, because the correlation simply indicates the strength between two variables, not the direction. As a result, there is no precise design for a study of this sort, except that a given number of variables is selected and then intercorrelated. For example, a researcher might be interested in studying the correlates of the perceived quality of life. Based upon past theoretical literature the investigator decides to select three variables assumed to be related to this variable, satisfaction with one's leisure, with work, and with personal income,—and then conducts the study by mailing to subjects a questionnaire planned to deal with the above four variables. Assuming that the instrument is valid and reliable, the hypothetical data could reveal a positive correlation between one's satisfaction with leisure and the perceived quality of life $(.50)$, suggesting that the more satisfied the person is with leisure, the better is the quality of life. A negative correlation $(-.50)$ between personal income and the quality of life would then indicate that the lower the personal income, the higher the quality of life. Finally, no correlation $(.00)$ between satisfaction with work and the quality of life would suggest that the two variables are unaffected by one another.

Although the above example is a simplified illustration of the use of this approach, it nevertheless demonstrates the main point, that is, the researcher collects data on numerous variables and then correlates them. Many examples of this design can be found in the literature (e.g., Schmitz-Scherzer and Strödel, 1971; Crandall, 1978). Investigators, however, do not usually stop their data analysis in "simple" correlations. One of the most popular methods of extending correlational analysis is to factor analyze data. An example might be a study in which subjects are asked to rate the importance of 40 reasons or considerations, as motives for their leisure participation. Since it is likely that these motives (variables) overlap, a researcher wants to determine their common characteristics or the basic dimensions underlying leisure motivation. For that purpose, factor analytical techniques can be used. The results of such analysis may reveal that four to five "factors" are sufficient to explain people's leisure motives. This result is plausible if many of the 40 reasons are to some extent intercorrelated (e.g., relaxation and "getting away from it all"). Thus, factor analysis would reduce overlapping between the variables and would make the explanation of leisure motivation more concise and complete.

Another extension of simple correlations which is often used is what might be called path analytic conceptualization. Unlike the general correlational or factor analytic approach, this design is based upon a preconceived causal analysis of the variables to be investigated. Again, the distinction between independent and dependent variables is crucial. An example will illustrate this. A researcher wants to determine the relationship between adult leisure participation and several social background variables, namely, youth participation, parental encouragement, and school friends' leisure participation. The following path analytic hypothesis may be formulated:

Figure 4   Path analytic conceptualization of determinants of adult leisure participation.

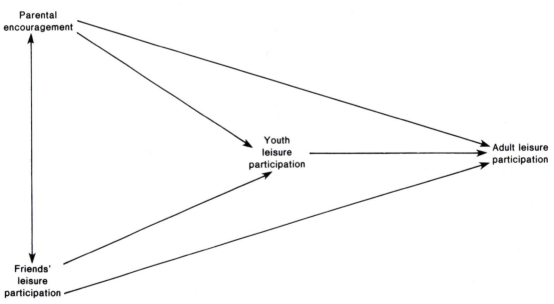

Tools of Social Psychological Inquiry

Leisure participation in youth, friends' leisure patterns, and parental encouragement have a *direct* effect on the rate of adult leisure participation; parental encouragement and friends' participation also have an *indirect* influence on adult leisure participation through their direct effect on youth participation. Conceptually and statistically, the testing of this overall hypothesis is divided into two classes. In the first case, the dependent variable is leisure participation in youth, and the independent variables consist of parental encouragement and friends' participation. In the second analysis, adult participation is the dependent variable, and youth participation, friends' participation, and parental encouragement comprise the independent variables. Note that this approach relies exlusively on one-way causal relationships between the variables, except in the case of the relation between parental encouragement and friends' participation.

The post hoc data for this type of study could be collected by various interview or questionnaire techniques. Once the data are available, the researcher proceeds to test the above hypotheses. Although the statistical analysis is beyond the scope of this book, we briefly note that "simple" correlations, though interesting, would not be sufficient in testing the above model. The researcher would have to determine by means of multiple regression analyses the "path coefficients" for each link between the variables. These coefficients would indicate whether or not the independent variables contributed significantly to the dependent measure, as well as their relative contributions. Path coefficients would allow causal inferences about the relationships between the variables, while simple ("zero-order correlations") correlation coefficients would not. A hypothetical result of the .50 path coefficient between youth and adult leisure participation would suggest that youth participation is an important factor in determining adult leisure participation. That is, if the person was active in leisure when young he is likely to be active in leisure when adult. Youth participation, therefore, would be a *causal* determinant of adult leisure participation. Examples of this type of study can be found in the literature (e.g., McPherson, 1976; Spreitzer and Snyder, 1976).

Another way of classifying nonexperimental studies is to group them according **types of methods** to types of methods used. Three major types of methods exist: field studies, surveys, and unobtrusive measures (Kerlinger, 1973; Webb, Campbell, Schwartz, and Sechrest, 1966; Wrightsman, 1972). These methods are general approaches rather than specific techniques of data collection. Field studies, for example, could be carried out by using various data-gathering techniques like interviews, questionnaires, objective tests and observation of behavior. For these specific strategies, the reader is referred to Kerlinger's (1973) and Selltiz', *et al.* (1976) texts, which are excellent sources. For the purpose of this book we focus on the aforementioned general methods and discuss field studies first.

Besides their ex post facto nature, *field studies* may be characterized as scientific inquiries that systematically explore and test relationships between variables. The word "field" implies that these studies are conducted in real life environmental situations like recreation centers, theaters and tennis courts. Although field studies are primarily concerned with social relevance, their main objective is not the representative character of the sample. Unlike surveys, field studies aim at in-depth analyses of social behavior in natural settings. This is usually achieved by thoroughly studying a few but potentially theoretically meaningful variables. Cialdini's, *et al.* (1976) investigation exemplifies field studies and their applicability to leisure-related problems. The investigators' purpose was to demonstrate that people have a tendency to publicly display their connection with others who are successful, "to bask in reflected glory." To test this hypothesis, the researchers covertly monitored the attire or garb of students enrolled in sections of introductory psychology courses every Monday following Saturday's collegiate football games. As predicted, students wore school-of-attendance apparel more after their university team's victories than after losses. In random telephone interviews (second study), subjects were asked to describe the outcome of their school's football team. As predicted, students exhibited a tendency to use "we" response more frequently following the successful Saturday in describing the team outcome than following an unsuccessful one. While the study clearly reveals its post hoc nature and thus its limitations in making causal inferences, it nevertheless provides new insights into the psychological antecedents and consequences of spectator sports as a form of leisure.

Surveys constitute the second major nonexperimental method in social psychological inquiry. Often, they deal with attitudes, beliefs, opinions and values, in short, what people think and do. Gallup's and Harris' nationwide polls are outstanding examples of such surveys. As noted above, surveys usually achieve great breadth but limited depth because they are designed to gather superficial information about many things, sometimes about hundreds of variables. Survey researchers are particularly concerned about the representative nature of their samples. Irrespective of how the population is defined, a sample(s) is drawn in such a way that the results are generalizable to the entire population. While the size of the population to be surveyed varies from one study to another, usually it is very large. As for the actual techniques of collecting data, personal interviews and mailed questionnaires are perhaps the two most often used. Telephone surveys are also relatively popular. For a detailed discussion of these techniques and their advantages and disadvantages, see Kerlinger (1973) and Selltiz, *et al.* (1976).

Surveys deal with descriptive information about relative frequencies, incidences, and distributions. In the area of leisure, a good example can be found in Szalai's (1973) monumental survey of actual time spent in various free-time activities. The survey provided a minute-by-minute account of everyday living-patterns of people from 12 different countries. The free-time usage was also classified by sex, age, and other variables. Similar studies are plentiful in the field (e.g., Burton, 1971); and it appears that surveys have been employed by leisure researchers more often than any other method. While the findings can be interesting, we contend, however, that they ordinarily are of little psychological value. For example, if people in Bulgaria spent 100 minutes per evening watching TV and people in the U.S. 200 minutes, so what? Such information does not tell us why they watch TV so much, with whom they watch, what psychological consequences this leisure expenditure has, etc. Furthermore, Bishop, Jeanrenaud and Lawson (1975) have shown that recall questionnaires yield information about people's leisure patterns similar to that revealed by tedious and cumbersome time-budget diaries. In sum, the major weakness of survey research appears to be its inability to penetrate the surface of descriptive information. On the other hand, it is possible that this problem may have more to do with the lack of skillful leisure scientists than with the unavoidable inadequacies of surveys.

Lastly, we consider *unobtrusive measures* as a major group of nonexperimental methods (Webb, *et al.*, 1966), focusing upon *archival research*. This set of methods refers to nonreactive investigations, which include the use of such techniques as public and private records, physical traces, or anything that human beings have left behind. The nonreactive nature of unobtrusive measures is an advantage which other social psychological methods do not possess. In using interview methods, for example, it is always possible that the researcher may change the phenomenon being studied, without being aware of it. Such a possibility does not exist when using unobtrusive measures. These methods are also advantageous because of the opportunity they provide for investigating trends in social behavior over a period of time. Other methods discussed earlier do not readily lend themselves to historical and time series analyses.

When judging from the standpoint of past and present research, archival investigations hold great promise for the future. In comparison to other social psychological inquiries, however, at the present time archival studies represent a minority. Despite reduced quantity, excellent archival research can be found in the literature of this subject. McClelland's (1961) classical study on the relationship between a nation's need for achievement and its later economic growth is perhaps the most famous. Based upon the contents of children's storybooks in 23 countries published around 1925, McClelland determined each nation's level of achievement motivation. He then correlated the need for achievement with economic growth (the latter was defined in terms of the amount of electricity output from 1925 to 1950). The high correlation ($+.53$) between the two variables suggested that the types of stories children read in school affected their need for achievement, which in turn had a significant impact upon the nation's future economic growth.

Another excellent use of archival material was reported by Suedfeld and Rank (1976). These investigators were able to demonstrate that the political fate of 19 revolutionary leaders (e.g., Thomas Jefferson, George Washington, V.I. Lenin, J.V. Stalin, Mao Tse Tung and Fidel Castro) was a function of their ability to change the degree of their conceptual complexity over time. More specifically, the long-term success of a revolutionary leader was characterized by single-minded and categorical approach (low conceptual complexity) in solving problems during the phase of revolutionary struggle, but this changed to a relatively flexible and integrated way of approaching problems during the post-revolutionary phase. Like McClelland, Suedfeld and Rank took great pains to read and score a vast amount of archival material to quantify their independent and dependent variables. These two studies clearly illustrate that archival research is not restricted to explorations and descriptions but can be used in testing hypotheses as well.

As for social psychological leisure research, to the best of this author's knowledge no archival studies have been conducted. However, the potential uses of this approach are many. Most recreation programs maintain public statistics about citizens' leisure patterns, and these provide material for closer inspection by leisure scientists. Similar data may be obtained regarding theaters, performing arts and sports centers, etc. Of course, the mass media (newspapers particularly) provide numerous possibilities for archival leisure research. Exploitation of these materials would considerably enrich our knowledge about human social behavior in leisure domains. After all, the future of social psychology of leisure as a science depends upon the heterogenous use of existing research methods as well as on the researchers' ability to create new methods.

social psychological leisure research

The above discussion has emphasized the principal methods employed by social psychologists. It is noted that experimental research is strongly overrepresented in this search for knowledge. The question arises whether the same is true for social psychological leisure research. The answer is unequivocally "no," because experiments are rare among the published leisure studies. There are probably two main reasons for this trend. First, it is difficult, if not impossible, to address "social problems" empirically in the laboratory. The higher the level of social relevance desired, the more difficult it may become to utilize the experimental method. By definition, the social psychological analysis of leisure is primarily concerned with social concerns, thereby limiting the applicability of this method. Second, studies in which leisure experiences are examined as either independent or dependent variables, are difficult to design and conduct. If, for example, one is to investigate the effects of leisure experiences on such psychological constructs as attitudes, self-perception and personality, the operationalization of leisure experiences in laboratories may easily disclose its artificiality and therefore may produce highly distorted findings. The problem of operationalization is further compounded by the fact that leisure experiences are to a major extent a matter of several hours and days. Inevitably, this creates a problem of finding subjects for studies which require hours, with the added problem of experimentally controlling lengthy leisure experiences in laboratory settings. Similar difficulties arise when leisure experiences are studied as dependent variables.

The above obstacles should not be taken to imply that experimental leisure research should not be conducted. On the contrary, the problems are to be solved, and some useful steps have already been taken to this end (Mannell, 1978a, b). The need for more experimental research is particularly evident because surveys and field studies (i.e., correlational studies) seem to dominate leisure research (Van Doren and Heit, 1973). As discussed earlier, correlational data may be variously interpreted, thus providing ambiguous evidence about psychological mechanisms underlying leisure behavior. Another reason for the need of more experimental leisure research is documented in a survey by Crandall and Lewko (1976). The area most often proposed for future research was the antecedents and consequences of leisure behavior. Unquestionably, this objective cannot satisfactorily be achieved by descriptive or correlational research alone. Both laboratory and field experiments are very much needed to attain such goals. The point, however, is not to argue for complete or even predominate replacement of surveys or field studies by experiments. Rather, both approaches should be utilized when investigating the same phenomenon. Many general social psychologists contend that their research has progressed very slowly, and is even slowing down, due to an excessive use of the experimental method. We suggest that the same decline will be the destiny of leisure research if nonexperimental methods dominate the field. The balanced use of a variety of methods is the best guarantee of success in attempts to explain human social behavior in leisure environments.

summary

In the present chapter we discussed the major methods of social psychological inquiry. They can be presented as in figure 5. While the difference between independent and dependent variables is crucial to all studies, it is particularly important in the case of experimental research. The former represents a presumed cause and the latter a presumed effect. From this distinction we proceeded to discuss the conceptual basis of experiments, with special emphasis on experimental and factorial designs. Examples of various factorials were given, and the two most fundamental experimental designs were described. The difference between field and laboratory experiments was briefly discussed, and leisure-related examples of both types of experiments were shown. Finally, in addressing the advantages and disadvantages of experimental research it was noted that this method is strong because of its high internal validity but weak due to its low external validity. When an investigator can exercise control over the independent variables and

Figure 5   Types of methods in social psychological inquiry.

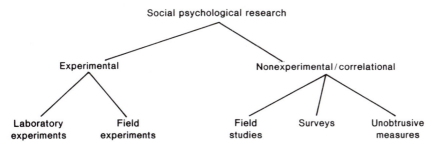

has confidence that the experimental variables/treatments indeed made a difference, the study is said to have high internal validity. On the other hand, when the experiment is so designed and executed that the findings are generalized and are representative of other than subjects and situations investigated, its external validity is defined as being high. Unfortunately, internal validity in social psychological experiments is frequently achieved at the expense of external validity.

The second part of this chapter dealt with nonexperimental and correlational research. First, the ex post facto character of nonexperimental studies was indicated, stressing the limitations of causal inferences about the relationships between variables. Next, the conceptual basis of correlational investigations was discussed, and the three most common correlational approaches were distinguished: (1) factorial designs, (2) simple correlations with their statistical extensions, and (3) path analytic conceptualization. The last section of this chapter was concerned with three major types of nonexperimental methods: field studies, surveys, and unobtrusive measures.

Field studies were characterized as scientific inquiries that systematically examine and test relationships between variables. These studies are conducted in "real life" situations (e.g., recreation centers). Surveys, unlike field investigations, are mainly directed toward providing a quantity of descriptive information about many things. Survey researchers are particularly concerned about the representative character of their samples. Since surveys usually yield superficial, descriptive information, their value as a major social psychological tool of research is doubtful. Finally, we considered the potential use of archival investigation in social psychological analysis of leisure and recreation. This unobtrusive and nonreactive method could be utilized in examining public and private records of citizens' leisure patterns. Such records are available in newspapers, recreation centers, theaters, sports stores, etc.

While social psychological research in general can be accurately described by one word, *experimental*, the same is not true of studies dealing with leisure and recreation from the social psychological standpoint. Experiments are rare, whereas field studies and surveys are common. The reasons for this trend were offered. Regardless of difficulties in designing and conducting effective experimental research in the domain of leisure behavior, use of the experimental method is highly desirable and should strongly be encouraged. The excessive use of correlational techniques may not only impede progress in the field but also may give a misleading and distorted picture of psychological processes underlying leisure behaviors. The scientific future of the social psychology of leisure lies in the diversified use of existing research tools as well as in the researchers' ability to discover new methods for systematic data-gathering.

developmental analysis of leisure and recreation

part 4

children's unorganized leisure: free play 5

One of the most important questions about leisure is how we are drawn into it socially. When, where, and how do we acquire the knowledge and skills needed in leisure participation? Is childhood recreation associated with adult leisure behavior? What is the character of children's play and how do the socialization agents (e.g., peers and parents) shape it? Do children play for intrinsic or extrinsic reasons? What is the role of play in the young's cognitive and social development? In an effort to answer these and related questions this unit examines leisure behavior from the developmental point of view. The first chapter focuses on the first five years of life, during which unorganized play is an important part. By the age of six to seven years, children's play becomes increasingly organized. Simultaneously, the desire for competitive encounters increases, reaching its peak around ten to twelve years of age (Eifermann, 1971). The following chapter is devoted to a social psychological analysis of children's organized leisure. Particular emphasis is placed upon Little League baseball, the climax of children's organized leisure. The third chapter of this part continues the developmental analysis, focusing on socialization processes. The final chapter is devoted to the examination of an aging individual and his leisure behavior.

Scientists have shown little theoretical and empirical interest in the concept of children's leisure. Child and Child (1973) suggested that this is probably due to the fact that the idea of leisure is not clear to preschool children. Unlike adults' time, children's daily hours are not institutionally divided into obligatory and nonobligatory activities, and consequently, children do not differentiate between work and leisure. Whether or not this is the reason, psychologists have paid little attention to children's leisure, but they have discussed play behavior at length. Although children may not be able to distinguish work from leisure, they certainly know the difference between obligatory and nonobligatory, attractive (motivating) and nonattractive, enjoyable and nonenjoyable activities. From

seeking and conquering challenges

adults' standpoint, it often looks as if children are "playing;" however, the children themselves may not think so. The question then arises: what is play? What factors are necessary and sufficient for defining play? What functions does play have?

Ellis (1973) has examined theories of play in detail. His review turned up five "classical" theories (i.e., surplus energy, instinct, preparation, recapitulation, and relaxation), six "recent" theories (i.e., generalization, compensation, catharsis, psychoanalytic, developmental, and learning) and two "modern" theories (i.e., arousal-seeking and competence/effectance motive) of play. Each one of these seeks to explain why people play. As Ellis noted, the problem is that they all focus on such narrow aspects of play that their explanatory ability is inadequate. These theories range from one extreme to another. At one end of the continuum is the instinct theory according to which play is caused by inherited factors. Learning theory represents the other end, and to the exclusion of inherited forces, it emphasizes the role of environmental factors in the development of play behavior. Other theories fall somewhere in between these two extremes.

optimal arousal

In an effort to reconcile the differences between these theories and to build a more comprehensive explanation of the causes of play, Ellis (1973) stressed the need for optimal arousal as a key motivator of play. He maintained that the optimal level of arousal (stimulation or level of interest) ranges from person to person. Due to this drive, an individual is in a continuous process of seeking and avoiding interactions with the environment, striving to sustain his optimal level of arousal. The continuum of the optimal arousal not only varies between individuals but also within each one. When interacting with the environment, a child constantly learns new things; the accumulative effect of such learning increases the complexity of interactions. This upward spiral in complexity, however, is not linear but rather occurs in developmental cycles. Most individuals go through similar phases at approximately the same time (Ellis, 1973, p. 118). Although the absolute level of arousal changes, due to the growth of an individual, nevertheless play is motivated by the optimal arousal both in childhood and adulthood. Thus, Ellis has clearly incorporated learning and developmental aspects in his arousal-seeking theory of play.

optimal incongruity

The idea of optimal arousal is not new. Based upon various lines of evidence, Hunt (1961, 1965, 1969) had earlier formulated essentially the same theory as Ellis. Accordingly, an organism's behavior is a function of its informational interaction with the environment. He called this "the problem of the match" and suggested:

> If encountering a given set of circumstances is to induce psychological development in the child, these circumstances must have an appropriate relationship to the information already accumulated in the child's mental storage from his previous encounter with circumstances (Hunt, 1969, p. 129).

Hunt (1969, p. 83) also noted that there is an optimum amount of arousal for each individual at any given time in all informational organism-environment interactions, and this optimum depends principally on individual experience. Instead of talking about arousal-seeking, Hunt referred to the motivated behavior as seeking "incongruity." When the environment provides too many inputs and stimuli for the child to handle (i.e., the situation is too incongruous in relation to the stored information), then the child withdraws from the environment. On the other hand, when the environmental inputs are overly similar to the coded and stored information and experience, the child becomes bored and seeks situations which offer more incongruity, uncertainty, novelty, and complexity. Thus, this tendency to seek the optimal incongruity channels the child's play.

Unfortunately, many children live in an environment that impedes their attempts to achieve the optimum amount of arousal or incongruity. This is particularly true for children in families with "low" social class levels. A number of studies have shown that throughout the world children of parents in poverty lack opportunities ("cultural deprivation") to acquire the fundamental skills, habits, values and standards necessary for the development of competence (cf. Hunt, 1969). Situations having few or no inputs create the conditions for "stimulus deprivation," which has been shown to have dramatic effects on both animals and humans. Rearing animals under the conditions of complete stimulus deprivation (i.e., in the dark) leads to changes in biochemical and anatomical structures of their central nervous system. Specifically, these animals are deficient in the production of RNA (ribonucleic acid), thereby suggesting that "the effects of experience may be stored as RNA within the glial component of retinal tissue and, perhaps, of brain as well" (Hunt, 1969, p. 11). In another paper, Hunt (1972) cited empirical evidence, reported by other researchers, indicating that the thickness of the cerebral cortex and the level of total acetylcholinesterace activity of the cortex (which are indicators of higher intelligence) increase as a function of complexity of the environment during early life. Harlow and Harlow (1962) found evidence that a longer period of stimulus deprivation (i.e., six months) renders the animals permanently inadequate, whereas the effects of shorter periods (e.g., 60–90 days) of deprivation are reversible. Bronfenbrenner (1972) took this to mean that there is at least one critical period for the effects of stimulus deprivation, probably occurring in middle infancy or "in those instances in which the infant is separated from the mother during the period of maximal dependency drive and placed in a situation in which physical and social stimuli are at a minimum" (p. 272).

Although identical studies concerning stimulus and sensory deprivation have not been made on human beings, a similar line of research on orphanage children lends credence to the above animal investigations. Dennis and his associates (1957, 1960) reported that stimulus deprivation in the form of continuous homogeneity of auditory and visual experience reduced children's capacity to interact with their environment, resulting in retarded locomotor performance. The orphanage environment (in Iran and Lebanon) was deprived, in the sense that children were provided with practically no stimuli during the first four years of their lives. For example, the sides of the cribs were so arranged that only the ceiling remained open, toys and playthings were very few, if any, and adult caretakers spent almost no time with the children. Investigators found that most of these orphanage-reared children failed to sit up alone at two years of age and failed to walk alone at four years of age. "Normal" children sit alone by the tenth month and walk alone by the 14th month.

The question then remains as to how lasting and permanent these detrimental effects are. Dennis and his associates' own studies, as well as Kagan's (1976) research, suggest that almost perfect recovery is likely, even following prolonged stimulus deprivation in infancy, provided that later a stimulating environment is offered. Similarly, Hunt (1969) reported that the enrichment of experiences through progressively complex environments increases the growth of central structures of the brain and augments the problem-solving ability. On the other hand, Hunt found evidence that "massive enrichment" is not necessary and may even be counterproductive. This is consistent with the idea about the need for the optimal amount of incongruity and arousal. Massive enrichment would probably provide too many stimuli and too much incongruity for the child to handle, thereby resulting in withdrawal.

The above studies indicate convincingly the importance of an appropriate match between the child and the environment. Situational encounters have to be suitable to an individual child, not offering too little or too much incongruity. The proper organism-environment interaction is also important from the standpoint of developing mastery over the environment. Stimulus deprivation, especially maternal deprivation, can result in the sense of lack of control. As Seligman (1975, p. 136–7) has shown, children's experience with controllable and uncontrollable events directly affects their perceptions and feelings of helplessness or mastery. Some environmental arrangements produce children who believe they are helpless, while other conditions induce children to believe they can control a private little world. The outcome of childhood experiences with the environment will determine the sense of helplessness or mastery, while this, in turn, is the underlying basis of an adult's self-concept, and thus the foundation for effective and satisfying living. In part this also explains why children tend to avoid too much or too little incongruity in environmental stimulation (i.e., stimuli that they cannot control), and approach play and games in which they can achieve the feeling of being effective human beings. Seligman (1975) calls such games "synchrony" games.

It is clear that the parents' role is crucial in meeting children's need for an optimally stimulating milieu in which to grow. As the above cited research convincingly illustrated, one cannot leave children to the mercy of inherited capacities and believe that the genes will take care of the unfolding. What is absolutely certain is that human intelligence and cognitive performance are not fixed or predetermined, but subject to critical influences of the environment. On the other hand, this does not imply that the environment is the only determinant of children's behavior. Matheny and Dolan (1975) reported evidence indicating that environmental influences are mediated through the individuals' innate tendencies to shape play behavior. Nevertheless, situational factors remain crucial in their effect; and one of the best means to provide children with a stimulating and enriching environment is play. While play may be fun, it is also a very serious business (Bruner, 1975; Sutton-Smith, 1971).

It follows from the above that exploration, investigation, and manipulation are at the heart of play. Berlyne (1960) has distinguished two types of exploration: specific and diversive. The former seeks to answer the question: what does this object do? The latter is directed toward the problem: what can I do with this object? Specific exploration involves behaviors dominated by the stimulus properties (across the children), whereas diversive exploration is mainly a function of an individual organism (Barnett, 1976; Hutt, 1971). Specific exploration refers to a perceptual-motor examination of an object, the desired outcome of such examination being a reduction in subjective uncertainty (Weisler and McCall, 1976). Through this examination the child acquires information which helps him to achieve greater control and mastery of the environment. Weisler and McCall (1976) reviewed empirical evidence on factors increasing the likelihood of exploratory behavior and found that salient stimulus properties (e.g., complexity dimensions), moderately discrepant, unusual and novel objects or events heighten subjective uncertainty, while this in turn prompts specific exploratory behavior. This aspect of exploration is more characteristic of the play of infants and the very young, rather than of older children. Play as diversive exploration, on the other hand, is principally manipulative activity which is often aimed at elevating to the optimal range the amount of arousal and incongruity. This aspect of play is based more upon imagination, creativity, and imitation, and less on information acquisition than is the former aspect of play.

exploration, manipulation and play

In sum, play consists of behaviors and activities which tend to reduce excessive uncertainty and to increase minimal incongruity to the level optimal for an individual. Since play comprises specific and diversive aspects of exploration interactively, neither should be excluded from the definition of play. Nor is it appropriate to study short periods of time empirically, because such segments are likely to give an erroneous picture of the character of play, indicating that the activity may be primarily either exploratory or manipulative (cf. Hutt, 1971). It is important to realize that optimal incongruity and arousal can be achieved *within* as well as *between* play activities. A given play activity may be less stimulating and more boring than the child would like to have it, but because of some external factors (e.g., peers) the child participates in it. Later, however, he may compensate by engaging in highly novel, complex, and dissonant explorations, with the net result that all the play activities of a day reach equilibrium in terms of the optimal stimulation and incongruity. Unfortunately, no research has been conducted regarding the nature and length of cycles within which the optimal arousal is defined individually.

Regardless of the type of exploration involved, play is organism dominated. An individual child seeks and responds to the environmental stimulation on the basis of his experiences. Thus, it is appropriate to define play as consisting of behaviors which are intrinsically motivated and engaged in for their own sake. Intrinsically motivated play is frequently very enjoyable and satisfying. Many theorists subscribe to this position (e.g., Csikszentmihalyi, 1975; Ellis, 1973; Weisler and McCall, 1976). It follows that children are playing when their behavior is largely under their control, that is, when it is not extrinsically rewarded and externally sanctioned. To make a given setting appropriate to play, one should eliminate as many external constraints as possible.

implications of optimal arousal and incongruity

What are the implications of the above theory of play in relation to the "real world?" Unquestionably, we can say that they are many and may even be considered revolutionary. Since such ramifications have been excellently put forth by Ellis (1973) in the last chapter of his book, we will cite his main points, augmenting them here and there with our views. First, the child should be given opportunities for exploration and manipulation in the home. He should be able to experience novelty, incongruity, arousal, increasing complexity and control. This can be achieved by providing arousing stimuli, e.g., playthings. For toys to be stimulating, they must be novel enough to induce exploration and sufficiently complex to puzzle the child and to prompt investigation; they should also be responsive so that manipulation is possible. In support of this notion, McCall (1974) found that 8½ and 11½ month old babies played longer, manipulated more and in general, had a richer form of free play when the toys were complex than when they were simple. In the laboratory setting, these children were also observed to play for the same amount of time with their "old favorite toys" as with the new play objects. This corroborates the claim about the need for optimal incongruity and arousal.

playthings

Unfortunately, many of the playthings commercially available today do not even come close to meeting these important criteria. All the child has to do in most cases is to push a button and see how the football moves through the air, or to wind a toy up and then look passively at its repetitive movement for a few minutes. On the other hand, good toys, such as legos, blocks, clay, playdoh and trucks are also available. These types of toys are psychologically beneficial because they provide (1) opportunities for a complex investigation of possible functions of an object, (2) lend themselves to unique activities, (3) reward creative interaction, and (4) can elicit imitated behavior (McCall, 1974).

But the toys should not be the only arousing stimuli at home. In fact, Ellis recommends that as many material objects as possible should be used as legitimate playthings. Even the best toys may not be able to satisfy children's need for novelty, dissonance, and complexity. Children want to work with real objects like tools, utensils and ornaments; and they should be allowed to do so under parental guidance. Another source for arousing stimulation consists of other adults at home. Most children exhibit a tendency to play at the adults' feet, between legs, on the back, and in the lap. In addition, adults should play "synchrony games" with children (Seligman, 1975), since these develop the sense of control over the environment. Critical to such games is the idea that the child makes some voluntary response, to which the adult then responds by repeating it. Whatever forms this play may take, the idea is to give the child an opportunity to control the action or resolve the problem by himself. Opportunities to practice such forms of play are very important for child development. Bishop and Chace (1971) have documented a significant increase in children's creativity as a result of a flexible and encouraging home play environment. This, of course, does not imply that children must have complete freedom to do whatever they wish. In fact, we recommend that clear and respectable boundaries ought to be established for children, so that they can realize the limits of their behavior. It is within these boundaries that flexibility and interaction are to be encouraged.

Next, we consider home itself as a place for stimulus seeking. As Ellis (1973) pointed out, living in modern apartments is very restrictive and therefore impedes arousal seeking. The physical height of apartments (e.g., in New York City) on the one hand, and streets and parking lots at their foot on the other, necessarily limit children's mobility and discourage play. Such an environment, of course, is also physically dangerous to those at play. Apartments are small in most cases, containing little space for adult needs. Children's play is not only curtailed by the lack of physical space but also by the fragile structure of apartments, especially in the United States. Children have to be continuously wary of making noise, to avoid disturbing neighbors. Unfortunately, due to lack of financial resources to support a single family home, this type of living is the fate of most young families. It is ironic that at the same time many people can afford to live in large and adequate houses only after their children have left home. Such living involves wasted space and suggests a need to reexamine societal priorities. Thus, the human tendency for the optimal arousal and incongruity is not only a psychological problem but an important social concern as well.

home

The theory of play as incongruity seeking has paramount implications for the design of playgrounds, too. Typically, playgrounds offer standard equipment, consisting of swings, slides, and a few other devices. These facilities are fixed, in the sense that they cannot be modified or manipulated, and hence provide little to be explored and investigated. This writer presently lives in a condominium complex which is adjacent to a corner with a playground. Yet, children (ages 3 to 6) living in the neighborhood seldom go to the playground, though they are allowed to do so. Instead, they choose to play in nearby sand and earth piles used for building new houses; or they play on the patches of green grass between the condominiums. The playground apparently is unstimulating, redundant and boring for these children, and not conducive to experiencing control over the environment.

playgrounds

What then is a good playground? Most importantly, it is one which changes and is open to continous modification by children; it cannot be fixed or standard.

Children have to be able to dig, build, and alter their playground. As this case study showed, there must be sand, dirt, earth, bricks, lumber, or other modifiable substance in the play environment. Ellis (1973) calls these places adventure and junk playgrounds, and strongly recommends them. Playgrounds like Disneyland are good for a few visits and explorations, but they soon become repetitive and boring because they offer the same thing time after time. Thus, the simplest and cheapest appears to be the best.

socialization

Finally, we consider the implications of the optimal incongruity theory of play in terms of socialization. Since play activities reflect the rudiments of adult leisure behavior (Yoesting and Burkhead, 1973), it is important to understand how the need for optimal incongruity is met through the child's play. What is optimally arousing for an individual as a child is likely to affect the optimum level of arousal when he is an adult. Consistent with this, Erikson (cited in Bruner, 1975) carried out a follow-up study 30 years later of persons who had been tested as children. He found that individuals who were able to keep a "sense of playfulness at the center of things" when they were children had the most interesting and fulfilling lives 30 years later. Thus, if an individual's play and recreation is poor in stimulation throughout childhood, the person may become accustomed to a low level of arousal and may regard it as optimal. This in turn may impair the tendency to seek novel, incongruous and complex leisure experiences in adulthood.

Since play is creative response (Ellis, 1973), it is important for the child to be able to exercise cognitive and behavioral flexibility in play. When a variety of play activities is encouraged, it is reasonable to expect leisure pursuits of adults to be creative and flexible, a condition which in turn is likely to improve subsequent psychological coping and mental health. If, on the other hand, children learn to satisfy their need for incongruity by one-sided play activity(ies) (e.g., predominantly sedentary or predominantly physical activity), they may never be able to value and experience a variety of leisure skills. It is not uncommon to find parents who, instead of encouraging the values of play, stress and facilitate only the acquisition of work-related skills such as reading, calculating, and writing. Many parents only impress upon their children the value of physical activities. When a child learns to pursue and reach an optimal arousal exclusively through such categories of activities, he or she will inevitably possess a reduced repertoire of leisure experiences as an adult.

There is another reason why, from the psychological standpoint, the lack of a variety of play experiences in childhood may be detrimental to adults. That is, if a person with limited early play experiences is paralyzed or suffers other physcial impairment due to an accident, his ability to cope with the trauma may be considerably less than that of the person with rich play experiences in childhood. This occurs because use of the few leisure skills possessed before the accident is no longer feasible, a situation which therefore impedes attempts to satisfy the need for optimal arousal. In contrast, a person with a variety of leisure skills *and* a learned predisposition to satisfy this need through diverse forms of leisure, can more easily find substitutes for now unattainable forms of leisure activities, thus providing arousal while coping with the trauma. An individual who has learned to satisfy the need for optimal arousal by means of a narrow range of play activities comes to view these one-sided forms of leisure as a necessity. It is believed that our culture is strongly biased toward this sort of socialization. It is frequently emphasized that certain types of play are socially desirable only for males. In this sense, football and baseball appear as standards for everything else. If so narrowly socialized respecting leisure, people are likely to overadapt to their environment, believing that these leisure activities are necessary for their psychological well-being. Modification of environment and lifestyle, or the changing society at large, become painful experiences for these individuals when familiar patterns are upset. Thus, the very early patterns of interacting with one's environment establish the foundations for being able to use leisure in a satisfying and rewarding manner in later life. How parents guide their offspring in meeting the need for optimal arousal and incongruity is therefore the ultimate challenge of child development.

In their attempt to provide an optimal play environment for their children, parents have to bear in mind that intrinsic motivation is the necessary condition for play to occur. As noted earlier, play consists of behaviors intrinsically motivated or performed for their own sake. Hence, play means the absence of external constraints. This, however, is often forgotten by parents and educators when guiding children's play behavior. Frequently, various rewards and sanctions are used and direct intervention in play is often taken for granted. Empirical data accumulated during the last ten years, however, suggests that adult intervention—be it in the form of extrinsic rewards or surveillance—undermines children's intrinsic motivation in free play, meaning that children's recreation is turned into children's work. This is confirmed when one reviews the relevant research in greater detail, and also indicates implications for child-rearing practices.

detrimental effects of extrinsic rewards on free play

As we discussed earlier, the absence of external constraints is not sufficient to define play as intrinsically motivated behavior. Based upon Ellis' (1973) and Hunt's (1961, 1965, 1969) idea about the need for optimal arousal or incongruity and Seligman's (1975) emphasis on exercising control or mastery over one's environment, this writer developed a position suggesting that the psychological foundation of intrinsically motivated play resides in the child's need to be a competent human being. An almost identical theory derived from different considerations has been advanced by Deci (1975a). He posits that intrinsically motivated behavior implies the human need for feeling competent and self-determining. Consequently, people look for optimally challenging situations (i.e., involving incongruity), and aim at responding to the challenge or reducing the incongruity. The need to seek and conquer individually optimal challenges is an ongoing process, the end product of which is satisfaction resulting from feelings of competence and self-determination. In this way, intrinsic motivation energizes and directs a child's interaction with the environment.

theoretical positions

But what happens when adults interrupt intrinsically motivated play by providing rewards? Deci (1975a) maintains that extrinsic rewards affect intrinsic motivation by two processes. One of them, which might be called an attributional explanation, focuses on a change in perceived locus of causality. This holds that when behavior is intrinsically motivated, its cause is perceived to reside in one's own intrinsic need, that is, the person is cognitively aware that he himself initiated the course of action. The opposite is true for externally motivated behaviors whose locus of perceived causality is in environmental factors. The second process involves alteration in feelings of competence and self-determination. Rewards which imply that the person is competent will increase intrinsic motivation, whereas rewards implying a lack of competence will reduce intrinsic motivation. Deci (1975a) further postulated that all extrinsic rewards have two aspects: a controlling and an informational aspect. If the former dominates, a shift in perceived locus of causality (from internal to external) ensues, resulting in decreased intrinsic motivation. On the other hand, the latter situation leads to a change in feelings of competence and self-determination, resulting either in increased or decreased intrinsic motivation depending on the feeling of competence or incompetence conveyed by the informational feedback. In sum, extrinsic rewards reduce the level of children's intrinsically motivated play if such rewards cause children to perceive that external sources are the reasons for their behavior, or if these rewards suggest a lack of competence.

That extrinsic rewards undermine children's intrinsic interest has also been proposed by Lepper, *et al.* (1973), and Lepper and Greene (1976). Their position, derived from Bem's (1967) self-perception theory and deCharms' (1968) theory of personal causation and called the "overjustification" hypothesis, states that when a person is induced to engage in an intrinsically motivated activity as an ulterior means to some extrinsic goal, his subsequent interest in that activity declines. Such undermining is due to the unnecessarily high external or psychologically "oversufficient" justification for engaging in an activity. Overjustification gives rise to external attributions and is therefore identical with Deci's idea of environmental locus of causality of behavior. It is important to note that these theorists predict detrimental effects of rewards only under the conditions where persons are originally intrinsically motivated in an activity and do not expect extrinsic rewards for their participation.

What are the effects of extrinsic rewards in a situation of insufficient justification, that is, when the task is dull and does not produce feelings of competence? On the basis of an experiment (Calder and Staw, 1975), Staw (1976) concluded that extrinsic rewards increase intrinsic motivation, satisfaction and performance when a task is neutral, or so uninteresting that individuals would not ordinarily perform it. Lepper and Greene (1976, p. 33) do not deny this possibility. An additional theoretical consideration is mentioned by Kruglanski (1975), who maintains that rewards must be exogenous to a task to produce decremental effects on intrinsic motivation. In other words, if external rewards are so inherent a part of play and game or have become so institutionalized that children expect them automatically, then rewards do *not* decrease intrinsic motivation; only when a task, not usually done for the sake of extrinsic rewards, is now performed for pay will the detrimental effects appear.

Despite some slight differences in wording and emphasis, the above theoretical positions are considered identical for present purposes. They all represent cognitive social psychology at best because of their assumption that it is not the rewards per se which cause detrimental effects, but rather the cognitive representation of rewards; cognitions (i.e., thinking and rationalization) mediate the effects. Thus, it is no surprise that the real opposition to the above theoretical positions comes from behaviorally (S-R)[1] oriented psychologists (Reiss and Sushinsky, 1975; Scott, 1975). The present writer rejects the S-R attempts to explain the "overjustification" hypothesis. He does this on philosophical grounds, believing that human behavior cannot be reduced to simple S-R accounts. Furthermore, he opposes behaviorists on conceptual and theoretical grounds, since cognitive social psychologists have been able readily and convincingly to dismiss Reiss and Sushinsky's (Lepper and Greene, 1976) and Scott's (Deci, 1975b) arguments. Finally, empirical evidence militates overwhelmingly against the behavioristic position (for recent reviews, see Condry, 1977; Ross, 1976), thereby providing additional reasons to favor social psychological theories. Of these approaches, Deci's theorizing (1975a) seems to be the most promising at the present, and therefore most adequate to explain the effects of extrinsic rewards on intrinsic motivation. Deci's theory also parallels the present discussion of play in terms of optimal arousal or incongruity and feelings of personal control or competence.

empirical findings

The idea that extrinsic rewards undermine exploration and intrinsic motivation is certainly not new. As Condry (1977) pointed out, several theorists (e.g., Berlyne, deCharms, Harlow, Hunt, Koch, and White) suggested this hypothesis in various forms in the 1950s and 1960s. Also, the statement about the effects of overjustification on behavior constitutes one of the critical tenets of Festinger's (1957) famous cognitive dissonance theory. But what is new is the systematic empirical testing of the hypothesis in the 1970s. Although a precise and comprehensive test of Deci's theory (1975a) has not been carried out, several studies generally support his reasoning.

lepper and associates

In one of their early experiments, Lepper, *et al.* (1973) divided nursery school children (3 to 5 years old) into three experimental conditions: (1) those who were asked to play to get an extrinsic reward ("expected reward"), (2) those who were asked to play but did not receive a reward ("no reward"), and (3) those who were asked to play and received the same reward unexpectedly ("unexpected reward"). To provide an intrinsically motivated playtask, the investigators placed felt-tip pens of various colors ("magic markers") on one of the tables in the playroom and recorded behind one-way mirrors the amount of time every

[1]The S-R approach attempts to explain human behavior only in terms of stimuli (S) and responses (R), thereby assuming that human beings are robots "whose behavior is determined by reinforcement histories and contingencies in the present environment" (Deci, 1975b).

child spent with the markers; only those who exhibited interest in the felt-tip pens were selected for the experiment and were randomly assigned to one of the experimental groups. Following this basic observation, experimental sessions began within two weeks. All children were asked to draw with the markers for six minutes, but depending on the experimental group, some of them were offered "Good Player Award" for doing so, while others not. One week later, the investigators returned and recorded the time the subjects chose to play with the markers when the pens were placed on the play table; none of the children expected to receive rewards for drawing. This period, free-time spent in playing with the markers, was taken to indicate subjects' intrinsic motivation.

As predicted on the basis of the overjustification hypothesis, the mean percentage of free-time spent with the markers during the post-experimental period was considerably ($p < .02$) less in the expected-reward condition (8.6%) than in either the no-award (16.7%) or the unexpected reward (18.1%) condition. In addition, three judges' evaluation of drawing revealed that the quality of pictures drawn in the expected-reward condition was lower ($p < .05$) than in the other two groups. These findings were later successfully replicated by two experiments, (1) using the magic markers again (Greene and Lepper, 1974a) and (2) using a novel task of solving puzzles (Lepper and Greene, 1975). Taken together, these experiments provided convincing evidence that the use of extrinsic rewards undermines children's intrinsically motivated play, turning children's recreation into children's work. Specifically, it is not the reward per se but cognitive representation of it, the expectation, which has detrimental effects on intrinsic motivation.

Before leaving the Lepper and Greene studies, one should also examine their latter experiment (1975). In accord with the 2×2 (reward expectancy X surveillance) factorial design, the investigators determined the effects of reward expectancy (expected vs. unexpected reward) and surveillance (yes vs. no) on children's subsequent intrinsic interest. The reward expectancy manipulation was identical to that of the earlier study (Lepper, *et al.*, 1973). In addition, one half of the subjects were told that they would be monitored through a closed-circuit TV system when working with the puzzles, whereas the other half was directed to play alone. A small light was used to remind the former subjects that they were being watched. Lepper and Greene hypothesized that such surveillance should decrease subsequent intrinsic motivation, because it might make children believe their play was being externally controlled. Thus, playing under surveillance should be the same as playing for extrinsic rewards. The results are displayed in figure 6. As can be seen, both reward expectancy and surveillance had a significant ($p < .05$) but independent impact upon children's subsequent interest in playing with the puzzles. Specifically, intrinsic motivation was lower in the expected reward situation than when reward was not expected, regardless of the surveillance situations. Similarly, intrinsic motivation was much less in the presence of surveillance than in its absence, irrespective of the reward expectancy conditions. Surveillance and expected reward, therefore, reduced intrinsic motivation independently.

Figure 6 Effects of reward expectancy and adult surveillance on children's free play. (From Lepper, M.R. and Greene, D. "Turning play into work: effects of adult surveillance and extrinsic rewards on children's intrinsic motivation." *Journal of Personality and Social Psychology,* 1975, 31, 479–486, Figure 1. Copyright © 1975 by the American Psychological Association. Reprinted by permission.)

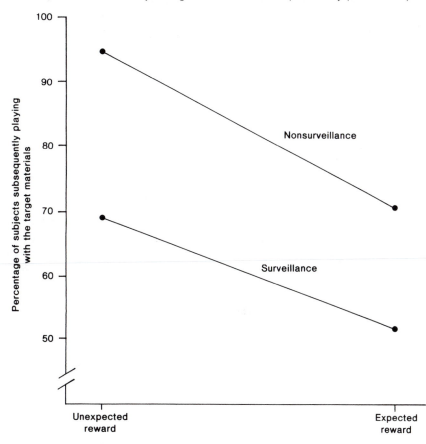

Although the above findings are theoretically ambiguous (i.e., they are confounded with the inhibitive effects of the presence of others; see "social facilitation" by Zajonc, 1965), they nevertheless are very important for practical considerations. Often parents and educators not only use extrinsic rewards to lure their children to engage in activities but also enhance the inhibiting effects of rewards by monitoring their behavior. Such external pressures take away a sense of personal control and produce feelings of distrust, thereby making external attribution for engaging in an activity the only possibility. By using external pressures parents often destroy opportunities for children to develop interest in household activities. For example, children are frequently asked to wash dishes for rewards or other external reasons. Perhaps the most common incidence, however, is the situation in which play is used as a reward for doing some household activities: "You cannot go out and play with your friends until you have cleaned this room, and I'll watch to see that you do it.'' This certainly destroys any chances of developing interest in home activities. On the other hand, many parents use reward systems and surveillance as tools of directing their children's play into the forms they consider appropriate. As we will discuss later, Little League baseball, for example, has become drudgery for some players, because their parents reward them, forcing them to participate. To resort to such external pressures is unfortunate because it undermines children's intrinsic interest in play, thereby hampering their attempts to seek and conquer challenges, to achieve optimal arousal and incongruity.

salience of rewards

Because it is unrealistic to expect that extrinsic rewards will always decrease intrinsic motivation, several experiments have recently been conducted to establish the boundary conditions for the ''overjustification'' phenomenon. One such condition appears to be the salience of rewards. Ross (1975) found that when nursery school children played with a drum to get an expected reward placed under the box in clear view (salient reward), their subsequent interest was markedly decreased as compared to subjects who anticipated and received a nonsalient reward or subjects who neither expected nor received a reward. It is notable that decreased intrinsic motivation to play with the drum was not only limited to the period of free-play immediately following the experimental session but persisted one month later. In his second experiment, Ross manipulated the salience of a reward in a different way by asking children to think about the reward (salient award) while playing, as opposed to the second situation in which subjects were invited, while playing, to think of something unrelated to the reward. The results were essentially the same as above. Thus, taken together, the above findings suggest that detrimental effects of rewards depend, to a large extent, on how conspicuous the reward is and whether the reward becomes the central focus of children's attention. If the reward is so salient that it constantly reminds them of its presence, then intrinsic interest will subsequently wane and the damage will probably last.

contingency of rewards

Another qualification has to do with the contingency of rewards. Two considerations arise in this respect. First, if the attainment of rewards is contingent only on performing a given playtask without regard to the quality of performance, the effects of extrinsic rewards on intrinsic interest are detrimental. Such awards are called task-irrelevant (Ross, 1976; Karniol and Ross, 1977) or exogenous (Kruglanski, 1975) rewards. In this case, children are asked to play with certain toys and are led to expect awards for doing so. These rewards are task-irrelevant, because children do not ordinarily anticipate awards for playing with toys used in an experiment; the use of toys therefore undermines intrinsic interest. If, on the other hand, rewards are a norm and thus an integral part of the play or the game, then the rewards do not decrease interest. The second consideration deals with the contingency of rewards in terms of the quality of performance. Several experiments have reported evidence indicating that contingent rewards which recognize an individual's competence in the task enhance rather than decrease intrinsic motivation. Since such rewards indicate competence, they produce feelings of mastery and control over the environment (Ross, 1976; Karniol and Ross, 1977).

Anderson, Manoogian and Reznick (1976) performed an experiment to compare the effects of various types of contingent rewards on 4–5 year old children's subsequent interest in the target activity of drawing. The results showed that positive verbal reinforcement increased subsequent interest in drawing, whereas symbolic award (Good Player) and money resulted in decrease of subsequent interest. This finding clearly supports the idea that if rewards convey information about one's competence they enhance intrinsic motivation. Children in the positive verbal-reinforcement condition were told after each 2-minute interval during the 8-minute period of experimental drawing that "you are pretty good at this," "you really did a good job," or "that picture is real nice." Children in other conditions were told that if they will draw some pictures, they will get a good *et al.* (1976) study was also important for another finding. This showed that the dren's interest in play. Combined with other studies (Anderson, *et al.*, 1976; et al. (1976) study was also important for another finding. This showed that the most powerful undermining effect occurred in a control condition where the experimenter sat "in absolute silence" for 8 minutes, thereby totally ignoring a child's play and attempts to interact with the experimenter. (This result parallels the Lepper and Greene (1975) study which demonstrated decrease in intrinsic motivation to play as a result of adult surveillance.) By completely ignoring the children, the experimenter created an unpleasant and awkward situation, which probably led these children to perceive the experimenter's behavior as surveillance or punishment and their drawing as externally controlled.

Similar to the above results, Swann and Pittmann (1977) found that verbal praise as compared to the material reward (good player award) increased children's interest in play. Combined with other studies (Anderson, et al., 1976; Karniol and Ross, 1977) this pattern of results lends credence to Deci's (1975a) theory which posits an enhancement of intrinsic motivation as a result of rewards which produce feelings of competence and self-determination. The Swann and Pittman experiment was also significant in that it revealed a decline in intrinsic motivation when an adult rather than the child chose the play activity. Again, it appears that when children's play is externally controlled it loses its characteristics of play and acquires those of work.

The above studies persuasively suggest that the use of extrinsic, task-irrelevant rewards undermine children's intrinsically motivated behavior, play. Such rewards not only decrease continued interest in play activity but also impair the quality of performance as well as creativity (Condry, 1977). These overall findings have been confirmed by numerous experiments on children as well as on adults of various ages, with different forms of toys, play and games; they have been shown to persist even one month after the experimental sessions. Thus, the detrimental effects of extrinsic rewards do not seem to be products of the labora-

rewards signaling competence

summary and implications

tory, or statistical artifacts which can be dismissed as academic trivia. The implications of these conclusions for child-rearing practices by parents and educators are of considerable importance.

To avoid negative effects, extrinsic rewards should be used only when absolutely necessary. Of course, there are situations where extrinsic rewards may be beneficial. They are useful, for example, in attempting to arouse initial interest in the activity or task to which persons would not otherwise be attracted. If extrinsic rewards have to be employed, they should be made as inconspicuous as possible (minimal salience), and they should be used in play activities where it is at least somewhat reasonable to expect rewards. Whenever possible, rewards should be given in a form or manner which permits the child to feel competent and self-determining. Adults should not compound the negative effects of rewards by watching children's activity by the use of surveillance or by ignoring their desire to interact with an adult. Children should be allowed to select their own play activities independently.

Unfortunately, the pace of life has become so hectic that people all but ignore children and their daily play activities. Based upon the studies reviewed, there are compelling reasons to conclude that an excellent environment for seeking optimal arousal and incongruity is provided by parents who do not use extrinsic rewards or otherwise force their children to engage in certain play activities, but rather spend considerable time in talking with them about their self-directed play experiences of the day. Interspersed with pieces of advice, encouragement and praise, such comments will create an atmosphere and interaction which can sustain high intrinsic interest in a variety of play activities, or may even increase it.

cognitive benefits from play

The psychological consequences of play may be many. One of them is satisfaction resulting from feelings of competence and self-determination achieved in intrinsically motivated play. Another includes the long-term socialization effects of the intrinsically motivating play environments. As indicated earlier, optimally stimulating play environments lay the foundations for satisfying and rewarding leisure behaviors of adults. In addition to these important functions, play also contributes to children's cognitive development. Traditionally, theorists have stressed the role of play in character and personality formation (e.g., Bowen and Mitchell, 1930), in intellect development and social growth (e.g., Curtis, 1924), in the development of moral judgment (Piaget, 1932), in psychic adjustment and adaptation to the outside world (Davis, 1938), as a means of coping with emotional stress (Erikson, 1950), to name but a few examples. Seldom, however, have these hypotheses or speculations been subjected to rigorous empirical test. It is not until recently that the cognitive functions of play have been systematically investigated. Next, some empirical studies dealing with the role of play in cognitive development will be examined. The main focus is the effects of play on children's problem-solving ability and creativity.

A child increases his understanding of the world by constructing and reinventing things. To be able to discover, invent, and create, the child must have opportunities for experimenting and research. Piaget (1972, p. 27) has noted that "every time we teach a child something, we keep him from inventing it himself." Although parents and educators can and should guide a child by providing stimulating play material and environment for experimentation, the child should be allowed to discover things himself. To highlight the importance of play in cognitive performance, Piaget (1972) gave the following example. A small boy played with stones and decided to count them. He first put them in a straight line and counted them from left to right, then from right to left, and each time found there to be ten of them. He next put them in a circle, once again finding ten stones. He discovered that the sum was independent of the order. As a result, the boy was very excited. Later he became a mathematician; today he attributes his career to this early play experience with stones and the accompanying discovery.

Another but more reliable piece of evidence about the seriousness of play comes from an experiment performed by Bruner (1975). He first speculated that play provides opportunity to combine and practice sequences of behavior that enhance problem-solving skills. Consistent with earlier discussion in this book, Bruner suggested that learning such skills through play requires the optimum amount of motivation arousal, not too much or not too little. To determine the effects of play on the problem-solving abilities of 3–5 year olds, children were given various kinds of training prior to attempting to solve the problem. The experimental task consisted of fishing a prize from a box which was out of the children's reach. For this, subjects were allowed to use only two sticks and a clamp. In order to accomplish the task the children had to discover that the two sticks must be tied together by the clamp to make a pole of sufficient length. Children were divided into five groups who received different training prior to working on the problem. One of them observed an adult demonstrate the principle of how to clamp sticks together. The second group watched the experimenter perform the entire task, thereby observing the complete solution of the problem. The third group were instructed to manipulate the materials in question; specifically, they practiced putting clamps together on a single stick, but not the actual solution. The fourth group simply played with the sticks and clamp without any instructions. The fifth group was comprised of those children who had no exposure to any of these materials. After the training, children were given the above task to be performed and asked to solve the problem with the tools (two sticks and a clamp).

play and problem-solving abilities

The results were quite startling. The percentage of successful solutions was equal (about 40%) among those who received no training but simply played with the materials, and those who observed the complete solution. It was 20 percent for those who were instructed to manipulate the tools, about 18 percent for those who observed the principle and less than 10 percent for the children who were not exposed to the materials at all. Thus, the play group did as well as those who were shown how to perform the entire task, and considerably better than the other groups. The implications of these findings are compelling. It is clear that an appropriately stimulating play environment enhances problem-solving ability in children. Children should be provided with various tools and playthings that allow them to explore, investigate, and manipulate. Allowing them to play alone with such materials is intrinsically motivating and psychologically satisfying; this seems to create a cognitively beneficial environment. When we compare the play group and the no-exposure group (40% vs. about 8% of successful solutions), the difference in the effects of the two environments becomes particularly evident. It appears that these findings clearly support the emphasis placed in the preceding discussion concerning the need to supply children with a stimulating environment which is optimally arousing and incongruous. In pursuit of optimal arousal and incongruity, the child learns skills which are helpful in becoming a more competent and effective human being. As the Bruner study indicates, problem-solving abilities learned while playing tend to transfer to other non-play situations involving the same play materials. It is an open question as to what extent these skills transfer to situations not involving the same play materials as were used in the original play task.

Sutton-Smith (1967) has addressed this question, claiming that play increases the child's repertoire of responses, which condition is later potentially useful for adaptive behaviors. Accordingly, the child plays with toys, investigates and manipulates them, and in so doing increases his range of responses for these particular toys. To prove his point, Sutton-Smith (1967) recorded kindergarten boys' and girls' responses to the question, "What can you do with this toy?" The toys that were used were either favorites (i.e., ones with which they played most often throughout the kindergarten year) or nonfavorites. It was hypothesized that children would have a greater range of responses to favorite toys than for those that were not favorite. The results confirmed this expectation. The total number of uses found for each object, as well as the number of unique usages, were greater for favorite than neglected toys. Citing other evidence to back up his findings, Sutton-Smith concluded that "play may not only increase the repertoire of available responses, but that, where encouraged, it may also heighten the ease with which representational sets can be adopted towards diverse materials." However, he was careful to point out that empirical evidence for such adoption to diverse materials and situations is not strong at the present time. In a way, similar to Sutton-Smith's idea of a repertoire of responses, many theoreticians (e.g., Piaget, 1950) stress the role of explorative manipulation of objects in the acquisition of a store of information. This wealth of information later forms the basis of the child's intellectual development.

play and creativity Further evidence about cognitively beneficial effects of play comes from several studies on play and creativity. Lieberman (1965) reported a positive relationship between kindergarten children's playfulness and their ability to perform creative tasks. Hutt (cited in Bruner, 1975) found that children who were inventive and exploratory in their early play had higher originality scores even four years later, than did non-exploring children. Using archival data, Simonton (1975) provided evidence that growth of creativity is affected by the availability of creative role models during the individual's developmental period. Though all of these findings appear consistent in pointing to the facilitating effects of play on the development of creativity, their value is lessened by the correlational character of the studies. It is the old problem: Does play in itself contribute to creativity or does play merely express the existing level of individual creativity? Of course, this questioning is too simplistic; it does not have to be "either—or." While the precise nature of this circular relationship remains to be shown, there are, nevertheless, compelling reasons to believe that the opportunity to play enhances creativity. Several experiments appear to confirm this conclusion.

Feitelson and Ross (1973) set out to test the hypothesis that teaching children to play thematically will increase their creativity. By thematic play they referred to a certain play theme which is the mainspring of activity. Subjects were 12 boys and girls who were on the average 5.6 years old. These children were randomly divided into four experimental groups: (1) those whose play was tutored with the purpose of guiding and encouraging combinational play and of decreasing dependence on ready-made toys, (2) those who came to the laboratory to play with the same toys as the tutored children but without any adult guidance, (3) those who were taught to play the tonette (nonthematic play); all the above subjects had ten 30-minute sessions; (4) those who were not exposed to any treatment but only took part in the pre- and post-testing. The results showed that the play-tutored group improved significantly ($p < .05$) more than the other three groups in combinational play. Most importantly, when measured by conventional tests of originality, innovation and exploration, the play-tutored children's creativity increased considerably more than that of the other groups.

Thus, the study succeeded in demonstrating a causal relationship between thematic play and certain aspects of creativity. Although the implications of these results are clear, one should keep in mind that the study does not deal with long-term effects of thematic play on creativity. It should not be concluded that improved creativity due to thematic play in childhood will appear as increased performance on tests of creativity in adult years. But, as Feitelson and Ross suggested, even the possibility that free and thematic play may provide an avenue for acquiring and rehearsing skills conducive to creative behavior should be taken into account by those who are responsible for child-rearing and educational practices. Hirshfeld and Hirshfeld (1977) have presented concrete examples of how educators can use play and games in developing analytical and combinatorial reasoning in children. A play of simple, physical manipulations can be turned into a cognitive challenge.

Another important study on play and creativity was performed by Bishop and Chace (1971). The purpose of this experiment was to test the hypothesis that abstractness of parents' cognitive functioning affects the type of home play environment they provide for their children, and that this in turn influences children's potential creativity. According to their cognitive style, parents can broadly be divided into two categories: (1) those who are abstract, flexible, unorthodox and nonauthoritarian in their thinking and (2) those who can be characterized as concrete, simple, rigid, and conventional in their cognitive performance. Bishop and Chace hypothesized that the former parents would show less restrictive and more favorable attitudes toward play; they would actually create a more stimulating

parents' cognitive style, home play environment, and children's creativity

and playfulness-engendering environment for their children than the latter type of parents. To test this conjecture, the investigators first determined parents' levels of conceptual development (abstractness-concreteness) on the basis of their open-ended replies to ten concept referents. In addition, a questionnaire was developed to measure parents' attitudes toward their children's play as well as the actual conditions of play in the home; more than 100 parents of 72 children (3–4 year-olds) participating in the study were interviewed. Parents expressed their attitudes toward such things as rights of children in play and types of toys provided. Parents were also asked to describe characteristics of the home play environment in terms of novelty, variety and exploration in play. The results supported the predictions. Abstract mothers' (but not fathers') attitudes toward their children's play were more flexible, and they encouraged play more than concrete mothers. The abstract mothers also reported actual conditions of the home play environment to be more conducive to play than the ones found in the homes of concrete mothers.

To investigate the relationship between the home play environment and potential creativity, an experiment was conducted. Bishop and Chace predicted that children of the "abstract" parents would exhibit higher potential creativity than children of "concrete" parents. The measure of potential creativity was made on the basis of children's performance on a laboratory play task which revealed their preferences for complexity and variety in play. Each child was presented with 54 geometric figures varying in color and complexity, and arranged on a stimulus board. In addition, an identical but blank board was provided. The task was to pick up figures from the stimulus board and use them to make any figures they wished on the empty board. As predicted, the children of the "abstract" mothers showed more complex and varied choice behaviors on the task. If performance on the complexity board task is viewed as analogous to creativity response, then the results clearly support the idea that children's creativity improves as the playfulness (i.e., greater complexity, variety, novelty, and autonomy for the child) of the home play environment is increased. Providing such a play environment calls for flexible and supportive attitudes toward play. Although it may be difficult to change parents' thinking patterns from concrete to abstract, it should not be difficult to modify their values and attitudes regarding the importance of play in children's cognitive development. Such attempts are needed, they are challenging, and they are most likely to pay off.

The above findings are consistent with previous discussion of the need for the optimal incongruity and of intrinsically motivated play. Why children of more abstract mothers preferred complex and varied choice behavior is understandable, because the home play environment was intrinsically motivated. It allowed and encouraged children to seek optimal incongruity. While continuously seeking and conquering incongruity in such a stimulating environment, these children developed a wide repertoire of responses, and these could later be utilized in a different situation with novel materials. Thus, a stimulating home play environment seems to form a stronger motivational base for children to fulfill their need for optimal incongruity in a variety of old and novel environments. As a result, children not only gain satisfying play experiences but also benefit cognitively through improved creativity. There is scarcely anything more important parents can hope to do for their children than enhance their creativity.

To summarize, intrinsically motivated play is both fun and serious business. It is summary fun because of the accompanying satisfaction stemming from feelings of competence and self-determination. It is serious, in the sense that problem-solving skills and certain other aspects of creativity may improve as a result of such play experiences. This probably occurs because enriched play environments widen the child's range of responses, and motivate him to utilize the repertoire in complex, innovative and varied ways in a variety of environments. Since parents and educators are interested in improving children's cognitive and intellectual performance, they should understand that it can only be done through intrinsically motivated play environments. By being flexible and supportive in their attitudes toward play and by providing novel, varied and increasingly complex play experiences (i.e., unstructured playthings and "junk" playgrounds) parents and educators contribute much to child development. Occasional encouragement and guidance are desirable, but at the same time teachers should be careful not to go too far in tutoring. Otherwise, there is a danger of turning children's recreation into work.

summary

Understanding children's leisure and recreation is important for several reasons. Two of them guided the writing of this chapter. First, by knowing the principles underlying children's leisure behavior, parents, educators, and practitioners of leisure services are in a better position to endow them with enjoyable play experiences. Such knowledge makes it possible to see things from children's perspective, thereby probably improving actions directed toward them. Frequently these things are taken for granted in dealing with the young, and educators simply give orders to them. But, as the preceding chapter showed, such negligence has severe psychological consequences. One should make every effort to understand children's psychological world and the role of leisure in it. Therefore, knowledge of children's leisure is needed for the sake of information and for improving the child-parent relationship. Second, understanding is important in order to comprehend the roots of socialization into leisure. This chapter clearly demonstrated that children's play experiences lay the foundations for future leisure. Although leisure behavior changes in a changing world throughout one's lifespan, early recreation experiences provide the setting and direction for individual changes in leisure patterns during the later stages of life. It is therefore essential to be cognizant of underlying psychological principles when providing play environments for children.

In discussing free-play, the chapter first considered children's tendency to seek and conquer challenges. Based upon theoretical and empirical evidence, it was shown that all human beings have a need for optimal arousal or incongruity. There is an optimum amount of arousal for each individual at any given time in all informational organism-environment interactions. An individual is in a continuous process of seeking and avoiding interactions with the environment, striving to sustain an optimal level of arousal. This "problem of match" theory holds that if the environment provides too many stimuli (too much incongruity) for the child to handle, the result is withdrawal. If the environmental inputs are overly similar to the stored information and previous experiences (too little incongruity), the child becomes bored and consequently seeks more incongruous, uncertain, novel, and complex situations. Thus, this tendency to seek optimal incongruity energizes and directs the child's play behavior.

Some environments, however, impede and restrict children's play and thus their attempts to achieve optimal incongruity. Situations having no or few inputs create the conditions for "stimulus deprivation;" this has been shown to cause dramatic effects in both animals and human beings. These include changes in biochemical and anatomical structures of the central nervous system, as well as retardation in ability to sit up and walk alone without adult support. On the other hand, the detrimental effects of stimulus deprivation can be reversed later by enriching one's experiences through increasingly complex environments. Massive enrichment, however, is not needed or desirable, because it provides too much incongruity for such a child to handle. Thus, "normal" development calls for an appropriate match between the child and the environment, neither too little nor too much incongruity. The responsibility of parents and educators is to provide optimally arousing and incongruous play environments for children. They should not leave children at the mercy of their inherited capacities, in the belief that the genes will take care of development.

In seeking novelty, dissonance, and complexity, children explore, investigate, and manipulate. Thus, play is defined as behaviors which are intrinsically motivated and engaged in for their own sake. Children are playing when their behavior is largely under their control. To make a given setting amenable to play, as many external constraints as possible should be eliminated. In support of this contention, ample empirical data reveal that expected external rewards undermine intrinsic motivation and free play, thereby turning children's recreation into children's work. Expected extrinsic, task-irrelevant rewards not only decrease continued interest in play activity but also impair the quality of performance and creativity. These detrimental effects are particularly discernible if the rewards are salient. The same undermining effects occur also when children play under surveillance. On the other hand, verbal reinforcement which makes children feel competent and self-determined increases children's interest in a play activity and therefore facilitates it. The above findings suggest that favorable conditions for seeking optimal arousal or incongruity are provided by parents who do not use extrinsic rewards or otherwise force their children to engage in given play activities, but instead spend time talking with them about the self-directed play experiences of the day.

Implications of the above theory of play are manifold. First, the child should be given opportunities for exploration and manipulation in the home. For toys to be stimulating, they must be responsive to manipulation; they should also be novel enough to invite exploration, sufficiently complex to puzzle the child and to incite to investigation. Furthermore, as many material, real objects (e.g., tools, utensils, ornaments) as possible should be made legitimate playthings in the home. As children often look to adults for stimulation, they should be allowed to play at the adults' feet, between legs, on the back, and in the lap. It has been shown that a flexible and encouraging home play environment is positively related to children's creativity. Unfortunately, many young couples are faced with a difficult problem, in that living in modern apartments is very restrictive physically, thereby limiting children's mobility, discouraging play, and impeding indulgence in arousal seeking. Second, playgrounds should be drastically altered to accommodate the principles of the need for optimal incongruity. A good playground is one which is not fixed or standard, but rather is susceptible to continuous modification by children. They must be able to dig, build, and alter their playground. Sand, dirt, earth, bricks, lumber and other substances which can be modified, should replace conventional and standard equipment (e.g., swings, slides).

The last part of the chapter discussed cognitive benefits arising from play. One of the most notable findings indicated that children who simply played on their own with the materials needed in solving a given problem did as well as children who were shown the complete solution of the task. This suggests, therefore, that an appropriately stimulating play environment enhances the problem-solving ability in children. Another study indicated that free and thematic play provides an avenue for children to acquire and rehearse skills conducive to creative behavior. Finally, it was shown that mothers with an abstract, flexible and unorthodox cognitive style tend to provide a playfulness-engendering environment for their children; this in turn is positively related to children's later cognitive performance, especially creativity. Presumably, these beneficial effects occur because enriched play environments widen children's repertoire of responses, and also their motivation to utilize this range in a complex, innovative and varied way in old and novel environments. Thus, play is not only fun but also serious business, in that children's problem-solving abilities and other aspects of creativity are here involved.

6 social play and organized games

social play

Much intrinsically motivated play takes place in groups. While social play has its role in all stages of child development, its importance increases with age (Britt and Janus, 1941; Millar, 1974). Social play may be defined "as a state of engagement in which the successive, nonliteral behaviors of one partner are contingent on the nonliteral behaviors of the other partner" (Garvey, 1974, p. 163). To put it more simply, social play is an activity in which one child influences and is influenced by other children. It is intrinsically motivated if a child does not perceive others' influence as external constraint. Before the child can be said to play socially, certain skills must have been acquired. Garvey (1974) suggested that three abilities are fundamental to social play: (1) to play with another, a child must understand the distinction between play and nonplay—what is and is not "for real;" (2) a child has to have an understanding of the abstraction of rules, because social play depends on mutually accepted rules. The most basic rule is reciprocity or "taking turns" ("You do it next"), that is, doing the same thing or doing a complementary thing, (3) a child must be able to identify a theme of the activity and interaction and develop it in a mutually satisfying way.

**developmental
analysis**

social play in infancy

The above definition clearly precludes infants from social play. Although "the human infant is a social organism as soon as he is born" (Caplan and Caplan, 1973), the baby does not have ready-made skills to engage in social play. These abilities (most notably the three listed above) have to be learned through encounters with the social environment. This is not to say that adult or peer social contacts with the very young children are unimportant. In fact, social interaction between a caretaker (usually the mother) and a baby is critical. Bronfenbrenner (1968) reported that a progressively more complex pattern of reciprocal interaction with the mother (or substitute caretaker) becomes essential to the psychological development of behavioral capacity in the infant. The importance of social interaction and social play is also reflected by the finding that in monkeys "infant-infant interactions can compensate for lack of mothering" (Harlow and Harlow, 1962). Such infants developed effective play patterns and strong affectional bonds to each other. On the other hand, if monkeys were raised with natural mothers but isolated from peers, they showed no tendency to play together when introduced to the company of other infant monkeys in a play environment. Although the issue is controversial and the long-term effects have not been studied (cf. Bronfenbrenner, 1972), there are some reasons to believe that in human beings also, infant-infant interactions can, to some extent, compensate for lack of mothering, though not completely. But what seems to be more crucial is that once a child has developed a dependency drive or attachment to a caretaker, subsequent maternal deprivation becomes very detrimental. These adverse effects include a reduced repertoire of responses and a decreased capacity for adaptation, problem-solving, and withstanding stress (Bronfenbrenner, 1972). But if an infant is isolated from the mother since birth, the baby does not *know* that such deprivation is abnormal, and therefore the motivation to explore the environment is not impaired by emotional disturbances.

Thus, social contacts are very important for an infant. While a mother's (or caretaker's) role in providing these contacts is critical, age mates are also needed for social stimulation. As Bronfenbrenner (1972, p. 266) stated, "there must be room and incentive for breaking the ties of contact comfort and dependency to engage in exploratory activity and interactive play." Although the infant-caretaker interactions might not be called social play as such, many "games" in infancy are played between mother and infant. Peek-a-boo, for example, is common and is psychologically meaningful, in that it gives the infant opportunities to separate himself from the caretaker and experience a delightful reunion again. Such games help the infant to deal with one of the basic human anxieties: the fear of losing human contact (Call, 1970).

Parten (1932) defined six sequential classes of social participation. According to the first category, a child's play is characterized as *unoccupied, onlooking,* or *solitary.* Unoccupied behavior consists of watching anything that happens to be of momentary interest or of playing with own body. Onlooking behavior is comprised of observing other children's play, without overtly entering into the play itself. Solitary play refers to playing alone with toys different from those of other children, and centering personal interest around one's own activity without regard to others' play. The second major category of social participation is characterized by *parallel* play. Here the child plays independently and beside rather than with other children; his toys are similar to those of others. The third classification of Parten's social participation involves *associative* play which represents a group play, with minimal or no organization of the common activity. All the children engage in a similar activity, each child acting according to his individual wishes. Participants exchange and share play materials. Finally, *cooperative* play emphasizes a division of labor and a highly organized form of group activity which is directed toward making some material product or attaining competitive goals. The group has a leader(s), subordinates, and various roles to be occupied by members.

Parten (1932) found that social participation largely depends on the age of children. In general, solitary or parallel play was typical of younger children, whereas older ones preferred integrated play groups. Solitary and parallel play were common at the age of two and two-and-a-half years, but declined markedly in importance among the 3- and 4-year-olds. Associative group play was popular among children aged 3½ to 4½. Similarly, cooperative play increased in popularity with age, with 3–4 year-olds cooperating partially when working toward a common goal. Some researchers, however, have found that cooperative behavior generally emerges around or after the age of five years. Based upon a series of experiments, Nelson and Kagan (1972) concluded that 5-year-olds often fail to cooperate, due to a lack of capacity to understand interdependency and of the need for mutual assistance. Thus, the above time-table concerning Parten's categories of social participation should be viewed as a general description rather than as a rule strictly followed by all children. Individuals of the same age differ in the rate at which they mature so as to participate in each type of play. What is more important than the time-table is the order in which these various forms of play appear. Eifermann (1975) reported that the order originally proposed by Parten tends to hold true: first solitary, then parallel, then associative, and finally cooperative.

the second year

If we subscribe to Garvey's (1974) definition of social play, then solitary and parallel play can hardly be referred to as social play. Rather, "associative" play (from 3–3½ years of age onward) may be taken to mark the beginning of social play. Before the skills for social play are developed, a child has to acquire experiences in interacting with peers. In light of recent studies it appears that the child becomes increasingly social during the second year of life. Thus, it then looks as though the first year lays the foundations for the development of social contacts during the second year, while this in turn serves as basis for enhancing social play after the third birthdate.

That children become more social in play during their second year was clearly demonstrated by Eckerman, Whatley and Kutz (1975). In this study, normal, home-reared children aged 10–12, 16–18, and 22–24 months were placed in a playroom with several toys on the floor. Play behavior of two children of the same age was monitored for 20 minutes. In addition to the two children (unknown to one another), their mothers sat in the playroom during the testing period but did not intervene with the toddlers' play. Thus, each child could initiate interaction with a peer, with one's own mother, with a new adult (the other mother), or simply play alone with the toys available. The results showed that watching the peer was a prominent activity at all ages. The frequency of contact with the shared playthings increased with age. Similarly, such forms of direct involvement in the peer's play as imitation of activity, taking a toy from him, struggling over a toy, and coordinating activities with the toys, significantly increased with age. Solitary play took slightly more than one-third of children's time in all age groups. Most important, play with the peer increased significantly as the age increased, occurring in 60 percent of the periods by two years of age. Play with the new adult was about zero in all groups; play with one's own mother increased from the period of 10–12 to 16–18 months, but declined to the 10–12 month level among the 22–24 month-olds.

Taken together, it is important to note that play in all age groups was more often directed toward the peer than toward the child's own mother, especially at the end of the second year. Thus, children in a novel play setting seemed to turn more and more to their peers and less to their mothers, suggesting that peers offer stimulation different from that of mothers. Although these children were socially active, their play with the peer was quite limited; they smiled and vocalized to each other, imitated one another, offered and accepted toys, and sometimes struggled over them. Nevertheless, these behaviors are clear signs of emerging social play among the three-year-olds. The second year seems to serve as a transitional, pretraining period for this unfolding skill. Development of social behavior across the second year is perhaps due to children's increased ability to combine the formerly separate segments of social contact.

Mueller and Brenner (1977) reported data consistent with the above findings and conclusions. In this longitudinal study, two groups of six boys, differing in the amount of peer acquaintance, participated for a total duration of seven months in a laboratory testing of free play. Results indicated that both groups exhibited a significant linear growth in peer interaction over the testing period. But more important, those toddlers who had 4½ months' acquaintance with their playmates more frequently engaged in sustained social interactions than the age-mates who were unacquainted. While the latter expressed vocalizing and smiling responses, they were not able to "turn the fun into a sustained game." The significant effect of peer acquaintance was entirely due to differences in "coordinated" social behaviors between the two types of play groups. "Coordinated" interaction referred to those instances where the child vocalized and waved while watching his peer. The findings also revealed that *parallel* play is an important activity enabling toddlers to discover and increase peer social interaction.

Mueller and Brenner (1977) interpreted these findings to indicate that the development of peer social interaction requires experience of 4½ months with age-mates. Social skills, therefore, are not the result of maturation or of immediate generalizations from child-parent interactions. All in all, these results indicate that peer interaction in play enhances the child's social skills, which is the source of coordinated peer-oriented behavior. Participation in peer interaction, therefore, is as much a cause as it is an effect of coordinated social behavior and social play. This conclusion is consistent with Smith and Connolly's findings (1972) that sociability in play behavior correlates more highly with nursery school experience than with age, thereby suggesting that peer interaction is a necessary and more important developmental factor of social skills than is chronological age.

From the age of three years (approximately) onward social (i.e., associative and cooperative) play becomes more frequent and prominent. This increase continues until children reach the age of 6 to 7 years, a milestone which seems to serve as a transitional period leading to the "gang-age," from about 8 to 12 years (Millar, 1974). Prior to such a transition, highly organized games with rules are rare. From 3 to 6 years, children's preference for social interaction increases, or remains at a relatively high level, but children often play social games without clear-cut rules. In addition to involving peer interaction, these social games provide children with opportunities to practice their physical and verbal skills, while this, in turn, increases feelings of personal competence and control over the environment. Children often repeat the same action over and over again, suggesting that games provide the challenge for the players to exercise their skills. In this context, Eifermann (1975) claimed that much of children's play is done "for the pleasure of being the cause of what is happening." However, all social play is not oriented toward practicing skills. The other aspect of social play during this period is what Piaget (1950) calls symbolic play. Children's play becomes imaginative, and they play "as if" they were something other than themselves. Thus, they may choose to imitate objects, animals or human beings. Children's symbolic play seems to become increasingly realistic from three years of age onward (Eifermann, 1975). Animal or human roles which children assume then become as close to real life models as possible.

The picture emerging from the past studies tends to demonstrate the developmental nature of children's free play behavior. Games and play tend to reflect children's actual level of development. Thus, younger children's play is cognitively and socially less mature than that of the older ones. "When children are younger they interact less in their play, play fewer games with rules, play fewer games of strategy, play for shorter periods of time, and play in smaller groups" (Eifermann, 1975, p. 56). The developmental view, however, should not be taken to suggest that children's play will automatically mature with age. As discussed earlier, the nonstimulating play environment and lack of peer interaction retard considerably the rate of evolution of both cognitive and social play. There is evidence to indicate that social and cognitive play of children of parents from middle socioeconomic status is of a more highly developed form than that of children from low socioeconomic status (Rubin, 1977). While children living in relatively impoverished play environments may be able to achieve these "higher" levels of play later, the unfortunate fact is that they will always stay behind their age mates, unless their play environment is changed dramatically. If so, cognitive and intellectual skills of these children will suffer, and they are likely to develop poor self-concepts perpetuated by their impoverished play styles.

**social interaction
versus playthings**

Children need a variety of increasingly complex playthings as well as peer interaction in their environment. The desire for social play increases with age, because repeated exposure to peers generally augments children's preference for peers, whereas among 4 to 5-year olds preference for play objects decreases as a function of repeated exposure (Scholtz and Ellis, 1975). Other things being equal, peers, therefore, seem to be more interesting and stimulating than play objects. In support of this contention, Wade and Ellis (1971) reported an experiment which showed that augmenting environmental complexity by increases in the size of play groups, facilitated kindergarten children's free play more than did augmented complexity of the play apparatus. Hence, it appears that social interaction is a more powerful stimulator of free play than physical play objects. This is presumably attributable to the novel, complex, and changing nature of the interaction with others. It is also important to know that while repeated exposure to peers enhances preferences for social interaction, the amount of this increase is lower when the external play setting is complex than when it is relatively simple and familiar. Although repeated exposure to play objects reduces children's preferences for them, this decrease is less if the play stimuli are complex than if they are not (Scholtz and Ellis, 1975).

Taken together these findings suggest that even familiar peers are more complex and stimulating than familiar play objects, once the immediate novelty of toys has worn off. Therefore, it is highly desirable to facilitate and encourage children's social interaction in play. If possible, peer interaction should take place in settings with increasingly complex play objects. It is believed that peers are more interesting and stimulating than physical play objects because they change continuously, whereas toys, regardless of their initial novelty and complexity, remain the same or change little. Children's minds grow and their experiences accumulate at a rapid rate, phenomena that involve continual changes in cognitive and behavioral patterns. In play groups of several children this results in increasing complexity and novelty. In contrast, the "brains" of play objects do not change and they do not change their capacity to respond to children's continuous need for novel and complex encounters. This is why peer interaction is the best single solution for meeting children's play needs. If parents try to satisfy the requirement for novelty and complexity through novel play objects, immense practical problems arise, such as the question of who can afford to buy new toys continuously. Peer interaction, on the other hand, is a practical, inexpensive, and in most cases a safe form of play.

Play objects vary in their capacity to stimulate social play. The Scholtz and Ellis findings show that when a child encounters novel and complex objects, social play decreases temporarily, until the objects become familiar. But familiar toys also differ in their capacity to enhance peer interaction. Britt and Janus (1941) found that clay led to more social and cooperative play than blocks. Parten (1933) had earlier reported that house and dolls, kiddie-car, and clay (in this order) more often led to social play than other toys. Trains, beads, swings, paints and sand (in this order) were least likely to facilitate children's social participation. In a more recent study, Rubin (1977) obtained both similar and dissimilar results when investigating behavior of 4-year-olds. Painting and using crayons, playdoh and clay, sand and water, or puzzle activities more often resulted in solitary and parallel play than in associative and cooperative behavior. On

social value of toys

the other hand, the most social interaction was prompted by house play and related themes, vehicle play, reading and number activities. These somewhat inconsistent results are probably due to individual differences in development as well as methodological discrepancies (e.g., various subject populations and differing toys) between the studies. Although there is some inconsistency in these findings, the studies nevertheless demonstrate that physical play objects vary in terms of their potential for social play. Thus, when providing children with toys, parents and teachers should carefully consider the value of various playthings for children's social play. If they are not aware of this concern, adults may unintentionally restrict children's repertoire of play responses. As we noted earlier, the reduced range of play behavior is likely to retard children's cognitive and social development.

The above studies indicated that toys differ quite consistently in their capacity to encourage social play. However, there is evidence that on a temporary basis the social value of any toy can fluctuate notably. It has been shown that children's interest in a given toy is affected by the immediate social environment, specifically, by their playmates' toy preferences. Costanzo, Grumet and Brehm (1974) performed an experiment which demonstrated that children rated the toy which was chosen and played with as more desirable than the one which was not selected or played with. In other words, a toy is much more interesting when others are seen to choose it and/or play with it, than when others do not express interest in the toy. While this is hardly surprising, the finding demonstrates that the value of playthings is influenced by the social environment of play.

sex related differences

Boys and girls differ in their play patterns. Goldberg and Lewis (1969) found considerable sex differences in the first year of life. In comparison to girls, boys exhibited more independence, exploratory behavior, and vigor; boys more than girls preferred toys requiring gross motor activity, and they tended to bang in their play. These findings parallel those obtained relative to children at later ages. Lehman and Witty (1927) presented a long list of play activities in which either boys or girls more frequently participate. Boys' activities were characterized as active, vigorous, and organized play and games, involving muscular dexterity, skill, and competition. Girls, on the other hand, more often engaged in sedentary activities and other forms of play with a more restricted range of action. These sex differences were most pronounced between ages 8½ and 10½, after which they tended to diminish. Britt and Janus (1941) reported similar results, in that boys preferred a greater specificity in the form of organized and physical play (ball games) and vigorous games, while girls were more interested in unorganized play and active social games, showing a breadth of play interests. In a similar vein, Smith and Connolly (1972) found that nursery school boys made more noises, their play was more rough and tumble, while their overall physical activity level was higher than that of girls. It has also been found that girls are more likely than boys to play house, that they engage in such activities as cutting, pasting and painting, whereas boys play more frequently with vehicles and blocks (Millar, 1974; Rubin, 1977). In sum, the play activities of boys seem to involve physical strength, a need for achievement and associating in groups to a greater extent than those of girls (cf. Eifermannn, 1975).

It also appears that most of the play groups are unisexual (Parten, 1933), indicating that children like to play with members of their own sex. Eifermann (1975) noted that this tendency increases from 3 to 8 years of age. While sex differences in play have changed somewhat within the last 40 years (Millar, 1974), a low rate of play involving both sexes is still the rule rather than the exception among preschool children. Serbin, Tonick and Sternglanz (1977), on the other hand, reported data indicating that cooperative cross-sex behavior can be markedly increased by adults' reinforcement of such behavior. In this study, a teacher reinforced cooperative cross-sex play approximately every five minutes during the free play session (30–45 minutes per day), for two weeks in a preschool. Reinforcement comments included statements like, ''I like the tower John and Kathy are building with the blocks.'' Such comments were made aloud so that all the children could hear them. This relatively simple manipulation was sufficient to double the rate of cooperative cross-sex play. Since this increase was achieved without a simultaneous decrease in the amount of solitary and single-sex play, it indicated that it is possible to enlarge children's repertoire of play responses and opposite-sex interaction, without interferring with their existing play experiences. Unfortunately, the increase in cross-sex play disappeared when social reinforcement was withdrawn. The results also showed that while the treatment (reinforcement) doubled cross-sex play, involvement in this play remained lower than in other forms of play. To summarize, the Serbin, *et al.* findings suggest that social reinforcement is an effective method of advancing cross-sex cooperative play, but that such positive effects are temporary at best.

That social reinforcement influences were limited in duration comes as no surprise. Since parents begin reinforcing sex differences from the first weeks of an infant's life onward (Goldberg and Lewis, 1969), it is clear that superficial reinforcement of opposite play patterns (i.e., cross-sex play) for a short period of time several years later is not likely to alter children's play behaviors permanently. By the age of 4 to 5 years (subjects in the Serbin, *et al.* study), sex differences may have already become firmly fixed in children's minds. Stein and Smithells (1969) found that sex-role standards become gradually more definite and more extreme with age. Children viewed artistic, social, and reading skills as the most feminine areas, whereas athletic, spatial, mechanical and arithmetic skills were rated as the most masculine or the least feminine domains. It follows, then, that if one seeks to eliminate these differences, emphasis should first be placed on changing parents' attitudes toward appropriate activities associated with the sex role. As Goldberg and Lewis suggested, parents should be held responsible for bringing about differences in boys' and girls' play patterns because of their reinforcement of those behaviors that they consider appropriate to the respective sex-role. There is absolutely no evidence to support the idea that boys and girls are born with differing innate *needs* to play with different toys and participate in different activities. Family attitudes and practices directly affect the amount of activity, originality and social content of children's play (Millar, 1974, p. 204).

organized games: the social psychology of little league baseball

Thus far we have focused on children's free play and games without rules. The remainder of this chapter is devoted to the other side of the coin: children's leisure behavior as reflected by their participation in organized games with clear-cut rules. This will first be considered from the developmental viewpoint, then the psychological benefits of structured play behavior will be analyzed, with special reference to Little League baseball. American children's organized play and games are often said to reach their climax in Little League baseball.

desire for organized games

As noted earlier, group play and games often are rather loosely organized before the beginning of the "gang-age," at about 7–8 years (Millar, 1974). Of course, because of considerable individual differences in the developmental rate, it is difficult and perhaps fruitless to call certain chronological periods "gang-ages" or other names. Nevertheless, there seems to be some truth in Millar's claim that gang behavior is most frequent between the ages of about 8 and 12. Britt and Janus (1941), for example, found that the maximum number of play activities engaged in by children occurs at the age of 10½ years. Similar results were obtained by Eifermann (1971). In this study, researchers observed children's play behavior once per week for several months during the ten-minute recess period in school. Figure 7 depicts the results in terms of percentages of players in competitive rule-governed games (e.g., ball games) by grade, considering all children in each grade.

Developmental Analysis of Leisure and Recreation

Figure 7 Percentage of play participants in competitive rule-governed games by grade, out of all children in each grade. (From Eifermann, R.R. "Social play in childhood," Figure 2, p. 279, in R.E. Herron and B. Sutton-Smith, Eds., *Child's Play.* Copyright ©1971 by John Wiley and Sons, Inc. Reprinted by permission.)

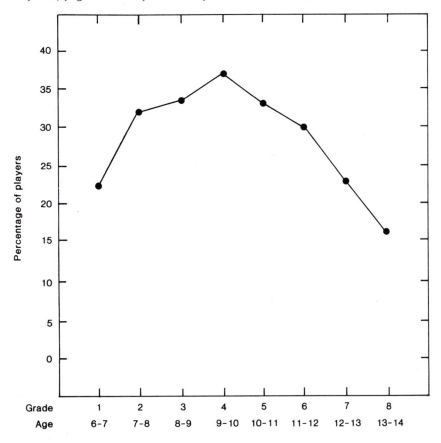

It can be seen that the percentage of play participants in these types of games increased from the age of 6–7 years onward, until reaching its peak among about 10-year-olds, after which the decline was strong and linear. Almost identical results were obtained in relation to *non*competitive rule-governed games (e.g., hand-clapping) by grade, thus showing similar increases in the lower school grades and the same decreases in the upper grades as those presented in figure 7. This study also revealed that these declines in participation in rule-governed games were not limited to play at school, but were also observed at play out of school, that is, on streets and neighborhood playing fields. In speculating as to reasons for a general decline in competitive activities after the age of 11 and 12 years, Eifermann conjectured that this is partly due to a lack of challenge posed by such games, and to the fact that because of social pressures, these games may turn into formal sports and athletics, which most children do not like. Besides, if games governed by rules approximate highly organized sport activities, many youngsters probably lose their interest in them, since they know that only a handful of the most capable individuals will actually participate on competitive teams.

Again, it seems that the young should be provided with the opportunity to participate in a wide variety of both competitive and cooperative games. Eifermann's (1975) other data indeed indicate that too much emphasis placed on either competitive or cooperative behavior may not be desirable, presumably because it limits children's repertoire of play responses. She found that the kibbutz young, who are raised in the spirit and letter of cooperation, exhibit a tendency to participate less frequently in purely cooperative games than do family-reared city children when given a chance to do so. Thus, it is plausible that the kibbutz children have received an overdose of organized cooperation during the childhood years, which may lead them to seek stimulation from more competitively oriented games and activities, in an effort to achieve optimal arousal. Certainly, this finding is consistent with the earlier conclusion that there is a universal human need to challenge and conquer incongruity. If too heavy doses of cooperation are not good, the same should be true of excessive participation in competitively organized games such as Little League baseball. To examine this assumption, it is useful to consider a social psychological analysis of Little League baseball and seek to determine the psychological consequences of participation in this popular form of children's leisure activity.

Social psychologists have paid very little attention to children's achievement behavior in athletic and sport contexts (Crandall, 1967). The lack of social psychological analyses is surprising, in that Little League baseball constitutes a major recreation and leisure "industry" for both adults and children alike. Each summer more than one million players participate in these leagues throughout the country, and the majority of parents come to see their children's games (Watson, 1973). It is also significant that most Little League baseball players (83%) reported that baseball takes half to most of their free-time during the entire year (Skubic, 1956). Although this may not be true objectively speaking, it nevertheless shows how important baseball is to the players. In view of such intensive involvement, it is reasonable to suppose that some psychological effects will result from this participation. Although the amount of empirical research on Little League baseball is not extensive, the literature warrants a review of possible psychological benefits and injurious effects which result from engaging in this activity. This analysis is mainly theoretical and considers four different but interrelated frames of reference: (1) competition and cooperation, (2) attribution of causality, (3) learning helplessness, and (4) intrinsic-extrinsic motivation ("overjustification" hypothesis).

competition and cooperation

It is no secret that competition is the basis of free-market capitalistic societies, notably that of the United States. Both Republicans and Democrats preach the values of competition. Mass media promote sports and athletics by reporting countless results of various forms of competition and by publishing photographs of winners on front pages. This approach is reflected in the time and effort parents spend in attending their children's competitive sports. Skubic (1956) found that practically all parents of Little League players believe such activities are useful to the participants. When asked why, parents responded that Little League imprints socially desirable characteristics (i.e., achievement motivation) on participants, builds their character, and helps players become "better citizens." Strong emphasis placed upon competition and organized games is consistent with a wide-spread belief that "unlimited, unorganized, unled, and uncontrolled leisure is the gravest danger to which any nation was ever exposed" (Cutten, 1926, p. 96).

When parents and the entire society have such strong faith in the superiority of competition, it is not surprising to learn that children exhibit highly competitive behavior in their play and games. The ample empirical evidence indicates that (1) American children are more competitive than children from other countries (Johnson and Johnson, 1974), (2) Anglo-American children are more competitive than are Mexican-American and Afro-American (Avellar and Kagan, 1976; McClintock, 1974), (3) urban children are more competitive than rural children (Thomas, 1975a), and (4) children of parents of the low socioeconomic status display more maladaptive competition than do children of parents from high socioeconomic strata (McKee and Leader, 1955; Thomas, 1975b).

Both competitive and cooperative behaviors increase with age, but the former emerges earlier (Cook and Stingle, 1974). At the age of two years, children do not yet exhibit competitive behavior, but by six years of age all children have done so; on the average competitive responses develop around age four. Cooperative behavior, on the other hand, does not usually emerge before the age of five years. This is due to the fact that the ability to understand interdependence and cognitive and emotional viewpoints of others (also called "social perspective-taking," Johnson and Johnson, 1974) does not normally develop before five years of age. Once a child has learned to compete, this behavioral tendency increases steadily, reaching its peak among children who are 10 to 11 years old. Besides Eifermann's data (1971) reported in figure 7, Nelson and Kagan (1972) found evidence of children's strong motive to compete at the age of ten years. They noted that 10-year-olds not only failed to cooperate in conflict-of-interest situations, but above all, their capacity for adaptive and cooperative problem-solving was critically reduced as a result of an increased spirit of competitiveness. This tendency even reached the point where children became "irrationally competitive" and "sadistically rivalrous," that is, they were willing to sacrifice their own rewards to reduce their opponents' rewards.

The above findings suggest that competitive goal structures adversely affect interpersonal behavior. In support of this view, Johnson and Johnson (1974) concluded that (1) competitive tasks lower the quality of interpersonal relationships (e.g., mutual liking and concern), whereas cooperative tasks increase it, (2) in competitive rather than cooperative situations children tend to be more anxious and tense and less secure, and (3) cooperative tasks enhance social perspective, which in turn is positively related to social adjustment, effectiveness of communication, personal identity and self-awareness, moral judgment, openmindedness, and acceptance of individual differences. In addition to these positive effects, it is clear that activities based upon cooperative goal structures teach children to coordinate their efforts, divide labor equitably, work together, and share burdens and rewards. In the light of this compelling evidence in favor of cooperation, it would be very difficult to advocate such competitive activities as Little League baseball for children.

intergroup
competition and
ingroup cooperation

But before one accepts this conclusion, he should bear in mind that the studies on which these inferences are based were usually done under fairly limited conditions. In a typical experiment, subjects are given a problem to be solved and told that individual rewards depend on the quality of the group performance (cooperation); or subjects working in a competitive goal structure are informed that the best performance is rewarded by a maximum reward and lower performance by a minimum reward. Intrapersonal and interpersonal behaviors of the two groups are subsequently compared (Johnson and Johnson, 1974). In another line of research, two children who face each other across a table participate in a marble-pull game for rewards (Nelson and Kagan, 1972). This task is so designed that if children cooperate by taking turns in pulling their strings they both will receive the same number of rewards, but if they do not, neither of them will obtain an award. Although both of these approaches may shed light on competitive and cooperative behavior in general, they do not necessarily prove anything about the effects of intergroup competition. However, some research has been reported which suggests that intergroup competition may be psychologically beneficial if it does not become too intense (Johnson and Johnson, 1974; Sherif, *et al.*, 1961). Ingroup cooperation and cohesiveness, work relations, member self-esteem and satisfaction tend to increase as a result of intergroup competition or external threat.

Thus, the positive or negative effects of competition seem to be relative. It depends on the types of competition involved and the alternatives to which the effects of competitive participation are compared. While individual competition within a group should be condemned, intergroup competition, with its emphasis on ingroup cooperation, should be encouraged. But even individual competition is good for children if the alternative is to "hang around in the streets." So, to say that competition is either good or bad is an oversimplification, because of the relative nature of the factors involved. Competition in itself is not bad; what is critical is how it is used and what its implications may be. The detrimental effects may be mitigated by selecting the best form: intergroup competition. But even intergroup competition has to be kept controlled by not allowing it to become too serious or dominant. More emphasis should be placed on ingroup cooperation than intergroup competition. With this sort of orientation, Little League baseball would not seem to be so bad after all, and might even be psychologically more beneficial than harmful. As Johnson and Johnson suggested, children ordinarily find games and sports pleasant, provided that they do not produce anxiety:

> When winning or losing does not create a great deal of anxiety for any of the participants there seems to be a sense of pleasure in matching one's skills and abilities against a peer's to see who will win (Johnson and Johnson, 1974, p. 231).

This, of course, is the core of the problem, which parents, coaches, and others unfortunately appear to forget in the context of Little League baseball, as will be noted later.

One of the key determinants of the degree of anxiety associated with competition is the outcome. Specifically, it has been found that failure impairs a person's intrapersonal and interpersonal behavior, whereas success creates "warm-glows" (Hurlock, 1927; Isen, Horn and Rosenhan, 1973; Johnson and Johnson, 1974; Sherif, *et al.*, 1961). The impact of these effects is likely to increase with the importance of outcome. If so, it is also reasonable to assume that the more important the outcome becomes, the higher the degree of anxiety associated with competitive participation. Since winning and losing are an integral part of Little League, while external pressures (i.e., from coaches and parents) have made the outcome increasingly important, players are faced with the problem of being able to cope with such intense experiences. One important coping mechanism deals with the attribution of causes for success and failure. It is appropriate, therefore, to examine whether players are capable of coping with winning and losing in Little League, as reflected by their causal attributions.

attribution of causality

In principle, winning and losing can be attributed to internal (e.g., one's ability) or external (e.g., luck) factors. It is generally established that people have a tendency to explain their success by internal factors (high ability and effort), and their failure by external factors (bad luck or intervening environmental variables) (Weiner, Frieze, Kukla, Reed, Rest and Rosenbaum, 1971; Miller and Ross, 1975). This tendency seems to become more prominent when less trivial tasks such as motor skills are used (Iso-Ahola, 1977b; Iso-Ahola and Roberts, 1977). The bias toward internal attributions suggests self-serving behavior on the part of subjects, that is, people are ready to give credit to themselves when they succeed, but tend to deny that their lack of ability is responsible for failure. There is evidence that this self-serving attitude is typical of people in competitive and achieving societies. If so, it may indicate that individuals employ causal attributions as a means of coping with a competitive world. If a person wants to survive and succeed in such a society, it is desirable to attribute successes to his ability rather than to good luck, and to ascribe failures to environmental causes rather than to lack of ability. Otherwise, motivation to continue and persevere is impaired, a condition which in turn may undermine zest for life. This does not imply that self-serving attributions should necessarily be promoted, but rather that they are an empirical reality reflecting human coping and adaptation to stressful environments.

It follows from the foregoing that Little League players' causal attributions for team outcomes should reflect self-serving biases. If team members believe that they succeeded because of good luck or lousy opponents and failed due to lack of ability, it is fairly certain that such a team will not succeed in the future. Consequently, the intrinsic interest, enjoyment and satisfaction which players associate with Little League, will probably be impaired by continuous failures. Therefore, to avoid such negative experiences, players' attributions for their team's performances should be positively biased. This hypothesis can also be advanced, if one accepts the idea that Little League players are generally high achievers. In this connection Weiner (1974) has provided evidence indicating that high achievers tend to be more self-serving in their attributions than low achievers. In addition, some earlier research (i.e., Friend and Neale, 1972) has indicated that children are inclined to make such attributions for success and failure.

little league players' causal attributions

To test the above hypothesis on Little League players, a field study was conducted (Iso-Ahola, 1975, 1977c), in the summer of 1974. In this investigation some 300 baseball players' team-attributions and self-attributions for their teams' performances were measured immediately after the conclusion of 11 different ball games. Subjects were taken to an appropriate place in the field to fill out a questionnaire which measured these attributions. In the case of team-attributions, players indicated the extent to which they believed that team ability, effort, luck, and task difficulty, (i.e., opponent team) separately were responsible for team outcome; also, through self-attributions players expressed how much they thought their own ability, effort, luck, and task difficulty contributed to team success or failure. As predicted, attributions of team success to team ability and effort were much greater than attributions of team failure to these factors. Although attributions to luck and task difficulty remained low and did not vary as a function of team outcome, it appeared that the lack of team effort and a "hard" opponent were seen to contribute more to team failure than the lack of ability. Attributions of those players whose team won by a clear margin did not differ from those of players who defeated their opponents narrowly, nor was a systematic difference between attributions made following clear loss or bare loss. This was interpreted to mean that the outcome in itself (i.e., either win or loss) rather than the margin of victory, is the critical determinant of players' causal reasoning about team performance. As for self-attributions, similar results were observed. Players thought their personal ability and effort contributed considerably more to team performance when they had been successful than when their team had lost, and they thought that their personal effort had improved team performance more following a clear win than following a bare win. It is also worth noting that lack of personal effort and a strong opponent were perceived to have played a more important part than lack of personal ability in affecting team failure. This suggests that players consider the effects of their personal ability and effort as being positive and important when their team succeeds but not when it fails.

Developmental Analysis of Leisure and Recreation

Another aspect of the same study (Iso-Ahola, 1977d) dealt with players' trait attributions, that is, how high they rated their team and themselves in terms of ability, effort, luck, and task difficulty, following winning and losing. These ratings represented trait judgments rather than causal ascriptions of the characteristics involved. The results showed that team failure decreased players' evaluation of team ability and effort, but did not reduce ratings of their personal ability and effort. That is, players judged their own ability and effort to be high, regardless of a team's present failure or its repeated poor performance in the past. These findings seem to indicate that players maintain a high and stable self-concept with regard to their ability and effort, irrespective of their team's present and past performance. If so, players' perception of internal qualities is not vulnerable to team failures.

In sum, these findings suggest that players perceive their team success to result from team ability and hard work, and they consider their personal ability and effort as contributing importantly to the team success. Team losses, on the other hand, are generally regarded as due to environmental factors (e.g., a lousy umpire). Although team ability and effort were judged lower following losing than following winning, these factors were not considered important for explaining failure in the absolute sense. And if something internal was to be blamed for failure, players chose lack of effort rather than lack of ability. Players rated their personal ability and effort high, regardless of team failure, and therefore did not consider their own ability to be responsible for the team's poor performance. These results may be interpreted as implying that players are capable of successfully coping with team outcomes. They seem to believe that to a considerable extent their own actions control team performance: their team succeeded because of their actions, and failed, in part, because of the inadequacy of their actions. Thus they seemed to know how to sail in blue waters and when to jump out of the sinking boat. This clearly illustrates one great advantage of team sports over individual sports: failure in the former can be explained relatively easily by reasons other than those stemming from personal qualities. Logically, the reverse should also be true, that is, it should be relatively difficult to claim personal credit for team success. Although players viewed their personal qualities as an important causal factor in team success, they nevertheless acknowledged the significance of team ability and effort for their success, thereby avoiding overly self-serving attributions.

summary of attributional findings

If one accepts the view that these attributions reflect players' capacity to cope with team failures and successes, what then is the cause of this capacity? It appears to be a sum of developmental factors and a self-selection process. The fact that children's desire for competitive activity reaches its peak at the time of Little League (Eifermann, 1971) and that practically all players like playing baseball "very much" (Fine, 1977; Iso-Ahola, 1976b) indicates that from the developmental standpoint children are maximally prepared for competitive activities. This general capacity is likely to be greater among Little League players than non-players, providing that players participate voluntarily in the game. It has been shown that before the baseball season, when compared to non-players, the self-concept and achievement motivation of players are higher, (Bowlsby, 1978; Seymour, 1956). It is therefore reasonable to assume that players with a general tendency toward competitive action, a liking for the game, and relatively high self-concept, are well equipped to deal with winning and losing.

learned helplessness

Although the above attributions point to the conclusion that players are capable of coping with team performance, a few words of caution are in order. The studies reviewed previously do not pertain to the whole baseball season and therefore do not necessarily indicate that the same findings would be obtained at the end of the season's last game. An important but yet unsolved question has to do with the effects of continuous failure on players' feelings and the inferences of helplessness. How long are players able to tolerate repeated failure before they conclude they have inferior ability and feel helpless? If such negative experiences lead to helplessness, does learned helplessness generalize to other aspects of players' life? In the absence of any directly applicable empirical data we have to rely on Seligman's (1975) theory, which is based upon a wide array of laboratory experiments. Of course, the difference between the laboratory and Little League has to be kept in mind when discussing the applications of this theory.

Helplessness is a psychological state that frequently results when events or behaviors are uncontrollable. It produces three deficiencies in humans (Seligman, 1975): (1) decreased motivation to initiate action, (2) retardation in ability to learn, perceive, and believe that one's behavior has been successful when it actually has been, and (3) disturbed emotional balance, with increased anxiety and depression. Seligman has demonstrated that once helplessness is felt, it tends to extend to circumstances other than those under which it was first learned, and thus to undermine a person's entire repertoire of adaptive behaviors. If continuous failures in Little League are sufficient to induce helplessness, it follows that players' other interests and behaviors will also suffer from such experiences. Although this hypothesis has not yet been tested, some relevant suggestions can be found in Skubic's (1956) data.

Based upon parents' reports, one-third of the players were too excited after winning, or too depressed after losing, to eat a normal-sized meal. But when questions were directed to boys themselves, over 80 percent of them said that the outcome does not make any difference to their appetite. On the other hand, they (over 80%) admitted they were generally quite disappointed following a team loss, and that winning the game means a great deal to them. To summarize, winning and losing seem to have strong emotional impact on all players and appear to interfere with some players' performance in activities unrelated to baseball. While it is probably safe to conclude that an outcome of one game does not harm players psychologically, the long-term effects are unknown. If one game has such strong emotional influence, do these effects add up during the season, or do they dissipate in time between the games? An answer to this question would be very important in light of Seligman's findings. That is, if the effects of the outcome (especially losing) accumulate, then players are likely sooner or later to feel helplessness. On the other hand, if in time, they dissipate, then Little League may serve as an excellent vehicle of equipping children to resist helplessness in the future.

An answer to the question whether Little League baseball can cause helplessness in players is important for theoretical and practical reasons. Robin Roberts (1975), for example, has publicly denounced Little League because it is supposedly conducive to generalized helplessness. Three principal factors have been shown to lead to learned helplessness in humans (Seligman, 1975): (1) experience of uncontrollability, (2) chance comments, in which a person is simply told that his attempts are futile, and (3) external personality; as opposed to internal persons, external individuals believe that the most important things in their lives are not under their personal control. As for the first factor, uncontrollability may be experienced in Little League if one's team loses continuously and decisively. This, however, does not necessarily and automatically follow, as players are able to cope with failure to a considerable extent.

It has been indicated elsewhere (Iso-Ahola, 1977d, e) that causal attributions mediate the effects of outcome and determine whether or not repeated failure turns into a state of helplessness. Theoretically, the relationship between causal attributions and helplessness can be presented as follows:

theoretical model

Figure 8 An attributional model of learned helplessness with particular reference to Little League sports.

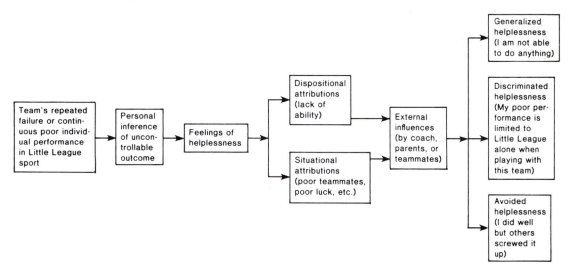

Following his team's continuous failures or poor individual performance (e.g., continuous strike-out), a player is confronted with an inference of uncontrollable outcomes, which in turn gives rise to initial feelings of helplessness. Then, the individual evaluates the locus of the cause of uncontrollable outcomes and thus of helplessness. Theoretical possibilities are twofold: the player may assume personal responsibility for failures and therefore think that lack of personal ability was one of the main causes of losing (dispositional attribution); alternatively, the player may assign the principal causality of failure to such situational factors as a lousy umpire or other teammates' poor performance. Other things being equal, dispositional attributions are likely to result in generalized or discriminated helplessness. In the former case, the person believes that personal inability to bring about positive outcomes holds true for most of life's activities, not just that of Little League. Although this is possible in theory, it is unlikely in practice. A more realistic possibility, following dispositional attributions, is discriminated helplessness; this means that the player believes personal inability to be limited just to Little League performance. Situational attributions, on the other hand, lead in most cases to avoided helplessness; in other words, a player ignores the initial feelings of helplessness on the ground that repeated failure is totally determined by factors other than those associated with his personal performance. In general, situational attributions are rarely followed by discriminated helplessness, not to mention generalized helplessness.

coaches' and
parents' role

The foregoing are possibilities when other things are kept constant. However, Little League does not exist in a vacuum, and other things are seldom equal. Parents, coaches, and other teammates shape an individual player's causal attributions. In theory, it is conceivable that because of these external influences, the player changes his dispositional attributions to situational ones, thereby avoiding helplessness. In addition, the coach may minimize the importance of the game that was lost. Seligman (1975) has suggested that helplessness tends to generalize from traumatic situations to less traumatic, from important to less important but not vice versa. Of course, it is also possible in principle that social agents lead a person to convert situational ascriptions into dispositional ones, thereby making him infer (discriminated) helplessness. Although this latter possibility may seem too theoretical or unrealistic, the present author has witnessed numerous coaches who get angry at players after losing, and condemn the players as unable. Such behavior puts the main blame for failure on individual players, who consequently are faced with dispositional attributions and perhaps helplessness. The writer, however, believes that the majority of coaches try to do the opposite, that is, making it clear to the players that their failure was due to bad luck, fortunate opponents, or other environmental causes, and that these things can be overcome in the next game. Parents can also alleviate players' negative feelings by reinforcing the coach's situational attributions. Since helplessness produced by uncontrollable outcomes undermines people's competitiveness and persistence (Seligman, 1975), coaches should try to do everything in their power to prevent players from making dispositional attributions for failure. Otherwise, the team is doomed to fail and players sink into a state of helplessness.

The above model and analysis show the psychological importance of the attitudes of parents and coaches when a team loses. As Seligman has demonstrated, a feeling of helplessness can be induced by simply telling human beings that their attempts are futile because the outcome is not under their control. Coaches who resort to this technique will not only destroy their team's future chances of winning, but above all will do considerable psychological damage to players. The fact that mere chance instructions can cause a sense of helplessness is frightening, because they can be so easily misinterpreted. On the other hand, if parents and coaches are aware of the probability of helplessness, they can prevent it by changing players' dispositional attributions. But even without the help of parents and coaches, the likelihood of helplessness can be minimized by certain arrangements prior to the baseball season. The main consideration is that players of various teams should be equal in their ability and motivation. If so, then there is good reason to expect equable games throughout the baseball season. When teams are matched in this way, the outcome of each game is uncertain, and all the teams will occasionally win and occasionally lose. Closeness and unpredictability of outcomes make it much easier for players to account for team failure by situational factors, and therefore reduce the likelihood of helplessness. **equal teams by random assignment**

To match the teams according to the suggested criteria, players should be *randomly* assigned to all the teams participating in a given league. No recruitment of ''good'' players should be allowed. This could be done before the season by simply putting the names of all players in one pile from which they would randomly be picked for each team. The law of randomness guarantees that every team would have about an equal number of good and not-so-good players *before* the baseball season starts. Besides equalizing teams according to ability, this procedure would also match teams in terms of their motivational levels. As Seligman has indicated, externally oriented persons are more likely to develop a feeling of helplessness than are ''internal'' persons. Therefore, if a team consists of ''internal'' players only, its probability of winning each game is much greater than that of a team manned with ''external'' players. This follows because ''internal'' players are inclined to resist failures by attributing losses or setbacks to situational factors. Consequently, failure does not eliminate the motivation to play well next time; regardless of losing, they still think that things are under their control. Thus, the random assignment of players to various teams before the season will distribute the internally and externally oriented players evenly among all teams.

The above discussion has focused on failure as a source of helplessness. How about repeated success and helplessness? Seligman suggested that too much success is not desirable because it undermines a person's ability to cope with inevitable failures in the future. In support of this contention, Jones, Nation and Massad (1977) found that a 50 percent immunization schedule of success produced a better result than either zero percent or 100 percent schedule of reinforcement. In other words, if a person succeeded every time, his motivation decreased and the likelihood of depression increased. Therefore, it seems that judicious use of failure, appropriately interspersed with success, will best maintain an individual's **is continuous success good?**

motivation, while effectively preparing him to confront his environment realistically and to handle failure satisfactorily (Jones, *et al.*, 1977). This view challenges the traditional position that winning is everything, that a person should win all the time. These findings lend considerable support to an earlier statement that Little League should be organized so as to guarantee virtually equal teams and unpredictable outcomes. *Ideally,* a team should win one half of its games and lose the other half.

early prevention of helplessness

The prevention of a sense of helplessness, with immunization against it, should begin in infancy and early childhood. Children should be provided with an environment which allows them to experience mastery and control, and also enables them to overcome anxiety and frustration *by their own actions.* Seligman states:

> Unless a young person confronts anxiety, boredom, pain, and trouble, and masters them by his actions, he will develop an impoverished sense of his own competence. . . . If we remove the obstacles, difficulties, anxiety, and competition from the lives of our young people, we may no longer see generations of young people who have a sense of dignity, power and worth (Seligman, 1975, pp. 158–159).

A child's experience of mastery over the environment is positively related to the development of ego strength and self-concept. Accordingly, the positive self-concept emerges after the child has confronted failures, frustrations, troubles and pain, and when he himself has overcome them. As Seligman puts it: "A sense of worth, mastery, or self-esteem can only be earned." Based upon his self-esteem studies, Coopersmith (1968, p. 106) makes a similar point: ". . . learning at an early age to respond constructively to challenges and troublesome conditions is essential to becoming a self-respecting individual."

In view of the above, Little League seems to be an excellent vehicle for immunizing players against helplessness. This, however, assumes that teams are relatively equal and that all of them both win and lose. If uncontrollable outcomes can be avoided, then Little League may be a desirable place to train children against helplessness. Under such circumstances, players are exposed to occasional failures, frustrations and pains, which they themselves can overcome by playing well in the next game. In light of the attribution studies (Iso-Ahola, 1975; 1977c, d), we are inclined to believe that this is what Little League seems to do best. Since self-concepts of players are higher than those of non-players (Bowlsby, 1978), it is possible that Little League reinforces participants' already-high ability to tolerate feelings of helplessness. But as remarked earlier, this presupposes that coaches and parents provide adequate psychological support when players confront repeated failure or repeated success. In addition, parents should not get too involved in their children's activities. Unfortunately, they seem to be doing just the opposite.

extrinsic rewards and sanctions

The earlier review of research on the "overjustification" hypothesis revealed that extrinsic rewards undermine children's free play and intrinsic interest. One implication of this conclusion is that the use of such extrinsic rewards as trophies decrease players' intrinsic motivation. Although the validity of the hypothesis has not been tested on Little League players, one is logically justified in accepting it, because there is much evidence to indicate that Little League baseball is an intrinsically motivating activity for children (Fine, 1977; Iso-Ahola, 1976b). In line with the previous discussion, one can also hypothesize that the more salient the extrinsic rewards are, the more likely are detrimental effects. Similarly, surveillance reduces intrinsic motivation, a fact which implies that the mere presence of a coach may make players perceive the locus of their participation to be extrinsic rather than intrinsic. This is especially the case if the coach is authoritative and constantly draws the players' attention to extrinsic rewards.

But the coaches are not the only instance of surveillance undermining players' interests. Watson (1974) reported that when parents were intensively involved in their children's Little League games, the players did not like it. Similar findings were recently documented by Horn (1977). Based upon the data of other researchers, he concluded that parents are the biggest problem in Little League because they not only urge their children to participate in the program, but above all "chew players out if they played poorly." Players also criticized their coaches for yelling too much and for taking the outcome too seriously. These findings convincingly indicate that trophies and other rewards, as well as the presence and conduct of coaches and parents, have made Little League an activity in which many players infer external motives and sanctions as reasons for their participation. Players become overly concerned about extrinsic rewards and reprimands following the team performance. This is unfortunate, because it has been found that as rewards increase in value, so does the tension and frustration of failure (Tseng, 1969). If this is true, then external rewards and surveillance not only undermine players' intrinsic motivation but also increase the likelihood of learned helplessness after failure.

There are compelling reasons to conclude that Little League competition, of itself and with its inherent outcomes, is intrinsically motivating. For one thing, children seem to enjoy the competitive interaction of a game more than the prizes to be gained by joint effort (Nelson and Kagan, 1972). Similarly, Watson (1974) reported that Little League players value intrinsic motivation ("having fun," "getting to play") more highly than extrinsic rewards. If a person places a high value on an activity, knowledge of results, without any tangible rewards, appears to be the most effective reinforcement type (Sorensen, 1976). Since spontaneity of game outcomes is the most attractive feature once involved in the game (Watson, 1974), it is perhaps justified to conclude that intrinsic motivation through outcomes is built into the game structure. Therefore, "the power of the attraction of game interaction, for its own sake, is stronger than the attraction of any adult-mediated extrinsic reward" (Watson, 1974). Ellis (1973, p. 143), has made a similar point: "To the extent that the reward ceases to lie in the processes of interaction with an opponent and depends on the extrinsic reward of the goal, the activity becomes less playful." Therefore, it is here advocated that Little League baseball should be left to the players! Adults' (coaches, parents) involvement should be minimized or perhaps totally eliminated.

**is little league
baseball good or
bad?**

What, then, are the conclusions about Little League baseball? Is it psychologically good or bad? The following conclusions appear justified in the light of our
present knowledge:

1. Other things being equal, cooperation is superior to competition, because of the positive effects of the former on interpersonal and intrapersonal behavior. However, intergroup competition along with ingroup
   cooperation is often more beneficial psychologically than no intergroup
   competition. With major emphasis on ingroup cooperation and minor
   emphasis on intergroup competition, Little League baseball is
   psychologically healthy, assuming that competition between the teams
   does not become too serious.

2. Self-serving causal attributions for team outcomes suggest that players
   are capable of coping with winning and losing. However, there are
   reasons to believe that repeated and uncontrollable failure gives rise to
   feelings and inferences of helplessness, which seem to interefere with
   players' other behaviors. To decrease the likelihood of such feelings,
   two courses of action are available: (a) players should be randomly
   assigned to all teams so that those with varying degrees of ability and
   motivation can be equally distributed among all the teams, thereby
   making games more equal and unpredictable; (b) parents and coaches
   should help players make situational attributions for their failure, and
   minimize the importance of games that were lost.

3. Intensive involvement by coaches and parents in Little League has
   turned children's recreation into work. The use of external rewards and
   sanctions has reached a point where players have to infer extrinsic reasons for their participation. This clearly reduces the players' intrinsic
   interest in Little League baseball and makes it seem more like work.
   The fact that parents and coaches take the game outcome very seriously
   increases the severity of winning or losing, while this, in turn, augments the likelihood of a sense of helplessness following failure.

4. Before and after the baseball season players rate higher than nonplayers
   on self-concept and certain socially desirable characteristics (e.g.,
   leadership and emotional adjustment) (e.g., Seymour, 1956). Thus,
   players retain the advantage on these characteristics over the season,
   although this does not increase during the playing experience. That
   players' self-concept does not improve more than that of nonplayers
   during one summer season may be due to the fact that extrinsic rewards
   and sanctions undermine players' intrinsic motivation and self-
   confidence. At the same time, nonplayers may spend their summer
   months in intrinsically motivated activities. (As we noted earlier, intrinsically motivated play increases one's sense of control and mastery
   over the environment, thus contributing to an effective self-concept).

   The principal psychological function of Little League is to provide
   one (but not the only) outlet for individuals who are oriented toward
   competition and achievement to seek and overcome challenges which

are commensurate with their needs and experiences. Thus they strive to satisfy their need for optimal arousal and incongruity. However, this objective is not realized when coaches and parents intervene in their children's recreation, or if Little League becomes a predominant form of leisure for these children. To sum up, Little League and similar activities are psychologically healthy insofar as intrinsic motivation guides players' interaction with teammates and opponents, and as long as players do not become obsessed by the activity due to external forces.

5. Parents encourage their children to participate in Little League because they believe that such activities provide players with socially desirable skills and characteristics (e.g., competitiveness), build character, and help players to become better citizens of the existing, achieving society. But, due to its highly structured nature, Little League does not provide players with skills and characteristics (e.g., creativity, innovativeness) needed for changing and improving the prevalent society; if anything, it will reinforce those traits that tend to maintain the status quo. From this point of view, Little League programs are contributing very little to child development.

---

summary

The chapter first discussed the development of social play. The research reviewed demonstrated that infants' interaction both with the caretaker (mostly mother) and peers is essential to the development of socially competent human beings. During the second year of life, children's play becomes increasingly social, though their behavior is not yet marked by cooperation and coordination of various activities. In a novel play setting children seem to turn more and more to their peers and less to their mothers. It is important to note that social skills are not the result of maturation or of immediate generalizations from child-parent interactions. Rather, peer interaction in play enhances children's social skills, which is the *source* of coordinated peer-oriented behavior. It has been shown that peers are more interesting than material playthings, because they offer more stimulation, dissonance, and complexity. Nevertheless, inanimate play objects are also important in providing variety. In this sense, playthings have been shown to differ in their capacity to stimulate social play.

From the age of three years onward social play becomes more frequent and prominent. This growth continues until children reach 6 or 7 years of age, a time which seems to serve as a transitional period leading to the "gang-age," from about 8 to 12 years. Evidence also shows that the percentage of players in competitive rule-governed games increases from the age of 6–7 years onward until reaching its peak among about 10-year-olds, after which the decline is strong and linear. There are, however, many sex differences in children's play patterns. To a greater extent than the activities of girls, boys' play activities involve physical strength, need for achievement, and ganging together. Most of the play groups are unisexual. While it has been shown that cooperative cross-sex play can be markedly increased by adults' reinforcement of such behavior, at best the effects appear to be temporary. Empirical research has indicated that the sex differences are due to socialization practices. That is, parents begin reinforcing sex-appropriate behaviors from the first weeks of an infant's life onward. Attempts to eliminate sex differences must therefore focus on changing parents' perceptions about sex-role appropriate activities.

The greater part of the chapter was devoted to the social psychological analysis of organized games, with particular emphasis on Little League baseball. The purpose was to evaluate the phsychological consequences of such participation, on the basis of research centering on competition and cooperation, attribution of causality, learned sense of helplessness, and intrinsic-extrinsic motivation. The conclusions are: (1) if major emphasis is placed upon ingroup cooperation and minor emphasis on intergroup competition, Little League baseball is psychologically healthy; (2) players' self-serving causal attributions for team success or failure are indicative of their capacity to cope with winning and losing. Repeated and uncontrollable team and/or individual failures may give rise to feelings and inferences of helplessness, which interfere with players' other behaviors; (3) intensive involvement by coaches and parents in Little League has turned children's recreation into children's work; (4) the principal psychological function of Little League is to provide *one* outlet through which individuals who are oriented toward competition and achievement may seek and conquer challenges, that is, satisfy their need for optimal incongruity. However, parents and coaches seem to be major obstacles to children's attempts to achieve this objective; (5) due to its highly structured character, Little League is not conducive to creativity and innovation in children, but rather solidifies those traits which correlate with maintaining the status quo of the prevailing social system. Viewed in this light, Little League programs contribute very little to child development.

the socialization process 7

Based upon past research it was asserted in the preceding unit that childhood play lays the foundations for leisure and recreation behavior in one's later life. The importance of the optimally arousing and incongruous play environments was stressed, with emphasis on the need for a large variety of play experiences. It was pointed out that limited opportunities for play in childhood tend to impair cognitive and behavioral flexibility in adult leisure pursuits, while this in turn may reduce one's capacity for psychological coping during the entire life span. If this reasoning is correct, there should then be a systematic relationship between early childhood recreation and adult leisure behavior, that is, if a person is active in play as a child then he is likely to be active in leisure as an adult. In a similar vein, inactivity in childhood foreshadows inactivity in adulthood. On the other hand, the concept of a changing individual in a changing world (due to social influence processes and the individual need for an optimal amount of novelty, incongruity and complexity) suggests that people are continuously looking for new leisure experiences by experimenting within the same recreational activities, and/or by switching to new ones.

The present chapter examines the empirical validity of these theoretical considerations. In addition, the chapter considers the influence of socialization agents (parents, peers, teachers) on the acquisition of various leisure skills and habits. Finally, this chapter shows that the socialization process does not always succeed in producing socially and psychologically competent individuals. To this end, there is a social psychological account explaining why some individuals become drug users and vandals. Such forms of free-time and their possible causes will be outlined in the latter part of the chapter. But before this, it is desirable to define socialization as a theoretical construct and to discuss its meaning in the context of leisure and recreation.

what is leisure socialization?

socialization

The concept of socialization is usually limited to the periods of childhood and adolescence. Typically, socialization refers to childhood learning experiences and the process of becoming a social being. It deals only with attitudinal and behavioral changes resulting from social learning and interaction with others. Thus, changes originating from biological growth are not considered part of the socialization process. Socialization involves learning norms of behavior and values in the group, community, and society to which an individual belongs. While everyone is expected to comply with such norms, it is important to note that norms are established by consensus and are shaped by the social environment, that is, their forms are variable and changeable. Adopting such norms provides psychological security, in that the social environment becomes predictable to a person, and he, in turn, becomes predictable to others who are part of that environment (Kelvin, 1970).

When speaking of socialization, there is always a danger of overemphasizing the importance of conformity to cultural norms (Zigler and Child, 1969). As noted earlier, Little League may be good because it teaches and strengthens certain values and norms needed in the highly competitive society (i.e., makes children conform to the system). At least the parents of most players believe so. But this immediately raises the question of the desirability of the "achieving" culture. If everyone agreed that such a society is healthy, then all would be willing to imprint on the young the norms of behavior and values central to such a system.

How about parents who believe in a more socialistic order? Should they refrain from teaching their children the competitive values and behaviors? Should they, therefore, prevent their children playing Little League baseball? One answer to these questions could be derived from Kelvin's (1970) argument, that children have to learn what to do before they are able to understand why they do it. Assuming that Little League players *have to* learn to play baseball before they are capable of understanding why they play, one could readily support Little League types of activities. This assumption, however, ignores the fact that children can be taught to evaluate norms, values and behaviors. Thus, one may ask: why can't children be taught to live with others through activities which do not put a premium on the competitive values and norms? Theoretically, it is possible. But because one of the main purposes of the socialization process is to help children form an orderly view of their social environment and world in order to be able to function in society as they grow older, compliance to norms cannot totally be avoided. Failure to understand the world one is living in may interfere with psychological development.

What perhaps is expected from socialization more than anything else is provision of a wide range of experiences, of which Little League is just one. As a result, a person may be expected to develop a general readiness for a changing environment, and an individual predisposition to contribute to environmental and societal change. But if activities like Little League, with their emphasis on extrinsic motives, make up an individual's principal form of leisure, then development of such individual predispositions may not be possible. This follows because "the values transmitted by structured athletics are more conservative than those of the society at large" (Goldstein and Bredemeier, 1977).

The above discussion suggests that socialization is a continuous, life-long process. But despite their common characteristics, the processes of childhood and adulthood socialization differ from one another in one important sense. Kelvin (1970) pointed out that children become socialized by accepting norms of behavior. In the first stage they watch and imitate the acting of others. Later, they want to identify themselves with others, repeating the behavior of others because they want to be like them. In the last stage of childhood socialization, the young "internalize" group and societal norms concerning behaviors and values, that is, they accept these norms as their own. Thus, socialization in childhood begins from behavior and ends with the internalized values. On the other hand, in adulthood, the process of socialization often starts with individually adopted values which are the *source* of certain behaviors (Kelvin, 1970). An example of this would be a person who, because of his religious values, voluntarily joins a church club, or a person who, due to his political convictions, spends his leisure in campaigning for a given candidate.

It follows from this that socialization is a broad term, which cannot simply be defined as conformity to cultural norms. Socialization refers to "the whole process by which an individual develops, through transaction with other people, his specific patterns of socially relevant behavior and experience" (Zigler and Child, 1969, p. 474). Thus, socialization involves the process whereby an individual acquires a self-image and perceived competence based on skills, knowledge, attitudes, beliefs, values, ideals, interests, habits, needs and motives (McNeil, 1969). The "processes" refer to the influence of socialization agents like parents, peers, and school teachers, who in turn are affected by cultural and societal forces (e.g., political climate, social class, race, ethnic background, and the community).

In focusing on leisure, the emphasis is placed on the processes through which a child acquires basic knowledge about leisure and recreation, forms fundamental attitudes and values associated with them, learns various leisure skills and motives. As noted above, much of this learning in childhood occurs through imitation, modeling, and identification with the behavior of others. It then follows that the socialization agents (e.g., parents) play an important role in transmitting behavioral patterns and basic values relating to leisure, that is, judgments as to which leisure activities are good and which are bad.

leisure socialization

While adults convey to children—knowingly or unknowingly—a notion of desirability of certain leisure forms, children often play and recreate without adopting the basic values attached to their activities by the parents. Children, for example, may play games which require sharing and cooperation, without understanding why such games are desirable. It is only in the later stages of childhood socialization that the young begin "internalizing" the values underlying their leisure participation. They may decline friends' offer to hunt because of a fundamental conviction killing animals is wrong. Or they may choose to spend a considerable amount of free-time in physical exercise, due to their strong belief in the beneficial influences of leisure (exercise) on psychological well-being. The internalization of certain values in later childhood, however, does not mean that these adopted values are permanent. It is conceivable, for instance, that as an adolescent a person is an avid hunter, but turns against this activity after being influenced by a liberal college education emphasizing environmental concerns. In sum, one way to define *leisure socialization* is to view it as *a process by which basic leisure knowledge, attitudes, values, skills and motives are learned and internalized, with the net result of socially relevant and psychologically rewarding leisure behavior*. Leisure socialization, like any other aspect of socialization, is a life-time process.

theoretical model   The basic idea of the process of leisure socialization is depicted in figure 9. Social and cultural forces (e.g., social system, race, ethnicity) establish the outer boundaries within which socialization processes occur. Accordingly, remote African tribes have different expectations concerning their members' participation in various activities than do such cultures as those in North America. These differences are in part due to the availability of certain forms of leisure, but also to the established societal norms. Within the cultural boundaries, social agents (mainly parents, peers and school teachers) constitute the major source of socialization influences. They directly affect an individual's range of leisure experiences by either providing him with certain models and encounters, or by

Figure 9   Process of leisure socialization.

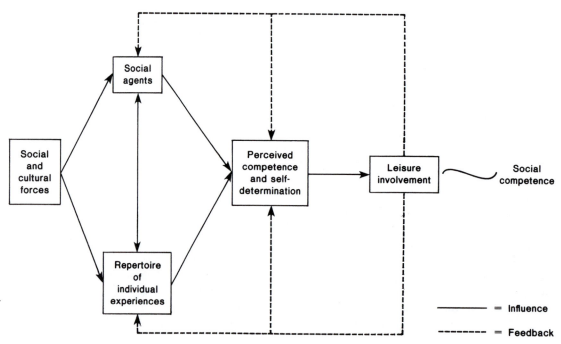

Developmental Analysis of Leisure and Recreation

encouraging participation in various leisure activities. Based upon their own experiences, competencies, and values, these socialization agents directly shape the perceived competence in a number of leisure activities. Of course, the individual's accumulated repertoire of leisure experiences also helps him determine the level of his subjective competence. In a broad sense, then, involvement in a particular leisure activity is a function of self-determination and perceived competence. (The effects of internalized values discussed earlier are reflected by the influence of self-determination).

In the diagram the continuing nature of leisure socialization is shown by the feedback from involvement. In other words, every leisure experience in itself directly modifies one's self-determination and perceived competence, either strengthening or weakening them. Similarly, leisure involvement increases the repertoire of individual experiences, while this, in turn, influences self-determination and perceived competence. Finally, in itself or through the enlarged repertoire of experiences individual leisure involvement also affects socialization agents' leisure participation, or their values and attitudes about leisure. Clearly, then, socialization is a two-way street in which an individual exerts influences and is influenced by others. Little League serves as a good example: while players are influenced by their parents, players may also alter their parents' leisure patterns by inducing them to attend games.

The above model clearly demonstrates the continuing nature of the socialization process. Earlier attitudes and values about leisure are being changed and new leisure skills are being acquired. Although the socialization process implies continuing change in leisure involvement, it does not mean that people constantly select and experiment with new leisure activities (*between* change). Change can also occur *within* the same activities. For example, a person may play golf throughout life, but may often change playing partners, golf courses, etc.

As a continuous process, leisure involvement is not simply a matter of consuming time, but rather, developing an individual's interpersonal competence. On the other hand, it should be realized that leisure socialization is only one component which contributes to social competence. School, work, and other experiences are also important in this respect. As noted previously, social competence can be viewed in two ways: (1) as a total conformity to the norms of leisure behavior of the group and society to which the individual belongs, or (2) as a predisposition to change the group's (society's) leisure patterns (for the better). Thus, to say that socialization processes produce socially competent human beings is not self-evident; it depends on value judgments and definitions of social competence.

So far this study has favorably presented the dialectical view of the changing individual in the changing social environment, and its applicability to explaining leisure behavior. Convincing evidence for this paradigm can be found in children's tendency to seek optimal arousal and incongruity through novel, dissonant, and increasingly complex experiences. At the same time, however, this presentation has stressed the need for change to be orderly. The child can absorb

early childhood recreation and adult leisure behavior

novelty, dissonance, and complexity only within individual confines; readiness for change is indicated only if the child is able to perceive and feel a degree of psychological structure and permanence in his little world. Seeing the environment as a chaos or anarchy cannot serve as a basis for change in behavior. Further evidence supporting this dialectical view of leisure is provided by several leisure researchers who have demonstrated a statistically significant link between early childhood recreation and adult leisure patterns on the one hand, and a significant difference in leisure participation between the two periods on the other. These studies are here reviewed.

empirical evidence   To test the relationship between early life experiences and adult leisure behavior, Sofranko and Nolan (1972) investigated the participation of some 700 hunters and fishermen in these leisure activities, both in their youth and at the present time. The level of their current participation was computed by adding up the number of times each sportsman had hunted or fished during the year prior to the study. Childhood participation was calculated by asking each sportsman to recall whether he had hunted or fished "Frequently," "Occasionally," or "Not at all," when he was young. In addition to correlating the level of participation in youth with current participation, the investigators determined the relationship of residence in youth (rural vs. urban) and the source of introduction (e.g., parents, friends) to hunting and fishing, with the two participation measures.

The results showed that participation in youth was directly related to current level of participation, that is, those who hunted and fished "frequently" in their youth did so also when they were adults. This association was somewhat stronger for hunters than for fishermen. Residence during youth and the source of introduction to the two activities were positively (significantly) related to participation in youth but not to current participation. Specifically, these relationships indicated that those who were from rural areas hunted and fished in their youth more frequently than those who were from urban areas; those who were introduced to these two activities by their parents hunted and fished more often as youths than those who were initiated by others, such as relatives and friends. Thus, the suggested link seems to be such that residence during youth and the source of socialization are associated with the level of leisure participation in youth, while this, in turn, is a significant contributor to the level of adult participation in the same activities. Insofar as hunting and fishing are concerned frequent youthful participation appears to predispose an individual toward frequent engagement as an adult. Other studies have shown that this relationship holds true also for such outdoor recreation activities as camping and hiking (Burch, 1969; Cicchetti, 1972; Hendee, 1969).

A similar but somewhat more elaborate study was reported by Yoesting and Burkhead (1973). The respondents' (137 rural inhabitants aged 20 or more) activity level was defined as a number of outdoor recreation activities they mentioned as having participated in during youth. When interviewed, each respondent was presented with a list of 35 outdoor recreation activities, and then was asked to recall the activities he had participated in (yes or no) when he was 6 to

11 years of age, ages 12 to 17, and at present; no measure of intensity of participation was secured. The results indicated that the level of individual participation both in childhood (ages 6–11) and in adolescence (ages 12–17) was positively related to the level of present participation. In other words, if the respondents participated in many outdoor activities when they were young they tended to do so later when they were adults.

But perhaps the most interesting finding was the fact that 12 (34%) out of 35 activities (e.g., tennis, tent camping, hunting, skiing, canoeing) were participated in similarly during ages 6–11 and the present time; 14 (40%) out of 35 activities (e.g., motorcycling, picnics, hunting, power boating, fishing) were engaged in both during ages 12–17 and the present time. Taken together, these data clearly demonstrate that there is a similarity between childhood and adult life recreation, since the respondents had participated in approximately 40% of all activities during both youth and adulthood. Thus, the childhood outdoor recreation activities of an individual seem to be *one* important predictor of his participation in the same activities as an adult. However, this conclusion is only one side of the Yoesting-Burkhead data.

Surprisingly, the authors failed to take notice of another aspect of these results. That is, more than 60% of all outdoor activities (e.g., football, baseball, bicycling, horseback riding, golf) were participated in *dis*similarly during childhood and adult years. Taken together, then, Yoesting and Burkhead's data indicate both similarities and discrepancies in leisure participation at various developmental stages. Therefore, one should not ignore the fact that leisure patterns change continuously over a life span, as well as within shorter developmental cycles. It appears that this continual change is due to the individual need to seek novel and arousing leisure experiences, and this, in turn, is the result of socialization influences; that is, socialization molds individual readiness and predisposition toward leisure. Some activities (e.g., football) are begun in childhood but dropped later, while others (e.g., golf) are added to one's leisure repertoire only in adulthood. Further evidence for the concept of the changing leisure behavior was seen in the fact that some activities (e.g., tennis) were participated in similarly when the period of childhood (ages 6–11) and adulthood were compared, but not when adolescence (ages 12–17) and adulthood were contrasted. Only five of the total 35 activities were participated in similarly throughout all three periods. Thus, change takes place not only between childhood and adolescence but also between adolescence and adulthood, that is, *continuously*.

This is in full concert with the dialectical view of leisure behavior, which holds that an individual continually changes leisure encounters, though within the confines of his psychological functioning. That is, an individual has a need for both stability (or security) *and* change (or variety) in leisure experiences and behavior. To understand this perspective, it is useful to consider stability and change separately. Always performing the same activity in the same manner provides psychological stability and security; but such leisure behavior soon becomes boring and unchallenging and may be psychologically detrimental in the

continual change in
leisure behavior

long run. The opposite pattern is characterized by leisure participation directed to new leisure activities all the time, or to new forms of the familiar activities. Such leisure behavior is also psychologically detrimental in the long run, because it does not allow the attainment of stability and security. Thus, leisure behavior or experience is the result of two opposite forces simultaneously influencing the individual: the need for stability and the need for change. It should be noted, however, that by looking at a single disparate leisure behavior one cannot reliably determine these influences. Stability and change should be considered in the light of the individual's leisure *patterns* and the total behavior. Change and novelty can be pursued in different (but often subtle) ways and through different dimensions which are not readily apparent, especially when a single leisure behavior is the source of one's analysis.

additional evidence for the dialectical view

The two studies here dicussed provide tentative data for understanding what might be called the between-stability and change in leisure behavior, that is, a degree of change from one activity to another over time. Further evidence for this dialectical view of leisure behavior comes from two studies reported by Kelly (1974, 1977). In the first investigation, respondents (persons from 21 to 64 years of age) were provided with a list of 77 different leisure activities and asked to check those activities engaged in during the previous 12 months, marking the ten most important to them. Among other things, subjects were then asked to indicate when they had started the ten activities which currently were most important to them.

The results bore a striking resemblence to the studies reviewed above. Of all the activities reported by the respondents, 49% were begun in childhood, and 51% in adult years. Upon differentiating leisure activities by form, identical results were obtained in that one-half of "recreation" activities were started as a child, and the other half as an adult; the same held true for activities classified as "cultural," "work-oriented," and "interactional." Kelly properly concluded that "learning new leisure activities, then, would seem to be as much an adult as a childhood process." The second study (Kelly, 1977) essentially replicated the first one. The same 50%-50% differential between the child and adult beginning of leisure activities again was found. These results were confirmed by the fact that the replication study compared a larger sampling of respondents, including three distinct communities. Thus, there are strong reasons to support the idea of continuously changing leisure behavior and life-long leisure socialization.

In reference to the Yoesting and Burkhead study, Kelly (1977) noted that "a childhood determination of adult leisure model of leisure socialization" is too simplistic and thus not worthy of additional testing. Although to some extent Kelly is right, it is also important to realize that the dialectical nature of the socialization process cannot be understood if an individual's previous recreation experiences are excluded. As Patrick (1945) concluded: "If a child is taught to follow a hobby, he is apt to pursue one when he becomes an adult, although its nature may change." Therefore, to grasp why an adult's leisure behavior has changed and what directions the change has taken, it is necessary to consider his childhood recreation behavior, as *one* but not as the sole determinant of adult leisure behavior. To reduce the socialization process into a simple childhood-adulthood link is, of course, inadequate in the light of Yoesting and Burkhead's own findings. That is, the young's leisure participation changed from the elementary school period (ages 6–11) to the time of junior high and high school (12–17), and again in adulthood.

Throughout childhood and adolescence there are several developmental stages in which leisure patterns take on very different forms. One of them is a transitional period at the time of entry into high school (i.e., 9th grade). Freeberg and Rock (1973) analyzed leisure behavior of over 1,000 students from 7th, 9th, and 11th grade levels and found marked similarities in recreation patterns between the 7th and 11th grades but considerable differences between the 7th and 9th and between the 9th and 11th grades. For boys, sports, general reading, TV-viewing, and artistic interests were at the highest among the 7th and 11th graders, and at their lowest in the 9th graders, whereas specialized reading interests and "feminine-esthetic activities" (e.g., cooking) showed the reverse pattern. For girls, the results were similar in relation to general reading, TV-viewing and artistic interests at the three grade levels, but were opposite with respect to participation in sports and feminine-esthetic types of activities. Thus, these changes clearly indicate discontinuity for a number of dimensions of leisure interests over time, and imply "transitional phenomenon" occurring approximately at the time of the high school entry, the onset of puberty (Freeberg and Rock, 1973). Since appreciable differences can already be observed during short periods of time, it is totally unjustifiable to reduce leisure socialization into the simple childhood-adulthood paradigm.

Although there may be similarities between early leisure experiences and adult leisure interests, this simplified conclusion regarding the relationship fails to consider what happened between the measured periods. As Freeberg and Rock showed, the young adopt certain leisure patterns, then drop them and again return to the original leisure activities. It is reasonable to assume that such shifts in leisure interests are also accompanied by changes in motives and expectations underlying the participation. For example, the 7th grade boys' participation in sports may have been motivated by their need to achieve success and to excel. But following a decline of sport interests among the 9th graders, the increased interest in sports at the 11th grade level may have been the result of the boys' desire for social interaction. In support of this speculation, Himmelweit and Swift (1977) found that while time spent in viewing TV changes (i.e., increases) considerably from adolescence to early adulthood, so also does individual taste in programs. Adolescents look for adventure, thrills and excitement in TV programs, whereas adults exhibit strong interest in the informative, the nonfiction, and "useful" television programs.

In sum, although there is a significant link between childhood leisure experiences and adult leisure behavior, this relationship does not explain the whole phenomenon. One also has to consider that there is a marked discontinuity in leisure interests between the two periods. This empirically established fact can be predicted from the dialectical view of leisure behavior.

substitutability

factor analytic
studies

The dialectical view of leisure behavior assumes an individual's readiness to change recreation patterns. One way of demonstrating the validity of this assumption is to provide evidence of willingness to replace present leisure activities by new ones. Indirect support for the idea about substitutability of leisure activities comes from factor analytic studies (e.g., Bishop, 1970; Witt, 1971). This line of research has demonstrated that only a few dimensions generally underlie people's leisure participation. In other words, various activities tend to cluster and intercorrelate when factor analyzed. Since those leisure activities (e.g., bicycling, basketball, swimming) that are clustered on the obtained "factors" (or dimensions) have common characteristics, it is reasonable to assume that a group of such activities overlap in their psychological meaning as leisure. If so, these overlapping or clustering forms of leisure must to a certain extent serve the same psychological function. It is logical therefore to suppose that such activities within a cluster can be substituted for one another without great loss in the psychological value which they presumably represent, but activities would not be substitutable from one cluster to another.

For example, Bishop (1970) found that activities like bicycling, picnicking, basketball, swimming, and driving for pleasure clustered together (Factor I); this suggested to him that movement and freedom from the routine typify all these activities. Consequently, he argued that the dimension underlying the activities (their predominant psychological function) is the active-diversionary factor. If so, the clustered activities might be substituted for each other without substantial loss in this psychological function. Of course, Bishop (or anybody, for that matter) has no way of knowing whether in fact the active-diversionary factor was also what subjects had in their minds when they responded to his questions. Nevertheless, this and other factor analytical studies (e.g., Witt, 1971) may provide tentative support for the idea about people's ability to substitute leisure activities, with little loss in the basic psychological values of activities.

direct evidence
about
substitutability?

But more direct support for the substitutability concept is also available. Inspired by Hendee and Burdge's (1974) theoretical writing, Christensen and Yoesting (1977) studied the ability of some 300 heads of households to replace, with similar satisfaction, their current recreation participation by other activities within the same "activity type." Subjects simply responded "yes" or "no" to the question whether they could substitute recreation activities with similar satisfaction. The four activity types were: games and sports, hunting and fishing, nature appreciation, and motorized activities. It appeared that 67% of those who participated in games and sports could substitute (vs. 33% could not substitute) within this activity group with little or no loss in satisfaction. The values for other activity types were as follows: hunting and fishing (45% could, 55% could not), nature appreciation (55% could, 45% could not), and motorized activities (62% could, 38% could not). Thus, on the average, 57% of all recreationists interviewed could substitute within their activity type. Hunters and fishers seemed to be the least willing to find a substitute for their activities, while game- and sports persons were the most flexible in this respect.

The above findings, however, should be treated with extreme caution because of conceptual flaws of the study. Of these the most serious is the fact that the authors provided a varying amount of activities within the four "activity types." That is, those who were supposed to substitute within the "games and sports" had 13 alternatives for doing so, while only six possibilities were offered in the case of "hunting and fishing," five for "motorized" activities and seven for "nature appreciation" activities. Thus, considered merely from the quantitative standpoint, it is no wonder why more sportsmen than hunters could substitute; the former had twice as many alternatives as the latter. Due to these quantitative differences alone the comparison between various types of recreationists' ability to substitute is meaningless and distorted in light of Christensen and Yoesting's study. Their findings clearly undermine hunters' and fishers' ability to substitute. While they may be correct, their interpretation does not warrant such biased conclusions.

The Christensen and Yoesting study is marked by other conceptual problems which stem from the authors' failure to consider psychological aspects of substitutability. Even if the investigators had kept the number of activities constant across the activity types, they should have also provided controls for the qualitative differences between the activity types in making comparisons. By the term *qualitative differences* is meant the psychological importance of the activities to be substituted. For instance, a person who is to substitute within, say, five hunting-related activities, may perceive these five alternatives as considerably less attractive than the five sport-related alternatives perceived by the person within the sports and game category. Social psychologists (e.g., Jellison and Harvey, 1976) have reported empirical data indicating that equally matched or attractive alternatives increase perceived freedom which, of course, increases one's tendency to substitute. If leisure alternatives are more attractive in the case of one activity type (sportspersons) as opposed to another (hunters), it is clear that these groups cannot be justifiably compared in their "ability" to substitute. No matter how oranges are colored they still differ from apples!

It is possible that differences in attractiveness between alternatives within the "activity types" may have stemmed from potential satisfaction. That is, sportspersons may have expected to extract more satisfaction from their alternatives than hunters from their own options (in part due to a greater number of alternatives). Liking for the alternative activities may also have been greater in the former than in the latter case. If so, the comparison of the two groups' willingness, or "ability," to substitute is quite meaningless. The problem is compounded by the inexact interpretation of the term "satisfaction." What specifically were the subjects supposed to think when faced with the question, "Just as satisfied to participate in other activities?" What aspect of satisfaction did they in fact have in mind when responding to the question? If the respondents' notion of

the psychology of substitutability

satisfaction was not uniform with respect to the activity types, how can their "ability" to substitute be compared—without having to compare apples and oranges?

It should also be noted that to begin with, the level of perceived satisfaction with the recreationists' *current* activity may have been different between the "activity types." Assume that sportspersons' recreation activity was baseball and that they were extremely satisfied with it. Then, assume that hunters' recreation activity comprised hunting water fowl with which they were relatively dissatisfied. Now, both groups are given, say, five alternative activities within their category and asked whether they could substitute or not. It is clear that these two groups differ in their readiness to substitute and therefore should not be compared. Specifically, we would hypothesize that those who are dissatisfied with their current activity are more inclined to substitute than those who are satisfied with it (because the former have more to gain).

Theoretically, the comparison of the four types of recreationists' "ability" to substitute is valid only when the alternatives are equally attractive to persons from each activity type. Had this been the case and had the equivalent difference been found between hunters (45% could substitute) and sportspersons (67%), could one then say that hunters have a lower ability to substitute? Even then the comparison would be relatively questionable, because it would not give information about *why* hunters were less willing to substitute. In such a case information about the psychological dimension(s) that the recreationists attach to their activities should also be gathered.

Slovic (1975) reported conclusive data indicating that of two equally valued alternatives, people systematically select one that is superior in terms of the more important dimension. For example, if trap shooting and fishing were equally attractive alternatives to a person who hunts small game and whose "more important dimension" is physical exercise, he will subsequently select one (e.g., fishing) which he assumes to be superior in this important dimension. Thus, it is clear that simply asking people whether or not they can substitute does not provide understanding of their tendency to change from one leisure activity to another.

It should also be noted that the psychological function of the *current* activity may have differed for the recreationists within the four activity types. That is, if the reasons why persons participated in the recreation activity (to be replaced) varied from one activity type to another, it is inappropriate and unjustified to compare these persons' tendencies to substitute. The more unique psychological value the current activity has, the less likely it is to be replaced. For example, assume that a sportsperson plays racquetball only for the sake of his physical fitness. He is then presented with alternative sport activities which he does not consider capable of providing avenues for physical exercise. Of course, his inclination to replace racquetball by other sport activities is then very low. This is in sharp contrast to a "hunting" person who also participates in his recreation activity to get physical exercise and believes that the alternatives offered provide opportunities for physical exercise; that is, he believes that his motives or rewards can be substituted from one activity to another. Consequently, his willingness to substitute is much greater than that of the person who engages in sports. This same principle applies to all motives underlying leisure behavior (e.g., motive to obtain social interaction). In sum, to understand why some people are willing to replace or change their leisure activities while others are not, it is necessary to know why they have participated in their current activity(ies) in the first place, and what they expect to derive from their participation.

Finally, when studies on substitutability are conducted one should note the effects of leisure repertoire. Leisure repertoire consists of all activities a person considers potentially usable during his daily leisure. Some persons' leisure repertoire may be broad but may lack in depth, while that of others may be narrow but deep. The former, therefore, participate in a great number of activities but perhaps more superficially in each of them; the latter in turn concentrate on a few activities requiring very intensive participation. Most people probably fall between these two extremes. If a person's current activity, which he is asked to replace, is part of a wide leisure repertoire, it is easier for him to substitute the activity, as compared to a person whose current activity is part of a narrow leisure repertoire.

Although the above points clearly invalidate the relative comparison of substitutability among the activity types in the Christensen and Yoesting study, the overall tendency of recreationists to substitute is nevertheless worth noting. That about 60% of the participants could substitute their current recreation activity with similar satisfaction (whatever it means!) implies that there is cognitive and behavioral flexibility in leisure participation. Such flexibility, moreover, is predictable on the basis of the dialectical view of leisure behavior and is consistent with the earlier survey of studies concerning the relationship between early childhood and adult leisure behavior. Substitutability supports the idea about the life-long leisure socialization. What seems clear in the light of the above studies is that people want familiarity and stability as well as novelty and change at the same time, in their leisure behavior.

It is notable how, from the standpoint of "between-change," these two propensities are almost evenly distributed. That is, about one-half of the adult leisure activities are familiar and the other half novel in comparison to childhood leisure. This finding may reflect that a tendency to substitute is also a matter of individual differences or past experiences. Some people look for more change and variety than do others. Thus, although everyone is seeking novelty and variety in leisure throughout the life span, this occurs within the confines of the *individual* need for optimal arousal and incongruity, while this is in part a result of childhood opportunities to play in stimulating environments. What is even more striking about the 50%-50% divergence for familiarity and change, is that it is already present in infants. As we noted earlier, McCall (1974) found that 8½ to 11½ month old babies spent about the same amount of time in playing with their "old favorite toys" as with the new play objects in the novel laboratory play setting.

biological basis of
substitutability

Even though empirical research has shown convincingly that the individual tendency for optimal incongruity is strongly affected by the environmental forces, the above finding that such tendency exists even in infants, may reflect the influence of biological, inherited factors in determining what is optimal for an individual. If so, one way of providing evidence for this contention would be to show that interest styles differ between the members of biological families and those of adoptive families. Grotevant, Scarr and Weinberg (1977) recently reported a relevant study. In this investigation, members of 114 biologically related families and members of 109 adoptive families were administered the interest style inventory. The inventory was designed to measure dimensions (e.g., social, artistic) which characterize individual orientation to the environment. Correlations were performed for all combinations of the family members (father-son, mother-daughter, brother-brother, etc.) concerning the dimensions of the interest inventory in the two family types separately.

The results were consistent and conclusive. The overall profile correlations showed that the biological parent-child and child-child relationships were all positive and significant, ranging from .19 (father-daughter) to .34 (sister-sister). On the other hand, none of the parent-parent, parent-child or child-child correlations for adoptive family pairs were consistent and significant. It appears therefore that the biological family members are moderately (but significantly) similar in the interest styles which were measured, whereas "adoptively related family members bear no more resemblance to each other than do parent-child pairs randomly selected from the population."

Interestingly, the data also revealed that the same-sex siblings (.36 on the average) were more similar to one another in the interest dimensions than were opposite-sex siblings (.08, on the average) and parent-child (.17, on the average) pairs. The difference between the biological child-parent and the like-sex sibling pairs became more conspicuous when the response patterns on the interest dimensions were measured. Since biological parent-child and child-child pairs share, on the average, half of their genes in common, theoretically the correlation between the interests of a biological father and son should be about the same as that between the brothers' interests. That the latter (child-child) pair resembled each other more closely than the former is apparently indicative of environmental effects. Like-sex pairs have more similar rearing environments than do the parent-child pairs.

Taken together, the above findings clearly suggest that genetic factors influence interest styles. As Grotevant, *et al.*, concluded, "there is a small but reliably heritable influence on the *patterning* of interests in individuals." As a word of caution, it should be noted that these genetic factors do not determine one's participation in specific activities. Rather, they set the stage for certain types of social experiences which subsequently direct an individual's participation in specific activities. Thus, the biological factors seem to provide an individual with general propensity toward some social encounters, as opposed to others. Hence the main tendency of socialization is bio-social (Helanko, 1957). As for the relationship between biological parents and their children's *leisure* patterns, the above study does not provide an explanation, because leisure interests were not specifically in question. But it promises to be a fascinating topic for leisure research in the future.

For the purposes of this discussion, however, the Grotevant, *et al.* study is important. Because genetic factors establish the overall orientation toward individual activity patterns, it then follows that the basis of need for optimal arousal and incongruity (and thus a tendency to substitute) is biologically determined, with the optimum amount varying from person to person. As empirical research has shown, a lack of environmental stimulation can destroy an individual's tendency to seek play and recreation encounters which are commensurate with his inherited tendencies. On the other hand, it was evident that enriched environments can enhance an individual's capacity to seek stimulating play and recreation experiences. In view of these facts, it is not surprising that even infants possess a 50-50 preference for familiarity and novelty. This reflects their tendency toward the optimally arousing play.

perceived competence and need for change

Since individuals are continually exposed to social influences, it is obvious that their need for optimal incongruity changes as a function of these influences, and that this is reflected by developmental and age differences in quantity and quality of leisure experiences. This change, however, occurs within the limits of an individual's *perceived* capacity. Consistently, too extensive and too rapid change is rejected, because the perceived competence to cope with it is lacking; only the optimum amount of change is accepted. This "problem of match" view posits that a set of circumstances must have an appropriate relationship to the information already accumulated in the individual's mental storage from previous encounters with the environment (Hunt, 1969). Therefore, it appears that the perceived competence (i.e., a person's subjective view of the level of his competence to perform given tasks or activities) is the key determinant of the speed and direction of change required in leisure encounters.

Whether or not an individual defines leisure behavior as having an appropriate amount of novelty and familiarity, depends on his perceived competence. For example, if a recreationist who plays tennis during his free-time wants more change and novelty, he replaces his old tennis partner for a new one of similar caliber. He does not choose to play with Wimbledon champions, because he knows that his capacity is far short of theirs. Similarly, a housewife who wants more variety in her daily activities may enroll in an evening class (e.g., needlepoint). In doing so, however, she selects the type of class on the basis of her perceived competence, which in turn is the result of her past experiences and social influences (see the model of socialization process, p. 132). In Christensen and Yoesting's terms, she selects or substitutes within the "activity type." This recalls the starting point of the present discussion and offers an explanation of *why* people find substitutes for leisure activities. To reiterate, when a need for change or substitution in leisure behavior arises, it stems from a relative lack of arousal or incongruity. The direction and speed of the subsequent change or substitution is principally determined by perceived competence to participate with satisfaction in various leisure activities.

If the above theory is correct, leisure involvement should significantly depend on perceived competence. To the best of our knowledge, only two studies have direct bearing on this hypothesis. In their survey, Spreitzer and Snyder (1976) sought to determine the childhood antecedents of adult sports involvement. Subjects (mean age of 42) responded to a mailed questionnaire which was designed to assess their behavioral (active participation), cognitive (e.g., following sports in mass media), and affective (meaning of sports in a person's life) involvement in sport as a function of such antecedent factors as perceived ability, youthful participation, and parental encouragement. As might be expected on the basis of the previously reviewed studies, youthful participation was positively (and significantly) related to the combined (behavioral, cognitive, affective) index of adult sport involvement. That is, those who participated in sport activities as part of formally organized programs in their youth were also involved in sports when they were adults. This was true for men (path coefficient = .25) but not for women (.01). However, perceived athletic ability was the strongest predictor of adult sport involvement for both men (.35) and women (.32). This indicated that if a person's perceived ability was high, sports involvement was also high, but if perceived ability was low so was sports involvement. It was also found that youthful participation was an overriding determinant of perceived ability for both men (.44) and women (.59).

Another study to substantiate the notion of intrinsic motivation (perceived competence in particular) as a determinant of leisure involvement was reported by Csikszentmihalyi, Larson and Prescott (1977). Besides its important findings, the study is noteworthy for its ingenious and unprecedented methodology. Adolescent subjects (ages ranging from 13 to 18) carried a pocket-size electronic paging device for a week, and self-reported at random times what they were doing, why they were doing it, etc. Based upon a predetermined random schedule, investigators sent radio signals to subjects through this device. Upon receiving audible beeps (5–7 per day) subjects started to fill out the self-report form.

The results showed that the activities which provided the most positive experiences were playing games or sports, and talking with peers. Based upon these self-reports, games and sports were enjoyable because they enabled subjects to perceive themselves as being strong, active, free, excited, and sociable. These activities were also considered desirable because they were perceived to offer the greatest amount of challenge, required a relatively high level of skills, and provided a strong feeling of control over their actions. The results also indicated that when talking with peers, subjects were the most happy, very friendly and sociable. This activity was also perceived to require a moderate level of skills and to offer strong feelings of control. At the same time, watching television was the activity associated with the least positive overall mood (e.g., weak, unhappy), offering virtually no challenge, requiring a very low level of skills, and providing the least amount of personal control. Thus, the most enjoyable forms of leisure were strongly associated with perceived competence. This does not mean that people will always participate in activities as prompted by perceived competence, because such is not possible for practical reasons alone and because these activities after a while would lose their stimulation value. But whenever they are participated in, activities that provide feelings of competence and control are likely to be most enjoyable.

Taken together, these findings lend strong support to previous theoretical derivations. While childhood leisure experiences have significant impact on an individual's adult involvement patterns, nevertheless, because of the need for novel, stimulating leisure encounters, they remain insufficient to adequately explain present engagement in leisure. The strong influence of perceived competence signals just that. It suggests that the subjectively defined ability regulates attempts to change and to replace familiar (and boring) leisure experiences by new and more stimulating ones. between- and within-changes

The persuasive influence of perceived competence tells the observer that this change-substitution process occurs mainly within "activity types" when adults change from one activity to another ("between-change"). This is relevant, because activities within "activity types" are similar in terms of competence involved. But perhaps more important, the changes may often take place within the same activities. In other words, rather than jumping from a familiar activity to a new one, individuals seek optimal arousal within the same activity ("within-change") by changing, for example, partners and courts in playing tennis, by meeting new people when socially interacting, or by visiting new places with old friends or old places with new friends. It is conceivable that the "between-changes" are more frequent among the young than among old people, while the reverse may be true for "within-changes." In general, there is tentative evidence that the older people become, the less willing they are to substitute "between" activities (Christensen and Yoesting, 1977).

Inasmuch as empirical research lends considerable support to the dialectical view of leisure behavior, what practical implications can be derived from this perspective? Since people continually substitute, whether between or within leisure activities, such a need for change appears to be a major consideration when leisure services are provided for the public. This certainly runs counter to the Yoesting and Burkhead (1973) statement that childhood experience is "a useful tool for prediction of outdoor recreation demand in the future," and that it is "possible to utilize school facilities for interviewing to determine leisure activities rather than using extensive personal interviews with adults." If so narrowly focused, this procedure would all but ignore the individual need to change leisure activities with age, and would therefore force all people to substitute within those activities that were learned in childhood. Inevitably, such an approach would restrict people's leisure environments and reduce the potential satisfaction to be derived from them. As Kelly (1977) pointed out, "no groups can be defined as past the possibility of new leisure learning or the potential of previously-untried kinds of activity." **implications**

One immediate implication, therefore, for practitioners is that a variety of leisure activities should be provided for the public. Further, practitioners should continually introduce and experiment with novel forms of leisure. A recreation program should also include activities which are "contextually familiar" (Kelly, 1977); that is, activities which are similar to past experiences and thus replaceable within the "activity types." As for the principle of change within one and the same activity, leisure programmers should experiment with new ways of implementing the process. For example, colleges which provide recreational evening classes should not only offer new classes every semester; they should also rotate teachers, try new materials, use novel methods, and encourage new ways of looking at the same phenomenon. Another example and practical procedure emerging from the within-change principle is to provide recreational tennis players with a list of the available players with their preferred playing hours. Such a list could include players' experience with tennis, so that when people want a new opponent they could generally match the competence levels. Recreation centers should make such lists available to the public.

The above are just a few potential applications of theory. To facilitate further derivation of practical implications, it may be useful to describe the types of changes in detail. As has been repeatedly pointed out, an individual can theoretically substitute between or within activities. Both major categories of change can further be broken down into three main components. Let us first consider "between-changes." A person can replace his current leisure activity by (1) another activity which is perceived as unrelated to the original in terms of required ability or other psychological dimensions, (2) by an activity which is perceived to be moderately related to the original, and (3) by an activity which is perceived to be very similar to the first one in certain characteristics. The last is similar to what Christensen and Yoesting called substitution within "activity type" (e.g., from racquetball to tennis). It should be noted, however, that the degree of similarity between the leisure activities is a matter of individual perception; thus, tennis and racquetball may be very similar in the eyes of one person, but quite unrelated in the opinion of another. Without such subjective information it is not possible for an observer to know what activities are replaceable or changeable, according to the views of different individuals.

The above breakdown also applies to the within-substitutions. Given a leisure activity (e.g., listening to symphony music in a performing arts center), a person may substitute within this same activity by attending (1) a very similar performance, that is, symphony concerts presented by different orchestras, (2) moderately related performances (e.g., operas) or (3) unrelated performances (e.g., pop music). Another example of the use of this breakdown would be a tennis player who changes or replaces opponents according to their ability levels, from similar to dissimilar. These theoretical possibilities for substitution reveal some of the dimensions that can (should) be considered when arranging alternate forms of leisure for the public. Unfortunately, it is not yet known at what level various leisure experiences are replaceable with little or no loss in satisfaction. On the other hand, the above model should provide an impetus and guideline for investigating the changing individual in the changing social leisure contexts.

It is often said that a decision to engage in a leisure activity is an individual matter. Individuality, however, is relative, as a person's choices of and preferences for certain forms of leisure are influenced by other people to a varying extent. In the course of his development and socialization, an individual accumulates experiences, which in turn have been shown to affect significantly his perceived competence (Spreitzer and Snyder, 1976). As noted earlier, perceived competence, in turn, influences or determines individual leisure involvement.

the influence of
social agents

The theoretical model of socialization presented previously (see p. 132) demonstrates that the effect of past experiences is only one side of the coin. By shaping the direction of leisure experiences, socialization agents indirectly affect an individual's perceived abilities. The impact of these agents upon the subjective definition of competence is direct, in that the participant is frequently given feedback about leisure performance. For instance, a boy in secondary school who decides to spend much of his out-of-school time singing in the school choir is soon told whether or not his voice is appropriate to the choir's needs. The literature distinguishes three major socialization agencies and agents: family (parents), reference group (peers) and school (teachers). The remainder of this section is devoted to an examination of the influence of these agents on the development of leisure interests and actual leisure participation. Since family, reference group, and school all affect the upbringing of children interactively, we focus on their combined effects.

Virtually everyone agrees that parents, peers, and teachers decisively shape the development of the young. If so, they must be "significant others" to children. It is important, however, to note that their significance lies in the eyes of the beholder; an individual by himself determines how significant these socialization agents are. Each person may value and respect the opinions and judgments of one agent more than those of another. This is particularly true in comparing various aspects of social influence. Thus, one may ask, significant for what? For molding self-concept, teaching social roles, shaping leisure patterns or what (Rosenberg, 1973)? A child's opinion of personal ability to play baseball, for example, may be more strongly influenced by his coach than by his father, if he attributes superior knowledge and experience to the former. Another child, on the other hand, may believe that his father's knowledge of baseball is more comprehensive than that of either a coach or a physical education teacher. Consequently, he is more affected by his father than by the others. It is reasonable to suppose that the relative impact of these agents on children changes with their age and psychological development. Parents probably exert their strongest influence when children are young, while the influence of peers and teachers may become more pronounced when children are older and more experienced.

**"significant
others"**

That there are such age differences in an individual's reliance on judgments of significant others was clearly demonstrated by Rosenberg (1973). When asked who "knows best what you are like deep down inside," (p. 843) the following data were obtained (percentages):

	Age			
	8–10	11–13	14–15	16–18
Mother	50	33	19	20
Father	6	5	4	2
Yourself	40	57	61	62
Best Friend	3	5	16	15
Total	100%	100%	100%	100%

Reproduced with permission.

Thus, the older children grow, the more likely they are to trust their own judgment and the less likely to rely on the opinions of others. Interestingly, the mothers' impact was much greater than that of the father and of friends, a fact which may reflect child-rearing patterns. A clear indication of reliance upon the judgments of others in the perception of one's abilities was observed when subjects were asked "how smart you are" and "how good you are." While 76% of 8–10 year olds trusted their mother and 24% of them relied on themselves in judging how smart they are, only 31% of 16–18 year olds trusted their mother and 69% trusted self. Despite this age-determined decline in reliance on the mother's judgment, however, the respondents trusted their mother more than themselves, on the average (58% vs. 42%). This difference in favor of mothers was even clearer when asked about how "good" they are in general (67% vs. 33%). Unfortunately, other social agents were not included in these comparisons.

To summarize, although confidence in personal judgments about what one is really like and how competent one is increases considerably with age, children and adolescents still seem to depend, to a major extent, on the explanations of others who are significant to them, especially parents. It is therefore not surprising that the leisure behavior of the young is strongly shaped by others who have significance for them, especially by family members, as will be considered next.

strong impact of family

As was observed earlier, Kelly (1974) reported that one-half of adults' ten most important activities were begun in childhood. The question then is: "With whom are leisure activities usually begun?" When this question was posed to the subjects, Kelly observed a striking influence of family. About two-thirds (63%) of all the activities reported were started with family; the remaining 37% reflected the combined influences of peer, school, and community. When distinguished by form, the results showed that 71% of all recreational (e.g., sports, games, water-based activities) and 82% of all interpersonal (e.g., conversation, "being

Developmental Analysis of Leisure and Recreation

together") activities were begun with family, whereas 61% of all "cultural" (e.g., reading, theatre, TV) activities started with school and other social agents combined. The problem with the latter results is that division of activities into such broad categories is highly arbitrary, because most activities involve many psychological functions and values at different times for different persons. For example, people often participate in "recreational" games for social interaction.

Nevertheless, these findings demonstrate the predominating importance of family over other social agencies, in establishing the foundations and directions for individual leisure pursuits. The above results become even more convincing when one considers that Kelly (1977) obtained essentially the same facts in a replication study with a larger and more representative sample than in the original study. Depending on the communities surveyed, 63% to 67% of all leisure activities reported were said to have begun with family. Kelly extended the earlier study by including additional categories of social contexts of starting leisure. When considered in terms of all activity types, it appeared that 14% of all activities were begun alone, 42% as a child with family, 8% as a child with friends, 6% at school, 20% as an adult with family, and 10% as an adult with friends. It is of interest to note that 69% of all activities that were started alone were "cultural."

Besides the overriding influence of family as a social context of initiating leisure patterns, another impressive finding is worthy of attention. Only 6% of all "important" leisure activities reported by subjects were begun at school; 62% of these were "cultural" such as reading and participation in various forms of arts and crafts. It is surprising that this small proportion of all the leisure activities which adults prefer and in which they participate have their roots in school. The finding certainly does not speak very favorably for school as a setting for teaching leisure activities which are important to adults.

In defense of schooling, however, it should be noted that even though the school system may not provide an impetus to many enduring leisure activities, it may advance, refine, and add variety to those activities which were begun in other social contexts. For example, if children first begin playing baseball with peers, they will learn new things about this activity in school, which in turn affects play in peer groups. Or as Csikszentmihalyi, *et al.* (1977) found, school serves as an important *physical setting* for various forms of recreation, especially sports and games. If so, Kelly's data give an over-simplified picture of the relative importance of various socialization agents. On the other hand, knowing teachers' lack of concern for leisure education, the above finding about the meager effect of school in this regard comes as no surprise. It is ironic and discouraging that despite the fact that the average adult has more "free-time" each day than he spends time in his work daily, educators continue to ignore education for leisure and persist in stressing work-related skills. In a way, when educating children they are ignoring more than half of an adult's life. Yet, at the same time we know from empirical research (e.g., London, Crandall and Seals, 1977) that leisure contributes more to an adult's quality of life than does his work.

ineffective schools?

If educators in secondary schools devoted more attention to the leisure needs of students, not only would the students' leisure repertoire be enlarged, with increased possibilities for more satisfying future experiences, but also the paramount objective of the school system (i.e., educational attainment) could be achieved to a greater extent. This follows from Spady's (1970) and Otto's (1975) findings which showed that the level of participation in high school extra-curricular activities was a more important indication of educational attainment than were such conventional and hard-stressed factors as family socioeconomic status, academic ability, or academic performance. Relevant to all this is a well-documented finding (e.g., Gordon, Gaitz and Scott, 1973) that education is a statistically more important determinant of leisure behavior than are many other variables. This implies that people can be educated to improve their leisure experiences and thus the quality of life. Thus, one is tempted to ask: How much more evidence is needed to convince policy-makers of the importance of leisure in the lives of young people, and hence its necessary place in the school curricula?

Of course, school cannot and should not be expected to provide all or even a majority of adult leisure skills, because the need for novel experiences continues throughout the life span. But what the school should do is to educate children to understand the importance to them of wholesome leisure (not just physical activities) during their entire life, thereby providing students with the fundamentally positive orientation to leisure, to learn that the need for self-esteem, for example, can be satisfied by meaningful leisure activities as well or better than by work accomplishments. Thus, children should be exposed to a wide variety of leisure experiences in school; later, they, by themselves, may refine and expand these experiences.

A critical problem of today's school system arises from the great emphasis placed on external rewards and sanctions. By an excessive use of various external factors (e.g., grades), students' tasks and learning experiences are made to resemble work, and little room is left for intrinsic motivation. This is evident because students perceive school-related activities as coercive (Csikszentmihalyi, *et al.*, 1977). It is then not surprising that under such conditions learning becomes drudgery. As Greene and Lepper's (1974b) research points out, failure to provide conditions for intrinsically motivated learning of various subject matter is the major reason for today's problems and upheavals at school. Even those activities that are supposed to be leisure and recreation to students (e.g., games) become work-like activities, by reason of the use of external sanctions. This is also the case with the numerous subjects in which students have minimal initial interest.

The use of extrinsic rewards and sanctions not only undermines learning but unfortunately it adversely affects interpersonal behavior (Garbarino, 1975). Knowing that social interaction is the single most important form of leisure to adults (Crandall, 1978), it is clear that the present school system is impairing the capacity of future adults to enjoy their leisure and thus improve the quality of life. In spite of poor environmental settings, students are always the main target of accusations that their behavior is deviant, rebellious, and indifferent, while in fact the system should be blamed for such behavior. Years of drudgery and boredom are likely to leave psychological scars on students. As Garbarino expressed it in conclusions drawn from the experiment on detrimental effects of extrinsic rewards on learning and interpersonal behavior:

> If one of the consequences of the imposition of social structures upon the child as he proceeds from infancy to middle and later childhood is the increasing suppression of intrinsic motivation and its replacement with extrinsically oriented motivation . . . then the puzzling discrepancy between the infant's seemingly boundless curiosity (exploratory drive, competence motivation . . .) and the developmental increase in cognitive lethargy and passivity among many adults may be partially accounted for (Garbarino, 1975, p. 428).

socialization into sport

In addition to Kelly, several other investigators have conducted research to determine the relative effects of the socialization agents on the leisure participation of the young, specifically, their involvement in sports. Based on a sample of some 300 high school students, McPherson (1976) set out to test the relationship between four social agencies (family, peers, school, community) and socialization in the role of sport consumer. The dependent variable, a degree of sport consumer role socialization, was composed of an index derived by summating three elements of socialization: (1) a degree of *behavioral socialization,* i.e., a sum of the number of sport events attended and the frequency of watching sports on TV, etc., (2) a degree of *affective socialization,* i.e., a sum of the frequency with which the person thinks about sports and the amount of loyalty felt toward individual athletes or teams, etc., and (3) a degree of *cognitive socialization,* i.e., a sum of various pieces of knowledge about sports. The relevant information about the four independent variables (the amount of family-induced, peer group-induced, school-induced, and community-induced propensities to consume sport) was obtained by asking the questions about a number of persons (e.g., of family members) who consumed sport, the frequency of sport consumption, the frequency of rewards received for consuming sports, the importance attached to sport consumption and the opportunities of consuming sports. The results can be summarized as follows:

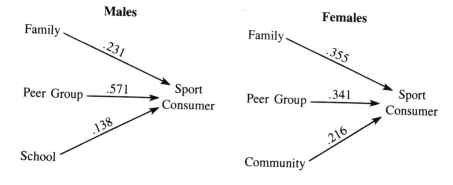

As determined by standardized regression coefficients, the numbers indicate the relative contributions of three significant social agencies to sport consumer role socialization. Statistically, the results were respectable since the four agencies as a whole explained a substantial portion of the total variance (100%) for both males (61%) and females (53%), a result which is quite rare in this type of study. The remaining amount of variance, which is unaccounted for, is due to methodological errors in the conduct of the study and/or failure to consider other relevant variables. It can be seen that peers were more important than family and school in affecting male subjects' tendency to "consume" or take advantage of sports as spectators; the effect of community (e.g., relatives, neighbors, coaches) was practically negligible. For females, family had a slightly stronger influence on sport consumerism than did peers or community, but the school had negligible influence. These positive relationships indicated that individual tendency to become a sport consumer increased with an increase in social agents' behavioral, affective and cognitive involvement. In other words, the more their peer group, family and school or community supported this participation, the more the high school students were involved in spectator sports.

It is of interest to note that more than any other agencies the peer group influenced males' spectator behavior. Peer influence was equally strong in all three aspects (behavioral, affective and cognitive) of involvement. On the other hand, this result is entirely congruent with Gordon's, et al. (1976, p. 320) conclusion, based upon their review of past research, that "late adolescents frequently use leisure activities to promote and maintain autonomy from their parents by first increasing degrees of solidarity with friends and then through intimacy with very close peers." In a similar vein, Rosenberg (1973) reported data which indicated that the influence of parents on an individual's self-perception decreased steadily from childhood to late adolescence. At the same time, it is well established that both in childhood and adolescence, the desire for social and interactive participation increases with age (cf. Sherif and Sherif, 1964). Csikszentmihalyi, et al. (1977), for example, found that in terms of absorbing their time and making them most happy, "talking with peers" was the single most important activity for adolescents. Viewed in the light of these results, it is not surprising that among the social agents, peers had the strongest impact on high school students' sport consumer behavior.

What is the significance of the fact that for females the family was most influential? When examining McPherson's (1976) findings more closely, it appears that the family was most important in the case of cognitive and affective socialization, whereas the peer group was the most significant determinant of *behavioral* socialization. This suggests, therefore, that female students' actual spectator behavior depended more on peers, while family contributed more to affective and cognitive socialization. These comparisons, however, should be treated with extreme caution, because the difference between the family and peer influences was minor. While one can conclude that peers are "significant" social agents for female adolescents as well, in this respect the family cannot be ignored. Further evidence of this can be found in a study reported by Snyder and Spreitzer (1973).

These authors found that for both sexes, the parents' interest in sports was positively related to all three dimensions of sport involvement of their children: behavioral, cognitive, affective. In other words, if parents participated frequently in sports, talked often about sports, and watched sports regularly (behavioral involvement), so also did the respondents (their children). If sports were of high affect and value to parents, e.g., a way to relax and achieve satisfaction, so were sports to the respondents. If parents had extensive knowledge of sports, so also had the respondents. Not surprisingly, the parents of the same sex tended to have somewhat more effect on the respondents' behavioral involvement than did those of the opposite sex. However, the mothers' interest was more strongly related to both their sons' and daughters' affective and cognitive involvement than was the fathers' interest in these two aspects of sport participation. In addition, parental encouragement was found to be positively related to children's sports involvement. In their later report, Spreitzer and Snyder (1976) observed that mothers' and fathers' interest in sports per se was not significantly related to their children's sports participation in youth. Rather, it was explicit parental encouragement which showed a strong and systematic relationship with youth participation.

Taken together, these findings suggest that models provided by parents' own involvement may not be enough for developing children's interest in sports. It looks as if parents also have to communicate to their children the positive values and benefits associated with sports involvement. Explicit encouragement may be needed. On the other hand, this is exactly what those parents who are involved in sports seem to be doing (Snyder and Spreitzer, 1973). In sum, even though family influence appears to wane, and peer effects to increase with age, parents nevertheless have a consistent and significant impact on their children's sports involvement. The importance of this effect is reflected by the fact that an individual's first encounter with games and sports is likely to be arranged by the family, that parental encouragement (or lack of it) shapes the direction of sports involvement throughout childhood and adolescence, and that adult sport participation in part follows early childhood experiences. Thus, there is no eluding the fact the family is a major source of one's present and future leisure behavior.

By encouraging participation in certain forms of leisure, parents not only give direction for their children's future behavior but more importantly, they affect children's psychological well-being as adults. Brooks and Elliott (1971) found in their longitudinal study that childhood leisure activities, and satisfactions derived from them, especially those during the age period 8 to 11 years, were positively related to psychological adjustment at age 30. In other words, those who were fortunate enough to have satisfactory leisure activities at the age of 8 to 11 were psychologically better adjusted 20 years later than those who did not have such leisure activities in their early years, but rather derived satisfactions from passive pursuits in childhood. Sex differences also emerged, since "for girls, early warmth followed by later independence and self-reliance and for boys, active pursuits carried out in the framework of a satisfying home life were associated with psychological adjustment at 30."

These findings are important, in that they support the earlier contention that a wide range of satisfactory childhood activities is essential for an individual to be able to pursue rewarding leisure experiences later in life. Instead of encouraging children to participate in few specific activities, it is desirable for parents and other socializing agents to provide a wide range of active, satisfying forms of leisure for their children. The Brooks and Elliott data indicate that if children learn to derive satisfaction from passive pursuits (e.g., watching TV), their psychological well-being as adults may suffer, presumably because they were denied opportunities to fulfill the need for optimal arousal and incongruity in early years. This childhood passivity may later turn into delinquent acts in adolescence, as the amount of TV viewing (passive leisure) is positively correlated with such antisocial behaviors as vandalism and stealing from stores (Csikszentmihalyi, *et al.*, 1977).

problems with past research

Regardless of these seemingly consistent and conclusive findings, a few words of caution are in order. The problem with studies like those reported by Kelly, McPherson, Snyder and Spreitzer is that they are all static in nature; they assume that the influence of socialization agents is relatively stable. But as Rosenberg (1973) showed and as can be predicted from the dialectical view of leisure behavior, these effects not only change steadily as a function of chronological age but they may fluctuate within a short period of time. If one is to understand why the socialization process also produces individuals who turn to drug abuse, juvenile delinquency and vandalism, it is necessary to know what sort of family influence is needed at different phases of child development, as well as how to react to and accommodate best the changing needs of the changing child. It is possible that there are certain "critical periods" in childhood and adolescence which require appropriate adjustment or matching of one's propensities with social influences, in order for the socialization process to be successful. For example, Brooks and Elliott (1971) reported data which implied that the timing and balancing of satisfactions may be the important factor for future psychological adjustment.

Unfortunately, the studies on leisure socialization reviewed above do not have bearing on these important issues. They have simply demonstrated the importance of various socialization agents. Here much work remains to be done. For example, Kelly's findings place great emphasis on the family as a social context of initiating leisure behavior. This, however, is open to question, since being introduced to certain forms of leisure by the family is only a beginning of a life-time socialization process. Following their initial leisure experiences with family, children have to be "properly" influenced by teachers, peers and others if they are to socialize successfully in leisure. In this light, Kelly's and others' findings are only a tip of the iceberg and therefore do not present a complete picture of the process of leisure socialization. It is inadequate to reduce the changing nature of socialization to such a simple formula as childhood-adulthood leisure. The starting point of research should be the changing individual in changing leisure contexts.

In addition to the above problems, past research can be criticized for not considering the interaction influences of various social agents. Although family, peer group, school, and community have their independent effects on children's socialization, they nonetheless operate jointly; that is, the effects of one depend on those of another, and one social agency should understand the influence of another in order to contribute positively to the development of leisure skills. The values and ideologies of these agencies are often contradictory and incoherent, at least in the United States (Bronfenbrenner, 1970). It is important to know how such inconsistencies and conflicting social pressures affect the development of leisure patterns.

Another consideration arises when one socializing agency is more deficient than others in providing stimulation for leisure experiences. For instance, if deficiencies stem from home, due to the parents' socioeconomic status, can stimulating peers and "good" schools compensate for such defects? This question is pertinent, because it is well established in educational literature (e.g., Walberg and Marjoribanks, 1976) that different patterns of stimulation in the family are related to the diverse developments of specific abilities. A clue is given by Himmelweit and Swift (1969) who reported that very good schools can compensate for the deficiencies of the home, provided these defects are not extreme. However, studies having direct bearing on the interactive effects of socialization agencies on the development of individual ability to pursue rewarding leisure experiences have not yet been conducted.

From the standpoint of value judgments, the results of leisure socialization may broadly be classified as desirable, acceptable, or unacceptable. It was noted earlier that there is a danger of overemphasizing the importance of conformity to cultural norms and conservative values in socializing children for adult life. Such conformity, however, seems to be acceptable to most parents, as they encourage their children to participate in leisure activities (e.g., Little League baseball) which are known to foster compliance with traditional norms and to transmit conservative values. This is understandable if parents believe in the "old system" and if they are generally not willing to take risks with their children by encouraging a critical attitude or deviation from accepted norms. Because variance from the standard patterns would generate uncertainty about the children's future and because, at the same time, most parents want their children to be successful, they tend to encourage participation in leisure activities known to contribute to successful socialization within the prevailing social system. To this end, they consider such forms of leisure as Little League to be acceptable and worth supporting.

It was argued, however, that the desirable product of socialization is a creative and innovative individual who is capable of viewing critically his social environment and the entire society, with the purpose of constructively changing it for the better. The word "constructive" here refers to the change emanating from within the system, the change thus being carried out by its own tools (democracy). Resorting to terrorism, vandalism, and drug abuse as methods of

drug abuse and vandalism as outcomes of leisure socialization

achieving change are therefore considered unacceptable. Unfortunately, the socialization process sometimes fails, with the undesirable consequence of drug abuse and vandalism. The unacceptable outcome of leisure socialization, therefore, is an individual who is destroying either himself or his social environment by or incident to his leisure activities. Drug usage and vandalism qualify as the major forms of destructive leisure; they are the failures of the process of leisure socialization. Possible antecedents of these unfortunate results will be discussed next. By drugs we refer to their nonmedical usage, or rather, their abuse.

drug usage
If personal experiences and social agencies can produce successful leisure socialization, they then must be the sources or determinants of destructive leisure participation as well. The question then arises as to what kind of combination of these factors is likely to lead to the abuse of drugs. An answer to this question can be found in Gorsuch and Butler's (1976) review of past research concerning the predisposing social psychological factors in drug use. The most obvious condition to be noted is that if drugs were not available at all or were difficult to obtain, no hypotheses would be needed for explaining their use. But in view of relatively easy access to various types of drugs today, personal and social factors must be taken into account in order adequately to explain this phenomenon. Thus, the mere availability of drugs does not reveal why some people resort to them while others do not. It appears that there are three types of initial drugs uses: (1) medically induced; (2) by the unsocialized person and, (3) by the person socialized into a pro-drug subculture (Gorsuch and Butler, 1976). For present purposes, the last two categories have immediate relevance and are therefore considered here.

The evidence of a greater use of drugs among "unsocialized" persons is two-fold. First, it has been found that the drug users tend to rate lower on the scales measuring social conformity; for example, those who consider themselves leftists in the political spectrum are more likely to experiment with a drug like marijuana than individuals who are more conservative. Viewed in this light, the finding that drugs are regarded by some people as a means of achieving a better social order (Davis, 1972) comes as no surprise. Second, drug users tend to be less socialized than nonusers; by a four-to-one margin, drug abusers report that "I never found a group where I belonged" (Yankelovich, 1975). Although it is a long way from this finding to reality, one could argue that organized sports like Little League, despite their apparent negative influence, as discussed earlier, may be beneficial, at least temporarily, in preventing drug use among the young. This is particularly true if participation in such organized activities becomes an intrinsically motivated form of leisure for the participants rather than a "time filler."

But socialization in the above sense is insufficient to explain drug usage satisfactorily. Some individuals are socialized into a pro-drug subculture. Gorsuch and Butler (1976) cited evidence to show that family and peers play a crucial role in this respect. As for the family, it appears that at least three family characteristics are associated with children's involvement with drugs. First, an

Developmental Analysis of Leisure and Recreation

ineffective parent-child relationship, which increases the likelihood of initial drug use. Specifically, less cohesive families characterized by self-indulgence and short-range goals are predisposing their children to drug usage. Second, if the family is relatively liberal in its political ideology and does not exhibit a great deal of respect for social institutions, it increases the probability of children's drug use. Third, by using drugs (e.g., alcohol) parents themselves provide a model which induces their children to sample drugs.

As for peers, Gorsuch and Butler noted that the relationship is unambiguous: the more children's friends use drugs, the more likely it is that they also will use them. Thus, combined with availability, peer modeling is an important factor accounting for initial drug experience. In 1978 Kandel reported a study which examined the similarity along a variety of characteristics in real-life adolescent (high school) friendship pairs. The results indicated that the second most important dimension at which similarity appeared was behavior, especially illegal drug use. Kandel interpreted this to mean that "deviant activities in particular need the support of the peer group for their initiation as well as their sustenance."

Although the foregoing factors considerably increase an individual's propensity to drug usage, even their combined presence does not necessarily indicate that a person will resort to drugs. Past experiences, attitudes, and psychosocial maturity have to be considered. In the context of drinking, for example, it has been found that a person's attitudes toward drinking (which reflect his stage of psychosocial maturity), and the social environment of drinking, influence interactively, not additively, a tendency to drink (Gorsuch and Butler, 1976). That is, if a person is an abstainer, it is obvious that he will not drink, no matter what the atmosphere, and therefore no further information is needed. However, since most people (about 65%) drink occasionally and since the single most often cited reason for drinking is sociability (Riley, et al., 1958), it is essential to take into account the social environment of drinking. Therefore, the person who is not opposed to drinking consumes more alcohol in a favorable situation (i.e., when his peers drink too) than in an unfavorable atmosphere (i.e., when his peers are against drinking). On the other hand, there is tentative evidence to suggest that drinkers seek those social groups and activities (e.g., associated with outdoor recreation) which are favorable or conducive to drinking (Young and Kronus, 1977). Taken together, these findings demonstrate that attitudes toward a drug as well as the social atmosphere which tolerates or encourages drug use are important interacting determinants of the individual decision to experiment with drugs.

Besides attitudes, another critical variable related to personal experiences is learned helplessness. Yankelovich (1975) found that drug abusers typically have a history of failures, while this leads to feelings of helplessness, then depression, and finally to antisocial behaviors like drug usage. More abusers (36%) than users (16%) of drugs reported failing courses and being expelled from school (70% vs. 41%); "things often seem hopeless" to abusers (43%) as opposed to nonusers (19%); more abusers (47%) are "unable to finish projects" once started than nonusers (26%); more abusers (47%) than nonusers (18%) feel that "every time I try to get ahead; something or someone stops me."

These findings clearly point to the preponderance of learned helplessness among drug abusers. Hence, it is not surprising to learn that non-medicinal drugs are commonly seen by their users "as a means of changing oneself, of becoming a better person or of achieving a better social order" (Davis, 1972). Some who abuse drugs, therefore, seem to resort to them in an attempt to escape their personal world and the social environment, both of which they perceive as hopeless. The situation gets worse if those who misuse drugs believe that there is something inherently wrong with them and that *they* are helpless to bring about the change (Lloyd and Salzberg, 1975). As discussed previously, early experiences of mastery and control over the environment play a determining role in preventing feelings of helplessness. To be sure, parents have the chief responsibility to provide their children with play and leisure environment which helps them to attain this desirable objective. The more parents fail in their mission, the more difficult it is later for others, such as recreation practitioners, to provide effective alternatives to drug abuse.

vandalism

A stereotyped view holds that vandalism is a product of senseless adolescents. However, such behavior is not a unified action, but rather has many facets, (Cohen, cited in Zimbardo, 1976, pp. 130–131):

1. *Acquisitive vandalism*—property damage done to acquire money or goods (e.g., breaking open vending machines)
2. *Tactical vandalism*—damage done intentionally in order to achieve some other objectives (e.g., prisoners destroying their cells to protest inadequate facilities)
3. *Ideological vandalism*—damage done to advance an ideological cause (e.g., slogans such as "Vietnam is bleeding" painted on public buildings)
4. *Vindicative vandalism*—damage done in revenge (e.g., students demolishing a classroom because of a seemingly unjust teacher)
5. *Play vandalism*—damage done in the context of a game (e.g., who can shoot out the most street lamps)
6. *Malicious vandalism*—property damage done as an expression of frustrations, often carried out indiscriminately against public and private property.

That vandalism is not necessarily the act of mindless adolescents was vividly illustrated by Zimbardo's (1976) field study. A used car in good condition, its license plate removed and hood raised, was placed a block from the New York University campus in the Bronx. The first strippers—a mother, father and young son—came only ten minutes after the car was abandoned. *Adults* continued vandalizing the car, to the extent that "in less than three days what remained was a battered, useless hulk of metal, the result of 23 incidences of destructive contact" (Zimbardo, 1976, p. 133).

Although social psychologists have paid very little attention to vandalism as a form of antisocial behavior, it seems that basically the same antecedents predispose individuals to vandalism as to drug abuse. Some support for this can be found in Yankelovich's (1975) data which showed that drug abusers damage property (e.g., parks) purposely more often than do others. Despite an apparent correlation between drug abuse and vandalism, individuals other than those who abuse drugs also engage in acts of vandalism. Nevertheless the same psychological mechanisms probably explain this deviant behavior, as well as drug abuse. It has been reported that those who feel powerless spend a considerable amount of their time in such passive forms of leisure as watching TV, especially thrillers (Himmelweit and Swift, 1977). At the same time, it is known that engaging in passive leisure activities (e.g., watching TV) is positively related to such antisocial behavior as vandalism and stealing in stores (Csikszentmihalyi, et al., 1977). Thus, feelings of powerlessness and helplessness, with accompanying depression and frustration, seem to be as much a cause of drug abuse as of vandalism. As Zimbardo (1976, p. 132) noted, those who commit acts of vandalism "lead lives with little hope of change or significant improvement, without feelings of ownership or relatedness to society, [because] social conditions have limited the availability to them of traditional means of 'making it,' of gaining status, prestige and social power."

Of course, other factors should also be considered. The socialization variables that were shown to predispose an individual to drug abuse may also be relevant to a social psychological theory of vandalism. Situational determinants form another group of pertinent factors, as demonstrated by Zimbardo (1976). In this study, graduate students were invited to smash and dent an old car. Although students were reluctant to do so at the outset, later, in the process of demolishing the car, they were aroused, to the extent of not wanting to stop it, presumably because of the exhilarating feeling of physically destroying something (Zimbardo, 1976). Another situational factor of vandalism is peer pressure. As Zimbardo pointed out, vandalistic acts are sometimes committed to build one's reputation, make one's mark, and to instill fear.

Regardless of these situation-specific determinants, it appears that the underlying cause of vandalism is learned feelings of helplessness and powerlessness, induced by failures during the socialization process. As noted earlier, parents play a critical part in preventing a sense of helplessness from developing. Disruption of the effective child-parent relationship, lack of opportunities for involvement in organized groups, and peers who commit acts of vandalism, are some of the probable factors predisposing to vandalism. Therefore, the core of the problem is how children are socialized, and how they are treated when they grow up. Zimbardo (1976, p. 134) put it aptly: "The real threat is not in what some deviants will do to the society, but what society is doing to turn an ever-increasing number of its once respectable citizens into deviants and 'mindless wanton vandals.' "

summary

Leisure socialization was defined broadly as the process through which a child acquires basic knowledge about leisure and recreation, forms fundamental attitudes and values toward them, and learns various leisure skills and motives. A dialectical perspective of leisure socialization was developed, emphasizing the continuing, life-time nature of socialization process. In the center of this theorizing is an individual with self-determination and perceived competence to perform various leisure behaviors. Empirical research supports the dialectical model, in that several investigators have demonstrated a statistically significant link between early childhood recreation and adult leisure behavior on the one hand, and a significant difference in leisure participation between the two periods on the other. Research indicates that learning new leisure activities is as much an adult as a childhood process. Tentative evidence shows that about 60% of leisure participants could replace their current recreation activity for new activity with minimal or no loss in satisfaction. This was taken to reflect cognitive and behavioral flexibility in leisure behavior. Although everyone is seeking novelty and variety in leisure throughout the life span, this occurs within the confines of the individual need for optimal arousal and incongruity, a condition which is in part a result of childhood opportunities to play in stimulating environments. While people at one and the same time desire stability and familiarity as well as novelty and change in their leisure behavior, the perceived (subjective) competence is a key determinant of the speed and direction of change desired in leisure encounters. Practical implications of the dialectical view of leisure behavior were discussed.

The next section focused on the role of social agents (parents, peers, teachers) in affecting an individual's socialization in leisure. Studies indicate that family has the strongest impact on the development of an individual's leisure patterns. When people were asked with whom leisure activities are usually begun, their responses indicated that about two-thirds of all activities reported began with family. At the same time, the influence of friends and school teachers in this respect, appears to be considerably less. In relation to sports, it has been found that if parents participate frequently in sports, talk often about sports, and watch sports regularly, so do their children. As the child grows older, however, the influence of parents seems to decrease, and that of peers to increase, so that by the high school years, peers play a more important role than other agents in socializing students as sports consumers. By encouraging participation in certain forms of leisure, parents not only give directions for their children's future behavior, but, more importantly, they affect children's psychological well-being as adults. It has been found that childhood leisure activities and satisfaction derived from them, especially those during the age period 8 to 11 years, were positively related to psychological adjustment at age 30.

The last section of the chapter dealt with failures of leisure socialization, most notably drug abuse and vandalism. Since the leisure socialization process does not always succeed in developing a socially and psychologically competent individual, some persons resort to such antisocial behaviors as drug abuse and vandalism. It appears that at least three family characteristics are associated with children's abuse of drugs: an ineffective parent-child relationship, liberal political orientation and disrespect for social institutions on the part of parents, and parents' own drug use. Research also suggests that typically those who misuse drugs have a history of failures, which leads to feelings of helplessness, then depression, and finally to antisocial behaviors like drug abuse. Feelings of powerlessness and helplessness seem to be as much a cause of drug abuse as that of vandalism. Zimbardo (1976) noted that those who commit acts of vandalism "lead lives with little hope of change or significant improvement, without feelings of ownership or relatedness to society, because social conditions have limited the availability to them of traditional means of 'making it,' of gaining status, prestige and social power."

8 aging and leisure

Socialization is a life-time process. To become a "successful adult" as a result of early social learning is not the end of the socialization process. Although the direction and rate of socialization in childhood and adulthood may differ, an individual nonetheless changes throughout the life span. When discussing leisure socialization, therefore, one has to consider the elderly as well as young children. The present chapter is devoted to analysis of a maturing individual and his leisure behavior. The emphasis is placed on examination of the changes in leisure patterns from adulthood to retirement. This will begin with observation of the anatomy of life cycles in general and then consider the role of leisure at various stages of the life cycle. The chapter concludes with an analysis of leisure and successful aging.

limitations of later-life socialization

Despite the fact that children and adults both represent "the changing individual in the changing world," childhood and adulthood socialization differ from one another. This is due to the limitations of later-life socialization. The biological capacities of an individual as well as the effects of early social learning (or lack of it) impose these limits, and together determine the effectiveness of socialization in later life (Brim, 1966). Biological forces restrict socialization by imposing the upper limits to an individual's capacity to perform and function, a capability which changes with age. For example, no matter how favorable and effective early socialization has been, a person may never become interested in leisure activities involving motor skills, if coordination is not well developed biologically. This is especially true with increasing age.

It has also been shown that some personality characteristics more than others are under biological constraints, and that these genetically "overdetermined traits" remain throughout a life-time (Shaie and Parham, 1976). If so, then such characteristics may be manifested in certain leisure activities, thereby predisposing a person to some leisure behaviors rather than to others. On the other hand, this life-long persistence of predispositions is relative, because it has been shown (Dworkin, Burke, Maher and Gottesman, 1976) that certain personality traits may be under significant genetic control in adolescence but not in adulthood, and vice versa. Consistent with this, Haan (cited in Casady, 1975) found that the personalities of well-adjusted young and middle-aged adults and older persons were similar, but that these people "relied upon different traits more heavily at specific stages of life." Taken together, this probably indicates that biological factors limit people's leisure behavior, or perhaps more appropriately, predispose them to certain leisure patterns, and that these influences are subject to change with age.

Another major class of limitations on later-life socialization stems from the influence of early childhood learning, or lack of it. For example, a person who has not learned waterskiing by the time of adolescence probably will not learn this leisure activity in middle or late adult life either. It appears that there are critical periods in the life cycle during which certain things have to be learned (Brim, 1966). If this is true, then some leisure skills have to be acquired in childhood, or adolescence at the latest. The same is true for the overall attitude toward leisure. If in adolescence or early adult years the Protestant work ethic becomes the determining principle, an individual may not be able to appreciate the value of leisure in later life. As was shown earlier, the acquisition of favorable attitudes toward leisure during formative years lays the foundations for satisfactory socialization in later stages of the life span. These considerations, however, remain to be confirmed by empirical research.

The above influences conform to the principle of durable qualities of early childhood learning (Brim, 1966; Schaie and Parham, 1976). But despite apparent limitations imposed by biological forces and early childhood learning, there is substantial opportunity for change in leisure behavior during later years. Even though change generally becomes more difficult and painful in the later stages of the life cycle, it is not impossible if the person is determined to experience such change. Viewed in this way, the evidence of "continuity of personality" does not mean that biological factors and early learning necessarily "limit" one's leisure behavior. Besides, change can be both "between" and *"within"* activities as noted earlier. Brim makes a similar point:

> The usual objective of socialization in the later-life stages is to get one to practice a new combination of skills already acquired, to combine existing elements into new forms, to trim and polish existing material, rather than to learn wholly new complexes or responses . . . (Thus) the content acquired in adult socialization is not so much new material as it is the aggregation and synthesis of elements from a storehouse of already-learned responses (Brim, 1966, p. 28).

Although old persons generally are inferior to young adults in learning, especially when the learning rate is increased (Witte, 1975), it is not justified to argue that "teaching an old dog new tricks" is inefficient from society's point of view. Each individual has important ideas about change, and everyone defines learning individually, with personal views ranging from "new material" to a "synthesis of old elements." More important, efficiency is not the criterion by which human beings should always be evaluated, but unfortunately, this is what Western societies are prone to do. One undesirable consequence of judging people in terms of their efficiency may be that the diminuation of some capacities and functions in the elderly is the result of society's negative and indifferent attitudes, or lack of concern for older persons. Despite physiological changes accompanying old age, "the remaining capacities are more than sufficient in millions of older persons . . . (and) a satisfying, physical, mental and emotional life is possible for the majority of older persons if society finds value in providing a reasonable framework" (Weg, 1977, p. 83). Thus, the "limits" of later-socialization are quite relative, and depend, to a large extent, on the support which is furnished by one's social environment. The social aspect of leisure behavior is as important for the elderly as it is for the young.

seasons of life

levinson's model

Later-life socialization cannot be looked at as one coherent segment of time. Like children, adults go through several stages during their life-cycle. Levinson (1978) has proposed a model dealing with the anatomy of the male life cycle. He divides the life cycle into four broad stages: childhood and adolescence, early adult age, middle adult period, and late adult era. Entry into each stage is preceded by a troublesome transitional period which is associated with chronological age and can therefore be rather reliably predicted. Transition to early adult life occurs around the age of 20 ($\pm$ 3) years, the middle life era starting at about 40 ($\pm$ 3) years, and the late adult life beginning at approximately 60 ($\pm$ 3) years. In addition to these critical transitions, a person passes through a sequence of stable periods, starting at about the ages of 30 and 50 years and lasting about four to eight years; during these periods the "individual life structure" is built or modified.

As Levinson points out, it is important to realize that all these periods are subject to individual variations, so that the prediction of the exact time of the stages for an individual is virtually impossible. Nonetheless, this variation has a pattern which enables one to anticipate the transitional periods as beginning within three years on either side of the 20th, 30th, 40th, 50th, and 60th birthday. In each transitional period, a person experiences psychological crises. For example, Levinson found that about 60% of the people in his study reported experiencing moderate to severe crises during the age-30 transition. Before discussing the implications of this model for leisure behavior it is useful to examine another concept of the life cycle.

gould's model

A somewhat similar model of adult life stages was proposed by Gould (1975) after probing the life experience of more than 500 men and women. Like Levinson, Gould found that the years between 22 and 28 constitute a time of entering the adult world, during which young people direct their energies to becoming personally and professionally competent. It is the "now generation:" now is the

Figure 10 Developmental periods in the life cycle. (From *The Seasons of a Man's Life,* by Daniel J. Levinson. Copyright © 1978 by Daniel J. Levinson. Reprinted by permission of Alfred A. Knopf, Inc.

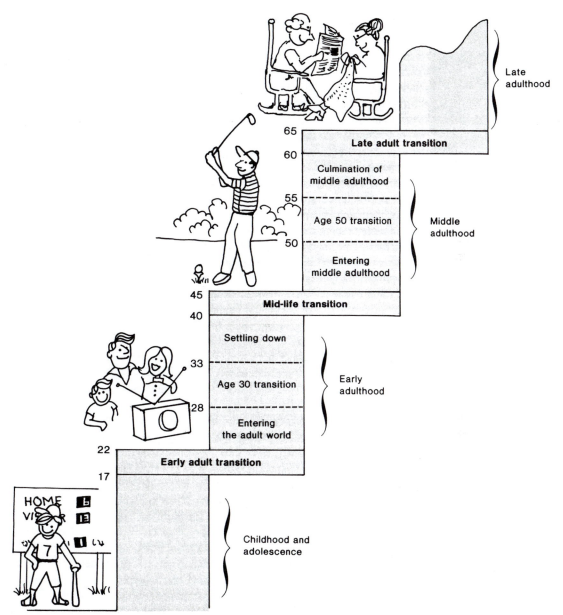

time to live and now is the time to build for the future. This era is followed by a period of self-questioning, varying roughly from 29 to 34 years of age and characterized by such self-examination as: what am I doing? why am I doing these things? This, then bears a striking resemblance to Levinson's "age 30 transition." Gould's data suggested that a young marriage both absorbs and reflects much of the stress and strain peculiar to this period. Statements like "I wish my mate would accept me for what I am as a person," become more common during the age 30 transition than at any other stage. In this phase another overriding change has to do with the importance placed upon children. These changes of attitude are understandable, in that they often coincide with the deaths of close relatives. In this sense, young adults are biologically forced to turn from the old generation to the future one. The age 30 transition, therefore, is in part biologically controlled.

In the 30's people "settle down" (Levinson) or continue "expanding their personality and life structure in a leisurely fashion" (Gould). However, they may become concerned about not making enough money to do what they want. By the same token, the feeling that marriage has been a good thing for them is at a lower level in the 30's than at any other period. The next stage, beginning at about the age of 40, is what Levinson called "mid-life transition," and Gould termed "quiet urgency." Now time is no longer perceived as infinite, thereby occasioning some worries. Comfort associated with marriage remains at a relatively low level; suddenly, people begin to regret their mistakes in raising children, to feel that life does not change much from year to year, to become concerned about their health, to feel that it is too late to switch their career, to feel that there no longer is plenty of time to do most of the things they want to do, and to worry relatively little about making enough money (Gould).

Following the mid-life transition, the 40's are spent in "entering middle adulthood," a time during which the marriage again gains in importance and personality is perceived to be rather fully developed. In this period, to a greater extent than during the earlier phases, people would feel lost without their friends. As a result, there is a sharp increase in the degree of preference for active social life during the 40's. This preference, however, declines considerably in the "age 50 transition." Although interest in "active" social life decreases, human experiences become especially precious through spouse, children and friends. At the same time, "self" loses its importance toward the end of the 50's. There is an increasing feeling that time to do what one wants to do is running out. Health becomes a greater concern, and such feelings as "I can't do things as well as I used to" and "I try to be satisfied with what I have," grow steadily (Gould).

Like Levinson, Gould was quick to point out that predicting the precise age of the individual stages is worthless because change is a function of individual personality (and thus individual biological background), the life style and subculture to which a person belongs at any given time. Nevertheless, Gould argued that the adult life cycle consists of a developmental sequence which the majority of people pass through in the same order. He further posited that with increasing age an adult inclines toward self-acceptance and self-tolerance; beliefs about one's self, the environment and the whole world become better organized and more stable. The process of change, however, is not smooth but rather is a matter of confrontations and contradictions: on the one hand, the person feels that the actions taken are correct, but on the other hand, he believes them to be inadequate or insufficient. This is the heart of the dialectical view of human development.

Although both Levinson's and Gould's models are based upon empirical data, one should be careful not to overgeneralize their applicability to all social groups and cultures. Whenever the life cycle is broken into various stages there is always a danger of oversimplifying the picture and of assuming that people from diverse socioeconomic classes and cultures experience the various life stages in the same way. For example, certain periods (e.g., "teenager" or adolescence) may be short or nonexistent in some cultures and long in others. Despite a need for caution in analyzing the data of developmental research, the fact remains that two investigators (independent of one another) reported strikingly similar models of the adult life cycle. This, therefore, lends credence to the proposed pattern of sequential stages of the life span and indicates that leisure behavior should be analyzed as a function of developmental phases and transitional periods.

Since both Levinson's and Gould's data lend clear support to the idea of the four seasons of the life span, it must then be true that there are "smaller seasons" within each of the four stages. By further reducing the length of the "season" or cycle one finally reaches the period of one day. Regarded from this standpoint, one may better understand the relationship between human development in the several stages, and the need for postulating an optimal amount of change. Just as there is a difference (contradiction) between day and night, so too is there a continuous confrontation between the novel and the familiar, between too much or too little incongruity in our daily encounters. The process of change as a global concept involves mutations from one developmental stage to another, or a confrontation between stability and novelty at that level. The same process can be seen in operation on a smaller scale in everyday activities. It is for this reason that leisure activities always have had (and always will have) a function of providing either stability or diversion (novelty), depending on how they relate to other contemporary behaviors. The need for optimal arousal and incongruity is therefore an important basic reason for most leisure activities. It should be noted, however, that optimal incongruity does not predict specific leisure behavior, because it only sets the outer boundaries within which more specific needs can be accommodated.

A key to the Levinson (1978) model is the idea that human beings are rational organisms who consciously shape their individuality. To prepare for an uncertain future, therefore, it is desirable that people in various transitional stages evaluate their past quite honestly and candidly. Building and modifying the basic structure of life is not only an external process but perhaps more important, these processes deal with "internal aspects" of the life structure. When

implications for
leisure behavior

transitional crisis periods force them to do so, people must redefine themselves in relation to their younger and older counterparts. Refusing or postponing such self-appraisal does not remove problems or help in reaching the next developmental stage in an orderly fashion. Levinson (1978) argues that pursuing youthful dreams and illusions should be replaced by seeking new sources of vitality.

This search for novelty is consistent with the idea of the need for optimal arousal and incongruity. While the optimum amount of incongruity changes as a function of the chronological age and fluctuates within a certain period of time, it nevertheless underlies one's behavior at any developmental stage. As we noted earlier, tomorrow's change is precipitated by today's stability. It is therefore natural at times to feel stagnated, or motionless (Levinson, 1978). While the transitional crisis periods make such feelings more pronounced, a person should not give in to these sensations, but instead, should fight against feelings of drying up and not growing. In this struggle toward "generativity" (Levinson), arousing and stimulating leisure activities can be of great help.

Levinson's (and Gould's) model should be viewed as a general description of the total life cycle rather than as a theory of human behavior. Levinson's stages constitute a general framework of human development and change in connection with which more specific behavioral changes occur. What is significant about his model is that there are several developmental stages and troublesome transitional periods through which all individuals have to pass. Thus, these change periods must be incorporated in the analysis of leisure behavior and considered separately. This model is particularly intriguing because it implies the differential role of leisure behavior at various points of adult development. It is possible that rewarding leisure experiences may, to a great extent, alleviate transitional problems. If so, it should be understood that it is not the leisure activity per se which may be important, but rather what a person does with leisure and why each individual behaves as he does. Although leisure behavior has not been examined empirically in light of Levinson's model, some research findings allude to the applicability of this approach.

Orthner (1975, 1976) found that participation in various types of leisure activities was significantly related to marital satisfaction in the first marital period (the first five years of marriage) and the fourth period (after children have left home), but not in the periods between these extremes. Orthner suggested that joint leisure participation enhanced marital satisfaction in these two periods, because it increased communication between the spouses. Although these findings do not have direct bearing on Levinson's model, they nevertheless point out that the psychological role of leisure participation varies during the several developmental stages of the life cycle. It appears that the function of leisure becomes more important during the periods of transitional crises. More direct evidence for this can be seen in Gould's (1975) data. As was remarked earlier, the desire for active social life took a sharp upward jump among the 42–48 year olds. Furthermore, DeCarlo (1974) found evidence to suggest that leisure-time pursuits were essential in reducing the impact of later-life crises, particularly after 60. These studies should be extended and further research be done on the basis of Levinson's and Gould's excellent theoretical frameworks.

Prior to the publication of the Levinson model, some descriptive research was undertaken to determine the rate of leisure participation throughout the adult life cycle. One of the most comprehensive studies was reported by Gordon, *et al.* (1976). A sample of 1,441 adults ranging from 20 to 94 years of age were interviewed in Houston. When the respondents' participation in all leisure activities was combined for the total leisure score, the following results were obtained (see figure 11).

Figure 11   Percentage reporting high leisure participation, by stage and sex. (From *Handbook of Aging and the Social Sciences,* edited by Robert H. Binstock and Ethel Shanas. Copyright ©1976 by Litton Educational Publishing, Inc. Reprinted by permission of Van Nostrand Reinhold Company.)

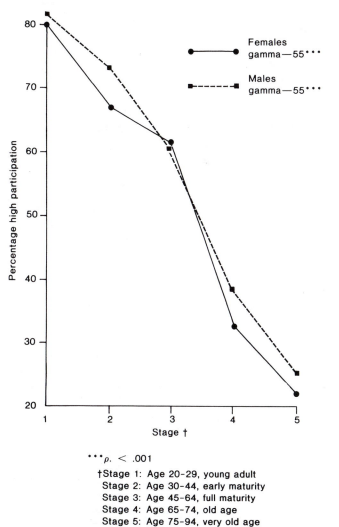

*** *p.* < .001
†Stage 1: Age 20-29, young adult
Stage 2: Age 30-44, early maturity
Stage 3: Age 45-64, full maturity
Stage 4: Age 65-74, old age
Stage 5: Age 75-94, very old age

As can be seen, there is a strong (significant) negative relationship between age and leisure participation for both males ($-.55$) and females ($-.55$). In other words, as age increased, general leisure participation decreased. Or, with increasing age the number of respondents reporting high levels of participation decreased linearly. That the average frequency of participation in leisure activities decreases with increasing age has been observed in other studies as well (Schmitz-Scherzer, 1976; Baley, 1955). Thus there seems to be no question about whether the intensity of leisure participation declines with chronological age.

However, it should be kept in mind that the Gordon, *et al.*, results were obtained when the respondents were divided into five broad categories of age. Had a more refined classification of age been used, the relationship might not have been as linear. Besides, the results shown in figure 11 represent an average participation in various leisure activities as a function of age, meaning that for some activities the relationship was more negative than for others. This can be seen in the coefficients (based upon the values of gamma, whose meaning is similar to correlation coefficient) expressing the strength and direction of the relationship between age and leisure participation for various activities separately (Gordon, *et al.*, 1976):

Activity	Males	Females
Dancing and Drinking	$-.77*$	$-.75*$
Movies	$-.67*$	$-.69*$
Sports and Exercise	$-.56*$	$-.54*$
Outdoor Activities	$-.43*$	$-.53*$
Travel	$-.38*$	$-.37*$
Reading	$-.36*$	$-.36*$
Cultural Production	$-.34*$	$-.25*$
TV-Viewing	$-.17*$	$-.19*$
Discussion	$-.16*$	$-.17*$
Spectator Sports	$-.14*$	$-.19*$
Cultural Consumption	$-.17*$	$-.08$
Entertaining	$-.17*$	$-.06$
Number of Clubs	$-.02$	$-.07$
Home Embellishment	$+.03$	$-.01$
Cooking	$+.59*$	$-.25*$
Solitary Activities	$+.26*$	$+.40*$

*Statistically significant at the .05 level or better.

It can be seen that with age the decline in leisure participation was strongest for dancing and drinking, movies, sports and exercise. The decrease was also substantial for activities such as outdoor recreation, travel, reading, and cultural production (e.g., painting and playing a musical instrument). Thus, it seems that leisure participation declines most in those activities that are carried on outside the home and those that require physical exertion (Gordon, *et al.*, 1976). Similarly, Schmitz-Scherzer (1976) reported that with increasing age family related contacts intensify but extrafamilial interactions decrease.

On the other hand, the above coefficients indicate that the decline was only moderate or minimal for activities like TV-viewing, discussion, spectator sports through TV, cultural consumption (e.g., belonging to social or civic organizations), and home activities (e.g., sewing, fixing or working in the yard). Hence, for these activities, participation was slightly reduced or remained the same across the life span. This is understandable as most of them are carried on at home and are sedentary in nature. It therefore appears that engagement in the high-intensity and the outside-home activities declines, whereas participation in "home-centered forms of sociability and media-based interaction" remains relatively stable across the life cycle.

Interestingly, as they grow older, the percentage of high participation in cooking increased notably for males (+.59) but declined for females (−.25). Regardless of these opposite trends, more females than males had high levels of participation in cooking still during the fifth stage. This is due to the fact that females' decline and males' increase with age started from the opposite ends of the participation rate in the first stage. Nevertheless, this finding is psychologically important because it clearly suggests that people change their leisure activity patterns throughout the life stages. More and more men switched to cooking and more and more women shifted away from it as they grew older. In addition, though it cannot be seen in the above gamma coefficients, the Gordon, et al., data revealed that participation in several activities increased from early adult years to the mid-life periods, after which it again declined in later years. For example, "clubs and organizations" and "discussion of important issues" peaked at the age range of 40–54 years; this is practically identical with what Gould (1975) found about preference for active social life in this period. Watching spectator sports peaked at 30–39 and home-centered activities reached their zenith both in early maturity and after retirement.

Such fluctuations and changes with age are consistent with the dialectical view of leisure behavior. The fact that cooking was the only "new" activity for men, while participation in many leisure forms declined or remained relatively stable, implies that with increasing age, changes occur primarily "within" activities rather than "between" them. Similarly, Schmitz-Scherzer (1976) reported that older persons seldom take up totally new leisure activities. While time spent in solitary activities (i.e., being alone and thinking, planning, or just doing nothing) increased considerably with age, such change can hardly be interpreted as learning of a new leisure activity. In sum, few older people show a tendency to acquire completely new forms of leisure. Rather, they change the pattern of leisure behavior within their existing leisure repertoire.

It follows from the foregoing that the desired level of change can be achieved by numerous ways within the scope of previously learned activities: by changing (1) intensity of participation, (2) the locus of participation (e.g., outside vs. inside home), (3) social company of participation, both quantitatively (few vs. many

dimensions of change

partners) and qualitatively (males vs. females; old vs. young; close vs. distant friends, etc.), (4) psychological reasons of participation (social interaction vs. physical exercise, etc.) and (5) time (morning vs. evening, etc.) of involvement. These various dimensions of change are used differently by different people in order to achieve optimal novelty, incongruity and complexity in all stages of the life cycle, and at any given time in a developmental stage. Such mechanisms (dimensions) of change regulate persons' involvement in various leisure activities. It is therefore inadequate to examine change in leisure behavior as a function of one dimension only. For example, Schmitz-Scherzer (1976) found little systematic change in numerous leisure activities at four different measurement points, and concluded that "constancy predominates." While the intensity of participation may have been relatively stable in his study, he failed to recognize that respondents may have changed their leisure encounters according to one or more of the remaining four proposed dimensions of change. Thus, the study does not shed much light on the patterns of change in leisure behavior of the aging individual.

It is clear that the five basic dimensions provide nearly an infinite number of combinations and possibilities for seeking variety. This is psychologically important; it shows that theoretically, all people can experience optimal change and variety, this optimum being essential to maintaining mental health throughout the life cycle. It is true that all people do not achieve this optimum nor do some people all the time. Nevertheless, the situation is satisfactory, in that the need for change and variety can be satisfied within one and the same activity. It would be intolerable if this need had to be satisfied each time by acquiring completely new leisure skills.

However, there is another aspect. That the need for change can be satisfied within one and the same activity with little variety is probably the main reason why human beings are capable of adapting to almost all conditions, including those that can be considered most inhumane (Proshansky, 1973). While ability to adapt to the environment (Dubos, 1965) has made it possible for people to survive, this capacity can also defy the very human values that have made survival possible. It follows then that the need for optimal arousal and incongruity may be satisfied in a manner which threatens the basic human values. Therefore, how the individual achieves the desired level of arousal and incongruity is significant for society, which has a responsibility to provide those forms of leisure experience that promote rather than depress human values. Unfortunately, Western societies seem to be doing just the opposite by exalting work and labor and discrediting leisure. Often one is left with the impression that decision-makers seem to think that granting permission to establish some new Las Vegas fulfills the "leisure needs" of citizens.

consequences of neglecting the elderly

A vivid example and a drastic consequence of the general neglect for leisure can be seen in what has happened (and is happening) to the elderly in institutionalized settings. Deprived of social contacts and personal responsibility (perceived control), they have dramatically declined in both physical and psychological well-being. At the same time, the mortality rate has increased among institutionalized aged (Schulz, 1976; Rodin and Langer, 1977). Thus, lack of concern for how the elderly should satisfy their need for optimal arousal and incongruity through leisure has not only dehumanized them with respect to their leisure values, but has prevented them from seeking optimal incongruity. In other words, people, by their capacity to overadapt, come to accept even the most dehumanizing forms of leisure as appropriate and sufficient to "satisfy" their need for novelty and variety. In the absence of social interaction, for example, people in a nursing home may think that their social input is no longer needed or desired, and as a consequence they isolate themselves from the social environment. They may accept their room as a sufficient source of stimulation and thereby reduce their range of leisure activities, as well as several possibilities for achieving optimal arousal. Such a deteriorating situation obviously undermines human leisure values. Thus, it appears that overadaptation to the environment does not occur without taking its toll; it reduces people's need for optimal arousal, which in turn affects their survival.

But institutionalized settings are not the only situations in which there is failure to satisfy the need for optimal incongruity. Due to the lack of opportunities many poor or undereducated people come to accept forms of free-time activity (e.g., drugs) which not only downgrade their values and disappoint their expectations, but which also threaten their existence as human beings. Thus one of their most basic psychological needs, optimal incongruity, is denied or distorted to destructive ends. It is well documented in the relevant literature (e.g., Bishop and Ikeda, 1972; Gordon, et al., 1973; Schmitz-Scherzer, 1976; White, 1975) that lack of education and income (or occupation) restricts people's leisure behavior and thus narrows the range and diversity of experiences needed for bringing about optimal arousal. Yet, at the same time it has been reported that active leisure participation throughout the life span is associated with high satisfaction and happiness (e.g., DeCarlo, 1974; Gordon, et al., 1973; Graney, 1975; Haan, cited in Casady, 1975; Nystrom, 1975; Palmore and Kivett, 1977). These results may be interpreted to indicate that a lack of recreational opportunities because of an impoverished social environment seriously impairs an individual's attempts to fulfill the need for optimal arousal; the result is decreased psychological well-being.

That public officials are little concerned about this human need is clearly demonstrated during crisis periods. When city budgets have to be cut due to the financial difficulties, it is the recreation department which is sacrificed first and suffers most. From the psychological standpoint, just the opposite should be done: if anything is to be saved it should be the recreation department. As noted earlier, the role of recreation may become critical during crisis situations; and empirical evidence tentatively supports this contention (DeCarlo, 1974). Yet public officials seem to be willing to sacrifice first the opportunities for seeking novelty and variety. It is paradoxical and ill-advised that they do so at a time when these opportunities are needed most. Financial reductions in the recreation budgets compel people to strive for optimal incongruity under limited conditions, like watching TV at home. These budgetary reductions, therefore, force people to make substitutions "within" a narrow scope of activities. Inevitably, a reduced leisure repertoire increases the likelihood of stress and tension and may thereby impair psychological well-being.

The role of public services in helping to meet the need for optimal arousal becomes even more important with the elderly. As people grow older they have a natural tendency to restrict their leisure encounters, and hence they seek novelty principally in a few activities they learned previously (cf. Gordon, *et al.*, 1976). Thus, their arsenal of leisure activities tends to shrink after mid-life, as illustrated in figure 12. This diagram shows that the scope of the leisure repertoire of an average person increases steadily from birth to mid-life, after which it begins to decline. Of course, there are individual differences in this pattern, so that the leisure repertoire may be at its most extensive earlier or later than depicted above. For some individuals an increase or decrease in the breadth throughout a life span may be more abrupt than the below average, whereas for others it may be gently sloping.

The leisure repertoire can be both objective and subjective. The former refers to the quantity of leisure activities and the latter to the quality of these pursuits. While the above diagram may hold true for both aspects, it is more likely to reflect the quantitative storehouse of activities. Thus, it is possible (and desirable) that an individual should perceive a broad personal repertoire during the retirement years, even if actual participation is limited to only a few activities. Such perception is possible, provided that the person is active in leisure and successfully makes substitutions "within" leisure activities. This is precisely the function of leisure service for the elderly; the services need not necessarily introduce new leisure activities. But they should provide opportunities for changing leisure encounters within the sphere of familiar activities.

In this process particular emphasis should be placed on facilitating social interaction among the elderly. Empirical research supports this contention. For example, Lemon, Bengtson and Peterson (1972) reported a statistically significant positive correlation between "informal activity with friends" and life satisfaction, thus indicating that life satisfaction increases with an increase in social

Figure 12   Individual leisure repertoire as a function of life span.

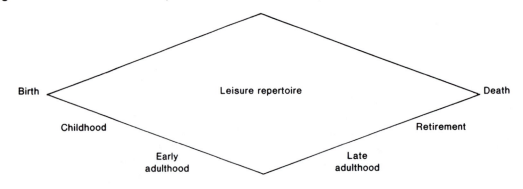

Developmental Analysis of Leisure and Recreation

activity with friends. Similarly, Graney (1975) found a significant positive relationship between happiness and social participation (especially face-to-face interaction) among elderly women aged 62 to 89 years. As a consequence of increasing social interaction up to the optimal level the elderly may perceive their leisure repertoire as wide. Other things being equal, it appears that the broader the perceived leisure repertoire, the better the psychological well-being.

The question is not whether old people will survive without recreation and leisure services. Of course they will, because of their enormous capacity to adapt to almost any condition. But in counter productive situations, they unfortunately lose sight of values that are characteristically human (Dubos, 1965). Thus, overadaptation occurs at the expense of the quality of their life and the length of their life expectancy. If this is desired, there should be no concern about cuts in the recreation budgets!

leisure
participation and
successful aging

The Constitution of the United States declares that pursuit of happiness is the right of every individual. Although the Constitution does not so state it, the primary function of the government is often said to be that of facilitating a happy life for everyone, regardless of sex, age, race, ethnic or other individual differences. This goal, however, becomes very difficult to attain because people do not generally agree upon what constitutes a happy life ("the pursuit of happiness"), and because definitions and expectations of happiness change as functions of age and social environment. Nevertheless, government has an obligation to pursue this difficult goal. Its responsibility is particularly vital in the case of individuals who, because of their minority status, may not be capable of pursuing happiness as vigorously as are more fortunate and privileged individuals. One group of such persons is the aged. Successful aging comprises high-level intellectual functioning, the maintenance of mental, physical and social health. Before it can be said what society in general and leisure agencies in particular should do to facilitate successful aging, it is necessary to understand the psychological processes which underlie such successful aging.

disengagement or
active participation?

During the past two decades the discussion of aging has concentrated upon the idea of increased disengagement in social participation as a result of increased age. Cumming and Henry (1961) proposed a theory of aging which holds that "aging is an inevitable mutual withdrawal or disengagement, resulting in decreased interaction between the aging person and others in the social systems he belongs to" (p. 14). They argue that because society is highly youth-oriented, it is not conducive to active social participation by the elderly, with the consequence that if old persons do not give up their role as an active social participant, psychological crises will be unavoidable. It is, therefore, necessary for the aging individual to become an increasingly passive observer of life. Not surprisingly, this theory has been challenged both on conceptual and empirical grounds, and in response, the opposite view of aging has been advanced (e.g., Havighurst, 1961; Atchley, 1977). This "continuity" theory of aging points out that "as the individuals grow older, they are predisposed toward maintaining continuity in habits, associations, preferences, and so on'' (Atchley, 1977, p. 27). Thus, if people are active during early and mid-adult years, they also are likely to be active in the later stages of life. The ''activity theory of aging'' (Lemon, *et al.*, 1972) further assumes that there is a positive relationship between activity and life satisfaction.

However, if this were the only interpretation of ''continuity,'' it would place an undue emphasis on the influences of biological factors or early childhood learning on leisure behavior of the elderly. But as Atchley (1977, p. 27) correctly pointed out, a predisposition toward certain activities and behaviors ''constantly evolves from interactions among personal preferences, biological and psychological capabilities, situational opportunities, and experience.'' In short, continuity means both stability and change.

need for stability and change

But what pattern of change and evolution is best for successful aging? To answer this question we first examine the general nature of change throughout the life span. When the entire life cycle is considered, the role of stability and change may have the following overall pattern and relative strength (see figure 13). In other words, soon after infancy the desire for novel play and recreation experiences becomes stronger than the need to participate in familiar forms of leisure. This desire for novelty continues its upward trajectory until it reaches a peak sometime in early childhood or adolescence, remaining at a high level for a number of years before starting downward in late adulthood. At the same time the need for familiar experiences has considerably less strength, except before retiring, when it begins its upward swing and becomes more insistent than the need for novelty. It is essential to realize that this model is based on the ''average'' person; there are many individual divergences from the general trends depicted above. Even though the absolute values of the two tendencies (novelty and

Figure 13   Relative strength of the tendencies to seek familiar and novel forms of leisure throughout the life cycle.

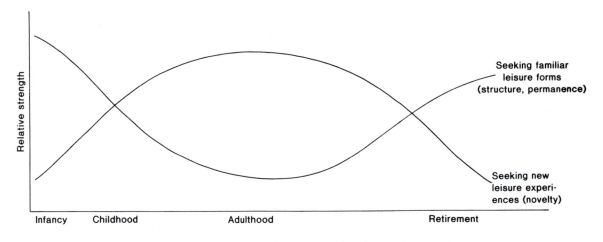

Developmental Analysis of Leisure and Recreation

stability) vary considerably for different individuals at different points of time, the overall configuration is likely to follow the same (above) pattern for the majority of people.

Since the tendency toward novelty and stability (and thus optimal arousal) is individual, the relative strength of these two forces cannot simply be tested by measuring the frequency of participation in various leisure activities. Leisure experiences are subjective, and thus their psychological values have to be known to indicate something about their contribution to gratifying the need for optimal arousal. It is also noteworthy that even though the desire for permanence, structure, and psychological stability is relatively weak during childhood, adolescence and adulthood, it nevertheless is important. For example, while expending most of his energy on exploring and investigation, a child can do so only if the environment is conducive to stability and security. In a way, the psychological stability and structure of the environment is in the back of the child's mind, but in a stable environment it does not dominate behavior. This is the principal reason why a stable and secure family life is critical for the child. It permits attention to exploration, investigation, and manipulation, which are essential to cognitive maturation.

The situation, however, is reversed in late adulthood, when the need for stability becomes the chief concern. This is due to increasing feelings of physical and mental malaise, a condition which is probably associated with the feeling that there is little to be explored in the world: "I know how it works, this is the way it has always been." On the other hand, the need for novelty does not disappear in later years; it merely assumes different forms and appears within a much more limited leisure repertoire. Rather than seeking totally new leisure encounters, people vary experiences within those activities they feel most capable of carrying out and which result in the most enjoyment. The responsibility of the social environment is to support the elderly people's inclination toward stimulating leisure experiences within their confines, rather than to promote such potentially devastating notions as "an old dog does not learn, or does not want to learn, new tricks." As Weg (1977) has noted, millions of older people have sufficient capacity for seeking new sources of vitality, until the last moments of life.

recreation and successful aging

The above observations indicate that successful aging requires opportunities for and encouragement in seeking "new" leisure experiences. It is reasonable to conclude that the more a person neglects this aspect of optimal arousal (either for personality or social reasons), the less successful will be his adjustment to the aging process. One consequence from this hypothesis is that those elderly persons whose leisure can be characterized as "active" are aging more successfully than those whose leisure behavior is passive. Several studies lend considerable support to this proposition.

DeCarlo (1974) investigated the relationship between subjects' (mean age = 85.5 years) recreative pursuits and the criteria of successful aging (SA). These criteria comprised mental and physical health, as well as intellectual performance. Recreation participation was defined in terms of frequency of participation and number of recreative pursuits throughout the total life cycle, as listed by the respondents. These activities were also differentiated by behavioral elements involved: sensory-motor, cognitive and affective. When the three criteria of SA were combined and correlated with the total score of recreational participation, a significant and positive relationship (.48) was found between recreative involvement and successful aging during later life and middle age. This indicated that as recreation participation increased, so did the quality of aging. It was also found that all three activity types (motor, cognitive, and affective) were positively related to mental health, but that cognitive (recreation) participation was the only one which was significantly related to intellectual performance and physical health. Finally, when participation in recreational activities "regularly" (i.e., from one life stage to another) was correlated with SA, the relationship was again consistent and positive, that is, those who participated regularly in leisure activities throughout their life-time had a higher score of SA than those who participated sporadically.

Thus, continued participation in recreational activities throughout the entire life cycle is characteristic of those who live long and age successfully. It is important to note that involvement in all three types of activities (motor, cognitive, and affective) was positively related to mental health. One implication of this result is that a variety of activities is needed for successful aging, and that those who follow this pattern are psychologically healthy. This reflects the importance of having opportunities to seek novelty through a variety of activities.

Another interesting finding of the DeCarlo study was that participation in cognitive activities ranked appreciably higher in terms of its effect on physical health than did other forms of recreational engagement. "Common sense" has always implied that participation in physical motor activities is the most dependable guarantee for staying physically fit in later life. While DeCarlo's data do not necessarily deny that, they nevertheless suggest that cognitive and mental exercises are urgently needed for maintaining physical health. One may, therefore, speculate that it is not motor activity per se which is important for physical health, but rather the kind of "thought processes" it stimulates in a participant. Such speculation, however, has to be taken with caution because of the correlational data and rather crude measures of participation used in the DeCarlo study. Nevertheless, one may tentatively conclude that active participation in a variety of recreational activities contributes significantly to successful aging. If so, it clearly indicates that for those individuals who are able to seek new leisure experiences (i.e., to maintain the optimal level of arousal relatively high), whether between or within activities, the aging process is more successful than for those who are not able to do so. This is consistent with Gordon's, *et al.*, (1973, p. 25) conclusion that ". . . active life styles tend to produce more pleasure and reduce the loneliness, depression, and anxiety of isolation."

The foregoing conclusions can also be drawn from a study reported by Nystrom (1974). In this investigation, 65 old persons, mostly females, with a median age of 76, were interviewed regarding their activity participation, leisure concepts, activity meaning, and their perceptions of free-time. In one form or another, social interaction was by far the most frequent use of their free-time. Social interaction had different forms, like phone calls to relatives and friends, card and bingo games, visiting relatives and friends, and participation in various types of social clubs. Watching TV and listening to the radio constituted the second major class of activities participated in by the subjects. In general, it appeared that these elderly people engaged in a wide range of activities, the intensity of involvement varying from activity to activity and from person to person. At the same time about a quarter of the respondents indicated that they would like to participate in various activities but could not do so because of deterrent factors like cost, safety, mobility, or opportunity in general. Such activities included taking rides, attending movies or theaters and concerts, and doing small handcrafts or needle arts. On the basis of these findings and other studies (e.g., Graney, 1975), it is then reasonable to conclude that many elderly people are active and that many more would be if their environment were conducive to activity.

the importance of social interaction

This, therefore, indicates tendency of older persons to satisfy the need for optimal arousal, by active leisure engagement both in familiar and "new" leisure encounters. Moreover, Nystrom (1974) found that the more active individuals were, the better satisfied they were with their free-time. Further evidence about the need for novelty and substitution within activities came from the finding that a given activity had several meanings and that the same meaning was attached to several activities. For example, social interaction was given four different meanings, of which "being in contact with my friends" was most frequently mentioned. On the other hand, the most often mentioned meaning, "enjoyment," ("I like it for the sheer pleasure of it") was associated with 12 different activities.

The above findings demonstrate that older people have a desire and tendency to be active, and that being able to be active is related to high life satisfaction. Especially, the role of social interaction seems paramount in this respect. Fox (1977) found that for retired women social contacts are much more significantly associated with psychological well-being than such contacts are for working females or housewives. In a similar vein, Palmore and Kivett (1977) observed in their longitudinal study of persons aged 46–70 that two types of social participation—sexual relations and organizational activity—were positively (significantly) correlated to present and future life satisfaction for both sexes. Subjective health, however, was a much better predictor of future life satisfaction than the above social variables, implying that it is important to maintain good health and remain socially active.

Taken together, it appears that occupational retirement does not reduce people's inclination to be active, to seek stimulating leisure experiences provided the social environment does not impede or discourage such efforts. Fox (1977), for instance, observed that although retirement decreased the perceived level of social interaction as a whole, specific types of social contact increased with retirement. That is, although retired women talked to fewer people each day than did women who worked, on the average the former knew more of their neighbors, had more close friends, maintained more contact with their neighbors, friends and relatives and enjoyed voluntary associations more frequently. Thus, retirement seems to enhance the quality of social interaction.

In sum, successful aging and high life satisfaction are associated with active life style among the elderly. To understand the implications of this relationship, it should be noted that this finding is not limited to old persons. As Palmore and Kivett (1977) reported, the best single predictor of a person's later life satisfaction is satisfaction at an earlier time, that active social participation is associated with life satisfaction at various points in time. It seems reasonable to conclude that active social participation is the single best guarantee of successful aging. Based upon Haan's research data, Casady (1975, p. 138) made a similar inference: "During the mainstream years from 20 to 50, those who are happiest and best adjusted are active participants in life. They are intellectually alert, socially assertive, engaged with environment and other people." Thus, more than anything else, adjustment to aging is a matter of individual differences. Those who have learned in their early years to be socially and otherwise active are very likely to continue this pattern throughout their life; as a consequence they are much better off mentally, physically and socially than are their inactive counterparts.

As has been stated repeatedly in earlier pages, these individual differences reflect variations in optimal arousal between persons. What becomes optimal for an individual is largely determined by early socialization experiences and biological predispositions. To avoid misunderstanding, it should be noted that the writer does not hold the deterministic view, because he sees no convincing evidence for it. The fact that some individuals are more active than others is indication of environmental influences. Individuals continue to develop, to change and grow through the life span; and the social environment is an important contributor to this process (for evidence, see Maddox and Douglass, 1974). But what should not be forgotten is that this continued change occurs within the individual limits, shaped principally by early socialization process. This conclusion is important not only for theoretical reasons but above all, for practical considerations.

implications   If the observer ignored individual differences as a contributing factor to continued development, he would immediately conclude that every old person should be brought into the realm of active leisure participation (because active participation may guarantee high life satisfaction). Directors of programs would make the elderly from all the corners of the country spend their free-time actively and effectively. They would set up countless new recreation programs with countless "active" activities. Why would all this be wrong? Principally because it would disregard the different experiences of different individuals, as these have in a sense predetermined the direction and rate of individual growth. Since it takes many years for a person to develop an individual, even a unique view of the world and how to function in it, this structure cannot quickly be obliterated by new recreation programs, without doing psychological damage to the person. The change should be gradual and adjusted to individual interests and capabilities. Too much and too rapid change brings too much incongruity for the person to cope with.

Due to social deprivation many persons have come to accept for themselves too low a level of arousal and stimulation optimal. When recreation professionals strive to raise this optimum with the intent of bringing about higher life satisfaction and more successful aging, they cannot assume that people are identical, that they are infinitely flexible in accumulating new leisure experiences. While professionals must promote change, they should recognize individual creativity and freedom (Bengtson, 1973). Undeniably, the human capacity for adaptation is very great, but it is not without its limits. This simultaneously is a challenge and warning to practitioners, not to impose too much or too little incongruity in helping the public pursue happiness through leisure encounters. After all, the need for optimal arousal and incongruity is an individual thing—at least so long as people differ in their genetic structure and socialization experiences.

---

summary

Socialization is a life-time process. Research indicates that the human life cycle can be divided into four broad stages: childhood and adolescence, early adult era, middle adult years, and the late adult period. While it appears that leisure participation generally decreases with age, this does not mean that the importance of leisure diminishes as age increases. There is some evidence to suggest that leisure participation plays an important role in solving problems which appear during transition from one stage to another. Furthermore, people change their leisure activity patterns throughout the several life stages, not necessarily by acquiring new forms of recreation but by substituting within the familiar activities. Five dimensions (ways) of achieving the desired level of change were presented. One of them, the quantity and quality of social interaction, seems to be a central factor in the pursuit of the optimal degree of arousal and incongruity, and thus also in maintaining mental health throughout the life cycle.

Leisure service for the elderly does not necessarily mean introducing new leisure activities, but rather providing opportunities for changing leisure encounters within the sphere of familiar activities. In this process, particular emphasis should be placed on facilitating social interaction among the elderly, for it appears that deprivation of social contacts and/or personal responsibility decrease their physical and psychological welfare. At the same time it appears that active leisure participation throughout the life span is associated with a high degree of satisfaction and happiness. It was noted that the more extensive the perceived leisure repertoire, the better the psychological state.

Several studies support the idea that those elderly persons whose leisure can be characterized as "active" are aging more successfully than those whose leisure behavior is typified by passivity. This difference is probably due to the fact that "active life styles tend to produce more pleasure and reduce loneliness, depression, and anxiety of isolation" (Gordon, *et al.*). In one form or another, social interaction is by far the most frequent use of the elderly's free-time. Occupational retirement does not seem to reduce people's need to be active and to seek stimulating leisure experiences, provided the social environment does not impede or discourage such efforts. This is particularly true if people have learned to be intellectually alert, socially assertive, involved with the environment and with other people during the mainstream years from 20 to 50.

social psychological determinants of leisure behavior

part 5

social psychological factors in the perception of leisure 9

**subjective
definition of leisure**

Everyone has a personal definition of leisure. To some leisure means participation in an activity, while to others it brings into mind an idea of not doing anything, or "getting away from it all." One person defines leisure solely in terms of success in competitive encounters, while another perceives leisure at its best when he is acquiring new skills. Whatever the individual definition, it is a product of personal experiences and situational/social influences, as shown in figure 14. Subjective definitions, in turn, are directly related to persons' leisure choices and actual leisure behavior. Of course, leisure behavior is also affected by situational factors at the time of participation. For example, a group of people wandering in a wilderness may decide to extend their stay by a day or two because of good luck in fishing. Or a person may have to play tennis whether or not he likes to because the boss asks him to play. It is important to realize the circular character of the above model. Leisure behavior is not only affected by personal experiences and social influences through subjective definition, but it also modifies

Figure 14   Relationship between personality and leisure. (Reprinted with permission of publisher from: Iso-Ahola, S. "On the theoretical link between personality and leisure." *Psychological Reports,* 1976, 39, 3–9, Figure 1.)

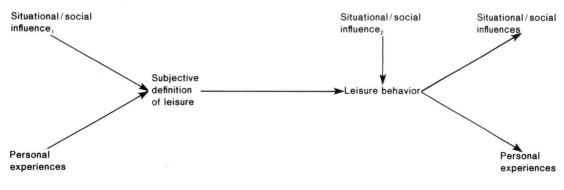

185

these two factors, while this, in turn, gives rise to change or maintenance of one's subjective definition.

Naturally, the above model is not a theory of leisure behavior as such, from which specific behavioral predictions could be derived. Rather, it is a theoretical framework intended to demonstrate the general relationship between the antecedents and consequences of leisure behavior. The model is important for three reasons. First, it acknowledges that an individual is continually changing in the changing world. Second, it accepts the principle that change is a result of interaction between personal experiences and social influences. Finally, it stresses the role of human beings as cognitive performers, rather than assuming that leisure behavior is determined by stimulus-response contingencies. Although these points may seem obvious, one finds, when looking at the reported research, that such is not the case. All too often investigators base their research on an assumption that the explanation of human behavior can be found in either personality or situational factors. Researchers have often forgotten the changing nature of behavior and have instead studied "frozen moments." And there are still a few investigators who adamantly deny the importance of cognitions in human behavior. Taken together, the model shows that theories of leisure behavior cannot ignore three key parameters: (1) person, (2) situation/social influence, and (3) time.

determinants of perceptions of leisure

Does this mean that individual cognitions and behaviors are person-situation- and time-specific? Can one make no generalizations about perceptions of leisure? Despite the three limiting conditions, individuals' subjective definitions of leisure share in common some characteristics that hold true of people, situations, and time. The most important of these is *perceived* freedom. If this characteristic or dimension is pervasive (i.e., not person-, situation- or time-specific), it means that a 50-year-old Iowa woman who goes to concerts during her "free-time," and an adolescent in Texas who plays tennis in his free-hours both have at least one thing in common: their subjective definitions of leisure are largely affected by perceived freedom to participate in various activities.

Thus, it comes as no surprise that the concept of freedom has been incorporated in practically all textbook and article definitions of leisure. Regardless of this apparent consensus, leisure authors differ in one important respect. Some of them (e.g., Kraus, 1971) stress the objective aspect of freedom, that is, time left over after work, while others (e.g., deGrazia, 1962) emphasize that the off-work hours are "free" only if the person so perceives them. To understand the effects of freedom on individual definitions of leisure, the term has to be analyzed as subjective (i.e., "perceived"). Thus, perceived freedom is high when a person attributes the initiation of leisure behavior to self, but it is low when he ascribes the source of behavior to external factors.

dimensions of leisure definitions

Besides perceived freedom, at least three other underlying dimensions of leisure definitions have been proposed. They are: intrinsic-extrinsic motivation, goal-orientation, and work-relation. Neulinger (1974) suggested that perceived freedom, intrinsic-extrinsic motivation, and goal-orientation (in the order of importance) are the paramount dimensions of individual leisure definitions. In a similar vein, Kelly (1972) considered perceived freedom and work-relation as the two critical ones. As for the specific meaning of these dimensions, Neulinger referred to intrinsic motivation as an activity done for its own sake, and to extrinsic motivation as an activity engaged in for some reward, like money. Goal-orientation comprises a distinction between instrumental and final goals. A person who paints a boat to be able to sail is engaged in a leisure activity with an instrumental goal; when the same individual is actually sailing later, this leisure activity is then said to be one with the final goal. Kelly's work-relation refers merely to the degree to which a person's leisure activities resemble work. Since these dimensions, in one form or another, have been proposed by leisure theoreticians for a long time, it is surprising that their validity has not been tested empirically. In an effort to improve the situation, two quasi-experimental studies were conducted (Iso-Ahola, 1977a, 1978).

In both studies, male and female undergraduates were presented with eight hypothetical situations and asked to rate on a scale from 1 (not leisure at all) to 10 (leisure at its best) what their participation in any given leisure activity would mean to them as leisure under each hypothetical condition. The situations were described in terms of the characteristics of three dimensions, with two levels in each. In the first study, the dimensions utilized were perceived freedom, intrinsic-extrinsic motivation, and work-relation. In the second study, the first two dimensions were the same as above; the third consisted of goal-orientation. For example, the first situation to be evaluated in terms of leisure in the first study was as follows: "You are not participating freely in the activity X (i.e., you did not have an opportunity not to participate)—the activity X is unrelated to your daily work—the activity X is intrinsically motivating." To test whether the three dimensions were indeed underlying and overriding factors in the perception of leisure, the effect of leisure activities was kept constant by not making a reference to any particular activity. The results are depicted in figure 15, in which the upper row pertains to the second study and the lower row to the first study.

two studies

As can be seen, the effect of perceived freedom was far greater than that of other variables. Although work-relation and goal-orientation had a statistically significant impact on the ratings of leisure, the above figure clearly shows that their effects were negligible in comparison to those of perceived freedom and intrinsic motivation. These findings were entirely consistent with Neulinger's and Kelly's theorizing, in that it was freedom rather than lack of it, intrinsic rather than extrinsic motivation, low work-relation rather than high work-relation and final goals rather than instrumental goals, which increased the subjects' perceptions of leisure. (Intrinsic motivation was operationalized by intrinsic rewards, such as feelings of competence, and extrinsic motivation by extrinsic rewards like money.) In addition to the above singular effects, several interaction effects were found.

Figure 15 Determinants of perceptions of leisure. (Upper panels from Iso-Ahola, 1977a and lower panels from Iso-Ahola, 1978.)

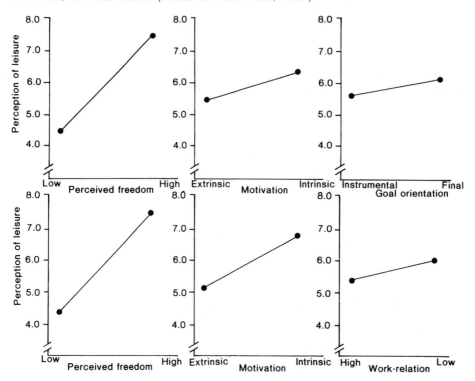

criticalness of perceived freedom

When free-time activities were unrelated to work, this low work-relation increased the male respondents' perception of leisure only when they had initially had freedom to participate in a given activity. In other words, if, for one reason or another, they felt that they were forced to participate, then low work-relation did not help turn the activity into a leisure-like activity. This is important, as it clearly shows that the perception of freedom prior to participation is critical to defining a given activity as leisure. Thus, even a highly work-related activity may become leisure if people perceive themselves as having an opportunity to participate or not to participate in it. Interestingly, this fact did not hold true for female respondents. That is, a free-time activity being unrelated to work increased female subjects' perceptions of leisure, regardless of whether they had had initial freedom to engage or not to engage in the activity.

This result was coupled by another sex difference found in the second study. While intrinsic motivation generally facilitated the perception of leisure, the effect was considerably greater for women than men. These two findings pertaining to sex differences can perhaps best be explained in light of the socialization process. Since men are typically socialized to be breadwinners and women housewives and homemakers, the latter may consequently become more open to and appreciative of leisure than the former. Thus, in the socialization process, women may learn to value the intrinsic aspects of leisure because leisure becomes a more important source of satisfying their need to be competent and self-determined, than does work. As was pointed out earlier, perceived competence regulates the direction and pace of leisure involvement within the confines of individually optimal arousal.

The perceived freedom and work-relation interaction for males clearly indicated that even a highly work-related activity may become leisure-like *if* a person has had an opportunity to select an activity before engaging in it. The importance of perceived freedom to the definition of leisure becomes more notable when considering the interactions of the second study. The significant interaction involving perceived freedom and motivation as well as perceived freedom and goal orientation demonstrated that when subjects had little or no freedom to participate in a given activity, even the fact that this activity produced feelings of competence (intrinsic reward) and was "final" in nature did not appreciably increase the perception of leisure, which remained at a relatively low level. However, when the participation was their own choice (i.e., high perceived freedom), then the perception of leisure associated with this participation not only became high but was further augmented by intrinsic motivation and by the "final" goal-orientation of activity. Thus, even extrinsically motivated and "instrumentally" oriented activities may become leisure-like if a person is able to exercise freedom before engaging in an activity. In this respect, men and women did not differ from each other.

In sum, the above results lend strong support to the idea of "threshold leisure," which states that perceived freedom is the critical regulator of what becomes leisure and what does not. In relation to leisure, perceived freedom involves the principle of all-or-nothing, a threshold, after which the effects of other variables can be seen. Since this conclusion is based on the results of two quasi-experiments utilizing hypothetical situations, one could argue that the findings do not necessarily hold true for actual leisure behavior. Mannell (1978a, b), however, has demonstrated in a laboratory setting that when subjects are given an opportunity to select a "leisure" activity they become considerably more involved in it than do subjects who do not have freedom of choice. Similarly, Wankel and Thompson (1978) reported a field experiment in which subjects (members of a commercial physical fitness club) were divided into two groups, and their perceived choice of activity was manipulated. Those who were told that the designed program was totally based on their own choices and preferences had a significantly higher average attendance than had those who were told that their program was based upon a "standardized exercise format rather than their expressed preferences." The difference in the average attendance between the choice and no-choice groups became greater as more time (i.e., 5–6 weeks) elapsed from the beginning of the program. In short, these studies demonstrated that actual activity choice (Mannell) and perceived choice (Wankel and Thompson) increased the subjects' involvement in free-time activities.

Thus, it appears that perceived freedom determines an individual's perception of leisure, which in turn directly shapes the extent of leisure involvement, as stated at the outset of this chapter. When translated into everyday living this means that if a person who usually plays tennis for its intrinsic rewards (its own sake) is suddenly forced to play (i.e., by the boss) or deprived of an opportunity to decide whether or not to play, this activity loses its leisure-like nature and gains a work-like character. This conclusion is in keeping with deCharms' conclusion:

> Man's primary motivational propensity is to be effective in producing changes in his environment. Man strives to be a causal agent, to be the primary focus of causation for, or the origin of, his behavior; he strives for personal causation (deCharms, 1968, p. 269).

Again, one sees that external sanctions have a determining property of turning play and leisure into work (cf. Deci, 1972; Greene and Lepper, 1974b). The critical nature of perceived freedom has been observed not only in the context of research on the "overjustification" hypothesis, but also in the case of the institutionalized aged. Schulz (1976), Langer and Rodin (1976), and Rodin and Langer (1977) have shown that deprivation of perceived freedom, choice, and responsibility not only decreases physical and psychological well-being of older persons, but may increase the mortality rate among the elderly. Consistent with this, Nystrom (1974) reported that about 50% of her subjects (women, with a median age of 76 years) agreed that leisure must have the element of freedom. Clearly, these findings point to the fact that perceived freedom retains its importance throughout the entire life cycle.

That perceived freedom is of such crucial value has important implications. As the above studies demonstrated, a lack of perceived freedom cannot be compensated for by introducing other aspects of leisure which have been shown to affect the subjective definitions. If, to begin with, a person is deprived of the opportunity to select free-time activities, very little can be done later to improve the situation. Unless one is able to increase perceived freedom, not only will a person's subjective definition of leisure notably decline, but more important, psychological well-being will deteriorate, and in the case of an old person, physical health may be damaged to a considerable extent. Thus, it seems imperative to augment feelings of perceived recreational freedom and choice.

Unfortunately, all too often societal norms and expectations disparage people's leisure repertoires and the quality of their leisure engagements by implicitly forcing them to participate in certain activities—without first giving them a choice. For example, many individuals, because of their occupation (e.g., bank officers), are expected to invest much of their "free"-time in community organizations—sometimes against their will and desire. In such circumstances, these activities are more work than leisure to them. Hence the conclusion would seem to be that of eliminating social norms, expectations, and even laws which impose constraints on leisure choices and behaviors. Of course, such suggestions are short-sighted and unrealistic. What, then, could be done, short of revision of norms, expectations, and laws? If perceived freedom is a matter of individual cognitions and if it can be cognitively disparaged, there must also be ways to enhance it at the cognitive level. To provide concrete methods for doing so one must understand the psychological mechanism of perceived freedom. Brehm's (1966, 1972) theory of psychological reactance offers a good starting point.

Freedom is so fundamental a concept that it is a cornerstone of modern international politics. All nations on earth have been classified in terms of those which seek to maintain individual freedom and those which more or less overtly oppose it. The Western world, the United States as its leader, bases its democracies on the idea of individual freedom, as that freedom is expressed in many ways (e.g., freedom to speak and to assemble) in the Constitution. When a person is socialized in such societies with this philosophy of life, it is no wonder why the individual feels that the foundations of life are removed when individual freedom, or even some part of it, are taken away. This may in part explain why people in general react strongly to more and more governmental involvement and "red tape."

perceived freedom and psychological reactance

Although the need for freedom is primarily an aspect of the socialization process, it also has some biological roots. That is, all humans have a need to understand their world and to exercise control over their environment; otherwise they could not survive. As Lefcourt (1973, p. 424) noted, "the sense of control, the illusion that one can exercise personal choice has a definite and positive role in sustaining life." A person who does not have perceived control does not have freedom either. Relevant to these considerations are Brehm and Weinraub's (1977) findings which showed that 2-year-old boys were, at that early age, sensitive to threats to freedom imposed by physical constraints, while girls of the same age showed less reactance and more acceptance of situational restrictions. Although it is not clear whether this sex difference resulted from biologically determined behavioral tendencies or of early socialization experiences, or both, the finding nevertheless demonstrated that psychological reactance to the threat or elimination of freedom "deals with motivational processes that are rather basic to the human organism" (Brehm and Weinraub, 1977).

It follows from this that each individual can be said to have a strong need to maintain behavioral freedom, and that, therefore, the threatened loss of that freedom generates psychological reactance manifested in various ways. This is the heart of Brehm's (1966) theory of psychological reactance. Attribution theorists (Heider, 1958; Kelley, 1967, 1971) have also claimed that people have a tendency to exercise control over their environment, as reflected by their tendency to attribute their own behavior to self rather than to situational factors. Based upon her review of past research, Wortman (1975) found definite support for the idea that people tend to believe that their behavior is under their own control and that their needs can modify their actions. Thus, it should be no surprise to find that people generally are prone to minimize the role of chance and external factors as determinants of their behavior. Such situational factors tend to impair one's perceived control over the environment and will therefore be maladaptive. Thus, perceived freedom can be equated with attribution of behavior (its initiation) to internal factors, and the absence of perceived freedom may be likened to external attributions of behavior.

Brehm (1966) postulated that a threat to one's behavioral freedom creates a state of motivational arousal, called reactance, leading to individual attempts to restore freedom. How strongly a person will react depends directly on several factors (Brehm): (1) expectation of freedom, (2) the importance of a particular freedom, (3) the strength of the threat, and (4) implications. First, the more a person has learned to expect to have freedom (due to socialization experiences), the more psychological reactance will be expressed in the case of threat or elimination of that freedom. Thus, a person who is used to playing tennis regularly at a municipal court reacts more strongly when the court is shut down than a person who plays tennis little or not at all.

Second, the person's reaction to the threat or to the actual elimination of freedom is stronger if a particular freedom is perceived as important. For example, if tennis is very important (i.e., the only form of physical exercise) to a person, that individual will react more vehemently to losing the opportunity to play than will the person to whom tennis is not important. Tennis is only one of the many forms of physical activities the latter person engages in during freetime. Having a large store of leisure skills, therefore, aids in coping with the loss of an opportunity to participate in one activity. This provides additional evidence for the necessity of including leisure education in the school system.

Third, if a particular freedom (e.g., playing at a municipal tennis court) is taken away entirely, the person will experience greater reactance than when there is only a threat to take away this freedom. Finally, if a threat to freedom has implications for a person's other (and future) leisure activities, then reactance is greater than if such implications do not exist. For example, if a tennis player frequently loses to opponents, the loser may conclude he lacks ability at tennis and generalize that conclusion with respect to a host of other activities involving motor skills. Thus, when failure has such implications, the psychological reactance is greater than when it does not have these implications. Unfortunately, failure in most competitive (even in "recreational") situations and events has such implications.

When a person is faced with an uncontrollable event preventing the pursuit of a given leisure activity that has been freely accessible previously, the resulting reactance generates certain effects which can be channeled in a number of ways and in various directions. The four most common consequences of psychological reactance are (Brehm, 1966; Wortman and Brehm, 1975): (1) increased attractiveness of the threatened or eliminated freedom or behavioral option; the reduced attractiveness of a forced alternative is greater than the increased attractiveness of a forbidden or lost option (Mazis, 1975); (2) direct attempts to pursue a threatened or eliminated behavior; (3) attempts to compensate for the loss by engaging in related behaviors and (4) hostile and aggressive feelings and actions.

It then follows that once a person's freedom to play tennis is threatened or eliminated (e.g., municipal tennis courts closed due to a fiscal crisis), the person is likely to view the activity more favorably afterwards and will therefore attempt to participate in this activity, for example, by tranveling to a nearby city where tennis courts are available. Another example can be observed in children's play groups. It has been demonstrated that the chosen toys are more desirable than the unchosen ones, and the toys which have been played with are more desirable than those toys which have not been played with (Costanzo, *et al.*, 1974). In other words, when a peer takes away a toy and plays with it, other children's liking of that toy immediately increases and they too want to play with it. The chosen toy thus diminishes their perceived freedom, thereby increasing the attractiveness of that toy and attempts to play with it.

The aforementioned parameters of reactance determine what a person is willing to undergo in a situation involving lost behavioral freedom. If direct attempts become too tedious and cumbersome, the person may change his evaluation of tennis as a leisure activity and may consequently deny or minimize its leisure value. Or the individual may restore and compensate for this lost freedom by participating in related activities which imply that pursuit of the threatened or eliminated activity is still possible. For example, when due to the lack of facilities, it becomes too difficult for a person to play tennis, the player may switch to similar activities, like racquetball, squash or badminton. Or a person who regularly goes to symphony concerts may compensate for the elimination of such concerts by attending other types of entertainment (e.g., opera).

Losing (or a possibility of losing) certain freedom may sometimes arouse aggressive feelings and in the most serious cases may even lead to physical attack. Such feelings and attacks are invariably directed at a person who is perceived to be responsible for the lost freedom. The likelihood of these feelings increases with the rising importance of a lost or threatened freedom. It is also conceivable that the perceived justice of the elimination of freedom affects the likelihood of hostile reactions. That is, if with little or no justification, recreational services are reduced, such "unjust" removal increases aggressive feelings on the part of those who used them. On the other hand, if the public is well informed about the necessity of eliminating certain programs and activities (e.g., due to a fiscal crisis), the inception and effects of psychological reactance may be avoided. It is important that blame for the elimination of programs be attributed to factors which are beyond the control of those who are responsible for executing it. Laboratory research (Worchel and Andreoli, 1976) has shown that such situational attributions reduce or inhibit reactance and therefore aid in restoring behavioral freedom. In a similar vein, Wicklund (1974) reported that when an action which reduces freedom is viewed as unintentional, negative consequences do not occur.

Finally, the correspondence or similarity of interests between an agent of freedom-reduction and an influencee mitigates psychological reactance (Friedland, 1976). In other words, if a person (e.g., recreation supervisor) who threatens or eliminates recreational freedom of service recipients is able to give an impression that the supervisor's interests are similar to those of recipients (the implication being that there will be joint distress from such elimination of recreational options), then compliance of the participant with freedom-reduction is increased and psychological reactance minimized. This "bailing-out" procedure may help those who receive recreational services to make situational attributions for freedom-reduction, therefore to decrease reactance and to increase attempts to restore the lost freedom through related modes of recreation. As a final note, it should be pointed out that if a person threatens or eliminates personal freedom (e.g., by voluntarily moving to a new community known to be deficient in certain recreation services), psychological reactance may not materialize. But if others are perceived to have caused the elimination of freedom, then, psychological reactance will be experienced, its strength and effects depending on the variables discussed above.

implications

Space limitations prevent a review of empirical research conducted to test the validity of the suggested antecedents and consequences of psychological reactance to the threatened or eliminated freedom. Brehm (1972), Wortman and Brehm (1975), and Wicklund (1974), however, have found several studies to support the theory. Given the face validity of Brehm's (1966) conceptualization, what are the implications of the theory? First and most important, a person who has a large store of leisure skills and experiences is much better equipped to handle psychologically a threat or the actual elimination of recreational freedom than is a person whose leisure consists of only one or two activities. This follows because the former individual has greater cognitive and behavioral flexibility to restore the lost freedom by implication, that is, by substituting "within" the activity types. When the young are socialized into leisure, it is extremely important to stress that physical, mental and social well-being can be achieved through many activities. No single activity should be viewed as irreplaceable or unique. Such training would prevent the young from building strong and enduring *expectations* about the need to satisfy certain psychological needs through one or two activities. Thus, the expectation would not be fostered that a given activity will be, or must be, available.

In addition to this training, with the expectation factor built in, children should be exposed behaviorally to a host of activities so that their leisure skills will become many-sided. Rodin (1976) reported tentative empirical evidence suggesting that if a child is not able (e.g., due to chronic environmental density) to develop a sense of prediction and control in the home, this deficiency leads to development of decreased expectancies to control behavior and to pursue certain outcomes, even in situations where control would be relevant and feasible. Such impairment of perceived control reduces perceived freedom and therefore impedes efforts to seek stimulating leisure experiences. Consequently, the leisure repertoire is reduced, and the prospective participant is very dependent on the availability of the few leisure activities of interest which remain. Viewed in this light, it seems that the present overwhelming and undue emphasis on a few physical activities like football and baseball in secondary schools is psychologically defective and even dangerous in terms of the students' future behavior. Finally, emphasis on winning should be reduced in recreational encounters, because failure often seems to imply a lack of personal ability, which in turn reduces one's perceived freedom. This is particularly important among the young, because they are in the process of developing leisure attitudes, motives, and skills, which will later form the foundations of their leisure endeavors. Failures experienced in selected activities certainly do not increase their attractiveness.

Since expectation is one of the key determinants of the perception of lost freedom it is obvious that the feeling of the lost freedom can never be eliminated as long as recreation services are provided. The mere presence of recreation services creates a need for them, and the longer the services have been available, the stronger are expectations about their availability. Thus, the provision of a wide variety of leisure activities does not eliminate the problem of lost freedom, but it makes it easier to restore reduced freedom through related, alternate activities. At the same time, however, program administrators have to be careful not to proceed too quickly in expanding the range of services. They must know beforehand that they will be able to provide and keep their activities in the future. If a number of services have to be decreased later (e.g., for financial reasons), psychological consequences may be severe because of heightened reactance and reduced attractiveness of forced alternatives. Thus, both private and public local agencies (and legislators) should, at all costs, avoid announcing administrative decisions and enacting ordinances which restrict freedom of recreational choice.

The above suggestions are more relevant to the prevention and coping with possible impairment of recreational freedom in the future. How about the present situation? Can anything be done to enhance perceived freedom? Can people be trained to perceive more freedom in their "real-life" decision-making situations? What makes people feel free? Based upon past research, several implications appear. The following suggestions stem from three reviews on the subject reported by Jellison and Harvey (1976), Harvey (1976), and Harvey and Smith (1977). As previously in this chapter, freedom is considered in the context of making decisions about leisure behavior. Perceived freedom is therefore used interchangeably with perceived recreational choice.

increasing perceived recreational freedom

Intuitively, it would seem that the more recreational alternatives people have, the more freedom they feel they possess. This common sense idea, however, appears to be misleading, since too many options become confusing rather than liberating. In an experiment (cf. Harvey, 1976), students were asked how much choice they felt was theirs in deciding which football team to select, and how much they enjoyed their decision. One group of students was given a small number of alternative teams (3), another a medium number (6), and the third group a large number (12). Not surprisingly, the ratings of perceived choice increased from the small number of options to the large one. However, those subjects who were told that they spent more time in evaluating the alternatives than others perceived the greatest amount of choice when faced with a moderate (6) number of alternatives. More interestingly, enjoyment of making decisions rose only slightly (1.5 units) from "medium" to "large" in comparison to the increase of three units from "small" to "medium" (Harvey, 1976).

These results suggest that perceived freedom cannot be indefinitely increased by augmenting the number of choices. There is an upper limit where the

a number of alternatives

number of choices becomes excessive and confusing. Rather than providing too much information (too many alternatives), it would be preferable to present a moderate, manageable number of choices. This conclusion must be comforting to those who are responsible for providing recreational services. Although too many choices may generally be confusing, it is difficult, however, to see that this is presently a problem in local recreation centers. Rather, the problem may have to do with too few services. If an overabundance of activities is the concern it can, in part, be avoided by providing services at different levels (beginners, intermediate, advanced) and at different times of the day and in the season, so that various activities do not have to appear as mutually exclusive alternatives.

similarity of choices
In addition to a sheer number of choices, the nature of choice options is important for attempts to augment perceived freedom. Laboratory research (Harvey, 1976) has shown that a sense of freedom is greater if alternatives are similar in attractiveness than if they are quite distinct from one another. Similarly, Steiner (1970) has suggested that "perceived decision freedom" is greatest when the alternatives are believed to offer approximately equal gains or benefits. It follows that anything which involves considerable inequality between the presumed benefits from mutually exclusive alternatives, will decrease freedom to choose. The principle of closely matched alternatives, therefore, calls for designing recreation programs in such a way that many similar activities are provided within an activity type or category. For example, when crafts are offered for evening class students in community colleges, various parallel activities should be included in the program: needlepoint, crochet, macrame, etc.; of course, this involves the assumption that these activities are close together in attractiveness.

While it is important to increase latitude within the activity type, this cannot be done at the expense of the number of activity categories, because "outcome freedom" (Steiner, 1970) would then be reduced. For example, it is conceivable that a recreation program provides many activities within two activity categories, say, physical exercise and arts. Such a program would be poor because it basically would allow only few outcomes or gains (e.g., physical exercise) to be achieved, thereby ignoring a large group of people not interested in these two outcomes. This is particularly relevant to industrial recreation. While an increasing number of companies are investing in recreational services for their personnel, most of them are doing so in the form of physical activities only, thereby ignoring other important recreational domains. Subsequently, satisfaction with "perceived outcome freedom" (and thus with the program) may be relatively low, because the total achieved gain is considerably less than the total desired gain. These suggestions, however, should be viewed with some caution, since it is possible that the outcomes resulting from participation in physical activities may be many-sided, not just physical exercise.

In sum, to enhance an individual's perceived freedom, one should be given an opportunity for both "outcome" and "decision" freedom. Outcome freedom is high if recreational alternatives are many and varied, thus enabling a person to expect to obtain all the outcomes or rewards (physical exercise, relaxation, social interaction, etc.) desired through recreational encounters. Decision freedom is high if there are many options in each activity category, and if these alternatives are closely matched in attractiveness. It is particularly important that options from which to choose should be equally attractive in the dimension(s) (e.g., physical exercise, relaxation, social interaction) which is considered important (cf. Slovic, 1975). For example, a company may provide only physical recreational activities for workers, although physical exercise is not important for all people; therefore their perceived freedom is low, regardless of a large group of activities offered in this category.

Besides the mere number of alternatives and equality in attractiveness of options, other dimensions other variables have also been shown to increase perceived freedom. Other things being equal, a sense of freedom is greater when choice decisions are made between pleasant alternatives than unpleasant ones (Harvey, 1976). In other words, if a person has many recreational activities from which to choose and these involve options a potential participant does not like, the perceived freedom is low in comparison to situations which permit selection from many pleasant activities. But this raises the question why some activities are liked and others not. The answer can be found in the earlier discussion of the socialization process. While recreational activities are pursued for a variety of reasons, the underlying cause is perceived competence within the individual confines of optimal arousal. Those activities which help to satisfy a person's need for competence are greatly preferred to those which are not congruent with individual competencies. Thus, instead of saying that the potential pleasure of activities increases perceived freedom, it is more accurate to state that competence-elevating activities enhance the sense of freedom. Leisure activities which bring about feelings of competence are those that enable one to make attributions for behavior and its consequences to dispositional factors. Thus, perceived freedom is directly related to perceived control over one's behavior and environment.

However, due to the costs involved many people cannot afford to participate in various competence-elevating activities. Thus, cost affects feelings of freedom. Specifically, it has been shown that expenses are inversely related to attributed freedom (Harvey, 1976). That is, other things being equal, perceived freedom decreases as costs increase. If a recreation program consists of expensive activities, most people's attributed freedom would be low, regardless of the potential feelings of competence, because they could not afford to pursue such forms of recreation. Flying may potentially elevate one's sense of competence but it certainly does not increase most people's perceived recreational freedom. Costs, of course, extend beyond those measured only in financial terms; time and effort required in certain recreational activities are types of cost which often prevent these activities from becoming acceptable recreational alternatives.

Unfortunately, the public is all too often misled by the media advertisement campaigns sponsored by private agencies which are interested only in profit-making. Countless media commercials paint a picture suggesting that the Bahamas, Miami Beach, and Las Vegas are *the* places where recreational needs can be satisfied. Or other advertisements point out the necessity of buying expensive recreational vehicles in order to have an enjoyable vacation. Some people argue that nobody is misled by such advertisements, because recreational choices are for an individual to make. However, they fail to note the well-established fact that continuous ("mere") exposure to an object changes people's attitudes about it (Zajonc, 1968). Under constant bombardment stressing the necessity and desirability of glamourous modes of recreation, people come to view these activities more favorably, and they begin to believe that their recreational need can only be satisfied in the Bahamas, for example. By contrast, local recreational services look less and less attractive. Rather than increasing attributed recreational freedom, advertisements in the mass media may reduce many people's sense of freedom, or leave them in a state of confusion.

implications   One of the problems in meeting people's desired level of freedom is that actors (service recipients) are generally prone to attribute less choice and freedom to themselves than do observers (e.g., recreation programmers and supervisors), who are inclined to attribute freedom to actors. While actors tend to underestimate their perceived freedom, observers are inclined to overestimate it. These opposite cognitive propensities make it difficult to create a situation where both providers and recipients of leisure services are in agreement as to the desired level of perceived recreational freedom. Nevertheless, the factors discussed above point out some of the implications for practitioners in their efforts to increase the public's attributed recreational freedom.

Providers should adhere to the principle of offering a relatively large number of alternatives. Since people prefer difficult, positive and closely matched choice options within activity types, a recreation program should offer a variety of leisure activities which are similar in selected areas. It follows that the current practice of simply responding to people's "leisure needs" is insufficient and hence inadequate, if the objective is to increase perceived recreational freedom, and thus satisfaction with leisure services. Information must be obtained about the benefits (outcomes) people expect to derive from recreational services, about the relative importance of these outcomes, equally valued alternatives, and perceived recreational competencies. Finally, activities requiring considerable monetary outlay should be avoided, if they exceed the capacity of most people to pay.

Although not previously discussed, there is some tentative evidence (Harvey, 1976; Steiner, 1970) that the more uncertainty people have concerning the alternatives from which to choose, the greater their feeling of freedom. This finding is consistent with the earlier analysis of human tendency toward incongruous, dissonant and novel leisure experiences, that is, toward change. Thus, recreation programs should provide participants with opportunities to choose not only between activities but also between times and places of participation, as well as the intensity (from beginners to advanced) of involvement. And as was suggested earlier, in the case of activities like tennis, recreation centers should offer a list of available players at various ability levels. If a person can choose his opponent from a group of, say, ten equally matched players, perceived freedom (and satisfaction) within this particular activity may be markedly enhanced. These examples, again, show the usefulness of the theoretical distinction of "between" and "within" activities. Attributed freedom can be maximized when both levels are considered in recreational planning. The above analysis clearly shows that the typical "cafeteria" approach of providing the standard package of leisure services is psychologically very short-sighted. Satisfaction with leisure involvement is not simply a matter of what is individually experienced during participation. Satisfaction can be increased considerably *before* engagement in various forms of leisure, and herein lies the challenge for recreation providers.

summary

Theoretically, an individual's subjective definition of leisure is a function of past experiences and social influences. Although this implies that subjective definitions are person-, situation- and time-specific, there are nevertheless dimensions that underlie most people's perceptions of leisure. The most important of these is perceived freedom. In addition, intrinsic motivation (i.e., feelings of competence), "final" goal orientation, and low work-relation of free-time activities are positively associated with the perception of leisure. However, the effects of these variables depend on perceived freedom. In other words, if a person by himself has not had an opportunity to decide whether or not to participate, intrinsic motivation and other factors cannot change the work-like character of an activity into leisure. But if the person has freedom to choose before participation, then, the above four factors further increase the perception of leisure. Thus, perceived freedom seems to be the critical determinant of perception of leisure, even to the extent of creating an all-or-nothing threshold.

If perceived freedom is so important, it should come as no surprise that a threat to or the elimination of freedom generates a state of motivational arousal called psychological reactance, resulting in attempts to regain freedom. The strength of an individual's reactance to such a threat to freedom is contingent upon (1) expectation of freedom, (2) importance of a particular freedom, (3) strength of the threat, and (4) implications of the threatened freedom. Reactance produces several effects, of which the following appear to be the most common: (1) increased attraction of a forbidden or lost option and reduced attractiveness of a forced alternative, (2) direct behavioral attempts to retain or to regain the threatened or lost freedom (or choice option), (3) attempts to compensate for the loss by participation in related activities which imply that a person possesses the lost freedom, and (4) hostile, aggressive feelings or actions. The implications of these facts were discussed in relation to leisure behavior. It was noted that a person with a wide variety of leisure skills and experiences is much better equipped to handle psychologically a threat or elimination of recreational freedom.

Because perceived recreational freedom is an integral part of enjoyable leisure experiences, it is necessary for professionals and practitioners to try to increase the public's sense of freedom. Based upon laboratory research, it has been shown that several factors may enhance attributed recreational freedom. First, as the number of alternatives increases so does the perceived choice. However, since too many alternatives become overwhelming and confusing, a "manageable" number of choice options guarantees the highest level of subjective freedom, other things being equal. Second, the perceived freedom is greater if alternatives are closely matched in attractiveness than if they are far apart. In particular, choice options should be equally valued on the basis of more important recreational dimension(s). Third, attributed freedom is greater if choice decisions are made among positive rather than negative alternatives. But because perceived competence determines liking and positive acceptance of leisure activities, it is more accurate to say that the sense of freedom is higher when choices are made among competence-elevating alternatives than among those which do not produce feelings of competence. Finally, costs are inversely related to perceived freedom, that is, the sense of freedom decreases as costs of participation increase. The question was raised, whether the private leisure industry may be grossly misleading the public by suggesting that "recreational needs" can be best satisfied in exotic places or by purchasing expensive recreational vehicles, thereby diminishing perceived recreational freedom.

personality and leisure 10

The preceding chapter showed that perceived freedom is a critical and pervasive determinant of people's subjective definitions of leisure and the degree of their leisure involvement. While the sense of freedom is an underlying dimension of leisure, it is not a determinant of participation in specific recreation activities. Although different people in different places at different times are concerned about their freedom to choose among leisure activities, among specific alternatives selection is a function of their past experiences and social influences. As discussed earlier, personal experiences establish and modify one's perceived competence which, within the confines of optimal arousal, determines which leisure activities are chosen (if freedom of choice is given). To be sure, there are situational factors which also affect leisure participation (e.g., a mother taking her son to a nearby playground in the evenings, weather and other situational factors permitting). But it should be kept in mind that the goal is to understand the causes of "leisure" behavior, which, by definition, is based upon an individual's subjective definition of leisure, as this, in turn, is influenced by personal experiences (see figure 14, p. 185).

In this chapter the relationship between a person's experiences, as reflected by his personality, and leisure behavior will be examined. It is important to bear in mind the level of causality here involved. Even though personality, perceived freedom, and optimal arousal are all causes of leisure participation, very different levels of causality exist in each case. That is, these causal factors differ in the degree of generality or specificity by which they are able to account for leisure behavior. This is precisely the reason why, for instance, "leisure needs" alone are insufficient and inadequate to help the observer comprehend the depth and breadth of the causes of leisure behavior. Although analysis of the relationship between personality and leisure seems self-evident, the task can (and should) be

201

approached from various perspectives. This analysis may be broken down as follows:

1. Objective causality:
   a. effects of personality on leisure choice and behavior.
   b. effects of leisure participation on personality.
2. Phenomenal causality:
   a. actor's self-perception of personality as a cause of his own leisure behavior.
   b. others' (observers') perceptions of actors' personality as a cause of the actors' leisure behavior.

The present chapter discusses the relationship between personality and leisure from these broad perspectives. Traditionally, the relationship has been analyzed in terms of objective causality. As the above classification shows, such an approach is too restricted and ignores the fact that personality also exists in the eyes of the beholder.

objective causality: effects of personality on leisure and vice versa

theories of personality

What is personality? If we seek an answer to this question from a lay person, we are most likely to get one of the following views (Hall and Lindzey, 1970): (1) personality refers to an individual's social competence, skills which enable him to interact successfully with a host of different people under different conditions. When a youngster is said to have a "personality problem" this definition implies that the individual is incapable of dealing adequately with other people; (2) personality refers to the impression an individual creates in others. In this context, one often hears people described as having a "creative personality," a "social personality," an "aggressive personality," etc. But when the above question is put to a psychologist, the answer is more likely to be there is no uniform or generalizable definition of personality, because it depends on which of the many theories is applied. Thus, the theoretical frame of reference has to be taken into account. Since many excellent reviews of personality theories are available, a few of the basic ideas of these theories are selected in order to represent a variety of explanations. The following overview is based upon the writings of Hall and Lindzey (1970) and Wiggins, Renner, Clore and Rose (1971), especially the latter.

According to the (Freudian) *psychoanalytic* approach, human behavior can be understood or explained only by simultaneously applying dynamic, economic, structural, genetic, and adaptive principles. Dynamic principles refer to the most important instincts, that is, sexual, aggressive, and competence drives. Economic constructs are associated with instinctual energies and their discharge. Instinctual energy operates on the basis of the pleasure principle ("least effort"), which aims at immediate discharge; it also operates on the basis of the reality principle which opposes the immediate discharge of instinctual energy. Structural constructs relate to the ego-structure, which is composed of the substructures called "super-ego" and "id." The principal task of the ego is to coordinate conflicting forces aroused by id, super-ego and external reality (Wiggins, *et al.*, 1971). Neo-freudians (e.g., Loevinger, 1976) emphasize the ego in terms of its development through stages rather than as a structural construct characterized by a slow rate of change. Genetic constructs refer to an individual's psychosexual and psychological development as determined by biological principles and "inner laws." Since each stage of psychosexual development creates social problems, an individual must solve them successfully to mature psychosocially. Finally, adaptive principles are related to coordination between instinctual drives and the external world.

It is quite obvious from this sketchy review that psychoanalysts do not give much credence to the notion of human beings as rational men and women. Behavior is primarily seen to be energized and directed by innate and subconscious forces. The heavy emphasis on instinctual energies in the form of sexual, aggressive and effectance drives stems from the fact that Freud's psychoanalytic theorizing was based on his clinical observations of neurotic patients.

By contrast, the *social learning* theory asserts that individual differences in behavior are due to "variations in the conditions of learning that the individuals have encountered" (Wiggins, *et al.*, 1971). Since the early works of Dollard and Miller, Bandura has become the champion of this approach. His theory (Bandura and Walters, 1963; Bandura, 1969, 1971) analyzes personality development in terms of observational learning and places emphasis on modeling in personality formation. Although reinforcement patterns play a crucial part in this quite behavioristically oriented theory, Bandura (e.g., 1971, p. 35) states that "actions are not always predictable from external sources of influence because cognitive factors (thought processes) partly determine what one observes, feels, and does at any given moment." Nevertheless, reinforcement and punishment are viewed as effective mechanisms of behavior modification and self-control. Like Bandura, Mischel (1968, 1973) places a premium on the situational specificity of behavior, and in this sense his approach is in sharp contrast to trait theories of personality. Social learning theorists maintain that a few traits are insufficient to explain complex and variable everyday behaviors, and that consistency in behavior is illusory.

While the proponents of the social learning theory view the growth of personality as a function of learning, *cognitive-development* theorists (e.g., Piaget, 1950) stress learning as a function of development. From Piaget's (1950) standpoint, personality develops through an invariant sequence of stages which everyone goes through in the same order, though not at the same rate. As we noted earlier, Piaget (1972) accentuates opportunities for individuals to create and invent events and experiences, because understanding is primarily achieved by such cognitive actions. Thus, personality should be viewed in the light of an individual's developmental stage as reflected by stage-typical cognitions about the process of acquiring and using information.

Rogers' (1959) humanistically oriented *self-theory* analyzes personality in terms of individual feelings and experiences. The focus is on the total individual whose ideal self is a state of being. "Self" integrates all forms of individual living under the sense of personal existence. Thus, personal skills and values as well as friends and possessions are components of the total personality. This theory approaches personality in terms of inner experiences and internal events rather than external forces. The basic tendency of growth is to actualize, to maintain and enhance an experiencing organism (Hall and Lindzey, 1970, p. 530). A closely related view of self has been forwarded by Maslow (1962).

Finally, the *trait* theory explains personality as a complex and differentiated structure of traits (Hall and Lindzey, 1970). In Cattell's (1950) conceptualization, a trait is a "mental structure" which accounts for regularity and consistency in behavior; it is a force within an individual, or an accumulation of personal experiences as a stable predisposition, from which personal action can be predicted for given situations. Allport (1968, p. 46) regards traits as motivational forces, examining them in terms of individual differences (called the nomothetic approach) and of personal dispositions (called the idiomorphic approach). It is perhaps accurate to state that most trait studies are nomothetic in nature, that is, personality traits of many people have been investigated in an effort to discover how traits are generally interrelated to certain behaviors. Such data give information about the generalizability of traits.

Cattell has classified traits in a number of different ways: common traits possessed by everyone versus unique traits possessed by a particular individual; surface versus source traits; environmental-mold traits versus constitutional traits, etc. In addition to a vast amount of theoretical work, Cattell's contributions include the development of a widely used personality instrument (Cattell 16-PF), as well as countless empirical studies conducted to test the validity of traits as predictors of behavior, and the empirical examination of clustering of traits. Cattell's trait approach is different from many other personologists, in that his focus is on the mental structure composed of numerous traits. Others, like Rotter (1966), have attempted to explain and predict behavior on the basis of one trait (internal-external control) only. In a similar vein, Eysenck has focused on the role of introversion-extroversion, and Guildford has extensively studied intelligence and creativity. A detailed examination of these and other works, however, is beyond the scope and focus of this book.

latest developments

Historically, emphasis during the 1950s was placed on "self" and "traits" as determinants of behavior. In the 1960s, the emphasis shifted to the advocacy of environmental factors, as shown by the popularity of the social learning theory of personality. More recently, the personality-environment interaction approach has dominated scientists' thinking in the 1970s (see Bowers, 1973; Endler and Magnusson, 1976). Of course, the idea of interaction is not new (see Ekehammar, 1974); it was indirectly proposed by McDougall (1908) and Allport (1924) and directly by Lewin in his famous formula, $B = f(P,E)$, where "f" means as a function of, "B" stands for behavior, "P" for personality and "E" for environment.

The interactionism, however, has changed its focus and has impelled trait psychologists to clarify their position. In his important paper, Golding (1975) demonstrated that while situational factors continuously change an individual's trait measures in absolute terms, the individual nevertheless maintains "rank order'' or position in relation to other individuals, with respect to particular traits in varied situations. Thus, there seems to be consistency in behavior in relative terms. Of course, Golding's argument is an empirical question, but as was noted earlier, recent research seems to support it. However, it remains to be shown which traits are more conducive to maintaining their consistency in varying situations, and which traits are more amenable to both absolute and relative change. What type of social influence, and how strong, must it be to lead to multiple, rapid and enduring changes in traits?

While there may be consistency in behavior, there is also much room for change due to social influences. What the Golding argument implies is that when change is studied, individual traits and tendencies must be considered as well. This view, however, is insufficient, because it fails to note that actual behavior is not simply a matter of the personality-situation interaction. While both components are at work, they are not independent of each other. Rather, personality and situation are *continuously* affecting one another in a two-way street, so to speak. This continuous-process nature of the effects was pointed out by Iso-Ahola (1976) (see figure 14, p. 185 this publication); Endler and Magnusson (1976) have also made a similar point. While it is interesting to know in general how personality and situational factors together affect a given behavior, one should continue this analysis by examining the effects of behavior on personality and situational factors. Again, one should stress that human behavior does not exist in a time vacuum in which only unidirectional causality is of concern. Given a social interaction situation, the observer should investigate how one individual affects others and is influenced in turn by others, in the *continuous* interaction process, and what changes in personality and social environment were observed as a result of this process.

This continuous-process analysis should be extended to cover a long period of time across situations to establish the extent to which patterns concerning consistency and change in human behavior can be generalized. Investigators should not lose sight of the basic tenet of cognitive social psychology (S-O-R): an individual is a rational human being who intentionally strives to influence personal behavior as well as the social environment. Thus, cognitions (thoughts, beliefs) and emotions about self and social environment have to be considered if one is to understand an individual's personality. In the continuous process of two-way causation, an individual affects others and is affected by others. Of course, this does *not* mean that people have as many personalities as they have interpersonal situations in which they behave. Identity exists in human behavior (Rychlak, 1976), and the origin of personality can be traced back to the beginning of an individual's life (Thomas, Chess and Birch, 1970). But to understand the role of personality in one's behavior, it is necessary to "treat the organism as truly active and dynamic rather than as the carrier of a stable dispositional reservoir of motives and traits" (Mischel, 1969, p. 1017).

Where does research on the relationship between personality and leisure stand in terms of the above theories? As might be expected, the volume of reported studies is very limited. As for the specific approaches, so far as is known to the author, no research has been undertaken from the psychoanalytic, social learning, cognitive-developmental, or self-theory standpoints. As in general psychology, most studies have been conducted in the frame of reference of trait psychology. One study (Bishop and Witt, 1970) has utilized the interaction (person-times-situation) framework based upon unidirectional causality. The lack of investigations designed to examine personality in light of "the continuous process in which person and situation factors interact in a multidirectional manner" (Endler and Magnusson, 1976) is not surprising, because such studies do not exist in general social psychology either. However, the dearth of such investigations should serve as a guideline for those who are contemplating studies in this area, since the process approach is the only feasible direction for research on the "objective" personality. Next, it is appropriate to consider studies dealing with the relationship between personality and leisure, though the above mentioned limitations of the trait approach and unidirectional interactionism should not be forgotten.

personality and leisure

In an effort to discover possible relationships between recreation behavior and "some common personality variables," Moss, Shackelford and Stokes (1969) asked undergraduates to fill out a questionnaire concerning their participation in various recreational activities. They also completed personality inventories designed to determine their traditionalism, intelligence, dogmatism, and rigidity. Some of the main results were:

1. As a whole, campers were more traditional than noncampers; group campers had a tendency (nonsignificant) to be more dogmatic than noncampers; family campers were more rigid than noncampers;
2. Hunters were more traditional and more dogmatic than nonhunters;
3. Golfers were less dogmatic and less rigid than nongolfers;
4. Basketball players were more rigid than nonparticipants.

The authors suggested that campers and hunters are more "closed minded" than the nonparticipants, that resource and camp managers should benefit from such information. The authors also claimed that the above information should in part explain why changing land-use patterns and land values are often in conflict with hunters' interests. Thus, one might take these results to suggest that the "closed mindedness" observed among hunters is consistent with Christensen and Yoesting's (1977) findings indicating hunters' relative unwillingness to replace their leisure activity by other forms of recreation.

But before a reader puts these findings into long-term memory, they should be scrutinized in detail. In fact, this study is presented here, not because of its scientific merits, but because it epitomizes the problems associated with studies emanating from the trait theory of personality. To avoid any misunderstanding, it should be pointed out that the following criticism is not directed at the researchers, but rather to indicate the problems of the theoretical framework which underlie their empirical data.

First, while Moss, *et al.* divided subjects into participants and nonparticipants in criticism various activities, they did not report the criteria for this procedure. No idea was given about how "participation" was operationalized, that is, whether it referred to the subjects' preference or actual participation; if the latter was in question, how many times did people have to participate before they were labeled "hunters," "golfers," etc.? This criticism is not just peculiar to the Moss, *et al.* study but is common to many similar investigations. The problem is that different studies have used different activities to be correlated with various personality traits, and if the same activity has been included in various studies, invariably it has been defined differently in each study. The problem becomes even worse when respondents are classified, on the basis of their participation in many activities, in such universal categories as athletes versus nonathletes, active versus passive participants. In no study have researchers offered any theoretical reasons why certain activities have been selected for their investigation.

But the problems do not end here. If diverse activities with different definitions of participation have been used in distinct studies, the divergences apply also to the personality traits selected. There are literally hundreds of personality instruments available which deal with such familiar constructs as self-esteem, self-concept, etc. In addition, countless inventories (e.g., Cattell's 16-PF) have been designed to examine many traits simultaneously, the so-called personality profiles. With this plethora of scales at one's disposal, it is little wonder that no uniformity or consistency exists in trait measurements. The problem is compounded by the fact that the numerous personality constructs for which countless instruments are available (e.g., self-esteem) have been defined differently by individual authors. Thus, even though two studies claim to measure the same trait concept by alternative measures, they may in fact be measuring quite different things. Besides, what does it mean when investigators call a group of responses to a number of comprehensive statements, by such labels as "dogmatic," "rigid," "traditional," etc.? These labels may be simply products of the trait psychologists' imagination, and so they may be!

The situation would be somewhat tolerable if investigators used well-established instruments instead of many obscure and unsatisfactorily validated scales (for an example of the use of obscure instruments, see Moss, *et al.*, 1969). Like the selection of leisure activities, the choice of traits to be correlated with activities has, without exception, been made for no apparent theoretical reasons. Thus, there is no way of knowing what the results of such studies mean theoretically. An undirected accumulation of facts, of course, is worthless and does not advance understanding of the relationship between personality and leisure. Perhaps the severest criticism directed against all personality traits studies arises from the fact that the traits measured are assumed to be stable and unchanged. But as noted above, a person's traits are subject to social and situational influences, and in the course of the years the evidence of a certain trait may change considerably. Thus, to label campers traditional, rigid and dogmatic ("closed-minded") on the basis of their responses to some obscure statements at a particular moment in specific circumstances does not mean anything, except that it creates stereotypes among those who read, without a critical eye, studies like that reported by Moss, *et al.* Unfortunately, this trend continues, as demonstrated by Martin and Myrick's (1976) study in which they found that skydivers, snow skiers, and scuba divers are socially abrasive and calm!

In addition to these problems, other criticism, e.g., heterogeneity of subject populations, statistical misinterpretations, could be leveled at many trait studies. However, these considerations suffice to demonstrate the numerous and complex problems connected with an interpretation of trait data. It is inadequate and insufficient to study traits alone. Social and situational factors have to be examined in a multidirectional manner, simultaneously with traits. If this is not done, one can only admit frustration, as did Driver and Knopf (1977) following their attempts to correlate selected outdoor recreation activities and numerous personality traits (p. 187): ". . . no definite conclusions can be drawn that personality disposition influences the choice of an activity in which a person participates actively. The weak associations suggest that other factors might influence choice more than personality trait does." Given the inevitable limitations of the trait approach, those who are researching leisure behavior may learn a lesson from psychologists and physical educators, and avoid studies which merely aim at correlating personality traits and participation in various leisure activities.

The danger of falling into the trap of trait studies, however, is immense. There is practically no easier way to conduct research than to use a ready-made personality instrument and administer it to a selected group of respondents, along with questions related to one's leisure participation. Such studies are convenient to use and require very little conceptually or intellectually from students. One might say that this approach provides the easiest and quickest way of getting an M.S. and Ph.D. This is precisely, the author believes, why the trait approach has been used extensively by physical educators. To avoid the same trap, it is recommended to those recreation researchers who advise students' theses, not to accept trait studies as a partial fulfillment of requirements for various degrees, unless theoretical reasons for conducting studies are presented, and unless situational factors are systematically investigated, along with traits. Almost any other approach or topic provides a better learning opportunity for students than time spent in correlating personality traits and leisure participation. The use of multivariate statistics (e.g., Howard, 1976; Schurr, Ashley and Joy, 1977) does not eliminate the aforementioned problems, but instead it discourages some students, due to the lack of their knowledge about multivariate statistics.

the interaction approach

Bishop and Witt's (1970) quasi-experiment marks an important departure from all other studies dealing with personality and leisure. The purpose of this study was to determine the relative effects of person, situation, modes of response and their interactions on the leisure preferences of subjects (undergraduates). Respondents were presented with various hypothetical situations based on classical theories of play: e.g., "you have just gotten results from the biggest exam of the year and you have either failed or not done as well as you expected to do" (compensation theory). They were then asked to indicate what they *would* do in each situation, assuming that they could do it. Subjects could choose from 13 alternatives (''modes of response''): e.g., watch TV, take a nap, play games, sit and relax, etc. As other similar studies had earlier revealed (for a review, see Endler and Magnusson, 1976), Bishop and Witt found that neither personalities nor situations accounted notably for reported leisure behavior. Rather, interactions involving persons, situations, and modes of response explained leisure behavior to a greater extent than did singular effects of these variables.

An important interaction was that involving persons and responses, which suggested that choice of leisure activities is an individual act, free from specific situational influences. This tendency was greater for males than females. But the effect of the interaction involving situations and responses was also significant, suggesting that choice of leisure ''responses'' (activities) depends on situational events. It is interesting that this effect was substantially greater for females than males, indicating that situations have a greater influence on women's leisure choices than men's. Bishop and Witt suggested that this sex difference may be due to the fact women are more emotionally responsive to situational events than are men. This explanation is congruent with the reported evidence (Hoffman, 1975, 1977) that females are more empathic and considerate of others than males, the differences stemming from the sex-role socialization.

Bishop and Witt's findings clearly support the idea of the importance of the interaction approach in analyzing the relationship between personality and leisure. It appears that different persons select different leisure forms under various situations. At the same time, the study lent considerable support to the contention that there is individual consistency and stability in leisure responses to different situations. Thus, persons may be characterized by the patterns of their leisure responses to various situations. Although the Bishop and Witt study is an important step in the right direction, it is not definitive in providing complete understanding of leisure behavior. Their study ignores the multidirectional causality of leisure behavior and neglects the fact that leisure experiences may alter an individual's personality, the situational forces, and the modes of responses.

Leisure behavior is determined by a continuous process in which individual and situational forces interact in a multidirectional manner (for a diagram of this idea, see p. 185). For example, a student's choice of a leisure activity as a response to exams may vary from time to time depending on personal experiences and a variety of situational factors at a given period of time. An individual selects a leisure response from a personal leisure repertoire, which changes as a function of age and development. But each person tends to select an activity which is optimal and also represents an appropriate match between personal needs and situational demands at a given time. Thus, the question of how personality affects leisure choices is not simple, because consistency and stability are relative concepts. This requires that the dimensions of individual change (as discussed in Chapter 8) have to be taken into account in analyzing personality and leisure.

effects of leisure participation on personality

One of the most popular themes in leisure writing is the positive effects of leisure experiences on personality. As noted earlier, practically every leisure author or textbook writer has considered the importance of leisure on personality formation and development. In particular, the role of leisure in the development of self-concept has been repeatedly emphasized. This is hardly surprising because the whole field and profession is based upon this very fundamental assumption, that is, if practitioners cannot produce positive effects through their programs, what else are they supposed to accomplish? But what is known about the effects of leisure experiences on personality? The answer is very simple: very little is known, because systematic research is conspicuously lacking. Merely to correlate participation in various recreation activities with selected personality traits does not reveal when, how, and why leisure creates the effects it does in various persons. Thus, the preceding criticism of past studies dealing with personality and leisure is applicable here as well. It is too simplistic to probe a relationship by posing the question of whether or not (i.e., yes or no) leisure participation affects the growth of one's personality.

To answer the question about the effects of leisure on personality, the following four parameters have to be considered as a part of a continuous process of change: (1) dimensions of personality, (2) situational social influences, (3) type and degree of leisure involvement, and (4) an individual's developmental stage. The effects, in turn, may be any one of three: (1) they may improve, (2) they may deteriorate, or (3) a person may maintain his present level at a given personality dimension. The resultant change in personality can be measured in absolute or relative terms; the former refers to change within a person, and the latter to a person's change in relation to other individuals on a particular personality dimension (e.g., self-esteem). Thus, depending on its strength, a given leisure program may improve a person's self-concept but not his sociability. If a person's self-concept is well developed but sociability poorly developed, it is likely that leisure participation will have a stronger effect on the latter than on the former in absolute terms. On the other hand, different forms of leisure participation may have different effects on the same dimension of personality. That is, while one person strives to improve self-esteem through baseball, another does it by means of playing a musical instrument. Each of these effects may be mediated by situational factors. For example, whether Little League improves players' self-concept depends not only on the outcomes of games but also on support given by significant others (i.e., parents, coaches and peers).

Finally, analysis of the effects of leisure on personality has to consider an individual's developmental stage. If the self-concept, for example, grows with age, then it is reasonable to suppose that leisure involvement has a relatively greater impact on the development of adolescents' self-concept than on that of persons in their late adulthood. It is also probable that there are some critical periods in the life cycle, during which leisure may appreciably affect various personality dimensions whereas during other periods the impact may be negligible. Finally, when the influence of leisure upon personality is studied, it is necessary to consider the transient nature and durability of the effects.

The above theorizing provides a general framework for investigating conditions under which leisure participation affects personality. It is important to realize that leisure involvement in itself does not lead to any changes in personality. Rather, what an individual is able to derive psychologically from leisure participation is critical. This is clearly illustrated in a study by Koocher (1971). The investigation was designed to demonstrate that increasing an individual's sense of competence over the environment by means of leisure skills will enhance the self-concept. For this purpose, swimming was selected as an activity because "simply daring to challenge the water in an attempt to gain control of oneself in the medium may carry powerful implications" (Koocher, 1971). Subjects were boys aged 7 to 15 years who were part of a YMCA summer program. The self-concept instrument was administered to the boys upon their arrival at the camp and at the end (i.e., 12 days later). The boys were divided into three groups: (1) those who learned to swim during the 12-day camping period, (2) those who refused to take the swimming test upon their arrival or failed in it, and (3) those who passed the test at the outset and spent the camping period in improving their swimming skills. The results showed that the first group (learners) improved their self-concept significantly between the pre-test and post-test period, while the other two groups did not.

These findings are important in two respects. First, they lend strong support to the hypothesis that *learning* new leisure skills improves one's self-concept because of the increased sense of *competence*. The result is clearly consistent with earlier theorizing about the role of perceived competence in regulating leisure involvement. In the light of Koocher's data, one is inclined to believe that those individuals who have a wide variety and a large number of leisure skills have a higher self-concept than those who possess only a few leisure skills.

Second, the fact that those who had the ability to swim before their camp experience did not initially have a higher self-concept than the other groups and did not improve significantly their self-concept, provides further evidence of the importance of new leisure skills in efforts to enhance the self-concept. That is, since the result seems to suggest that the improvement is not lasting but limited to those periods during which new skills are acquired, there is an implication that the frequency of experiencing a high self-concept increases directly with the number of new leisure skills acquired and the number of higher levels of skills achieved in familiar activities.[1] The Koocher data imply that practicing the already-learned skills helps maintain the present level of self-concept but does not significantly increase it. If this is true, it would seem to be important for practitioners to expose their clients to new leisure experiences occasionally, or to help them attain higher levels of skills in familiar activities. Such attempts, however, must increase a person's sense of competence to enhance the self-concept.

[1] To explain the reason why the positive effect of learning new skills on self-concept does not appear to last, one may have to consider the influence of social environments. It is possible that the effect fluctuates as a function of how much the social environment values the learned leisure skills. Thus, one could argue, other things being equal, that a person's self-concept is higher in the social environment where the learned leisure skill is valued than where it is not valued.

While the task of increasing the self-concept via leisure participation is important for all age groups, it would seem to be particularly advantageous for the young. As discussed earlier, the need for a sense of competence is especially strong among 10–12 year-olds. This is reflected in their interest in sports and recreational activities. In an innovative study on "spontaneous self-concept," McGuire and Padawer-Singer (1976) found that when sixth graders were requested to "tell us about yourself," the greatest proportion of their total responses fell in the category labeled "own activities." The two most important items of this category were hobbies—amusements and sports. This finding suggests that recreational and sports activities are an essential part of these youths' self-concepts. In view of Koocher's (1971) data, this finding is not surprising, because recreational activities provide avenues for the young to attain intrapersonal and interpersonal competence.

leisure involvement and psychological adjustment

Besides such widely assumed benefits as "building character," increasing self-concept and other personality characteristics, it is frequently claimed that leisure activities participation improves one's psychological adjustment (e.g., Davis, 1938; Ferriss, 1970). Psychoanalytically oriented authors (Slavson, 1948) even go so far as to state that recreation helps discharge energies and repressed emotions as well as release hidden and unconscious motivations, with the result of enhanced mental health. Since a positive relationship between recreation and psychological adjustment (and mental health) has been recognized by nearly all leisure authors, one would expect that such a popular hypothesis has been put to vigorous test. However, as in many other areas of recreation only few preliminary attempts have been made to test this hypothesis.

Cavanaugh's (1942) study was one of the first investigations dealing with the issue. In this study, the recreation participation of college students in various activities was related to their psychological adjustment as assessed by a personality inventory measuring neurotic tendencies. The results showed that as neurotic tendencies increased, the number of recreation activities participated in (especially sports and hobbies) decreased. Cavanaugh, therefore, concluded that psychologically well-adjusted students tended to participate in more recreational activities than their less well adjusted fellows. This conclusion, however, is clouded by the "trait" methodology used in the study. Thus, the limited empirical definitions of recreation participation and psychological adjustment have to be considered before any generalizations are made. For example, it would be grossly misleading to interpret these results as implying that the problem of mental health and psychological maladjustment can be resolved by making everyone participate in a large number of recreation activities. It is important to note, again, that involvement in leisure activities in itself is meaningless; it is critical what people do *psychologically* with their participation, and whether their psychological expectations and achievements are properly accommodated in recreational engagements.

In defense of Cavanaugh, however, it must be acknowledged that his findings are consistent with research done about 30 years later. For instance,

Cavanaugh found a positive relationship between a number of recreation activities participated in and a degree of extroversion. The same result was reported by Hendry and Douglass (1975), indicating that those university students who were active in either competitive or recreational sports tended to be more extroverted and stable than nonparticipants. In a similar vein, much earlier McKinney's (1937) data had shown that well-adjusted college students exhibit a greater tendency toward athletic participation and extracurricular activities than their less well-adjusted fellow students. Taken together, these findings imply that active recreation participation, extroversion, and psychological adjustment are positively related, at least insofar as college students are concerned. Further evidence indicates that the positive relationship between adjustment and active participation goes back to early childhood experiences. Namely, Brooks and Elliott (1971) found that those who were able to derive satisfaction from their leisure participation in early childhood (8 to 11 years of age) were psychologically better adjusted 20 years later than those who did not have satisfying leisure experiences, or derived their satisfaction from passive pursuits in their childhood years.

But, this seemingly consistent conclusion is not without its discordant notes. Bishop (1973) reported that psychologically well adjusted people spent more of their free-time in passive and relaxed activities in a home-like atmosphere. On the other hand, the low-adjustment group participated in activities demanding more physical energy and special skills, was less social and intellectual, and more tension-inducing and mobile. In this study, psychological adjustment was defined on the basis of subjects' (community residents) responses to five subscales of the California Psychological Inventory, and leisure time was measured according to the respondents' actual participation.

The same report (Bishop, 1973) included another study in which community residents' leisure choices in hypothetical situations were related to their typical feelings and moods. Subjects were given a list of feelings and moods which included such items as bored, happy, lonely, humorous, and upset stomach. Subjects then indicated whether they felt that way "fairly often," "once in a while," or "almost never." Based upon their responses, the subjects were divided into high, middle, and low adjustment groups. The results showed that the high-adjusted group tended to select more passive, relaxing and home-centered activities, in comparison to the "low-adjusted" respondents. Thus, the well-adjusted exhibited stronger preferences for such activities as watching TV, reading, relaxing alone, and engaging alone in competitive modes of leisure (e.g., golf, bowling). The less well-adjusted showed stronger preference for activities like fishing and hunting, spending time on a favorite hobby, playing tennis and similar activities in a competitive way.

Bishop's findings run counter to earlier studies which reported a positive relationship between psychological adjustment and leisure involvement. Despite the apparent contradiction, the discrepant results can in part be explained by the differences in subject populations and definitions of psychological adjustment between the studies. Bishop's subjects were community residents in the rural midwestern area, while subjects in other studies were college students. Since leisure patterns between these groups differ, it is fairly obvious that psychological adjustment is also sought through different activities among these subjects. Students are prone to active leisure participation, because of the university life style in general and the availability of facilities in particular. While students are required to participate in a variety of physical recreational activities, the rural community residents are not. In rural areas, residents do not have to take examinations which induce tension or write term papers under time pressure. Also, rural residents are generally older and apparently have less vigor to pursue activities demanding physical energy and skills. Combined with a relative lack of recreational facilities, it should not be surprising that more community residents than college students meet their psychological adjustment through "passive" and "relaxing" leisure activities.

These considerations probably do not give the whole story. For example, early childhood recreation experiences have to be considered, that is, whether one has learned to derive satisfaction from predominantly active or from passive forms of leisure (Brooks and Elliott, 1971). Another factor to be taken into account is differing definitions of psychological adjustment in the reviewed studies. All the researchers cited can be criticized for arbitrarily defining psychological adjustment. Bishop, for example, defined adjustment by choosing five subscales of a well-known instrument. His results might have been quite different had he selected other subscales of the same instrument or had he used a totally different instrument designed to measure psychological adjustment. In all fairness to Bishop and other researchers, however, it must be emphasized that no matter what instrument or scale was chosen the investigator could always be criticized for somewhat arbitrarily defining psychological adjustment. Again, this reflects problems associated with the trait methodology in studying the relationship between personality and leisure.

In sum, regardless of apparent differences in the results of the reviewed studies, there is little doubt as to whether psychological adjustment and leisure behavior are significantly related to one another. They are interrelated, but it is important to realize that at different times different people achieve psychological adjustment through different leisure or other kinds of activities. Therefore, it should come as no surprise that studies using different subject populations, different leisure activities, and different definitions produce considerable variation in the observed relationship between psychological adjustment and leisure participation.

The above discussion clearly demonstrates that any generalization about a person's psychological adjustment made on the basis of participation in a given leisure activity is not only unjustified but also highly misleading. For example, Bishop (1973) found that those who prefer playing tennis are relatively poorly adjusted. Does this mean that every time we see tennis players in a park we can say that there they are—the maladjusted? Of course not. Unfortunately, however, such generalizations are not rare, because the trait approach readily lends itself to misinterpretations. Researchers should not be exonerated from these mistakes because, after all, they selected the trait methodology for their studies.

In the absence of other systematic research, this section concludes by presenting Bishop's conclusion; but at the same time the reader should be cautioned that this conclusion probably holds true for only a few people under specific conditions at a specific time of their development:

> The kinds of time use that are related to improved adjustment are those in which the person can relax with activities that make a minimum of physical and mental demands on him and that are somewhat withdrawn from the demands of other people and the structure imposed by skilled or technically involved tasks (Bishop, 1973, p. 22).

The preceding section examined the causal relationship between personality and leisure from the "objective" standpoint. It is characteristic of this approach that an investigator "objectively" classifies people according to selected personality traits and subsequently relates their leisure participation to the traits. It is then assumed that either personality causes leisure participation or leisure behavior is a cause of personality. But as was noted above, studies based upon this approach have been quite unsatisfactory. One of the main reasons for the inadequacy of past research is the omission of subjects' self-perceptions of causes of their behavior (self-attribution). This is clearly reflected by recent findings which indicate that the relationship between personality and leisure has to be seen as a continuous process in which persons, social influences, and situational forces interact in a multidirectional manner. The multidirectional causation, of course, would not be needed if people's cognitions (self-perceptions) were stable and unaffected by situational and social influences. To understand the relationship between personality and leisure, it is therefore necessary to know the principles of self-perception concerning causes of one's behavior. The attribution theory deals with this issue.

phenomenal causality: actors' and observers' causal attributions of leisure behavior to personality

Attribution refers to the process by which a person (either an actor or an observer) obtains information about an act and then makes causal inferences about the source of the act (Iso-Ahola, 1976). In general, the sources can be found in either a person or an environment. Attributional analysis of leisure behavior, therefore, centers on the conditions under which the causes of behavior are ascribed to internal (personality) or external (situational) factors, and on the behavioral implications of these attributions. Heider (1958) was the first to propose a distinction between personal and situational causality and to infer that people are inclined toward causal analysis of their behavior. This tendency toward causal perceptions has subsequently been proven by experimental research (e.g., Michotte, 1963).

attribution theory

Heider (1958) also gave an account of why the tendency toward causality exists in humans: if a person is able to analyze causally his own behavior as well as that of others, inferences can be made (whether correct or incorrect) about why people behave in certain ways under certain conditions. Consequently, the world appears more orderly and predictable, and a person is able to make some sense out of the environment. In the absence of such a causal analysis, an individual is not able to exercise control over the environment (deCharms, 1968; Kelley, 1971). Thus, the mentally ill are sometimes described as persons whose subjective causal analyses are chaotic and disorganized. Besides this overall explanation of human tendency toward causal perception, attributions can, of course, be used for specific reasons as well. For example, Little League players seem to be making causal attributions as a way of coping with success and failure, or by way of enhancing and protecting their self-esteem following game outcomes.

self-attributions

When applying attribution theory to leisure behavior, one must distinguish between attributions made *before, during* and *after* leisure participation. The before-attributions refer to the case in which a person ascribes the initiation of participation to either personal, social/situational factors, or their combinations. Based upon earlier theorizing about the role of perceived competence in leisure involvement and attributed recreational freedom, the author postulates that as a whole, the origin of subjectively defined *leisure* activities is attributed to internal factors, while the initiation of less leisure-like activities is attributed to external factors. Those activities which a person defines as leisure are identical with those for which internal attributions are made and for which perceived competence is high.

By contrast, if a person feels that participation is required in certain activities because of some social pressures or other situational inducement (external attribution), then such forms of free-time do not become leisure nor enjoyable experiences. Since everyone has to participate in certain activities which are outside of internal control, a question arises as to how to turn such external attribution to internal attribution. For example, some people have to participate in social parties because of their occupation, or others have to play volleyball in a housing complex because everyone else is playing (otherwise, they would be labeled antisocial and odd individuals). One implication of the above proposition is that such persons should first be given a chance to decide by themselves whether or not to participate, thereby facilitating their internal self-attributions. Furthermore, these people's self-perceptions concerning their interpersonal competence in social parties and their ability to play volleyball should be enhanced by others. Such attempts are likely to facilitate attributions of leisure participation to self.

internality and
stability of attributions

To make this analysis conceptually as clear as possible, it may be useful to present causal attributions of leisure behavior as shown on the following page adapted from Weiner, *et al.,* 1971). The two extreme causes of attributions for leisure participation were discussed above: stable-internal (competence) and stable-external (social obligation). People also make unstable internal and unstable external attributions for their leisure involvement, as shown in figure 16. As for the former, a person admits little competence at a given activity, but wants to improve it by trying hard. Or an individual wants to learn new leisure skills which are somewhat similar to those activities that yield a feeling of competence, in other words, this is a sub-

Figure 16 Two fundamental dimensions of causal attributions of leisure behavior. (Adapted from Weiner, *et al.*, 1971.)

Internality

	Internal	External
Stable	I participate because I am good at this leisure activity.	I participate because I have to do so due to my social obligations.
Unstable	I participate because I want to learn new leisure skills and improve old ones.	I participate because of some incidental reasons (e.g., my friends happened to ask me to come along).

(Left axis label: **Stability**)

stitution "within" the activity type. These are examples of leisure participation attributed primarily to personal effort (internal-unstable causality). External-unstable attributions involve leisure activities participated in because of relatively incidental social/situational reasons, for instance, an invitation from personal friends to attend a movie.

In sum, *before* people participate in leisure activities they have a priori causes for doing so. The above 2 × 2 table classifies these causes into four major types. When a person attributes free-time participation to internal factors, such involvement is considered leisure at its best. Although this may be particularly true for attributions to ability, it also holds for ascriptions to effort to improve one's competencies, to learn new leisure skills. On the other hand, when a person attributes free-time participation to stable-external factors, such engagement becomes worklike. But when participation is attributed to unstable-external factors, participation may be defined as either leisure or work—depending on a person's perceived competence in the activity, and the subsequent opportunities to make internal attributions during and after the participation.

An individual who attributes the origin of leisure participation to personal competence is inclined to make similar attributions during and after involvement. For example, a person who plays tennis during free-time because of subjective perceptions of being good at it is most likely to attribute good shots during the game and winning to personal ability and bad shots and losing to such external factors as bad luck or a poor racquet. Otherwise, one could not maintain the personal belief that he is playing tennis because of high personal ability. There are, of course, many people who play various games in a noncompetitive manner. In such situations, it is considerably easier to maintain belief in one's personal competence, because the objective criteria of measuring competence are not applied.

Another example would be a person who goes to a concert to listen to a symphony orchestra. Such an individual participates in this activity because "I like that sort of music;" as we noted earlier, people like activities at which they are good or can excel. Since this person attends concerts of classical music because of personal ability to understand such music, one can expect behavior which implies expertise. That is, during the intermission and after the concert, he converses with friends and may evaluate (be it praise or criticism) an orchestra's performance in a way which leaves little doubt about personal expertise in classical music. If one confessed that he lacked ability to understand the music, that would be highly inconsistent with beliefs about personal competence to understand the music, and of course, such a confession would make one look strange in the eyes of others.

Thus, attributions of leisure behavior to ability before participation set the stage for similar ascriptions during and after leisure participation. The above implies that attributions of leisure behavior to ability before, during and after participation are relatively unchanged because of the stable nature of the ability factor and because of the initial impact of ability attributions before participation. Of course, it is possible that leisure participation can undermine perceived ability (e.g., continuously losing when playing tennis). This, however, is not likely to occur, because people seek those leisure activities (and levels of performance) which allow them to make ability attributions, as we suggested earlier.

If there is a relative similarity in a person's ability attributions throughout leisure participation, the same probably holds true for stable-external attributions of leisure participation; that is, if a person participates in an activity during free-time predominantly because of certain social obligations, these attributions are likely to remain the same both during and after participation, regardless of what happens during involvement. The situation, however, is theoretically much more interesting in the case of unstable-internal and unstable-external attributions, since these ascriptions are open for change. For example, unstable-internal attributions of a person who plays tennis because of a genuine attempt to learn a new leisure skill are subject to experiences during participation. After trying hard for several weeks, this person may advance to the level which permits personal ability-attributions for playing tennis. If so, the participant has been able to add a new skill to a personal leisure repertoire and therefore has increased possibilities for satisfactory leisure. Thus, while it is important to learn technical skills associated with a given leisure activity, it is perhaps more important to be able to make internal attributions (especially to ability) during and after such leisure involvement. This is particularly critical in the process of acquiring totally new leisure skills, because such learning experiences occasionally create moments of personal incompetency and inadequacy. The attributional help and support of others ("attributional therapy"), therefore, is needed in this process. It is time for recreation professionals and practitioners to realize that technical leisure skills are useless unless the appropriate psychological meaning is attached to them.

The above analysis suggests that a person who starts with unstable-internal (effort) attributions may change these attributions to stable-internal (competence) ascriptions following successful leisure experiences under a supportive leisure environment. How about a person whose attributions are originally unstable-external? It is reasonable to suppose that the change in attributional patterns (from external to internal) is possible if one has an opportunity to make internal attributions during such an incidental leisure engagement. Using the earlier examples, consider a person who decides to play tennis or attend a symphony concert for the first time at the request of friends. For these activities to become a part of an established leisure repertoire, it is essential that the person be given opportunities to temporarily feel competent during the first encounter (i.e., to make internal attributions). If so, the next time when he is involved in these activities, attributions may change from unstable-external to unstable-internal and perhaps finally to stable-internal, with the accompanying change in the patterns of leisure behavior.

Although the above analysis is tentative, it is logically consistent with theoretical and empirical research on attribution processes (Heider, 1958; Jones and Davis, 1965; Kelley, 1967; Jones, *et al.*, 1971; Harvey, *et al.*, 1976). Thus, the preceding theorizing implies that attributional analysis does not support the continuation of the past and present research attempts to relate personality traits to leisure participation. What is critical is how a person perceives the total personality (in relation to the environment) causally affecting leisure choices and participation. In this regard, the role of personality reduces to two dimensions: (1) perceived competence and (2) perceived effort to participate in a given leisure activity. Depending on the leisure activity in question, different aspects of perceived competence and effort have to be considered. For example, social recreation requires interpersonal competence, many physical activities demand motor abilities, etc. In sum, to advance our understanding of the relationship between personality and leisure, it is necessary to analyze how self-attributions of leisure participation to personal and environmental causes affect the quantity and quality of leisure involvement, and how leisure involvement in turn affects these self-attributions. Such an analysis should take into account the idea of the changing individual in the changing world.

It has been shown, by a method of deduction, that leisure participation attributed to internal factors is a source of enjoyable and satisfying experience. This then raises a question about the factors that facilitate internal attributions or decrease external ascriptions. Hastorf, Schneider and Polefka (1970) have proposed that "attribution of external causality is enhanced when (1) external forces are strong and (2) the power of the perceiver to resist external forces is low." By turning this around one can state that internal attribution ensues if external forces are nonexistent or of minimal strength, and when the attributor's power to resist external forces is high. Furthermore, using Kelly's (1967, 1971) "discounting principle" one can conclude that one's confidence in internal attribution is higher, the fewer hypotheses about external causes one has in mind. It is also logical to assume that the power to resist external attribution is strong when evidence supports internal attribution. Perhaps the single most important factor to corroborate a person's internal attribution is past experiences.

If the person participates *consistently* in a certain type of activity with subjectively defined success, attribution of such leisure behavior is predominantly

factors facilitating
internal attributions

internal. For example, physical exercise may be one of the main objectives of the person's leisure participation. If one has consistently (over a period of time, in diverse situations) been engaged in activities involving physical exercise, such experience confirms a contention about personal competence and desire to exert effort in these types of leisure activities, thereby bolstering internal attribution.

Another characteristic which might support internal ascriptions is *distinctiveness* of these activities in the leisure repertoire. That is, even though a person may participate in many types of leisure activities, only one class (e.g., activities involving physical exercise) may produce feelings of competence. If so, these forms of leisure would be distinctive and would therefore enhance the internal attribution assigned to participation in them. Finally, internal attribution can be supported by *social agents* (e.g., friends, parents, therapists). In fact, the main purpose of recreation therapy is to help clients participate in activities which enable them to make internal attributions. As noted previously, the role of social agents in providing attributional support is critical when a person is in the process of learning new leisure skills or improving old ones. As a final note, it holds true generally that men are more prone to make internal attributions than are women, because men's belief in personal forces is stronger than women's, the difference probably resulting from sex-role socialization (cf. Deaux, 1976).

observers' causal attributions

The above discussion has focused on an individual's self-attributions for leisure participation to personality and situational factors and on their behavioral implications. But personality as a causal force exists not only in the actor's eyes but also in the eyes of those who observe that actor's behavior. People constantly make inferences about the causes of others' behavior, as reflected by such everyday expressions as, "He is no good at it," "He is just plain stupid," "She is always such a nice person." These statements indicate people's beliefs that various aspects of personality have caused certain behavior.

When observing the participation, behavior, and performance of others, people have to decide whether their acts are person-induced or enviroment-induced. Depending on the locus of causality (person vs. environment), these attributions have important interpersonal consequences. For example, if a person's attack on another person is interpreted as an attempt at defense, rather than being due to an aggressive personality, observers will ignore such violent behavior on the ground that everyone else would have done the same thing in a similar situation. Consequently, they continue to interact with this "attacker." By contrast, interpersonal behavior would be very different if observers *believed* that the attack was the result of an aggressive personality. Whether correct or not, observers' beliefs and perceptions of causes of an actor's behavior shape their impressions and consequently their interpersonal encounters.

When people observe a neighbor playing tennis regularly, they are inclined to ask: why does he do that? This pervasive search for causality results from a need to find meaning in human behavior. If one does not understand (correctly or incorrectly) why people do various things, one is not able to exercise control over the environment. Therefore, people are "biased" so as to perceive causality in their own and others' behavior to increase their understanding of the world in general and to predict others' behavior in particular. Hastorf, *et al.,* (1970) have compiled evidence suggesting that perceivers view personality traits as causal and organize them into coherent groups, which together constitute one's observed personality.

In deciding why a neighbor plays tennis, the first thing that observers are likely to do is to make a judgment of intentions (Heider, 1958). They ask: "Is Tom doing it intentionally, of his own will, or is his wife forcing him to play in order to make him lose weight?" In the absence of specific information, observers rely, to a varying degree, on their personal knowledge about the neighbor, his other leisure behaviors, external influences (e.g., his wife) associated with playing tennis. They may also compare their own leisure patterns to that of the neighbor. If the actor is judged to play tennis *intentionally,* this behavior is then attributed to personality; environmental attribution follows if the person is judged to participate without intention.

Attribution theorists (Jones and Davis, 1965; Kelley, 1967) have proposed several factors, which they believe facilitate observers' dispositional (personality) attributions for actors' behavior. It has been proposed (Jones and Nisbett, 1971) and shown (Nisbett, Caputo, Legant and Marecek, 1973) that as a whole, observers are biased toward dispositional attributions. That is, in comparison to actors, there is a pervasive tendency for observers to attribute behaviors to actors' stable personal dispositions. This bias should be particularly relevant to leisure behavior, because leisure is typically viewed as a matter of individual freedom. Thus, it may be formally stated that *people have a pervasive tendency to attribute others' (actors') leisure behavior to their stable personal dispositions.*

factors facilitating personality attribution

Besides this overall tendency toward dispositional attributions, other factors have been shown to influence the general bias. Jones and Davis (1965) theorized that *social desirability* of a person's actions reduces the strength of observers' dispositional attributions concerning those actions. In other words, if a person participates in leisure activities that are considered socially desirable, such leisure pattern provides little information about personality, because one is simply going along with the mass. Consequently, observers are more likely to make situational rather than dispositional attributions for leisure participation. For example, since tennis has become an extremely popular form of leisure, a person's participation in this activity may be perceived to be a result of social influence more than dispositional tendencies to play the game. The situation, however, would be quite different if an observer knew that the person also participates in leisure activities which are not generally considered socially desirable and popular. In such a case, the observer would probably assign causality of the tennis-playing to dispositional factors.

Social desirability is similar to the idea of social norms. People occupy various roles (e.g., housewife, teacher), and these roles set up general expectations about what people are to do in their roles. The more a person departs from such norms in his leisure participation, the more likely the observer is to attribute it to the individual's disposition. If, for instance, the president of the United States went fishing every weekend, most people would probably make dispositional attributions for such leisure behavior and would attribute certain characteristics to him, because people are not used to the idea of fishing presidents. As leisure behavior deviates from the role requirements, it is interpreted as reflecting underlying personality. These suggestions are similar to the idea previously proposed, that *distinctiveness* facilitates dispositional attributions. In other words, when a leisure pattern is unique and peculiar to an individual, it is seen to indicate dispositional (personality) tendencies.

Other principles to be considered include *consistency* of a person's leisure behavior and *consensus* among observers (Kelley, 1967). If an observer knows that an individual maintains a leisure pattern over time and over situations, the observer is likely to make dispositional attribution. This is even more likely when other observers are in agreement about that individual's leisure behavior. But if consistency is not observable, the actor's leisure behavior is interpreted as having been determined by social and situational influences rather than by personality. Empirical research (e.g., McArthur, 1972) indicates that observers tend to use consistency information more than consensus one.

While the preference for dispositional attributions may be beneficial in trying to make some sense out of one's environment, it may make an observer lose sight of other situational influences. If people over-emphasize the role of "personality" to the exclusion of environmental forces, they fail to see that the force of circumstances in fact may have created the undesirable free-time patterns. For example, one often blames the deviant personality of drug abusers for the destructive use of their free-time. In so doing, the observer fails to recognize that the detrimental social environment may be the primary reason for such free-time behavior. Or consider the case of the widely spread view that black youths spend most of their free-time playing basketball. Due to the tendency toward dispositional attributions, observers assign causality of this interest to the black's ability to play the game and to the lack of their capacity to engage in other free-time activities. Thus, people overlook the fact that black people generally live in neighborhoods where facilities for other forms of leisure are minimal or nonexistent, or that they simply cannot afford anything else but basketball. Of course, the same principle applies to anybody who uses public recreational facilities, not just to the black. With their emphasis on personal causation, observers seem to be saying that the problem lies in the person, not in the system. Consequently, they try to resolve it by changing people rather than conditions.

impression formation

When people are in a position to say that a person's leisure behavior is caused by personality, they are in the process of forming impressions about the person. The end products of this process are personality traits attributed to others. When observers learn that a person spends free-time in climbing mountains, they may attach to the individual such labels as sensation-seeker, risk-taker, brave, lonely, etc. Asch (1946), in his classic research, showed that impressions are based on central traits; other traits are organized in a coherent manner around these central characteristics. Asch found that "warm" and "cold" were such central traits and that they decisively influenced subjects' impression formation. In addition to central traits, impressions consist of a host of other traits, a "correlation matrix" of traits, often called the implicit personality theory (Hastorf, *et al.*, 1970; Schneider, 1973). In other words, people have intuitive ideas about which traits are closely related and which are unrelated; and they carry such correlation matrices in their minds. It then follows that if somebody is perceived, for instance, as cold, this immediately brings to mind other characteristics about that person as well.

Hastorf, *et al.* (1970) noted that in the final analysis, implicit personality theories are equal to stereotypes people hold about others. The authors defined a stereotype as "a set of characteristics which is assumed to fit a category of people." People learn stereotypes through the socialization process, and they retain them for a long time. Empirical research has shown (for a review, see Wyer, 1974) that first impressions tend to be lasting; this is referred to as "primacy effect." Thus, people may be told in their early years that boys are physically active and competitive, and that baseball is therefore inappropriate for girls. Such stereotypes are, unfortunately, most likely to endure; to change them may require strong measures. For example, a few years ago when girls entered Little League for the first time, many boys and men became upset, even to the extent of refusing to accept girls playing on their teams and leagues. The issue had to be settled in court, which ruled in favor of the girls' constitutional right to participate along with boys.

Stereotypes are not limited to leisure patterns of the two sexes. People have come to expect that businessmen play golf in private clubs, college students assemble in bars to drink beer, etc. It then follows that observers have a tendency to correlate not only various personality traits but traits and leisure activities as well. In principle, leisure participation may serve as a primary or secondary source of impression formation. In the former case, impression formation begins with the actor's leisure behavior; these initial impressions are subsequently matched with the actor's other behaviors or characteristics (e.g., occupation). In the latter case, impression formation begins with other behaviors and characteristics, which are subsequently related to the actor's leisure behavior.

Observers may first learn either directly from others that an actor possesses certain traits, or indirectly, by being informed about the actor's social role (e.g., occupation). If observers know that an individual is a business person, they immediately form an "implicit theory" of personality, and consequently expect the person to participate in those leisure activities (secondary source) that are congruent with their implicit personality theory. If the business person plays golf, as might be expected, this reinforces their idea about this individual's personality. On the other hand, if leisure patterns are opposed to stereotypes, such leisure participation may lead them to revise their implicit personality theory about the actor, or to disregard the inconsistent information (for how such inconsistencies are resolved, see Wyer, 1974; Hastorf, *et al.*, 1970). Alternatively, they may first come to know a person's leisure interests; on the basis of such known leisure interests they may immediately form an implicit personality theory about the individual (primary source). Subsequent information about other aspects of the actor's life (e.g., occupation) may or may not confirm the initial impression derived from leisure pursuits.

Unfortunately, studies pertaining to the above theorizing are almost nonexistent. So far as the author knows, only one such research attempt has been reported. Paluba and Neulinger (1976) asked about 500 volunteers, primarily at beaches in the New York City area, to rate a number of adjectives in terms of "how well the word describes a person whose favorite free-time activity is bowling, golf, or tennis." Although the study was quite limited in its approach, it nevertheless demonstrated that leisure activities and personality traits are implicitly correlated. For example, golfers were seen as more extroverted and higher in "ego organization" than bowlers and tennis players. Rather than relating all specific activities to all personality traits (there are some 18,000 different trait names in the English language), it would be better in the future to examine this relationship by correlating the underlying personality dimensions with the activity dimensions. Central traits should be correlated with central activities. Osgood, Suci and Tannenbaum's (1957) work suggests that three independent factors (evaluation, activity, and potency) can account for most of people's thinking about others, regardless of (or because of) the 18,000 trait names. Undoubtedly, people's thinking about others is simpler than might generally be suspected, and it is often based on a priori causal theories or stereotypes provided by the culture or subculture where people live (Nisbett and Wilson, 1977).

When people form impressions about the personality of others, they do so on the basis of the actors' leisure *patterns*. Bishop (1970) reported tentative evidence that participation in leisure activities tends to cluster along Osgood's, *et al.* (1957) three dimensions. It is then conceivable that in their minds people categorize leisure participation according to these same dimensions. If so, observers are likely to relate implicit personality theories and leisure behavior to one another on the basis of evaluation, potency, and activity. As did Bishop (1970), one might then expect that those persons whose leisure involves "evaluation" are perceived by others as "good, pleasant, interesting, intelligent," and in terms of other traits that characterize this dimension. If persons are considered outstanding on the "potency" dimension in their leisure, they are perceived as "tough, rugged, strong, masculine," etc. Finally, those whose leisure participation is "activity" oriented are perceived as "active, quick, excitable, energetic," etc.

---

summary

In examining the relationship between personality and leisure from the standpoint of objective causality, the major theories of personality were reviewed, and all were found to be narrowly focused. Some theories have emphasized unconscious forces or cognitive development in the formation of personality, while others

Social Psychological Determinants of Leisure Behavior

have stressed the role of environment or stable traits as affecting personality. Recent studies, however, have made such theorizing suspect and have commended interactional approach. This examines personality in light of a continuous process in which personal and situational factors interact in a multidirectional manner. Unfortunately, past research on personality and leisure has been carried out in the limited framework of selected traits, which has led to such questionable conclusions as, "campers are rigid, dogmatic and traditional." Only one study has simultaneously taken into account persons, situations, and modes of leisure responses. Its findings indicated that different persons select different leisure activities under different situations. At the same time, it appeared that there is some individual consistency and stability in leisure responses to different situations.

Studies dealing with the effects of leisure experiences on personality lend support to the hypothesis that *learning* new leisure skills improves one's self-concept because of the increased sense of competence, thereby supporting the idea that perceived competence regulates leisure involvement. Empirical research has also revealed that leisure participation is significantly related to one's psychological adjustment, though different people pursue psychological adjustment through different leisure activities at different times.

The relationship between personality and leisure from standpoints of phenomenal causality was examined in two ways: (1) a person's self-attributions of leisure behavior to dispositional and environmental causes, and the behavioral implications thereof, (2) observers' perceptions concerning personal and environmental causation of the actor's leisure behavior. It was shown that people have a tendency to attribute their own *leisure* participation to internal (dispositional) causes. When attributions are internal, behavior on which these attributions are based is considered leisure at its best. But when attributions are external, the underlying behavior resembles work. In this analysis, however, one has to distinguish between attributions made before, during, and after leisure participation. In general, it appears that internal attributions are made if external forces are minimal and/or if the attributor's power to resist external causation is high. Consistently successful leisure experiences form the basis for internal self-attribution.

When people observe others playing tennis, for example, they are inclined to ask: why do they do it? Depending on the causal attributions which observers assign to actors' leisure participation, the observers behave differently toward them. Attributions are made to personality (dispositions) if observers perceive actors to engage intentionally in their leisure activities. It was suggested the observers have a pervasive tendency to attribute the leisure behavior of others to their stable personal dispositions. This overall tendency becomes more pervasive in proportion, as the actors depart from social norms, expectations, and desirability in their leisure participation. An observer is more confident about dispositional attributions to the actor, if the actor's leisure behavior is consistent over time, place, and modalities, and if the observers are in agreement concerning the actor's leisure behavior.

Attribution of causality is important not only for understanding and explaining why others participate in certain leisure activities but also for forming impressions about others. Impressions are based upon certain central traits or dimensions around which other traits are organized into coherent clusters. These clusters, correlation matrices of personality traits, are called implicit personality theories or stereotypes which people form about others. Research has shown that leisure participation and implicit personality theories are related to one another. Thus, the leisure behavior of those observed may serve as a primary or secondary source in determining the perceivers' impressions of others. People's thinking about others, however, is relatively simple, in that it is based upon comparatively few dimensions of leisure activity and traits at a time. This is understandable in the face of countless leisure activities and 18,000 trait names in the English language.

leisure needs and motives 11

Besides its theoretical relevance, the concept of leisure (recreation) need is important for practical considerations. In a way, the future of the entire field of leisure studies as well as the recreation profession depends on the construct of leisure need. That is, if it could not be shown that people have a need for leisure and recreation, professionals and practitioners might as well give up and begin searching for new jobs. As will be seen (and has already been alluded to), the problem is not whether people need leisure and recreation but rather, whether professionals are able to "sell" "leisure need" to those who make decisions about the development of our profession and thus affect people's psychological well-being. The purpose of this chapter, however, is not to present specific strategies for "selling" leisure need, but rather to examine psychological foundations of the concept. This analysis, therefore, aims at demonstrating the importance of leisure need in human behavior. Needs and motives as psychological constructs will be discussed first, and then their relation to leisure behavior. The social nature of leisure motivation is delineated next with a detailed review of empirical studies done in this area. The following section focuses on social interaction as a leisure need. Finally, the chapter outlines new directions for future research concerning leisure motivation.

But, before embarking on this task, it is desirable to examine the concept of levels of causality in leisure behavior. Students (or other observers) often are confused when they are confronted by various theories of play and leisure. They ask: "Which one is right?" This confusion is a result of the authors' failure to point out the limits of their leisure theories. Any given theory has been described as if it were *the* theory of leisure behavior. For example, Sapora and Mitchell (1963) posited that people play because of their need for self-expression, and Patrick (1916) claimed that relaxation is the cause of pleasure participation. These and other theoreticians have failed to recognize that causality of leisure

levels of causality of leisure behavior

and play behavior is multifaceted, that it cannot be explained by a single concept or factor. This is not to say that past theories are totally inadequate. But the problem is that they are limited in scope because they do not consider that different persons participate in the same activity for different reasons under different conditions. The picture becomes even more confusing when sociological and psychological variables and theories are compared in providing answers to the above question. This sort of comparison between apples and oranges becomes "fruitless," as the causes of leisure behavior operate on different conceptual levels.

To make this point more concrete, consider figure 17. The diagram is supposed to illustrate how the "whys" of leisure participation can be explained at different levels of causality. As the figure shows, the most fundamental cause of a person's leisure behavior is his biological make-up, his inherited background. As was discussed in chapter 7, Grotevant, *et al.,* (1977, p. 673–75) reported empirical evidence indicating that "there is a small but reliably heritable influence on the *patterning* of interests in individuals . . . (so) that genetic differences among individuals contribute to interest differences among them." Biological factors, however, are insufficient to explain leisure behavior, because such factors only set the stage for leisure pursuits.

Figure 17   An illustration of levels of causality of leisure behavior.

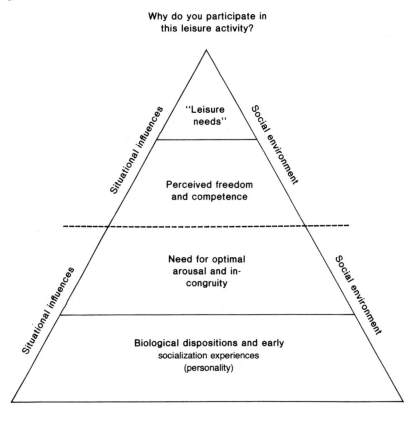

Social Psychological Determinants of Leisure Behavior

Within one's biological dispositions, early socialization or social learning experiences influence what specific activities a person becomes interested in. Biological forces and early socialization experiences jointly shape an individual's personality, which perhaps best summarizes the foundations of all human behavior, including leisure behavior. It should be stressed that while one part of personality is fixed (biological factors), another part of it is open to social influences and thus to change. For example, even though a person biologically may not have much talent for playing musical instruments, he may, however, develop talent in a strongly supportive and encouraging social environment, and thus playing piano may become his favorite leisure activity. Or, consider the fact that many, if not most, people have biological tendencies toward many different types of activities. Since one person cannot participate in all the activities he is capable of doing, he has to select which activities to engage in. Such selection is determined by his socialization experiences and the social environment he is living in.

The importance of the joint influence of biological dispositions and early socialization experiences is that they form the foundations for the individual need for optimal arousal and incongruity. As was pointed out earlier in detail (chapter 7), too little or too much stimulation is damaging to an individual, both physiologically and psychologically. Thus, leisure behavior takes place within a framework of optimal arousal and incongruity. The person does not participate in one and the same activity, in the same manner, in the same place, with the same friends, etc. Even if he spends most of his free-time in one leisure activity, he seeks variety "within" this activity in order to meet the need for optimal arousal or incongruity. While this need has its biological roots, it is also influenced by one's social environment. Thus, what becomes optimally arousing may appear as "active" leisure participation to one person and "passive" leisure engagement to another, depending on social influences.

At the next level of causation, leisure behavior can be explained in terms of intrinsic motivation. Specifically, people have a tendency to participate in leisure activities for such intrinsic rewards as feelings of self-determination and competence. As stated previously, one derivation of this explanation is that people have a tendency to participate in those leisure activities that permit them to make dispositional causal attributions. Thus, perceived freedom and competence are at the heart of intrinsically motivated leisure behavior. It is important to note, however, that the influence of these factors is exerted within the framework of the need for optimal arousal. For example, a person who plays tennis during free-time because he feels he is good at it, does not always play with the same opponent nor does he select an opponent he can beat easily. This is because such an opponent soon becomes repetitive, boring and unchallenging.

Finally, there appears the top of the pyramid or iceberg in the illustration of levels of causality of leisure behavior. Perhaps the most popular way of explaining the reasons why people participate in various leisure activities is to pose this question directly to them. As will be shown in this chapter, a typical leisure researcher provides subjects with a large number of reasons ("leisure needs") and asks them to rate the importance of each of them for their participation in various activities. This is the most direct way of explaining the "whys" of leisure behavior, but as figure 17 illustrates, it is also the most simplistic approach. In a sense, it could be said that those researchers who are studying so-called "leisure needs" based upon this approach are scratching the surface or exploring the tip of the iceberg. When a person is asked, "why do you participate in this leisure activity?," he does not, of course, say that it is because of "optimal arousal." Yet the concept of optimal arousal is essential for understanding and explaining the causes of leisure behavior. The same holds true for other concepts of figure 17.

Two additional points should be noted about figure 17. The "iceberg" depicted in the figure can be likened to an individual. Thus, the person has both hidden and open reasons for participating in a given activity. Those under the dotted line represent hidden causes, meaning that they are not clearly observable, or causes of leisure behavior which are not readily tested. Also, the diagram shows that situational variables and social factors operate at each level of causality. For example, perceived competence is determined not only by past experiences but also by such social influences as the performance and evaluation of others. Similarly, when the person is asked why he plays tennis ("leisure needs"), his response is not only affected by perceived competence but also by culturally learned stereotypes of why people *generally* play tennis.

The above diagram is presented to emphasize the point that leisure behavior cannot adequately be understood by such isolated concepts or theories as childhood-adulthood socialization, personality, optimal arousal, etc. Leisure behavior must be analyzed at different levels of causality. When one examines leisure motivation in this chapter, it is important to keep in mind the specific level of causation. This is particularly true in the case of "leisure needs" because one is only "exploring the tip of the iceberg."

motivation as a psychological construct

As might be expected, there is no uniform theory of human motivation (Berkowitz, 1969; Madsen, 1973; Weiner, 1973). Regardless of variations in approaches to motivation, most scientists agree that "a motive is an internal factor that arouses, directs and integrates a person's behavior" (Murray, 1964). Much of the controversy about the concept "motivation" has centered around the idea that motivation is an internal factor. The controversy is not surprising, because a motive cannot be observed but must be inferred from one's behavior. In simple terms the controversy is the question whether drives are physiologically aroused or based upon cognitive processes. In the influential Hullian theory of motivation, psychological drive is likened to physiological need. Since a physiological need is strictly a biological process, this theory essentially states that conditions creating a homeostatic imbalance give rise to psychological motives. A person is in a state of homeostatic disequilibrium, for example, when the water level of the blood is below the required amount internally. Consequently, the individual becomes motivated to restore the equilibrium by finding water.

Although the homeostatic motives (hunger, thirst, etc.) are primarily based upon biological processes, they are also influenced by environment. For example, when a person smells or sees good food the result may be a sudden feeling of hunger, even if the system is homeostatically balanced. It is then logical to suppose that motives other than homeostatic ones are strongly affected by social (environmental) forces. Earlier, empirical evidence was reviewed indicating that optimal incongruity or arousal is biologically determined, but the directions and forms it takes in individual behavior are socially shaped. Even if a person is biologically predisposed to certain behaviors, these behaviors do not materialize unless the social environment is conducive to them.

The above reasoning implies that it is inadequate and misleading to equate psychological motives with physiological needs. Basically, various psychological motives or needs are *learned* through the socialization process, and thus primarily social in nature. As shown previously (Part 4), the origin of social interaction goes back to the very early relationship between a parent (mostly mother) and an infant. It was observed that early social deprivation from the caretaker or peers has detrimental and, in some cases, even irreversible effects not only on a child's social behavior but also on total functioning. On the other hand, an affectionate and stimulating parent-child interaction in early years is likely to develop strong and healthy psychological motives (e.g., achievement, self-esteem, "self-actualization") in a person. Instead of turning inward, the individual becomes socially oriented. When a person takes others' behaviors and preferences into account in making choices about personal behaviors, this is said to manifest a social motive (MacCrimmon and Messick, 1976). The reported research clearly suggests (see Part 4) that the person who is capable of interacting with others is well equipped to meet a biologically determined predisposition toward optimal incongruity. The issue, therefore, is not whether psychological motives are social or genetically inherited. All psychological motives have their biological roots, but they are strongly shaped by the socialization process. Thus, psychological motivation can better be understood by viewing it as social motivation.

social motivation

Apart from homeostatically motivated behaviors, human actions are motivated by subjectively defined goals and rewards. Motives and actions terminate when the previously set goals and rewards are achieved. Motives (and thus behaviors) may be continuous or short-lived. A person may spend a part of daily free-time in jogging throughout the life span. Thus, the goal of being in good physical shape is continuous, never-ending. Or, a person may want to see a highly publicized movie. The goal of seeing the movie is short-lived, lasting only two hours.

intrinsic-extrinsic motivation

Theoretically, goals and rewards can be either intrinsic or extrinsic. When an activity is performed to obtain a reward which is extrinsic to the activity, it is said to be extrinsically motivated. When no apparent extrinsic rewards underlie one's behavior (i.e., an activity is engaged in for its own sake) it is said to be intrinsically motivated. The major line of demarcation between work and leisure is the difference between extrinsic and intrinsic motivation. Even though there are exceptions, the rule, however, is that people's work is primarily motivated by extrinsic reasons (i.e., money), whereas leisure is chiefly motivated by intrinsic factors. In some cases, rewards are built into activities (e.g., winning and losing in various recreational games), so that they have become intrinsic to them. If so, the behavior may be considered intrinsically rather than extrinsically motivated. Of course, it is a different story if extrinsic rewards (e.g., trophies for winners) are offered in addition to intrinsic rewards.

Finally, it should be noted that while some activities are engaged in for either intrinsic or extrinsic reasons, many activities are participated in for both intrinsic *and* extrinsic rewards. It is important to realize, however, that continued participation in such half-intrinsic, half-extrinsic activities is severely hampered if extrinsic rewards are taken away. As shown earlier (Part 4), extrinsic rewards undermine intrinsic motivation. Of course, a person can be made to engage in almost any behavior by extrinsic rewards, but once the rewards are removed interest dies. Thus, removal of extrinsic rewards erodes not only the extrinsic aspect of motivation but more importantly, the intrinsic aspect as well. It is for this reason that leisure activities should be engaged in for intrinsic rewards *to begin with,* if they are to become lasting and enjoyable forms of recreation.

It should be emphasized that intrinsic and extrinsic rewards are subjectively defined. No matter how obvious extrinsic rewards may look to an observer, one cannot say for sure whether a person is engaged in an activity for extrinsic or intrinsic reasons. For example, when one sees a student attending classes at a university the observer is inclined to say that the individual is motivated to do so in order to obtain a degree which then, hopefully, provides good employment. Although this may be true in many cases, there are also students who enroll in courses for sheer learning and acquisition of knowledge. Or, many people play games (e.g., volleyball) in recreational leagues for which the recreation department has offered trophies. At first glance, their participation may seem to be extrinsic, but a closer inspection might reveal that the participants are playing volleyball for mere enjoyment and social interaction. Again, this also works the other way around. For example, many people spend their free-time in various organizations to accumulate points which they can later cite as evidence of their vast experience when they become political candidates.

Accordingly, it is critical how a person by himself perceives personal leisure behavior as being motivated. This leads to the subject of self-attributions of behavior. As noted earlier (chapter 10), when the perceived locus of causality of participation is internal, then leisure behavior is intrinsically motivated, but when it is external, leisure behavior is extrinsically motivated. But as the diagram (p. 217) showed, there is a difference between internal-stable and internal-unstable attributions. Thus, intrinsic motivation is enhanced when a person attributes leisure participation to perceived competence (internal-stable), as opposed to an effort to acquire competence (internal-unstable). If participation increases one's feelings of competence in a given leisure activity, it also increases attributions to personal competence and thus contributes to the perception of intrinsic motivation. By contrast, attributions to stable-external causes increase extrinsic motivation, in comparison to attributions to unstable-external factors.

Although external rewards generally decrease intrinsic motivation, there is at least one important exception to this rule. When rewards convey feedback that a person is competent they enhance rather than reduce intrinsic motivation (Deci, 1975a). Recent empirical research supports this proposition (see chapter 5). For practical considerations, such a finding is valuable because it suggests that "significant others" can ameliorate a person's intrinsic motivation by transmitting feedback about personal competence in the participated leisure activities. It is an essential device for those who teach leisure skills and who provide recreation therapy. In sum, for leisure activities to become intrinsically motivated a person has to be able to participate in them freely (high perceived freedom or self-determination) and must be able to obtain feelings of competence from such engagement. This is reflected by individual attributions of leisure behavior to internal factors. Because intrinsic motivation is positively correlated with satisfaction, the above theorizing constitutes the basis of a theory of leisure satisfaction.

The idea of intrinsic motivation and Maslow's (1943) need hierarchy theory of motivation are in some respects similar. But there is another reason to note carefully Maslow's (1943, 1970) need hierarchy theory: it is perhaps the most popular theory of motivation used by leisure authors. Maslow categorized human needs in "five sets of goals," and pointed out that they arrange themselves in a relative hierarchy of prepotency, that is, the appearance of one need depends on the satisfaction of the lower-order need(s). From the lowest to the highest, the order is as follows:

1. Physiological needs (e.g., homeostatic imbalance as reflected in hunger, thirst, etc.)
2. Safety needs (e.g., children's desire for justice, fairness, and consistency in their parents' behavior; adults' desire for a savings account, insurance, and a job with tenure)
3. Love needs (i.e., people's desire for affectionate relations with others and preference for belonging to a group)
4. Esteem needs (i.e., desire for stable, high evaluation of oneself, self-esteem, self-respect, achievement of independence and freedom as well as prestige and status)
5. Need for self-actualization (i.e., desire "to become everything that one is capable of becoming," self-fulfillment) (Maslow, 1943, p. 382).

Maslow (1943) contends that when one need is fairly well satisfied the next higher need becomes a dominant motivator of "the conscious life." As one moves up the hierarchy, the percentage of non-satisfaction increases. To illustrate this he pointed out that the average citizen is satisfied perhaps 85% in physiological needs, 70% in safety needs, 50% in love needs, 40% in self-esteem needs, and 10% in self-actualization. Maslow stressed that gratified needs are not active motivators of behavior; rather, it is an unsatisfied need which energizes and directs human action. He also emphasized that any thwarting of one's attempts to achieve the basic goals is viewed as a psychological threat to oneself. He maintained that psychopathology has its roots in such threats.

Although Maslow emphasized the hierarchy of basic needs, he (1943, p. 386) was aware of the limitations of the model. At one point, he noted that the hierarchy is "not nearly as rigid as we may have implied" and went on to give examples of exceptions to the basic idea. While the hierarchy notion and his other points implied that one set of five goals at a time motivates behavior, he was careful to point out that behavior is multi-motivated (p. 390): ". . . any behavior tends to be determined by several or *all* of the basic needs simultaneously rather than by only one of them . . . not all behavior is determined by the basic needs." These considerations, however, do not exclude the basic tenet of the theory (hierarchy) nor do they make it immune to conceptual and empirical criticism.

Unfortunately, Maslow's work has been taken at its face value, with slight questioning about its conceptual and empirical validity. While the theory is intuitively appealing, its basic tenet (hierarchy of needs) remains highly suspect (Brockett, 1976; Wahba and Bridwell, 1976). An excellent example of how writers are convinced by Maslow's theorizing is seen in Mitchell's (in Murphy, 1975, p. 179) application of the basic idea. He asserted that security was the dominant need in the 1900–1930's, belonging in the 1940–50's, ego-self-esteem in the 1960–70's, and self-actualization in the future. Poor Plato!

In an effort to clarify Maslow's theorizing, Brockett argued that (1) each need has its own qualitative hierarchy ("a series of hierarchically arranged hierarchies") and (2) there is an interdependence or a two-way relationship among the basic needs. Instead of advocating a motivational sequence, Brockett emphasized qualitatively distinct forms of gratification; how one need is satisfied affects gratification of the other. Brockett's criticism is borne out by empirical research designed to test the theory. Wahba and Bridwell (1976) reviewed all past studies and found "little clear or consistent support from the available findings." None of the past studies using the factor analytic approach verified all of Maslow's five need categories as independent factors. There was some evidence for the existence of two types of need sets as lower-order and higher-order needs tended to cluster together independently of one another. But overall, the results showed that need categories overlap between both adjacent and nonadjacent sets of needs. When rank order studies were reviewed no consistent support was obtained for the idea of the need hierarchy. As for the notion that the percentage of non-satisfaction should increase when going up in the hierarchy, it generally appeared that self-actualization and security are the least satisfied and social needs the most satisfied; Maslow's theory predicts that security needs, not social needs, should be the most satisfied.

Taken together, the results provide very limited support for Maslow's theory. This, of course, is assuming that the research methods used have been adequate to test the theory. For example, one could criticize the methodology on the grounds that it is static, while the theory is dynamic. But, since at least two types of approaches have been used in many studies and yet no consistent evidence has materialized, more than weak methodology must be involved. Besides, Maslow (1943, p. 395) himself said that the hierarchy principle can be "empirically observed" in terms of the decreasing percentages of satisfaction as one moves up on the ladder. That the empirical studies do not support this is not surprising, in the light of suggestions like those of Brockett (1976). As the amount of money in one's savings account varies from day to day so does the level of satisfaction of security need. Furthermore, if a person does not feel psychologically secure, it is difficult to satisfy other needs; the degree to which other needs are satisfied in part determines the extent of satisfaction of the security need. In short, basic needs are interdependent, and the gratification of one affects that of another.

One of the major problems with Maslow's theory arises from the idea of self-actualization. Since self-actualization is peculiar to every individual, how do we know specifically what it means to each one of us? What is it that we have to do to be able to self-actualize? Maslow refers to it as "becoming what one is capable of becoming" and states that the self-actualizing person's behavior is inner-directed rather than socially motivated. But what does "inner-directed" mean? If it denotes some mechanism built into a human being, everyone should then be able to self-actualize automatically. If it does not, then the only thing it can refer to is one's free will to do what one is capable of doing, which is another way of saying *intrinsic motivation*. This, in turn, assumes that objective criteria exist for determining one's competence. Such is often not the case, and the social comparison theory (Festinger, 1954) and research (Suls and Miller, 1977) indicate that in the absence of the objective criteria, a person seeks to evaluate personal abilities by comparing them with abilities of those persons who are thought to be close to one's perceived competence level. Thus, while the self-actualizing person's behavior is inner-directed, it is also socially motivated.

Indeed, it is practically impossible to avoid social influences on behavior. In fact, Berkowitz (1969) inferred that self-actualization is a result of the socialization process and cultural values rather than of basic needs. Apparently, by self-actualization, Maslow meant to refer to those forms of behavior that are engaged in pursuant to one's free will and result from perceived competence rather than from the latest social fads. But consider a person who is extremely capable of doing things in needlework. She spends much of her free-time in needlepoint, knitting, and macramé. One day, however, crochet becomes popular in her town, and she decides to try it because many of her friends do so, also. Although this may look like following the latest fad, it is hard to see anything wrong with this sort of social motivation so long as she enjoys crocheting and feels competent to do it. Of course, it would be a different story should most of her leisure participation be based upon the latest fads. In this context, Brockett's (1976, p. 81) observation is relevant: "Pursuit of happiness is contradiction—the more vigorously happiness is pursued, the further from reach it recedes. Once this pursuit is forsaken for involvement in some personally meaningful activity, however, happiness becomes a possibility." Personally meaningful activities do not follow the newest fads.

Personally meaningful activities are those that are conducive to feelings of self-determination and competence. Thus, pursuit of happiness and self-actualization come close to what was earlier defined as intrinsic motivation. The use of such a unitary motivational concept, in lieu of several sets of basic needs, is clearly justified by Wahba and Bridwell's (1976) findings, because higher-order need categories clustered together. This, therefore, suggests that self-actualization is a highly abstract concept which does not exist independently from other psychic needs in people's minds, unless it is made, by implication, a socially desirable response. Intrinsic motivation (i.e., an individual's desire to do what he wants and what he is capable of doing) is characteristic of higher-order needs. It is logical, therefore, to suggest that those persons whose leisure is intrinsically motivated are in fact "self-actualizing" and come close to reaching personal happiness.

the social nature of leisure motivation

Thus far it has been argued that intrinsic motivation constitutes the basis of an individual's leisure behavior. In so doing, the role of perceived freedom (self-determination) and perceived competence in leisure motivation were stressed. Despite the emphasis placed on an individual, it would be audacious to state that intrinsic motivation exists in a social vacuum. Intrinsic motivation has its own social character. To a considerable extent, environmental forces determine how intrinsic motivation develops to influence human behavior. For example, the effects of environmental factors are immediate and negative when they (extrinsic rewards, sanctions, norms, etc.) induce a person to conclude that participation in an activity is externally motivated. Unfortunately, much leisure behavior seems to be externally motivated; Kelly (1976) found that 26% of all leisure activities were perceived as having "some obligation" and 29% as having "considerable obligation." Environmental factors can reduce the role of intrinsic motivation in leisure behavior either by minimizing an individual's perceived recreational freedom or by limiting perceived competence to perform certain leisure skills.

The effect of social factors can also be less apparent. Many activities (e.g., tennis, concerts, spectator sports) require the presence of others. Thus, people often seem to direct their intrinsic motivation to social recreational activities. Another case of less apparent social influence are people who jog during their free-time. Even though they may be highly competent to jog, they would not do it if they were the only people in the world to do so. They have seen others jogging and have learned through the socialization process that such exercise is good for their hearts and their psychological well-being. Thus, their intrinsic motivation clearly operates in the social milieu, though they are not necessarily aware of it. In sum, intrinsically motivated leisure behaviors are social in that (1) they involve activities in which others participate, which also require the presence of others, and (2) they are sometimes affected by external factors like trophies, sanctions, and norms.

Another way of considering the social nature of leisure motivation is one reported by Mercer (1973). Based upon Bradshaw's work, Mercer distinguished between normative and comparative recreational needs. Even though Mercer talked more about these needs at the societal level, the distinction is applicable at the individual level as well. Normative need refers to the norms of leisure participation established by outside sources. For example, physiologists contend that to maintain the heart in good condition one should exercise at least three times a week for half an hour at a time so that the heart is beating about 150 times per minute. This, then, clearly sets a norm as to how many free-time hours should be spent weekly for physical exercise if a person is concerned about keeping the body in good shape. Such norms, however, are a matter of subjective interpretation rather than external sanctions.

Comparative leisure need refers to "the relative abilities or disabilities of individuals to make use of recreation opportunities for one reason or another" (Mercer, 1973). For instance, if a teenager gets a motorcycle, this is likely to arouse a comparative need for motorcycling among friends. Or, a physically handicapped person who has not learned to swim may develop a comparative need for swimming when seeing friends swimming. Viewed in this light, the comparative leisure need is characteristic of those people who change their leisure interests according to the newest fads. But the comparative need has another aspect. Festinger (1954) called it a drive to achieve an accurate appraisal of one's abilities. He posited that if non-social means are not available for comparison, a person will evaluate personal abilities by comparison with those of others, especially with abilities of a person whose abilities seem to be similar to one's own. Thus, to have an enjoyable and stimulating tennis game (i.e., one which is conducive to feelings of competence), a person selects an opponent who is similar in ability.

In sum, the comparison need refers to a situation in which people decide to pursue a leisure activity because others do so or because they want to compare their leisure skills to those of similar others. Even if a person's participation is promoted by comparative or normative "needs," it is possible that such extrinsically motivated leisure behaviors become intrinsically motivated. For that to occur, however, the person has to be able to derive feelings of self-determination and personal competence from leisure participation.

As noted earlier, the question of why people engage in one recreation activity rather than another can be answered at different levels of causality. The most superficial level is a sociological analysis based on such variables as socioeconomic status and residence. The present author contends, however, that examination of social forces in terms of variables like residence is quite meaningless if the objective is to understand why people participate in the available activities, what they expect to obtain psychologically from their leisure engagement, and how they strive to meet these expectations. It takes little insight to know that "residence influences the kinds of recreation environments available" (Mercer, 1976). If a community does not have a theater in a radius of, say, 50 miles, it is evident that theater-going is not a frequent leisure activity among people living in the community. It is the same as finding that people do not go for a picnic when it rains as opposed to when it does not rain. If all one can conclude is that there are differences between extreme urban and rural areas in people's leisure patterns due to the availability of leisure services (Mercer, 1976), very little indeed has been learned about the "whys" of leisure behaviors.

research on leisure needs

need theories and leisure involvement

To find out why people participate in various leisure activities, researchers have typically used a procedure according to which subjects are given a series of motivational statements (reasons) and then asked to evaluate the importance of each reason for their participation in various activities. In one of the first studies, Witt and Bishop (1970) presented subjects (college students) with 13 different activities and asked them to rate the degree to which they would feel like participating in each of them, after having been in ten situations characteristic of five need theories (surplus energy, relaxation, catharsis, compensation and task generalization). The results showed that surplus energy, catharsis, and compensation were more useful than other "need theories" in explaining the relationship between antecedent situations and subsequent leisure participation. The surplus energy theory refers to leisure involvement prompted by a need for stimulation. This need results from excess energy left over after gratification of biological demands. Catharsis refers to leisure participation initiated by a need to release emotional tension and anxiety. According to the compensation theory, leisure engagement results from a need to compensate for unattained goals in other domains.

A further examination of the Witt and Bishop data reveals that the subjects' responses along the "restoration-relaxation" dimension were similar to their responses along the catharsis and compensation dimensions, whereas "diversionary-relaxation" bore resemblance to surplus energy. Restoration-relaxation referred to passive leisure involvement (e.g., TV-watching, napping) following activities that caused fatigue because a person had been busy and under pressure. Diversionary relaxation referred to participation in active leisure activities (e.g., partying, playing competitive games) following situations that have not necessarily caused fatigue in a person, but provided only few opportunities for escape from routine (Witt and Bishop, 1970).

Taken together, this study clearly supports a contention that leisure provides an important avenue for gratifying the fundamental need for optimal stimulation and arousal. If work and other daily activities are perceived as requiring relatively little energy, persons tend to use their leisure for burning up that "surplus" vitality through active pastimes in order to maintain optimal incongruity. If, on the other hand, daily activities are viewed as strenuous and energy-consuming, persons exhibit a tendency to engage in less energetic activities. It is important to realize, however, that "surplus energy" is entirely an individual matter, which is strongly shaped by the socialization experience (see Part 4). While "surplus energy" has its biological roots, it is primarily determined by social learning.

The Witt and Bishop findings provided evidence for an individual tendency to use leisure in a manner commensurate with one's need for optimal incongruity, but the results do not justify predictions as to people's participation in specific activities. For example, it is common for people to plan for social parties many days beforehand. At the time a person is supposed to leave for a party he may be extremely tired, both mentally and physically, due to the prior activities of the day. The optimal incongruity theory prediction that the individual would spend that evening quietly and passively would not hold true because of an earlier commitment to to a party. High use of energy during the day, however, could reduce the activity level of one's behavior at the party so that one might be more passive, less talkative and less social than usual.

The final point to be noted about the Witt and Bishop findings is that the way a person chooses to relax depends in part on prior situational and social experiences. At any given time, a person tends to select that activity from an individual leisure repertoire, which best meets the demand for relaxation. Since all activities in the person's *leisure* repertoire (not free-time repertoire) are intrinsically motivated, they are also activities which produce feelings of competence and self-determination. These are activities which are expected to provide enjoyment, and of course, these activities vary in the amount of required energy. Since all enjoyable activities are also relaxing activities, selection of one activity can be reduced to choosing from intrinsically motivating activities, the choice in part depending on the desired energy expenditure.

The above reasoning is strongly supported by a recent study. Kelly (1976) found that reasons intrinsic to the activity dominated subjects' leisure choices. Even with the most popular reason ("because I like it") removed from the intrinsic category, intrinsic reasons outweighed the second most important category ("relational or social") by about a 2-1 margin. This finding becomes even more important when it is considered that the study involved adults from three communities from the East and West coast. To be sure, the above reason ("I like it") should not be removed from the intrinsic category, because it is based upon feelings of competence and self-determination which are the basic ingredients of intrinsic motivation.

intrinsic leisure motivation

By way of criticism, however, it should be pointed out that the importance of one motivational category over another depends on how each category is defined. Unquestionably, Kelly's methodology was biased toward "intrinsic" motivation, because this category included many more motivational statements than did other categories. Nonetheless, the total effect of intrinsic reasons was so striking that its importance is undisputable. Besides, other studies are in keeping with these findings. Copp (1975), for instance, reported that escape ("diversionary-relaxation") was the common theme among the replies made by hunters when asked why they hunt. In addition, they cited reasons directly pertaining to perceived competence: mastering a difficult skill and overcoming the challenge of nature. This, then, supports the contention that different forms of relaxation (restoration or diversionary) are pursued in intrinsically motivated activities.

Data consistent with the above findings have been found in several factor analytical studies. Hollender (1977) reported that various forms of escape were important motivational factors in a decision to go camping. Also, such skill-oriented motives as building campfires and cooking outdoors were closely associated with a factor called "primitive life style," thereby supporting the idea that various forms of relaxation are sought in activities which produce feelings of competence and self-determination. These results, however, are not totally un-ambiguous. That "escape" was an important theme (three of seven factors were escape-related) in the study was not surprising, because the number of motiva-tional escape-oriented statements to which subjects responded was considerably greater than the number of other motivational dimensions. Such a bias is undesir-able, since factor analysis as a statistical tool can only produce "factors" (mo-tives) which are based upon the items included. In other words, if all the motiva-tional items which the subjects are supposed to evaluate are socially oriented, the extracted "factors" can only be social in nature. Or, if all the items are escape-oriented, only escape-factors will emerge from the analysis. Thus, Hollender clearly weighted his results in favor of the "escape" motive even before he collected his data.

individual differences and leisure needs

In a different approach, Tinsley, Barrett and Kass (1977) asked college students to rate each of five popular leisure activities in terms of their importance in relation to 45 predetermined leisure needs. The results showed that 42 needs were specific to leisure activities, indicating that different activities were per-ceived to satisfy the same need to a different degree, and that the same activity was perceived to satisfy different needs. For example, bicycling was highly rated in response to the needs called independence, catharsis, and ability-utilization. Or considered the other way, reading, bicycling, attending plays, concerts and lectures, and drinking and socializing were perceived to satisfy the "ability-utilization" need to a relatively high degree; bicycling and drinking (and socializ-ing) were expected to do the same for the "catharsis" need.

In a design which is much better conceptually, London, Crandall and Fitzgibbons (1977) not only considered activities and the needs they satisfy but also individual differences in the degree to which various activities are perceived to satisfy given needs. The results showed that subjects (college students) per-ceived leisure activities in terms of three basic need dimensions: (1) the extent to which they provide "feedback" about one's competence, (2) the degree of one's "liking" to perform the activity, and (3) "positive interpersonal involvement." These findings lend considerable support to the concept of intrinsic motivation underlying leisure behavior. Because the "leisure needs" statements, like those provided by Tinsley, *et al.* (1977), overlap considerably, leisure motivation can best be explained by using such a terse concept as intrinsic motivation.

As shown in table 1, London's *et al.* (1977) data also revealed individual differences in perceptions of leisure activities and their need-satisfying qualities. Leisure activities clustered in three groups labeled as "productive-intellectual," "sports," and "cultural-passive." Based upon their responses, subjects could be divided into three groups of individuals who perceived the activity dimensions differently in terms of their need-satisfying qualities. For example, one group (I) could be categorized as individuals who perceived sports and productive-intellectual activities as high in "feedback" but viewed all activities as low in "positive interpersonal involvement;" they also "liked" all leisure activities. Another group of individuals (III) was similar to the above except that they

Table 1

Relationships Among Leisure Activity Dimensions,
Leisure Need Categories and Individuals

Groups of Individuals	Activity Dimensions	Need Categories		
		Feedback	Liking	PID*
I	Sports	60.1	45.5	9.9
	Cultural-Passive	−53.2	58.0	−16.4
	Productive-Intellectual	59.9	38.3	−34.5
II	Sports	−17.1	37.0	−35.4
	Cultural-Passive	−94.3	25.3	−66.1
	Productive-Intellectual	− 8.1	8.9	−86.4
III	Sports	77.2	65.8	64.0
	Cultural-Passive	−47.7	40.6	−14.9
	Productive-Intellectual	61.3	29.4	−10.9

*Positive Interpersonal Development

Note: Numbers represent factor scores derived from a three-mode factor analysis. The more positive the score, the higher the ratings made by the individuals on the need categories for the activity dimension.

Source: Manuel London, Rick Crandall and Dale Fitzgibbons, "The Psychological Structure of Leisure: Activities, Needs, and People." *Journal of Leisure Research,* 1977, 9, 252–263. Copyright © 1977 by the National Recreation and Park Association. Reprinted by permission of the National Recreation and Park Association.

perceived sports as high in positive interpersonal involvement. In short, the first group was clearly competence-seeking while the second was seeking both competence and social interaction. Still another group (II) was characterized by individuals whose liking for all activities was relatively low, who saw all activities as low both in feedback and positive interpersonal involvement.

The London, *et al.* study is important in several respects. It clearly demonstrates that people do not walk with 45 leisure needs in their minds from which, all of sudden, they extract such obscure need dimensions as "deference" (for these, see Tinsley, *et al.,* 1977) before participating. Rather, leisure needs tend to cluster together in people's thinking; this can perhaps most concisely be described as intrinsic motivation. While feelings of competence and self-determination (and thus enjoyment) are common to everyone's intrinsic motivation, individuals differ in the degree to which they view these elements as important to their leisure involvement. They also differ in terms of activities through which these feelings are sought and in the degree of social interaction desired. For example, the London, *et al.* findings demonstrated that one group of individuals regarded sports as primarily competence-producing, another group viewed them as both competence-producing and social interaction-involving, and yet another group saw them as low in both aspects. Although the London, *et al.* study was done on college students, similar results have been obtained when testing other subject populations as well (e.g., McKechnie, 1974; Ritchie, 1975). McKechnie's study, for example, produced such competence-oriented factors as mechanics, crafts, intellectual, and neighborhood and glamour sports.

Finally, one should note the practical importance of London's, *et al.* findings. To provide leisure services that best satisfy most people's intrinsic motivation, it is essential to acquire information about how well a given recreation program meets the intrinsic leisure needs of those surveyed. Simply asking people to state their leisure preferences, as is conventionally done, is insufficient. For example, two groups of individuals may express strong preferences for playing volleyball but they may differ considerably in the reasons for participation. One group of players may be primarily interested in volleyball because of the accompanying feelings of competence. If so, they are likely to want feedback about their performance in the form of a competitive league. The other group may be interested in volleyball mainly because of positive social interaction involved, preferring less competitive and more informal games. It would, therefore, be a mistake to mix these two groups of individuals when organizing volleyball games. In many recreation centers the only method of evaluating the effectiveness of various programs has been to keep statistics on participants in terms of their demographic (e.g., sex, age) qualities. In the light of the studies reviewed above, such practice is inadequate for designing and providing leisure services.

social interaction as a leisure need

As pointed out earlier, intrinsically motivated leisure behavior often takes place in social contexts. This is possible because (1) many leisure activities are so structured that they require the presence of others, and (2) many people define their perceived competence in terms of interpersonal competence. Therefore, social interaction can be both a cause and an effect of leisure involvement. Empirical evidence in favor of social interaction as a leisure motive is strong and unambiguous. Somewhat depending on the population studied and the way in which social interaction is operationalized in past studies, this variable reportedly emerges as one of the leading reasons for leisure participation when subjects are given a list of leisure motives from which to select.

As discussed above, London, *et al.* (1977) found positive interpersonal involvement (e.g., developing close friendships, cooperating with other people) to be one of the three basic dimensions of leisure needs. Other factor analytical studies (e.g., Ritchie, 1975) have also shown that social leisure is one of the key dimensions of leisure participation. Kelly's (1976) data revealed that the "relational" category was the second most important group of reasons for leisure participation; "enjoy the companions" and "it strengthens relationships" were the two most important items under the category of "relational." The subjects of the study by Neulinger and Raps (1972) ranked affiliation ("chance to be with others, meet new people and cooperate with others") as the most important category of leisure involvement.

Even if social interaction is not ranked as *the* most important reason for leisure involvement, it nevertheless is considered an important one. This is clearly evident in Grupp's (1975) data, which revealed that 76% of the assembly line workers interviewed rated the reason, "it allows me to be with people I like," as very important or important for participation in their favorite leisure activity. At the same time, however, this motive was ranked no better than the fifth most important among other motives. Rather obviously, social interaction is rated as an unimportant leisure motive when a person participates in an activity (e.g., hiking) to avoid social contacts. Knopp (1972), for example, reported that solitude was one of the leading motives of participation in outdoor recreation for urban residents, whereas social interaction served the same function for people in rural farm areas. While social interaction is an essential part of everyone's leisure experience throughout the life span, it seems to be particularly critical to the elderly. Thus, it has been demonstrated (Graney, 1975; Schulz, 1976) that physical and psychological well-being of old persons depends on their opportunities for social interaction.

Crandall (1978) reviewed past research on social interaction and reported some relevant data. On the basis of his review, he concluded that "the case for the importance of social leisure based on the literature is a strong one." He also reported data which comprised two large samples, one of them being a national probability sample. These studies explored the relationship between social leisure and total leisure experience. This was done by correlating subjects' affective ratings of various aspects of leisure. Although the correlations were generally smaller in the national sample, a similar pattern of results emerged in the two reports. It appeared that the items designed to estimate social leisure were related to total leisure (median = .35) about as closely as items measuring other aspects of leisure. The social item that was correlated more highly to total leisure feelings than other items was: "the feelings about things you do and the times you have with your friends."

An important finding was that the subjects' feelings about the social aspects of leisure were equally as or even more important than such often-stressed aspects as feelings about sports and recreation facilities. This implies that people are as much (if not more) concerned about social interaction during their leisure participation as they are about recreational facilities. Yet the main emphasis is still placed upon facility management when leisure services are provided.

The only item that was as important as "things done with friends" was "the feeling about the amount of time you have for doing the things you want to do." Since "things done with friends" was the best social item, Crandall concluded that the best leisure activities seem to be those that involve both friendly interaction *and* an activity. Consistent with this conclusion, Wheeler and Nezlek (1977) found that the most predominant interaction for both males and females (college students) was with one person of the same sex, and that the bulk of social interaction fell into the activity category labeled *conversation*. On the above basis, it appears that if a leisure activity which is expected to bring about feelings of interpersonal competence provides avenues for social interaction, then social interaction is rated as an important motive for leisure involvement. Needless to say, things done with friends very often provide feelings of interpersonal competence. These feelings are an integral part of intrinsic leisure motivation.

The above findings about the importance of social interaction have far-reaching implications for the practice of the recreation profession. Typically, practitioners have been concerned with people's feelings about sport and recreation facilities, the idea being that if good facilities are provided then leisure feelings have been taken care of. Unfortunately, this mentality has spread even to academic circles, to the extent that the first and most important courses in recreation curricula around the country are those involving recreation and park facility management, administration, and courses of similar kind. Yet, the above results persuasively imply that enhancement and maintenance of intrinsic leisure motivation should be the chief target of recreation management. Inevitably, this calls for social psychological analysis of leisure and recreation behavior, which should become the focal point of leisure studies in the academic departments. Only then can we expect changes in the field. *The management of intrinsic leisure motivation* requires that both academicians and practitioners investigate how to facilitate the service recipients' feelings of self-determination and competence.[1]

As was seen, social interaction and interpersonal competence constitute an essential part of this process. Crandall's (1978) findings clearly point out that practitioners ought to pay at least as much attention to improving social interaction among leisure participants as to improving physical facilities and other nonsocial aspects of involvement. It is contended by this writer that instead of focusing on activities, professionals and practitioners should exert major effort on finding out how various facilities and programs could be changed and reorganized so that they would encourage and support social interaction. In addition, practitioners should know *why* people participate in their programs. The London, *et al.* (1977) study clearly suggested that those persons who are compatible in their leisure needs and activities should be grouped together. The practitioners' task, therefore, goes far beyond the usual cafeteria-style approach of providing standard activities and facilities and keeping simple statistics of participants' characteristics.

new directions for research on leisure needs

It appears that the above evidence is unambiguous in suggesting that future research should be carried out in the proposed theoretical framework of intrinsic leisure motivation. When researchers embark on this task, several principles should be kept in mind. The foremost of these is the *dialectical* nature of human leisure behavior. That is, if people change so do their leisure needs. All past research, however, is based upon the assumption that leisure needs are static. As

---

[1]By way of criticism one could ask: How do you manage something which is intrinsic? Although this may look like a contradiction in terms, such is not the case, because the management of intrinsic leisure motivation involves facilitation of people's acquiring of intrinsic rewards through leisure participation. Thus, practitioners should be concerned with the enhancement of perceived recreational freedom (chapter 9), perceived competence (chapter 10), social interaction and other intrinsic rewards. Clearly, such management is possible and urgently needed. At the same time, however, it should be emphasized that those who are responsible for the management of intrinsic leisure motivation have to understand that this process is a subtle one, that is, external intervention and influence can easily turn leisure into work. But a difficult task should not be confused with the impossible one. In short, although a new term is coined, much more is involved than re-phrasing cliches. One of the purposes of this entire book is to offer the principles for the management of intrinsic leisure motivation.

noted (Part 4), such an assumption is grossly invalid because human behavior (and, thus, "leisure needs") is dynamic. A person's leisure needs may change in several respects:

1. *Change over time across the life span.* For example, a person in the teens may play golf for competitive reasons (i.e., to be competent in the eyes of others) and may be little interested in social company. But when age 50 years is reached, the principal motive for playing golf may no longer be competition, but rather feelings of mastering a skill, social interaction, or physical exercise. Thus, perceptions of leisure activities and their need-satisfying properties change across the several stages of life, the change occurring both between and within activities.

   Some "needs" become more salient while others decrease in their subjective value with age. For example, it is common that as people grow older they become more concerned about their physical well-being and consequently add physical exercise to the repertoire of their leisure needs. Although the scope of leisure needs may change over a period of time, there is one thing common to all newly-added or strengthened "needs": they (e.g., physical exercise) are pursued in leisure activities which are expected to provide feelings of self-determination and competence. In short, they are intrinsically motivated. Finally, when leisure needs are studied it should be realized that change can occur not only across the major life stages but also within a given stage, which may be a short period of time.

2. *Change across persons and places.* When a person moves to a new community, the entire pattern of leisure needs may change, depending on the individuals associated with and recreation facilities available. Within one's leisure need repertoire some needs may be added or strengthened, others dropped or weakened.

3. *Change across situations.* This aspect of change in needs has two elements: (1) *Improvised Leisure Needs* and (2) *A Priori—A Posteriori Needs.* Improvised Leisure Needs refers to the situational or social factors that influence a person to participate in an activity without planned reasons. For example, in the midst of work an executive looks through the window, sees beautiful weather and sunshine outside, and immediately decides to spend the rest of the afternoon playing golf. Or, following a long and tiring examination several students decide to go and drink beer rather than attending the next class.

   Most improvised leisure needs are not new but are based on existing needs. The executive, for example, may play golf regularly (i.e., to exercise), even though a decision to do so had not been made the day when the beautiful weather or the need for exercise suddenly appeared. Of course, the improvised leisure needs may be directed toward activities which take place in novel physical and social settings. In the above case, the students might have decided to go and drink beer in a tavern where they do not usually go.

Improvised leisure needs often interfere with leisure behavior planned on the basis of stable leisure needs. For example, a person may have made a commitment to attend a party several days ahead because of a desire for social interaction. When it is time to leave for the party, the party goer may be mentally or physically tired due to the requirements of daily activities so that the participant would much rather do something else than spend the evening at a social party. Successful recreation programs not only consider people's stable leisure needs but also provide opportunities for them to satisfy improvised leisure needs. As an example, "challenge courts" for playing tennis and racquetball serve that function in many university settings. It remains the task of future research to show how vital the gratification of such improvised leisure needs is to one's psychological well-being, in comparison to the gratification of stable leisure needs.

The other aspect of the principle of "change across situations" involves change in leisure needs from *before* to *after* participation. An individual's primary reason for going to symphony concerts may be appreciation (i.e., understanding) of the music; but when one meets good friends there with whom one has enjoyable interaction, the need for social contact via concerts may increase considerably. In other words, if the person is asked before the concert why attendance is planned, social interaction may receive a low rating, but if the same question is asked afterwards, the result might be very different. In short, leisure needs vary, depending on whether people are interviewed before, during, or after participation. These other reasons (e.g., interaction) are likely to become much more salient when the primary need (liking of the music) is not satisfied by participation (e.g., the orchestra is thought to play badly).

Of course, this also works the other way around. That is, the person's liking and understanding of the music as a motive to attend the concerts probably increases with the excellence of the orchestra performance. A person's judgment of how well the orchestra performed in turn is affected by others' appraisal of it (e.g., standing ovation). Similar examples can be found in other recreation activities. Consider a tennis player enrolled in a men's singles tournament who, before the game, informs an interviewer that he plays because he feels he is relatively good at tennis. But after losing several games, he may tell the interviewer that he actually does it because of physical exercise. Such change in the expressed leisure needs is self-serving and may be important for one's self-concept.

Finally, it should be noted that the a priori reasons also change. That is, one day a person may say that he plays primarily for physical exercise, the next day the reason may be for social interaction, etc. This follows from the principle of improvised leisure needs, which in turn has its psychological basis in the need for optimal incongruity. Whether current recreation programs provide adequate opportunities for such sudden changes in leisure needs should be examined.

Finally, there is a question about the origin of leisure needs. It was argued above that intrinsic motivation is the underlying motive of all leisure (but not free-time) behavior, that reasons like "escape," "relaxation" and "being with friends" are popular expressions of this fundamental tendency. What becomes intrinsically motivated is determined through the socialization process; a person learns competencies and what sort of leisure activities are compatible with his perceived capacities. It is for this reason that an individual does not have to go through a list of 45 leisure needs before deciding to participate in a given activity. Insofar as an activity is perceived (expected) to provide feelings of self-determination and competence it fulfills the principal criteria of intrinsic motivation, and therefore constitutes the basis for meeting such popular "leisure needs" as relaxation and escape. It should be emphasized that no matter what need a person expresses as the important cause of leisure participation, he is not able to satisfy it in activities he dislikes, because such activities do not produce feelings of self-determination and competence. This is why some people seek escape and relaxation in hunting while others turn to arts and crafts.

are "leisure needs" nothing but culturally learned stereotypes?

On the above basis, it is inferred that people do not rationalize to themselves before their leisure participation why they decide to get involved; they do not go through Tinsley's, *et al*. (1977) list of 45 leisure needs to decide why they should play tennis today. (In fact, such review would be cognitively impossible, because research indicates that an individual is capable of attending to or processing only five to nine pieces of information at a time; Miller, 1956). This, of course, does not mean that a person does not have a priori reasons for leisure participation, but that they are concealed in intrinsically motivated leisure, which one does not have to consciously repeat. Besides, due to the cognitive limitations in information processing a person has to group leisure needs in the mind as a coherent package with only a few underlying dimensions.

When intrinsic leisure motivation is violated or when the person is asked (e.g., by a researcher) to describe them, the participant becomes immediately aware of the a priori reasons. Typically, researchers provide subjects with a list of motivational statements and ask them to rate each "need" in terms of its importance for participation in various leisure activities. But what are those motivational statements of leisure needs? Are they nothing but cultural labels often used by others to describe their participation? In the light of Nisbett and Wilson's (1977) conclusions, the answer is affirmative. They stated that when people are asked to make judgments about causality they first resort to culturally supplied explanations for the behavior in question. A person's culture and subculture provide explicit rules and implicit theories about causal relationships. Nisbett and Wilson (1977) gave the following example. If we ask a person why a particular party was enjoyed and the answer was "I liked the people at the party," the question is then how the conclusion was reached. According to Nisbett and Wilson, the person first thought *Why People In General Enjoy Parties*.

By relying on culturally furnished rules or theories the individual decides that individuals generally like parties if people at the party are likable. This, then, forms the basis of the response to the question why the participant enjoyed the party. Nisbett and Wilson (1977) suggested that such responses are more stereotypical (i.e., culturally supplied explanations), the more they are removed in time from actual participation.

Looking at it from the standpoint of intrinsic motivation, the reader will probably not quarrel with the Nisbett and Wilson conclusion. The prime mover of leisure behavior is intrinsic motivation, and "leisure needs" statements are popular ways of tapping this fundamental force. For example, when a woman is asked why she went hiking in a wilderness, the response ("solitude" and "escape from routine") may be strongly shaped by cultural explanations of why people generally hike. However, it would be misleading to state that these responses always and merely reflect typical stereotypes and thereby are inaccurate. For example, in an earlier case in which the executive improvised and played golf in the afternoon, one would probably have gotten a stereotypical answer (exercise, relaxation, etc.) if asked for the reason. The point, however, is that at this time the response might have been quite accurate, reflecting basic leisure needs: intrinsic motivation and optimal incongruity or arousal. It remains to be determined when the expressed leisure needs are accurate indicators of underlying leisure motivation and when they simply mirror cultural explanations. The idea of improvised leisure needs may prove a good starting-point.

summary

The chapter began by illustrating the levels of causality needed to explain the "whys" of leisure behavior. It was shown that the most fundamental motivator of leisure participation is a need for optimal incongruity or arousal, as determined by biological dispositions, early socialization experiences, and social/situational influences. Intrinsic motivation, however, more specifically regulates leisure encounters. A more superficial level of analysis consists of attempts to determine people's "leisure needs" by asking them to indicate how important such popular reasons as "escape" and "relaxation" are for their participation in various activities. The discussion proceeded to examine motivation as a psychological construct and concluded that it is in essence socially determined. It was inferred that intrinsic motivation provides the best theoretical framework for understanding the motivational basis of leisure behavior. It was argued that the best leisure activities are those which are performed for their own sake, because they offer such intrinsic rewards as feelings of self-determination and competence.

Maslow's need hierarchy theory was next presented and discussed in relation to intrinsic motivation. Research has shown that high-order and low-order needs form their own clusters. An individual's desire to do what he wants and is capable of doing is characteristic of higher-order needs. Intrinsically motivated leisure equals "self-actualizing" leisure. Intrinsically motivated behavior, however, is not free of social influences, since most leisure behavior takes place in social contexts and is directed at social recreational activities. The social nature of leisure motivation is also manifested in behavior prompted by normative and comparative recreation needs.

Research has shown that reasons intrinsic to the activity dominate subjects' leisure choices. Studies have also revealed that various "leisure needs" tend to cluster together in people's thinking about the causes of their leisure behavior, which can best be described as intrinsic motivation. Individuals, however, differ in terms of the activities through which feelings of competence and self-determination (intrinsic motivation) are sought, and in the degree of social interaction desired. Past research has provided evidence that the best activities are those that involve both friendly interaction *and* an activity, thereby implying that social interaction is rated an important motive for leisure participation if it is expected to provide feelings of interpersonal competence. "Things done with friends" is a major source of such feelings and thus an important contributor to the perception of intrinsic leisure motivation. The observation that feelings about social interaction are equally or even more important than feelings about sport and recreation facilities has far-reaching implications for the design of the recreation curricula at universities and for recreation management in practice. These implications were discussed.

The chapter concluded with discussion of new directions for research on leisure needs. It was emphasized that future studies should be done within the theoretical framework of intrinsic leisure motivation when taking into consideration the *dialectical* nature of human behavior. Leisure needs should not be viewed as static and stable but rather as changing qualities. It was shown that leisure needs change with time during the entire life span, and in relation to persons, places, and situations. A distinction was made between the improvised and stable, as well as between the a priori and a posteriori leisure needs. Finally, the question of the origin of leisure needs was considered. It was pointed out that people do not walk with numerous leisure needs in their minds and do not rationalize specific causes of participation if their involvement is intrinsically motivated. There are strong reasons to argue that frequently expressed leisure needs (e.g., escape and relaxation) represent culturally learned stereotypes or explanations for leisure behavior. Sometimes, however, these needs accurately reflect a person's basic motivational force: the need for optimal incongruity as regulated by intrinsic motivation.

12 leisure attitudes

The preceding chapter showed that intrinsic motivation is a basis of leisure behavior. When a leisure activity is performed for its own sake (i.e., for intrinsic rewards) it is said to be intrinsically motivated. Such activities are expected to produce feelings of self-determination and competence. Thus, they are seen potentially high in satisfaction and enjoyment. But when people are asked why they participate in given activities, they seldom, if ever, give answers such as intrinsic motivation, self-determination, and competence. Rather, responses like, "because I like it," "relaxation" and "escape from routine" are common. As noted, these reasons (or "leisure needs") are in part culturally learned labels used to express what were termed intrinsic leisure motivation. Of course, not all such labels are expressions of intrinsic motivation; only those designations that are intrinsic to an activity reflect this basic motivation.

Depending on an individual, some activities give rise to certain labels more readily than do others. For example, activities like hunting and hiking may involve the category "escape from routine" more often than does, say, a social party. What is important is that all such activity-intrinsic labels are different expressions of the same thing, intrinsic motivation.[1] As Kelly (1976) reported, the most frequently offered label (reason) is "because I like it." It is this concept of *liking* that constitutes the core of the present chapter. Liking, or feeling, or affect is the heart of the construct called "attitude." A positive leisure attitude toward an activity is interpreted as an aspect or a special case of intrinsic leisure motivation. That is, a person who is engaged in an activity for intrinsic rewards

[1]This, of course, is not to say that all free-time activities are motivated by intrinsic rewards, but merely to state that the two most fundamental intrinsic rewards (feelings of self-determination and competence) of leisure participation can be expressed by different (culturally learned) labels such as liking, relaxation, escape, etc. As was seen earlier, activities that provide feelings of self-determination (or freedom) and competence are likely to be most enjoyable.

also has a positive attitude toward that activity. On the other hand, a positive attitude toward an activity does not necessarily mean that the individual will actually participate in it, though participation is likely. The chapter begins by discussing attitude as a psychological construct, and continues by focusing on attitude formation and attitude change. It concludes by examining the attitude-behavior relationship.

Allport (1969) stated that attitude is "the most distinctive and indispensable concept in contemporary American social psychology." Just by looking at the contents of the leading journals it is easy to understand why Allport made his famous statement. Amid an incredible volume of attitude studies it is hardly surprising that a diversity of attitude definitions exists. Fishbein and Ajzen (1975) found that research published within three years (1968–1970) alone was based on 500 different operations of attitude measurements, including standard scales (e.g., Likert, semantic differential); various indices; single statements of feelings, opinions, knowledge, or intentions; observations of overt behaviors; and physiological measures. Therefore, Fishbein and Ajzen's report that 70% of recent studies (using more than one attitude measure) produced different results is hardly surprising.

attitude as a psychological construct

Despite a lack of agreement concerning the conceptual and operational definitions of attitude, most researchers agree that attitude is "a learned predisposition to respond in a consistently favorable or unfavorable manner with respect to a given object" (Fishbein and Ajzen, 1975, p. 6). To some researchers (e.g., Triandis, 1971, p. 3), the definition of attitude consists of three components: (1) cognitive, (2) affective, and (3) behavioral. The cognitive component refers to a certain general category (i.e., belief or idea) which is a part of the human thinking process; leisure can be such a category. The affective component denotes emotions or feelings expressed toward the category, its degree varying from positive to negative. The behavioral component refers to a predisposition toward action, like participating in a leisure activity.

definition

At a general level, then, attitude is a product of one's past learned experiences. Attitude predisposes to action, and if this action materializes it is consistently favorable or unfavorable toward an object (Fishbein and Ajzen, 1975). Of these three components, the affective one stands out as it distinguishes attitude from other related concepts. When applying the Fishbein and Ajzen conceptualization one may broadly define a *leisure attitude as the expressed amount of affect toward a given leisure-related object*. Although this definition emphasizes the "affect" component, it does not preclude the cognitive and behavioral components, as will be seen. The object of an attitude can be leisure itself or some of its components like a leisure behavior, a leisure activity, a person or a group participating in leisure activities, a leisure program or policy, and a place where leisure participation takes place. Thus, a leisure attitude can be both general and specific, depending on how the object is defined.

beliefs, intentions, and behaviors

Fishbein and Ajzen (1975) distinguished attitude from beliefs, intentions, and behaviors. While attitude refers to "affect," belief is used to describe the information a person has about an object. Belief is therefore similar to the term "cognition." Individuals differ in "belief strength," which indicates the perceived probability of the relationship between an object and an attribute. For example, the following is a belief, because it links an object (recreation program) with some attributes (good): "The Iowa City recreation program is good." However, not everyone agrees with this statement. People differ in the extent to which this belief is perceived to be true, as reflected by such everyday expressions as "I believe so," and "I think so." The concept "intention," sometimes called conation, simply refers to one's intention to perform various acts, like an intention to attend a concert tomorrow. Again, individuals differ in terms of the strength of intention to participate in leisure activities. This strength is equal to a subjective likelihood of performing a given behavior. Finally, behavior refers to an observed overt action. To understand attitude formation and change as well as the relationship between behavior and attitudes, it is therefore useful to distinguish between beliefs, attitudes, intentions, and behaviors.

Fishbein and Ajzen maintain that beliefs constitute a person's informational base and are therefore the fundamental "building blocks" which determine a person's attitudes, intentions, and behavior. They emphasize that attitudes do not predispose the person to engage in any specific behavior, because they are related to a *general* behavior *pattern*. If the purpose here is to predict participation in a specific leisure activity, the prediction should be made from intentions to engage in it rather than from an attitude toward that leisure activity. To make an accurate behavioral prediction, it is essential that intentions are measured at the same level as behavior. In other words, if the purpose is to predict whether a person will go to a specific movie at a specific time it is imperative to measure intention with respect to that particular movie and that particular time, not intention to attend movies in general. If this requirement is met, intentions are good predictors of behavior. Those intentions which are formed in close temporal proximity to the onset of behavior are the best predictors of the behavior. For example, it is known that the Gallup Poll prediction about the outcome of the election of political candidates improves as the voting time draws near. Based upon Fishbein and Ajzen's reasoning, one may conclude that if the purpose is to *predict* leisure behavior one should focus on measuring intentions, but if the objective is to *understand* leisure behavior, then efforts should be expended on studying factors which affect intentions.

According to the above conceptualization, intention toward an object is determined by a person's attitude toward that object, which in turn is a result of beliefs about the object. Various antecedents (e.g., situational and social influences, past experiences and individual differences) in turn give rise to beliefs. This chain of events is presented in figure 18 (adapted from Fishbein and Ajzen, 1975). Based upon past experiences and situational influences (e.g., advertisement), a person develops beliefs about the consequences of attending a symphony concert and about other things (e.g., crowded conditions) associated with

Figure 18   Conceptualization of leisure attitude. (Adapted from Fishbein and Ajzen, 1975.)

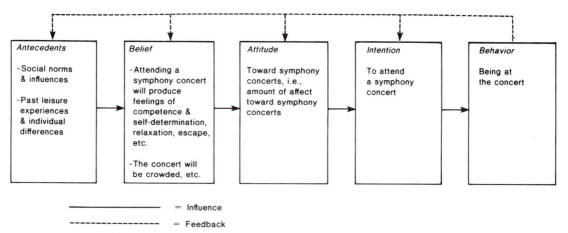

the attendance. While a person may hold several beliefs about a symphony concert, the attitude toward the concert is based upon only a few salient beliefs. Since activity-intrinsic characteristics (e.g., escape from routine in the case of wilderness hiking) are conspicuous consequences of participation, these intrinsic rewards associated with an activity become salient beliefs about an object. If the person has reason to believe that participation in a leisure activity will lead to intrinsic rewards, then the attitude toward that activity is highly positive.

Sometimes, however, other beliefs affect salient beliefs and thus mold attitudes. Consider a person who is told that Yellowstone is supposed to be very crowded at the time of a proposed visit there. Since the visitor expects to find relaxation and escape from routine while hiking in the national park, it may now be reasonable to believe these outcomes cannot be achieved. Consequently, the attitude toward Yellowstone becomes much more negative when compared to the attitude before obtaining knowledge of its crowded condition. This, of course, need not permanently change the attitude toward *hiking;* the hiker may still expect to achieve relaxation and escape from routine when hiking, though not in Yellowstone. Fishbein and Ajzen (1975) noted that in general, beliefs about the consequences of participation or about a person vary considerably. If beliefs vary, so also do attitudes and intentions. As a final note, it should be emphasized that the aforementioned conceptualization is dynamic, in that it takes into account change in human behavior. Participation in a leisure activity affects the person's experience, which in turn influences beliefs. Participation can also directly affect beliefs, attitudes, and intentions.

In everyday language attitudes are expressed by such statements as "I like swimming," "I hate symphony concerts," "I love movies." These attitudes are based on a few salient beliefs we hold about swimming, symphony concerts, movies, etc. Without beliefs attitudes cannot be formed. Occasionally someone

formation of leisure attitudes

says, "I don't like to make judgments before I know more about the case." In other words, the person has not formed an attitude toward the object (person), because information about the object is lacking. The informational base is low due to the absence of salient beliefs about the object. But as soon as one forms or acquires beliefs about the object, he simultaneously forms an attitude toward it (Fishbein and Ajzen, 1975). This follows because each belief links an object (swimming pool) to some attribute (crowded).

A person may ask a friend whether he likes to swim in the pool at the city park. The friend may answer: "Well, I don't know, I have not been there." In other words, the friend is not able to form an attitude toward the swimming pool because of lack of information about what attributes are associated with it. In the mind of the friend, however, there are certain attributes which are relevant to attitudes about swimming pools and which have been evaluated in positive terms. For example, the friend generally evaluates crowded conditions negatively and good-looking girls positively. But because he does not know whether the city swimming pool is crowded and whether there are good-looking girls he is not able to form an attitude toward the pool. However, when he is told, or he finds out by himself, that the pool is not particularly crowded and has a lot of good-looking girls (i.e., the connection between the object and attributes is made), he simultaneously forms an attitude toward the pool, which in this case, is presumably a positive one.

a theory of attitude The above examples illustrate that at least two things should be considered when people's attitudes are examined: (1) belief strength indicating the subjective likelihood that an object has certain attributes, and (2) general evaluation of these attributes. This follows from Fishbein's theory of attitudes (Fishbein and Ajzen, 1975, p. 29):

$$Ao = \sum_{i=1}^{n} b_i e_i, \text{ where } A = \text{attitude toward some object O}$$

$$B = \text{belief i about O}$$
$$e = \text{evaluation of attribute i}$$
$$n = \text{number of beliefs}$$

In other words, a person's attitude toward any object is a function of belief (belief strength) about the object's attributes and a personal evaluation of these attributes. According to the above formula, an attitude can be numerically computed by multiplying a person's evaluation of each attribute by subjective probability that the object has the attributes in question. Then, the products are simply summed up. An example illustrates this. Assume that one is interested in residents' attitudes toward the city's recreation program developed by the municipal recreation center. Then compute a girl's attitude toward the recreation program. (Of course, the same should be done for everyone in this probability sample, in order to determine the attitude of an entire community.) For the sake of simplicity, assume that through a questionnaire, information has been obtained about four attributes. Her attitude could be computed as follows:

Attribute	Belief Strength (b)	Evaluation (e)	be
Variety of activities available	.80	+4	3.20
Good facilities	.60	+3	1.80
Competent personnel	.60	+2	1.20
Limited access to various activities	.90	−4	−3.60

$$Ao = \sum b_i e_i = +2.60$$

On the whole, the girl had a positive attitude toward the city's recreation program. She held four beliefs, and these varied in the extent to which she perceived them to be true: (1) the recreation program has a variety of activities available, (2) it has good facilities, (3) its personnel are competent, and (4) due to a great number of participants, there is limited access to various activities of the program. Sample residents were asked to indicate on a scale from +5 to −5 how high they generally evaluate each attribute without reference to the city program. Similarly they were asked, on a scale from .00 to 1.00, to rate how likely it is that the recreation program possesses each attribute. By simply multiplying each belief strength by the appropriate attribute evaluation one obtains a product for each belief. By adding the products for the total set of beliefs one determines her attitude, numerically expressed as +2.60. This value indicates that her attitude toward the recreation program is positive. In a similar vein, the observer would have calculated each sample resident's attitude. By averaging them one could arrive at the attitude of the total community. If desired, the researcher could have compared males' and females' attitudes, the attitudes of people from various occupations, or the attitudes of those who have used the services of the program frequently and those who have used them seldom. Thus, the principal value of the above formula is that it provides a good quantitative measure for comparing leisure attitudes of different groups of leisure participants, rather than for making precise predictions about leisure attitudes.

belief formation

The above examples illustrate that attitudes are formed immediately at the time when a person learns that an object (recreation program) is linked to a certain attribute (variety of activities). But how does a person make these links and what makes one connect objects with attributes? As derived from the model (p. 185), it can be stated that there are two major sources of belief formation: (1) situational/social influences, and (2) personal past experiences. This distinction can be specified by considering the types of beliefs. Fishbein and Ajzen (1975) suggested three kinds of belief: (1) informational, (2) descriptive, and (3) inferential.

When beliefs are formed on the basis of externally provided information they are called "informational." For example, by reading newspapers and magazines or by watching television a person acquires information about Disneyland and subsequently may decide to spend a vacation there next year. Descriptive beliefs refer to directly observable relationships. For example, when a person goes to the city's recreation center and sees its sports facilities, such direct experiences lead to the formation of descriptive beliefs about the recreation program. Finally, beliefs can be formed, without outside sources and without direct observations, by making logical inferences. Such inferential beliefs may utilize the rules of logic or may simply be based on culturally provided explanations. For instance, swimming pools are often expected to be crowded; a person who jogs regularly is assumed to be fit, etc. An example of the use of a simple logical rule (deductive reasoning) could be as follows: the recreation program in Iowa City has a greater variety of activities than that in Charles City, which in turn has a greater variety than the program in Solon. The person could make an inference that the variety is greater in Iowa City than in Solon. Fishbein and Ajzen (1975) noted that most inferences are based upon descriptive beliefs. For further discussion of the relationship between the rules of logic and belief information, see Wyer, 1974.

Beliefs differ not only in terms of how they are formed but also how long they endure. Beliefs about social institutions tend to be relatively stable; institutions include such concepts as democracy, capitalism, church, school. On the other hand, beliefs about consequences of behavior and about persons are quite unstable (Fishbein and Ajzen, 1975). This, then, implies that beliefs about leisure activities may vary considerably. These are commonly evaluated in terms of consequences of participation. As illustrated earlier, a person may generally expect to feel solitude when hiking. But twenty years later the same hiker may primarily expect physical exercise from hiking. This evaluation of consequences may even vary from time to time. One day a person may think that participation provides social interaction, the next day solitude, then relaxation and escape, etc. If evaluations of consequences vary, so do beliefs and attitudes. On the other hand, beliefs about the recreation programs are likely to be relatively stable, since recreation centers and their programs are like institutions. The same probably holds true for the beliefs about the total leisure.

developmental approach to belief formation

The above demonstrated that personal experiences play an important part in belief formation (descriptive beliefs). Previously (Part 4), evidence was presented indicating that early childhood recreation experiences set the stage for one's basic orientation toward leisure. Thus, how a person evaluates the consequences of leisure involvement and what one expects from leisure participation are notably affected by early recreation experiences. It has been demonstrated that if a person learns to derive satisfaction from active leisure pursuits in the early years, psychological adjustment is greater in later years than if satisfaction is derived from passive pursuits (Brooks and Elliott, 1971). In a similar vein, Neulinger (1974) has discussed attitude formation in terms of developmental stages from childhood to adolescence. Based on Maier's work, he divided child development into five phases and speculated about the importance of each stage to the formation of leisure attitudes (pp. 117–120):

Phase	Years	Overall Theme	Importance to Formation of Leisure Attitudes
I	1–2	Establishing primary dependence	"Of crucial importance in the development of a basic attitude of openness, optimism and confidence, that allows one to fully experience leisure."
II	2–4	Establishing self-care	"Critical in terms of the amount of energy a person might feel he has available for nonsurvival-related activities."
III	4–8	Establishing meaningful secondary relationships	"The phase when the child develops the attitudes which he will later express in, and which will determine in part, his choice of specific free-time activities."
IV	8–12	Establishing secondary dependence	"Most critical in determining what a person will seek in his job; a means to an end or an end in itself."
V	12–18	Achieving balance between dependence and independence	"The phase during which environmental factors outside the family have their strongest effect on the developing leisure attitudes; it is a period of great changes in leisure attitudes."

For several reasons the reader should view the above theorizing with caution. First, while there is some evidence for the existence of five phases, the ages attributed to each stage have been chosen very arbitrarily. Even if everyone goes through the above stages in the same order, the time when a person reaches each stage varies from individual to individual. Furthermore, the phases are not separate and distinct from each other. That is, a person does not, all of a sudden, jump into the next stage and begin concentrating only on the theme of that stage. For example, the child who is in the second phase not only establishes self-care but also meaningful secondary relationships, secondary dependence, etc.; and the establishment of self-care continues throughout adolescence. The designations simply indicate the general and perhaps dominant aspect of development in each stage.

As to the role of the five phases in the formation of leisure attitudes, Neulinger can be criticized for being too general in his description. Every stage seems to be critical. Following this line of reasoning, one would say that each day is critical in a person's life, with respect to later leisure attitudes. Moreover, asserting that a given stage is crucial in certain respects does not provide any practical advice. For example, how should parents treat their children during the first phase to help them develop a basic attitude of openness, optimism, and confidence? If everything is so critical in the early stages, how is it that in the fifth stage, leisure attitudes change "greatly?" Unquestionably, the above description is highly speculative. In defense of Neulinger, however, it should be noted that in the absence of any empirical test it is difficult to do more than offer general descriptions and speculations. Besides, the above model is not entirely misleading, because it parallels the previous discussion of children's leisure (Part 4) which was based on *empirical* research. Neulinger's description is important, because it shows that a person's basic orientation toward leisure has its roots in childhood recreation experiences. Early experiences increase one's informational base which serves as a foundation for forming descriptive and inferential beliefs.

leisure attitude change

One of the most important questions recreation professionals are frequently faced with concerns attitude change. How to change people's attitudes toward leisure in general and toward a given recreation program in particular? It is often assumed that by being able to change individuals' attitudes it is possible to influence their behavior, improve interpersonal relations, and produce social change (Freedman, Carlsmith and Sears, 1974). Viewed in this light, it is easy to understand why attitude research has become "the most distinctive and indispensable concept in contemporary American social psychology" (Allport). Practically all textbooks on social psychology include chapters dealing with attitude and attitude change. Numerous theoretical frameworks have been developed to account for the psychological mechanisms underlying attitude change.

At present, the writer is convinced that Fishbein and Ajzen's information processing approach best explains attitude change. This conviction is based on the logic of their analysis and the empirical research supporting their model. Their theory is also one which lends itself to practical applications much more readily than does any other theoretical position. Another important theoretical framework is provided by the cognitive consistency models, of which Festinger's (1957) dissonance theory and Heider's (1958) balance theory are the two most prominent. Although support for Festinger's theory is controversial, the theory is reviewed here because it has stimulated a vast amount of research and because it can explain changes in leisure attitudes under some conditions. The bulk of this section, however, follows Fishbein and Ajzen's theorizing.

cognitive consistency

Festinger (1957) proposed that when a person has two opposite cognitions, dissonance exists. Since dissonance is unpleasant, a person is motivated to reduce it; and this tendency is greater, the more dissonance is felt. If the inconsistent cognitions are important, more dissonance is experienced than if these cognitions are unimportant. More dissonance is also aroused as the proportion of dissonant cognitions increases. The level of dissonance can be estimated by the following formula (Sherwood, Barron and Fitch, 1969, p. 58):

$$\text{Dissonance} = \frac{\text{Importance} \times \text{number of dissonant cognitions}}{\text{Importance} \times \text{number of consonant cognitions}}$$

It follows from the above that in theory, dissonance can be decreased by reducing the importance of the dissonant cognitions, by reducing the proportion of dissonant cognitions in relation to the total number of cognitions in a situation, by adding consonant cognitions, and by changing dissonant cognitions into consonant ones.

To illustrate this, consider an example. A person may have two inconsistent cognitions: (1) "I dislike the recreation program of our city" and (2) "I play basketball regularly in a league organized by the city's recreation center." Assuming that these two incongruent elements are important cognitions, the person is in a state of dissonance. To eliminate it by changing one of the dissonant cognitions, the person can either stop playing basketball or start liking the recreation program. If one is fond of basketball, he is unlikely to drop that activity from the preferred leisure repertoire. Consequently, he ends up changing his attitude toward the recreation program, from unfavorable to favorable.

In general, how consistent are our attitudes? Freedman, *et al.* (1974) cited evidence suggesting that on issues dealing with domestic policy, about 80% of the public has unstable and inconsistent attitudes across the policy areas. They also reported that consistency is common in relation to "the early socialized, high commitment attitudes" such as racial and political attitudes. This is parallel to the Fishbein and Ajzen finding, which indicated that beliefs about various institutions are stable. Freedman, *et al.* (1974) further indicated that consistency in attitudes is common if people are highly involved in the issues in question. Finally, educated people generally have more consistent attitudes than the uneducated.

How about leisure attitudes? Unfortunately, no statistics are available about consistency among leisure attitudes. But it is not difficult to find representative examples of inconsistency in this area as well. For instance, people often say that physical exercise is good for them, thereby suggesting that their attitudes toward activities involving physical recreation are favorable. Yet many of them do not participate in any such activities. If they do not change their attitudes or participation patterns, the seemingly dissonant situation can be tolerated by assuring oneself that many people lived to old age without any exercise. Moreover, a neighbor does not seem to be doing any exercise and yet appears to be feeling fine!

Another example can be derived from Festinger's (1957) proposition that following a decision between two or more alternatives dissonance almost always exists. Thus, one might predict that the purchase choice for a camper creates post-decision dissonance, which can be reduced by using the purchased camper intensively (a behavioral justification) or by being highly satisfied with it and by decreasing liking for the camper which was not chosen (a cognitive justification). This is exactly what camper owners seem to be doing (Marquardt, McGann, Ratlift and Routson, 1972). Millions of vacation travelers are faced with post-decision dissonance every summer when choosing their vacation targets. Yet, one seldom hears anybody complaining about the selected route, perhaps because of post-decisional justifications. This, of course, is speculation, since it is difficult to tell when attitude change originates from dissonant cognitions; people differ in the way they reduce dissonance. They also differ in their ability to tolerate dissonance; and what is dissonant for one person may be consonant for someone else (Aronson, 1971).

information
processing
approach

A very different approach to explaining attitude change is provided by the theoretical framework based upon information processing. Implicitly, this approach was already explained in the discussion of attitude formation. In that exposition attitude was said to be a direct function of the evaluation of certain attributes and a few salient beliefs (or belief strengths) that an object (e.g., swimming pool) has given attributes (e.g., crowded). It then follows that in principle, attitudes can be changed by changing salient beliefs or evaluations of the attributes in question (Fishbein and Ajzen, 1975). To change beliefs about an object, one has to first identify the salient ("target") beliefs associated with that object. Based upon Miller's (1956) classic finding that an individual is capable of cognitively handling only five to nine pieces of information at a time, Fishbein and Ajzen (1975) suggested that people hold 5–9 salient beliefs about a given object at the most. These primary beliefs can be identified by asking people to list qualities and attributes about the object or the consequences of participating in a leisure activity. It has been found that using an open-ended (free response) format, people usually express their salient beliefs first.

Once the salient beliefs have been identified they are then chosen as the targets of external attack designed to bring about change in attitudes. To succeed in this, it is imperative that the object of the target (salient) beliefs should be the same as the object of the attitude to be changed. In sum, if one wishes to change a person's attitude toward the city recreation program, one should attempt to change beliefs that the recreation program has certain attributes. For example, the public may believe that their city's recreation center has poor facilities, uncooperative personnel, unmotivated instructors, and offers a narrow range of activities. If these were the salient beliefs, it is obvious that to alter the public's attitude toward the center, recreation personnel should launch a major attack on these target beliefs. Various strategies and techniques exist for making such an attack; they will be discussed a little later. Viewed in the above light, it is easy to see why the information processing approach is considerably more practical than the cognitive dissonance theory for attempts to change the leisure attitudes of other persons.

In addition to attacking beliefs about an object, the Fishbein and Ajzen conceptualization suggests that attitudes can be changed by changing attribute evaluations. For example, a person's attitude toward the city swimming pool may be negative, chiefly because of a belief (salient belief) that it is crowded, which is evaluated rather negatively. In this type of situation it would be unrealistic to try to change a belief that the pool is crowded, because it is in fact crowded and everyone knows it. Instead of attacking the belief that the swimming pool is crowded, it would be better to try to change the evaluation of the attribute "crowded." For example, one might tell the person that a crowd is not so bad at the pool after all, because the number of good-looking girls and boys increases with a crowd. If one changed his evaluation of the attribute "crowded," one would then also change his attitude toward the swimming pool. Notice that by attacking the evaluation of the attribute "crowded," in essence, the critic attacked the belief that crowded (object) possesses certain characteristics. This is why Fishbein and Ajzen noted (p. 398) that "in the final analysis, attitude change involves changing a person's beliefs, whether they are beliefs about the object or beliefs about its attributes."

The above exposition suggests that when recreation professionals and practitioners are planning to change the public's attitude toward leisure—be it total leisure or a specific program and activity—the best overall strategy is to attack people's salient beliefs about the object. But, how should this be done more specifically? Since a vast volume of research has been accumulated relevant to this question, it can be answered quite fully. Rather than reviewing past studies in detail, it is useful to cite the principal conclusion put forth in various sources (e.g., Baron, *et al.*, 1974; Bem, 1970; Fishbein and Ajzen, 1975; Freedman, *et. al.*, 1974; McGuire, 1969; Kiesler, Collins and Miller, 1969; Triandis, 1971; Wyer, 1974; Zimbardo and Ebbesen, 1969). The first factor to be considered is active participation.

strategies of attitude change

It has been shown that, other things being equal, active participation is a more effective method of attitude change than passive exposure to information. This implies that if a practitioner is intent upon improving the public's attitudes toward the program, he should invite them to tour and personally examine the program, its facilities, and the staff. It also follows that those who use services of a given recreation program actively have a more positive attitude toward it than those who do not participate in the program. Implicit in this strategy, then, is the fact that persons acquire new information (i.e., descriptive beliefs) about the program, or they change their prior descriptive beliefs while actively participating. Of course, active participation has to succeed in modifying salient beliefs, if attitude change is to be expected as a result of involvement.

active vs. passive participation

Since people evaluate leisure activities primarily in terms of intrinsic rewards which they are expected to provide, it is therefore important for the practitioners to know what individuals are expecting ("leisure needs" = salient beliefs) from various programs. If the practitioners really want to "sell" their programs, they would do well to organize participants according to the similarity of their "leisure needs," and then attempt to affect their salient beliefs ("needs"). For example, if a group of people is looking for possibilities for social interaction through a recreation program, a practitioner should emphasize and highlight those aspects of the program that provide opportunities for enjoyable social contacts.

The second major strategy of attitude change consists of persuasive communication. Freedman, *et al.* (1974) have suggested that the variables in this category can be described under two general headings: (1) trust in the persuasive message, and (2) the strength of the message itself. It has been found that the more

persuasive communication

trustworthy the persuasive communication appears, the more likely the target person is to accept the message and consequently to change beliefs and attitudes. The source of communication (communicator) may increase this trustworthiness (1) if one is respected or perceived to be an expert, (2) if one is liked, (3) if one is perceived to be honest, intelligent, and well-informed, and (4) if one is like the audience he is addressing (Baron, *et al.*, 1974). Freedman, *et al.* (1974) add to this list one more factor: a reference group. The more highly members value the group to which they belong, the more likely it is that their beliefs are influenced by the group's attitudes. The trustworthiness of communication can be decreased by delivering an extreme or a clearly biased message.

In addition to trustworthiness, the strength of the message increases the persuasiveness of communications. The more powerful the message, the more likely the target person is to accept it and thus to change an attitude. But, how can the message be made powerful? Freedman, *et al.* (1974) reviewed evidence indicating that if arguments are weak and are presented in an unimpressive manner, little change can be expected to occur. Zajonc (1968) reported that "mere repeated exposure" to a message is a sufficient condition to induce attitude change, presumably because it makes the presented communication more powerful. It certainly looks as if television advertising is solely based on this principle!

Other factors should also be considered. Freedman, *et al.* (1974) suggested that two-sided communication is more effective under most conditions than the one-sided message. For example, when a recreation practitioner is selling a program to a group of people who value social interaction highly, the "pitch" would do well to advertise other intrinsic rewards which can be obtained when participating in the program. Two-sided communication is probably advantageous because it makes the communicator appear relatively well-informed, objective, and less obvious in an attempt to persuade the audience (Freedman, *et al.*, 1974).

Other factors that increase the effectiveness of a persuasive communication include various characteristics of information contained in the message. Wyer (1974) has shown that in most circumstances favorable, important (relevant), unambiguous, consistent, and novel information tends to maximize the power of communication to change a person's attitudes. He also noted that when a large amount of information about an unfamiliar object is presented, more attention is directed to the first items of information, and relatively less to later information. The relatively greater influence of the first information is called "primacy effect." For a detailed discussion of these variables, see Wyer, 1974.

Finally, it should be noted that if information arouses fear, under many conditions it tends to increase the power of a persuasive communication (Baron, *et al.*, 1974; Freedman, *et al.*, 1974). The American Cancer Society has used this principle in advertising the deadly effects of smoking (see Freedman, *et al.*, p. 294–295). Recreation practitioners could also make use of this technique by demonstrating to their audience strong evidence of the detrimental effects of lack of stimulating recreational experiences on mental and physical well-being. Conversely, the beneficial impact of physical exercise and social interaction could be shown to be undisputable.

Recently, there has been much discussion of the importance of cocktail lunches to the businessperson. Judging by the anger of businesspeople which was directed against the President's tax proposal, it seems that the tax-deductible business lunch creates an atmosphere in which a partner can be persuaded and good deals made. There is some empirical evidence that a recreational (non-tax deductible?) atmosphere does indeed "soften up" people and make them ready for attitude change.

does a recreational atmosphere facilitate attitude change?

Galizio and Hendrick (1972) performed a study which examined the effects of a relaxed and pleasant atmosphere on persuasion. More specifically, subjects were exposed to the lyrics of four folk songs which were concerned with social issues like water pollution and the mistreatment of mine workers. The experiment was so arranged that the lyrics were either sung or spoken, accompanied by guitar music or not. As predicted, the guitar music facilitated subjects' acceptance of the persuasive communications contained in the songs. Since the guitar music also increased subjects' positive feelings, Galizio and Hendrick (1972) inferred that the arousal of such feelings makes people more susceptible to the intended message, thereby leading to changes in attitudes. These results provide tentative evidence that recreational atmosphere is conducive to attitude change, at least temporarily. As was noted earlier, positive feelings are characteristic of most leisure experiences, implying that recreational atmosphere is common and places for attitude change are therefore many.

Finally, it is necessary to consider some qualities of the audience as factors influencing the effectiveness of persuasive communication. Freedman, et al. (1974) found that it is more difficult to change the attitudes of those who are highly committed to their attitudinal position than of those who are not. Some personality factors have also been found to be associated with attitude change. Freedman, et al. noted that people of high intelligence are less influenced by inconsistent or illogical communication, and are more influenced by complex, difficult messages than are persons of less intelligence. McGuire (1969) proposed that there is an inverted-U-shaped relationship between self-esteem and attitudinal change. In other words, persons with moderate self-esteem are more receptive to persuasive communications and thus, attitude change, whereas persons with either a very low or high self-esteem are the least impressionable. Resistence to persuasion and change can be increased by "innoculating" (McGuire, 1969) persons against persuasive messages, thus increasing their ability to refute, distort and ignore arguments or by forewarning them about the forthcoming exposure to a persuasive communication (Freedman, et al., 1974).

attributes of the audience

As a final note, it should be emphasized that the above strategies do not always guarantee attitude change. They simply increase its probability. For any of these and other possible techniques to be successful it is essential that persuasive communication be directed at the target persons' salient beliefs. It makes little, if any, difference how trustworthy and powerful the source of communication and the message are perceived to be, if the attack is oriented toward remote or irrelevant beliefs. Nevertheless, the above strategies of change provide good suggestions for recreation practitioners and professionals in their efforts to change the public's leisure attitudes and behavior.

persuading people
to be physically
active

An example of the applicability of the above approach was recently reported by Wankel and Thompson (1977). This study examined the effectiveness of various persuasion techniques in motivating people to be physically active during their free-time. Inactive female members of a commercial physical fitness club were randomly divided into three experimental groups and one control group, with the experimental subjects undergoing different treatments during a telephone interview. The age of the subjects ranged from 18 to 62.

One group received phone calls (lasting about 5–8 minutes) normally used by the health club to follow up inactive members, in an effort to find out why they have not utilized the club and then to encourage them to use their membership more often in the future. The second group received telephone calls which asked them to think of and write down the gains and losses expected to result from participating in exercise sessions at the health club; gains and losses were recorded in relation to self and to "significant" others. After completing this "decision-balance-sheet" grid, subjects were asked to read the gain-loss items aloud, to which the experimenter responded with "encouraging positive feedback." At the conclusion of the interview, the subjects were encouraged to utilize the services of the club. The third group received the same treatment as subjects in the decision-balance-sheet group, except that they were asked to think of and record only the positive outcomes (gains, but not losses) expected to result from their participation. The inactive members assigned to the control group received no treatment.

The effects of the above approaches were measured in terms of subjects' attendance over a one month period. The results showed that the attendance of subjects following the decision-balance-sheet procedure and that of subjects following the positive-only condition was significantly greater than the attendance of the control subjects. In addition, the attendance of the positive-outcome-only group was significantly greater than that of the standard follow-up call condition (first group). These results are important in several respects. First, they indicated that the health club's currently used call-up procedure was ineffective. In other words, simply calling people, asking them why they did not attend, and then encouraging them to participate is an ineffective and useless strategy because it does not result in a greater turn-out than the procedure of not calling at all. One explanation for this can be found in the Freedman, *et al*. (1974, p. 289) findings that "stating explicitly a conclusion" is detrimental under many conditions because it makes the intent of persuasion too obvious and apparently reduces the communicator's credibility. They suggested that when the audience is encouraged to reach the conclusion by itself, the effectiveness of a persuasive communication is likely to increase. "Too obvious" persuasion makes a person's behavior overly and externally justified, and as we saw earlier (Part 4), the attribution research on "overjustification" has convincingly shown that the externally attributed behavior loses its qualities of intrinsic motivation.

Thus, it would seem that a cautiously and prudently administered self-persuasion treatment is needed to motivate recreational participation. Wankel and Thompson accomplished this by asking their subjects to think of, record, then report to an interviewer the expected positive outcomes of the participation. That such an externally initiated self-persuasion strategy was effective in bringing about changes in leisure behavior is not surprising in the light of the previous discussion. As noted, beliefs about the consequences of participation in leisure activities amount to the same as intrinsic rewards expected to emanate from leisure behavior. Assuming that intrinsic rewards ("leisure needs") are also salient beliefs, the Wankel and Thompson findings come as no surprise, because the self-persuasion treatment in essence modified the subjects' salient beliefs about the object of engaging in a physical fitness program. The treatment might have been even more effective had two or three most salient beliefs (intrinsic rewards) been distinguished for each individual, and had the experimenter then emphasized that these intrinsic rewards can best be achieved through their physical fitness program.

Because the Wankel and Thompson treatment was not able to persuade everyone to become active again, and because the overall frequency of attendance still remained low among those who resumed the activity, these facts imply that other strategies might also be effective in attacking the subjects' salient beliefs in the context of physical recreation activities. It would, for example, be interesting to know how the use of other techniques (e.g., the arousal of fear for the consequences of not doing any physical exercise) might affect the attendance rate. Zajonc's (1968) finding about the efficacy of "mere repeated exposure" might prove useful in changing inactive members' attitudes and in maintaining continued interest in physical recreation. In sum, Wankel and Thompson's self-persuasion treatment was effective because it did not impair the subjects' intrinsic motivation (i.e., it did not turn internal attributions into external ones), and because it successfully modified (or more appropriately reinforced) their salient beliefs about the consequences of participating in the leisure activity. It is reasonable to assume that the Wankel and Thompson results could be obtained in other recreational contexts as well.

attitude-behavior relationship

Persuasive communication is based upon an implicit assumption that changing attitudes toward an object will lead to changes in overt behavior or behavioral patterns. Thus, it is assumed that Wankel and Thompson were able to increase their subjects' recreation participation because they succeeded in changing subjects' attitudes toward physical exercise or managed to reinforce subjects' already-learned predisposition toward physical activity. Of course, it is not known whether attitude change or reinforcement indeed took place, because beliefs and attitudes were not measured in the study. But there are strong reasons to believe that salient beliefs about (and thus attitudes toward) the object were influenced by their experimental treatment.

Another way of looking at the attitude-behavior relationship is to ask: can behavior be changed without attitude change? Frequently people have to engage in behavior (for extrinsic reasons) which is inconsistent with their attitudes, thereby suggesting that behavior is changed without attitude change. As for the intrinsically motivated leisure behaviors, attitudes and behaviors are usually consistent. This means that continued involvement in a leisure activity is preceded by change in attitude toward that activity. For example, assume a person who has not been to church before, but now, all of a sudden, becomes an avid participant in church services. The author contends that such behavioral change cannot be sustained by external stimuli alone. Attitude change must have preceded it.

correspondence of
attitude-behavior
measures

If attitudes and behaviors are so consistent, why is it then that one often finds empirical studies suggesting that attitudes are poor predictors of actual behavior? Wicker (1969), for example, reviewed the literature and found attitudes and behaviors to be unrelated. This apparent lack of correlation can, however, be explained in the light of Fishbein's theory of attitude. In short, "attitude is a *general* predisposition that does not predispose the person to perform any specific behavior. Rather, it leads to a set of intentions that indicates a certain amount of affect toward the object in question. Each of these intentions is related to a specific behavior, and thus the overall affect expressed by the pattern of a person's actions with respect to the object also corresponds to his attitude toward the object" (Fishbein and Ajzen, 1975, p. 15).

The fact that the past studies have not found a strong relationship between attitude and behavior, therefore, is attributable to different levels of measurement, or expressed in another way, it is due to comparing apples and oranges. If one is to *predict* a person's specific leisure participation it should be done from intentions, not from attitudes. Even when behavior is predicted from intentions one has to ensure that the specificity of intention is the same as that of behavior. In other words, if one has to predict accurately whether a man will go to the movies to see "Turning Point" in Iowa City next Sunday starting at 7:30 p.m., one should ask the person specifically how likely he is to attend that particular showing. If his intention was measured at a more general level by asking him whether he intends to go to the movies, the prediction would be much more inaccurate than in the above case. The prediction would weaken even more if one measured his attitude, that is, the amount of affect he has for the movies in general.

Thus, leisure attitudes and leisure behavior may be highly consistent even though the correlations may indicate something quite different. To improve correlations between leisure attitudes and behaviors, one should measure participation at a general level, because of the generality of attitudes. Thus, instead of asking whether a person will go to a specific movie at a specific time, one should ask how often the person *generally* goes to the movies, if the inquiry is to relate it to attitudes toward the movies. A correlation between attitude and behavior can, therefore, be improved in two ways: by measuring both concepts at the specific level or at the general level. The issue is not one of specificity but one of correspondence.

It follows from the above that leisure attitudes are good predictors of intentions to engage in leisure activities (and actual leisure behavior), provided that they have been measured on the same level as intentions. In the study which involved numerous free-time activities Ajzen and Fishbein (1969) reported strong empirical evidence for this contention. Depending on an activity in question, correlation between the subjects' attitudes toward a leisure activity and their intention to engage in it was quite high, with the numerical values ranging from .52 to .67.

leisure attitude-intention

It appears that these correlations would have been even higher had the authors included in their analysis only those individuals who were intrinsically involved in the free-time activities. Because most of these free-time activities (e.g., going to a concert, a party, a movie, or playing poker) were such that they are often rated both intrinsically and extrinsically motivated, it is likely that the subjects did not see these activities as predominantly intrinsically motivating. If so, correlation between attitudes and intentions may have declined. This is in part reflected by a relatively high correlation (average = .54) between "social norm" and intention to engage in leisure activities; social norm referred to the subject's perception of his friends' expectations about participating in the leisure activities. By definition, when the person's leisure participation is highly motivated intrinsically, the contribution to leisure behavior of such external influences as social norms is nil. But the more these external factors affect leisure involvement, the lower the correlation between leisure attitudes and intentions (as well as behavior). It should be remembered that leisure attitudes are based upon salient beliefs about the consequences (intrinsic rewards) of participation in given activities.

leisure attitude-behavior

Murphy (1975a) investigated the relationship between attitude toward a lake and the number of visits to it made by recreational boaters. The results showed a very modest relationship between the two variables. This finding, however, has to be treated with caution because of the statistical problems (the questionable use of the stepwise regression in the data analysis and failure to report zero-order correlations). But even if the finding were statistically correct one would not expect the correlation between the two variables to be particularly high, because attitudes toward the *activity* were not measured, thereby suggesting that the object of attitudes was different from the behavior to be correlated. Attitudes toward facilities (e.g., the lake), while interesting in their own right, have little to do with attitudes toward a leisure behavior. It is essential that both a person's salient beliefs about the consequences of participation in a given leisure activity and the evaluations of these consequences are measured. Murphy, himself, made a similar point (p. 223): "Personal satisfaction with the visit appeared to be a major element of site attraction rather than the physical characteristics and amenities of the lake."

In a related study, Wicker (1971) examined attitudinal and "other variables" as determinants of church attendance: attitude toward one's church (.31), evaluation of attending church services (.31), perceived consequences of behavior (.19), and extraneous variables (.42) all systematically (significantly) correlated with behavior, that is, the number of Sundays the respondent attended church during a 39-week period. Although the three attitudinal measures had a relatively low relationship to church attendance in general, and lower than the extraneous variables, the relationships nevertheless were positive and significant. Thus, for example, the first correlation (.31) indicated that the more positive the attitude toward church, the more frequently the respondent attended church services.

That extraneous variables were relatively closely related to church attendance is not surprising, especially because this category of independent variables was operationalized by how the subjects judged the influence of such variables. That is, subjects were asked to rate whether intervening events (e.g., weekend guests) would interrupt their church attendance. Therefore, it should not be surprising that what was judged to be the influence of "other variables" was related to the church attendance as closely as it was. This relationship, however, is psychologically quite meaningless, because no theoretical framework has been proposed to specify how these extraneous variables should be considered in examining the attitude-behavior relationship. As for the relatively low but significant correlations between the attitudinal measures and the church attendance, much of the blame has to be placed on the methodological problems. For example, the subjects were asked to evaluate whether church attendance would help them achieve the nine suggested consequences (e.g., "providing inspiration and help in coping with problems"). Yet, no indication was given as to how subjects perceived these consequences. Thus, there is no way of knowing whether these were salient or trivial beliefs. The problem is compounded by the fact that the subjects' estimates of the perceived likelihood of achieving each consequence were grouped together so as to form one index, the psychological meaning of which is not very clear (Fishbein and Ajzen, 1975).

Despite the above problems, the conclusion remains that there is a positive and significant relationship between leisure attitudes and leisure behavior. In other words, the more positive a person's attitude toward a leisure activity, the more likely it is that the individual will participate in it regularly. This linear relationship is not perfect, but it is strong enough to indicate that leisure behavior can be successfully predicted from leisure attitudes. In fact, Ajzen and Fishbein's (1977) recent review of research showed that the attitude-behavior relationship may reach correlations as high as .80 if the measures of attitude and those of behaviors correspond to each other. Thus, there is nothing wrong about the concept of attitude. If somebody or something is to be blamed, it is the researcher, not attitude. This should be understood by those (e.g., Heberlein, 1973) who attack such "innocent" psychological constructs as attitude.

It should be reiterated that the strong attitude-behavior relationship emerges invariably (for a review of evidence, see Fishbein and Ajzen, 1975; Ajzen and Fishbein, 1977) if leisure attitude toward a behavior, rather than toward a related object (e.g., toward a lake by Murphy, 1975a), is correlated with a given leisure behavior. Because attitude is a general concept (even if it is expressed in a specific behavior), behavior to be correlated with the attitude has to be measured at the same level of generality. If this is done, the attitude-behavior relationship emerges as strong, positive, and significant. The issue, however, is not one of specificity but rather of correspondence between attitudes and behaviors. This correspondence is said to exist, to the extent that attitude is identical to behavior in terms of "the *action* and the *target* at which the action is performed" (Ajzen and Fishbein, 1977, p. 889). An example of attitude toward an action that specifies both action (playing) and target (tennis) would be: attitude toward playing tennis. A behavioral measure corresponding to this attitudinal entity would be the frequency of playing tennis. A high correlation between attitude and behavior can be obtained if the correspondence is achieved in terms of action and target element alone. It follows from the above that the correspondence has to be considered also in the context of attitude change.

If the task is to predict specific leisure behavior at a specific time in a specific place, the researcher should obtain a measure of the subject's intention to perform that particular behavior. In the context of leisure, this has been demonstrated by a study by Holman (1956), who provided students with a list of football games and asked them to indicate their intentions to attend each game. At the end of the season, subjects reported the number of games they had attended. Subsequently, a correlation was computed between the number of games subjects said they would attend and the number of games they actually had attended during the season. The result, a correlation of .80, lends strong support for the contention that intention is the best predictor of a given leisure behavior. The intention-behavior correlation approximates perfection if the measure of intention is taken in an immediate proximity to the predicted behavior (Fishbein and Ajzen, 1975).

In addition to the studies reviewed above, several other investigations bearing the title of leisure attitudes have been reported. Among them is a series of studies by Neulinger and his associates (1969, 1971, 1972). These studies, however, do not deal with attitudes in the sense in which they were discussed earlier in this chapter. Neulinger gave subjects a number of opinion statements or questions to be answered, (e.g., "How long could you stand a life of leisure?"); some of these specified the target and action, others did not. Some of them seemed to deal with the evaluation of attributes, others with the evaluation of consequences of leisure participation. In such a mixed package with a little bit of everything, it is difficult to tell from the attitudinal standpoint what these studies have accomplished.

This is not to deny the value of Neulinger's studies. His results, for example, were interesting and valuable in revealing that one's "self-definition" (self-esteem) is still a matter of work, not leisure. But because the opinion statements were unsystematic and atheoretical, it is unclear what they are supposed to mean to the attitudinal explanation of leisure behavior. Admittedly, Neulinger appropriately submitted his data to factor analysis which was expected to sort out the basic dimensions underlying the subjects' responses to the opinion state-

a final note about studies on leisure attitudes

ments. But, it should not be forgotten that the "dimensions" emerging from the factor analysis depend on the kinds of opinion statements fed into the computer in the first place. That is, had Neulinger omitted some of his items, or added others, the extracted "basic dimensions" might have been quite different from those presently obtained. It is for these reasons that more weight is not assigned here to the Neulinger studies, regardless of their apparent relevance to this discussion of leisure attitudes.

Other studies have also been reported. Groves, Kahalas and Bonham (1977) investigated the functional nature of leisure attitudes and found that "selection process, needs, and expectations tended to be associated." This then reinforces the previous statement that leisure attitude is a special case of intrinsic leisure motivation. In other words, leisure activities are evaluated in terms of the consequences they are expected to produce through participation. The extent to which intrinsic rewards can be derived from participating in these activities is directly related to the amount of affect (i.e., attitude) expressed toward an activity. Perceived positive consequences are "salient beliefs" which are building blocks of leisure attitudes.

Finally, a few words of caution are in order. When the determinants of leisure behavior are investigated, the level of causality of the independent variables should be kept constant. Combining all kinds of variables together in one analysis (e.g., Christensen and Yoesting, 1973) does not increase the understanding of leisure behavior but rather confuses the picture. It is conceptually and theoretically inappropriate to combine such variables as occupation, income, education, age and leisure attitudes in one analysis. The problem is compounded statistically if one of these variables is measured at the individual level and others at the group level, and if a variety of measurement scales is used. Variables like occupation are not the actual determinants of leisure choices and behaviors, but rather the outer boundaries within which an individual operates and makes decisions about leisure behavior.

It is important to understand why a person spends leisure within personal "boundaries." In such analysis, variables like occupation are of little use, nor are simplistic comparisons of the relative importance of occupation and attitudes. As was repeatedly noted in the earlier pages, the real determinants of leisure choices and behavior are human social cognitions. In an effort to understand leisure behavior, one can learn little from variables like occupation and income. Unfortunately, researchers who have utilized these variables have assumed that occupation, income, and other variables actually influence people's decision-making about their leisure involvement.

The most unfortunate procedure is that some investigators have gone so far as to declare the supremacy of variables like income against cognitive variables. If this comparison has to be made for some particular reasons, one would expect that each variable be given at least a fair chance to explain leisure behavior. Christensen and Yoesting (1973), for example, measured subjects' attitudes toward leisure in general (or leisure orientation) and correlated this with the number of participants in outdoor recreation activities. This is an excellent example of what Fishbein and Ajzen call a lack of correspondence between the measures of attitude and behavior. It is, therefore, no wonder that attitude did not explain much of the variance in comparison to other variables. A review of past research (Ajzen and Fishbein, 1977), however, showed that the relationship between leisure attitude and leisure behavior can even reach a correlation of about .80 when a study is *conceptually* sound. The author has never seen occupation, income and variables of a similar kind approximate this level of prediction.

summary

Leisure attitude was defined as the expressed amount of affect toward a given leisure-related object. This attitude is a multiplicative function of a person's beliefs that an object (e.g., swimming pool) has certain characteristics (e.g., crowded), and a personal evaluation of these characteristics. Attitude is formed simultaneously when a person learns that an object (swimming pool) is linked to a certain attribute (crowded). Since beliefs are "building blocks" of attitudes, the question is how they are acquired. It was shown that externally provided information often gives rise to beliefs (informational beliefs). Descriptive beliefs in turn are based upon personal observations of certain relationships. Finally, beliefs can be formed without outside sources and without direct observations by making logical inferences or utilizing culturally learned explanations (inferential beliefs). In a broad sense, then, belief formation is a function of personal experiences and social influences. The foundations of attitude formation, therefore, are laid in early childhood play experiences.

While attitude change can sometimes be explained in terms of human tendency to cognitive consistency, it was shown that a better explanation is provided by the information processing approach, which focuses on belief change. In principle, attitude can be changed by altering salient beliefs about an object or by changing evaluations of the attributes in question. Once salient or target beliefs have been identified these beliefs should be attacked and changed if a change in attitude is to be expected. For example, if a person holds a negative attitude toward a swimming pool chiefly because of the salient belief that it is crowded, one should change this person's belief that the pool is crowded, or that such a crowded condition is undesirable; otherwise the attitude toward the pool cannot be expected to change.

To accomplish this objective, various strategies can be employed. Two major types of strategies are active participation and persuasive communication. Perceived trust in persuasive communication and the power of the message, in turn, are the two general factors determining the effectiveness of persuasive communications in changing salient beliefs and thus attitudes. Tentative empirical evidence indicates that persuasive communication can indeed be effective in changing people's leisure attitudes and actual leisure behavior. It was pointed out that this strategy is effective, to the extent that persuasion does not impair intrinsic leisure motivation and does change salient beliefs about the perceived consequences of participating in a leisure activity. Because intrinsic motivation is the force underlying leisure behavior, intrinsic rewards (perceived consequences) are therefore the salient beliefs associated with participation in leisure activities. To modify a person's attitude toward a leisure activity, beliefs about consequences should be changed. That is, if a person holds a negative attitude toward swimming because of beliefs that through swimming one cannot achieve those intrinsic rewards (e.g., relaxation and escape from routine) which are valued highly, then these beliefs should be changed to change one's attitude toward the activity.

Attitudes, because they are linked to a *general* behavior *pattern,* do not predispose a person to engage in any specific leisure activity. It has been shown, however, that leisure behavior can be predicted from leisure attitudes very successfully (.80), provided that the measures of attitude and behavior correspond to one another. At a minimum, this correspondence is said to exist if attitude is identical with behavior in terms of the action and in terms of the target at which the action is directed. The best predictor of a specific behavior is a person's intention to engage in that behavior.

a social psychological perspective on outdoor recreation

perceiving and experiencing outdoor recreation environments

Social psychology examines leisure and recreation in terms of (1) an individual and his personal cognitions, (2) the social context where behavior is observed, (3) the time at which behavior occurs, and (4) the physical environment where behavior occurs. Thus far this study has considered individual leisure behavior as a developmental or dialectical process and has pointed out its social character and context. This study, however, would be incomplete if it did not consider the physical environment of leisure involvement. Whether the physical environment is an end in itself or a means toward an end, it nevertheless is an inseparable part of leisure behavior. Millions of people every year spend their vacation with the intent of seeing and experiencing different physical environments (an end in itself), and millions of recreationists play tennis in various environments (a means toward an end).

Even when the physical setting may appear merely incidental to the main activity (e.g., tennis), it makes a difference where the activity takes place. Therefore, the contribution of a physical environment to leisure experience has to be subjected to a systematic analysis directed toward establishing theoretical and empirical relationships between the leisure behavior and experience of the individual and the physical environment. The purpose of the present chapter is to discuss the perception and experience of physical environments with particular reference to outdoor recreation environments. Outdoor recreation refers to "those recreational activities which occur in an outdoor (natural) environment and which relate directly to that environment" (Jensen, 1977, p. 8). The chapter focuses on environmental perception and experience. It concludes with a discussion of the environmental crisis in human dignity.

Craik (1973) distinguished between several related aspects of environmental perception: (1) environmental assessment, which refers principally to assessment of the relationship between the physical-spatial properties of places and the frequency of use of these places, though it can also refer to the assessment of traits

environmental perception

of places; (2) environmental perception, the focus of which is on the influence of psychological and environmental factors on the impressions people form about places; (3) cognitive representation of the large-scale environment, which refers to the way in which people conceptualize or cognitively perceive the physical environments too large to be seen all at once; (4) public attitudes toward the physical environment, like parks and wilderness areas. The focus in this chapter is on what Craik termed environmental assessment and perception.

perceived physical correlates of outdoor environments

As in the context of any human behavior, people develop certain expectations before they visit various outdoor recreation places. But what specifically are some of the perceived requirements of outdoor recreation environments? A good deal of research relevant to this question has been reported and has recently been reviewed by Brush (1976), Heimstra and McFarling (1974) and Zube (1976). It appears that when natural landscapes and scenes are evaluated, there is a high degree of consensus among people, whereas the least agreement in evaluations occurs with regard to those landscapes which are predominantly urban (Brush, 1976). Utilizing Clawson's (1963) classification of outdoor recreation areas into "user-oriented" (daily leisure), "intermediate" (weekend leisure) and "resource-based" (vacation time) areas, it appears that this agreement upon scenic quality increases from user-oriented to intermediate and to resource-based areas. This ensues because the number of natural elements increases and the number of urban elements decreases from user to resource-based recreation environments.

As for the perceived physical characteristics of natural landscapes, it has been shown (cf. Brush, 1976) that landforms, water, agricultural features, and natural vegetation affect positively the evaluation of natural environments, but on the other hand, urban development and the presence of a large number of people have a negative impact on scenic evaluations; Chamber (1974) found that perceived density influences the perceived quality of a recreational environment. In a similar vein, Zube's (1976) findings suggest that physical environments can be placed on a continuum "ranging from the most natural through various stages of management to the more nearly total man-made landscape."

When a number of photographs about varied environments were arranged according to the subjects' ratings, four qualitatively distinct groups emerged (from the highest to the lowest): (1) a group of photographs featuring open water and topography in natural settings, (2) a group consisting of a diversity of vegetation, (3) a group characterized by various signs of man-made elements, and (4) a group comprised of strip commercial developments. Further evidence that certain environments create cognitive images or maps in persons is found in another study by Zube and his associates. Based upon cluster analysis, seven groups of scenes were identified (Zube, 1976, p. 110–111):

1. *Farms*—rural lands under management, including rural housing, farm buildings, agricultural fields, and pastures.
2. *Meadows and Woods*—natural-appearing open areas, including abandoned fields, natural meadows and surrounding woods.

3. *Forested Hills*—landscapes dominated by dense woods, including obvious topographic variation.
4. *Open Water*—landscapes dominated by large areas of open water, including reservoirs, lakes, and rivers.
5. *Wetlands and Streams*—natural-appearing landscapes that include visible wetlands and small streams or rivers.
6. *Towns*—intensive-use areas, including surburban residential developments, town centers, and commercial areas.
7. *Industry*—areas influenced by the presence of heavy industrial developments.

On the basis of the above findings, one may conclude that the perceived quality of an outdoor recreation environment is positively related to its perceived naturalness. This is particularly pertinent because "naturalism" is the strongest predictor of subjective scenic values (Zube, 1976). Further support for the above contention can be found in Heimstra and McFarling's (1974) review of research on the natural environment and behavior. On the other hand, the hypothetized correlation may vary, depending on the prevailing culture and the education which the observer has received.

Since aesthetic and emotional aspects rate much higher than other aspects among wilderness hikers (Shafer and Mietz, 1972), the problem is to find out the characteristics that give rise to aesthetic feelings. Litton (1972) suggested that *unity, vividness,* and *variety* are the underlying dimensions of the perceived landscape. Unity refers to the "quality of wholeness, a single harmonious unit;" vividness to distinctive and "visually striking" characteristics of the environment; and variety to a number of different objects found in a landscape. In support of Litton's conceptualization, Shafer and Mietz (1972, p. 214) reported hikers wanting "variation in trail scenery more than anything else." Hikers reported that the most scenic enjoyment will be obtained from the trails that (1) "include large rock outcrops where the hikers can observe the surrounding landscape; (2) go through natural openings in forest stands where there is variability in lighting, color, temperature, and the distance one can see through the forest; and (3) follow stream courses whenever possible so that waterfalls and rushing water are part of the natural beauty along the trail." By contrast, when people walk through big cities (e.g., New York, Boston) they judge the urban environment along the following ten dominant but interrelated attributes: beautiful, ordered, fresh, smooth, rich, vivid, pleasant, clean, likeable, and light (Lowenthal and Riel, 1972).

In a related study by Muriam and Amons (1968), hikers, horseback riders, and roadside campers were asked to indicate the criteria they personally use in defining wilderness. The following were given: undeveloped natural country, difficulty of access, few people, the absence of improvements introduced by civilization. Interestingly, hikers were much more specific than were campers in pointing out what constitutes wilderness to them. While hikers said that they should be at least three miles from the nearest road or guided tour before feeling that they were in the wilderness, campers considered themselves as being in the wilderness at the edge of the campground. Similarly, Lucas (1964) found that wilderness users were more specific than casual users (e.g., weekend campers) in describing the difference between wilderness and non-wilderness on the map. These results imply that the perceived naturalness of an outdoor recreation environment increases with the perceived degree of wilderness of the environment. But they also indicate that environmental perception is influenced by the *expectations* of what a given recreation environment is and what it can provide psychologically.

perceived quality of outdoor recreation environments

When people camp and hike in national parks or simply visit a neighborhood park, they have expectations about the scenic (environmental) features of these places *and* about their potential to satisfy their recreational needs. Based upon this assumption, the author proposes that the subjective quality of an outdoor recreation environment (PQRE) may be determined by the formula:

$$\text{PQRE} = \frac{\begin{array}{c}\text{observed quality}\\\text{of recreation}\\\text{environment}\end{array}}{\begin{array}{c}\text{expected quality}\\\text{of recreation}\\\text{environment}\end{array}} = \frac{\left(\begin{array}{c}\text{observed}\\\text{environmental}\\\text{quality}\end{array}\right) \times \left(\begin{array}{c}\text{observed}\\\text{psychological}\\\text{quality}\end{array}\right)}{\left(\begin{array}{c}\text{expected}\\\text{environmental}\\\text{quality}\end{array}\right) \times \left(\begin{array}{c}\text{expected}\\\text{psychological}\\\text{quality}\end{array}\right)}$$

To state it simply, the above formula indicates that the perceived quality of a recreation environment (PQRE) amounts to the same as reporting whether a person derived from the recreation environment what was expected from it. When the individual has experienced (''observed'') an outdoor recreation environment, the question then is whether that actual experience fulfills the preconceived environmental and psychological expectations. Thus, PQRE is defined by comparing actual experiences over expected experiences, taking into account both environmental and psychological aspects of recreation experiences. The mathematical development of the above formula is explained and an example to illustrate its use is provided in the Appendix, pp. 397–399.

The above theory is based upon the assumption that the person has two basic kinds of expectations when entering an outdoor recreation environment. First, environmental or aesthetic expectations refer to scenic characteristics (e.g., undeveloped natural country, forested hills, open water) which the visitor expected to observe with a certain likelihood in a given environment. Mentally, the person has evaluated each such characteristic in terms of its positive nature, and also has formed a subjective probability of finding these characteristics in the environment. Second, psychological expectations refer to the psychological entities or intrinsic rewards (''leisure needs,'' e.g., escape from routine and relaxation) which a person expected to obtain with a certain probability through an encounter with an outdoor environment. The person has evaluated each intrinsic reward according to its positive character, and has developed a subjective probability of obtaining it in the environment. Then, the environmental and psychological qualities of the environment have to be estimated also following the person's visit to a given environment. Thus, the perceived environmental quality of a recreation environment simply involves comparing the observed quality with the expected one.

The above formula is useful, in that it takes into account the interaction between a person and the physical environment, enabling one to identify the relative contributions of the environment and person (psychological) components to the PQRE. The example (see Appendix) showed that if one only considered the environmental component $\left(\dfrac{3.1}{1.3} = 2.4\right)$, the PQRE would have been much greater than if the observer only considered the psychological component $\left(\dfrac{2.5}{6.6} = .38\right)$. In other words, the person achieved environmentally much more than he expected, but gained considerably less psychologically than expected, with the net result of the PQRE being slightly less than expected (.90). Thus, it is clearly insufficient to consider only one of these components in estimating the PQRE.

The above formula (PQRE) is comprehensive, in that it incorporates time as a factor in the basic formula. That is, it takes into account revisions in one's perceptions of recreation environments. The formula estimates the degree to which these perceptions change as a function of actual recreation experiences. Consequently, it also allows for changes over time in the individual expectations of environmental and psychological qualities. It is also useful, in that it enables one to point out exactly what aspects (and how much) of the environmental and psychological component are contributing to the expected and observed qualities of a recreation environment and to their change. The formula also makes it possible to compare the PQRE of various groups (e.g., males vs. females) to determine, among the components here compared, what contributes to the differences in the PQRE between the contrasted cohorts.

This conceptualization clearly demonstrates that in the final analysis, the PQRE is a psychological construct which is a matter of individual cognitions. Thus, it is possible in theory to change the PQRE by manipulating expectations about the environmental and/or psychological quality of a recreation environment. Direct evidence for this supposition can be found in a study by Leff, Gordon and Ferguson (1974). The results showed that judgment as to the pleasantness of an actual scene was unaffected by the subjects' paying particular attention to such environmental elements as shapes and lines. The evaluated pleasantness, however, was decreased when subjects were specifically asked to observe the human influence in the scene, or when they were asked to imagine how the landscape could be improved. This cognitive manipulation thus reduced the environmental quality observed by subjects, presumably because it changed their evaluations of certain environmental characteristics and their subjective likelihood of observing these characteristics in the environment. It is conceivable that the entire perceived quality of the recreational environment was changed by this cognitive manipulation.

Does the above formula mean that the PQRE cannot be estimated without persons actually having been on the scene or without having experienced the environment? Theoretically, the observed quality of a recreation environment can be estimated by presenting respondents with photographs of the landscape and environment to be evaluated. (In fact, this strategy has been the primary method of research on environment and behavior.) But there are both conceptual and empirical reasons to question the use of this procedure in estimating the PQRE. Since it has been shown that the physical environment generally has a relatively strong psychological impact on human beings (e.g., Mehrabian and Russell, 1974; Russell and Mehrabian, 1976; Proshansky, Ittelson and Rivlin, 1970), it is reasonable to assume that the actual experience of a physical environment affects its perceived recreational quality differently from the impacts of photographs of the same environment. Furthermore, Lowenthal and Riel (1972) reported a study in which one group of subjects walked through four cities and subsequently made their environmental judgments, while the other group gave their judgments without the actual environmental experience. The authors concluded (pp. 199, 205): ". . . striking differences emerged between the nature of the environment as it invariably *looks* to people, and as they invariably *believe* it to look . . . What we *think* we like or should like (or dislike) about certain kinds of environments is often not what we *do* like (or dislike) when we actually experience them."

psychological correlates of outdoor recreation environments

Although the above formulation has not been tested as such, several past studies lend indirect support for it. Earlier, evidence was reviewed indicating the relationship between certain physical characteristics of the environment and the perceived aesthetic quality of the scene. Research has also shown that some of these environmental characteristics increase the participants' satisfaction with the environment, while others reduce it. Peterson (1974a) reported that the satisfaction of canoeists with their recreation environment was enhanced by such physical characteristics as being able to drink water directly from the lake, natural noises (e.g., waterfalls) and mature virgin forests. Qualities that undermined canoeists' satisfaction were of the following kind: litter, trees damaged by cutting, and the use of motors. From the standpoint of the above theory, this analysis was only partial because it did not consider the contribution of the "perceived psychological quality" of the environment to the satisfaction of the subjects, nor did it take into account their expectations.

That participants see outdoor environments in terms of potential psychological rewards has been documented in several studies. Stankey (1972) asked wilderness users to rate a number of items according to their desirability in the context of wilderness. It appeared that 82% of the total sample rated solitude as an important feature of wilderness; this was even more evident among those who were classified as the "strong purists," as 96% of them evaluated solitude as desirable. Similarly, Shafer and Mietz (1972) found that hikers rated aesthetic and emotional values as the most important aspects of wilderness experience, followed by physical, educational, and social values. Aesthetic and emotional values were approximately ten times more favored than were social values. These findings point out unequivocally the importance of escape from others or from routine as a psychological reward for wilderness users. Other intrinsic rewards possibly include relaxation and psychological well-being because emotional experiences ranked very high.

Further evidence of the relationship between the expected psychological rewards and perception of outdoor recreation environments was reported by Kaplan (1977). When subjects' responses to the environmental preference questions were related to their reasons of participation in favorite activities, several positive correlations emerged. The preference for nature correlated positively both with desire to be alone, away from other pressures (.34), and with "liking doing things outdoors or close to nature" (.53). Thus, those who seek peace and quiet prefer nature as well. Taken together, these findings lend strong support to the contention that what people seek psychologically from outdoor recreation environments affects their perceptions of quality of these environments.

If expectations of obtaining psychological rewards from environmental encounters are an important factor in the perceived quality of a recreation environment, the question then arises about the determinants of such expectations. Although this was not discussed specifically in relation to environmental perception and outdoor recreation, the question was dealt with in the previous chapters concerning past individual experiences and social influences. In theory, the individual's personality/past experiences and situational/social factors in combination determine expectations about the perceived environmental and psychological quality of outdoor recreation environments (cf. the model of page 185). A similar point has been expressed elsewhere (e.g., Kameron, 1973). When arguing from the standpoint of environmental knowing, Moore (1976, p. 163) expressed the same idea: "To understand how people come to know the environment and how they come to organize their knowledge of the environment, it is necessary to understand the transactions of persons in environments and the interactions between interorganismic variables, like values and aspirations." Empirical data in support of this position have also been documented. Cicchetti (1972) found that those who had hiked or camped frequently as children had a more positive preference for the wilderness than did those who had not hiked or camped often when young.

Cicchetti also found that education had a positive effect on wilderness preferences. Specifically, the degree of the computed purism in respondents' attitudes toward the wilderness increased steadily for each year of education after the eighth grade. Education, however, is such a global variable that it does not tell us precisely what made these preferences positive. Did it have to do with educational materials, the school atmosphere, teachers, or peers? Or, was it simply due to the "contrast effect;" that is, students have to spend almost all their time in visually monotonous buildings with a minimum of opportunities to experience

contrast effect

the unity, vividness and variety of the nature. If such a contrast effect is a valid explanation, it follows that those who grow up in urban areas should show a stronger preference for wilderness than those who spend their childhood in rural areas. This is exactly what Cicchetti's findings indicated. Thus, it is not surprising that conservationism is positively related to education (Craik, 1973); needless to say, more educated persons reside in urban than rural areas. Natural outdoor environments provide a contrast to people living in urban areas, and such contrasting experiences are needed to satisfy individual tendency toward optimal arousal and incongruity through novelty, variety and dissonance.

In exhibiting strong preferences for conservation of natural resources, educated urban dwellers are in effect trying to preserve conditions suitable for meeting their need for optimal arousal. Of course, they could seek novelty and dissonance (contrast) also in their urban environments, but wilderness and other rural outdoor places provide an obvious and natural contrast to their urban surroundings. Thus, the conservation of natural outdoor environments expands their leisure space in meeting the basic need. Diminished natural outdoor areas reduce urban dwellers' *perceived* opportunities for experiencing optimal arousal, which in turn may pose a perceived threat to their survival. It should also be remembered that human thinking and behavior are dialectical in character; that is, they form a continuous process which is marked by contrasts and contradictions (Riegel, 1976). Since optimal arousal or incongruity is both a cognitive and behavioral matter, it is not necessary to experience and visit wilderness places. In other words, many educated and urban residents may be staunch conservationists and express strong preferences for wilderness areas perhaps without ever visiting such places. The mere existence of such contrasting environments, however, is psychologically valuable and healthy to them because of awareness that they can *potentially* return there should they so desire.

If the above theorizing is correct, urban residents should seek solitude in outdoor recreation to a greater extent, and social encounters to a lesser extent, than people living in rural areas. Knopp (1972) has reported tentative empirical support for this contention. He asked residents in urban, rural non-farm, and rural farm areas to indicate, among other things, the outdoor recreation activities in which they participated during the preceding year, in terms of the opportunity to (from 1—very little to 10—a great deal):—(1) "allow me to get away from the crowds and congestion of the city" (solitude) and (2) "give me the opportunity to meet and associate with friends" (social). The mean of the solitude statement was much higher for urban (6.67) than for either rural non-farm (5.85) or rural farm (3.67) residents. But it would have indeed been surprising had this result not been obtained. This follows because solitude was defined as "getting away from the city." It is impossible for the farmers to get away from the city because they do not even live in the city!

Despite this conceptual lapse the fact remains that outdoor recreation provides an important avenue for urban residents to find solitude. When the means of the three groups for the "social" statement were compared, it appeared that people living in rural farm areas (6.44) perceived their outdoor recreation activities as being of a greater social value than did rural non-farm (5.6) or urban (5.6) residents. Taken together, these findings seem to indicate that urban residents seek more solitude and less social company through outdoor recreation than do their rural counterparts, presumably because the city provides too much incongruity for the former, while rural areas offer too little incongruity for the latter (for a detailed discussion of optimal incongruity, see Part 4).

The above theorizing and evidence imply that an individual's past experiences and social influences give rise to expectations of psychological (intrinsic) rewards to be derived from outdoor recreation environments. In the final analysis, the desire to obtain certain rewards (e.g., escape, relaxation, solitude) arises from an individual need for optimal arousal and incongruity. Thus, it should not be surprising that users and managers of outdoor recreation environments differ considerably in their ratings of the quality of a recreation environment. For example, Peterson (1974b) found that canoeists were more in favor of the untouched natural environment than managers. It has also been found that campers rate the natural environment more positively than do managers (Brush, 1976). It is likely that these differences simply reflect variation in users' and managers' motives for coming to the natural environment.

differences in perceived quality of environments as viewed by users and managers

Since canoeists and campers usually spend only a few days per year in the wilderness (as opposed to the managers' continuous presence there), these users expect to receive substantial psychological rewards because of their brief environmental experiences. Consequently, they do not come just to see the landscape. Since most of these users are from areas where they do not have access to the wilderness, the actual encounter with wilderness does not visually disappoint them. They expect to observe and experience aesthetic and psychological contrasts to their home environment, and indeed they develop this expectation before starting on the trip. It may, therefore, be the contrast effect that dominates their rating of the natural environment and diverts their attention from details (e.g., litter) impairing the objective quality and attraction of the environment.

At the same time, the managers are not seeking any contrast in their encounters with the environment, but are instead paying particular attention to environmental details so that the perceived quality of the landscape could be improved. In fact, Peterson's (1974b) data indicated that canoeists were less aware than managers of such human influences as motors, seaplanes, logging, and forest fires. In a similar vein, campers, to a lesser extent than managers, thought litter and noise to be a problem (Brush, 1976). Brush also reviewed evidence indicating that the environmental "design professionals are more sensitive to differences in natural scenic quality than non-experts," due to the superior training and experience of the experts. That the experts (e.g., managers) and nonexperts (users) perceive and rate the natural environment differently is, therefore, of little wonder. While the former rate the environment on the basis of its specific features, the latter do so on the basis of their overall impression of the environment.

One should not, however, forget Leff's, *et al.* (1974) finding, discussed earlier. When respondents were asked to take note of human influences in the landscape, the rated quality of the natural environment decreased substantially. Therefore, managers should not interpret the earlier results to mean that they do not have to worry about the man-made elements (e.g., litter) in the environment, on the pretext that users worry about them less than they do. There may always be something that causes users to focus their attention on environmental features, and if so, their perceived quality of the environment declines. It is conceivable that as environmental knowledge increases, people will pay more and more attention to the scenic characteristics of recreation environments, a reaction which then poses a growing challenge for managers of outdoor recreation environments. A set of guidelines on management techniques (e.g., clear-cutting, single trees or group tree selection for harvesting, clean-up operations after logging) has been developed, directed toward improving the visual qualities of the natural scenes and thus augmenting the users' environmental experience (Brush in Zube, 1976). But as Zube (1976) noted, "the prudent decision maker (e.g., resource manager and planner) would be well advised to carefully consider the perceptual processes of the public to be served by a proposed planning program."

littering

Although the perceived quality of an outdoor recreation environment is an individual matter, for most people certain phenomena demean quality. One such characteristic is the presence of litter in the natural scene. Admittedly, littering is mainly a problem of big cities, but it also has become a source of increasing concern among managers of outdoor recreation environments. Littering is a concrete example of human influence, and clearly it is a problem only where human beings exist. To some extent, it is safe to say that littering increases with the number of people in a given environment. This, of course, is an insufficient explanation of the phenomenon, as large crowds of human beings can coexist with a minimal amount of litter. Many large cities in Europe attest to this fact; and the lack of litter there does not only, or even mainly, reflect more efficient clean-up operations. Again, it appears that the best explanation of this phenomenon is a social psychological one. After all, littering is obviously a product of human interaction with nature.

In a series of intriguing field experiments conducted in New York City, Krauss, Freedman and Whitcup (1978) found that sex, race, and age were related to a propensity to litter. Specifically, males were observed to litter more frequently than females at the time of the first experiment and in a replication experiment one year later. The first experiment showed no significant difference between whites' and non-whites' tendency to litter, but the replication a year later indicated that a higher percentage of whites than non-whites litter. Finally, age was strongly and consistently associated with the littering propensity. Specifically, passersby estimated to be 20 years or less were much more likely to drop their waste material on the ground than were the remainder of the sample; and this was observed both in the original and the follow-up study.

But Krauss', et al. (1978) study went far beyond demonstrating the relationship between the selected demographic variables and littering. The field experiments revealed that littering was related to the rated cleanliness of the studied areas on the days of the data collection. This, therefore, suggested that littering occurs less frequently in relatively clean areas than in dirty ones, thereby indicating that "clean environments deter littering and dirty ones encourage it." Since this result was obtained in a real-life setting in a big city, it could have been affected by some extraneous variables. However, controlled laboratory experiments subsequently performed confirmed the direction of causality, again indicating that people do not litter clean streets as frequently as they do the streets which already are littered. Thus, litter seems to invite litter. This implies that the simple solution of cleaning streets may be the most effective method of preventing people from damaging the visual quality of their immediate environment.

The question then arises as to why litter seems to invite litter. If one approaches this question from the attributional perspective, one concludes that people are more likely to litter when they can attribute causality of littering to others than when they themselves have to take responsibility for it. It is easier for a person to avoid assuming responsibility for littering in a littered environment than in the clean environment. In the former case, the person can rationalize to himself that: "I did not start it; what difference does it make if I add one more leaflet to the trashpile!" But if nobody else has littered before, it is much more difficult to blame others for littering, because the individual is the first one to commit this act. Thus, it appears that litter invites litter, because the existing litter increases opportunities for external justification for littering and thus decreases the necessity of assuming personal responsibility for this behavior. The more clearly the environment points its finger to personal causation of littering (whether it is done through cleanliness or posted signs, etc.), the less likely is the individual to litter.

It remains to be investigated whether the relationship between the amount of existing litter and the likelihood of an individual littering is linear. For example, it is conceivable that a relationship consists of certain steps or thresholds which trigger littering. If an environment is completely clean, it is possible that the first piece of litter serves to trigger this behavior. The additional few pieces of litter may not increase the littering rate, but if there are ten of them then the likelihood of littering may escalate considerably. This step-by-step hypothesis, of course, is a speculation which is subject to rigorous verification through empirical testing.

The Krauss, *et al.* (1978) study demonstrated that the rate of littering can be reduced by increasing the conspicuousness of social norms concerning littering behavior, or, as this author explained it, by decreasing external justification of littering while increasing the need or inducement to assume personal responsibility for personal littering. Passersby in New York City were approached and asked to sign a petition for "clean streets," aimed at increasing state aid to the Sanitation Department so that it could do a better job of cleaning streets. After signing the petition subjects were given a handbill by a second experimenter stationed about 100 feet farther down the block. The experimenter observed how people disposed of the handbill. The control subjects were only given a handbill but not stopped to sign the petition. The results showed that the control subjects littered twice as often as did those who signed the petition. Thus, signing a petition which denounced littering considerably reduced subjects' tendency to drop the leaflet on the street. In a sense, subjects made an internal commitment not to litter when they signed the petition. Krauss, *et al.* (1978) theorized that this procedure made the social norms against littering more obvious and therefore decreased people's tendency to litter. This author would like to extend this explanation by adding that an increase in the conspicuousness of social norms relating to littering increases awareness of personal causation and responsibility for such behavior; it also reduces external justification of littering, with the net result of a decreased rate of littering.

Other phases of their data lent some support to the idea that the rate of littering may decline due to the modeling or exemplary effect. That is, if a person observes others throwing a leaflet into a container the observer is likely to do the same, presumably because the behavior of the other persons (non-littering) provides a model or a reminder of the social desirability of not littering, the norm against littering, and personal causation and responsibility of personal littering. Since people have a tendency to avoid attributing causality of negative behaviors (e.g., littering) to themselves, they have two options: (1) not to commit such behavior or (2) to place the blame for such behavior on factors other than themselves. Thus, others' non-littering behavior reduces chances of attributing individual littering to external factors, thereby encouraging the first option.

As a final point, one should take notice of the authors' suggestion that public campaigns against litter in the form of posted signs may not be productive, because these signs are overlooked in the midst of hundreds of other signs in the cities, and because they have not been directed specifically at the young people who are mainly responsible for litter. Federal money would be better spent in classrooms and on children's television programs than in public campaigns. Since children are in the socialization process of developing cultural norms, they are open to learning and can therefore be taught to adopt pro-social acts. In support of this idea, Miller, Brickman and Bolen (1975) reported data indicating that fifth graders reduced their littering behavior drastically when a teacher attributed neatness to them on several occasions.

By coincidence, when this section was being written the author observed the utilization of the above principle in a children's popular TV program. He went downstairs to have a cup of coffee and see what his four-year-old son was doing. As expected, he was watching Sesame Street. While drinking coffee he also started to watch the program, and as if it had been prearranged, one of the short segments in the program showed a little boy walking in the street, picking up three different pieces of litter and pitching them into the container! Clearly, the scene presented children with a model, which suggested that it is undesirable to litter. Although young children watching the program probably did not rationalize why not littering is desirable, the scene nevertheless provided them with a model which depicted littering as an antisocial act. Such models are likely to serve as a basis of forming negative attitudes toward littering.

Although all the above discussion has revolved around littering in the city, there are reasons to assume that the findings would hold true for similar behavior in recreational settings as well. If litter invites more litter, it follows that cleanliness feeds on cleanliness. This implies that if, for example, managers succeed in making their campgrounds clean, it is likely that campers will help by not littering. Furthermore, managers could alleviate the problem of litter by asking every visitor to sign a "clean camping" pledge before erecting a tent. Finally, while the posted signs may not be productive in big cities, they may be useful in the campgrounds and other recreational environments if they are made highly conspicuous.[1] In practice, these strategies are successful in reducing litter to the extent that containers are available and conveniently located.

In the preceding pages it was noted that the perceived quality of an outdoor recreation environment is based on both perception and experience of the environment. Although environmental perception and environmental experiences are interdependent conceptually and empirically, studies dealing with these two processes focus on different phases of the problem. While the former is directed at how people form impressions about various environments, the latter analyzes the modes of environmental experiences and the relationship between desired and achieved psychological rewards of environmental experiences. The distinction is analogous to the difference between *specific* and *diverse* exploration in children's play. Specific exploration poses questions such as: "What kind of environment is this?" "What does this environment have and what does it do to me?" "Does it have forested hills, streams and waterfalls?" On the other hand, diverse exploration asks: 'What can I do with this environment?" "Can I get relaxed and can I reach peace of mind here?" "Will I meet other people here?" Novel environments typically invite specific exploration, while familiar surroundings give rise to diverse exploration.

Nevertheless, both types of exploration are present in all environmental encounters. The outcome of environmental exploration is an individual way of experiencing various environments. Ittelson, Franck and O'Hanlon (1976) have distinguished five different but overlapping modes (ways) of experiencing the environment: (1) environment as an external physical place, (2) as self, (3) as social system, (4) as emotional territory, and (5) as setting for action. These modes will be examined next.

psychological experience of outdoor recreation environments

To some extent everybody experiences the environment as an external physical place, because such a mode is based on the psychological development of an individual. A person who cannot separate self from environment does not have cognitive capacity to function in the world. Achieving a sense of an autonomous self represents an important step in cognitive and personal development. It has been shown that infants are not capable of distinguishing between themselves and their surroundings (Altman, 1975; Ittelson, *et al.*, 1976). Even though all adults may be able to experience the environment as a physical place, they vary, however, in the extent to which this tendency affects their experiences. Environments

environment as an external physical place

[1]However, there is a problem with posted signs in that they themselves constitute an intrusion into the natural landscape.

also differ in their capacity to facilitate this mode. It is probably safe to say, other things being equal, that because of their highly distinctive characteristics Colorado's Rocky Mountains enhance the mode of experiencing them as an external place more than many other scenes.

Other factors possibly increasing people's tendency to experience the environment as an external place include novelty, expectations, and orientation. That is, when a person visits the Rocky Mountains for the first time (novelty) the visitor is more likely to view the place primarily in terms of its physical characteristics than is the person who visits the mountains for, say, the tenth time (familiarity). But even the familiar environment can be experienced as an external physical place if the person visits it with the expectation of viewing it as an external place. Finally, when a person is in the process of establishing an orientation toward the environment, experiencing it as an external physical place is likely because lacking effective orientation would make the person lose his way in the environment. The need for orientation is apparent within novel and complex environments. As a result of the orientation process, the person forms a cognitive map on which certain places are marked according to their physical properties alone; thus he experiences them as external physical characteristics. The cognitive organization of an environment into various categories is essential for a person to be able to function in any surroundings. All the above indicates that the mode of experiencing the environment as an external physical place is parallel to what we termed above as ''specific exploration'' of the environment.

In his provocative essay, Proshansky (1973) asserted that the ideology of modern capitalism encourages people to view and to experience the environment not only as an external physical setting, but above all as an external enemy which has to be conquered, mastered, and controlled. He claimed that ''the physical environment is to be manipulated, exploited and used exclusively to serve man. There seemed to be no reason why he has to serve it, except in the sense of killing the goose that lays the golden eggs'' (p. 4). The recent controversies between American industry and the Environmental Protection Agency (EPA) indeed attest the validity of Proshansky's assertion. Rather than trying to comply voluntarily with the EPA standards, industry has spent millions of dollars in lobbying and fighting against regulation. The business community argues that the environmental standards are too strict to be followed without enormous losses in profits and without massive layoffs. Thus, those directing industry have resorted to the scare tactics by saying that it is *either* the environment *or* employment, work or free-time.

But the problem does not end there. Since capitalism is based upon the idea of continuous growth, economists contend that it is essential to continuously expand industry, and therefore it is necessary to use more and more natural resources, including wilderness areas. There is evidence that the environment takes second place, not only in the minds of economists and industrialists but also among workers, at least when a person loses his job due to the enactment of environmental regulations. In sum, there is some truth to the statement that the capitalistic social order induces the individual to view and experience the environment as an external physical setting. The author, however, contends that this explanation is far too simplistic and general, because it is the individual who ultimately is the source of modes of experiencing the environment, though he is also influenced by the social system he lives in.

This mode refers to the situation in which "a total merging of self and environment is accomplished . . . environment becomes self, and self, environment" (Ittelson, *et al.*, 1976). The person is therefore likely to view a change in the environment as a change in the self. Injury to the environment is experienced as injury to self. Factors likely to facilitate one's experiencing environment as self include those suggested above. Thus, variations in personal experiences as well as in the types of environments are likely to influence the degree to which this mode dominates an individual's environmental experiences. Furthermore, the more often one visits a given environment, the more familiar one becomes with it and thus the more likely one is to experience it as self. Other things being equal, increased familiarity develops expectations that the environment will be a source of self-identity and self-concept, and this in turn facilitates experiencing the environment as an inseparable part of one's self. Ittelson, *et al.* (1976) reported that personal possessions and personalized space tend to enhance the association and identification of self with the environment. Finally, increased environmental knowledge is essential to forming the fundamental attitudes which make it possible for a person to experience the environment as self. Needless to say, such ecological consciousness may pose a severe threat to modern capitalism.

environment as self

To increase environmental awareness, Leff (1978) suggested that three general forms of education should be implemented: (1) environmental, (2) synergistic, and (3) confluent education. The first aims at increasing environmental knowledge and ecological consciousness, for example, "by environmental issues and concerns pervasive throughout the educational curriculum" in most subject matter and at all grade levels. This also calls for student involvement in environmental action projects and participation in outdoor nature study. Synergistic education stresses cooperation (instead of competitive individualism) and creativity at all levels of human activity and transcending grade levels. Since the ideology of modern capitalism with its emphasis on competitive individualism is one of the major obstacles to increasing ecological consciousness, synergistic education is designed to penetrate to the core of this ideology. Finally, confluent education refers to the integration of affective and cognitive domains. Leff (1978) suggests that the purpose is to expand self-awareness in general, to clarify feelings, enhance aesthetic sensitivity and expression, encourage imagination, etc. Such education strives to enhance self-identity and self-concept by integrating affective and cognitive elements.

However, no one form of education can achieve the objective of making most people experience the environment as self, but it certainly can help in this respect. One might indeed say that the majority of outdoor recreationists experience the environment as self, particularly in the wilderness. This contention was indirectly confirmed by Shafer and Mietz's study (1972), which showed the aesthetic experience ranked highest out of other experiential modes among wilderness hikers.

environment as social system

According to this mode of Ittelson's, *et al.* (1976) schema, social interrelation-ships become the major element of environmental experience for some people. These persons describe environments chiefly in terms of the people whom they know there or with whom they are associated in some capacity. Studies, how-ever, indicate that the environment as social system may not be the dominant mode of experience among outdoor recreationists. Shafer and Mietz's (1972) data revealed that wilderness hikers ranked social experience the least important of all the listed modes, and ten times less favorably than aesthetic experience, the leading mode. Consistent with this, Stankey (1972) reported that 82% of all wilderness users studied considered solitude an important feature of wilderness. It should be emphasized, however, that these studies were done on wilderness hikers, so that any generalizations of the above findings to apply to all outdoor recreationists are premature.

The idea of solitude is a relative concept. Stankey found that only two percent of all wilderness hikers were traveling alone. Thus, solitude is defined in terms of one's own social company, especially because only a small fraction of the respondents indicated they enjoyed meeting others on the trail. Heimstra and McFarling (1974) suggested that large groups disturb wilderness users more than small ones. Another indication of the relative nature of solitude and social experi-ence in the minds of outdoor recreationists is the finding that a single motorboat threatens canoeists' feelings of solitude more than do several other canoes (Lucas, 1964). Finally, there is one important social dimension of solitude which has been overlooked in the past. That is, even though a person may hike com-pletely alone in the wilderness, the hiker talks about it to others before and after the actual experience. In this sense, then, a person's wilderness experience is clearly social, even if solitude was ranked as the main mode of the actual en-vironmental experience. As Shafer and Mietz (1972) asked: "How many of the wilderness users would continue to like it if there was no opportunity to share their experience?"

Although most wilderness hikers do not experience environment as "social system," there are many outdoor recreationists to whom the social aspect is important. If persons do not find opportunities for social interaction in their everyday living they are likely to look for such experiences in outdoor recreation. In support of this contention, Knopp (1972) reported that outdoor recreation ac-tivities are of higher social value to residents in rural farm areas than to residents in urban areas. Apart from these findings, the fact remains that by a sizeable margin a majority of wilderness hikers prefer solitude over sociability as a way of experiencing the outdoor environment.

This conclusion, however, may not be true for all outdoor recreationists (e.g., campers), because some outdoor environments are more conducive to the social/solitude experience than others. Fridgen and Hinkelman (1977) reported the following data on the relationship between outdoor sites and their capacity for providing certain experiences and activities. The means below are based upon subjects' judgments on a 9-point scale as to how well (9) or poorly (1) each site is "suited to provide for this activity/experience."

Site	Solitude	Challenge	Relaxation	Playing Sports
Wilderness Area	8.4	8.3	7.9	2.8
National Parks	6.0	6.2	7.2	4.0
State Parks	5.5	5.4	6.4	5.4
City Parks	2.4	2.5	4.8	7.8

It is evident that the value of solitude increases strongly and steadily from city parks to wilderness areas. In fact, an identical trend occurred with regard to "challenge;" the correlation between "solitude" and "challenge" was .64. The mean of relaxation also rose, though not as sharply as that of solitude or challenge. As could be expected, the value of playing sports strongly declined from city park to wilderness. Assuming that perceived natural attractiveness increases from city parks to wilderness areas, the above data clearly indicate an inverse relationship between the perceived natural attractiveness of the environment and the experience of the environment as a "social system." In other words, the more natural one views a given environment, the less one expects to experience it as a social system and the more as solitude. In this light, then, it is evident why the past studies of wilderness users (e.g., Stankey, Shafer and Mietz) have shown that solitude ranks very high, and the social aspect extremely low, as modes of experiencing an outdoor environment.

Implicit in the foregoing discussion is the idea that experiencing outdoor environment as a social system can be internally or externally induced. When one visits a crowded city park, he may not perceive any alternatives, and experiences it as social (externally induced) because of the crowd. By contrast, another person visits the same park merely to watch people or to meet friends (internally induced). It may then be proposed that if the environmental experience as social system is internally caused, such experience is enjoyable and psychologically rewarding. But if it is externally caused the environmental experience becomes less enjoyable.

This mode conveys the idea that the environment may be experienced predominantly in terms of affect and emotions. Ittelson, *et al.* (1976) suggested that most people know some familiar environments which they experience principally as emotional territories. It is likely that former places of residence are environments which become such territories. For example, after having lived in a new community for a while people have a tendency to return to their previous places of residence to remember "the good old times and places." For these individuals the old environment emotions become the dominant mode of experience.

environment as emotional territory

Another variable that has to be considered is the effect of continuous exposure to a given environment on the individual's tendency to experience it as an emotional territory. In general, it appears that any environment loses its affect- and arousal-inducing qualities after repeated exposure to it. If novelty, uncertainty, dissonance and incongruity are associated with an object (environment), these internal responses give rise to arousal and affect toward that object. But the longer the person remains near a given environment, the more familiar but less uncertain, dissonant and incongruous it becomes. Consequently, over a period of time one is likely to become more analytical and less emotional in his orientation toward familiar environments.

Besides these tendencies which are rather universally observed among all persons, individuals also differ in their propensity to experience environments as emotional places. Ittelson, *et al.* (1976) suggested that poets and artists in general are more inclined to experience the environment as an emotional place than do other people. Emotions are a more dominant mode of environmental experience for "purists" and environmentalists than for the public in general, because the attitude of the former (amount of affect) toward the environment is more favorable. It is conceivable that those who experience the environment as self also experience it as an emotional territory.

Mehrabian and Russell's (1974) review of past studies led to the conclusion that "emotional reactions represent the common core of human response to all types of environments." In an effort to analyze this universal emotional response, the authors conducted studies which indicated that an emotional experience has three dimensions: *pleasure, arousal,* and *dominance.* Pleasure is a feeling or state which a person describes with the adjectives *happy, pleased, satisfied, contented, hopeful* and *relaxed.* Arousal is a feeling state characterized by the adjectives *stimulated, excited, frenzied, jittery, wide awake,* and *aroused.* Dominance is a feeling state which reflects the subjects' responses to the adjectives *controlling, dominant, influential, important, autonomous,* and *in control.* Thus, an individual's feeling of pleasure associated with an environment is in part based upon the extent to which he feels happy, pleased, etc. An individual's feeling of arousal toward an environment is based upon the extent to which that person feels stimulated, excited, etc. And the feeling of dominance stems from the degree of perceived freedom to behave in a variety of ways in an environment. In a similar vein, Proshansky, *et al.* (1970) have proposed that "the individual attempts to organize his physical environment so that it maximizes his freedom of choice."

Are outdoor recreation environments experienced as emotional territories? Based upon Shafer and Mietz's (1972) findings the answer is strongly affirmative. The reader may recall that when an attitudinal scale was used in their study, emotional experience ranked as the second highest of the five listed modes, immediately after aesthetic experience. The results were even more in favor of "emotions" when the respondents' (wilderness hikers) answers to the question, "What is the most important thing you enjoy about wilderness recreation?", were considered. It appeared that 47% of the hikers rated emotional experience as the most important category followed by aesthetic experience (37%). Such things as "the roaring flush of a ruffed grouse, the splash of a leaping trout, or a simple curve in the trail that promises something new or challenging beyond the bend" were mentioned as the encounters which constitute the emotional experience.

Although these findings stress the emotional experience, the limitations of the study should be kept in mind. That is, the Shafer and Mietz investigation was conducted on wilderness hikers whose outdoor setting represents the extreme point on a continuum ranging from the least natural to the most natural. The Fridgen and Hinkelman data (see above) clearly showed that the rated value of various aspects (e.g., relaxation) of emotional experience increased steadily from the least natural outdoor environment (city park) to the most natural (wilderness). In other words, city parks were perceived to be much less suitable for providing emotional experience than the wilderness. Thus, even though all outdoor environments may be a source of emotional experience, it is clear that such feelings are more likely to peak in the wilderness than in other outdoor recreation settings.

Theoretically, outdoor recreation environments can be categorized according to Mehrabian and Russell's (1974) three emotional dimensions: pleasure, arousal, and dominance. In the absence of empirical data one can only speculate about possible relationships, but it is plausible that in the wilderness all three states of feeling are relatively high and evenly represented. However, it is unlikely that city parks can provide all these emotional dimensions to the same extent as wilderness-oriented environments, especially feelings of dominance.

The relationships between outdoor recreation environments and the three emotional dimensions, therefore, remain to be explored empirically. When such efforts are undertaken researchers should exercise extreme caution in classifying outdoor environments according to the emotional dimensions, because feelings are very unstable, changing, and above all individual. Another approach would be to investigate various people's tendency to approach and to avoid outdoor environments, evaluating this tendency as a function of the emotion-eliciting qualities of various environments. Mehrabian and Russell's work (1974) provides an excellent base for such research. For example, Russell and Mehrabian (1976) reported data indicating the desire-to-stay, desire-to-explore, desire-to-affiliate and desire-to-drink were differently affected by the degree of the rated pleasantness, arousal, and dominance of varied environments. The results, therefore, clearly demonstrated some behavioral effects of the physical environment.

This final mode (Ittelson, *et al.*, 1976) suggests that the environment may be experienced primarily as a setting for action. Accordingly, a person's view of a given outdoor environment may be based exclusively on participation in various activities and on achieving the desired goals through participation. Ittelson, *et al.* (1976) noted that those laymen and professionals who plan and create environments typically view them in terms of providing for actions. Planners often assume that they can do little other than providing a setting for action to affect the individual's experience in terms of various modes. It is probably safe to say that this mode is the prevalent one among recreation professionals. When recreational places are designed, the chief concern seems to be space for certain activities.

environment as setting for action

Environmental psychologists (e.g., Altman, 1975; Ittelson, *et al.,* 1976; Mehrabian and Russell, 1974), however, have reported ample evidence indicating that some physical arrangements may facilitate social interaction, while others may discourage it. The same is probably true for other ways of experiencing the environment. For example, the environment where tennis courts are placed could encourage emotional experience if the courts were surrounded by an aesthetically pleasing landscape (palm trees, small lake, etc.). Or, consider the ingenious and brilliant design of the Washington Art Gallery. Critics, professionals, and everyday visitors, all were overwhelmed by the feeling they experienced inside the building. Some of them even said that paintings and other pieces of art take a secondary place in the visitor's experience. Thus, it is clear that recreational environments can be designed to emphasize various modes of experiences, not just to provide a setting for action. Unfortunately, the other modes have often been forgotten when recreational places are planned.

Outdoor recreation environments, on the other hand, are better suited to provide for many modes of environmental experience. The Fridgen and Hinkelman data (see above) suggested that the more natural the outdoor environment is perceived, the less it is experienced as a setting for action. For example, the city park was rated well suited to provide for playing sports, whereas wilderness areas rated poor in this regard. Of course, this is not an impressive insight in itself, but it nevertheless attests the principle that outdoor environments vary in their capacity to encourage viewers or visitors experiencing the environment as setting for action. Based upon these findings, the implication would seem to be that the less natural environments (e.g., city parks) should be designed with a variety of leisure modes in mind. To maximize people's experiencing these environments as settings for action, however, creates a self-fulfilling circle. That is, it may very well be that people generally perceive city parks as settings for action because no room has been provided for other modes of experience in these places. The author contends that undue emphasis has been placed on the action mode when user-based recreation environments are planned and built. All one has to do is to walk to city parks and observe how many of them look alike, consisting of such standard features as baseball diamonds. After all, who said that a baseball diamond has to be in a city park?

phases of the outdoor recreation experience

The above discussion has focused on the five modes (ways) of experiencing outdoor recreation environments. But the discussion was general, in the sense that it did not specify the time or phase when the environment is experienced. Theoretically, the modes of experience could be measured *before, during* and *after* the environmental encounter. In this vein, Clawson (1963) has conceptualized outdoor recreation experience in terms of five phases: (1) anticipation or planning phase, (2) phase involving travel to the recreation site, (3) phase of the on-site experience, (4) phase consisting of the travel back home from the site, and (5) the recollection phase. It is conceivable that the prevalence of the mode of experiencing the outdoor recreation environment varies from stage to stage. Moreover, each environmental encounter affects the total recreation experience, whether the environment is viewed as "self," "emotional territory," etc. These effects may reinforce the dominant mode or change it. For example, as mentioned earlier, the more familiar a person is with a given wilderness area, the

A Social Psychological Perspective on Outdoor Recreation

more likely he is to experience it as "self." Thus, changes in the environmental experience should be investigated as functions of one's life span, as well as in terms of shorter periods of time like one recreational trip. Ittelson, *et al.* (1976, p. 206) put it aptly: "Environmental experience is the continuing product of an active endeavor by the individual to create for himself a situation within which he can optimally function and achieve his own particular pattern of satisfaction."

As the above discussion showed, the environment may be experienced in many ways, and in varying degrees this experience can be psychologically rewarding. To the extent that environmental experience is a subjective thing, it can be enhanced by environmental design which focuses on the individual. On the other hand, the experience can be impaired by poor environmental design which ignores human aesthetic and psychological needs. This chapter concludes by presenting Proshansky's (1973) philosophical (arm-chair) speculation about environmental crisis in human dignity and its implications.

environmental crisis in human dignity?

In his stimulating essay, Proshansky (1973) has vividly and convincingly argued that the design and organization of physical settings have ignored and oversimplified the *human* characteristics of the individual, conceiving of him as a simple "machine man." When environments were being designed and built, how individuals experience them apparently has meant very little to the planners. The environmental crisis in human dignity, therefore, represents the crisis in the values placed on *human* life. It is reflected by such physical indicators as polluted air and waterways and is marked by the failure "to maintain and enhance all of the human qualities that distinguish human beings from lower organisms." This failure "confirms the very restricted, vacuous, and undifferentiated nature of our built environment" as testified by "the monotony of gas stations, billboards, shopping centers, trailer camps, and hamburger stands" (Proshansky, 1973, p. 2). He poignantly but aptly continued:

> Some may disagree, but in my judgment it is hard to make a case for technological improvements or advances in human life in the name of electric toothbrushes and shoeshine kits, remote-control home TV sets, gas-lit garbage pits, disposable clothes, electric pencil sharpeners; and certainly no case at all for the annual change in car models, for clothes styles, equipment design, food packaging, patent medicine remedies, and so on" (p. 5).

One is tempted to suggest (knowing the danger of oversimplification) that the above points are clear signs of the crisis in human dignity in the *instant society*. The principal concern of such society is that most of the things can be done instantly and effortlessly. In this pursuit the environments are standardized, as evidenced by monotonous hamburger stands in urban areas and baseball diamonds in city parks. This environmental design concedes little value to human ways of experiencing the environment. The biggest problem with the instant society is the human being; that is, many people have accepted or internalized the inhuman values of the instant society. Due to their enormous capacity to adapt to almost any conditions, human beings have "overadapted" (Dubos,

1965, 1971) to the environment created by this society. Overadaptation can even reach the point where the values characteristically human are destroyed (Proshansky, 1973). Thus, the question is not whether people are able to get by without outdoor recreation environments. Of course, they will, because of their capacity to overadapt. But they do so at the expense of the values and dignity that make them characteristically human. Herein lies the dilemma and challenge for the recreation professional.

---

summary

The chapter began with a discussion of environmental perception. It was shown that the perceived quality of the outdoor recreation environment is determined by physical characteristics of the environment as well as by psychological rewards expected from outdoor environmental encounters. Based upon these two elements, a theory and an index of the perceived quality of the recreation environment was presented. This theory was developed by relating the observed quality of the recreation environment (nominator) to its expected quality (denominator). To arrive at these two components, expected and observed evaluations, as well as subjective probabilities relating to environmental characteristics (e.g., undeveloped country, open water), have to be assessed. Similarly, expected and observed evaluations as well as subjective probabilities regarding psychological entities (e.g., escape from routine, relaxation) have to be estimated. It was postulated that satisfaction with an outdoor recreation environment is a direct function of the perceived quality of that environment.

Consistent with this theorizing, research has shown that some physical characteristics enhance, while others undermine, the perceived aesthetic (environmental) quality of the scene. It generally appears that the more natural the environment, the higher is its perceived aesthetic quality. Also congruent with the theory is evidence indicating that what people seek and achieve psychologically from outdoor recreation environments affects their perceptions of the quality of these environments. The individual's personality or past experiences, his situational or social factors, determine expectations about the perceived aesthetic and psychological quality of outdoor recreation environments. The contrast-effect hypothesis was developed to explain differences in preferences for outdoor environments. To people living in urban areas, natural outdoor environments provide a contrast, and such contrasting experiences are needed to satisfy the human need for optimal arousal and incongruity.

Past research has shown that the users and managers differ in their assessments of perceived quality of outdoor recreation environments. Psychologically, this finding is not surprising, because these differences simply reflect variation in the users' and managers' motives for being in the natural environment. It has been found, for example, that campers rate a given natural environment more positively than do managers, presumably because the latter have been trained to pay particular attention to the characteristics (e.g., litter) that degrade the perceived quality of the environment. At the same time, the users (mostly urban residents) expect to see and experience aesthetic and psychological contrast to their home (urban) environment, therefore paying less attention to specific features of the environment. Despite these differences, litter is one of the characteristics that reduces the perceived quality of an outdoor recreation environment in the eyes of most people. The latter part of this section of the chapter was devoted to the discussion of research on the social psychological determinants of littering.

The second half of the present chapter focused on the psychological experience of outdoor recreation environments. It centered on reported distinction between five interrelated ways of experiencing the environment: (1) environment as an external physical place, (2) as self, (3) as social system, (4) as emotional territory, and (5) as setting for action. The chapter concluded with the thesis that there is an environmental crisis in human dignity. The designing and organization of physical settings have ignored and oversimplified the *human* characteristics of the individual, conceiving of the human being as a simple "machine man." Environmental design has contributed to the development of the instant society and has thereby failed "to maintain and enhance all of the human qualities that distinguish human beings from lower organisms."

14 privacy, crowding, and outdoor recreation

As was repeatedly stated before, too much or too little incongruity provided by the leisure environment is psychologically abnormal and unhealthy. Thus, the individual strives to maintain an optimal level of incongruity through recreation participation. An individual approaches and avoids social interaction so as to achieve the desired social contact. He avoids and pursues crowds. It is for this reason that crowding or privacy in itself is neither good nor bad. The most important consideration is an appropriate match between the expected and achieved level of social interaction. When people go to a football game they are disappointed if nobody else is attending the game. This follows because people have come with the expectation to see thousands of spectators at the stadium. Or, consider a woman who was asked by a TV broadcaster about her favorite in this year's Kentucky Derby: "Oh gosh, I haven't seen a single horse yet, but, I don't mind as I came to watch and enjoy these people." On the other hand, when people hike in the wilderness they are annoyed if the area is full of other hikers. This reaction ensues because they have come to expect to see nobody or only a few people in the wilderness. Satisfaction with social interaction results when the expected level of interpersonal contacts equals the desired one.

In the preceding chapter, the role of social interaction in outdoor recreation was surveyed. The present chapter is devoted to a more detailed analysis of human tendency to pursue and avoid interrelationships in outdoor recreation environments. It begins with a discussion of privacy and crowding as theoretical constructs, and continues by focusing on outdoor recreation as a means of coping with crowding and environmental stress. It then proceeds to analyze behavioral and cognitive mechanisms for controlling crowding in outdoor recreation settings. The chapter concludes with an examination of psychological benefits of outdoor recreation participation.

According to Altman (1975), privacy is an *"interpersonal boundary-control process"* which regulates social interaction with others to provide a person with a desired level of privacy. Thus, privacy is *"an optimizing process"* which aims at an optimal amount of contacts with others; too much or too little interaction is unsatisfactory. To achieve the optimum, a person has to restrict and seek contacts with others. Privacy is, therefore, *"a dialectic process,"* a continuous interplay of opposing forces, to shut oneself off from others at one time and to open oneself up to interpersonal contacts at another time. The desired level of social interaction is not stable but rather dynamic, changing with circumstances and time.

To achieve the desired level of privacy, various techniques are commonly used. Altman (1975) suggested that these mechanisms include verbal or paraverbal behavior, personal space, territory, and cultural mechanisms. Verbal behavior simply refers to such everyday phrases as "keep out" and "come in." Often, non-verbal behavior (body language) can be as effective in regulating privacy as the actual words. One place where people's body language daily demonstrates discomfort with the invasion of privacy is an elevator. Altman (p. 35) observed: "In a crowded elevator where we are forced to be close to strangers, we typically keep our hands at our sides, hold our bodies rigid and immobile, breathe quietly, and look up at the floor designation numbers, look down at the floor, or stare blankly ahead."

Privacy can also be regulated by such environmental mechanisms as clothing and adornment and personal spacing. Clothes, or lack of them, are sometimes used to protect one's privacy or to express the need for more interaction. An example of protecting privacy by clothes would be a woman wearing a veil to cover her face. From personal experience, the writer can mention a Saudi-Arabian couple who were living as neighbors in a married-student apartment in Champaign-Urbana, Illinois. For several months after coming to the U.S., the wife still had difficulties in adjusting to the "naked culture." She said she felt nude whenever she went outside because she could not cover her body to the extent she was accustomed to. The Western way of dressing did not give her a sufficient feeling of privacy. A totally different way of signaling the desire for privacy through clothing can be seen during the hot summer days in the streets of Copenhagen, where one may meet women going topless. For some men this may be confusing because they do not know what kind of privacy the topless women have in mind!

Personal space refers to "the invisible boundary surrounding the self" (Altman, 1975). A person decides situationally the desired distance for social interaction so as to regulate interpersonal contacts. In his classic text, Hall (1966) distinguished four distance zones to indicate the type of interaction sought: (1) intimate distance (0 to about 18 inches), including lovemaking and fondling, (2) personal distance (1½ to 4 feet), referring to the protective sphere, (3) social distance (4 to 12 feet), involving most interpersonal behaviors and encounters, and (4) public distance (more than 12 feet), found in official and formal meetings; for example, royal etiquette in Great Britain requires Prince Philip to walk several feet behind Queen Elizabeth during official state visits. The four distance zones are not important in terms of physical distance per se but rather in terms of affecting interpersonal communications.

Attempts to protect one's personal space can be seen everywhere. Houses are often built so that each family member can have a room or at least a corner of personal space; houses are frequently surrounded by walls, hedges, or fences. Working space is often so arranged that a person can have a private office or corner in which to carry out tasks and duties. Ways of regulating personal space and privacy, however, differ from culture to culture. Altman (1975) noted that in an effort to control interpersonal boundaries Englishmen speak less loudly than Americans. Americans, on the other hand, tend to secure their privacy by territorial behavior, that is, through ownership of areas and objects. The Japanese are noted for their moveable separators in their houses as a means of achieving different privacy for different situations. Thus, it appears that most societies have mechanisms for maintaining privacy, though specific techniques may vary from one culture to another.

The above conceptualization stresses the interpersonal function of privacy. In addition to regulating social interaction with others, privacy serves to maintain and enhance a person's self-identity. Altman (1975) noted that if privacy-protecting mechanisms fail to control access to the self, the person becomes "nothing." Self-identity is also lost if a person cannot make a distinction between self and the environment; the self becomes "everything." The absence or reduction of privacy, therefore, poses a menace to self-identity and psychological well-being. It also threatens human dignity (Proshansky, 1973). Since privacy regulation is an interpersonal process, the solution to the problem of lack of privacy has to come from this (social) domain. Thus, it is more important to educate people to respect others' need for privacy than to establish physical boundaries. Such respect should be based upon the idea that privacy is an individual thing, defined personally and not by others.

crowding

Crowding is a concept closely related to privacy. Like privacy, crowding is an interpersonal, optimizing, and dialectical process. In short, crowding is felt when the privacy-controlling mechanisms fail, producing more social interaction than is desired. Or stated differently, crowding occurs when achieved privacy is less than desired privacy (Altman, 1975). The dialectical nature of crowding is seen in that people both approach and avoid crowds; they experience them positively and negatively. For example, a person who goes to a stadium to watch a football game expects to see thousands of people there, and probably enjoys the crowd. But the same individual who tries to get close to a hot-dog stand during an intermission becomes frustrated by the crowd and if asked at that moment, would probably say he hates the crowd. The distinction between density and crowding draws the line between a sociological and a psychological approach to this phenomenon. While density strictly speaking refers to a physical quality (a number of people per space unit), crowding is a psychological concept since it is personally experienced. Thus, the concept "density" regards people simply as numbers and does not consider subjective reactions to the presence of others.

altman's model of crowding

Altman (1975) has proposed a theoretical model which seems to be the best and most comprehensive conceptualization of the phenomenon available today. As can be seen in figure 19, a person situationally defines the desired level of privacy. This definition results from the combined influences of personal factors, interpersonal forces, and situational conditions. Predicated upon an individual's desired degree of privacy, one then attempts to achieve this objective through various privacy-controlling mechanisms, as discussed above. Following these efforts one evaluates their effectiveness and decides whether the achieved privacy equals the desired condition. If what is achieved is less than desired, crowding occurs. But if what is achieved is more than the desired, a feeling of social isolation results. Altman postulated that this assessment is accompanied by "a subjective, motivational state of stress," which induces the person to readjust privacy-controlling behaviors in the case of over- or under-shooting the mark. This readjustment continues as long as the desired privacy is achieved.

In the writer's opinion, however, the feedback arrow should go all the way back to the "situational definition" and the antecedents. Altman's original model implies that the person continues to engage in "coping behaviors" (privacy-controlling mechanisms), until the desired degree of privacy is achieved. There are, however, many situations where the individual cannot be so stubborn. Consider a football stadium where the person attempts to buy a hot-dog during the intermission. No matter what verbal or body language is used, one may not be able to reach the stand. Rather than continuing these coping behaviors, one may have to redefine the desired level of privacy and forget the hot-dog. Privacy-controlling mechanisms or coping behaviors affect personal experiences and possibly also "interpersonal characteristics." Thus, the employment of coping behaviors becomes a two-way street in which the person influences others and in turn is influenced by them. These possibilities are not considered in the original model, and therefore the feedback line should be extended to "situational definition" and antecedents in the model.

To achieve the desired level of privacy "costs" the individual psychological and physiological energy. If one travels to Yellowstone Park from New York City to experience privacy, it is obvious that he has to pay for it, not only financially but physically and psychologically. Altman suggested that if this energy expenditure leads to extreme "costs," it adds to the subjective feeling of overcrowding, thereby contributing to social pathology in the extreme case.

The final link to be considered in the model is an hypothesized possibility that density sets in motion such interpersonal processes as intrusion and social interference. To the extent that this occurs, density undermines privacy-controlling mechanisms. Thus, density in itself does not interfere with coping behaviors, but only intervenes through its power to initiate or reinforce psychological processes. Altman's model also involves time as an element of the crowding phenomenon, but it does not go beyond this superficial acknowledge-

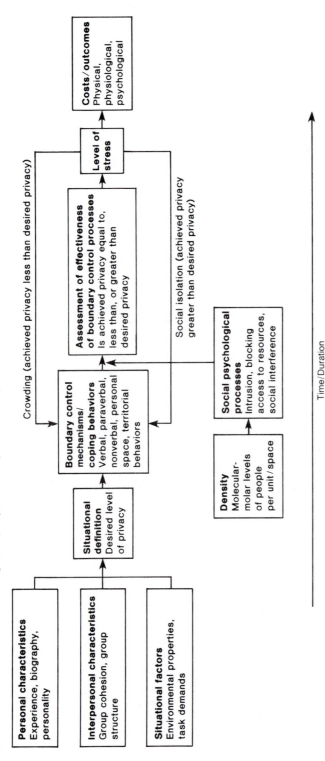

Figure 19 A model of crowding. (From *The Environment and Social Behavior*, by I. Altman. Copyright ©1975 by Wadsworth, Inc. Reprinted by permission of the publisher, Brooks/Cole Publishing Company, Monterey, California.)

ment. As a final note, it should be made clear that Altman's model is not the only conceptualization of crowding. For example, Proshansky, *et al.* (1970), Stokols (1972), and Wohlwill (1974), have discussed crowding in a manner somewhat similar to Altman's optimizing process. In addition, Choi, Mirjafari and Weaver (1976) have developed a list of potential variables affecting crowding and ways of adapting to it. Nonetheless, Altman's model retains the basic ideas presented in other conceptualizations and places a premium on crowding as an interpersonal process, an approach which is necessary for understanding crowding as a social psychological phenomenon.

According to the above theorizing, crowding is experienced as an unpleasant cognitive situation. To avoid this unpleasantness, people have developed various ways of coping with it. The Altman model suggested that individuals resort to verbal, non-verbal, and environmental mechanisms to attain the desired level of privacy and interaction. Evidence of successful coping can be seen in many different cultures. As Altman (1975) noted, the Japanese have developed ways of using their homes and rooms for a variety of purposes (e.g., recreation, eating) with the help of movable walls and separators. These flexible physical arrangements provide opportunities to cope with limited space. Another approach to coping with the lack of space is seen in the Japanese obsession for some recreational activities, especially gardening. Altman also cited evidence indicating that coping behaviors designed to regulate social interaction are present in more primitive cultures like those of East African tribes and societies.

ways of coping with crowding

Hong Kong is another densely populated culture which is often cited as an example of the successful management of crowded living. A low rate of various indicators of social pathology (e.g., juvenile delinquency, crime, admissions to mental hospitals) in Hong Kong has been attributed to such cultural coping mechanisms as styles of family functioning and social organization in general (Altman, 1975). This raises an interesting and important question about the role of recreation in preventing and reducing social pathology. Only one study has explored the relationship between recreation and social pathology. Craig (1976) reported that as recreation opportunity increased, the rate of various indicators of social pathology decreased. This finding, however, has to be treated with extreme caution because of the definitions and indicators of "recreation opportunity" (full-time staff, per capita expenditures, and open space) and "social pathology" (poverty, income, serious crime, robbery, physical health, education, unemployment, and mental health), and because of the correlational nature of the study, and because of the "subjects" of the study, that is, subjects were 30 U.S. cities with population over 250,000 in 1970, with no individual and psychological measures being taken. The value of the study lies in the suggested inference that leisure and recreation activities may play an important role in reducing social pathology. This tentative conclusion should be subjected to rigorous empirical testing at the *individual* level.

But what are some of the specific coping responses to ongoing social interaction and overcrowding? Milgram (1971) has systematically studied the experience of living in cities, particularly New York City, and has theorized that city dwellers are repeatedly exposed to stimulus overload. Because there are too many inputs for the individual to process and cope with in the city, adaptation occurs. He (p. 668) put forth six adaptive responses that people use to handle cognitively the stimulus overload: (1) allocation of less time to each input; (2) disregard of low-priority inputs like the drunk and the sick; (3) redrawing of boundaries in certain social transactions; e.g., harried bus drivers do not make change for customers (riders) any more; (4) blocking the reception of stimulus inputs, for example, by unlisted telephone numbers; (5) diminishing the intensity of stimulus inputs by filtering devices; (6) creation of specialized institutions (e.g., welfare departments) to absorb inputs which otherwise overwhelm the individual. Of course, the above list is not exhaustive. Altman, for example, reported that people have "systematic transit rhythms" in cities, that they walk more rapidly under crowded conditions.

Another list concerning ways of adaptation to crowding has been reported by Choi, et al. (1976). The authors divided the coping mechanisms into three major categories: (1) behavioral, (2) perceptual and cognitive, and (3) biophysiological. Behavioral modes include, among other things, withdrawal and leaving the crowding situation, increasing personal space, and resorting to such behaviors as aggression. Altman (1975, p. 182), however, reviewed past research and concluded that "it is simply not possible to make universal statements such as 'crowding produces aggression' or 'crowding produces social withdrawal.' " Perceptual and cognitive modes in the model of Choi, et al. are similar to Milgram's (1971) adaptive responses, and include perceptual and cognitive withdrawal, avoiding visual attention to crowding situations, day dreaming, etc. Finally, biophysiological modes bear resemblance to Altman's physiological "costs" of crowding, and refer to increased heart rate, blood pressure, adrenal secretion, muscle tension, sweating, and decreased appetite.

A question then arises about the effectiveness of these and other measures in helping one to cope with crowding in cities. One way of measuring the success of adaptation is to determine the relationship between population density and various indicators of social pathology. In a directly relevant study, Freedman, Heshka and Levy (1975) investigated this relationship in New York City and concluded that when the effects of income and ethnicity are removed, the population density is insignificantly and negligibly related to such indicators of social pathology as juvenile delinquency, admissions to state mental institutions, unmarried births, infant mortality, and venereal diseases. This conclusion, however, is hampered by the correlational nature of the study, by a lack of psychological measurements of density or crowding, and by a somewhat arbitrary selection of indicators of social pathology.

Nonetheless, the study provides tentative support to the idea that adaptive responses used by city dwellers in coping with crowding are relatively successful. Further evidence of this was found by McCauley and Taylor (1977), who reported that city dwellers (Montreal) did not feel more overloaded with interpersonal contacts than small-town people. The majority of respondents in the city and the small-town felt that they had "just enough friends to be happy."

Although city dwellers did not feel over-endowed with friends and acquaintances, however, there was indication that they felt crowded with respect to strangers. Taken together, these results indicate that cities provide an overload of interpersonal contacts but that urban dwellers have developed ways of minimizing psychological impact and optimizing the amount of social interaction.

The above theorizing showed that there are many ways of adapting to crowding, and that this adaptation has been relatively successful from the psychological standpoint. In the past, much of the emphasis has been placed on perceptual and cognitive modes of coping (Milgram, 1971), while relatively little attention has been paid to behavioral modes, like "leaving the crowding situation." In fact, no research has been undertaken to determine specifically what modes are necessary and sufficient for successful adaptation. There are, however, reasons to conclude that leisure behavior serves as a major mode of coping with crowding. For city dwellers, outdoor recreation often becomes the dominant form of imagined and actual leisure involvement. Heimstra and McFarling (1974) reported that "a disproportionate percentage of the users of national parks and wilderness areas have a college or postgraduate degree, belong to one of the professions, and have an above average income;" one study found that about 80% of all wilderness visitors had at least some college education and 27% of these had received some postgraduate training. Since most of the educated people live in cities, it then follows that visitors of national parks and wilderness areas are predominantly city dwellers.

Driver (1972) stated that recreation areas provide opportunities for coping with crowding. Specifically, he postulated that crowding contributes to the environmental stress felt in everyday urban living, and that outdoor recreation becomes "an important means of temporary escape and recovery for men under stress" (p. 236). As evidence for the stress-alleviating value of outdoor recreation, Driver (1972) reported that about 50%–70% of the users of recreation areas generally mention "peace and tranquility," "get away from the city" or "from it all," and "change from routine" as reasons for visiting these areas. This is consistent with the research reviewed earlier. Stankey (1972) found that 82% of the sampled subjects regarded solitude as an important feature of wilderness. Similarly, Knopp (1972) observed that, to a great extent, outdoor activities allow urban residents to get away from the crowds and congestion of the city. Copp (1975) reported that escape from frustrating or boring work, as well as escape from routine or stiffling family life, were important self-expressed reasons for hunting. Hollender's (1977) data revealed that escape from routine, the familiar, and urban stress are important factors in motivation toward camping. All these findings are highly consistent and seem to support Driver's idea about stress-mediating value of outdoor recreation.

The question then may be raised about the irreplaceability of outdoor recreation in alleviating environmental stress experienced by urban residents. Can urban stress be escaped by means of leisure activities other than outdoor recreation? Or, does outdoor recreation alleviate stress to a greater extent than other

outdoor recreation as a means of coping with crowding and environmental stress forms of leisure? To answer these questions, it is important to keep in mind that more than anything else, environmental stress is a psychological or cognitive condition, though it has physiological correlates. It then follows that an individual's past experiences must play an important role in determining what kinds of situational pressures are experienced as stress. This, therefore, forces one to study the above questions in the light of social learning, the socialization process, and the adaptation theory.

It appears that learning and past experiences cause some people to view outdoor recreation as an important, perhaps irreplaceable mode of coping with crowding and urban stress. That is, an individual who has learned in childhood and adolescence to "get away from it all" through outdoor recreation, expects to be able to do the same later in life. In general, the more important outdoor activities become in the early years, the more irreplaceable this mode of recreation will become as a means of coping with environmental stress in the adult stages of life. This does not imply that outdoor habits can be learned only in childhood. Many people become aware of outdoor and natural environments in the later stages of their life span. However, other things being equal, the more an individual has learned to derive satisfaction from outdoor activities in the early years, the more important this form of recreation becomes as a mode of escaping urban stress.

It should also be emphasized that the foregoing does not mean that the young always internalize the values of outdoor recreation. Yet (Part 4) this internalization becomes a reality for most individuals during later phases of the childhood socialization. However, if the foundations are laid out in early years, outdoor recreation will be of unique value to the individual as a tool of maintaining and improving psychological well-being. The opposite is also true, that is, a person who has not been socialized to experience and appreciate outdoor recreation, is likely to resort to other leisure activities as a means of coping with environmental stress. One popular form of leisure in cities, which apparently has important stress-alleviating value, is spending free-time at home with the family or watching TV. In fact, escape from urban stress may be one of the major reasons why TV-watching is the most popular leisure activity in the United States.

Another implication of this view of socialization is that is is not necessary to use leisure activities for coping with crowding and stress if the person has learned to "put up" with the stressful environment. As Altman's (1975), Choi's, *et al.* (1976), Milgram's (1971), and Wohlwill's (1974) works suggest, people develop various adaptive responses or cognitive and behavioral modes of becoming accustomed to the stimulus overload in cities. While living under crowded conditions, they continuously redefine their standards of crowding and privacy, with the result of adapting to environmental stresses.

Altman, Choi, *et al.,* Wohlwill and others maintain, however, that the individual has to pay a psychological and physiological price for this adaptation to crowding and resultant stress. Glass, Singer and Pennebaker (1977), on the other hand, have questioned whether disruptive after-effects of environmental stressors occur "in spite of adaptation or because of the effort entailed in the adaptive process." Their own research on urban stress does not provide a clear-cut answer to this problem, but they incline toward explaining harmful after-effects as the result of continued exposure to environmental stressors in spite of adaptation. Aside from this theoretical issue, Glass and Singer's (1972) and Glass', et al. (1977) studies have clearly demonstrated adverse effects of uncontrollable environmental events on human behavior. It even appears that the stressful impact of uncontrollable aversive events (i.e., noise stressors) contributes to the development of coronary heart disease.

Glass, et al. (1977) accounted for these adverse after-effects in terms of Seligman's (1975) theory of learned helplessness, inferring that if a person's self-perception is lack of ability to control the onset and/or offset of a stress-producing environmental feature, the person becomes helpless. Since inferred helplessness has profound motivational, emotional, and cognitive consequences, it severely undermines an individual's capacity to cope with adverse situations. Specifically, feelings of helplessness interfere with the motivation and ability to learn to escape from environmental stress-producers when they in fact are controllable. Thus, to the extent that crowding and environmental stresses induce helplessness, the individual becomes passive and unmotivated to develop or search for ways of escaping adverse events. There is tentative empirical evidence to suggest that prolonged or habitual residence in high density sectors during one's childhood leads to feelings of lack of control, and thus to decreased expectancies for personal control in other situations (Rodin, 1976). It is generally true that the more control, the better (Sherrod, Hage, Halpern and Moore, 1977).

Although these conclusions follow from experimental studies on the effects of noise (Glass, et al., 1977), they also have implications for recreational participation as a means of coping with urban stress. It appears that if the urban environment produces feelings of helplessness in human beings, it impairs persons' leisure motivation in general and outdoor recreation participation in particular. Instead of active forms of leisure, an individual is likely to adopt such passive modes as watching TV. Consistent with this, Edney and Buda (1976) found that the home, with the people around oneself, is the preferred setting for the majority of "relaxing activities," like "watching TV," "just relaxing, being yourself," "relaxing after a hard day" and "casual conversation with one friend." Spending the bulk of one's free-time in watching TV or in activities of similar kind may, therefore, be an indicator of helplessness and/or of attempts to cope with environmental stress caused by crowding and other forms of stimulus overload.

If urban environments are conducive to feelings of helplessness, it is likely that absence or lack of available recreation services in cities, especially those services associated with the outdoors, deepens these negative feelings. Just to reach a city park may require an excessive amount of effort on the part of many city dwellers, not to mention traveling to state or national parks. Because of the cities' polluted air and water and the overcrowded condition of the parks, urban people are left with few practical opportunities for outdoor recreation. Consequently, the relative lack of availability of outdoor recreation may contribute to feelings of helplessness. On the other hand, it would be too simplistic to assume that urban environments cause helplessness in all residents. Some people find the city an exciting and stimulating place filled with various opportunities; besides, those who have been raised in the inner city may find outdoor and wilderness environments menacing. Again, this shows that it is the individual's perception which determines whether a given environment is over- or understimulating, psychologically healthy or detrimental.

cognitive spacing of outdoor recreation

Although lack of adequate outdoor recreation services may frustrate city dwellers, a theoretical possibility of participating in outdoor recreation sometimes in the future may partially solve the problem of environmental stress. In other words, *cognitive awareness* of outdoor places where one might go may in itself provide a way for coping with city stress factors. The person may say, ''If things get worse, I can always leave this place and go fishing.'' Such a cognitive opportunity or viewpoint expands a person's cognitive leisure repertoire of potential coping behaviors, thereby alleviating the experience of environmentally induced stress. On the other hand, a person can also do the opposite and confine himself to the city. In other words, one may not see any alternatives to those presently provided by the city and therefore may not be cognitively aware of various recreational opportunities for coping with urban stress forces. Such a situation is psychologically dangerous because it does not leave any escape route open in psychological emergency situations. It then follows that simply informing the public about the psychological value of outdoor recreation, or increasing people's cognitive awareness of various opportunities for outdoor recreation, may of itself help them cope with environmental stressors.

Another psychological function of expanded cognitive space of outdoor recreation is to provide means and sources for daydreaming or fantasizing. For many people, simple daydreaming is sufficient to satisfy their desire for outdoor recreation. Actually, for millions of city dwellers this may be the only way of engaging in outdoor recreation. Rossman and Ulehla (1977) reported data indicating that the use of outdoor recreation facilities in wilderness areas would double if money were no obstacle and would triple if distance were no object. The results also showed that people expected to obtain most of the psychological rewards (e.g., tranquility) *only* in the wilderness. If so, *cognitive spacing* of outdoor recreation may indeed play an important role in helping urban residents cope with their stressful environment. In sum, expanding cognitive awareness or the cognitive space of outdoor recreation, is psychologically beneficial because (1) it provides a psychological safety valve to escape urban stress when the environment becomes excessively stressful, and because (2) it enhances imagination and daydreaming through outdoor recreation. To what extent and under what conditions imagined outdoor recreation can be substituted for actual experience remains to be determined.

A Social Psychological Perspective on Outdoor Recreation

The above discussion showed that urban residents have developed effective, but often costly ways of adapting to their stressful environment. For them, outdoor recreation serves as an important mechanism for coping with crowding and other stressors. When people decide to set out on trips to outdoor recreation places they generally expect to meet relatively few people. Since solitude or privacy is a central psychological quality of outdoor recreation, it then becomes imperative to avoid overpopulated service behavior settings. If possible, the overcrowding of outdoor recreation places has to be prevented, not only for psychological but also for environmental reasons. Otherwise visitors would destroy the natural resources. The simplest solution to the problem of overpopulation would be to acquire more land and reduce the number of visitors to the minimum. Simplicity, however, is not often the best and the most practical solution, at least in this case. There are, however, other methods which recreation professionals can use to reduce the overcrowding of city, state and national parks, or other outdoor recreation spots. These methods can broadly be categorized as behavioral and cognitive. Wicker and Kirmeyer's (1977) conceptualization of behavioral mechanisms for controlling the overpopulation of outdoor recreation environments involves a practical approach.

These authors (pp. 92–93) postulated that at least three basic mechanisms exist for regulating the number of visitors: (1) controlling the entrance of clients into the setting, (2) controlling the capacity of the setting, and (3) controlling the length of time clients spend in the setting. Wicker and Kirmeyer suggested a number of ways of achieving these three basic types of control:

A. Regulation of the entrance of clients into the setting
   1. Scheduling entrances
      Example: Popular parks might require campers and hikers to make reservations beforehand for specific times.
   2. Varying recruiting activities
      Example: Popular outdoor places might stop advertising.
   3. Adjusting standards of admissions
      Example: Popular wilderness areas might require all backpackers to demonstrate a knowledge of how to minimize the environmental impact of their visit before issuing them wilderness permits.
   4. Channeling clients into holding areas
      Example: Visitors to popular wilderness spots might be directed to a "lounge" area to wait until the actual hiking place is free.
   5. Preventing unauthorized entrances
      Example: Park visitors might be asked to enter only through certain gates, and park personnel might be given the right to remove and fine unauthorized visitors.

behavioral and cognitive mechanisms for controlling crowding in outdoor recreation places

behavioral mechanisms

B. Regulation of the capacity of the setting
1. Altering physical facilities and spaces
Example: More trails in a wilderness area might be opened for public use so as to accommodate a large number of campers and hikers during the peak periods.
2. Adjusting duration of visits and occurrences in the setting
Example: A popular park, like Yellowstone, might extend or cut down the hours and/or the days of the week it is open.
3. Adjusting size of staff
Example: Additional employees might be assigned to duty during peak periods in camping areas.
4. Varying assignments of nonservice tasks to staff
Example: Lifeguards at a beach might be asked to suspend all equipment maintenance tasks during heavy visitation periods.
C. Regulation of the amount of time clients spend in the locale
1. Varying rate of processing clients
Example: Camp personnel with a number of customers waiting might spend less time orienting each camper.
2. Varying limitations on the length of stay
Example: A public campground might allow campers to stay only seven days during the summer, but 21 days during the rest of the year.
3. Imposing a graduated fee structure based upon time spent in the locale
Example: Campers in a public campground might be charged a higher fee each successive night they spend there.
4. Establishing priorities among clients on such bases as time of arrival, waiting costs, service time required
Example: A popular campground might give priority to those who stay a short period of time.
5. Altering the standing patterns of behavior by means of procedures, rules, and/or physical facilities which affect the rate of flow of clients into and out of the locale
Example: A popular campground might be redesigned with separate entrance and exit gates.

cognitive
mechanisms

In addition to the above behavioral or physical techniques, the congested state of outdoor recreation places can be reduced cognitively by manipulating visitors' perceptions and experiences of crowding (Wicker and Kirmeyer, 1977). This viewpoint is, of course, the same as the one discussed earlier on the basis of Altman's (1975), Choi's, *et al.* (1976), and others' theorizing. It emphasizes that crowding exists in the eyes of the beholder, with personal perceptions and experiences ultimately determining the degree of congestion. Numerous experiments have demonstrated that feelings of crowding can indeed be manipulated effectively (Baum and Greenberg, 1975; Baum and Koman, 1976; Greenberg and Firestone, 1977; Langer and Saegert, 1977). One of these studies is particularly relevant to the present discussion, and is reviewed next.

Langer and Saegert (1977) reasoned that the use of behavioral mechanisms is often difficult in crowded situations and that negative consequences of crowding may be reduced through cognitive means. They hypothesized that increasing cognitive control by providing information about the effects of crowding would ameliorate the adverse influence of crowding. Eighty women were recruited outside two New York grocery stores at crowded and uncrowded times. Their experimental task was to choose (not to buy) the most economical product corresponding to each item on a list of 50 familiar household items located throughout the store; they were allowed 30 minutes to make as many selections as possible. One-half of the subjects were given information about how people generally react and feel when supermarkets are crowded (cognitive control), while the other half received no information regarding the effects of crowding (no control). As expected, crowding decreased the subjects' shopping efficiency and performance, reduced their satisfaction with the supermarket, and made them feel less comfortable. The authors hypothesized that these and other negative effects of crowding could be reduced by increasing their cognitive control over crowding (increased information).

The results clearly supported this expectation. Subjects who were given information about the effects of crowding before shopping were more effective in their task and had more positive feelings than subjects who were not given such information. Significantly, these beneficial effects of prior information were observed under both crowded and noncrowded conditions, though they were expected to occur only among those who shopped at the crowded times. The results, therefore, indicated that the adverse impact of crowding can be ameliorated by appropriate information, and that this information is desirable even when conditions of crowding do not exist. Langer and Saegert interpreted these results to mean that information increased subjects' cognitive control over crowding and therefore produced positive effects. This interpretation is in keeping with other studies (Baum and Greenberg, 1975; Baum and Koman, 1976) which have revealed that subjects who are informed about a forthcoming crowded situation begin preparing themselves for and adapting to crowded conditions. It is also conceivable that such prior information increases the sense of control over the environment, since it creates realistic expectations about the upcoming environmental events and therefore allows the individual to make a relatively accurate situational definition of crowding. If the expected level of crowding equals the observed one, unpleasant surprises can be avoided.

Although the above study was not conducted on recreationists in a natural environment, it is believed that the findings have important implications for the professionals concerned with outdoor recreation. The study strongly implies that crowding can psychologically be controlled through cognitive means. This does not mean that behavioral mechanisms should be rejected or substituted for cognitive ones. That large crowds of people visit places like Yellowstone National Park is an objective fact which has to be accepted and should be the basis of lessening the environmental impact of wilderness users. But what the Langer and Saegert findings clearly show is that the visitors' psychological experience of outdoor recreation can be enhanced even under crowded conditions. Achieving the desired level of privacy is, therefore, possible even at crowded times, provided that campers' and hikers' cognitive control over crowding is increased prior to their visiting outdoor recreation settings. One way of increasing cognitive control for users of outdoor recreation places might be to disseminate information about the degree of density in these environments, showing the average rate of visitation each weekday throughout the season and how people usually behave under crowded conditions.

psychological benefits of outdoor recreation

It has been argued throughout the text that leisure behavior can best be understood as an optimizing and dialectical process. In other words, the individual seeks to attain and maintain optimal amount of incongruity and arousal through environmental and interpersonal encounters, and in so doing, is constantly faced with the contradiction of simultaneously seeking and avoiding inputs. This becomes readily apparent when one attempts to account for antecedents and consequences of outdoor recreation. In essence, this raises the question of the causes and effects of outdoor recreation. For example, is "escaping urban stress" more of a cause or an effect of wilderness hiking? According to the dialectical view of leisure behavior, it is both a reason for and benefit of outdoor recreation. This dialectical quality of leisure motivation has totally been overlooked by leisure researchers in the past. But it appears to be the only meaningful approach to understanding leisure behavior, because it is the dynamic individual who decides when, where, and why to recreate outdoors.

It follows from the above theorizing that the causality of outdoor recreation has two dimensions (or two poles on one continuum): attempts to achieve something and attempts to avoid something. Although outdoor recreation is motivated by the interplay of these two forces, it is conceivable that one is more dominant than the other. For example, a person who is setting out for a trip to a national park may be primarily concerned about leaving everything (i.e., city life) behind, rather than achieving certain psychological rewards. The visitor is aware of challenge, adventure, aesthetic experience and other psychological rewards accompanying wilderness hiking, but places secondary value on them. In contrast, another person is also happy to leave city crowds and stress behind, but is mainly motivated by various psychological rewards which may be achieved from wilderness hiking.

This theoretical distinction has practical implications for the conduct of outdoor recreation services. A person who visits an outdoor recreation place for the sake of "leaving everything behind" probably does not care so much about the aesthetic and psychological quality (see chapter 13) of the environment so long as the visit permits getting away from it all. On the other hand, a person who vigorously pursues aesthetic and emotional experiences through outdoor recreation is likely to be concerned with the environmental as well as the psychological quality of the outdoor settings. Thus, it may be more difficult to satisfy the latter person's need for privacy than that of the former.

In a broad context the above conceptualization helps to explain psychological benefits of outdoor recreation. Theoretically, outdoor recreationists may be categorized as follows:

1. Those who primarily seek psychological rewards (e.g., emotional experience), and secondarily tend to avoid their daily living environment (e.g., crowded and stressful cities)
2. Those who primarily tend to avoid their daily living environment and secondarily seek psychological rewards
3. Those who primarily seek both psychological rewards and avoidance of the living environment
4. Those who secondarily seek both psychological rewards and avoidance of the daily living environment.

It should be noted that the same individual can be classified in different groups at different times. The major psychological benefit of outdoor recreation for the first group equals the sum of the achieved intrinsic rewards. Shafer and Mietz's (1972) data indicated that aesthetic and emotional experiences are such rewards. Similarly, Rossman and Ulehla (1977) found that emotional or spiritual experience, challenge and adventure, and aesthetic enjoyment of natural settings were among the five main categories of psychological rewards to be gained in wilderness.

The major psychological benefit of outdoor recreation for the second group is "leaving everything behind" or escape from urban stress. Such rewards as emotional experiences are of secondary importance, that is, extra bonuses achieved while escaping the everyday environment. The third group perhaps includes more outdoor recreationists than any other because it comprises those who actively seek to escape the daily living environment *and* vigorously pursue psychological rewards via outdoor recreation. Finally, the fourth group consists of those who do not particularly seek psychological rewards nor attempt to escape environmental stresses through outdoor recreation. An example would be a person who annually takes the family to various national parks because of social obligation. Such extrinsically motivated outdoor recreation, however, is not likely to offer psychological benefits. In sum, two major types of psychological rewards emanate from outdoor recreation: (1) those obtained by leaving the everyday environment behind oneself, and (2) those obtained by pursuing a contrasting (new or old) outdoor environment.

In support of the above theorizing, "escape from urban stresses" has indeed emerged as a unique dimension of outdoor recreation in several studies. The most recent one (Rossman and Ulehla, 1977) found that subjects' ratings of the 30 common reward items produced five major categories ("factors") of rewards gained in wilderness:

1. Emotional or spiritual experience
2. Challenge and adventure
3. Aesthetic enjoyment of natural settings
4. Escape from urban stresses
5. Escape from the familiar

The authors labeled the fifth factor differently, i.e., "anti-societal influence." However, the author believes that "escape from the familiar" better describes the items that constituted this factor: "chance to avoid different types of sports," "don't meet other people who have similar recreational interests," and "doesn't make me more appreciative of the comforts of civilization." By drawing a line between the first three factors and the remaining two, Rossman and Ulehla's findings lend strong support to this author's theorizing that psychological benefits of outdoor recreation emanate from the interplay of two forces: avoidance of stressful environments and seeking outdoor recreation places for certain psychological rewards.

Rossman and Ulehla's results also showed that outdoor recreation environments differ in their capacity to help the individual seek psychological rewards and avoid urban stresses. When subjects were asked how likely it is that they would achieve the listed psychological rewards in different environments, it appeared that expectations for obtaining the rewards increased, proceeding from indoor facilities to outdoor recreation environments, and eventually to roadless wilderness. Subjects expected to obtain many of the rewards (e.g., tranquility) only in a natural environment. As reported in the preceding chapter, Fridgen and Hinkelman (1977) obtained practically identical results, indicating that solitude, challenge and relaxation increased regularly from city parks, through state and national parks, to wilderness areas. Similarly, the Rossman and Ulehla data indicated that rewards pertaining to "emotional or spiritual experience," "challenge and adventure," "aesthetic enjoyment of natural settings" and "escape from urban stresses" were strongly expected only in two natural environments: roadless and untouched wilderness, and improved mountain country.

The relative importance of this latter environment ("improved") implies that a complete wilderness is not necessary in order to obtain psychological rewards, though it maximizes the expectations for realizing them. Nevertheless, it appears that the availability of wilderness areas in general is of extremely important psychological value. It is debatable at this point whether the wilderness experience is so important that people use "mind-expanding" drugs to substitute for it, as Rossman and Ulehla would like us to believe. Substitute or not, their data indicated that "leisure time spent in wilderness would more than double if money were no object, and would more than triple if distance were no object."

short-term or
long-term effects?

The above evidence leaves no doubt about the psychological benefits of the outdoors. But are the beneficial effects temporary or lasting? In the absence of systematic research one can only speculate. There are conceptual reasons to presume that the effects do not endure for months and years after the actual outdoor experiences. This is particularly relevant when one recalls that people often recreate outdoors to leave environmental stresses behind them. When they return from outdoor recreation trips they are again faced with the stressful reality they escaped. Furthermore, the studies reviewed above indicate that psychological rewards are mainly affective and emotional in nature. It is generally true that emotions are situation- and time-specific. Also, since the aesthetic enjoyment associated with the experience of natural environments is one of the major psychological rewards of outdoor recreation, it is clear that this benefit is limited in space and time. On the other hand, the "recollection phase" is an important part of an outdoor recreation experience (Clawson, 1963) and may provide some lasting psychological benefits. One could argue that outdoor recreation charges the psychological battery, which then helps an individual live through environmental stresses in the everyday settings. Empirical evidence of this battery-charging hypothesis and of possible enduring effects of the recollection phase, however, remains to be shown.

Kaplan (1974) reported a study of the psychological benefits of an outdoor challenge program in which high school students participated. Although, because of methodological weaknesses (i.e., lack of the necessary experimental control), the data do not allow one to draw firm conclusions about the long-term effects of the program, they nonetheless raised a possibility that participants "gain a more realistic outlook with respect to their strengths and weaknesses," that they develop their concern for others. If so, outdoor recreation may help a person maintain and perhaps enhance intrapersonal and interpersonal behavior as well as psychological well-being, though the specific psychological rewards discussed earlier may not be lasting. This, of course, is sheer speculation which must be subjected to empirical testing.

As for the immediate benefits of the outdoor program, Kaplan (1974) found that the participants' feelings improved significantly from the pretest to the post-test period. Similarly, the learning of specific outdoor skills (e.g., rock-climbing, using a compass, setting up camp, finding their own food in the woods) improved significantly as a result of participation in the program. Kaplan concluded (p. 108) that "the outdoor program makes a definite difference in the lives of these people. They enjoy it, learn from it, and come to see the world around them in a new light." If indeed so much can generally be said about the psychological benefits of outdoor recreation, then the evidence for the implementation of these programs is compelling.

Although in themselves the psychological rewards of outdoor recreation may generally be short-lived, in one sense outdoor recreation (wilderness hiking particularly) has long-term effects: for many years after their hiking and camping, people often talk about their outdoor experiences with others. These experiences frequently provide a source of conversation in social gatherings and parties. Thus, they offer a stimulant which enhances the individual's intrapersonal and interpersonal behavior. In this sense, outdoor recreation widens the scope of a person's social interaction and thus expands his leisure repertoire. Although social psychologists have entirely overlooked this benefit of outdoor recreation in the past, it does not mean that it is an insignificant consequence of outdoor recreation. In fact, that may be one of the most important benefits. This speculation should be subjected to rigorous empirical testing.

As a final point, the question about the effects of outdoor recreation on a person's self-concept or self-esteem should be considered. There are several reasons to believe that outdoor recreation trips are not likely to augment self-esteem. First and most importantly, campers and outdoor visitors seldom expect to improve their self-concept when they set out for trips. Their main concern seems to be to leave the stressful urban environment behind them and to gain such temporary psychological rewards as aesthetic and emotional experiences in natural settings. Furthermore, as noted in the case of Little League baseball, it is unreasonable to expect changes in personality as a result of participation that usually lasts two to three weeks at the most. Since millions of people take these short vacations each year, one would have little reason to worry about people's self-concepts were these trips indeed able to change people's self-concepts that readily.

This is not to say that outdoor recreation may never improve self-esteem. As in the case of Little League, it appears that the self-concept of those who participate in a given outdoor recreation program for the first time is affected more than that of old-timers. This is particularly true if new skills and experiences are acquired during the first encounters (Koocher, 1971). It is equivalent to a situation in which a child learns to ride a bicycle. Upon acquiring this new skill the self-concept undoubtedly jumps up several units. But soon after learning to ride the bicycle the skill becomes routine, part of a total repertoire, and therefore no longer advances the self-concept. Self-concept may improve slowly, step-by-step, influenced primarily by the acquisition of new intrapersonal and interpersonal skills. Of course, it is conceivable that an outdoor recreationist develops mastery (e.g., rock-climbing) over the environment further and further each time (i.e., conquering more and more difficult mountains), thereby increasing the self-concept every time. While this is possible in theory, it is unlikely in practice, because there is a limit to how much each specific skill can contribute to one's total self-concept. Outdoor recreation, rock climbing particularly, is just one aspect of the total repertoire of human behavior. As Neulinger (1974) has shown, today people still derive their self-esteem from work rather than leisure. It may, however, be proposed that the more important leisure (outdoor recreation) is to an individual, the more likely one is to define one's self-esteem in terms of leisure-skills and performance.

summary

The chapter began with a discussion of privacy, which was viewed as an "interpersonal boundary-control process." People strive to achieve the desired level of privacy by simultaneously seeking and shutting off environmental and interpersonal stimuli. Privacy, therefore, is both an optimizing and dialectic process. Mechanisms used to achieve the desired level of privacy include verbal and paraverbal behavior, personal space, territory, and cultural techniques. Crowding is felt when the privacy-controlling mechanisms fail, producing more social interaction than desired. Often the expected level of privacy is not obtained, and therefore, the individual has to develop ways of coping with and adapting to crowding. These modes are behavioral and cognitive in nature and lead to psychological and physiological "costs" to the individual. Research suggests that city dwellers have been relatively successful in coping with crowding, though they have paid a psychological price for it and will continue to do so in the foreseeable future.

Empirical evidence indicates that outdoor recreation, wilderness hiking particularly, serves as a means of coping with environmental stress caused by crowding and other factors. It was stated that the more the individual has learned to "get away from it all" through outdoor recreation in the early years, the more important this form of recreation becomes as a way of coping with crowding. A person who has not learned to derive satisfaction from active forms of leisure may resort to such passive modes as TV-watching as a means of adapting to environmental stress. There is some evidence to suggest that chronic high density living during childhood leads to feelings of lack of control, and thus to decreased expectancies of personal control in other situations. The resulting sense of helplessness may be reflected by participation in passive leisure activities like TV-watching. However, it was proposed that although city living often compels residents to spend their free-time passively because of unavailability of outdoor recreation (i.e., distance and cost), such residents are cognitively aware that they can resort to outdoor recreation if things get worse. Using outdoor recreation as a cognitive escape device may serve to help city dwellers to cope with urban stress. Besides this function, expanded cognitive space of outdoor recreation provides a source of daydreaming or fantasizing about outdoor and wilderness. For many people, daydreaming is sufficient to satisfy their desire for outdoor recreation.

The next section discussed some behavioral and cognitive mechanisms for controlling crowding in outdoor recreation places. There are at least three basic behavioral mechanisms of regulating the number of visitors to recreation locales: (1) controlling the entrance of clients into the setting, (2) controlling the capacity of the setting, and (3) controlling the length of time clients spend in the setting. Since overpopulation or crowding exists in the eyes of the beholder, another useful mechanism is to reduce it cognitively by manipulating visitors' perceptions and experiences of crowding. Cognitive control can be increased by providing information about the crowded condition of outdoor recreation places, and people's behavior under crowded conditions.

The chapter concluded with a discussion of psychological benefits of outdoor recreation. It was shown that the causes and effects of outdoor recreation cannot be separated. For example, "escaping urban stress" is both an antecedent and consequence of outdoor recreation, because recreationists are in a dialectical process of simultaneously seeking psychological rewards and avoiding environmental stresses. Individuals, however, differ to the extent that they primarily seek psychological rewards (e.g., emotional experience) or try to avoid the stressful environment through outdoor recreation. Practical implications of this theoretical distinction were briefly noted. In support of the above theory, research has shown that escape from urban stress and from the familiar, emotional or spiritual experience, challenge and adventure, and aesthetic enjoyment of natural settings are the major types of psychological benefits derived from wilderness hiking. However, people expect to gain these rewards only in natural environments, that is, roadless and untouched wilderness or improved mountain country. Some authors have speculated that "mind-expanding" drugs are used as a substitute for the wilderness experience in cities if natural environments are not accessible.

The chapter concluded with a note that although psychological benefits of outdoor recreation are essentially temporary in nature, they improve the person's intrapersonal and interpersonal behavior over a longer period of time. One neglected benefit of outdoor recreation experience is that it provides a source of personal recollection and also stimulation for interpersonal behavior (e.g., a topic of discussion in social parties) for many years afterwards. As for the effects of outdoor recreation on personality, especially self-concept, it is unreasonable to expect appreciable or enduring changes, because people usually spend only a short time in natural environments while vacationing. The only possible exception is the case in which individuals acquire new, personally important skills through outdoor recreation.

A Social Psychological Perspective on Outdoor Recreation

a social psychological perspective on therapeutic recreation

attributional analysis of therapeutic recreation 15

The relationship between social psychology and leisure studies can be seen perhaps more clearly in therapeutic recreation than anywhere else. The grand design of both fields is the same and may be expressed as follows (see figure 20). Although this schema is a simplified representation of the two fields, it demonstrates the fundamental similarity between the two. Social psychology strives to understand how an individual influences and is influenced by others. Therapeutic recreation as a specialized field within the recreation profession aims at increasing knowledge of how a therapist can ameliorate a client's psychological functioning and quality of life. While therapeutic recreation recognizes a two-way or reciprocal interaction between the specialist and the client, the emphasis is placed on the influence of the former (specialist) upon the latter (client). In theory, therapeutic recreation seeks to improve a client's physical, physiological and psychological functioning and well-being. The writer contends, however, that therapeutic recreation is in fact a social psychological endeavor, and that physical disabilities are technical matters which should not dominate the practice of the profession and training of students. This is not to discount physical disabilities but rather place them in a different perspective. Even if a patient has difficult physical or physiological problems they can be overcome, provided that the person has a "proper attitude." The main task of therapeutic recreation specialists is, therefore, to improve patients' psychological and social well-being.

This chapter delineates the social psychological relationship between therapists and clients and describes what therapists have to know about their clients' cognitive performance in order to improve their psychological well-being. Specifically, it is pointed out that therapists have to base their services on the attributional analysis of clients' behavior, thereby considering clients' self-attributions in the context of abnormality, and their beliefs about others' attributions, and learned sense of helplessness. The chapter begins with a discussion

Figure 20 Relationship between social psychology and therapeutic recreation.

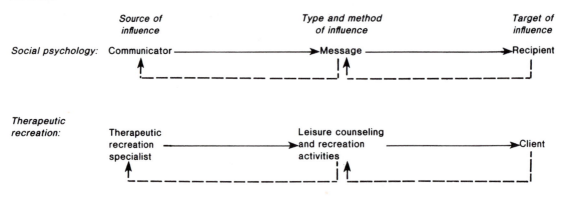

of general definitions of the field and continues by focusing on labeling processes. The bulk of the chapter, however, is devoted to an attributional analysis of therapeutic recreation, including discussion of the relationship between learned helplessness and therapeutic recreation.

what is therapeutic recreation?

According to the National Recreation and Park Association (NRPA) Therapeutic Recreation is "a specialized field within the recreation profession and generally refers to those recreation services that are provided in relation to recovery or adjustment to illness, disability, or a specific social problem. Although therapeutic recreation service is frequently recognized as an adjunctive component of treatment modalities, it primarily endeavors to promote the *positive health* and *functional aspects* of the ill, disabled and disadvantaged." Professionals working toward this objective are called therapeutic recreation specialists; they use such techniques as leisure counseling and recreation activities to improve their clients' quality of life. Although they strive to contribute to the recovery or adjustment of an illness, disability, or specific social problem, they are not exclusively concerned with limitations and dysfunctions. Therapeutic recreation is related to other professions, like physical therapy, occupational therapy, and correctional therapy; but it differs from them in terms of philosophy, goals and objectives, education and preparation, as well as treatment modalities.

In addition to the above NRPA view of therapeutic recreation, other definitions have been put forth by various textbook writers:

1. "Therapeutic recreation is a process which utilizes recreation service for purposive intervention in some physical, emotional, and/or social behavior to bring about a desired change in that behavior and to promote the growth and development of the individual" (Frye and Peters, 1972, p. 41).
2. "Therapeutic recreation serves patients or clients who because of mental, physical, social, or chronological limitations are inhibited or prohibited from utilizing existing recreation resources. The purpose of a therapeutic recreation service system is to provide opportunities for individuals with limitations to gain

leisure skills and attitudes, and/or to exercise recreative abilities within a framework of preventive, sustaining, or remedial services in order to enable or encourage recreative experience'' (Avedon, 1974, pp. 130–131).

3. "Therapeutic recreation can certainly be considered a process wherein recreative experiences are used to bring about a change in the behavior of those individuals with special needs and problems. The focus of the process is on the use of recreative experiences to (a) enhance growth and development of the individual and (b) enable the individual to meet his responsibility for fulfilling his own leisure needs'' (O'Morrow, 1976, p. 121).

4. "The aim of therapeutic recreation is to help the ill, disabled, aged, or retarded person help himself or herself to live the fullest physical, mental, social, psychological, and economic life possible within the limits of his or her illness or disability'' (Kraus, 1978, p. 4).

With different words, all the above definitions express the same thing: purposeful intervention designed to improve the clients' quality of life through recreation and leisure. All of them agree on the type of influence (recreation or leisure) to be exerted, but they differ somewhat in an emphasis placed on the focus of influence; some definitions are more specific in referring exclusively to the disadvantaged, while others are more general in that they seem to view all recreation as therapeutic. In fact, as noted throughout this text, people generally expect their leisure and recreation participation to be psychologically therapeutic. In this sense, then, it is justified to say that all recreation is aimed at being therapeutic. Here, however, the term ''therapeutic recreation'' is restricted to the process whereby a person (''therapist'') actively and intentionally strives to remove the psychological barriers hindering clients (''the disadvantaged'') from experiencing satisfactory leisure and recreation. Participation in a free-time activity in itself is meaningless. The most important consideration is what the clients by themselves and with the help of a therapeutic recreation specialist are able to derive psychologically from their recreational involvement.

The upcoming pages will specifically demonstrate that the main task of the therapist is to increase the patients' perceived control and mastery over the environment and to prevent them from inferring helplessness. The most critical challenge to the therapist is a client who views the world as uncontrollable and infers personal helplessness to do most anything. It is in this process of increasing the clients' perceived control and avoiding a feeling of helplessness that recreation activities are used as a treatment modality. Participation in leisure activities is therapeutic to the extent that it enables a person to make attributions of leisure behavior to personal abilities and improves self-perception of personal capabilities. It is then clear that simply providing recreational services to special populations is psychologically insufficient. What is needed is attribution therapy aimed at conquering helplessness and improving the self-concept.

This task often turns out to be very difficult, not only because of patients' state of mind but because society does not support the therapists' endeavors. That is, the disadvantaged are frequently reminded of their abnormality and led to believe that they are more disabled than they in effect are. Moreover, they are categorized, labeled, and stigmatized. These practices, however, have been shown to have harmful psychological consequences. Before discussing learned helplessness and therapeutic recreation, it is desirable to review research concerning the effects of labeling and categorization on patients and therapists. Although this research has not been carried out in the context of therapeutic recreation, it has clear implications for such therapeutic endeavors.

the insane in sane places or the sane in insane places?

In his widely publicized and now-classic study, Rosenhan (1973a) set out to determine whether the sane can be distinguished from the insane. In reviewing past research he found that evidence showing that the sane individual can be distinguished from the insane context is conflicting, and therefore he came to question the purpose and usefulness of such designations as "insanity," "mental illness," and "schizophrenia." If the procedures used by psychiatrists and others in diagnosing mental illness are unreliable, then such psychological categorization of individuals with such labels as mentally ill is misleading and harmful. Therefore, a study was planned to determine whether "the salient characteristics that lead to diagnoses reside in the patients themselves or in the environments and contexts in which observers find them." For this purpose, eight normal people were instructed to seek admission into psychiatric hospitals. It was reasoned that if the admission personnel detected the sanity of these pseudopatients, there would be clear evidence that the sane can be distinguished from the insane context.

Subjects who secretly gained admission to 12 different hospitals were five men and three women; three psychologists, a pediatrician, a psychiatrist, a graduate student in psychology, a painter, and a housewife. They used pseudo-names and falsified only their occupation and employment. The twelve hospitals into which these subjects were admitted were located in five different states, from the East to the West coast. Some of them were old and shabby, others new; some research-oriented, others not; some had a good staff-patient ratio, others did not. This variety was sought to achieve as representative a sample of hospitals as possible. Subjects made an appointment with the admissions office of the hospitals and during the examination, complained about hearing voices. Specifically, all of the pseudo-patients were instructed to tell that the voices seem to be saying "empty," "hollow," and "thud." These were the only symptoms the pseudo-patients described to the examiner. Aside from occupation and employment, past events and life histories were presented as they actually were. Nobody had a pathological background. When the subjects entered the hospitals they had no foreknowledge of the time of possible discharge. The hospital staff, of course, did not know anything about this experiment or the presence of pseudo-patients.

It is striking that the three self-announced symptoms (empty, hollow, and thud) were enough for the examiners to admit the subjects to the psychiatric wards. Not only were they admitted but their conditions diagnosed as schizophrenia! And most amazingly, they never got rid of this label. That is, when they were finally discharged following the average length of hospitalization of 19 days (ranging from 7 to 52 days) they left the wards with the diagnosis of schizophrenia "in remission." Subjects were told before the experiment that they have to get out of the hospitals by their own resourcefulness in convincing the staff that they were sane. Consequently, they ceased showing any symptoms of abnormality immediately following their admission. They reported that they felt fine and revealed no symptoms when asked by the staff. They cooperated with the personnel and were friendly. A later inspection of the nursing reports confirmed these behaviors and in fact showed that the pseudo-patients "exhibited no abnormal indications." Regardless of their strong motivation as well as actual attempts to behave in a sane manner, it took 19 days, on the average, for the subjects to get out of the hospitals! This is particularly striking in light of the fact that the pseudo-patients' normal behavior went so far that for research purposes they openly wrote down notes about the staff and actual patients. While actual patients did detect the pseudo-patients' sanity ("you are not crazy, you are a journalist or professor"), the staff viewed the notetaking as a symptom of abnormality.

The above data provided unequivocal evidence about the staff's failure to detect sanity and their inability to make correct diagnoses. To explain this, Rosenhan suggested that "physicians are more inclined to call a healthy person sick than a sick person healthy," because it is "more dangerous to misdiagnose illness than health." This may be so from the physician's standpoint, but certainly not from the psychological viewpoint. Diagnosing a healthy person as sick carries with it personal and social stigmas which often have severe and lasting psychological consequences. Such labeling, however, may be advantageous to psychiatrists for financial reasons. That is, if they designate everyone healthy, they lose their patients and thus perhaps employment and income. Scheff (1975, p. 12) has made a similar point in arguing that the label *mental illness* may have an "ideological function; that is, it may help to reaffirm the current cultural, and thereby the political, status quo in our society." Whatever the reasons, it seems clear that the diagnostic process is not very reliable when it can lead to such inaccurate diagnoses.

Further evidence of this unreliability was found in the second experiment (Rosenhan, 1973a). The staff of one research and teaching (psychiatric) hospital was informed about the above findings and told that at some time during the following three months, one or more pseudo-patients would show up and try to be admitted. Actually, no pseudo-patient was sent to the psychiatric hospital. Nevertheless, at least one staff member was highly confident that 41 of the total 193 admitted patients were pseudo-patients; at least one psychiatrist considered 23 patients "suspect" and one psychiatrist *and* one other staff member were suspicious about 19 patients. These data, then, clearly demonstrated that the inclination to label the sane insane can be reversed with relative ease. Consequently, the results cast doubt about the usefulness of psychological categorization of people when such classification is based on the diagnostic process that leads to such "massive errors" (Rosenhan, 1973a). Labeling someone "schizophrenic," "insane," "crazy," etc. leaves psychological scars not only on the person so described, but also on relatives and friends. Rosenhan suggested that this may eventually lead to a self-fulfilling prophecy, with the person accepting the tag and behaving accordingly. Having once been labeled by "experts" there is very little a person can do, because labels stick (for a related analysis of "stigma," see Coffman, 1963).

It should come as no surprise that Rosenhan's article led to an uproar among psychiatrists and raised considerable controversy among scholars. He was strongly attacked, accused of conceptual errors and failure to provide hard-data evidence to back up his claims. In the judgment of this author, however, Rosenhan's evidence is largely indisputable. In his response, Rosenhan (1973b, 1975) has successfully dealt with his critics and has spelled out more clearly the contextual nature of psychiatric diagnosis (1975). As for the empirical criticism, attribution research has provided abundant laboratory ("hard-data") evidence consistent with Rosenhan's contentions. For example, Langer and Abelson (1974) reported an experiment showing the powerful effect of a context on attribution of mental illness. Clinicians were presented with a videotaped interview of a young man, describing his job history and difficulties. Those clinicians who were led to believe that it was a job interview rated the man considerably better adjusted than did those who were told that the person was a patient.

biased to detect insanity

By the virtue of their professional role, diagnosticians are biased toward designating the sane as insane. They are more inclined to say that there is something wrong with the patient (dispositional attribution) rather than with the environment (situational attribution). This, of course, is contrary to what attribution therapy is hoping to accomplish. But why should they be biased in such a manner? Rosenhan (1973a) implied that diagnosticians think it is less dangerous to wrongfully diagnose health than illness. This supposedly inclines them to find the causes of a possible illness in the person rather than in the environment. However, as noted above, such a bias serves the diagnostician's personal interests and supports the status quo of the prevailing society. This bias is also consistent with an attributional proposition which states that "there is a pervasive tendency for actors (patients) to attribute their actions to situational requirements, whereas observers (diagnosticians) tend to attribute the same actions to stable personal dispositions" (Jones and Nisbett, 1971, p. 80). This hypothesis has been verified by empirical data (e.g., Nisbett, et al., 1973). Snyder, Shenkel and Schmidt (1976) found that those subjects who assumed the counselor's role in a laboratory situation attributed a person's problems to personality to a greater extent than did subjects who were instructed to assume the client's role.

It appears that physicians' and psychiatrists' educational training widens the gap between the observers' and actors' causal attributions. That is, diagnosticians are exclusively educated and trained to focus attention on personal rather than situational causes of human disorders. Thus, when someone consults them for help they immediately assume that there is something wrong in the person because otherwise, why should one consult a doctor? Accordingly, it is not surprising that the patient is perceived to be the cause of the presumed illness and is so labeled. But what is surprising is that the staff in the Rosenhan study was ready to go so far as to "unintentionally" distort patients' past history in order to fit it into a popular theory of the illness in question, that is, to find the causation in the person.

Further evidence of the influence of the diagnosticians' educational training on their bias toward attributed personal causation was reported by Snyder (1977). The data indicated that the psychodynamically trained clinicians are more inclined to attribute the cause of a patient's problems to personal abnormality than are the behaviorally trained clinicians. If diagnosticians are biased toward finding something wrong in the patient rather than in the environment, how is personal causation then treated? Rosenhan's data again serve as an excellent example. He reported that the pseudo-patients were administered a wide array of drugs, totalling nearly 2,100 pills! Certainly, medication was an easy way out, especially because the staff spent, on the average, 6.8 minutes in daily contact with the patients. Dehumanization and depersonalization could hardly be carried farther.

All the above, to be sure, is not to claim that psychiatric diagnoses (or any other diagnoses for that matter) are useless. The point is that more attention should be devoted to the weaknesses and severe limitations of these diagnoses, so that they could be made more reliable. The crux of the matter is to recognize that the outcome of diagnoses (i.e., labeling)—whether correct or incorrect—is psychologically potent, because labeling has far-reaching intrapersonal and interpersonal consequences. It is important, therefore, for persons (e.g., therapeutic recreation specialists) who work with the categorized individuals to be aware of the psychological effects of labeling. The diagnoses are useful only to the extent that they result in treatments which cannot be determined or implemented without the diagnoses (Rosenhan, 1975).

labeling interferes with attribution therapy

The problem of psychological categorization is that it not only affects the targets of labeling but also interferes with the type of treatment given to the clients. For example, having once been labeled mentally ill, the person is placed in the category of people who are under heavy medication and whose interpersonal contacts are minimized. By excluding a variety of possible treatments, labeling, therefore, leads to the implementation of a certain type of care, often the wrong one. Another way in which labeling interferes with therapy is that it reduces the therapist's expectations concerning the patients' ability to perform various behaviors. Yaffe and Mancuso (1977) reported that once a given problem is attributed to a client's abnormality, the patient is perceived to be less potent, less active, and less capable of functioning in a wide variety of social situations.

Severance and Gasstrom (1977) investigated the effects of the label "mentally retarded" on observers' causal attributions for actors' success and failure. The results showed that observers attributed the "mentally retarded" performers' failure to ability, to a greater extent than their success, whereas, the reverse was true for those who were not labeled "mentally retarded." In other words, when the mentally retarded failed, their failure was ascribed to lack of ability, but their success was attributed to their effort rather than to their ability. In contrast, lack of ability was considered less important to "normal" people's failure, and effort less essential to their success. Taken together, these findings clearly point out the observers' bias against the labeled persons' capacity to function.

To the extent that therapeutic recreation specialists exhibit similar attributional biases toward their patients, it would not be surprising to see many therapeutic recreation programs fail. Thus, it is extremely important for therapists to be cognizant of these attributional biases. After all, therapists, by the very definition of their profession, seek to improve the psychological well-being of the clients so labeled. They must believe in their patients' capacity to engage in a variety of behaviors, and in their ability to restore the patients' belief in their control of personal actions in the world. If not, learned helplessness in patients is an inevitable consequence.

learned helplessness and therapeutic recreation

Seligman (1975) has proposed a theory which states that "helplessness is the psychological state that frequently results when events and behaviors are uncontrollable." Behavior is uncontrollable when something happens, regardless of a person's attempts; that is, whatever the person does makes no difference. It is important to note that helplessness is *learned* through environmental encounters; it is not a result of inherited traits. Seligman (1975) reviewed past research and concluded that three major classes of factors are responsible for learned helplessness in human beings: (1) laboratory experience of uncontrollability; by using various techniques such as insoluble problems, helplessness has rather easily and successfully been induced in laboratory settings, (2) a cognitive set brought about by chance instructions, that is, when subjects are told that their performance in a task is governed by chance, they become helpless, (3) external personality, that is, those whose personality is predominantly external tend to feel helpless more easily than those whose personality is predominantly internal. ("External" people are characterized by their belief that the most important things in their lives are controlled by forces outside themselves, whereas "internal" individuals believe that the most important things are under their personal control).

Probably the first experiment to demonstrate the helplessness phenomenon was conducted by Richter (1957). He squeezed wild rats in his hand until they ceased struggling and then placed them in an inescapable water tank. These rats drowned within 30 minutes, whereas unsqueezed rats swam for 60 hours before drowning. Richter discovered that he could prevent sudden death by holding the rat for a while and then putting it in the water tank, rescuing it, holding it again, putting it back in the water, etc. He suggested that this procedure, in contrast to holding the rat until it stopped struggling and then putting it in the water, induced a sense of control in the rat, and therefore prevented sudden death. Since it seemed that the procedure immunized the rat against inescapable trauma, Richter suggested that "hopelessness" was the crucial factor in causing sudden death.

consequences of helplessness

Past research has shown that the consequences of learned helplessness are threefold (Seligman, 1975): motivational, cognitive, and emotional. Once the person has inferred helplessness, motivation to escape the conditions that lead to helplessness is drastically reduced, and consequently, one becomes passive. An example of this would be a person whose legs have been amputated due to an automobile accident. Many of the leisure activities that used to be readily available are now totally out of reach, and as a consequence, motivation to participate in various forms of recreation may have disappeared completely. Thus, it is possible that a person who learns that skills in a given leisure activity are inadequate, is apt to generalize this uncontrollability as applicable to other leisure skills, and in the worst case, to the entire leisure repertoire. However, in the absence of empirical data this remains speculation at best.

As for the cognitive consequences of helplessness, it has been shown that once a person has experienced uncontrollability, it is difficult to accept a conclusion that personal performance has been successful, even if it has indeed been successful. By reducing perceived control, helplessness hinders the person from believing that the same activity can be performed successfully again. Generally it appears that it is more difficult to repudiate a state of helplessness than to surrender to it (Seligman, 1975). Such cognitive inadequacy, due to helplessness, poses a great challenge to therapeutic recreation specialists, especially in the case of severe helplessness. Recreation programs are successful in meeting this challenge, to the extent that they are able to alleviate and perhaps to overcome the negative cognitive consequences of helplessness. It is then clear that of itself recreational activity does not do any good. What is important is the extent to which recreational activities can increase the client's perceived control. The task of future research is to discover what forms of recreation (and under what conditions) can best be used to alleviate learned helplessness and its negative consequences.

Helplessness also has emotional consequences, in that uncontrollable events tend to heighten emotionalism. Seligman (1975) reported that *one* experience of uncontrollable trauma produces an effect that dissipates in time. But if the person is repeatedly exposed to an uncontrollable trauma without opportunities to escape it, chronic emotional effects, in the worst case, severe depression, will result. For example, if a person persists in participating in a leisure activity which leads to feelings of lack of control, that individual probably experiences trauma following each participation, with the result of becoming more and more depressed. Or if the scope of a person's leisure repertoire is dramatically reduced due to an accident, it is likely that the resulting sense of helplessness will be accompanied by strong emotional retardation. In the absence of research evidence these possibilities, however, have to be viewed as speculation.

attributional analysis of helplessness

Although uncontrollable events are likely to lead to helplessness, this does not occur all the time. Some people are more resistant to helplessness than others. Some situational events, though uncontrollable, may not be viewed as uncontrollable, or may be dismissed as coincidence, or unimportant. The point is that helplessness does not automatically follow uncontrollability. It has been suggested elsewhere (Iso-Ahola, MacNeil and Szymanski, 1977) that causal attributions mediate learned helplessness. This is pertinent because people have a tendency to search for meaning in human behavior. That is, people are continuously looking for explanations for their own behavior and that of others, so as to understand the determinants of behavior and to be able to predict human actions in the future. Knowing why something happened and whether it will happen again makes one's world orderly and predictable, an outlook which is necessary for maintaining mental health. The attribution theory (Bem, 1972; Harvey, *et al.*, 1976; Heider, 1958; Jones and Davis, 1965; Jones, *et al.*, 1971; Kelley, 1967, 1971) describes the processes by which causal explanations are made. It deals with the principles of assigning causality of behavior to the qualities of an actor (dispositional attribution), to the situational factors (environmental attribution), and with the implications of these attributions for one's future behavior.

Causal attributions of action to personal dispositions (ability, competence, or effort) imply personal control. They reflect a person's "tendency to exercise control over his environment" (Kelley, 1971) or a desire to be "origin" rather than "pawn" (deCharms, 1968). Thus, it is logical to assume that people tend to persist in those leisure activities that allow dispositional attributions. The author postulates that *people have a pervasive tendency to prefer and participate in those leisure activities that enable them to make predominantly dispositional causal attributions.* They do this because such attributions imply personal causation and control over one's behavior and feelings of adequacy and competence on the one hand, and because of potential satisfaction from participation in such activities on the other (Iso-Ahola, *et al.*, 1977).

Situational attributions are opposite to dispositional causal ascriptions. In the former category, the person believes that personal behavior and its outcomes are (were) determined by factors external to self. The person who makes situational attributions has two possibilities: (1) to withdraw from a leisure activity and/or find new recreation activities which allow dispositional attributions, or (2) to admit that there is nothing he can do but remain passive and accept helplessness (Iso-Ahola, *et al.*, 1977). The latter alternative is the last option which is adopted if the former is blocked relatively permanently. Such is the case only when situational attributions imply personal abnormality or lack of personal competence. Often, however, behavior is imputed to situational factors, without the accompanying inference of helplessness. That is, the person admits that there is nothing he can do, but views the situational determinants as unsystematic and temporary or limited to a particular behavior and situation.

attributions of one's own and others' leisure behavior

It follows from the above reasoning that helplessness is preceded by causal attributions to personal abnormality, inadequacy, or incompetence. Since therapeutic recreation specialists often work with clients who feel helpless and depressed (e.g., recent amputees or cancer patients), their main task is therefore to deal with these people's self-destructive attributions through recreational services. If the patient's situational attributions stem from feelings of personal incompetence in leisure activities, the therapist's objective is to change the attributions from environmental to personal causation (i.e., to personal competence), or to advise the patient to seek recreational activities which will make possible dispositional attributions for leisure involvement. In striving to remove psychological barriers to rewarding recreation behavior, therapeutic recreation

Perspective on Therapeutic Recreation

specialists must not only know whether the client attributes leisure behavior dispositionally or situationally, but also how the client attributes the same behavior performed by other people. Theoretically, four different possibilities exist (Iso-Ahola, *et al.*, 1977):

1. The person attributes a given leisure behavior to situational factors (e.g., difficult task or activity) which imply incompetence and abnormality, or directly to personal incompetence, and simultaneously attributes the same leisure behavior performed by others to their incompetence or abnormality (no deviance or "universal helplessness"). Thus, the person thinks that his personal performance is not any worse than that of others. In this sense, attributions are adaptive. However, they are maladaptive because they imply personal abnormality. Therapeutic recreation services are needed to change this negative view of self.

2. The person attributes a given leisure behavior to those situational factors which imply incompetence and abnormality, or directly to personal incompetence, but by the same token he attributes the same leisure behavior performed by others to their competence (negative deviance or "personal helplessness"). This attributional pattern is psychologically dangerous, not only because the person has a distorted view of self, but also because of isolation from others induced by regarding his personal performance worse than that of social counterparts. Such a view of self is most likely to require therapeutic recreation services.

3. The person attributes a given leisure behavior to personal competence and ascribes the same behavior performed by others to the lack of their competence or to their abnormality (positive deviance or "personal competence"). This case is psychologically healthy, because the person believes in his personal capacity to participate successfully in a leisure activity and even thinks that his personal performance is better than that of others. These attributions, however, may be maladaptive to interpersonal behaviors if one makes these attributions known to others.

4. The person attributes a given leisure behavior to personal competence and imputes the same behavior performed by others to their competence (no deviance or "universal competence"). As in the third situation, this person has a healthy view of self and is therefore not likely to need therapeutic recreation services.

In addition to the knowledge about the client's self-attributions and attributions of performance of others for the same behavior, therapeutic recreation specialists should be aware of the client's beliefs about how "significant others" perceive his leisure behavior as having been caused. Theoretically, the following four possibilities exist (Iso-Ahola, *et al.*, 1977):

beliefs of others' attributions

1. The person attributes a given leisure behavior to situational factors which imply abnormality and incompetence, or directly to personal in-

competence, and by the same token believes that significant others also view him as incompetent to perform the leisure behavior in question. This pattern is psychologically damaging to self and likely to benefit from the services provided by therapeutic recreation specialists.

2. The person attributes a given leisure behavior to incompetence (or situational factors implying it), but is led to believe that others attribute the behavior to his personal competence. The attributions of others, therefore, constitute a therapeutically supportive environment. This therapeutic value, however, depends on the weight the person assigns to the opinions of others in general. If the individual decides to ignore personal attributions and to rely on those of others, positive consequences may be expected; but if the individual insists on personal attributions and ignores those of others, negative outcomes may be expected.

3. The person attributes a given leisure behavior to personal competence but believes that others perceive his behavior as having been caused by abnormality and incompetence. Whether this person can benefit from the services of a therapeutic recreation specialist depends on how long the client is able to rely solely on personal attributions and to ignore the beliefs of others' attributions of his personal leisure behavior. In such a situation, a therapeutic recreation specialist would do well to reinforce the person's own attributions and to discredit attributions of others.

4. The person attributes a given leisure behavior to personal competence and believes that others do the same. Such attributions and expectations are psychologically healthy and are not likely to need a therapeutic recreation specialist.

an attributional model of helplessness

The above theorizing has clearly shown that the person's causal attributions mediate helplessness. It is now feasible to schematically combine Seligman's idea of learned helplessness with the attributional analysis. Figure 21 presents a theoretical model which extends and modifies Seligman's theory of helplessness. It is evident that exposure to uncontrollable events and outcomes leads to unstable, variable feelings and inferences of helplessness. It is at this point of initial feelings of helplessness that the person's cognitive processes come into the picture and determine the type and degree of helplessness. As figure 21 shows, others' (therapists') role is critical in influencing how the person will interpret exposure to uncontrollable events and outcomes. Confronted with initial feelings of helplessness, the person attributes this helplessness to either personal incompetence/abnormality or to some situational (i.e., temporarily intervening) factors.

If the former attributional pattern dominates, it is very likely to result in a stable inference of generalized helplessness, meaning that the person's leisure participation diminishes drastically because he does not believe in his personal capacity to participate successfully in any leisure activities. The resultant withdrawal is probably accompanied by apathy and depression. If the therapist is successful, this attributional pattern may be altered and the person may be saved

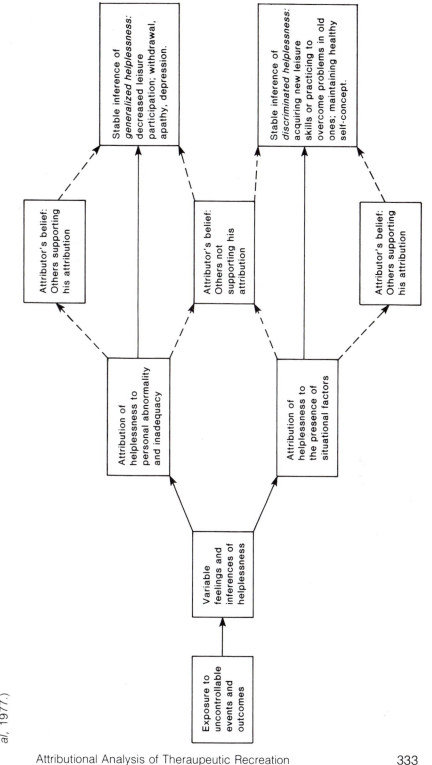

Figure 21 An attributional model of learned helplessness. (From Iso-Ahola, *et al*, 1977.)

from sinking into a generalized helplessness (as the dotted arrow indicates). If the person fails to consult a therapist or others in this attributional phase, little can be done to save the individual from generalized helplessness. This is especially true if one consults somebody who agrees with one's self-destructive attributions.

If situational attributions dominate, the person is likely to make a stable inference of discriminated helplessness, meaning that the uncontrollable events are dismissed as trivial; he thinks that personal competence has little to do with it. Rather, the person concludes that some unusual situational conditions interfered with behavior and resulted in uncontrollable outcomes. Consequently, the person continues to engage in the same leisure activity and tries to overcome problems in such a way that attribution of behavior to personal competence is creditable. Alternatively, one may turn to new leisure activities and acquire new skills which are more congruent with personal talents, and which more readily allow dispositional attributions. The inference of discriminated helplessness is psychologically healthy, because it enables the person to maintain a self-concept and helps coping with uncontrollable events. The probability of discriminated helplessness becomes even greater when the person believes that others accept the same situational attributions of the causes of helplessness, especially if "others" are perceived as important. But if the person believes that others do not share situational attributions, generalized or discriminated helplessness ensues, depending on how significant "others" are thought to be. If one has high regard for their opinions in general, one is likely to accept their attributions and ignore one's own, with the consequence of generalized helplessness. Alternatively, one may totally reject the attributions of others and rely solely on personal attributions, thereby inferring discriminated helplessness.

generalized helplessness

It is the group of "generalized helpless" people who therapeutic recreation specialists often encounter, and therefore, it is this group in which they may confront the most difficult problems. After having experienced helplessness in one leisure activity, a person may firmly believe that he is abnormal, inadequate, and lacks basic skills in that activity. As a consequence, the person believes that he is handicapped to participate in this activity; and this belief may then generalize to personal performance in other areas of leisure behavior. The total repertoire of leisure behavior is therefore in jeopardy. If helplessness generalizes to total leisure and if leisure is important to the person, helplessness and depression may extend to one's work life and in the worst case, to the entire life. While it has to be borne in mind that these are theoretical possibilities without empirical justification, they are not illogical and certainly not unrealistic. Therefore, social psychologists will make important contributions by investigating the questions raised above.

Potential examples of persons falling into the category of the generalized helpless can be found anywhere. A person who has unexpectedly been restricted to a wheelchair may find that his personal feelings of uncontrollability are impossible to overcome in a given leisure activity; and the resultant dispositional attributions to personal incompetence may make him generalize the feelings of helplessness to include all leisure skills the person has possessed and thought about. The same may also be true for "normal" persons who spend their leisure in competitive athletics but continually lose because they compete with higher caliber persons than they actually should. Similarly, "normal" persons may become helpless in the area of social interaction skills. People may feel helpless because they believe that they cannot relate effectively to others. Consequently, they may withdraw from all the contacts and activities requiring social skills.

These latter examples are important in demonstrating that all of us should be therapists to our fellow men and women, because there is not a single person on this earth who is free from occasional feelings of helplessness. This is especially true in the Western world, where the emphasis is placed upon competition and achievement. To stretch the point to the extreme, it could be argued that only one person (the winner) is normal, everybody else (the loser) is abnormal. To this end, it might be argued that helplessness is a product of a highly "achieving" and competitive society. If so, helplessness can never be totally eliminated until the entire system has been modified. On the other hand, helplessness can be alleviated if the right measures are taken. So far, it has been shown that therapeutic recreation specialists can do wonders if they are able to use the power of attribution therapy through recreation services. But much more than recreation is needed to prevent and cure the feeling of helplessness. No one should be afraid to seek help from others when he feels helpless; and all should be ready to furnish attributional therapy whenever it is needed and whoever needs it. Such universal comradeship and concern for the psychological well-being of others is likely to do much more than any kind of formal therapy.

helplessness is a symptom of the achieving society

Beyond this global effort, what should therapists specifically do to alleviate helplessness? First, as figure 21 suggests, the therapist should attempt to discover what factors initially have led to the client's helpless feelings and inferences; how the client has formed attributions of helplessness; whether these attributions were subsequently influenced by personal beliefs of others' attributions of his helplessness. This information serves as a basis for diagnosing the client's state of helplessness. The next task is to find methods and techniques to overcome the client's inference of helplessness.

how to alleviate helplessness?

In this task, the most obvious objective is to try to change dispositional attributions (to incompetence and abnormality) to situational ones. Dispositional attributions should be discredited as being false or inappropriate. This could be done by pointing out that anyone would feel helpless under similar conditions because of strong external influences. The implication, therefore, is that it is the environment, not so much the client himself, which is responsible for unsuccessful leisure experiences. The second strategy is to minimize the importance of the leisure activity in which uncontrollability was experienced in the first place. If the client is known to be good at one leisure activity, then this should be emphasized. For example, "It's much more important to be able to play piano than baseball," or, "Everyone can play baseball, but it's only a few who can play the piano.'' The implication, then, would be that the person does not really need the leisure activity (baseball) that caused helplessness.

The third strategy is to attack those experiences which gave rise to uncontrollability, with the purpose of changing the client's expectation of uncontrollability to one of controllability. This could be done by exposing the person to positive experiences in the original leisure activity in such a way that uncontrollability will not be inferred. This might be accomplished by training the person to perform the activity "correctly" and/or by decreasing the standards of excellence in the activity. Alternatively, the client could be advised to participate in a different but similar leisure activity, which would more easily allow him to infer controllability and more readily and realistically permit the therapist to attribute the person's performance to personal ability and competence.

These principal techniques, then, should be used to deal with the client's history of personal control in leisure behavior, for the purpose of changing his expectations of uncontrollability to those of controllability. Because therapeutic recreation specialists, by the very definition of their profession, deal with persons who have been exposed to uncontrollable events and outcomes, their main objective is to prevent the client from sinking into generalized helplessness, and to induce him to accept that helplessness is limited to a particular leisure activity under these specific conditions only (e.g., "While you did not play baseball especially well *today*, you are a good player, not to mention your highly talented piano-playing'').

prevention of helplessness

The above principles are directed toward providing immediate cure when someone is in danger of inferring generalized helplessness, but they do not deal with the early prevention of generalized helplessness. Since the feeling of helplessness is a product of one's *learning* experiences, it should then be possible to prevent helplessness long before it occurs. Seligman (1975) has suggested that "behavioral immunization'' ought to be started in childhood, that parents should play "synchrony games'' with their children to enhance their feelings of personal control. Since the principles of early prevention of helplessness were previously discussed in the context of Little League baseball (Part 4), the reader should consider here some possibilities suggested by the idea of behavioral immunization.

In short, competition should generally be deemphasized and one should learn to establish realistic personal goals and expectations. Because both success *and* failure (about 50% each) are needed for successful immunization, continuous failure and continuous success should be avoided (Jones, *et al.*, 1977). Educators and parents ought to teach children to deal with failure (and success) directly and realistically. Instead of passive, spectator-types of participation, personal involvement and active participation should be emphasized and encouraged in recreational sports and other leisure activities. It should be stressed that there are no uniform or standard leisure activities in which everyone has to participate. In childhood, the young should be provided with a wide variety of leisure skills. The application and implementation of these principles aid in immunizing against helplessness in the future.

Perspective on Therapeutic Recreation

Although the above theorizing presents one conceptual analysis of helplessness, it has indirectly been supported by other researchers. *After* the above model was developed and made public (Iso-Ahola, *et al.,* 1977), Seligman and his associates (Abramson, Seligman and Teasdale, 1978) also proceeded to revise the original theory of helplessness by incorporating causal attributions into the model. In a similar vein, Wortman and Dintzer (1978) discussed helplessness from the attributional standpoint. Consequently, these other attempts are viewed as confirmation of our previous theoretical analysis. This is emphasized, not for self-serving purposes but rather to lend support to the attributional approach in enhancing the understanding of learned helplessness. A reader who is interested in a detailed discussion and debate of the theory is referred to Maier and Seligman's (1976) review article, and the February issue (1978) of the *Journal of Abnormal Psychology* which was devoted to learned helplessness in its entirety.

support for attributional model of learned helplessness

The similarity between the author's model and Abramson's, *et al.* (1978) subsequent theorizing is striking. In fact, with the exception of differing terminology, table 1 in the Abramson, *et al.* paper (p. 53) is identical to figure 1 in the Iso-Ahola, *et al.* paper (here: page 331). For example, according to situation number one (presented here on page 331), the person attributes a given leisure behavior to incompetence and abnormality and does the same for others' performance of the same leisure behavior. This situation was termed "no deviance," and designated as a form of helplessness. Abramson, *et al.* called it "universal helplessness." The second situation involves attribution of a leisure behavior to personal incompetence/abnormality, and the same behavior to others' competence. The author termed this "negative deviance" and stated that it is likely to lead to the most severe form of helplessness. Abramson, *et al.* called it "personal helplessness." Another striking similarity between the two papers can be seen in relation to generality of helplessness. The author postulated two types of helplessness: generalized and discriminated (see figure 21). Abramson, *et al.* made the identical distinction, calling them "global" and "specific" helplessness, respectively.

The above examples illustrate similarities between the two attributional models of helplessness, and therefore, indicate that this author's theory has been verified conceptually. But more important, Abramson, *et al.* reviewed past attribution experiments and found them to be consistent with the reformulation of learned helplessness in attributional terms. Further support comes from more recent research. Kuiper (1978), for example, reported that depressed subjects attributed failure to internal factors (e.g., lack of ability), whereas nondepressed subjects made self-protective, external attributions for failure. In a similar vein, Diener and Dweck (1978) found that helpless children tend to attribute failure to their lack of ability, while the mastery-oriented children focus on remedies for failure rather than on the cause of their failure. Furthermore, past studies have indirectly supported the above theorizing, in that helpless subjects reveal impaired expectancy changes in skill tasks (Abramson, *et al.,* 1978). Although none of these studies was specifically designed to test the above attributional theory of helplessness, they certainly are consistent with it and therefore warrant more systematic testing in the future. Since both theoretical and empirical literature seems to support the author's theorizing, it is tentatively proposed that the above attributional model should be the basis of delivering therapeutic recreation services. It is the task of future research to point out the conditions under which the attributional therapy is most effective and least effective in alleviating and curing learned helplessness.

causal attributions for severe accidents and subsequent coping behavior

Many of the therapeutic recreation specialists deal with victims of various types of accidents. One of the main purposes of a recreation program is to help such patients acquire new leisure skills so that they can once more lead lives which are mentally, socially, and physically satisfying. Based upon the previous analysis, one might expect that these patients feel helpless and, therefore, suffer from motivational, cognitive, and emotional consequences. They probably think of themselves as being unable to participate in most leisure activities, due to their disability. As a result, they are likely to attribute a given leisure behavior to their personal incompetence and abnormality, the inevitable consequence of which is generalized helplessness.

For accident victims to infer helplessness, however, is not an automatic response. Bulman and Wortman (1977) reported that the manner in which patients attribute (i.e., blame themselves or others) the causes of an accident is critical for these persons' subsequent coping. If this is correct, then these attributions affect patients' orientation toward the recreation services provided by therapists. Thus, it appears that two types of causal attributions are linked to coping behavior: (1) attributions for the cause of uncontrollability (i.e., what or who caused the accident?), and (2) causal attributions for feelings of helplessness experienced while performing leisure behaviors during the therapeutic or healing process (i.e., Why am I so poor at performing these leisure activities?). So far, the discussion in this chapter has focused on the role of the latter attributions. The former attributions and their implications for coping behaviors will now be considered.

Bulman and Wortman (1977) conducted a field study to determine the best predictors of successful coping following severe accidents. Specifically, the purpose of their investigation was to examine the relationship betwen attributions of blame for an accident and effective coping. The subjects were 29 (23 males and 6 females) victims of spinal cord injuries, their ages ranging from 16 to 35 years with an average of 22.7 years. The sample consisted of 11 paraplegics and 18 quadriplegics, these subjects being full-time patients at the Rehabilitation Institute of Chicago. Of the 29 injury cases, 11 were caused by automobile accidents, 6 by diving accidents, and 4 by shooting. The remaining 8 injury cases varied from a private plane crash and a hang-gliding accident to a dive into a haystack and a tackle in a high school football game. In the interview, the subjects were asked questions about their perception of the cause and avoidability of the accident, and the amount of self-blame for it. In addition, subjects' perceived happiness was measured, and the interviewer administered three scales relative to subjects' perceptions of internal-external control, justice in the world, and their religious attitudes. Finally, the degree of coping was determined on the basis of one social worker's and one nurse's rating of how well the patient to whom they were assigned was coping with personal disability.

The results revealed that attribution of blame to others for the accident, perceived avoidability, and self-blame were the best predictors of coping. Specifically, it appeared that the more a victim blamed another person for the accident, the worse he coped; the more the victim believed he could have avoided the accident, the worse he coped with it later. Self-blame, however, was related to coping in the opposite manner: the more a victim blamed himself, the better he coped with the accident. The victim was most likely to blame himself (1) if he believed he could have avoided the accident, (2) if he was alone at the time of the accident or without any adversary, and (3) if he was religious. While perceived avoidability was positively related to self-blame, it was negatively correlated with effective coping. Consequently, good copers were those victims who felt that they could *not* have avoided the accident but, nevertheless, blamed themselves for it. On the contrary, poor copers were those who blamed others for the accident and believed that they could have avoided it.

Not surprisingly, subjects felt that their condition of victimization was practically the worst thing that could happen to them. It appeared, however, that the more educated the respondents were, the less negatively they perceived their victimization. When the subjects were asked whether they had asked themselves the question "Why me?," all of them responded "yes", and their answers fell into six categories (the number of subjects who expressed a given reason is presented in the parentheses): "God had a reason" (10), "Chance" (8), "Predetermination" (7), "It could have been worse" (6), "Probability" (4), and "Deservedness" (2). These findings showed a relatively strong tendency toward a fatalistic position or a belief in external causation of the accidents.

Perhaps the most interesting result from our standpoint was that the character of the activity in which the subjects had been engaging at the time of the accident affected their decision of whether they could have avoided the accident. If the activity was unusual for them (e.g., riding with a stranger), the victims tended to view the accident as avoidable, but if it was "common" or one in which they had participated frequently, they were inclined to regard the accident as unavoidable. It appeared that six of the eight most successful copers had been engaging in enjoyable leisure activities at the time of the accident, while the same was true for only one of the eight worst copers. These observations, then, suggest that "people who are involved in freely chosen leisure activities when an accident occurs may cope better than those who are victimized in other ways" (Bulman and Wortman, 1977, p. 361). If taken literally, this provides an additional reason why all persons should engage in intrinsically motivated leisure activities and why they should attempt to increase perceived freedom for their own as well as the leisure activities of others. (For a discussion of factors that facilitate perceived freedom, see chapter 9.) It is paradoxical, however, that by participating in intrinsically motivated leisure activities one may simultaneously increase the chances of having a severe accident and ability to cope with it afterwards.

The above findings have important implications for therapeutic recreation specialists. Clearly, it is essential for therapists to know how patients view the origin of their disability. Since the objective is to enhance patients' coping, it would seem logical to minimize through therapy those factors that are known to contribute to poor coping and, in turn, maximize those factors that are likely to enable the patient to cope successfully. Thus, if a patient thinks that the accident was avoidable and blames others for it, the therapist's task is to alter this thinking pattern so that the client accepts that the accident was largely unavoidable and that nobody else except himself was responsible for it. The therapist should stress that it was he (the patient) who decided to engage in the activity that led to the accident, even if the activity was unusual for the patient. It should also be emphasized that the outcome could have been worse, so that in the final analysis, the patient was lucky. Therapists could then proceed to show that the patient can still continue ''normal'' life and do things that others do. In this endeavor, therapeutic recreation specialists place special emphasis on their patients' leisure skills which allow causal attributions to personal competence. The specialists should do this not only as professional duty, but especially so as to demonstrate the importance of leisure to one's total life experience.

---

summary

This chapter began by defining the field of therapeutic recreation. Based upon the sample of existing definitions, the term ''therapeutic recreation'' was limited to the process whereby a therapist intentionally and actively strives to remove the psychological barriers which prevent clients from experiencing satisfactory leisure and recreation. In this process of increasing clients' perceived control and avoiding helplessness, recreation activities are used as a treatment modality. This task, however, often turns out to be difficult, because the disadvantaged are categorized by labels (e.g., ''mentally ill'') which endure and which have disparaging social implications. Thus, labeling interferes with recreational attribution therapy. Having once been labeled, the person is perceived to less potent, less active, less capable of functioning in a wide variety of intrapersonal and interpersonal situations. Consequently the person is placed in the category of people who are believed to be capable of only a limited array of behaviors.

In this sense the practice of labeling would seem to be highly prejudicial. In an effort to assess the usefulness of labeling, Rosenhan's now-classic study ''on being sane in insane places'' was reviewed in detail. The study showed that psychiatrists not only failed to distinguish the sane from the insane, but they also showed strong bias to call a healthy person sick rather than a sick person healthy. This bias is based upon the principle that it is more dangerous to make a faulty diagnosis of illness than of health. But such a tendency fails to consider that diagnosing a healthy person sick involves personal and social stigmas which often have severe and lasting psychological consequences. And those who, for example, are labeled mentally ill are placed in various institutions where they are sometimes dehumanized and depersonalized. On this ground, the author strongly questioned the usefulness of labeling in general, arguing that therapeutic recreation specialists should be aware of labeling biases. If therapists do not believe in their clients' capacity to function, their attempts to prevent or alleviate helplessness may be ineffective.

The next section of the chapter focused on the theory of learned helplessness and its implications for therapeutic recreation. After discussing antecedents and consequences of helplessness as derived from Seligman's theory, a new attributional model of helplessness was developed, with a special reference to therapeutic recreation. It was postulated that people have a pervasive tendency to prefer and participate in those leisure activities which enable them to make predominantly dispositional causal attributions. If this tendency is impeded, negative dispositional attributions follow, implying personal abnormality and incompetence. The person who makes such attributions can (1) either withdraw from a leisure activity and/or find new leisure activities which allow him to make dispositional attributions, (2) or admit that there is nothing he can do but to remain passive and accept helplessness. In attempting to alleviate helplessness, therapeutic recreation specialists have to know what factors are initially responsible for clients' helpless feelings and inferences, how they have formed attributions of their helplessness, whether attributions are predominantly dispositional or situational, and whether their attributions were subsequently influenced by their beliefs of others' attributions of their helplessness. Using this information, the therapeutic recreation specialist has the task of finding methods and techniques to overcome clients' inferences of helplessness. These strategies were discussed.

The therapist plays an important role in affecting his clients' interpretation of uncontrollable events, that is, whether they will attribute helplessness dispositionally or situationally. If the clients attribute helplessness to their abnormality or incompetence, generalized helplessness is likely to follow. This would then mean that their leisure participation diminishes drastically because they do not believe in their capacity to participate successfully in any leisure activity. If clients attribute helplessness to situational factors (i.e., variables not implying personal incompetence), discriminated helplessness is likely to follow, meaning that they dismiss the uncontrollable events as trivial and as products of unusual environmental conditions. Consequently, they continue to engage in the same leisure activity and try to overcome their difficulties in such a way that they can attribute the behavior to their competence. Alternatively, they may acquire new leisure skills which are more congruent with their talents. Both theoretical and empirical research has indirectly supported this attributional theorizing of learned helplessness.

The therapeutic recreation specialists often deal with victims of various kinds of accidents. Research has shown that attributions of blame for the accident are linked to subsequent coping. Specifically, research indicates that when patients think that the accident was avoidable and when they blame others for it, the therapist's task is to reverse this attributional pattern into one in which clients accept the fact that the accident was largely unavoidable and that they themselves were responsible for it. Bulman and Wortman have proposed that ''people who are involved in freely chosen leisure activities when an accident occurs may cope better than those who are victimized in other ways.'' If so, it is paradoxical that by participating in intrinsically motivated leisure activities people may simultaneously increase the chances of having a severe accident and their ability to cope with the accident afterwards.

therapeutic recreation, perceived control, and the institutionalized aged

16

The previous chapter demonstrated that perceived control is the critical variable in the practice of therapeutic recreation. It is not the recreational activity in itself that is crucial, but rather the extent to which such activity provides a sense of control and predictability with respect to one's environment. Increasing perceived controllability through recreation activities becomes especially important for those people who have been deprived of opportunities to regulate their own lives. One such group is comprised of the institutionalized aged. The present chapter is devoted to a discussion of the potential role of recreation among the institutionalized aged, with a special emphasis on patients in nursing homes. These individuals are cited, because they are prime examples of how far dehumanization or depersonalization have been extended, and what disastrous influence deprived uncontrollability may exert on people. Since institutions or homes for the aged are increasingly employing therapeutic recreation specialists, it is important for students to understand that much more than recreational activity is involved when various services are provided for the institutionalized aged.

To test the effects of a sense of personal control in successful aging, Langer and Rodin (1976) conducted a field experiment on 91 ambulatory adults (aged from 65 to 90) in a nursing home. These subjects, mostly females, were divided into two groups: a responsibility-induced group and a comparison group. The two differed from one another in one important respect. The nursing home administrator held a meeting and told the former subjects that they have responsibility for themselves, while the comparison group was told that the staff has responsibility for patients. Accordingly, the "responsibility-induced" subjects had freedom to choose and decide what recreational activities they wanted and when, how they wanted their rooms to be arranged, whether or not they wanted a plant, what kind of plant, etc. On the other hand, the staff made all these decisions for those subjects who were assigned to the comparison group. The dependent variables

effects of choice and enhanced personal responsibility for the aged

consisted of various questionnaire and behavioral measurements made one week prior to, and three weeks after the treatment.

The results showed that the responsibility-induced subjects exhibited greater increases in happiness, activeness and alertness than the comparison group. Further, nurses' ratings regarding each patient's general improvement revealed that 93% of the former subjects had progressed, while only 21% of the control subjects improved; 71% of the control subjects were rated as having become more debilitated during the testing period, which lasted only three weeks. But most important, the treatment (i.e., enhanced personal control) increased the subjects' activity level in general and their interpersonal activity in particular. That is, from the pre- to post-test measure the responsibility-induced subjects exhibited greater increases in terms of time spent visiting other patients, visiting people from outside the nursing home and talking to the staff, than did the control subjects. At the same time, the former subjects spent less time in such passive forms of recreation as watching TV than did the control group. The behavioral measures were consistent with the above findings, in that following the treatment participation in recreational activities (i.e., jelly-bean guessing contest and movies) was higher in the responsibility-induced than in the control subjects.

In short, the data implied that enhancing nursing home residents' perceived control over their lives increases their activeness, interpersonal activity, mental alertness and psychological well-being. It is noteworthy that these positive results were obtained by a simple procedure which stressed a sense of personal responsibility and personal control in decision making regarding matters of everyday living.

In an effort to increase the reliability of the above findings, Rodin and Langer (1977) continued their field experiment and collected long-term data on several variables using the same patients. While the nurses' ratings were based upon 52 patients in the original study (Langer and Rodin, 1976), there were 26 of them left for the 18-month follow-up data. When nurses' evaluations of patients' psychological functioning before and 18 months after the treatment were compared, it appeared that the decline was considerably less for the responsibility-induced subjects than for the comparison group. Health ratings based upon medical records indicated that the responsibility-induced subjects maintained their health or increased it slightly over a period of 18 months, whereas the health status of subjects in the comparison group decreased significantly.

But the most dramatic finding concerned the mortality rate of the two groups. The average death rate in the nursing home was 25% prior to the experimental treatment, but this rate was increased to 30% for the comparison group and declined to 15% for the responsibility-induced subjects during the 18-month period following the experimental intervention. Thus, those nursing home residents whose responsibility for themselves was emphasized by the experimental treatment had a significantly lower mortality rate than those subjects whose personal responsibility and perceived control were deprived by the staff. The reliability of these findings was established by the fact that before the study began, the length of time of institutionalization and the overall health status were the same for those patients who subsequently died and those who were still living after the 18-month period. Thus, the significant difference in the mortality rate between the two groups cannot be attributed to differing health status or institutionalization among the patients.

Significantly, nurses' evaluations prior to the study were lower for patients who subsequently died than for patients who were still living 18 months after the experimental intervention, thereby suggesting that the nurses' evaluations of the patients rather than the overall health ratings were better predictors of subsequent life and death. This raises a possibility that the nurses acted in accordance with their own evaluations and treated patients with higher ratings better than patients with lower evaluations. If so, the nurses contributed to the death rate. While this is pure speculation, it may very well be that the patient-nurse interaction plays a critical part in the patients' physical and mental health, especially in those nursing homes where other avenues for social interaction are absent. In sum, the results showed that a manipulation suggesting how patients might increase their choice and their personal control over everyday living in a nursing home had strong and lasting positive effects. Those residents who were given opportunities for personal choice, self-control, and their own responsibility were more active, healthier, more sociable, in a better mood and had lower mortality rates 18 months later than did patients who did not have such opportunities.

The concept of the importance of controllable environment for the aged is not new. Ferrari (1962), for example, reported a study dealing with the lethal effects of lack of perceived freedom of choice in a home for the aged. When subjects (55 females with an average age of 82) were asked how much freedom of choice they had felt in moving to the home, 17 women said they had no alternative but move. Of these 17 subjects, 8 persons died within four weeks after moving and only one was alive 10 weeks later. In another sample, Ferrari found that if the elderly of their own volition applied for admission to the home, only a minor proportion (4 out of 18) of them died by the end of the first month; but if these persons' families made the application for them, the death rate reached a dramatic proportion (19 out of 22) within the first month. Seligman (1975, p. 185) interpreted these data to "reflect the lethal effects of helplessness on old people."

In reviewing studies on stressful environmental events as prognostications of death for the elderly, Rowland (1977) found evidence to suggest that death of a person close to the patient, and relocation, but not retirement, are "fairly accurate" predictors of the elderly persons' death. Rowland argued that these factors, especially death of someone close to the patient, are stressful life changes that produce helplessness, which thus increase considerably the risk of death. Parallel to this, Mehrabian and Ross (1977) observed that extremely arousing or unpleasant life changes are more conducive to illness. Taken together, it appears that life changes for the elderly are psychologically hazardous to the extent that they produce uncontrollability and thus helplessness. A predictable and controllable environment is a prerequisite for successful aging. In a similar vein, Schulz and Brenner (1977) have argued that relocation of the aged from home to institution is not in itself psychologically harmful, provided that the environmental change does not bring about perceived unpredictability and uncontrollability. But as Ferrari's data indicated, if relocation occurs against the person's will, the subsequent physical and psychological deterioration is rapid and most lethal.

controllable and predictable social interaction

The Rodin and Langer findings suggested that social interaction is important for nursing home residents. The effects of social interaction, however, were specifically investigated in a field experiment by Schulz (1976). This study was planned to determine the influence of control and the predictability of a positive outcome (i.e., visitation by a friendly college student for a two-month period) on the psychological and physiological well-being of the aged. Subjects were 36 women and 6 men in a private, church-affiliated retirement home, with a mean age of 81.5 years. They were randomly assigned to one of four situations. In one case ("control-visitor group"), subjects had the opportunity to exert control over the frequency and duration of visits they received. The second experimental group ("predict-visitor group") was informed concerning the exact time and the length of visits, but was not allowed to modify and regulate the visits. The third group of subjects was visited randomly and, therefore, was not given any control over or information about the visits. The fourth group of subjects were not visited at all, with the exception of data collection during a pre- and post-test interview. Schulz hypothesized that controllable and predictable visits would enhance subjects' physical and psychological well-being more than would random or no visits.

The results showed that the subjects in the "predict-visitor group" and "control-visitor group" were rated healthier than subjects in the random-visit or no-treatment groups. The former also used a smaller quantity of medication than subjects who were visited randomly or not at all. These health status indicators, however, revealed that the procedures effectively inhibited a progressive physical decline, rather than actually improving residents' health. The indicators of psychological status, on the other hand, reversed the pattern of progressive decline; that is, the first two experimental groups increased, while the random-visit or no-visit group experienced decreased psychological well-being from pre-test to post-test measures. Specifically, the former groups were rated as having more "zest for life;" they perceived themselves as happier, as having a higher level of hope, than did the latter groups. It also appeared that the subjects of the two experimental groups became more active and future-oriented as a result of the treatment (i.e., controllable and predictable visits) than did the subjects of random or no visits. Overall, there were no differences between the "predict-visitor" and "control-visitor" subjects on the one hand and between the random and no-visit subjects on the other, with respect to the indicators of physical and psychological well-being.

Together, the findings imply that the simple procedure of increasing social interaction through visits paid to the institutionalized aged is an effective technique of improving the aged residents' physical and psychological health. It should be borne in mind, however, that these beneficial effects seem to materialize only if patients can control and predict their social interaction. Theoretically, the Schulz data leave unanswered the question of the relative importance of predictability and controllability; but from the practical standpoint, they clearly reveal the critical nature of the combined impact of predictable and controllable social interaction on the institutionalized aged.

It should be kept in mind that the above results were based upon the data which were collected at the conclusion of a field experiment, thereby reflecting short-term effects. In an effort to determine the long-term effects of the experimental treatments, Schulz and Hanusa (1978) did a follow-up study on the same subjects 24-, 30-, and 42-months after completion of the manipulation phase. The results showed that the experimental subjects' ("predict-visitor" and "control-visitor" groups') health status and "zest" for life declined significantly by the time 24 months had elapsed after the completion of the manipulation; this decline was still evident, though not very strong, at the 30- and 42-month follow-up intervals. On the other hand, those subjects who were randomly visited by college students (unpredictable and uncontrollable social interaction) and those who were not visited at all, maintained their health status and zest for life at the same level 24 months after the end of the experiment; but by the time 42 months had elapsed these two indicators had considerably declined for persons in the random and no-treatment groups. When all the groups were compared it appeared that the health status and zest for life of the "predict-visitor" and "control-visitor" subjects dropped to the level of the "random" and no-treatment subjects on these indicators; that is, there was no statistically reliable difference between the four groups at the 24-, 30-, and 42-month follow-up intervals.

Notwithstanding methodological and statistical problems,[1] these results imply that the previously noted positive effects of controllable and predictable social interaction for the institutionalized aged are temporary. Once the predictable and controllable visits were terminated, subjects' health status and zest for life dropped to the level of subjects who were not exposed to such visits or who were exposed to them randomly. Thus is appears that predictable and controllable social interaction has to be continued once it has been started, if the resultant positive effects are expected to last. Assuming that predictable and controllable visits raised the subjects' perceived control over their environment, it is then likely that the termination of the visits lowered subjects' perceived control and thus decreased their health status and zest for life. Alternatively, as Schulz and Hanusa noted, it is possible that the visits "resulted in strong personal attachment between the subject and visitor," suggesting that the termination of the predictable and controllable visits severed personal attachment and thus caused the decline in health status and zest for life.

[1]Schulz and Hanusa's results should be viewed with caution, because of several methodological and statistical problems. For example, no reliability measures of the activities director's ratings of subjects' health status and zest for life were reported. The fact that only one person (activities director) rated all the subjects on the criterion measures is in itself questionable. Furthermore, the data analyses were based upon the "repeated measures" analyses of variance and yet, homogeneity of covariances between repeated assessments was not checked.

The above findings suggest that the predictable and controllable social interaction has to be continued in order to maintain its positive psychological and physiological effects. In an indirect support of this contention, Graney (1975) reported a 4-year longitudinal study on the elderly women. The study revealed that social participation and happiness were positively and significantly related to one another in old age. Specifically, participation in such social recreation activities as visiting friends and relatives, attending religious services, attending meetings of voluntary associations, and making telephone calls to friends and relatives, were significantly related to happiness. Most of the activities which were highly associated with happiness seemed to involve face-to-face interaction. By the same token, participation in relatively passive activities like watching TV and reading were not associated with happiness.

All the above findings are persuasive indications that aging is not simply a biological process. Social psychological variables may precipitate unsuccessful aging or enhance successful aging. However, there is no denying the fact that the natural events (e.g., death of a spouse) make the elderly susceptible to physical and psychological illness. But what is critical is that physical and psychological decline due to aging can be slowed down or even reversed, if the right measures be taken. The common denominator of such measures is avoidance of uncontrollability and helplessness on the one hand, and maintenance of social activity level optimal to an individual on the other.

implications   One of the immediate implications of these studies would seem to be arranging opportunities for older people to live as normal a life as possible, rather than excluding them from the mainstream of society. Inasmuch as human beings are "social animals" (Aronson, 1972) and since the elderly lose their social partners or significant others more frequently than do younger persons, the need for social interaction among the elderly is particularly important. This should be the starting point in planning activity programs for older persons in institutionalized settings. It is imperative that their need for personal responsibility, choice, and control over their lives be respected, not only in theory but above all in practice. Because perceived unpredictability or uncontrollability contributes to many of the negative consequences of aging (Schulz, 1976), "institutionalized patients should be given maximum control over all of their daily lives: choice of omelets or scrambled eggs for breakfast, blue or red curtains, going to the movies on Wednesdays or Thursdays, whether they wake up early or sleep late" (Seligman, 1975, p. 183).

The fact that the termination of predictable and controllable social interaction seems to reverse the benefits of this treatment, has important implications for the conduct of activity programs in institutionalized settings. First, if nurses and activity therapists constitute the main source of patients' social interaction, the patients should be able to regulate this interaction according to their personal desires, rather than the staff imposing it. Second, once a program for predictable and controllable social interaction is established it should not be disrupted. Here, however, a problem arises because of the constant and frequent turnover of the staff in institutionalized settings (Moss and Halamandaris, 1977). A replacement of one staff member by another often means change in the program, if not quantitatively then qualitatively. Nevertheless, this problem can be avoided if the transition from one therapist to another is smooth and if the new staff member continues the program of predictable and controllable social interaction at the same qualitative level as the person whom he replaced.

The above suggestions are principles upon which therapeutic recreation specialists should build their activity programs. Recreation programs in the institutionalized settings are not to be means of simply filling patients' time. The objective is to make the residents look forward to their future and enjoyable living. Arts and crafts, for example, are activities that lend themselves readily to rewarding personal and interpersonal activity. They enable the elderly to be creative and productive, not productive because of productivity but because of the delight and enjoyment the older persons are likely to experience in being able to give self-made articles to their grandchildren, to other relatives and friends. Such activities can be sources of continued, predictable, and controllable social interaction for the institutionalized aged.

The need for therapeutic recreation specialists to plan and implement programs which promote the elderly's personal responsibility and social activity becomes urgent in light of the extensive operation of nursing homes in contemporary America. In their book (*Too Old, Too Sick, Too Bad*) based upon the U.S. Senate hearings on aging and nursing homes in America, Moss and Halamandaris (1977) showed how some nursing homes have become "services to the needy by the greedy." The authors claimed that welfare of the patients is of trivial concern to those who run the nursing home industry because they are involved in an immense program of profiteering, perjury, and kickbacks. They went on to show that some 80% of America's 23,000 nursing homes operate for profit and that there was an increase of 2,000 percent in revenues received by the industry between the years 1960 and 1976! At the same time, the number of individuals aged 65 and more increased by 23%, and the number of patients in nursing homes by 245%. Because the elderly are nonproductive members and thus an embarrassment to society, but also because they remind younger people of their own mortality, Moss and Halamandaris argued, social policy seemed to demand the removal of the elderly from the view of productive citizens. Free enterprise was invoked to solve the problem of a large number of the elderly; it responded by taking over nursing homes and by making the nursing home industry "big business." It is then little wonder that patients are physically and psychologically abused in such a profiteering atmosphere (Moss and Halamandaris, 1977).

As Moss and Halamandaris pointed out, due to its profiteering objectives, the nursing home industry has exploited the very people it is supposed to serve. Profits are being made at the expense of the patients' welfare. Opportunities for the elderly's personal responsibility and social activity have become negligible. A profile of America's one million nursing home patients reveals that more than

nursing homes: the warehouses of the aged?

50% of them have no close relatives, and more than 60% have no visitors at all (Moss and Halamandaris, 1977). Saddest of all is the fact that in some homes patients are physically and psychologically abused, even deliberately injured. To become floor favorites of the staff, patients have to offer "tips" to the personnel to help them use such basic facilities as a bathroom. In describing typical nursing home abuses, Moss and Halamandaris (1977, p. 22) put it as follows: "If a patient is not on the 'good side' of the staff, it means no bath or shave, fewer clean clothes and linens, no socks, no help going to and from the bathroom, and sitting in urine longer."

The lack of concern for patients' well-being on the part of the staff is also seen in what Moss and Halamandaris called "pharmaceutical Russian roulette." That is, control of nursing home drugs is almost totally inadequate, meaning that as much as 50% of these drugs are administered in error. On the average, patients take 4.2 different drugs each day, with daily average of 13 doses. It is astounding that one-half of all tranquilizers and 10% of all drugs used in the nursing homes consist of the two most powerful tranquilizers (Moss and Halamandaris, 1977). Knowing the big business character of the nursing home industry it is no surprise that drugs constitute the principal, in some cases the only form of treatment for the patients. Those who are running this industry can make immense profits from the drugs but not from recreational activities. Furthermore, drugs make it extremely easy for the staff to take care of the patients. The use of recreational activities, by contrast, is much more demanding, and if some recreation service is provided, residents pay for it out of their own monthly personal allotment (Moss and Halamandaris, 1977, p. 22).

In view of the above facts, it is hardly surprising to learn that over 50 percent of the nursing homes in the U.S. are substandard, and that 80 to 90 percent of the care is being given by untrained and unlicensed aides and orderlies. Consequently, it is understandable, but not acceptable, that the incompetent staff should attempt to control every aspect and every detail of the clients' lives. As the New York Civil Liberties Union observed:

> They (nursing homes) virtually abolish privacy, stifle individuality, defy the values of order and discipline and enforce arbitrary and discretionary rules. Viewed as a polity, these institutions can only be described as totalitarian. And indeed, those unfortunates who are confined to such institutions have much in common with residents of a totalitarian political regime (Moss and Halamandaris, 1977, p. 12).

In view of this situation, then, it is clear why enhanced personal responsibility, freedom of choice or control have had such powerful effects on physical and psychological well-being of institutionalized patients, as reported by Langer and Rodin, 1976; Rodin and Langer, 1977; Schulz, 1976. In short, human dignity of such older persons has been eroded and debased by institutionalized care. Although the problem is particularly acute in nursing homes, it is by no means limited to these settings.

Rosenhan's data (1973a) for example, showed that the sense of powerlessness and de-personalization is the rule rather than the exception in psychiatric hospitals. Patients are deprived of most of their legal rights; their freedom of movement is restricted; their personal privacy is minimized; and they cannot initiate contact with the staff. Rosenhan reported that not only are the staff and patients strictly segregated, but patients are sometimes beaten by the staff "for the sin of having initiated verbal contact." He reported that practically no mingling time with patients was allotted by nurses; the time they spent talking or playing games with patients was almost nonexistent. The hierarchical structure of the psychiatric hospitals aggravated de-personalization, in that physicians and psychiatrists were even less available for social contacts than were nurses and other residents.

These observations show that the solution to the clients' problem in both mental hospitals and nursing homes seem to be the same: prescribe and administer powerful drugs, avoid social contacts, and do not recognize the human dignity of patients. Unquestionably, such institutionalization of the aged and the mentally ill serves to facilitate rather than hinder helplessness. Thus, it is little wonder that the nursing home is the greatest fear of the elderly (Moss and Halamandaris, 1977). It is ironic that they are called "homes."

In the light of the above-described state of affairs in nursing homes, it becomes urgent to take immediate action to correct the situation and to restore human dignity to the institutionalized. In this task therapeutic recreation specialists can play a major role. The first need is for the staff of each nursing home to recognize and become aware of the possibility that the personnel may be fostering helplessness. Second, the staff should adopt a new philosophy which is directed toward maximizing human dignity. In so doing, the staff should establish new therapeutic programs planned to remove the exising learned helplessness and to prevent helplessness from occurring in the future. This assignment calls for individualized treatment, in which each patient becomes a focus of the staff's attention (Moss and Halamandaris, 1977).

how to improve institutionalization

To maximize human dignity and thus to foster physical and psychological well-being, it is imperative to strive vigorously to enhance the patients' personal responsibility and to increase their freedom of choice. In other words, the elderly should have the feeling that they themselves are in control of their lives. They should be made to feel important and needed. They should always have something to look forward to. The programs based on these principles should never become routine. The staff must be innovative, constantly looking for new ways of maintaining and improving patients' zest for life. The more routine recreation programs become and the more routinely they are carried out, the less valuable they are psychologically.

Thus, it is clear that the mission of therapeutic recreation specialists is much more than to entertain or to provide activities for patients. The challenge is great because the patients' physical and psychological well-being is at stake. To

maximize the human dignity of the institutionalized does not mean that everything should be done for patients. It has been said that total care for the aged is
just as bad as no care at all (Bengtson, 1973). Thus, the purpose of recreation
programs should be to help patients to help themselves. In this task, predictable
and controllable social interaction through various activities is the single best
medicine to guarantee psychological well-being of the institutionalized elderly.

Because each patient should be the focus of attention and since the treatment
should be individualized, it is not possible to suggest specific activities that are
universally applicable to all nursing home residents. One and the same activity
may be used in many ways for many specific purposes, and different activities
can be used for one and the same purpose. Nonetheless, there are some common
and generalized elements in patients' interests; and good nursing homes are
marked by certain types of activity programs. Moss and Halamandaris (1977)
presented a long list of activities offered by the administration of the Iowa Sol-
diers Home in Marshalltown, Iowa. Among them were the following: band concerts, shuffleboard tournaments, the annual Easter egg hunt, parties and picnics,
birdwatching, a fashion show, costume parties, a foreign food fair, adult education in such activities as painting, dancing and secretarial work, and a monthly
supper club activity. In addition, the Little League baseball team plays on the
grounds of the home in summer, residents prepare Christmas cards and send
them to relatives and friends and they run a Santa Claus answering service,
residents' birthdays are commemorated on bulletin boards and birthday parties
are arranged, patients repair appliances and participate in woodwork, leather-
work, sewing, quilting, residents try to prepare their own meals in a rehabilitation kitchen, and the residents choose an employee of the month and give him/her
a $25 savings bond.

It should also be mentioned that Senior Citizens Olympic Games have been
organized in some places. Moss and Halamandaris (1977) noted that the idea of
these Olympics has been very well accepted even by those who can only watch.
In general, competition has been therapeutic. It is obvious that losing does not
pose a threat to the elderly's self-concept as it does to that of the young. Consequently, there is hardly any reason to worry about psychologically detrimental
effects of competition on the elderly.

In addition to the Olympics, other forms of interpersonal activity have been
employed to enhance psychological well-being of the institutionalized aged. One
of them is to encourage nursing home patients to participate in self-government.
For this purpose, many homes have established "residents' councils." Another
approach is to enhance the relationship and closeness of nursing homes and the
community. Thus, nursing homes might sponsor a Little League baseball team,
establish scholarships to help students in fields related to the care of the elderly,
sponsor a free day care program, contribute to bazaars and county fairs, attract
volunteers to help out in the nursing homes and start an "Adopt a Grandparent"
program. These are some examples of how nursing homes can aid the community, as presented by Moss and Halamandaris (1977). Community residents, in
turn may help the patients in many ways. While such mutual understanding and

cooperation is good for both parties, it is particularly beneficial to the institutionalized aged because they have been excluded from the mainstream of society.

No systematic research has been undertaken to assess the impact of activity and recreational programs based upon the aforementioned principles. Some case studies, however, exist, and these clearly point out the patients' relatively high physical and psychological well-being in homes where activity and recreational programs have been employed. Hudson (cited in Moss and Halamandaris, 1977) reported that 67 patients (i.e., over two-thirds of all patients admitted) were classified as "heavy care" at the time of their admission into her activity program, but that the number of patients so classified a year later was reduced to nine. Hudson attributed this success largely to the operation of the activities program.

psychological impact of activity programs

Menninger (cited in Moss and Halamandaris, 1977) obtained similar results. He exposed 88 patients in the geriatric ward to the activities program. According to Menninger, prior to his recreational treatment, these 88 patients were "hopeless people, waiting to die;" 59 of them were bedridden and 41 were spoon fed at every meal. Physical and psychological amelioration resulting from the activity program reached the extent that within a year only nine were still bedfast and only six of them were still incontinent. Amazingly, four of these patients were gainfully employed and self-supporting one year later, six had gone out to live by themselves, twelve had gone home to live with their families, and four had found comfortable nursing homes. Only five had died by the end of the year. All this was achieved by a relatively simple program which emphasized individualized treatment and human dignity. For example, birthday parties were held for everyone, social activities were instituted and a social center was established. Activities such as suffleboard, bingo games, finger painting, leather-tooling, music, and television were introduced. Also, the setting was made homey by installing drapes and by placing cages of canaries, aquariums and potted plants around the rooms.

Although the above findings are highly suggestive of the positive effects of activity programs, it should be kept in mind that the results are based upon case studies. To what extent these findings can be generalized is therefore an open question. Similarly, lack of systematic research impedes determination of the specific aspect(s) of the activity programs which caused the beneficial effects. It is possible that the positive consequences have emerged because the case studies were conducted under extreme conditions, that is, on patients who had been deprived of all their basic human rights. Thus, an increase in perceived control and responsibility may lead to an increase in physical and psychological well-being of the patients who have been in the state of helplessness. But how are the patients' well-being and zest for life maintained in those nursing homes that have established controllability and predictability for their clients? Once perceived control and freedom are restored in patients, does this automatically guarantee continued well-being?

Based upon earlier theorizing, it is assumed that the need for optimal arousal and incongruity exists in the elderly as well as in the young, though there are obvious differences in magnitude between the two groups. If so, individualized treatment based upon respect for the human dignity of the institutionalized aged has to be based on the elderly's need for novel, dissonant and incongruent experiences. However, therapeutic recreation specialists and others who are responsible for planning and carrying out activity programs on the basis of this principle have to exercise caution in providing such experiences. It is clear that the elderly's desire for novelty and incongruity is considerably less than that of the young (see figure 13, p. 176). This, however, does not mean that perceived control and freedom in the institutionalized aged could or should be pursued through routine programs; although routine programs may be predictable and controllable, there is a danger that they become boring and unmotivating. In this sense, complete controllability may be just as bad as no control at all.

The above suggestions show theoretical ambiguities that arise from the aforementioned case studies. Both empirical and theoretical research is needed to improve understanding of the effects of activity programs on patients' physical, social and psychological well-being. But regardless of theoretical obscurity, implications for practitioners are unequivocal. The human dignity of the institutionalized aged must be the main concern of therapeutic recreation specialists in planning activity programs. This demands that the elderly be given rights and opportunities to exercise personal responsibility and freedom of choice in their everyday living. Based upon individualized treatment, therapeutic recreation specialists should exert every effort to make their patients' life as normal as possible. Striving to maximize human dignity in the institutionalized aged is *the* principle that will prevent helplessness and restore zest for life.

---

summary

The chapter dealt with therapeutic recreation, perceived control and the institutionalized aged. It was argued that it is not recreational activity in itself which is crucial but rather the extent to which such activity provides a sense of control and predictability over one's environment and entire life. In support of this inference, research has shown that enhancing nursing home residents' perceived control increases their activeness, interpersonal activity, mental alertness, and psychological well-being in general. Most dramatically, a procedure which demonstrated how patients in a nursing home might increase choice and personal control over their everyday living significantly reduced the mortality rate among the institutionalized aged. Other research has also been consistent with these findings, in that a simple procedure of increasing social interaction through visits to the institutionalized aged is an effective technique of improving the patients' physical and psychological health. However, these beneficial effects materialize only if patients can personally control and predict their social interaction. Yet there is some tentative evidence to suggest that such effects are temporary if the program for predictable and controllable social interactions is discontinued.

It follows from the above that recreation programs in the institutionalized settings are not to be means of simply filling the patients' time. The objective is to induce residents to look forward to their future and enjoyable living. A need for personal responsibility, choice, and control should be of paramount importance in planning recreational activities for the institutionalized aged. The implementation of recreation programs based upon these principles, in institutional settings like nursing homes, is urgent because privacy is commonly abolished, individuality stifled, and the basic human rights denied in these settings. To maximize human dignity in the elderly requires individualized treatment in which each patient is a focus of attention. Therapeutic recreation specialists' commitment to this principle is likely to prevent helplessness and to enhance zest for life in the aged. Then, and only then, can nursing homes be called homes for the aged.

on the social psychology

of work, leisure and quality of life

the interrelationship between work and leisure 17

In keeping with the purpose of this book the preceding chapters have focused on the antecedents and consequences of leisure and recreation behavior. While it is important to study leisure and recreation for their own sake, one should remember that leisure is not the only aspect of life. No matter how important leisure is to an individual, people nevertheless have to work in modern society, in other words, work and leisure are the two major components of the cognitive and behavioral repertoire. Therefore, leisure should not only be analyzed as an isolated aspect of life but also as an interdependent element of total human behavior. This calls for an examination of the interrelationship between work and leisure, that is, the effects of work on leisure and vice versa. The purpose of the present chapter is to examine such interrelationships between work and leisure. The underlying theme of this analysis is an individual who influences and is influenced by others in social leisure and work environments. The role of leisure in total behavior can also be analyzed by determining its contribution to the quality of life. In universal yet simple terms, it may be stated that quality of life is a function of work *and* leisure. This leads to an analysis which seeks to determine the relative contributions of work and leisure to the quality of life. The final chapter examines determinants of the perceived quality of life, with particular emphasis on work and leisure satisfaction.

Though sociologists have paid considerable attention to the relationship between work and leisure, psychologists and social psychologists have almost entirely ignored this area of research. Thus, it is not surprising that an individual (and thus individual differences) have been overlooked in the past when the work-leisure relationship has been subjected to theoretical and empirical investigation. Faithful to their characteristic approach, sociologists in their theoretical analyses have lumped individuals together, and in doing so, have assumed that the effects of work on leisure (and vice versa) are so pervasive that individual differences do not matter. This assumption, however, has been unfortunate, because it has retarded the progress in the area, as evidenced by frequent contradictory findings in the relevant literature (Champoux, 1975). The conflicting results are an indication of the influence of the omitted "third" factors. The neglected fact is that it is the individual who defines what becomes work and leisure; work or leisure in itself does not make any decisions. Therefore, an individual and his personal cognitions cannot be disregarded when the interrelationship between work and leisure is examined.

the effects of work on leisure

three hypotheses

The literature (Parker, 1971; Wilensky, 1960, 1961) distinguishes three major hypotheses to explain the effects of work on leisure. The first of these is the idea that working experiences tend to carry or "spill over" into free-time. That is, people choose leisure activities that are characteristically similar to their jobs—"the long arm of the job reaching out into life away from work" (Meissner, 1971). If their jobs are monotonous, unchallenging, and provide little or no autonomy and control over work, their leisure behavior becomes passive, idle amusement. The second hypothesis proposes the opposite effects, stating that work experiences are compensated for by the choice of free-time participation. In other words, people compensate for the negative aspects of their job in their free-time. If, for example, their job is constraining and socially isolating, they will participate in free-time activities which allow them to exercise control over life and to interact socially. Finally, the third hypothesis (Bacon, 1975; Meissner, 1971; Parker, 1971) posits that work and leisure are independent of each other, one having no discernible effect on another.

While Wilensky (1960, 1961) is typically credited for proposing the first two hypotheses, the spill-over and compensation ideas were already put forth by such classic authors as Adam Smith and Karl Marx. Smith (1937, p. 734) noted that a factory worker "whose whole life is spent in performing a few simple operations . . . becomes as stupid and ignorant as it is possible for a human creature to become," thereby supporting the "spill-over" hypothesis. As discussed earlier (pp. 33–34), Marx argued that class society makes workers feel alienated and helpless in regard to their work, with the consequence of the working-day spilling over to their free-time. But Marx also asserted that "the development of human personality for its own sake" can begin only after work. This implied that bad working experiences may be compensated for by the wise choice of free-time activities. On the other hand, he was skeptical about the possibility of compensation, because capitalistic society creates "false" consumer (leisure) needs and lures people to participate in activities which are mainly geared toward meeting these false needs rather than toward developing human personality for its own sake.

on the testing of the hypotheses

In testing the effects of work on leisure participation, it is essential that subjects under different working conditions do not differ in their leisure skills and leisure motivation to begin with. On the other hand, subjects who have objectively discernible working environments and whose leisure patterns are therefore compared should differ in the *perceptions* of their work. If subjects with different jobs or occupations perceive their work equally alienating or equally rewarding, there is no reason to compare their leisure behavior. It is therefore necessary that these two requirements be met when attempts are made to validate the above hypotheses.

This may be illustrated by an example. Iowa City has a toothpaste factory, whose workers come from all corners of the country; some of them might even be from foreign countries. Hence, these workers were raised in different social environments, and consequently their leisure values, attitudes, motives and skills may differ. If they do, it is impossible to determine the extent to which the factory work is responsible for their leisure participation, unless discrepant leisure motives and skills are systematically taken into account. Observed differences in their leisure patterns may simply reflect variations in socialization experiences, rather than working conditions. The danger of making erroneous conclusions is particularly imminent when the effects of work on leisure are tested by comparing leisure participation of individuals with different occupations. Unfortunately, this has been the main approach in testing the validity of the aforementioned hypotheses (cf. Champoux, 1975). If one compares leisure preferences and patterns of dentists and factory workers and finds some differences between the two groups of workers, the researcher is in no position to claim the differences to be due to the influence of work, unless leisure attitudes, motives and skills were kept constant between dentists and workers.

The above rationale applies to the generally established finding that individuals in relatively high level occupations are more active, involved, and diversive in their participation than individuals in relatively low level occupations (cf. Champoux, 1975). Again, these differences in leisure behavior cannot be interpreted as reflecting the influence of work on leisure, to say nothing of the relevance of these findings to the spill-over and compensation hypotheses. The differing leisure patterns may simply be the result of variations in socialization experiences (and the resultant differences in leisure attitudes, motives and skills) and/or perceptions regarding working conditions. To place dentists, for example, in the category of non-constraining work without ascertaining their own perceptions of the degree of constraint in the job is the same as doing an experiment without reporting "manipulation checks" regarding the validity of independent variables. Such a failure is a major error on the part of a researcher. It simply cannot be assumed that the researchers' and the subjects' perceptions of working conditions are identical. Unfortunately, all the past research claiming to test the effects of work on leisure or purporting to validate the aforementioned hypotheses appear guilty of this failure. Therefore, little or no credence can be given to the past investigations on the relationship between work and leisure.

The above criticism indicates that workers' socialization experiences (and thus, leisure attitudes, motives and skills) and their perceptions regarding the work should be identified and controlled in empirical studies. It also points out that the effects of work on leisure should be examined within one and the same occupation rather than lumping all occupations together. Even when these aspects have been considered in research, it would be desirable to obtain information about subjects' own reasons for their leisure participation; such information would help to determine whether subjects are actually "compensating," "spilling-over," etc. To simply collect data on minutes and hours people with various jobs spend in a number of leisure activities is inadequate for making inferences about psychological mechanisms (e.g., compensation) mediating the effects of work on leisure behavior. This is particularly relevant because bad work experiences can be compensated in various ways, "between" and "within" leisure activities (see Part 4). Without knowledge about what different leisure activities in different places at different times mean for different people, one is not justified in drawing conclusions about the existence of such underlying psychological processes as compensation.

In the past, both spill-over and compensation hypotheses have been presented in simple but rather vague terms. For example, the idea of compensation is typically presented by saying that the constraints and social isolation of the job are compensated for through discretionary free-time activities and activities involving social interaction. But what are such activities? How intensively should one participate in such activities before he can be said to be compensating? The point is that any free-time activity has elements of constraint and freedom, social isolation, and social interaction. Activities in themselves are not socially isolating or interactive, but rather it is the individual who attaches certain meanings to various activities. Thus, the result of simply comparing leisure participation of individuals in different working conditions or occupations (or comparing leisure behavior of one group of workers before and after their job experience) does not necessarily indicate anything about compensation or spill-over.

As pointed out earlier (Part 4), individual need for change, variety, and substitution (thus, "compensation") in leisure behavior manifests itself in different ways, because the change can occur along several dimensions. For example, social isolation on the job can be compensated for by participation in leisure activities involving a varying number of persons, or involving the same number of individuals but a varying degree of intensity of social interaction, or involving a varying extent of duration and frequency of social interaction. Thus, if social isolation on the job is to be compensated for by social interaction off the job, this can occur in countless ways, not to mention the fact that social isolation on the job may be compensated for by participation in strenuous physical exercise, or by intellectual activities during free-time, etc. Or, the negative aspects of work can simply be compensated cognitively by denying the importance of the negative qualities and by emphasizing positive characteristics of the job. After all, who is to determine, and on what grounds, that social isolation must be offset by social interaction?

The above criticism demonstrates the conceptual problems and limited perspective revealed in explaining the relationship between work and leisure by such simplistic notions as spill-over and compensation. Does this then mean that no compensation or spill-over is taking place? Not necessarily, because for some people certain leisure activities in certain places at certain times may be compensatory. Thus, what researchers should do is to establish the *conditions under which* work experiences are compensated and under which they tend to spill over to free-time participation. They should also consider that the effects of work on leisure (whatever they are) are not stable. Rather, these effects are likely to fluctuate as functions of time and environment. Furthermore, it is misleading to simply combine all the diverse aspects of work and then to examine the effects of work on leisure. A person's job is composed of many elements, such as salary, fringe benefits, freedom, social interaction, social atmosphere, peer relations, etc.

To understand how work affects leisure requires that the relationship between work and leisure be examined separately in each of these various aspects. Owing to the conceptual shortsightedness of the spill-over, compensation, and no-relationship hypotheses, it is not surprising to learn that past empirical research is confusing and contradictory. Following his thorough review of the past research, Champoux (1975, p. 56) concluded that "the empirical research directed at the work-nonwork relationship is best described as inconclusive." He attributes this to the fact that almost all theoretical and empirical work has been done by sociologists and proposes that an interdisciplinary approach to the issues would improve the quality of future research.

The failure of empirical research to provide consistent support for either compensation or spill-over does not necessarily mean that the third hypothesis (no-relationship) must then be correct. But it does imply that leisure behavior can be understood better by considering leisure socialization processes (including relationship between personality and leisure), leisure attitudes, and motives. If so, then earlier attempts (Parts 4–5) to account for leisure and recreation in terms of these constructs are further justified. As noted above, individual differences (as manifested in leisure experiences, attitudes, motives, and skills) mediate the effects of work on leisure. That is, work experiences may or may not affect a person's leisure attitudes, motives, and skills, which in turn may or may not influence actual leisure behavior. In short, to determine the effects of work (W) on leisure (L) and vice versa one must take cognitive variables (O) into account, the basic paradigm therefore being: W-O-L.

Some of the work-related variables that might influence a person's leisure behavior are success in daily work and the leisure interests of co-workers. As for the first variable, job satisfaction in distinct occupations varies as a function of a person's job performance each day. If, for example, a businessman has made excellent sales on one day, the good mood resulting from his successful job performance is likely to carry over into his leisure behavior. He may improvise (see the discussion of improvised leisure needs, chapter 11) and take his family to a good restaurant and perhaps to the movies afterwards. It is therefore reasonable to suggest that those factors that lead to the feelings of successful job performance have a positive influence on an individual's leisure behavior and leisure satisfaction.

successful job
performance and
leisure behavior

Like the feelings of successful job performance, the second variable—co-workers' leisure interests—has been totally overlooked in the past. This is surprising because its effects are potentially quite strong. On most jobs, workers are able to talk about their leisure experiences and thereby influence each other's leisure preferences and participation. It would be important to determine the extent to which co-workers' leisure patterns are similar in various occupations and the degree to which co-workers are in fact affecting—intentionally or unintentionally—the leisure behavior of others. It may be argued that lack of similarity between workers' leisure interests prevents cohesiveness from developing among workers in a given work unit. If so, dissimilar leisure interests might decrease workers' job performance and productivity, since it is known that the cohesiveness is positively related to productivity (e.g., Bakeman and Helmreich, 1975). It may also be proposed that workers' similar leisure interests help develop friendships which in turn may increase social atmosphere, cooperativeness, and cohesiveness among workers. These latter factors, in turn, have been shown to increase job satisfaction (Argyle, 1972).

Other questions may be raised about the influence of co-workers' leisure interests. It is reasonable to expect that in certain professions and jobs, there is social pressure for workers to engage in leisure activities considered appropriate for them. Because of the social status or norm implied by job a person may feel strong social pressure to participate in those leisure activities that other workers typically engage in. For example, if other factory workers watch television during their free-time and drink beer after work, a person may feel pressure to do the same, even though he dislikes these activities. Otherwise, the individual might not be able to communicate and interact with his fellow workers, thereby possibly creating a negative working environment. If he continued his preferred personal leisure habits (e.g., going to performing arts centers and reading novels), he might be mocked and told that those are leisure activities of the bourgeoisie, not appropriate for the workers.

Similar social pressure might be exerted at the other end of the social class continuum. That is, a businessman may feel pressure to join an elitist social club and to play golf with other businessmen. He might fear that his business would suffer due to customers' boycott if he does not participate in certain public service activities during his free-time. Another businessman may conform to this principle and spend his free-time in visible forums (e.g., serving as a chairperson of the United Way fund raising) in order to implicitly promote the sales of his business. A different type of social pressure may arise from social parties given by fellow workers. In many white-collar occupations, workers give social parties which everyone is expected to attend. A person who does not show up may be labeled weird or deviant, and this in turn may affect how others treat the individual on the job. Finally, when the effects of co-workers' leisure preferences and interests are examined, one should also consider the possible mediating influence of social status and power of a co-worker, that is, whether the leisure interests of superiors have more effect on a person's free-time participation than the interests of subordinate co-workers.

Of course, it is possible that co-workers alter a person's leisure behavior patterns without any social pressures. The *mere* existence of different leisure interests on the part of other workers may make a person change his free-time habits. A person may first participate in the activities of others out of curiosity, but may subsequently develop a liking for them. Or others may be able to persuade an individual to participate (e.g., go to a stadium to watch games) by presenting the positive aspects of these activities. One way in which working partners often temporarily influence each other's daily leisure participation is through evaluation of present leisure occurrences like movies, theater, and musical performances, etc. By telling fellow workers about a trip to the movies last night and by evaluating the movie a person influences the other person's probability of attending it. In a similar vein, working partners often remind each other about the forthcoming free-time happenings such as daily television programs.

In short, it is obvious that, whether directly or indirectly, co-workers affect one another's leisure behavior. In addition, due to their social status, many jobs apparently have implications for leisure participation. Unfortunately, the extent of these influences is not known because no research has been conducted on this subject. This area thus remains an important target for future research. For both practical and theoretical reasons it is essential to investigate these influence processes, because they are connected with job and leisure satisfaction and thereby with the quality of life.

The interrelationship between work and leisure includes not only the effects of work on leisure but also the influence of leisure on work. Unfortunately, however, both theoretical and empirical investigations have failed almost entirely to examine the latter relationship. This is surprising, since there are no apparent reasons to assume that job performance and satisfaction are unaffected by leisure behavior. In fact, precisely the opposite may be true, as indicated by many examples of how work performance and satisfaction are shaped by prior leisure participation. Perhaps the most obvious of these is concerned with the influence of physical fatigue. That is, if a person spends free-time in watching TV late in the evening or partying and drinking until the small hours of the morning, work motivation is most likely to suffer the next day, or at least early in the morning.

the effects of leisure on work

When the effects of leisure on work are being examined, some caution should be exercised. The fact that leisure affects work does not mean that it is possible to classify *activities* according to their ability to contribute to good job performance and high job satisfaction. This follows because different activities mean different things to different people, because the reasons for leisure participation even in the same activity differ from individual to individual, and because the effects of leisure participation are not stable with respect to time and space. Therefore, an examination of the leisure-work relationship should consider subjective perceptions of leisure. Simply to correlate objective indicators of leisure participation with job performance and job satisfaction does not account for the effects of leisure on work. Again, the concept leisure or work in itself is meaningless, because it is the individual who attaches certain values and meanings to these concepts, and personal cognitions then determine the effects of leisure behavior on work. Human cognitions, in turn, are socially influenced.

leisure behavior and job satisfaction

It is well established in the literature of the subject that job performance or productivity is positively (though moderately) related to job satisfaction (Argyle, 1972; Vroom, 1964). To increase productivity, it is therefore necessary to enhance job satisfaction. Thus, the fact that job satisfaction has been a favorite subject of research among American industrial psychologists is hardly surprising. A long list of variables assumed to affect job satisfaction has been subjected to empirical research. Among them are variables dealing with intrinsic nature of work (variety, autonomy, use of skills and abilities), hours of work (flextime), incentive conditions (pay and fringe benefits, occupational status, promotion aspects, security), the work group (cohesiveness, popularity, group size, opportunities for interaction), supervision (leader's warmth in personal relations, participation in decision-making), the company (size and type), as well as individual differences (personality, sex, age, orientation to work, etc.). For a review of research on the effects of these variables, see Argyle (1972), Locke (1976), and Warr and Wall (1975).

Despite the multitude of variables investigated, past research on job satisfaction can be criticized on several grounds. First, as the above list indicates, it has been assumed that the determinants of job satisfaction reside in the job only. In this approach, researchers have totally overlooked the contribution of the off-the-job and leisure-related factors to job satisfaction. Second, researchers have invariably assumed that job satisfaction is a stable trait. Although job satisfaction has a degree of stability, it also changes from time to time and from place to place. Third, past research has failed to consider that job satisfaction is a relative concept, the foundations of which lie in social comparison processes. These considerations indicate that people's expectations about job satisfaction tend to change. If certain factors and conditions led to high job satisfaction 50 years ago, today they may be totally inadequate to provide such satisfaction, because standards of excellence and also of expectations have changed dramatically over the period. These points of criticism will now be examined in greater detail, in order to better understand the causes of job satisfaction and thus the interrelationship between work, leisure, and the quality of life.

leisure environment and job satisfaction

The first point of criticism was that the industrial psychologists have failed to consider influences of leisure-related factors on job satisfaction. This neglect is apparently based upon an assumption that work is entirely isolated from other spheres of life. Such an assumption is incredibly short-sighted, because it is evident that the job does not exist in the environmental vacuum. Consider a person who is paid a large sum of money (say $80,000 per year) for work which is challenging and competence-producing, but which is performed in an environment (say, somewhere in the Sahara desert in Africa) where no leisure services are provided. Undoubtedly, this person's job satisfaction would be lower than that of a person whose job is equally rewarding extrinsically and intrinsically but which is performed in an environment where numerous and variable leisure services are available. Accordingly, it appears that, other things being equal, leisure environments which are perceived to be satisfying are more conducive to job satisfaction than are poorly rated leisure environments.

It is conceivable that many people do not describe their job satisfaction without considering the leisure environment of their work. To simply ask people how satisfied they are with their job, therefore, does not necessarily mean that the respondents are thinking only of on-the-job aspects of their work when they respond. This may in part explain the fact that 80% or more of Americans surveyed are satisfied with their jobs (Taylor, 1977). That is, the respondents might have considered both on-the-job and off-the-job aspects of their work when answering the questions dealing with overall job satisfaction.

Consistent with the above reasoning, it is not uncommon to find people who say that they are able to "put up" with their lousy job because of good off-the-job and leisure opportunities in their community. Although they may dislike their work, the excellent leisure opportunities offered in the community may compensate for low job satisfaction. There are many people who can endure their uninteresting jobs so long as they can live in big cities, while for others a "good" leisure environment means a small rural town away from the "action." It is clear, then, that the leisure environment may serve as an incentive for work, and leisure activities may become an aspect of life which people are looking forward to. Consequently, they are able to continue to work even on jobs which they dislike. If this is true, then it is surprising that relatively few companies and corporations have paid attention to their workers' views of leisure services in their community. It is possible that job satisfaction is lower, and various indicators (labor turnover, absenteeism) of reduced productivity higher, among workers in those communities where leisure services are perceived to be poor than where they are viewed as excellent.

In a study which is directly relevant, Hulin (1969) investigated the role of the community in workers' job satisfaction. The study was done in a town of about 10,000 people which is dominated by one company. Subjects consisted of personnel ranging from the first line supervisors to the plant manager. The results showed that satisfaction with adult recreational facilities and children's recreational facilities had strong positive relationships to satisfaction with work, pay, co-workers, and supervisors. This implied that the more satisfied workers are with recreational opportunities provided by their community, the more satisfied they are with these aspects of their job.

It is apparent, then, that people do not view their job as independent of other spheres of their lives and do not consider that their job exists in an environmental vacuum. Clearly, investigations of job satisfaction should take into account community characteristics, particularly recreational features, in determining the stable and variable causes of job satisfaction. Such research is important not only for theoretical reasons, but also for its practical implications. As the Hulin results indicate, one way of augmenting the stability of a company's work force and perhaps increasing productivity is to match the workers' leisure interests with the leisure services of the community where the company is located. This could be done by employing workers who are satisfied with, or even enthusiastic about the leisure opportunities provided by a community.

employers' interest in workers' leisure

An alternative is that a company itself may provide leisure services for its workers. This option has recently become rather widespread in private industry. An increasing number of companies are hiring recreation professionals to plan, organize and administer leisure services to the employees. Pioneering corporations like IBM have built their own jogging tracks, tennis courts, recreation areas, country clubs, and even hotels for their employees (Mayer and Ruby, 1977).

But why are corporations becoming interested in their workers' well-being off the job? Such interest, which appears to be very humane, is not characteristic of the business world. As might be expected, the interest has not grown as much from altruistic concern as from concern for profit-making. The chairman of IBM expressed it bluntly (Mayer and Ruby, 1977): "It's good business. The more satisfied your employees are, the better they'll perform." To keep its employees happy, IBM spends an estimated 2.3 billion dollars a year (14% of its 1976 gross revenues) on various benefit and service programs. In addition to such customary fringe benefits as pension, life insurance, and medical coverage, IBM provides day-care centers for its employees' children, pays most of the costs resulting from adopting children, supports employees' favorite charities, rebates the tuition of those who go back to school after retirement, and provides education, entertainment, and recreation services. As a result of all this, IBM is rated the best company to work for (Mayer and Ruby, 1977). The corporation has become a way of life for its employees, in short, a family firm.

While IBM may be exceptionally generous in its off-the-job services to its employees, the example of this corporation nevertheless illustrates what is happening in other companies as well, though probably on a smaller scale. The IBM case is typical, in that recreation services constitute an integral part of off-the-job benefits provided for the employees. Thus, recreation is one important aspect, but not the only or even the major off-the-job aspect catered to by companies. In view of other off-the-job services, it is difficult to say the extent to which recreation services contribute to the employees' job satisfaction and job performance. Some people may value their company's recreation services while others may be pleased because of medical expenses covered by the company.

One thing, however, is sure. By providing a wide variety of services and benefits, a company is likely to satisfy the needs, desires, and concerns of most employees. In doing so the company maximizes the positive impacts of the off-the-job variables on job satisfaction and job performance. To this end, recreation and other off-the-job factors are used as the tools to increase work satisfaction and productivity. Because of the policy of the company chairman that the services and benefits are offered because "it's good business," one might say that corporations are exploiting employees' recreation interests to make profits for the company. However, it would be too shortsighted to condemn corporations for such an attitude, because the employees' quality of life has improved as a result of carrying out this policy.

The fact remains, however, that the employer and employee view the basis of these services and benefits quite differently. While corporate chairmen provide recreational activities solely for the sake of good business, employees seem to think that their company is personally interested in them when it offers services and benefits. One IBM employee said that, "I do feel that the company takes a personal interest in me and my children, that the company provides me with security and cares about us" (Mayer and Ruby, 1977). Thus, employees seem to think that their company is interested in them as total human beings rather than as working machines. Consequently, they develop deep appreciation and demonstrate their loyalty to the company by working hard; and this is what the company is interested in. Although employers and employees may have differing ideas about the purpose of the off-the-job services and benefits provided by the company, the outcome may be one and the same: sustained or enhanced job satisfaction and productivity. This hypothesis, however, remains to be proven.

What IBM and other corporations are doing is psychologically effective, and this is the reason their off-the-job programs are successful in increasing workers' overall job satisfaction. By giving an impression that a company cares for its employees, not only as workers but as total human beings (whose life is composed of many other things besides work), off-the-job benefits and services penetrate to the psychological core of the workers. As noted earlier (chapter 16), respect for individual rights and potentials enhanced perceived personal responsibility and control, while this in turn, increased physical and psychological well-being, and lowered the mortality rate among the institutionalized elderly. Basically the same thing seems to be happening in the case of IBM, though here the respect for individual rights and capacities is directed to different ends. By providing various off-the-job benefits and services, IBM conveys the *impression* that it respects workers' individual rights and competencies, thereby enhancing employees' feelings of worthiness and importance. This, of course, is based upon the well-established social psychological fact that when others respect a person and cause him to feel important or needed, these others, whether employers, directors, or teachers, are viewed much more positively than those who do not show such individual respect.

The above reasoning implies that if a company provides recreation services to its employees, their job satisfaction and performance improve. Because of its strong psychological impact the provision of these services in itself appears to be sufficient for increasing job satisfaction. These inferences, however, are principally based upon the experiences of one corporation. Scientifically, therefore, the evidence leaves much to be desired. It would be useful to subject the above theorizing to rigorous empirical testing in order to determine the influences of recreation services as compared to vis-a-vis other off-the-job services and benefits, in affecting job satisfaction and performance. Although the subject lacks systematic and directly relevant research confirmation, some studies lend support to the above theorizing. Krech and Crutchfield (1948) reported that satisfaction with off-the-job factors is positively related to satisfaction with on-the-job factors. In a similar vein, Dwivedi and Pestonjee (1976) found that adjustment in social and personal life affected the overall job satisfaction of blue collar factory workers.

effects of shortened weekend

Thus far tentative evidence has been presented to show that workers' satisfaction with recreational opportunities in a community and a company's interest in workers' leisure life affect both their job satisfaction and performance. While these findings are important in themselves, they are also significant, in that they shed light on some related issues. One such issue is the impacts of a shortened workweek (i.e., 4 days, 40 hours) on job satisfaction and performance.

To test the widely held view that 4-40 scheduling is superior to the traditional worktime pattern (i.e., 5-40), Ivancevich and Lyon (1977) performed a field experiment which compared job satisfaction and performance of 4-40 workers to those of 5-40 workers. The company's executive committee agreed to establish two experimental groups, both working on the 4-40 schedule, but one of them for a period of 13 months, and the other for 25 months. The control group consisted of conventional 5-40 workers. As a whole, the results were mixed, in that the short-term effects (13 months) were positive, while the long-term effects (25 months) of the shortened workweek were negligible. When comparing the pre-test-post-test changes between the experimental (13 months) and control group, it appeared that both overall job satisfaction and overall job performance were significantly higher for the 4-40 workers than for the 5-40 workers. But these differences were not significant when the same comparison was made between the two groups for a period of 25 months.

Provided that the above findings generally hold true and do not reflect methodological problems in the study, why should the effects of the shortened work week be mixed? Methodologically it is known (e.g., Kerlinger, 1973) that whenever an independent variable does not have a powerful effect on a dependent variable, individual differences account for the "weak" findings. If the shortened work week were a very potent independent variable, it would increase everyone's job satisfaction and performance, regardless of the individual differences. But when it is not potent, individual differences become a major source of variance. That is, for some people the shortened work week is appropriate and beneficial while for the others it is not. In direct support of this, Ivancevich and Lyon (1977) cited studies showing that in some cases the shortened work week shows an incremental effect, in others a decremental effect, and still in others no influence.

To understand how individual differences are related to the shortened work week, one should consider socialization processes and the need for optimal arousal and incongruity. Depending on their socialization experiences, individuals differ in their need for stability and variety in leisure behavior. For some the shortened work week provides a better avenue to satisfy their leisure "needs," while for others the conventional schedule is more suitable. Thus, if the young learn to spend their leisure according to the shortened work week, they, as adults, will also support the policies which will enable them to do so.

It follows from the above that sudden changes in adults' worktime patterns may not lead to modifications in job satisfaction and performance, unless workers' leisure behavior is significantly altered by the new working schedule. If the shortened work week considerably improves a person's leisure satisfaction, then the new worktime pattern is likely to improve job satisfaction as well. But when workers' work week is shortened, nothing is usually done to change or improve recreational services in communities. Consequently there is no reason to assume that people will change their leisure patterns as a result of the shortened work week, implying that no changes should be expected in job satisfaction and performance without significant improvement in recreational services. Of course, better services in themselves are meaningless, unless people make use of them and *perceive* services to be better. Taken together, it seems that a study of the influences of the changed worktime pattern on job satisfaction and performance should take into account the mediating influence of leisure behavior and satisfaction. In itself the shortened work week is meaningless. What matters is the psychological impact of the shortened work week.

But how about the positive short-term influences of the shortened work week on job satisfaction and performance, as found by Ivancevich and Lyon (1977)? Based upon the above reasoning, one explanation would be that the shortened work week significantly changed workers' leisure patterns and thus perhaps increased their leisure satisfaction; if so, the workers' job satisfaction and performance increased. Alternatively, and more plausibly, however, the positive influences can be explained by the "novelty effect," which can best be illustrated by children's play behavior. That is, when a child is given a new toy, his enjoyment of the toy is much greater than his enjoyment of old toys, and the child plays with the new toy more frequently than with older ones. But when the new toy has been around long enough, it becomes familiar and old, thereby losing its attractiveness. The same with the new worktime pattern. The changed work schedule presents a person's job in a new light, makes it more interesting and likeable, and thereby probably improves job satisfaction and performance. After a while, however, novelty wears off and the worker realizes that the 4-40 schedule is nothing but old wine in a new bottle. As a result, after the initial novelty impact,[1] job satisfaction and performance of the 4-40 and 5-40 workers do not differ.

The effect of novelty is likely to be even stronger if workers receive the impression that the company has changed the worktime pattern *in order* to improve their quality of life. As pointed out earlier, when a company shows personal interest in its workers' off-the-job behavior, for example, by providing recreation services, the job satisfaction and performance of the employees tend to improve. However, it is reasonable to assume that by providing recreational services the com-

[1]In addition, the 4-40 schedule may lead to such drawbacks as fatigue and interference with family roles and family leisure, drawbacks which may become evident soon after novelty starts wearing thin.

pany is expressing more clearly and strongly its personal interest in its employ-ees' well-being than by simply rearranging worktime. To the extent that the shortened workweek is not psychologically as meaningful and important as the provision of recreational services, it is not surprising that, except in the short-run, the shortened work week has negligible influence on workers' job satisfaction and performance.

Inasmuch as leisure satisfaction mediates the effects of the shortened work week, a question arises about the determinants of leisure satisfaction. The answer can be found in previous discussion (Parts 4 and 5), more specifically in the chapter dealing with leisure motivation. As research indicates persuasively, in-trinsically motivated leisure behavior is the major source of leisure satisfaction. The main elements of intrinsic motivation consist of perceived freedom or self-determination, and perceived competence. If a person participates in certain ac-tivities without any external constraints and expects to receive such intrinsic re-wards from participation as feelings of competence, that individual is said to be intrinsically motivated in leisure behavior. As pointed out earlier, intrinsically motivated leisure behavior is frequently directed at activities involving social interaction. This means that if the shortened work week leads to an increase in a person's intrinsically motivated leisure behaviors, the new worktime pattern is likely to increase leisure satisfaction and thereby job satisfaction and perfor-mance. In sum, it is not the shortened workweek in itself that is critical to job satisfaction and performance, but rather the psychological impact of the new worktime pattern and its ability to facilitate intrinsically motivated leisure be-havior.

interpersonal leisure behavior and job satisfaction

Since social interaction and interpersonal relations are an important part of intrin-sically motivated leisure behavior, it is essential that these variables be taken into account when the impacts of leisure on job satisfaction and performance are examined. Consider two persons on the same job, one whose family life is happy and rewarding, the other whose family relations are bad. It is likely that the former individual is more satisfied with his job and more productive in his work than is the latter. If this is true, then it becomes imperative to try to ameliorate people's interpersonal relations off-the-job, so as to increase job satisfaction and performance.

One way of doing this is through leisure behavior. Orthner (1975, 1976) has shown that participation in "joint" leisure activities is positively and, participa-tion in individual activities is negatively, related to marital satisfaction, especially in the first five years of marriage and after a marriage of 20 years. Thus, partici-pation in those activities which provide avenues for interpersonal communication will improve the spouses' interpersonal satisfaction, but participation in individ-ual activities seems to deteriorate these relations. Other studies (e.g., Ragheb, 1975; West and Merriam, 1970) are consistent with this conclusion. If above hypothesis about the positive relationship between satisfaction with interpersonal relations on the one hand and job satisfaction and/or performance on the other is correct, it then becomes important for the industry to provide sufficient opportunities for work-ers to have satisfying interpersonal leisure experiences.

A strong, positive relation between "leisure time cohesion" and work performance was reported by Bakeman and Helmreich (1975). In that field study, the investigators examined ten teams of aquanauts in an undersea environment. These groups, comprised of four scientists and one engineer, spent 182 days altogether conducting marine science in a four-room underwater habitat. This habitat consisted of two 12-foot cylinders connected by a tunnel, and had a "laboratory compartment, an engine room, a control and communications center, and a crew quarters with kitchen." Since there was a TV-camera and an open microphone in each compartment, surface-stationed observers were able to monitor continuously the subjects' "work" and "leisure" behavior. Work was defined by activities related to the conduct of marine science such as making observations, collecting data, and preparing research reports. In contrast to this, leisure was defined as participation in activities involving social interaction or "solitary recreation" (e.g., listening to tapes or radio) or "relaxation." Since the observers recorded the subjects' behavior (whether work or leisure) at 6-minute intervals, the definition of team work performance was based upon the percentage of time the team, on the average, was observed to engage in "work," in relation to the total number of times observed. Cohesiveness was defined in terms of the percentage of time team members were observed in "leisure time conversation," in relation to the total number of times such interaction was observed.

The principal result of this study was that group cohesiveness, as defined by the degree of social interaction in leisure, was highly correlated ($r = .64$) with work performance. This result implies that as leisure time cohesion increased so did team work performance. This then raises the question about the direction of causality; that is, whether leisure cohesiveness caused work performance or vice versa. Additional data analyses (cross-lagged panel correlations) indicated that work performance was more the cause than the effect of leisure cohesiveness. But even if work performance contributed more to leisure cohesiveness than leisure cohesiveness to work performance, this result does not necessarily rule out the possibility of circular causation between the two variables. As a whole, the study demonstrated that leisure cohesiveness is highly associated with work performance, thereby providing support for the earlier suggestion that leisure behavior and satisfaction may play an important role in job satisfaction and performance. Since Bakeman and Heimreich investigated the relationship under the very special conditions, their study should be replicated in more "natural" situations and with more natural subjects, before firm conclusions can be drawn about the contribution of leisure cohesiveness to work satisfaction and performance.

Finally, the influence of leisure experiences on the development of interpersonal behavior and relations on the job are to be considered. It has been argued (e.g., Schrank, 1978) that employers should recognize the human "need to socialize" and take this basic need into account when designing the work structure. Such requirement is strongly supported by Colligan and Stockton's (1978) results, which showed that lack of opportunities to communicate with one another on the job contributes to the development of psychogenic illness (characterized by stress, muscular tension and depression) among workers. If workers are provided

leisure experiences and subsequent interpersonal relations on the job

with opportunities to socialize and share their experiences on the job (''to schmooze,'' Schrank, 1978), then their leisure experiences become important in the development of interpersonal relations on the job. Co-workers' leisure interests may be particularly critical in this regard. If workers have common leisure interests, they have much to talk about. Increased interpersonal communication in turn is likely to enhance interpersonal satisfaction. If so, similar leisure interests may give rise to cohesiveness among workers, and this in turn is known to be positively related to job satisfaction and performance (e.g., Argyle, 1972; Bakeman and Helmreich, 1975).

Moreover, recollection is an important part of multi-phase recreation experiences (Clawson, 1963; Hammitt, 1978). That is, leisure engagement consist not only of the ''on-site'' activities, but also in recollection of earlier experiences. Often this phase is the most enjoyable one. If people did not have chances to reminisce and talk to anybody, how many of them would continue, for example, to go to stadiums and watch football games? While many possibilities and places exist for sharing recreational experiences (e.g., social parties, family and friends), one of the most common of them is talking to co-workers on the job. It might even be argued that recreational participation is incomplete until previous experiences have been shared with others, particularly with co-workers. If so, it indeed becomes imperative for employers to provide opportunities for their workers to socialize and to talk about their leisure experiences. As a reward, employers may see workers to be more satisfied with their jobs. Again, this is speculation which should be subjected to rigorous empirical testing.

social comparison and job satisfaction

The above discussion has shown that the impacts of leisure behavior cannot be overlooked when the determinants of job satisfaction and performance are examined. But as noted previously, this omission is not the only deficiency in the literature on job satisfaction. One striking oversight is researchers' failure to consider implications of the idea that job satisfaction is a relative rather than absolute concept. This relativity means, for one thing, that social comparison processes are an integral part of the formation and modification of job satisfactions, suggesting that job satisfaction does not exist in an environmental or social vacuum. Everyone who holds a job knows that almost everybody else is also working. A person compares his job to that of others and finds it similar or different, better or worse. The person can hardly avoid comparing his job to other people's work on certain dimensions. It is common to hear statements like ''My job does not pay as well as his, but unlike him, I have freedom to decide when I do whatever I do.'' Or, ''My job is lousy in comparison to his job, but who cares because I get paid much more than he.''

Thus, a person can arrive at a sense of job satisfaction by simply comparing and weighing the importance of intrinsic and extrinsic aspects of the work. Often, however, this comparison is social in that the person evaluates the qualities of the job in relation to those of relatives, friends, neighbors, community residents and co-workers. This comparison is *lateral* if one directly compares the intrinsic or extrinsic qualities of the work to those of other persons who are "significant." For example, a person's job may not be particularly prestigious or well-paid on the national scale, but in comparison to the jobs of others in the community, it is both prestigious and well-paid. Consequently, the individual may be very content with his work.

The comparison is *vertical* if the person compares the job on the basis of various criteria (e.g., salary, prestige) in terms of improvement or deterioration from the past achievements of "significant others." For example, a person may compare his job to that of the father or mother. If he feels that his job achievement is better than that of his father, then job satisfaction is likely to be high, regardless of what others think of the job. But if he feels that his job is considerably worse than his parents' jobs, the individual may be very dissatisfied with the job, regardless of how high the job ranks in other people's eyes. Or the person may be dissatisfied with the job until he is able to fulfill the parents' expectations of the suitable position for him.

Social comparisons can occur downward or upward. That is, a person can always find people who have intrinsically (e.g., freedom on job) or extrinsically (e.g., salary) better or worse jobs than he has. The individual who compares *upward* thinks that most people have better jobs than he has, and the person who compares *downward* finds his job to be better than the jobs of those who have been his comparison source. Other things being equal, it is conceivable that the person who compares upward is more dissatisfied (or less satisfied) with his job than the person who compares downward.

These social comparison processes are psychologically important, in that they enable people to adapt to their jobs and find satisfaction in them. That is, if people compare downward, they rationalize that their job is not so bad after all, especially in relation to other people's work. On the other hand, these processes may be psychologically injurious in that they cause some people to set unrealistically high expectations about obtaining certain jobs. Failure to achieve the high-level objectives may lead to continued dissatisfaction with the present job and to such harmful psychological consequences as depression. It is conceivable that a tendency to make "downward" comparisons increases and a tendency to make "upward" comparisons decreases with age. This follows because it is known that job satisfaction increases with working experience (cf. Taylor, 1977). Thus, it seems that people adapt to their jobs with age and in the long run become more satisfied with them.

The above theorizing should demonstrate that social comparisons have to be taken into account when determinants of job satisfaction are investigated. It is not sufficient simply to relate various intrinsic and extrinsic aspects of work to feelings of job satisfaction, without knowledge of the social comparisons underlying these feelings. It remains the task of future research to determine specifically the role of social comparison processes in job satisfaction. Hopefully, the above theorizing provides an incentive for such endeavors.

In passing, attention should be directed to another theoretical area for future research on job satisfaction. This deals with attribution processes. Any person who holds a job has an idea about the causes of obtaining the job or of remaining on a certain rung of the ladder. For example, consider a housewife who thinks that the reason why she is not working outside the home is because she is not capable of doing any other work (i.e., she attributes her being a housewife to the lack of personal ability). Most likely, her work satisfaction differs from that of another housewife who believes that the reason why she does not work outside the home is because of such external reasons as her husband's opposition to her working.

Besides these self-attributions, job satisfaction may be affected by beliefs of others' attributions to personal work. That is, if a housewife believes that others think that the reason why she is a housewife is because of lack of her talent to do anything else, her work satisfaction and work motivation are probably impaired by such interpretation of the attributions which others make. A similar example can be found in regard to promotions in most jobs. If an individual is passed over for promotion, job satisfaction and performance are affected by self-attributions of failure to get a promotion and by the individual's conception of other peoples' attributions of why he failed to get the promotion. Finally, it is likely that individuals high in need for achievement attribute their work successes to their ability and effort, and their job failures to various external factors. Such attributions are probably associated with affect expressed toward job.

the changing nature of job satisfaction

The final point of criticism on the past research relates to the changing nature of job satisfaction. Like many other theoretical constructs, job satisfaction has two dimensions: stability and change. In the past, however, attention has been directed to job satisfaction as a stable characteristic, and thus its dialectical nature has been overlooked. It looks as if researchers have singlemindedly assumed that by adding one variable after another to the already-long list of factors investigated, they must finally be able to fully explain the causes of job satisfaction. This approach, however, is over-simplified, because it implicitly assumes that the effects of different variables (i.e., various intrinsic and extrinsic aspects of job) are additive, and ignores the observation that when rating their job satisfaction people assign different weights to different aspects of work, implying that the effects of these variables are nonadditive.

But perhaps the chief criticism of past research on job satisfaction has to do with the neglect of the fact than an individual is living in a changing society. Standards of excellence concerning job change—be it slowly or rapidly, and so do people's expectations about "good" jobs. What was considered a good job, both extrinsically and intrinsically, 200 years ago is likely to be an extremely poor job by today's standards. People never seem to be entirely satisfied with their jobs, because of their need to have better and better positions, both in absolute and relative terms—absolute in the sense that there is always room for improvement, and relative in the sense that somebody always seems to have a better job in certain respects. (However, as suggested, this tendency to compare "upward" may decrease with age.) Since people live in a social environment they can hardly avoid comparing their jobs to those of others, and consequently their definitions of the "good" job influence, and are influenced by, those of others. Continuous interaction among people leads to continuous social change—be it slow or rapid. Thus, while job satisfaction is a stable characteristic it is also one which changes over short and long periods of time. This is why in research on the antecedents and consequences of job satisfaction the dialectical nature of job satisfaction should not be overlooked.

The above discussion has shown the interdependence which exists between work and leisure. There is no doubt that job satisfaction affects leisure satisfaction, and vice versa. From this conclusion it is a short step to a hypothesis that job and leisure satisfaction are important determinants of the perceived quality of life. In the final chapter, quality of life will be examined, first focusing on the concept of the pursuit of happiness, and then reviewing empirical evidence concerning the determinants of perceived quality of life, with particular reference to the relative contributions of job and leisure satisfaction.

summary

In an effort to place leisure behavior in a broader perspective, the present chapter examined the interrelationships between work and leisure. The first section focused on the effects of work on leisure and reviewed the conceptual and empirical validity of the three popular hypotheses proposed to account for the relationship: (1) spill-over, (2) compensation, and (3) no-relationship. It was concluded that all of these hypotheses are inadequate to explain the influences of work on leisure. The reported empirical research has been inconsistent and contradictory, chiefly because the workers' socialization experiences (and thus, their leisure attitudes, motives and skills) as well as their perceptions of their work have not been controlled in past studies. Because individual differences mediate the influences of work on leisure, they must be considered when the relationship is analyzed. Furthermore, past research has ignored the potentially powerful impact on leisure behavior of such work-related variables as success in one's daily work and co-workers' leisure interests. Finally, when the effects of work on leisure are discussed, one should not assume that these effects are static or stable, but rather dynamic and changing.

Although much has been written about the influence of work on leisure, relatively little attention has been devoted to the other side of this relationship (effect of leisure on work). There is, however, tentative evidence to indicate that a person's leisure environment affects his job satisfaction and performance. Specifically, very satisfactory leisure environments seem to be conducive to job satisfaction and perhaps also to improved job performance. It appears that if a company provides recreation services to its employees, their job satisfaction and performance increase. Thus, workers' satisfaction with recreational opportunities in a community and a company's interest in workers' leisure life are important determinants of job satisfaction and performance. On this basis, it was inferred that changes in adults' worktime patterns (i.e., shortened work week) are not likely to improve job satisfaction and performance, unless the new worktime pattern facilitates intrinsic leisure behavior and improves leisure satisfaction.

It was also indicated that interpersonal relations off-the-job may influence job satisfaction and performance. If so, it is important to improve people's interpersonal relations off the job, and one way of doing this is through leisure behavior. Finally, leisure experiences and interpersonal relations on the job were discussed. Research indicates that lack of opportunities to communicate with others on the job contributes to the development of psychogenic illness. At the same time, it appears that people feel that recreational participation is unfinished until previous experiences have been shared with others (e.g., co-workers). In combination, these two separate findings suggest that it is important for employers to let their workers socialize and "schmooze" on the job.

the perceived quality of life 18

Thomas Jefferson wrote that the pursuit of happiness is an inalienable right of every human being and insisted that this be recognized in the Constitution. Jefferson and others who believed in the importance of this basic right implied that the pursuit of happiness is not only a right but the goal of all human behavior. To facilitate the attainment of this goal the primary task of the government is to provide conditions that enable most, if not all, people to pursue happiness. Translated into politicians' language and campaign promises, Jefferson's words have come to mean such things as: "I will make our country a better and safer place for our children to live." In campaigning for the presidency in 1932 Herbert Hoover was more specific about achieving happiness as he promised "a car in every garage and a chicken in every pot" (Campbell, Converse and Rodgers, 1976).

the pursuit of happiness

It is generally agreed that the first steps in pursuing happiness consist of satisfying the basic needs (physiological, safety and financial). But in addition to these lower-order or material needs, people have needs of a higher order, such as self-esteem, social relations and self-actualization (e.g., Maslow, 1943). This means that economic and other basic satisfactions are only one aspect of the pursuit of happiness. The other aspect, often ignored by politicians, deals with psychological needs and their satisfactions. Like Tolman (1941), Campbell (1976), and many others, the author asserts that Western societies should cease to be dominated by the concept of the *economic person* and be replaced by the concept of the *psychological person*. This follows because the pursuit of happiness is not promoted by the oversatisfaction of economic, materialistic, and other basic needs. This conclusion is not simply a matter of personal value judgments, because the verdict of empirical research is the same: money cannot buy happiness (Shaver and Freedman, 1976). In a similar vein, Campbell (1976) reported a steady decline in personal happiness from 1957 to 1972 while at the same time most of the economic indicators registered considerable improvement. The message then is clear: promising and delivering more and better cars in garages and more and better chickens in pots does not insure happiness.

determinants of perceived quality of life

on the concept of quality of life

Better to understand the pursuit and achievement of happiness, discussion will now turn to research on determinants of the perceived quality of life. In this analysis, particular attention is directed to the independent and the joint contributions of job and leisure satisfaction to the perceived quality of life. But before beginning a review of relevant research, it should be pointed out what is meant by the quality of life. The most important fact to note is that the quality of life is in the mind. No matter how much or little a person owns or does, he can be happy and satisfied with the life if he so decides. Material things do not determine decisions about happiness, psychological well-being, or the quality of life. It is the individual whose own perceptions (though influenced by those of others) underlie the personal definition of the quality of life. While many objective facts (owning a car, environmental pollution, etc.) may affect the quality of life, it is the individual who decides and determines the importance of such contributing factors to his quality of life. The psychological meaning of the objective facts of life is more critical to the perceived quality of life than is their economic function. The person whose quality of life is high can be characterized as one with feelings of happiness, life satisfaction, and psychological well-being.

contribution of job satisfaction

extrinsic aspects

Because men and women have been working since the beginning of the human race, both reason and experience corroborate that work must be related to the quality of life. That is, job satisfaction must be positively associated with life satisfaction. Indeed, this assumption is well borne out by empirical research (e.g., Argyle, 1972; Kornhauser, 1965; Rogers, 1977; Warr and Wall, 1975). The question then is what aspects of job satisfaction contribute to the quality of life. As noted above, the first step in pursuing the quality of life is to satisfy the lower-order needs.

Having a permanent job which brings in enough money to satisfy basic human needs is a prerequisite to attempts to gratify such higher-order needs as self-esteem and self-actualization. To this end, satisfaction with the material aspects of work (e.g., pay) should correlate positively with life satisfaction; and in fact this correlation has been confirmed (Hulin, 1969; Iris and Barrett, 1972). However, it may be argued that pay and other extrinsic aspects of work are essential but not necessarily sufficient conditions for attaining the high quality of life. In other words, there is a certain maximum point, a threshold, in job and life satisfaction, to which salary and other extrinsic rewards can contribute. In direct support of this contention, Renwick and Lawler (1978) found that, "If pay falls below this (threshold) level, then money becomes more important than interesting work. If wages or salary are above this level, then whether they consider their job interesting assumes more importance." In a similar vein, Shaver and Freedman (1976) concluded, based upon a survey of about 52,000 respondents, that money cannot buy happiness.

What is critical for increasing life satisfaction after the threshold level is attained, is the psychological meaning of work. For work to attain its level as a personally meaningful activity it must be intrinsically motivated. As demonstrated earlier (chapter 11), intrinsically motivated activities can be characterized principally by perceived freedom or control and feelings of competence. The importance of these factors to job and life satisfaction has been demonstrated in numerous studies (e.g., Renwick and Lawler, 1978). It is fairly obvious that when basic human rights (perceived freedom and control over life, perceived responsibility and perceived competence) are denied in work, a person becomes dissatisfied and even depressed with such work. Factory workers serve as a persuasive example of persons whose basic human rights have been impaired or denied. They must arrive and leave their place of employment at a prescribed time; they are not allowed to exercise any control over their work except to perform the same repetitive and monotonous task; they are given no responsibility in their work, but instead are told to carry out their mentally unsatisfying and unchallenging tasks efficiently; they are seldom given indications or recognition of their competence to carry out their tasks, except the weekly or monthly standard salary; and of course, they are rarely given an indication that their work is important or needed.

If a person is to continue to work under such dehumanizing conditions, he has to adapt to these circumstances. That millions of people have indeed so adapted is not surprising in the light of people's capacity to overadapt to almost any dehumanizing situations (Dubos, 1965). Such adaptation is reflected by the observation that workers are more satisfied with their jobs, the longer they have been working (Taylor, 1977), and by the fact that "those who have given up any thoughts of advancing beyond the assembly line appear to have better mental health than those who are still hoping for something better in life" (Iris and Barrett, 1972, p. 303). Thus, it is paradoxical, even contradictory, that their adaptation to work is psychologically both demeaning and healthy. But the problem is that people are willing to go too far in their adaptation, and in this process, they are led to accept values that are not characteristically human (Proshansky, 1973).

The question why people are able to overadapt to dehumanizing work conditions can only be answered in psychological terms, specifically by the idea of compensation. Those individuals whose work is not intrinsically rewarding can compensate for this deprivation by emphasizing extrinsic aspects of their jobs and by denying the importance of intrinsic values of work. They may say: "I get paid $15 per hour, I don't have to care about anything else in my work." Another way of compensating is to spend one's free-time in intrinsically rewarding activities. However, this behavioral compensation through actual participation can simply be substituted for cognitive compensation. That is, workers are cognitively aware that they are free to participate in any activities they wish, and it is this *cognitive awareness* of the possibility for intrinsically motivated leisure that may be sufficient to compensate for many people's dehumanizing work.

Despite some of its psychological virtues, adaptation to work is no substitute for an intrinsically motivated job in its contribution to job and life satisfaction. Russell (1930, p. 212) contended that ''the exercise of skill'' and ''construction'' are the two chief elements that make work interesting. Empirical research supports this hypothesis. Renwick and Lawler (1978) conducted an extensive survey in which they asked respondents to indicate the degree of importance of each job feature given. The following were the top six qualities, in order of importance: (1) opportunities to do something that makes you feel good about yourself, (2) opportunities to accomplish something worthwhile, (3) chances to learn new things, (4) opportunity to develop your skills and abilities, (5) the amount of freedom you have on your job, and (6) opportunities you have to do things you do best. The amount of pay ranked only as the twelfth most important feature.

It might be contended that these results are due to the fact that blue-collar workers were under-represented in the sample. Other studies, however, have revealed similar findings in that ''chance to use abilities'' in the work is important to the assembly-line workers' job satisfaction and to their mental health (Kornhauser, 1965). It has also been found that low-skilled and unskilled jobs lead to poorer mental health among workers than do skilled jobs (*Work in America*, 1973), presumably because of lack of opportunities to use abilities in low-skilled jobs. This is consistent with the finding that ''assembly workers attach great importance to their role in producing needed, high-quality products'' (Nord, 1977). In a similar vein, Iris and Barrett (1972) reported that if workers consider their work important, their life, family and leisure satisfaction are much higher than if they perceive their work as unimportant. Taken together, these results clearly reveal the significance of intrinsically motivated work (specifically, feelings of competence and worthiness ensuing from work) to job and life satisfaction.

perceived control
and responsibility

It follows from the above findings that the opportunity to exercise freedom and control over work should contribute importantly to job and life satisfaction. This supposition is well borne out by empirical research. Renwick and Lawler (1978) found that within certain limits an overwhelming majority of people would like to be able to set their own working hours. This emphatically supports the efforts of about 1,000 companies and government agencies that are presently implementing the idea of ''flextime.'' Flexible working hours improve not only the workers' job and life satisfaction but also their productivity, by decreasing absenteeism, sick leave, tardiness, and overtime (Stein, Cohen and Gadon, 1976). These positive effects are due to the fact that ''flextime'' recognizes a basic human need to exercise control over one's environment, or stated differently, ''flextime treats employees like responsible adults rather than children to be watched'' (Stein, *et al.*, 1976). Attribution theorists and researchers (e.g., Heider, 1958; Kelley, 1971), among others, have argued and provided evidence that people have a need or tendency to exercise control over their environment, or to be ''originators'' rather than ''pawns'' (deCharms, 1968). Although flextime also contributes indirectly to life satisfaction by allowing workers to juggle their work schedules to accommodate their family duties (e.g., child care) and leisure interests, its primary contribution to life satisfaction stems from the accompanying psychological benefits: increased perceived freedom and control.

In addition to perceived control, the quality of working life and thus overall life satisfaction can be enhanced by increasing employees' perceived responsibility in their work. Following the Western European example, particularly that of West Germany, many companies in the United States strive for job enlargement and enrichment through various programs. One of the most common forms of job enrichment is to provide workers with the opportunity to take part in the various decision-making processes concerning the development of their company and improvement of the work environment. Perhaps the most dramatic result of this experimentation is the finding that workers can set their own wages responsibly when given an opportunity to do so. Lawler (1977) found that the employee-designed pay plans are carefully thought out and conservative in the amount of salary set for oneself, and they tend to increase employees' pay satisfaction, their commitment to the company, attendance, and organizational effectiveness. Thus, it appears that increasing employees' personal responsibility contributes to an improved quality of work life. Lawler concluded that workers "are more likely to trust a system of their own design because they have more control over it. They become committed to it because they have contributed to its development." This conclusion is entirely congruent with our previous discussion in chapters 9 and 11.

Lawler's findings again demonstrate the importance of being able to exercise effective control over one's life, particularly over one's work life. Work can be made a personally meaningful activity if employees' basic human rights are here respected. Unfortunately, all too often this is not the case, as confirmed by Kornhauser's (1965) finding that about 50 percent of assembly-line workers feel that they have little control or influence over the future course of their lives. To this end, his finding that feelings of helplessness, withdrawal, alienation, and pessimism are widespread among workers, is not at all surprising. Clearly, the time has come to treat employees as individuals with the same basic human rights as employers. This means that working conditions should be made conducive to the development of intrinsic work motivation. Hence all jobs should lead to feelings of personal freedom, control, responsibility, and competence. These ingredients of intrinsic motivation are important, not only because of their capacity to improve job satisfaction, but also because of their strong contribution to overall life satisfaction, psychological well-being and mental health.

Perhaps the most common theme running through the literature is an assumption of the positive effect of leisure behavior on life satisfaction (e.g., Davis, 1938; Greenbie, 1940). It is indeed easy to find texts in which authors speculate that leisure satisfaction is the principal source of the perceived quality of life. This, of course, is understandable in the light of the traditional meaning of work. That is, work is done to earn a living, the implication being that quantity of life is a matter

contribution of leisure satisfaction

of work and quality of life is a function of non-work activities. The importance of leisure to life satisfaction has been recognized, not only by leisure philosophers and authors, but also by other social scientists. For example, under the auspices of a committee (on leisure time and its uses) of the American Psychiatric Association, psychiatrists produced a book (*Leisure and Mental Health: A Psychiatric Viewpoint*) in which the relationship between leisure and mental health was explored at length.

Predicated upon an assumption of the importance of leisure to life satisfaction, what does the empirical research indicate about this relationship? Although relevant studies are not many, they all support the notion of a positive association between leisure satisfaction and the perceived quality of life (e.g., Campbell, *et al.*, 1976; Flanagan, 1978; Haavio-Mannila, 1971; London, *et al.*, 1977). But to understand the meaning of this relationship it is essential to know what factors contribute to leisure satisfaction. As noted in earlier chapters (Part 5), people view leisure as optimum when leisure participation is intrinsically motivated. For a person to be able to participate in an activity for its own sake he has to have freedom to choose activities, to be the "origin" (originator) rather than the "pawn" (deCharms, 1968). In addition, intrinsically motivated leisure activities are characterized by accompanying feelings of competence—be it personal or interpersonal. Social norms, extrinsic sanctions and rewards undermine intrinsic leisure motivation and thus leisure satisfaction. Leisure satisfaction cannot be improved merely by increasing the number and variety of services available. It is the individual who, either by himself or with the help of others, has to make some of the available services personally meaningful activities before they can contribute to personal leisure satisfaction. Only intrinsically motivated leisure activities can become personally meaningful ones.

"active" recreation and quality of life

Although it is theoretically possible for any free-time activity to become personally meaningful, there are strong reasons to believe that passive forms of recreation are not likely to do so. Kornhauser (1965) found that workers with high mental health scores were active in their non-work behaviors, whereas workers with the lowest mental health scores tended to be escapist or passive in their free-time engagements, that is, they spent a lot of time in watching television and did not participate in community organizations. Brooks and Elliott (1971) reported that those who learned to derive satisfaction from active forms of leisure in early years were psychologically better adjusted 30 years later than those who learned to derive their leisure satisfaction from passive activities like TV-watching. In a similar vein, Flanagan (1978) found in his nation-wide survey that "active recreation" was one of the six areas showing the largest correlation coefficients with the overall quality of life. Taken together, these findings strongly imply that active recreational participation contributes to the perceived quality of life and psychological well-being.

This is not to deny the recreational value of any specific passive or observational leisure activity, but merely to infer that if a person's leisure behavior *pattern* is characterized by participation in passive activities, his life satisfaction is likely to be lower than that of the person whose leisure behavior is dominated by active participation. This conclusion, of course, is obscured by the ambiguity of activity and passivity. That is, what is active for one person may be passive for another. This is the case because individuals differ in their need for optimal arousal and incongruity. Nevertheless, it is possible to distinguish between some active and passive forms of leisure. In the Flanagan study, for example, "active recreation" consisted of such activities as playing games, participatory sports, traveling, etc., whereas "passive recreation" included activities like watching TV and observing sporting events or entertainments.

But why should active recreation be more conducive to life satisfaction than is passive reaction? The answer to this question lies in the idea of optimal arousal and incongruity. As was theorized and as the research has clearly shown (Part 4), too much or too little arousal and incongruity is detrimental to human functioning. Thus, an individual strives to attain and sustain the optimal level of arousal and incongruity in leisure behavior. The need for this optimum is evident because an individual is seeking both novelty and familiarity, stability and change, variety and similarity in leisure encounters. "Active recreation" is more consistent with the pursuit of optimal incongruity than is "passive recreation." While the optimal level varies from individual to individual, some activities provide so little incongruity and arousal that they can meet few people's (if anyone's) need for optimal arousal. Activities categorized as "passive recreation" are such activities (see Flanagan, 1978).

If the above reasoning is correct there should be an inverted-U relationship between the perceived quality of life and/or leisure satisfaction and the level of arousal in leisure participation. That is, life and leisure satisfaction should be at their highest when leisure behavior is optimally arousing or incongruous, and at their lowest when leisure behavior provides too little or too much arousal. This hypothesis is emphatically supported by data based upon a national probability sample of households in 48 states (Campbell, et al., 1976, p. 357). Figure 22 shows the inverted-U relationship between pressure on time use or the availability of discretionary time and life and leisure satisfaction. In other words, people are most satisfied with their life and leisure when they feel they have an optimal amount of discretionary time available for their activities. But when there is a feeling of little time pressure or feeling of plenty of free-time available their satisfaction with leisure and life in general decreases dramatically. A similar decline occurs when they feel too much time pressure to carry on their free-time activities or that too little free-time is available. Clearly, these data indicate that optimally arousing leisure is conducive to psychological well-being. Thus, the data further corroborate our previous theorizing throughout the book about the human need for optimally arousing and incongruous leisure behavior.

The data presented in figure 22 are also important in that the findings are consistent with the idea about a personally meaningful activity as a source of life satisfaction. As the figure shows, having little or nothing to do during free-time results in dissatisfaction with life and leisure. Although the figure does not point this out, it is reasonable to assume that personally meaningful activities are more

Figure 22 Variations in the index of well-being and satisfaction with nonwork time as a function of reported time pressure. (Figure 11-1 from *The Quality of American Life: Perceptions, Evaluations and Satisfactions,* by Angus Campbell, Philip E. Converse, and Willard L. Rodgers. p. 357, ' 1976 by Russell Sage Foundation, New York. Printed by permission.)

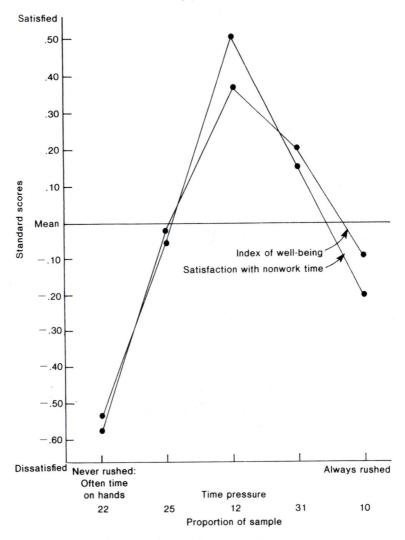

involving than simply "never rushing, having often time on hands;" in other words, personally meaningful activities are likely to involve an optimal level of time pressure. It is difficult to see how idleness could be personally meaningful activity to anybody. Moreover, since personally meaningful activities are intrinsically motivated, they are participated in for their potential to produce feelings of competence. Certainly, idleness or overabundance of discretionary time does not bring about feelings of personal or interpersonal competence. It appears,

Work, Leisure and the Quality of Life

therefore, that life satisfaction is significantly derived from intrinsically motivated and optimally arousing leisure activities.

The data in figure 22 also have implications for the concept of "leisure society." Some people have interpreted the idea of a leisure society to mean that the goal of humankind is to create societies in which nobody has to do anything. Hence leisure is likened to idleness or just doing nothing. If the above figure is any indication of human nature it would appear to indicate that such a society is psychologically lethal. Every human being is born with an enormous amount and variety of talent. To prevent or discourage the individual from using personal capacities and competencies is to deny the meaning of human life. Therefore, we agree with Argyle who stated:

> People will (always) seek activities of a certain kind, whether they are called work or leisure, because these are the conditions for human satisfaction: completing interesting and meaningful tasks, which use basic skills and abilities, giving adequate recognition and social status, performed under considerate and democratic-persuasive supervision (or no supervision), in cohesive groups and in small organizations with full participation (Argyle, 1972, p. 262).

If a personally meaningful activity (as defined above) is the main source of life satisfaction, psychological well-being, and mental health, one might ask whether work or leisure is equally important in providing opportunities for the development of such activity. There is empirical evidence in the literature that leisure is gaining in importance and may become the more important of the two in the future. Yankelovich (1978) reported that when Swedish men, 18 to 44 years of age, were asked in 1955, "What gives your life the most meaning—your family, your work, or your leisure?," the following results were obtained: 13% of the respondents rated leisure as giving the most meaning to their life, 33% answered work and 45% family. But when the same question was posed to a new cross-section of Swedish men 22 years later (1977), dramatic changes were observed: 27% answered leisure, 17% work and 41% family. Thus, the proportion of men who indicate leisure as the main source of meaning in life had doubled during the 22 years, while the number of men who regarded work as primary source of meaning in life had been reduced to half in the same period. The family was still the most important of the three, though its value had declined slightly. Yankelovich (1978) found the same phenomenon occurring in the American samples, in that only 21% of the respondents stated work to mean more to them than leisure.

Other researchers have obtained similar results. Campbell, *et al.* (1976, p. 76) reported that satisfaction with non-work activities was the most important variable of all the satisfaction domains which were related to life satisfaction. Satisfaction with non-work activities explained 29% of the total variance of the index of psychological well-being, whereas work satisfaction accounted for only 18% and "family life" 28%. Based upon a national probability sample, London, *et al.* (1977) found that when the total sample was considered, feelings about leisure behavior were better predictors of the perceived quality of life than job-

relative contributions of work and leisure satisfaction

related feelings, though both contributed significantly but independently to life satisfaction. There were, however, individual differences in these relative contributions. For example, job-related feelings contributed more to males' perceived quality of life than did leisure-related feelings, whereas the opposite was true for female respondents. But for most sub-groups, the contribution of leisure to life satisfaction was greater than that of job.

When the relative contributions of job and leisure satisfaction to the quality of life are compared, the findings should be interpreted with extreme caution for several reasons. First, the questionnaire items used to assess job and leisure-related feelings and satisfactions are likely to affect the relative importance of work and leisure. London, et al. (1977), for example, found that of all leisure-items, satisfaction with "the things you and your family do together" (r = .37) and with "the things you do and the times you have with friends" (.32) were the two most important items contributing to the perceived quality of life. Had these items not been used, the contribution of leisure satisfaction would have been less than that of job satisfaction. On the other hand, if London, et al., had included items relevant to perceived freedom, control and competence, the relative contributions of work and leisure would have been quite different.

One definite way of increasing the importance of leisure satisfaction over job satisfaction is to include family or marriage satisfaction in the leisure category when the relative contributions are compared (as London, et al. did). Past research has consistently shown that satisfaction with family life is more important to the perceived quality of life than are leisure and job satisfaction (e.g., Campbell, et al., 1976; Medley, 1976; Yankelovich, 1978). The only exception to this rule is unmarried men, as evidenced in the data reported by Haavio-Mannila (1971, p. 593) in Table 2.

The data below are based upon table 5 in Haavio-Mannila's paper (p. 593) and were obtained by averaging the percentages reported separately for urban and rural residents. In this study, 444 urban and 504 rural residents were interviewed and asked to indicate which of the three life sectors gives them presently most satisfaction. It is immediately clear that "family life" is overwhelmingly the

Table 2

Sources of Central Life Satisfaction by Sex and Marital Status*

Sources of Central Life Satisfaction	Unmarried		Married	
	Men	Women	Men	Women
	(in %)		(in %)	
Home, Family Life	12.5	33.5	63.0	82.5
Occupation, Work	30.0	36.0	22.0	12.0
Leisure Activities	47.0	21.0	8.0	1.5
No Answer	10.5	9.5	7.0	4.0
Total	100	100	100	100

*Computed on the basis of the data reported by Haavio-Mannila (1971, p. 593).

Work, Leisure and the Quality of Life

main source of life satisfaction to the married, particularly to married women. On the other hand, "leisure activities" become more important to the unmarried, especially to unmarried men, than to the married. A similar trend can be seen with regard to "work." The importance of family life to the quality of life and happiness has also been found in national polls. The Louis Harris poll in 1978 showed that a substantial 92% of the American public stated that family life is very important to the quality of their lives. Finally, Flanagan (1978) reported that "having and raising children" was "important" or "very important" to the quality of life of 83%–93% of the respondents, the exact percentage depending on the age group in question.

Taken together, these results provide undisputable evidence about the strong impact of a gratifying family life on the perceived quality of life. Therefore, if one is to include "family life" as a part of leisure satisfaction when comparing the relative contributions of leisure and job satisfaction to the quality of life, it should not be surprising to find that leisure satisfaction is more important than job satisfaction. Of course, this is not to criticize such an inclusion (because "family life," for the most part, is experienced during one's free-time), but simply to remind researchers of the probable reason for such findings. The above research demonstrates another fact why it is hazardous to compare directly the relative importance of job and leisure satisfaction, that is, there are considerable individual differences which mediate the relative effects of job and leisure satisfaction on the quality of life. Haavio-Mannila's (1971) findings clearly attest to this by indicating that the relative importance of leisure, work, and family depends on whether a person is married or not. The London, et al. study (1977) revealed the influence of some other individual differences.

Despite these methodological and conceptual problems in comparing the relative contributions of work and leisure satisfaction to life quality, the trend is apparent. More and more people are discovering that free-time can be a source of personally meaningful activities (Yankelovich, 1978). If the trend continues observers will see a steady increase in the proportion of people naming leisure as the main source of meaning in life. This does not mean, however, that people are expecting work to disappear from the scene or become unimportant, as evidenced by Lundberg and Ellonen (1977). When subjects were asked to indicate the likelihood of work becoming unnecessary in the future due to industrial efficiency and automation, the mean probability for women was .19 and .16 for men. Females estimated that it would take about 600 years before work will become totally unnecessary; males were more pessimistic, since they thought that about 1,000 years will elapse before mankind is completely freed from the need to work! But with regard to "meaningful leisure," the respondents, particularly the men, were much more optimistic. Men estimated that only about 20 years would elapse before the condition (i.e., "meaningful leisure") will occur, whereas women thought it would take approximately 50 years for "meaningful leisure" to materialize.

Another indication of the inevitability of work can be seen in the fact that most people would continue working even if they had enough money to live as comfortably as they would like for the rest of their lives (e.g., Renwick and

Lawler, 1978; Rodgers, 1977). This is psychologically understandable for two major reasons. First, since people have worked throughout the history of humankind, work has become a stable institution in the course of years, and therefore it is difficult to break the tradition. Parents keep on emphasizing the necessity of work, if not for any other reason than for the sake of tradition. Once custom is broken, however, it then is easy for parents to introduce their children to the concept of non-work. But until that departure from the need to work is achieved, work will be stressed as essential. Nevertheless, it is apparent that sooner or later one generation of parents will have to accept the idea of leisure as a primary source of personally meaningful activities for their children, a situation which undoubtedly will be painful for the parents to digest. In sum, because of its long history and tradition, work appears to have a psychologically stabilizing effect (Argyle, 1972, p. 260). As Freud (in Martin, 1967, p. 8) wrote, stressing the importance of work is more effective than any other technique in keeping the individual close to reality. Since everyone else seems to be working, a person is connected with reality through the work. Moreover, it is still socially unacceptable not to work, meaning that social pressure makes many people work even though they do not need money.

The second major reason why people would continue to work, even if unnecessary, is because many of them are fortunate in having intrinsically motivating and rewarding jobs. In such cases work has become a personally meaningful activity for them, producing feelings of personal or interpersonal control/competence, responsibility, worthiness, and rewarded by adequate social recognition. For the reasons noted, there seems to be no avoiding the fact that work will remain for the foreseeable future. In fact, it looks as if work is extremely healthy psychologically. The world of work is an important aspect of reality in modern society, thereby safeguarding people's mental health. But as pointed out earlier, work can become dysfunctional and destructive if the basic human rights are overlooked on jobs. Therefore, it is not enough simply to provide jobs for people. Past research indicated that work should be made intrinsically motivated so that it would become a personally meaningful activity. Since the same holds true for leisure behavior, one is justified in concluding that intrinsically motivated work *and* leisure are the main sources of life satisfaction and happiness.

To test this hypothesis a quasi-experiment was conducted (Iso-Ahola, 1977f). In this study, 76 undergraduate students were provided with hypothetical information of the character (intrinsic or extrinsic) of their work and leisure and were then asked to indicate their life satisfaction by answering the question, "In general, how satisfying would you find the way you are spending your life?" (from "not satisfying at all"—1—to "completely satisfying"—10). In accord with the 2 × 2 (work motivation × leisure motivation) design, subjects were randomly placed in one of the four conditions: (1) intrinsically motivated work-intrinsically motivated leisure, (2) intrinsically motivated work-extrinsically motivated leisure, (3) extrinsically motivated work-intrinsically motivated leisure, and (4) extrinsically motivated work and leisure. For example, subjects who were in the first situation were asked to assume that both their daily work and leisure behaviors are mainly motivated by intrinsic rewards like feelings of competence and self-determination, and then were asked to evaluate their life satisfaction under such condition. The results of the study are presented in figure 23.

It appeared that the ''main'' effects of both work motivation ($p < .03$) and leisure motivation ($p < .009$) were highly significant, meaning that these two

Figure 23   Effects of work and leisure motivation on life satisfaction. (From Iso-Ahola, 1977f.)

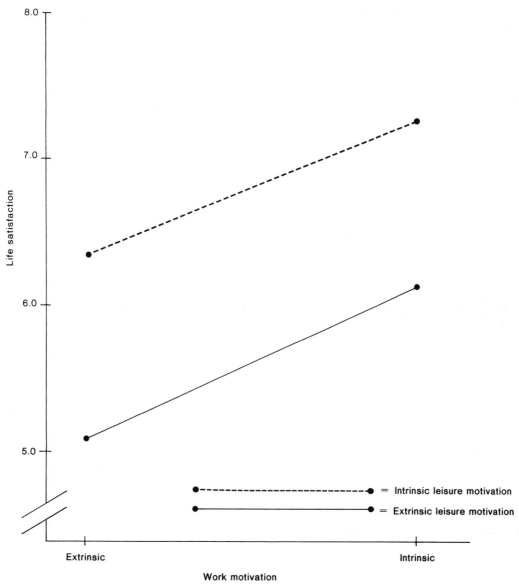

variables affected life satisfaction independently and additively. That is, the rating of life satisfaction was much greater when work was predominantly intrinsically motivated than when it was predominantly extrinsically motivated. Similarly, intrinsic leisure motivation significantly enhanced life satisfaction as compared to extrinsic leisure motivation. Thus, life satisfaction was at its highest when both work *and* leisure were intrinsically motivated and at its lowest when they were extrinsically motivated. Thus, these findings strongly support an earlier contention that intrinsic motivation in work and leisure is the main source of the perceived quality of life and happiness. As shown earlier, intrinsically motivated behaviors are psychologically potent because they provide for feelings of control over life and are conducive to feelings of personal and interpersonal competence. People are in a continual process of seeking and conquering challenges (see chapter 11) in a manner which is optimally arousing to them. If the principal spheres of life (leisure and work) offer opportunities for seeking and conquering challenges, it is obvious that people are very satisfied with their lives.

The above findings are also important as indicating that the enrichment of both work *and* leisure is needed to enhance people's quality of life. The enrichment of leisure is not an alternative to boring and unchallenging work, or vice versa. Based upon the results in figure 23, the author concurs with Gardell's (1976, p. 901) conclusion that "a change of work to make it more humane and democratic is vital and necessary, but must coincide with a trend toward shorter and more flexible working hours, and a more flexible relation between work-leisure activities considering different needs in different stages in life." For leisure to become a source for personally meaningful activities, it is not sufficient to simply expand leisure facilities. Education and training for leisure is of the foremost importance.

social psychologists' contribution to advancement of the quality of life

The dilemma of the quality of life and happiness is its relative and changing character. Although much can be done externally to enhance the pursuit of meaningful activities in leisure and work, for psychological reasons many people fail to achieve the state of life satisfaction and happiness. Much of this failure stems from the fact that life quality or happiness is not an absolute entity (which can be said to exist when certain things have been done), but rather a subjective and relative concept. People define their quality of life in terms of expectations and hopes which are chiefly the result of the social environment in which they live. Shaver and Freedman (1976) found that almost 70% of their subjects expected to be happier in the future than at the present time. People seem to revise continuously their definitions and expectations concerning their quality of life on the basis of what they have seen and heard others to have or to be. This revision process, then, is endless as long as human beings are "social animals," one influencing and being influenced by others.

Past research indicates that social comparison indeed is the principal psychological obstacle to achieving life satisfaction and happiness. Shaver and Freedman (1976) found that the happiest respondents in their survey were "those who feel in control of their lives, and who compare their progress against their own standards, not those of others." They concluded that "happiness is a matter of setting personal standards, not chasing after other people's." Unfortunately, competitive and achievement-oriented societies encourage individuals to set their personal standards in relation to others, especially in the world of work. Although it is possible to establish and pursue personal standards in the competitive system, these standards have implications for the goals of others. On many jobs, people have to set higher objectives for themselves than they might want to, because otherwise, they would lose their position to someone else. In a competitive system, one person's success is another's failure. When an individual sets personal standards higher than those of others', he forces everybody else to follow him. Once the chain-reaction is started, people keep on revising their standards, and the reaction continues so long as they can tolerate the competitive system.

Thus, the problem with an achievement-oriented system is that it seldom allows one to set standards which have no implications for other people's behavior. If, for example, a person enjoys the work and therefore performs much better than expected and better than other workers, such performance is psychologically threatening to others. Their performance is soon compared to his performance standards, and consequently they are—directly or by implication—forced to revise their norms, even though the individual might have never intended such consequences to result from his intrinsically motivated performance. All too often the same thing can be observed with regard to leisure behavior. It frequently happens that when a person changes standards and goals for leisure (e.g., starts to play tennis), others soon follow this example, because they have to be able to say that they too can do it. Fortunately, however, leisure does not lend itself to such revisions in personal standards due to others' interests as often as does work. When awareness of the potential of leisure in the future increases, then leisure participation may be more and more determined by personal standards having little or no relationship to the personal leisure goals of others.

It appears from the above that a highly competitive system is not conducive to the pursuit of happiness, since it encourages and compels people to conform to the standards of others. But it should not be forgotten that systems are created for people, not vice versa. If so, competitiveness should be lowered to a level which allows for the pursuit of happiness. Herein lies the challenge for social psychologists. The question is how to encourage people to set their personal standards and expectations without reference to the expectations and implications of the norms of others,—how to get people to compare "downward" socially rather than "upward." In short, *how to induce or convince people to be satisfied with what they are and what they have now.*[1] Social psychological research is required to answer these questions.

Nobody is perfect, everybody is missing something. Thus, if you are healthy, be happy because millions of people would give everything they have to be

[1]To avoid any misunderstanding, this is not to suggest that people should be taught to be satisfied with the status quo of the prevailing society.

healthy. If your family life works, be happy because millions of people are failing and have failed in their marriages. If you have a good job, be happy because millions of people are unemployed. If you enjoy leisure activities, be happy because millions of people are unable to participate in any leisure activity, etc. Your life provides many reasons to be happy; but you will never discover them unless you stop to think of them. Among others, social psychologists are called upon to help people initiate this thinking process and aid them by providing guidelines for setting personal standards for personally meaningful work and leisure activities.

Finally, it should be noted that despite social comparison and competition between people, human beings need each other to maintain and enhance their quality of life. The fact remains that interpersonal relations in one form or another constitute the fundamental pillar of happiness and life satisfaction. Feelings of mutual respect mean much more than any technology can ever provide. This can clearly be seen by the importance people place on interpersonal relations in rating their quality of life. As noted earlier, Haavio-Mannila (1971) found that social interaction in the form of family life is the source of life satisfaction for the overwhelming majority of the married couples. On the other hand, single men and women rate ''friends and social life'' as the most important pillar of their happiness (Shaver and Freedman, 1976). This evidence leaves little doubt about the critical nature of interpersonal behavior and leisure in relation to the quality of life in modern society.

> The secret of happiness is this: let your interests be as wide as possible, and let your reactions to the things and persons that interest you be as far as possible, friendly rather than hostile (Russell, 1930, p. 157).

---

summary

The first part of the chapter focused on the pursuit of happiness. It was argued that the concept of ''economic person'' should be replaced by the concept of ''psychological person,'' because happiness cannot be achieved by oversatisfaction of economic and materialistic needs. Empirical research has shown that money cannot buy happiness. Since the ''economic person'' is not sufficiently equipped for the pursuit of happiness and because our education system is directed toward the economic person, it follows that the objectives of education should be changed so that they would be derived from the concept of the psychological rather than economic person. As a part of this change, education for leisure should be introduced as an integral part of the school curricula, along with education for intrinsically rewarding work.

Better to understand the pursuit and achievement of happiness by the psychological person, the bulk of the chapter was devoted to a review of research on the determinants of the perceived quality of life. To this end, both independent and relative contributions of job and leisure satisfaction to the perceived quality of life were discussed. Past research has shown that in order for a person's job to enhance his life satisfaction, working conditions have to be conducive to the development of feelings of personal freedom, competence, control and responsibility. In a similar vein, intrinsically motivated leisure activities contribute substantially to the perceived quality of life. Although it is theoretically possible for any free-time activity to become intrinsically motivated and personally meaningful one, empirical research has shown that "active recreation" is more likely to accomplish this than passive recreation, and thus to contribute to life satisfaction.

When the relative contributions of work, leisure and family to life satisfaction are compared, it appears that the role of leisure has become increasingly important during the last twenty years. On the other hand, the importance of work and family has declined during the same period, though the family is still the most important of the three. This, combined with the finding that single men and women rate "friends and social life" as the most important pillar of their happiness, leaves little doubt abot the critical roles of interpersonal behavior and leisure in relation to the quality of life in modern society.

appendix: a theory of perceived quality of recreation environment

The fundamental assumption of the following conceptualization is that people have expectations about the scenic (environmental) features of recreational places *and* about their potential to satisfy participants' recreational needs. To the extent that this assumption is true, the following formula may provide a useful vehicle for measuring the perceived quality of recreation environments (PQRE):

$$(1)\ \text{PQRE} = \frac{\substack{\text{observed quality} \\ \text{of recreation} \\ \text{environment}}}{\substack{\text{expected quality} \\ \text{of recreation} \\ \text{environment}}} = \frac{\substack{\text{observed} \\ \text{environmental} \\ \text{quality (OEQ)}} \times \substack{\text{observed} \\ \text{psychological} \\ \text{quality (OPQ)}}}{\substack{\text{expected} \\ \text{environmental} \\ \text{quality (EEQ)}} \times \substack{\text{expected} \\ \text{psychological} \\ \text{quality (EPQ)}}}$$

The expected environmental quality (EEQ) of a recreation environment may in turn be obtained from the following:

$$(1a)\ \text{EEQ} = \sum_{i=1}^{n} e \cdot p = \sum \left(\begin{array}{c} \text{evaluation of an} \\ \text{environmental} \\ \text{characteristic} \end{array} \right) \times \left(\begin{array}{c} \text{subjective probability} \\ \text{of the characteristic} \\ \text{in a given environment} \end{array} \right)$$

The observed environmental quality (OEQ) is obtained *after* an actual environmental encounter. Thus,

$$(1b)\ \text{OEQ} = \sum_{i=1}^{n} e \cdot o = \sum \left(\begin{array}{c} \text{evaluation of an} \\ \text{environmental} \\ \text{characteristic} \end{array} \right) \times \left(\begin{array}{c} \text{observed occurrence of} \\ \text{the characteristic in} \\ \text{the environment} \end{array} \right)$$

The expected psychological quality of a recreation environment (EPQ) may be expressed as follows:

$$(1c)\ \text{EPQ} = \sum_{i=1}^{n} e \cdot p = \sum \left(\begin{array}{c} \text{evaluation of a} \\ \text{psychological} \\ \text{entity} \end{array} \right) \times \left(\begin{array}{c} \text{subjective probability} \\ \text{of obtaining the entity} \\ \text{through the environ-} \\ \text{mental encounter} \end{array} \right)$$

The observed psychological quality (OPQ) is obtained *after* an actual environmental encounter. Thus,

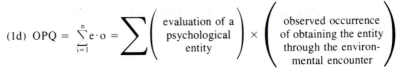

$$(1d) \ OPQ = \sum_{i=1}^{n} e \cdot o = \sum \left(\begin{array}{c} \text{evaluation of a} \\ \text{psychological} \\ \text{entity} \end{array} \right) \times \left(\begin{array}{c} \text{observed occurrence} \\ \text{of obtaining the entity} \\ \text{through the environ-} \\ \text{mental encounter} \end{array} \right)$$

By multiplying the evaluation of each characteristic by the appropriate probability and by adding the products up one obtains the expected environmental quality (EEQ, formula 1a). Other indices (1b–1d) are computed in the same manner, using the same basic formula. In this formula, "e" stands for evaluation, whether it is the evaluation of environmental characteristics or psychological entities; "p" stands for probability, whether it is the probability of observing certain environmental characteristics or of obtaining psychological rewards (entities); "o" refers to the degree to which environmental characteristics were observed to actually occur in the environment or to the extent to which psychological entities were actually observed to have been achieved.

As an example to illustrate the computation of the PQRE, assume that a person has three environmental characteristics and three psychological entities in mind relative to wilderness areas in general. Assuming that the following were the evaluations and probabilities/occurrences before and after hiking in one wilderness area, one can calculate the environmental and psychological qualities as follows:

	Environmental			
	Before		After	
Environmental Characteristics	Evaluation (e)	Probability (p)	Evaluation (e)	Observed Occurrence (o)
Undeveloped Country	+3	.70	+3	.80
Open Water	+2	.50	+3	.50
Presence of People	−3	.60	−2	.40

$$EEQ = \sum_{i=1}^{n} e \cdot p = +1.3 \quad ; \quad OEQ = \sum_{i=1}^{n} e \cdot o = +3.1$$

	Psychological			
	Before		After	
Psychological Entities	Evaluation (e)	Probability (p)	Evaluation (e)	Observed Occurrence (o)
Escape	+3	.90	+2	.60
Relaxation	+3	.90	+2	.50
Exercise	+2	.60	+1	.30

$$EPQ = \sum_{i=1}^{n} e \cdot p = +6.6 \quad ; \quad OPQ = \sum_{i=1}^{n} e \cdot o = +2.5$$

Thus, $\quad PQRE = \dfrac{OEQ \times OPQ}{EEQ \times EPQ} = \dfrac{3.1 \times 2.5}{1.3 \times 6.6} = PQRE = \dfrac{7.75}{8.58} = .90$

Appendix

In this instance, an individual's perceived quality of recreation environment was slightly less than was expected (.90). The higher the numerical value of PQRE, the higher the perceived quality of a given recreation environment. Numerically, PQRE can, of course, be less or more than 1.0 unit. If it is more than one, the perceived quality of a recreation environment is then higher than expected. The researcher also postulates that the higher the PQRE, the greater the satisfaction with an environment, that is,

Satisfaction with a recreation environment = f (PQRE)

references

Abramson, L.Y., Seligman, M.E.P. and Teasdale, J.D. Learned helplessness in humans: critique and reformulation. *Journal of Abnormal Psychology*, 1978, *87*, 49–74.

Ajzen, I. and Fishbein, M. The prediction of behavioral intentions in a choice situation. *Journal of Experimental Social Psychology*, 1969, *5*, 400–416.

———. Attitude-behavior relations: a theoretical analysis and review of empirical research. *Psychological Bulletin*, 1977, *84*, 888–918.

Allport, F.H. *Social psychology*. Boston: Houghton Mifflin Co., 1924.

Allport, G.W. *The person in psychology: selected essays*. Boston: Beacon Press, 1968.

———. The historical background of modern social psychology. In G. Lindzey and E. Aronson (Eds.), *Handbook of social psychology*, Vol. 1 (2nd ed.). Reading, Mass.: Addison-Wesley, 1969, 1–80.

Altman, I. *The environment and social behavior: privacy, personal space, territory, crowding*. Monterey, Calif.: Brooks/Cole Publishing Co., 1975.

Anderson, B.F. *The psychology experiment: an introduction to the scientific method*. Belmont, Calif.: Brooks/Cole Publishing Co., 1966.

Anderson, N. *Work and leisure*. New York: Free Press, 1961.

Anderson, R., Manoogian, S.T. and Reznick, J.S. The undermining and enhancing of intrinsic motivation in preschool children. *Journal of Personality and Social Psychology*, 1976, *34*, 915–922.

Argyle, M. *The social psychology of work*. Baltimore: Penguin Books, 1972.

Aronson, E. Dissonance theory: progress and problems. In E.P. Hollander and R.G. Hunt (Eds.), *Current perspectives in social psychology*, (3rd ed.). New York: Oxford University Press, 1971, 359–371.

———. *The social animal*. San Francisco: W.H. Freeman and Co., 1972.

Aronson, E. and Carlsmith, J.M. Experimentation in social psychology. In G. Lindzey and E. Aronson (Eds.), *Handbook of social psychology* (2nd ed.), Vol. 2. Reading, Mass.: Addison-Wesley, 1969, 1–79.

Asch, S.E. Forming impressions of personality. *Journal of Abnormal and Social Psychology*, 1946, *41*, 258–290.

Atchley, R.C. *The social forces in later life*, (2nd ed.). Belmont, Calif.: Wadsworth Publishing Co., 1977.

Atkinson, J.W. Motivational determinants of risk-taking behavior. *Psychological Review*, 1957, *64*, 359–372.

Avedon, E.M. *Therapeutic recreation service: an applied behavioral approach.* Englewood Cliffs, N.J.: Prentice-Hall, 1974.

Avellar, J. and Kagan, S. Development of competitive behaviors in Anglo-American and Mexican-American children. *Psychological Reports,* 1976, *39,* 191–198.

Bacon, A.W. Leisure and the alienated worker: a critical reassessment of three radical theories of work and leisure. *Journal of Leisure Research,* 1975, *7,* 179–190.

Bakeman, R. and Helmreich, R. Cohesiveness and performance: covariation and causality in an undersea environment. *Journal of Experimental Social Psychology,* 1975, *11,* 478–489.

Baley, J.A. Recreation and the aging process. *Research Quarterly,* 1955, *26,* 1–7.

Bandura, A. *Principles of behavior modification.* New York: Holt, Rinehart and Winston, 1969.

———. *Social learning theory.* Morristown, N.J.: General Learning Press, 1971.

Bandura, A. and Walters, R.H. *Social learning and personality development.* New York: Holt, Rinehart and Winston, Inc., 1963.

Barker, R., Dembo, T. and Lewin, K. Frustration and repression: an experiment with young children. *University of Iowa Studies: Studies in Child Welfare,* 1941, *28,* (No. 1), 1–314.

Barnett, L. Current thinking about children's play: learning to play or playing to learn? *Quest,* 1976, *26* (Monograph), 5–16.

Baron, R.A., Byrne, D. and Griffitt, W. *Social psychology: understanding human interaction.* Boston: Allyn and Bacon, 1974.

Baum, A. and Greenberg, C. Waiting for a crowd: the behavioral and perceptual effects of anticipated crowding. *Journal of Personality and Social Psychology,* 1975, *32,* 671–679.

Baum, A. and Koman, S. Differential responses to anticipated crowding: psychological effects of social and spatial density. *Journal of Personality and Social Psychology,* 1976, *34,* 526–536.

Bem, D.J. Self-perception: an alternative interpretation of cognitive dissonance phenomena. *Psychological Review,* 1967, *74,* 183–200.

———. *Beliefs, attitudes and human affairs.* Belmont, Calif.: Brooks/Cole Publishing Co., 1970.

———. Self-perception theory. In L. Berkowitz (Ed.), *Advances in experimental social psychology,* Vol. 6. New York: Academic Press, 1972, 1–62.

Bengtson, V.L. *The social psychology of aging.* Indianapolis: Bobbs-Merrill, 1973.

Berkowitz, L. Social motivation. In G. Lindzey and E. Aronson (Eds.), *The handbook of social psychology* (2nd ed.), Vol. 3. Reading, Mass.: Addison-Wesley Publishing Co., 1969, 50–135.

Berlyne, D.E. *Conflict, arousal and curiosity.* New York: McGraw-Hill, 1960.

———. Laughter, humor, and play. In G. Lindzey and E. Aronson (Eds.), *The handbook of social psychology* (2nd ed.), Vol. 3. Reading, Mass.: Addison-Wesley Publishing Co., 1969, 795–852.

Bishop, D.W. Stability of the factor structure of leisure behavior: analyses of four communities. *Journal of Leisure Research,* 1970, *2,* 160–170.

———. *Psychological adjustment and leisure-time activities.* Final Report for Grant MH 17913, Department of Recreation and Park Administration, University of Illinois, Urbana-Champaign, 1973.

Bishop, D.W. and Chace, C.A. Parental conceptual systems, home play environment, and potential creativity in children. *Journal of Experimental Child Psychology,* 1971, *12,* 318–338.

Bishop, D.W. and Ikeda, M. Status and role factors in the leisure behavior of different occupations. *Sociology and Social Research,* 1970, *54,* 190–208.

Bishop, D.W., Jeanrenaud, C. and Lawson, K. Comparison of a time diary and recall questionnaire for surveying leisure activities. *Journal of Leisure Research*, 1975, *7*, 73–80.

Bishop, D.W. and Witt, P.A. Sources of behavioral variance during leisure time. *Journal of Personality and Social Psychology*, 1970, *16*, 352–360.

Bowen, W.P. and Mitchell, E.D. *The theory of organized play.* New York: A.S. Barnes and Co., 1930.

Bowers, K.S. Situationism in psychology: an analysis and a critique. *Psychological Review*, 1973, *80*, 307–336.

Bowlsby, R.A., II. *Summer baseball programs as developers of self-concept.* Unpublished master's thesis. University of Iowa, Recreation Education Program, 1978.

Box, G.E.P. Science and statistics. *Journal of the American Statistical Association*, 1976, *71*, 791–799.

Brehm, J.W. *A theory of psychological reactance.* New York: Academic Press, 1966.
———. *Responses to loss of freedom: a theory of psychological reactance.* Morristown, N.J.: General Learning Press, 1972.

Brehm, S.S. and Weinraub, M. Physical barriers and psychological reactance: 2-year-olds' responses to threats to freedom. *Journal of Personality and Social Psychology*, 1977, *35*, 830–836.

Brightbill, C.K. *The challenge of leisure.* Englewood Cliffs, N.J.: Prentice-Hall, Inc., 1960.

Brim, O.G. Socialization through the life cycle. In O.G. Brim and S. Wheeler, *Socialization after childhood: two essays.* New York: John Wiley and Sons, 1966, 1–49.

Britt, S.H. and Janus, S.Q. Toward a social psychology of human play. *Journal of Social Psychology*, 1941, *13*, 351–384.

Brockett, C. Toward a clarification of the need hierarchy theory: some extensions of Maslow's conceptualization. *Interpersonal Development*, 1976, *6*, 77–90.

Bronfenbrenner, U. When is infant stimulation effective. In D.C. Glass (Ed.), *Environmental influences.* New York: The Rockefeller University Press and Russell Sage Foundation, 1968, 251–257.
———. *Two worlds of childhood: U.S. and U.S.S.R.* New York: Russell Sage Foundation, 1970.
———. Early deprivation in monkey and man. In U. Bronfenbrenner (Ed.), *Influences on human development.* Hinsdale, Ill.: The Dryden Press, Inc., 1972, 256–301.
———. Toward an experimental ecology of human development. *American Psychologist*, 1977, *32*, 513–531.

Brooks, J.B. and Elliott, D.M. Prediction of psychological adjustment at age thirty from leisure time activities and satisfactions in childhood. *Human Development*, 1971, *14*, 51–61.

Bruner, J. Child's play. *New Scientist*, 1974, *62*, 126–128.
———. Play is serious business. *Psychology Today*, 1975, *8*, (January), 81–83.

Brush, R.O. Perceived quality of scenic and recreational environments: some methodological issues. In K.H. Craik and E.H. Zube (Eds.), *Perceiving environmental quality.* New York: Plenum Press, 1976, 47–58.

Bulman, R.J. and Wortman, C.B. Attributions of blame and coping in the "real world:" severe accident victims react to their lot. *Journal of Personality and Social Psychology*, 1977, *35*, 351–363.

Burch, W.R., Jr. The social circles of leisure: competing explanations. *Journal of Leisure Research*, 1969, *1*, 125–147.

Burton, T.L. *Experiments in recreation research.* Totowa, N.J.: Rowman and Littlefield, 1971.

Calder, B.J. and Staw, B.M. Self-perception of intrinsic and extrinsic motivation. *Journal of Personality and Social Psychology, 1975, 31,* 599–605.

Call, J. Games babies play. *Psychology Today, 1970, 3,* (January), 34–37, 54.

Campbell, A. Subjective measures of well-being. *American Psychologist, 1976, 31,* 117–124.

Campbell, A., Converse, P.E. and Rodgers, W.L. *The quality of American life: perceptions, evaluations, and satisfactions.* New York: Russell Sage Foundation, 1976.

Campbell, D.T. and Stanley, J.C. *Experimental and quasi-experimental designs for research.* Chicago: Rand McNally and Co., 1966.

Caplan, F. and Caplan, T. *The power of play.* New York: Anchor Press, 1973.

Carlsmith, J.M., Ellsworth, P.C. and Aronson, E. *Methods of research in social psychology.* Reading, Mass.: Addison-Wesley Publishing Co., 1976.

Cartwright, D. and Zander, A. (Eds.) *Group dynamics: research and theory* (2nd ed.). New York: Harper and Row, 1960.

Casady, M. Character lasts: if you're active and savvy at 30, you'll be warm and witty at 70. *Psychology Today, 1975, 9,* (November), 138.

Cattell, R.B. *Personality: a systematic, theoretical, and factual study.* New York: McGraw-Hill, 1950.

Cavanaugh, J.O. The relation of recreation to personality adjustment. *Journal of Social Psychology, 1942, 15,* 63–74.

Chamber, A.D. Assessment of environmental quality in relation to perceived density in recreational settings. *Man-Environment Systems, 1974, 4,* 353–360.

Champoux, J.E. Work and nonwork: a review of theory and empirical research. *Technical Report No. 31.* University of California, Irvine: Graduate School of Administration, 1975.

Child, E. and Child, S. Children and leisure. In M.A. Smith, S. Parker and C.S. Smith (Eds.), *Leisure and society in Britain.* London: Allen Lane, 1973, 135–147.

Choi, S.C., Mirjafari, A. and Weaver, H.B. The concept of crowding: a critical review and proposal of an alternative approach. *Environment and Behavior, 1976, 8,* 345–362.

Christensen, J.E. and Yoesting, D.R. Social and attitudinal variants in high and low use of outdoor recreational facilities. *Journal of Leisure Research, 1973, 5,* 6–15.

————. The substitutability concept: a need for further development. *Journal of Leisure Research, 1977, 9,* 188–207.

Cialdini, R.B., Borden, R.J., Thorne, A., Walker, M.R., Freeman, S. and Sloan, L.R. Basking in reflected glory: three (football) field studies. *Journal of Personality and Social Psychology, 1976, 34,* 366–375.

Cicchetti, C.J. A multivariate statistical analysis of wilderness users in the United States. In J.V. Krutilla (Ed.), *Natural environments: studies in theoretical and applied analysis.* Baltimore: John Hopkins University Press, 1972.

Clawson, M. *Land and water for recreation.* Chicago: Rand McNally and Co., 1963.

Colligan, M.J. and Stockton, W. The mystery of assembly-line hysteria. *Psychology Today, 1978, 12,* (June), 93–99, 114, 116.

Condry, J. Enemies of exploration: self-initiated versus other-initiated learning. *Journal of Personality and Social Psychology, 1977, 35,* 459–477.

Cook, H. and Stingle, S. Cooperative behavior in children. *Psychological Bulletin, 1974, 81,* 918–933.

Cook, T.D. and Campbell, D.T. The design and conduct of quasi-experiments and true experiments in field settings. In M.D. Dunnette (Ed.), *Handbook of industrial and organizational research.* Chicago: Rand McNally, 1976, 223–326.

Coopersmith, S. Studies in self-esteem. *Scientific American, 1968, 218,* 96–106.

Copp, J.D. Why hunters like to hunt. *Psychology Today, 1975, 9,* (December), 60–62, 67.

Costanzo, P.R., Grumet, J.F. and Brehm, S.S. The effects of choice and source of constraint on children's attributions of preference. *Journal of Experimental Social Psychology*, 1974, *10*, 352–364.

Craig, D.W. *A study of the relationship between local public recreation opportunity and social pathology in selected large cities in the United States.* Unpublished doctoral dissertation, Temple University, 1976.

Craik, K.H. Environmental psychology. *Annual Review of Psychology*, 1973, *24*, 403–422.

Crandall, R. Social interaction, affect and leisure. *Journal of Leisure Research*, 1978, in press.

Crandall, R. and Lewko, J. Leisure research, present and future: who, what, where. *Journal of Leisure Research*, 1976, *8*, 150–159.

Crandall, V.C. Achievement behavior in young children. In W.W. Hartup and N.L. Smothergill (Eds.), *The young child.* Washington, D.C.: National Association for Education of Young Children, 1967, 165–185.

Crano, W.D. and Brewer, M.B. *Principles of research in social psychology.* New York: McGraw-Hill, 1973.

Csikszentmihalyi, M. *Beyond boredom and anxiety.* San Francisco: Jossey-Bass, 1975.

Csikszentmihalyi, M., Larson, R. and Prescott, S. The ecology of adolescent activity and experience. *Journal of Youth and Adolescence*, 1977, *6*, 281–294.

Cumming, E. and Henry, W.F. *Growing old.* New York: Basic Books, 1961.

Curtis, H.S. *Education through play.* New York: The MacMillan Co., 1924.

Cutten, G.B. *The threat of leisure.* New Haven: Yale University Press, 1926.

Davis, J.E. *Play and mental health.* New York: A.S. Barnes and Co., 1938.

Davis, K.E. Drug effects and drug use. In L.S. Wrightsman (Ed.), *Social psychology in the seventies.* Belmont, Calif.: Brooks/Cole Publishing Co., 1972, 517–546.

Deaux, K. Sex: a perspective on the attribution process. In J.H. Harvey, W.J. Ickes and R.F. Kidd (Eds.), *New directions in attribution research*, Vol. 1. Hillsdale, N.J.: Lawrence Erlbaum Associates, Publishers, 1976, 335–352.

DeCarlo, T.J. Recreation participation patterns and successful aging. *Journal of Gerontology*, 1974, *29*, 416–422.

DeCharms, R. *Personal causation: the internal affective determinants of behavior.* New York: Academic Press, 1968.

Deci, E.L. Work—who does not like it and why. *Psychology Today*, 1972, *6* (August), 57–58, 92.

———. *Intrinsic motivation.* New York: Plenum Press, 1975. (a)

———. Notes on the theory and metatheory of intrinsic motivation. *Organizational Behavior and Human Performance*, 1975, *15*, 130–145. (b)

DeGrazia, S. *Of time, work and leisure.* New York: Twentieth Century Fund, Inc., 1962.

Dennis, W. Causes of retardation among institutionalized children: Iran. *Journal of Genetic Psychology*, 1960, *96*, 47–59.

Dennis, W. and Najarian, P. Infant development under environmental handicap. *Psychological Monograph*, 1957, *71*, No. 7.

Deutsch, M. A theory of cooperation and competition. *Human Relations*, 1949, *2*, 129–152.

Deutsch, M. and Krauss, R.M. *Theories in social psychology.* New York: Basic Books, 1965.

Diener, C.I. and Dweck, C.S. An analysis of learned helplessness: continuous changes in performance, strategy, and achievement cognitions following failure. *Journal of Personality and Social Psychology*, 1978, *36*, 451–462.

Dollard, J., Doob, L.W., Miller, N.E., Mowrer, O.H. and Sears, R.R. *Frustration and aggression.* New Haven: Yale University Press, 1939.

Driver, B.L. Potential contributions of psychology to recreation resource management. In J.F. Wohlwill and D.H. Carson (Eds.), *Environment and the social sciences: perspectives and applications*. Washington, D.C.: American Psychological Association, 1972, 223–244.

Driver, B.L. and Knopf, R.C. Personality, outdoor recreation, and expected consequences. *Environment and Behavior*, 1977, *9*, 169–193.

Dubos, R. Man overadapting. *Psychology Today*, 1971, *4*, (February), 50–53.

———. *Man adapting*. New Haven: Yale University Press, 1965.

Dumazedier, J. *Toward a society of leisure*. New York: The Free Press, 1967.

Dwivedi, N. and Pestonjee, D.M. Off-the-job factors and job satisfaction: some evidence for the interactional model. *Psychological Studies*, 1976, *21*, 11–14.

Dworkin, R.H., Burke, B.W., Maher, B.A. and Gottesman, I.I. A longitudinal study of the genetics of personality. *Journal of Personality and Social Psychology*, 1976, *34*, 510–518.

Eckerman, C.O., Whatley, J.L. and Kutz, S.L. Growth of social play with peers during the second year of life. *Developmental Psychology*, 1975, *11*, 42–49.

Edney, J.J. and Buda, M.A. Distinguishing territoriality and privacy: two studies. *Human Ecology*, 1976, *4*, 283–296.

Eifermann, R.R. Social play in childhood. In R.E. Herron and B. Sutton-Smith (Eds.), *Child's play*. New York: John Wiley and Sons, Inc., 1971, 270–297.

———. Free social play: a guide to directed playing. In S. Coopersmith (Ed.), *Developing motivation in young children*. San Francisco: Albion Publishing Co., 1975, 25–58.

Ekehammar, B. Interactionism in personality from a historical perspective. *Psychological Bulletin*, 1974, *81*, 1026–1048.

Ellis, M.J. *Why people play*. Englewood Cliffs, N.J.: Prentice-Hall, Inc., 1973.

Elms, A.C. The crisis of confidence in social psychology. *American Psychologist*, 1975, *30*, 967–976.

Endler, N.S. and Magnusson, D. Toward an interactional psychology of personality. *Psychological Bulletin*, 1976, *83*, 956–974.

Erikson, E.H. Clinical studies in childhood play. In R.G. Barker, J.S. Kounin and H.F. Wright (Eds.), *Child behavior and development*. New York: McGraw-Hill, 1943, 411–428.

———. *Childhood and society*. New York: W.W. Norton and Co., Inc., 1950.

Feitelson, D. and Ross, G.S. The neglected factor—play. *Human Development*, 1973, *16*, 202–223.

Ferrari, N.A. *Institutionalization and attitude change in an aged population: a field study and dissidence theory*. Unpublished doctoral dissertation, Western Reserve University, 1962. (Cited in M.E.P. Seligman, 1975; see reference).

Ferriss, A.L. The social and personality correlates of outdoor recreation. *The Annals*, 1970, *389* (May), 46–55.

Festinger, L. A theory of social comparison processes. *Human Relations*, 1954, *7*, 117–140.

———. *A theory of cognitive dissonance*. Stanford, Calif.: Stanford University Press, 1957.

Fine, G.A. *Look at the monkey playing' first!: Little League baseball and the development of the male sex role*. Unpublished manuscript, University of Minnesota, 1977.

Fishbein, M. and Ajzen, I. *Belief, attitude, intention and behavior: an introduction to theory and research*. Reading, Mass.: Addison-Wesley Publishing Co., 1975.

Flanagan, J.C. A research approach to improving our quality of life. *American Psychologist*, 1978, *33*, 138–147.

Foote, N.N. Sex as play. In E. Larrabee and R. Meyersohn (Eds.), *Mass leisure.* Glencoe, Ill.: The Free Press, 1958, 335–340.

Fox, J.H. Effects of retirement and former work life on women's adaptation in old age. *Journal of Gerontology,* 1977, *32,* 196–202.

Freeberg, N.E. and Rock, D.A. Dimensional continuity of interests and activities during adolescence. *Human Development,* 1973, *16,* 304–316.

Freedman, J.L., Carlsmith, J.M. and Sears, D.O. *Social psychology* (2nd ed.). Englewood Cliffs, N.J.: Prentice-Hall, 1974.

Freedman, J.L., Heshka, S. and Levy, A. Population density and pathology: is there a relationship? *Journal of Experimental Social Psychology,* 1975, *11,* 539–552.

Freud, A. *The psycho-analytic treatment of children.* London: Imago, 1946.

Freud, S. Beyond the pleasure principle. In J. Strachey (ed. and trans.), *The Standard edition of the complete psychological works of S. Freud, 1920–1922,* Vol. 18. London: Hogarth and the Institute of Psychoanalysis, 1955.

Fridgen, J.D. and Hinkelman, B.E. Recreation behavior and environment congruence. Paper presented at the *NRPA Research Symposium,* National Recreation and Park Association, Las Vegas, Nevada, October 1977.

Friedland, N. Social influence via threats. *Journal of Experimental Social Psychology,* 1976, *12,* 552–563.

Friend, R.M. and Neale, J.M. Children's perceptions of success and failure: an attributional analysis of the effects of race and social class. *Developmental Psychology,* 1972, *7,* 124–128.

Frye, V. and Peters, M. *Therapeutic recreation: its theory, philosophy, and practice.* Harrisburg, Pa.: Stackpole Books, 1972.

Galizio, M. and Hendrick, C. Effect of musical accompaniment on attitude: the guitar as a prop for persuasion. *Journal of Applied Social Psychology,* 1972, *2,* 350–359.

Garbarino, J. The impact of anticipated reward upon cross-age tutoring. *Journal of Personality and Social Psychology,* 1975, *32,* 421–428.

Gardell, B. Reactions at work and their influence on nonwork activities: an analysis of a sociopolitical problem in affluent societies. *Human Relations,* 1976, *29,* 885–904.

Garvey, C. Some properties of social play. *Merrill-Palmer Quarterly,* 1974, *20,* 163–180.

Gergen, K.J. Social psychology as history. *Journal of Personality and Social Psychology,* 1973, *26,* 309–320.

Gerstl, J.E. Leisure, taste, and occupational milieu. In E.O. Smigel (Ed.), *Work and leisure: a contemporary social problem.* New Haven, Conn.: College and University Press, 1963, 146–167.

Gilmore, J.B. Play: a special behavior. In R.N. Haber (Ed.), *Current research in motivation.* New York: Holt, Rinehart and Winston, 1966, 343–355.

Glass, D.C. and Singer, J.E. *Urban stress: experiments in noise and social stressors.* New York: Academic Press, 1972.

Glass, D.C., Singer, J.E. and Pennebaker, J.W. Behavioral and physiological effects of uncontrollable environmental events. In D. Stokols (Ed.), *Perspectives on environment and behavior: theory, research, and applications.* New York: Plenum Press, 1977, 131–151.

Glasser, R. *Leisure: penalty or prize?* London: MacMillan and Co., Ltd., 1970.

Goffman, E. *Stigma.* Englewood Cliffs, N.J.: Prentice-Hall, 1963.

Goldberg, S. and Lewis, M. Play behavior in the year-old infant: early sex differences. *Child Development,* 1969, *40,* 21–31.

Golding, S.L. Flies in the ointment: methodological problems in the analysis of the percentage of variance due to persons and situations. *Psychological Bulletin,* 1975, *82,* 278–288.

Goldstein, J.H. and Bredemeir, B.J. Socialization: some basic issues. *Journal of Communication*, 1977, *27*, 154–159.

Gordon, C., Gaitz, C.M. and Scott, J. Leisure and lives: personal expressivity across the life span. In R.H. Binstock and E. Shanas (Eds.), *Handbook of aging and the social sciences*. New York: Van Nostrand Reinhold Co., 1976, 310–341.

Gordon, C., Gaitz, C.M. and Scott, J. Value priorities and leisure activities among middle-aged and older Anglos. *Diseases of the Nervous System*, 1973, *34*, 13–26.

Gorsuch, R.L. and Butler, M.C. Initiated drug abuse: a review of predisposing social psychological factors. *Psychological Bulletin*, 1976, *83*, 120–137.

Gould, R. Adult life stages: growth toward self-tolerance. *Psychology Today*, 1975, *8* (February), 74–78.

Graney, M.J. Happiness and social participation in aging. *Journal of Gerontology*, 1975, *30*, 701–706.

Gray, D.E. Exploring inner space. *Parks and Recreation*, 1972, *7*, 18–19, 46.

Greenberg, C.I. and Firestone, I.J. Compensatory responses to crowding: effects of personal space intrusion and privacy reduction. *Journal of Personality and Social Psychology*, 1977, *35*, 637–644.

Greenbie, S. *Leisure for living*. New York: George W. Stewart, 1940.

Greene, D. and Lepper, M.R. Effects of extrinsic rewards on children's subsequent intrinsic interest. *Child Development*, 1974, *45*, 1141–1145. (a)

———. Intrinsic motivation: how to turn play into work. *Psychology Today*, 1974, *8* (September), 49–54. (b)

Greenwald, A.G. Transhistorical lawfulness of behavior: a comment on two papers. *Personality and Social Psychology Bulletin*, 1976, *2*, 391.

Groos, K. *The play of man*. (Trans. E.L. Baldwin from original publication in 1898). New York: Appleton-Century-Crofts, 1901.

Gross, E. A functional approach to leisure analysis. In E.O. Smigel (Ed.), *Work and leisure: a contemporary social problem*. New Haven, Conn.: College and University Press, 1963, 41–52.

Grotevant, H.D., Scarr, S., and Weinberg, R.A. Patterns of interest similarity in adoptive and biological families. *Journal of Personality and Social Psychology*, 1977, *35*, 667–676.

Groves, D.L., Kahalas, H. and Bonham, T.D. Social psychology—a functional approach to recreation. *Social Behavior and Personality*, 1977, *5*, 93–111.

Grupp, E.A. Assembly line boredom and individual differences in recreation participation. *Journal of Leisure Research*, 1975, *7*, 256–269.

Gulick, L.H. *A philosophy of play*. New York: Charles Scribner's Sons, 1920.

Haavio-Mannila, E. Satisfaction with family, work, leisure and life among men and women. *Human Relations*, 1971, *24*, 585–601.

Hall, C.S. and Lindzey, G. *Theories of personality* (2nd ed.). New York: John Wiley and Sons, Inc., 1970.

Hall, E.T. *The hidden dimension*. Garden City, N.Y.: Doubleday, 1966.

Hall, G.S. *Adolescence: its psychology and its relations to physiology, anthropology, sociology, sex, crime, religion and education*, Vol. 1. New York: Appleton-Century-Crofts, 1916.

Hammitt, W.E. Outdoor recreation: is it a multi-phase experience? Paper presented at the *NRPA Research Symposium*, National Recreation and Park Association, Miami Beach, Florida, October, 1978.

Harlow, H. and Harlow, M.K. Social deprivation in monkeys. *Scientific American*, 1962, *207*, 136–146.

Hartley, R.E., Frank, L.K. and Goldenson, R.M. *Understanding children's play*. New York: Columbia University Press, 1952.

Harvey, J.H. Attribution of freedom. In J.H. Harvey, W.J. Ickes and R.F. Kidd (Eds.), *New directions in attribution research*, Vol. 1. Hillsdale, N.J.: Lawrence Erlbaum Associates, Publishers, 1976, 73–96.

Harvey, J.H., Ickes, W.J. and Kidd, R.F. (Eds.). *New directions in attribution research*, Vol. 1. Hillsdale, N.J.: Lawrence Erlbaum Associates, Publishers, 1976.

Harvey, J.H. and Smith, W.P. *Social psychology: an attributional approach.* Saint Louis: The C.V. Mosby Co., 1977.

Hastorf, A.H. and Cantril, H. They saw a game: a case study. *Journal of Abnormal and Social Psychology*, 1954, *49*, 129–134.

Hastorf, A.H., Schneider, D.J. and Polefka, J. *Person perception.* Reading, Mass.: Addison-Wesley Publishing Co., 1970.

Havighurst, R.J. The leisure activities of the middle-aged. *American Journal of Sociology*, 1957, *63*, 152–162.

———. The nature and values of meaningful free-time activity. In R.W. Kleemeier (Ed.), *Aging and leisure.* New York: Oxford University Press, 1961, 309–344.

Heberlein, T.A. Social psychological assumptions of user attitude surveys: the case of the wildernism scale. *Journal of Leisure Research*, 1973, *5*, 18–33.

Heider, F. *The psychology of interpersonal relations.* New York: John Wiley and Sons, Inc., 1958.

Heimstra, N.W. and McFarling, L.H. *Environmental psychology.* Monterey, Calif.: Brooks/Cole Publishing Co., 1974.

Helanko, R. Sports and socialization. *Acta Sociologica*, 1957, *2*, 229–240.

Helmreich, R. Applied social psychology: the unfulfilled promise. *Personality and Social Psychology Bulletin*, 1975, *1*, 548–560.

Hendee, J.C. Rural-Urban differences reflected in outdoor recreation participation. *Journal of Leisure Research*, 1969, *1*, 333–341.

Hendee, J.C. and Burdge, R. The substitutability concept: implications for recreation research and measurement. *Journal of Leisure Research*, 1974, *6*, 157–162.

Hendry, L.B. and Douglass, L. University students: attainment and sport. *British Journal of Educational Psychology*, 1975, *45*, 299–306.

Himmelweit, H.T. Studies of societal influences: problems and implications. In M. Deutsch and H.A. Hornstein (Eds.), *Applying social psychology.* Hillsdale, N.J.: Lawrence Erlbaum Associates, Publishers, 1975, 67–85.

Himmelweit, H.T. and Swift, B. A model for the understanding of school as a socializing agent. In P.H. Mussen, J. Langer and M. Covington (Eds.), *Trends and issues in developmental psychology.* New York: Holt, Rinehart and Winston, 1969, 154–181.

———. Continuities and discontinuities in media usage and taste: a longitudinal study. *Journal of Social Issues*, 1977, *32*, 133–156.

Hirshfeld, S.F. and Hirshfeld, S.L. The use of games in developing analytical and combinatorial reasoning. *Journal of Creative Behavior*, 1977, *11*, 101–104.

Hoffman, M.L. Sex differences in moral internalization and values. *Journal of Personality and Social Psychology*, 1975, *32*, 720–729.

———. Sex differences in empathy and related behaviors. *Psychological Bulletin*, 1977, *84*, 712–722.

Hollander, E.P. *Principles and methods of social psychology* (2nd ed.). New York: Oxford University Press, 1971. (3rd ed., 1976.)

Hollander, E.P. and Hunt, R.G. (Eds.). *Current perspectives in social psychology* (3rd ed.). New York: Oxford University Press, 1971. (4th ed., 1976.)

Hollender, J.W. Motivational dimensions of the camping experience. *Journal of Leisure Research*, 1977, *9*, 133–141.

Holman, P.A. Validation of an attitude scale as a device for predicting behavior. *Journal of Applied Psychology*, 1956, *40*, 347–349.

Horn, J.C. Parent egos take the fun out of little league. *Psychology Today,* 1977, *11,* (September), 18, 22.

Hovland, C., Janis, I. and Kelley, H.H. *Communication and persuasion.* New Haven: Yale University Press, 1953.

Howard, D.R. Multivariate relationships between leisure activities and personality. *Research Quarterly,* 1976, *47,* 226–237.

Huizinga, J. *Homo ludens: a study of the play element in culture.* London: Routledge and Kegan Paul, Ltd., 1949.

Hulin, C.L Sources of variation in job and life satisfaction: the role of community and job-related variables. *Journal of Applied Psychology,* 1969, *53,* 279–291.

Hunt, J. Mc.V. *Intelligence and experience.* New York: The Ronald Press, 1961.

———. Intrinsic motivation and its role in psychological development. In D. Levine (Ed.), *Nebraska Symposium on Motivation,* Vol. 13. Lincoln: University of Nebraska Press, 1965, 189–282.

———. *The challenge of incompetence and poverty.* Urbana, Ill.: University of Illinois Press, 1969.

———. *Heredity, environment, and class or ethnic differences.* Paper prepared for the 1972 Invitational Conference on Testing Problems, 1972.

Hurlock, E.B. The use of group rivalry as an incentive. *Journal of Abnormal and Social Psychology,* 1927, *22,* 278–290.

Hutt, C. Exploration and play in children. In R.E. Herron and B. Sutton-Smith (Eds.), *Child's play.* New York: John Wiley and Sons, 1971, 231–251.

Iris, B. and Barrett, G.V. Some relations between job and life satisfaction and job performances. *Journal of Applied Psychology,* 1972, *56,* 301–304.

Isen, A.M., Horn, N. and Rosenhan, D.L. Effects of success and failure on children's generosity. *Journal of Personality and Social Psychology,* 1973, *27,* 239–247.

Iso-Ahola, S.E. A test of the attribution theory of success and failure with little league baseball players. *Mouvement,* 1975, *7,* 323–337.

———. Evaluation of self and team performance and feelings of satisfaction after success and failure. *International Review of Sport Sociology,* 1976, *11,* 33–46. (b)

———. On the theoretical link between personality and leisure. *Psychological Reports,* 1976, *39,* 3–10. (a)

———. *An attributional analysis of effects of perceived work and leisure motivation on psychological well-being.* Unpublished manuscript, University of Iowa, Recreation Education Program, 1977. (f)

———. Effects of self-enhancement and consistency on causal and trait attributions following success and failure in motor performance. *Research Quarterly,* 1977, *48,* 717–726. (b)

———. Effects of team outcome on children's self-perception: Little League baseball. *Scandinavian Journal of Psychology,* 1977, *18,* 38–42. (d)

———. Immediate attributional effects of success and failure in the field: testing some laboratory hypotheses. *European Journal of Social Psychology,* 1977, *7,* 275–296. (c)

———. *A social psychological analysis of little league baseball.* Invited paper prepared for the Conference on Sport, Physical Activity and People: An Application of Ideas. Iowa City, Iowa, October, 1977. (e)

———. Social psychological determinants of perceptions of leisure. Paper presented at the *NRPA Research Symposium,* National Park and Recreation Association, Las Vegas, Nevada, October, 1977. (a) (An abridged version of the paper to appear in *Leisure Sciences,* 1979.)

———. Basic dimensions of definitions of leisure. *Journal of Leisure Research,* 1978, in press.

Iso-Ahola, S.E., MacNeil, R. and Szymanski, D. Social psychological foundations of therapeutic recreation: an attributional analysis. Paper presented at the *NRPA Research Symposium*, National Recreation and Park Association, Las Vegas, Nevada, October, 1977.

Iso-Ahola, S.E. and Roberts, G.C. Causal attributions following success and failure at an achievement motor task. *Research Quarterly*, 1977, *48*, 541–549.

Ittelson, W.H., Franck, K.A. and O'Hanlon, T.J. The nature of environmental experience. In S. Wapner, S.B. Cohen and B. Kaplan (Eds.), *Experiencing the environment*. New York: Plenum Press, 1976, 187–206.

Ivancevich, J.M. and Lyon, H.L. The shortened workweek: a field experiment. *Journal of Applied Psychology*, 1977, *62*, 34–37.

Jellison, J.M. and Harvey, J.H. Give me liberty: why we like hard, positive choices. *Psychology Today*, 1976, *9* (March), 47–49.

Jensen, C.R. *Outdoor recreation in America*. (3rd ed.). Minneapolis, Minnesota: Burgess Publishing Co., 1977.

Johnson, D.W. and Johnson, R.T. Instructional goal structure: cooperative, competitive, or individualistic. *Review of Educational Research*, 1974, *44*, 213–240.

Jones, E.E. and Davis, K.E. From acts to dispositions: the attribution process in person perception. In L. Berkowitz (Ed.), *Advances in Experimental Social Psychology*, Vol. 2. New York: Academic Press, 1965, 219–266.

Jones, E.E., Kanouse, D.E., Kelley, H.H., Nisbett, R.E., Valins, S. and Weiner, B. *Attribution: perceiving the causes of behavior*. Morristown, N.J.: General Learning Press, 1971.

Jones, E.E. and Nisbett, R.E. *The actor and the observer: divergent perceptions of the causes of behavior*. Morristown, N.J.: General Learning Press, 1971.

Jones, S.L., Nation, J.R. and Massad, P. Immunization against learned helplessness in man. *Journal of Abnormal Psychology*, 1977, *86*, 75–83.

Kagan, J. New views on cognitive development. *Journal of Youth and Adolescence*, 1976, *5*, 113–129.

Kameron, J. Experimental studies of environmental perception. In W.H. Ittelson (Ed.), *Environment and cognition*. New York: Seminar Press, 1973, 157–179.

Kandel, D.B. Similarity in real-life adolescent friendship pairs. *Journal of Personality and Social Psychology*, 1978, *36*, 306–312.

Kaplan, M. *Leisure in America: a social inquiry*. New York: John Wiley and Sons, Inc., 1960.

Kaplan, R. Some psychological benefits of an outdoor challenge program. *Environment and Behavior*, 1974, *6*, 101–116.

———. Patterns of environmental preference. *Environment and Behavior*, 1977, *9*, 195–216.

Karniol, R. and Ross, M. The effect of performance-relevant and performance-irrelevant rewards on children's intrinsic motivation. *Child Development*, 1977, *48*, 482–487.

Karpf, F.B. *American social psychology*. New York: McGraw-Hill Book Co., Inc., 1932.

Kelley, H.H. Attribution theory in social psychology. In D. Levine (Ed.), *Nebraska symposium on motivation*. Lincoln: University of Nebraska Press, 1967, 192–240.

———. *Attribution in social interaction*. Morristown, N.J.: General Learning Press, 1971.

Kelly, J.R. Work and leisure: a simplified paradigm. *Journal of Leisure Research*, 1972, *4*, 50–62.

———. Socialization toward leisure: a developmental approach. *Journal of Leisure Research*, 1974, *6*, 181–193.

————. Two orientations of leisure choices. Paper presented at the *Annual American Sociological Association Convention,* New York, 1976.

————. Leisure socialization: replication and extension. *Journal of Leisure Research,* 1977, *9,* 121–132.

Kelvin, P. *The bases of social behavior.* U.K.: Holt, Rinehart and Winston, 1970.

Kerlinger, F.N. *Foundations of behavioral research* (2nd ed.). New York: Holt, Rinehart and Winston, 1973.

Kiesler, C.A., Collins, B.E. and Miller, N. *Attitude change.* New York: John Wiley and Sons, Inc., 1969.

Klinger, E. Development of imaginative behavior: implications of play for a theory of fantasy. *Psychological Bulletin,* 1969, *72,* 277–298.

Knopp, T.B. Environmental determinants of recreation behavior. *Journal of Leisure Research,* 1972, *4,* 129–138.

Koocher, G.P. Swimming, competence, and personality change. *Journal of Personality and Social Psychology,* 1971, *18,* 275–278.

Kornhauser, A. *Mental health of the industrial worker: a Detroit study.* New York: John Wiley and Sons, Inc., 1965.

Kraus, R. *Recreation and leisure in modern society.* New York: Appleton-Century-Crofts, 1971.

————. *Therapeutic recreation service: principles and practices* (2nd ed.). Philadelphia: W.B. Saunders Co., 1978.

Krauss, R.M., Freedman, J.L. and Whitcup, M. Field and laboratory studies of littering. *Journal of Experimental Social Psychology,* 1978, *14,* 109–122.

Krech, D. and Crutchfield, R.S. *Theory and problems of social psychology.* New York: McGraw-Hill Book Co., Inc., 1948.

Kruglanski, A.W. The endogenous-exogenous partition in attribution theory. *Psychological Review,* 1975, *82,* 387–406.

Kuiper, N.A. Depression and causal attributions for success and failure. *Journal of Personality and Social Psychology,* 1978, *36,* 236–246.

Lana, R.E. *Assumptions of social psychology.* New York: Appleton-Century-Crofts, 1969.

Langer, E.J. and Saegert, S. Crowding and cognitive control. *Journal of Personality and Social Psychology,* 1977, *35,* 175–182.

Langer, E.J. and Rodin, J. The effects of choice and enhanced personal responsibility for the aged: a field experiment in an institutional setting. *Journal of Personality and Social Psychology,* 1976, *34,* 191–198.

Langer, E.J. and Abelson, R.P. A patient by any other name . . .: clinician group difference in labeling bias. *Journal of Consulting and Clinical Psychology,* 1974, *42,* 4–9.

LaPiere, R.T. and Farnsworth, P.R. *Social psychology.* New York: McGraw-Hill Book Co., Inc., 1936.

Larrabee, E. and Meyersohn, R. (Eds.). *Mass leisure.* Glencoe, Ill.: The Free Press, 1958.

Lawler, E.E. Workers can set their own wages—responsibly. *Psychology Today,* 1977, *10* (February), 109–112.

Lefcourt, H.M. The function of the illusions of control and freedom. *American Psychologist,* 1973, *28,* 417–425.

Leff, H.L. *Experience, environment, and human potentials.* New York: Oxford University Press, 1978.

Leff, H.L., Gordon, L.R., Ferguson, J.G. Cognitive set and environmental awareness. *Environment and Behavior,* 1974, *6,* 395–447.

Lehman, H.C. and Witty, P.A. *The psychology of play activities.* New York: A.S. Barnes and Co., 1927.

Lemon, B.W., Bengtson, V.L. and Peterson, J.A. An exploration of the activity theory of aging: activity types and life satisfaction among in-movers to a retirement community. *Journal of Gerontology*, 1972, *27*, 511–523.

Lepper, M.R. and Greene, D. Turning play into work: effects of adult surveillance and extrinsic rewards on children's intrinsic motivation. *Journal of Personality and Social Psychology*, 1975, *31*, 479–486.

———. On understanding "overjustification:" a reply to Reiss and Sushinsky. *Journal of Personality and Social Psychology*, 1976, *33*, 25–35.

Lepper, M.R., Greene, D. and Nisbett, R.E. Undermining children's intrinsic interest with extrinsic rewards: a test of the "overjustification hypothesis." *Journal of Personality and Social Psychology*, 1973, *28*, 129–137.

Levine, N. On the metaphysics of social psychology: a critical review. *Human Relations*, 1976, *29*, 385–400.

Levinson, D.J. (with C.N. Darrow, E.B. Klein, M.H. Levinson and B. McKee). *The seasons of a man's life*. New York: Alfred A. Knopf, 1978.

Lewin, K. *A dynamic theory of personality*. New York: McGraw-Hill Book Co., Inc., 1935.

———. *Resolving social conflicts*. New York: Harper and Row, 1948.

———. *Field theory in social science*. New York: Harper and Row, 1951.

Lewin, K., Lippitt, R. and White, R.K. Patterns of aggressive behavior in experimentally created "social climates." *Journal of Social Psychology*, 1939, *10*, 271–299.

Lieberman, J.N. Playfulness and divergent thinking: an investigation of their relationship at the kindergarten level. *Journal of Genetic Psychology*, 1965, *107*, 219–224.

Lippitt, R. and White, R.K. The "social climate" of children's groups. In R.G. Barker, J. Kounin and H. Wright (Eds.), *Child behavior and development*. New York: McGraw-Hill, 1943, 485–508.

Litton, R.B., Jr. Aesthetic dimensions of the landscape. In J.V. Krutilla (Ed.), *Natural environments: studies in theoretical and applied analysis*. Baltimore: Johns Hopkins University Press, 1972, 262–291.

Lloyd, R.W., Jr. and Salzberg, H.C. Controlled social drinking: an alternative to abstinence as a treatment goal for some alcohol abusers. *Psychological Bulletin*, 1975, *82*, 815–842.

Locke, E.A. The nature and causes of job satisfaction. In M.D. Dunnette (Ed.), *Handbook of industrial and organizational psychology*. Chicago: Rand McNally College Publishing Co., 1976, 1297–1349.

Loevinger, J. *Ego development: conceptions and theories*. San Francisco: Jossey-Bass Publishers, 1976.

London, M., Crandall, R. and Fitzgibbons, D. The psychological structure of leisure: activities, needs, people. *Journal of Leisure Research*, 1977, *9*, 252–263.

London, M., Crandall, R. and Seals, G.W. The contribution of job and leisure satisfaction to quality of life. *Journal of Applied Psychology*, 1977, *62*, 328–334.

Lowenthal, D. and Riel, M. The nature of perceived and imagined environments. *Environment and Behavior*, 1972, *4*, 189–207.

Lucas, R.C. User concepts of wilderness and their implications for resource management. In *Western Resources Conference Book—New Horizons: Issues and Methodology*. Boulder: University of Colorado Press, 1964. (Cited in N.W. Heimstra and L.H. McFarling, 1974; see reference.)

Lundberg, G.A., Komarovsky, M. and McInerney, M.A. *Leisure: a suburban study*. New York: Columbia University Press, 1934.

Lundberg, U. and Ellonen, E. Involvement in potential future events estimated by males and females. *Scandinavian Journal of Psychology*, 1977, *18*, 333–338.

Lykken, D.T. Statistical significance in psychological research. *Psychological Bulletin*, 1968, *70*, 151–159.

MacCrimmon, K.R. and Messick, D.M. A framework for social motives. *Behavioral Science*, 1976, *21*, 86–100.

Maddox, G.L. and Douglass, E.B. Aging and individual differences: a longitudinal analysis of social, psychological, and physiological indicators. *Journal of Gerontology*, 1974, *29*, 555–563.

Madsen, K.B. Theories of motivation. In B. Wolman (Ed.), *Handbook of general psychology*. Englewood Cliffs: Prentice-Hall, Inc., 1973, 673–706.

Maier, S.F. and Seligman, M.E.P. Learned helplessness: theory and evidence. *Journal of Experimental Psychology: General*, 1976, *105*, 3–46.

Manis, M. Is social psychology really different? *Personality and Social Psychology Bulletin*, 1976, *2*, 428–437.

Mann, L. On being a sore loser: how fans react to their team's failure. *Australian Journal of Psychology*, 1974, *26*, 37–47.

Mannell, R.C. The effects of perceived choice and task competitiveness on time perception, situational awareness and affective states during leisure experiences. Paper presented at the *NRPA Research Symposium*, National Recreation and Park Association, Miami, Florida, October, 1978. (b)

———. Leisure research in the psychological lab: leisure a permanent and/or transient cognitive disposition? Paper presented at the *Second Canadian Congress on Leisure Research*, Toronto, Canada, April, 1978. (a)

Marquardt, R.A., McGann, A.F., Ratlift, J.C. and Routson, J.C. The cognitive dissonance model as a predictor of customer satisfaction among camper owners. *Journal of Leisure Research*, 1972, *4*, 275–283.

Martin, P.A. (Ed.). *Leisure and mental health: a psychiatric viewpoint*. Washington, D.C.: American Psychiatric Association, 1967.

Martin, W.S. and Myrick, F.L. Personality and leisure time activities. *Research Quarterly*, 1976, *47*, 246–253.

Marx, K. *Capital: a critique of political economy*. Vol. III: The process of capitalistic production as a whole. (Edited by F. Engels, originally published in 1894 and translated from the first German edition by E. Untermann.) New York: International Publishers, 1967.

Marx, M.H. (Ed.). *Learning: theories*. New York: The MacMillan Co., 1971.

Maslow, A.H. A theory of human motivation. *Psychological Review*, 1943, *50*, 370–396.

———. *Toward a psychology of being*. Princeton: Van Nostrand, 1962.

———. *Motivation and personality* (2nd ed.). New York: Harper and Row, 1970.

Matheny, A.P., Jr. and Dolan, A.B. Persons, situations, and time: a genetic view of behavioral change in children. *Journal of Personality and Social Psychology*, 1975, *32*, 1106–1110.

Mayer, A.J. and Ruby, M. One firm's family. *Newsweek*, 1977, November 21, 82–84, 87.

Mazis, M.B. Antipollution measures and psychological reactance theory: a field experiment. *Journal of Personality and Social Psychology*, 1975, *31*, 654–660.

McArthur, L.A. The how and what of why: some determinants and consequences of causal attribution. *Journal of Personality and Social Psychology*, 1972, *22*, 171–193.

McCall, R.B. Exploratory manipulation and play in the human infant. *Monographs of the Society for Research in Child Development*, 1974, *39*, (No. 155).

McCauley, C. and Taylor, J. Is there overload of acquaintances in the city? *Environmental Psychology and Nonverbal Behavior*, 1976, *1*, 41–55.

McClelland, D.C. *The achieving society*. Princeton, N.J.: D. Van Nostrand Co., Inc., 1961.

McClelland, D.C., Atkinson, J.W., Clark, R.A. and Lowell, E.L. *The achievement motive*. New York: Appleton-Century-Crofts, 1953.

McClintock, C.G. Development of social motives in Anglo-American and Mexican-American children. *Journal of Personality and Social Psychology*, 1974, *29*, 348–354.

McDavid, J.W. and Harari, H. *Social psychology: individuals, groups, societies.* New York: Harper and Row, 1968.

McDougall, W. *An introduction to social psychology.* London: Methuen and Co. Ltd., 1908.

McGuire, W.J. The nature of attitudes and attitude change. In G. Lindzey and E. Aronson (Eds.), *The handbook of social psychology* (2nd ed.), Vol. 3. Reading, Mass.: Addison-Wesley, 1969, 136–314.

————. The yin and yang of progress in social psychology: seven koan. *Journal of Personality and Social Psychology*, 1973, *26*, 446–456.

McGuire, W.J. and Padawer-Singer, A. Trait salience in the spontaneous self-concept. *Journal of Personality and Social Psychology*, 1976, *33*, 743–754.

McKechnie, G.E. The psychological structure of leisure: past behavior. *Journal of Leisure Research*, 1974, *6*, 27–45.

McKee, J.P. and Leader, F.B. The relationship of socio-economic status and aggression to the competitive behavior of preschool children. *Child Development*, 1955, *26*, 135–142.

McKinney, F. Concomitants of adjustment and maladjustment among college students. *Journal of Abnormal and Social Psychology*, 1937, *31*, 435–457.

McNeil, E.B. *Human socialization.* Belmont, Calif.: Brooks/Cole Publishing Co., 1969.

McPherson, B.D. Socialization into the role of sport consumer: a theory and causal model. *Canadian Review of Sociology and Anthropology*, 1976, *13*, 165–177.

Mead, M. The pattern of leisure in contemporary American culture. In E. Larrabee and R. Meyersohn (Eds.), *Mass leisure.* Glencoe, Ill.: The Free Press, 1958, 10–15.

Medley, M.L. Satisfaction with life among persons sixty-five years and older: a causal model. *Journal of Gerontology*, 1976, *31*, 448–455.

Mehrabian, A. and Ross, M. Quality of life change and individual differences in stimulus screening in relation to incidence of illness. *Psychological Reports*, 1977, *41*, 267–278.

Mehrabian, A. and Russell, J.A. *An approach to environmental psychology.* Cambridge, Mass.: The MIT Press, 1974.

Meissner, M. The long arm of the job: a study of work and leisure. *Industrial Relations*, 1971, *10*, 239–260.

Mercer, D.C. The role of perception in the recreation experience. *Journal of Leisure Research*, 1971, *3*, 261–276.

————. The concept of recreational need. *Journal of Leisure Research*, 1973, *5*, 37–50.

————. Motivational and social aspects of recreational behavior. In I. Altman and J.F. Wohlwill (Eds.), *Human behavior and environment: advances in theory and research*, Vol. 1. New York: Plenum Press, 1976, 123–161.

Michotte, A. *Perception of causality.* New York: Basic Books, 1963.

Milgram, S. The experience of living in cities. In E.P. Hollander and R.G. Hunt (Eds.), *Current perceptives in social psychology* (3rd ed.). New York: Oxford University Press, 1971, 667–674.

————. Behavioral study of obedience. *Journal of Abnormal and Social Psychology*, 1963, *67*, 371–378.

————. Some conditions of obedience and disobedience to authority. *Human Relations*, 1965, *18*, 57–76.

Millar, S. *The psychology of play.* New York: Jason Aronson, 1974. (Reprint of the edition published by Penguin Books in 1968.)

Miller, D.T. and Ross, M. Self-serving biases in the attribution of causality: fact or fiction? *Psychological Bulletin*, 1975, *82*, 213–225.

Miller, G.A. The magical number seven; plus or minus two: some limits on our capacity for processing information. *Psychological Review*, 1956, *63*, 81–97.

Miller, N.P. and Robinson, D.M. *The leisure age*. Belmont, Calif.: Wadsworth Publishing Co., Inc., 1963.

Miller, R.L., Brickman, P. and Bolen, D. Attribution versus persuasion as a means for modifying behavior. *Journal of Personality and Social Psychology*, 1975, *31*, 430–441.

Mischel, W. *Personality and assessment*. New York: John Wiley and Sons, Inc., 1968.

———. Continuity and change in personality. *American Psychologist*, 1969, *24*, 1012–1018.

———. Toward a cognitive social learning reconceptualization of personality. *Psychological Review*, 1973, *80*, 252–283.

Moore, G.T. Theory and research on the development of environmental knowing. In G.T. Moore and R.G. Colledge (Eds.), *Environmental knowing: theories, research, and methods*. Stroudsburg, Pa.: Dowden, Hutchinson and Ross, Inc., 1976, 138–164.

Moss, F.E. and Halamandaris, V.J. *Too old, too sick, too bad: nursing homes in America*. Germantown, Md.: Aspen Systems Co., 1977.

Moss, W.T., Shackelford, L. and Stokes, G.L. Recreation and personality. *Journal of Forestry*, 1969, *67*, 182–184.

Mueller, E. and Brenner, J. The origins of social skills and interaction among play group toddlers. *Child Development*, 1977, *48*, 854–861.

Muriam, L. and Amons, R. Wilderness areas and management in three Montana areas. *Journal of Forestry*, 1968, *66*, 390–395. (Cited in Heimstra, N.W. and McFarling, L.H., 1974, see reference.)

Murphy, G. and Murphy, L. *Experimental social psychology*. New York: Harper and Row, 1931.

Murphy, J.F. *Recreation and leisure service: a humanistic perspective*. Dubuque, Iowa: Wm. C. Brown Co., Publishers, 1975.

Murphy, P.E. The role of attitude in the choice decisions of recreational boaters. *Journal of Leisure Research*, 1975, *7*, 216–224.

Murray, E.J. *Motivation and emotion*. Englewood Cliffs, N.J.: Prentice-Hall, Inc., 1964.

Nash, J.B. *Philosophy of recreation and leisure*. Dubuque, Iowa: Wm. C. Brown Co., Publishers, 1960.

Nelson, L.L. and Kagan, S. Competition: the star-spangled scramble. *Psychology Today*, 1972, *6* (September), 53–56, 90–91.

Neulinger, J. *The psychology of leisure*. Springfield, Ill.: Charles C. Thomas, 1974.

Neulinger, J. and Breit, M. Attitude dimensions of leisure. *Journal of Leisure Research*, 1969, *1*, 255–261.

———. Attitude dimensions of leisure: a replication study. *Journal of Leisure Research*, 1971, *3*, 108–115.

Neulinger, J. and Raps, C.S. Leisure attitudes of an intellectual elite. *Journal of Leisure Research*, 1972, *4*, 196–207.

Neumeyer, M.H. and Neumeyer, E.S. *Leisure and recreation* (rev. ed.). New York: A.S. Barnes and Co., 1949.

Nisbett, R.E., Caputo, G., Legant, P. and Marecek, J. Behavior as seen by the actor and as seen by the observer. *Journal of Personality and Social Psychology*, 1973, *27*, 154–164.

Nisbett, R.E. and Wilson, T.D. Telling more than we can know: verbal reports on mental processes. *Psychological Review*, 1977, *84*, 231–259.

Nord, W.R. Job satisfaction reconsidered. *American Psychologist*, 1977, *32*, 1026–1035.

Nystrom, E.P. Activity patterns and leisure concepts among the elderly. *American Journal of Occupational Therapy*, 1974, *28*, 337–345.

O'Morrow, G.S. *Therapeutic recreation: a helping profession*. Reston, Va.: Reston Publishing Co., Inc., 1976.

Orne, M.T. On the social psychology of the psychological experiment: with particular reference to demand characteristics and their implications. *American Psychologist*, 1962, *17*, 776–783.

Orthner, D.K. Leisure activity patterns and marital satisfaction over the marital career. *Journal of Marriage and the Family*, 1975, *37*, 91–102.

———. Patterns of leisure and marital interaction. *Journal of Leisure Research*, 1976, *8*, 98–111.

Osgood, C.E., Suci, G.J. and Tannenbaum, P.H. *The measurement of meaning*. Urbana, Ill.: University of Illinois Press, 1957.

Otto, L.B. Extracurricular activities in the educational attainment process. *Rural Sociology*, 1975, *40*, 162–176.

Palmore, E. and Kivett, V. Change in life satisfaction: a longitudinal study of persons aged 46–70. *Journal of Gerontology*, 1977, *32*, 311–316.

Paluba, G.V. and Neulinger, J. Stereotypes based on free-time activities. *Society and Leisure*, 1976, No. 3, 89–95.

Parker, S. *The future of work and leisure*. New York: Praeger Publishers, 1971.

Parsons, T. *The social system*. Glencoe, Ill.: The Free Press, 1951.

Parten, M.B. Social participation among preschool children. *Journal of Abnormal and Social Psychology*, 1932, *27*, 243–269.

———. Social play among preschool children. *Journal of Abnormal and Social Psychology*, 1933, *28*, 136–147.

Patrick, C. Relation of childhood and adult leisure activities. *Journal of Social Psychology*, 1945, *21*, 65–79.

Patrick, G.T.W. *The psychology of relaxation*. Boston: Houghton Mifflin Co., 1916.

Peterson, G.L. Evaluating the quality of the wilderness environment: congruence between perception and aspiration. *Environment and Behavior*, 1974, *6*, 169–193. (a)

———. A comparison of the sentiments and perceptions of wilderness managers and canoeists in the Boundary waters canoe area. *Journal of Leisure Research*, 1974, *6*, 194–206. (b)

Piaget, J. *The moral judgment of the child*. New York: Harcourt, Brace and Wold, 1932.

———. *The psychology of intelligence*. London: Routledge and Kegan Paul, 1950.

———. *Play, dreams and imitation in childhood*. London: Routledge and Kegan Paul, Ltd., 1951.

———. Some aspects of operations. In M.V. Piers (Ed.), *Play and development*. New York: W.W. Norton and Co., Inc., 1972, 15–27.

Proshansky, H.M. The environmental crisis in human dignity. *Journal of Social Issues*, 1973, *29*, 1–20.

Proshansky, H.M., Ittelson, W.H. and Rivlin, L.G. (Eds.). *Environmental psychology: man and his physical setting*. New York: Holt, Rinehart and Winston, Inc., 1970.

Ragheb, M. *The relationship between leisure time activities and family cohesiveness*. Unpublished doctoral dissertation, University of Illinois at Urbana-Champaign, 1975.

Rappoport, L. Symposium: towards a dialectical social psychology: introduction. *Personality and Social Psychology Bulletin*, 1977, *3*, 678–680.

Reiss, S. and Sushinsky, L.W. Overjustification, competing responses, and the acquisition of intrinsic interest. *Journal of Personality and Social Psychology*, 1975, *31*, 1116–1125.

Renwick, P.A. and Lawler, E.E. What you really want from your job. *Psychology Today*, 1978, *11* (May), 53–65, 118.

Richter, C.P. On the phenomenon of sudden death in animals and man. *Psychosomatic Medicine*, 1957, *19*, 191–198.

Riegel, K.F. The dialectics of human development. *American Psychologist*, 1976, *31*, 689–700.

Riesman, D. *The lonely crowd: a study of the changing American character.* New Haven: Yale University Press, 1950.

————. *Individualism reconsidered, and other essays.* Glencoe, Ill.: The Free Press, 1954.

————. Work and leisure in post-industrial society. In E. Larrabee and R. Meyersohn (Eds.), *Mass leisure.* Glencoe, Ill.: The Free Press, 1958, 363–385.

Riley, J.W., Jr., Marden, C.F. and Lifshitz, M. The motivational pattern of drinking. In E. Larrabee and R. Meyersohn (Eds.), *Mass leisure.* Glencoe, Ill.: The Free Press, 1958, 327–334.

Ring, K. Experimental social psychology: some sober questions about some frivolous values. *Journal of Experimental Social Psychology*, 1967, *3*, 113–123.

Ritchie, J.R.B. On the derivation of leisure activity types—a perceptual mapping approach. *Journal of Leisure Research*, 1975, *7*, 128–140.

Roberts, J.M. and Sutton-Smith, B. Child training and game involvement. *Ethnology*, 1962, *1*, 166–185.

Roberts, R. Strike out little league. *Newsweek*, 1975, July 21, 11.

Rodgers, W.L. Work status and the quality of life. *Social Indicators Research*, 1977, *4*, 267–287.

Rodin, J. Density, perceived choice, and response to controllable and uncontrollable outcomes. *Journal of Experimental Social Psychology*, 1976, *12*, 564–578.

Rodin, J. and Langer, E.J. Long-term effects of a control-relevant intervention with the institutionalized aged. *Journal of Personality and Social Psychology*, 1977, *35*, 897–902.

Rogers, C.R. A theory of therapy, personality, and interpersonal relationships, as developed in the client-centered framework. In S. Koch (Ed.), *Psychology: a study of science,* Vol. 3. New York: McGraw-Hill, 1959, 184–256.

Rosenberg, M. Which significant others? *American Behavioral Science*, 1973, *16*, 829–860.

Rosenhan, D.L. On being sane in insane places. *Science*, 1973, *179*, 250–258. (a)

————. Letters to the editor. *Science*, 1973, *180*, 365–369. (b)

————. The contextual nature of psychiatric diagnosis. *Journal of Abnormal Psychology*, 1975, *84*, 462–474.

Rosenthal, R. *Experimenter effects in behavioral research.* New York: Appleton-Century-Crofts, 1966.

Rosenthal, R. and Rosnow, R.L. (Eds.). *Artifact in behavioral research.* New York: Academic Press, 1969.

Ross, E.A. *Social psychology: an outline and source book.* New York: The MacMillan Company, 1908.

Ross, M. Salience of reward and intrinsic motivation. *Journal of Personality and Social Psychology*, 1975, *32*, 245–254.

————. The self-perception of intrinsic motivation. In J.H. Harvey, W.J. Ickes and R.F. Kidd (Eds.), *New directions in attribution research,* Vol. 1. Hillsdale, N.J.: Lawrence Erlbaum Associates, Publishers, 1976, 121–141.

Rossman, B.B. and Ulehla, J. Psychological reward values associated with wilderness use: a functional reinforcement approach. *Environment and Behavior*, 1977, *9*, 41–66.

Rotter, J.B. Generalized expectancies for internal versus external control of reinforcement. *Psychological Monographs*, 1966, *80*, (No. 1, whole no. 609).

Rowland, K.F. Environmental events predicting death for the elderly. *Psychological Bulletin*, 1977, *84*, 349–372.

Rubin, K.H. Play behaviors of young children. *Young Children*, 1977, *32*, 16–24.

Russell, B. *The conquest of happiness*. New York: Horace Liveright, Inc., 1930.

Russell, J.A. and Mehrabian, A. Some behavioral effects of the physical environment. In S. Wapner, S.B. Cohen and B. Kaplan (Eds.), *Experiencing the environment*. New York: Plenum Press, 1976, 5–18.

Rychlak, J.F. Personality theory: its nature, past, present and—future? *Personality and Social Psychological Bulletin*, 1976, *2*, 209–224.

Sampson, E.E. Psychology and the American ideal. *Journal of Personality and Social Psychology*, 1977, *35*, 767–782.

Sapora, A.V. and Mitchell, E.D. *The theory of play and recreation* (3rd ed.). New York: The Ronald Press Co., 1961.

Schaie, K.W. and Parham, I.A. Stability of adult personality traits: fact or fable? *Journal of Personality and Social Psychology*, 1976, *34*, 146–158.

Schlenker, B.R. Social psychology and science. *Journal of Personality and Social Psychology*, 1974, *29*, 1–15.

Schmitz-Scherzer, R. Longitudinal change in leisure behavior of the elderly. *Contributions to Human Development*, 1976, *3*, 127–136.

Schmitz-Scherzer, R. and Strödel, I. Age-dependency of leisure-time activities. *Human Development*, 1971, *14*, 47–50.

Schneider, D.J. Implicit personality theory: a review. *Psychological Bulletin*, 1973, *79*, 294–309.

Scholtz, G.J.L. and Ellis, M.J. Repeated exposure to objects and peers in a play setting. *Journal of Experimental Child Psychology*, 1975, *19*, 448–455.

Schrank, R. How to relieve worker boredom. *Psychology Today*, 1978, *12* (July), 79–80.

Schulz, R. Effects of control and predictability on the physical and psychological well-being of the institutionalized aged. *Journal of Personality and Social Psychology*, 1976, *33*, 563–573.

Schulz, R. and Brenner, G. Relocation of the aged: a review and theoretical analysis. *Journal of Gerontology*, 1977, *32*, 323–333.

Schulz, R. and Hanusa, B. H. Long-term effects of control and predictability-enhancing interventions: findings and ethical issues. *Journal of Personality and Social Psychology*, 1978, *36*, 1194–1201.

Schurr, K.T., Ashley, M.A. and Joy, K.L. A multivariate analysis of male athlete personality characteristics: sport type and success. *Multivariate Experimental Clinical Research*, 1977, *3*, 53–68.

Scott, W.E. The effects of extrinsic rewards on "intrinsic motivation:" a critique. *Organizational Behavior and Human Performance*, 1975, *14*, 117–129.

Secord, P.F. and Backman, C.W. *Social psychology*. New York: McGraw-Hill Book Co., 1964.

Seligman, M.E.P. *Helplessness: on depression, development and death*. San Francisco: W.H. Freeman and Co., 1975.

Selltiz, C., Wrightsman, L.S. and Cook, S.W. *Research methods in social relations* (3rd ed.). New York: Holt, Rinehart and Winston, 1976.

Serbin, L.A., Tonick, I.J. and Sternglanz, S.H. Shaping cooperative cross-sex play. *Child Development*, 1977, *48*, 924–929.

Severance, L.J. and Gasstrom, L.L. Effects of the label "mentally retarded" on causal explanations for success and failure outcomes. *American Journal of Mental Deficiency,* 1977, *81,* 547–555.

Seymour, E.W. Comparative study of certain behavioral characteristics of participant and non-participant boys in little league baseball. *Research Quarterly,* 1956, *27,* 338–346.

Shafer, E.L., Jr. and Mietz, J. Aesthetic and emotional experiences rate high with northeast wilderness hikers. In J.F. Wohlwill and D.H. Carson (Eds.), *Environment and the social sciences: perspectives and applications.* Washington, D.C.: American Psychological Association, 1972, 207–216.

Shaver, P. and Freedman, J. Your pursuit of happiness. *Psychology Today,* 1976, *10* (August), 26–32, 75.

Shaw, M.E. and Costanzo, P.R. *Theories in social psychology.* New York: McGraw-Hill, 1970.

Sheff, T.J. (Ed.). *Labeling madness.* Englewood Cliffs, N.J.: Prentice-Hall, 1975.

Sherif, M. *The psychology of social norms.* New York: Harper and Brothers Publishers, 1936.

Sherif, M., Harvey, O.J., White, B.J., Hood, W.E. and Sherif, C.W. *Inter-group conflict and cooperation: The Robber's Cave experiment.* Norman, Okla.: University of Oklahoma Book Exchange, 1961.

Sherif, M. and Sherif, C.W. *Reference groups.* New York: Harper and Row, 1964.

Sherrod, D.R., Hage, J.N., Halpern, P.L. and Moore, B.S. Effects of personal causation and perceived control on responses to an aversive environment: the more control, the better. *Journal of Experimental Social Psychology,* 1977, *13,* 14–27.

Sherwood, J.J., Barron, J.W., and Fitch, H.G. Cognitive dissonance: theory and research. In R.V. Wagner and J.J. Sherwood (Eds.), *The study of attitude change.* Belmont, Calif.: Brooks/Cole Publishing Co., 1969, 56–86.

Signorelli, A. Statistics: tool or master of the psychologist? *American Psychologist,* 1974, *29,* 774–777.

Simonton, D.K. Sociocultural context of individual creativity: a trans-historical time-series analysis. *Journal of Personality and Social Psychology,* 1975, *32,* 1119–1133.

Singer, J.L. *The child's world of make-believe: experimental studies of imaginative play.* New York: Academic Press, 1973.

Skubic, E. Studies of little league and middle league baseball. *Research Quarterly,* 1956, *27,* 97–110.

Slavson, S.R. *Recreation and the total personality.* New York: Association Press, 1948.

Slovic, P. Choice between equally valued alternatives. *Journal of Experimental Psychology: Human Perception and Performance,* 1975, *1,* 280–287.

Smith, A. *An inquiry into the nature and causes of the wealth of nations.* New York: Modern Library, 1937.

Smith, M.B. Is experimental social psychology advancing? *Journal of Experimental Social Psychology,* 1972, *8,* 86–96.

Smith, P.K. and Connolly, K. Patterns of play and social interaction in pre-school children. In N.B. Jones (Ed.), *Ethological Studies of Child Behavior.* Cambridge: The Cambridge University Press, 1972, 65–95.

Suedfeld, P. and Rank, A.D. Revolutionary leaders: long-term success as a function of changes in conceptual complexity. *Journal of Personality and Social Psychology,* 1976, *34,* 169–178.

Snyder, C.R. "A patient by any other name" revisited: maladjustment or attributional locus of problem? *Journal of Consulting and Clinical Psychology,* 1977, *45,* 101–103.

Snyder, C.R., Shenkel, R.J. and Schmidt, A. Effects of role perspective and client psychiatric history on locus of problem. *Journal of Consulting and Clinical Psychology,* 1976, *44,* 467–472.

Snyder, E.E. and Spreitzer, E.A. Family influence and involvement in sports. *Research Quarterly,* 1973, *44,* 249–255.

Sofranko, A.J. and Nolan, M.F. Early life experiences and adult sports participation. *Journal of Leisure Research,* 1972, *4,* 6–18.

Sorensen, R.L. Attainment value and type of reinforcement: a hypothesized interaction effect. *Journal of Personality and Social Psychology,* 1976, *34,* 1155–1160.

Spencer, H. *Principles of psychology,* Vol. 2, Part 2 (3rd ed.). New York: Appleton-Century-Crofts, 1896.

Spady, W.G. Lament for the letterman: effects of peer status and extracurricular activities on goals and achievement. *American Journal of Sociology,* 1970, *75,* 680–702.

Spreitzer, E. and Snyder, E.E. Socialization into sport: an exploratory path analysis. *Research Quarterly,* 1976, *47,* 238–245.

Stankey, G.H.A. A strategy for the definition and management of wilderness quality. In J.V. Krutilla (Ed.), *National environments: studies in theoretical and applied analysis.* Baltimore, Md.: Johns Hopkins University Press, 1972, 88–114.

Staw, B.M. *Intrinsic and extrinsic motivation.* Morristown, N.J.: General Learning Press, 1976.

Stein, A.H. and Smithells, J. Age and sex differences in children's sex role standards about achievement. *Developmental Psychology,* 1969, *1,* 252–259.

Stein, B., Cohen, A. and Gadon, H. Flextime: work when you want to. *Psychology Today,* 1976, *10* (June), 40–43, 80.

Steiner, I.D. Perceived freedom. In L. Berkowitz (Ed.), *Advances in experimental social psychology,* Vol. 5. New York: Academic Press, 1970, 187–248.

Stokols, D. A social-psychological model of human crowding phenomena. *Journal of the American Institute of Planners,* 1972, *38,* 72–83.

Streufert, S. How applied is applied social psychology? *Journal of Applied Social Psychology,* 1973, *3,* 1–5.

Strickland, L.H., Aboud, F.E. and Gergen, K.J. *Social psychology in transition.* New York: Plenum Press, 1976.

Suls, J.M. and Miller, R.L. (Eds.). *Social comparison processes.* Washington: Hemisphere Publishing Corp., 1977.

Super, D.E. *Avocational interest patterns.* Palo Alto, Calif.: Stanford University Press, 1940.

Sutton-Smith, B. The role of play in cognitive development. *Young Children,* 1967, *6,* 364–369.

———. Child's play: very serious business. *Psychology Today,* 1971, *5* (December), 67–69, 87.

Sutton-Smith, B., Roberts, J.M. and Kozelka, R.M. Game involvement in adults. *Journal of Social Psychology,* 1963, *60,* 15–30.

Swann, W.B. and Pittman, T.S. Imitating play activity of children: the moderating influence of verbal cues on intrinsic motivation. *Child Development,* 1977, *48,* 1128–1132.

Szalai, A. (Ed.). *The use of time.* The Hague, Netherlands: Mouton and Co., 1973.

Taylor, J.C. Job satisfaction and quality of working life: a reassessment. *Journal of Occupational Psychology,* 1977, *50,* 243–252.

Taylor, S.E. Developing a cognitive social psychology. In J.S. Carroll and J.W. Payne (Eds.), *Cognitive and social behavior.* Hillsdale, N.J.: Lawrence Erlbaum Associates, Publishers, 1976, 69–77.

Thibaut, J.W. and Kelley, H.H. *The social psychology of groups.* New York: John Wiley and Sons, Inc. 1959.

Thomas, A., Chess, S. and Birch, H.G. The origin of personality. *Scientific American,* 1970, *223,* 102–109.

Thomas, D.R. Cooperation and competition among Polynesian and European children. *Child Development,* 1975, *46,* 948–953. (a)

————. Effects of social class on co-operation and competition among children. *New Zealand Journal of Educational Studies*, 1975, *10*, 135–139. (b)

Tinsley, H.E.A., Barrett, T.C. and Kass. R.A. Leisure activities and need satisfaction. *Journal of Leisure Research*, 1977, *9*, 110–120.

Tolman, E.C. Psychological man. *Journal of Social Psychology*, 1941, *13*, 205–218.

Triandis, H.C. *Attitude and attitude change*. New York: John Wiley and Sons, Inc., 1971.

Tseng, S.C. *An experimental study of the effect of three types of distribution of reward upon work efficiency and group dynamics*. Unpublished doctoral dissertation, Columbia University, 1969.

Tunnell, G.B. Three dimensions of naturalness: an expanded definition of field research. *Psychological Bulletin*, 1977, *84*, 426–437.

Van Doren, C.S. and Heit, M.S. Where it's at: a content analysis and appraisal of the Journal of Leisure Research. *Journal of Leisure Research*, 1973, *5*, 67–73.

Veblen, T. *The theory of the leisure class*. New York: Viking Press, 1899.

Verhoven, P.J. and Goldstein, J.E. *Leisure activity participation and handicapped populations: an assessment of research needs*. Arlington, Va.: National Recreation and Park Association, 1976.

Vroom, V. *Work and motivation*. New York: John Wiley and Sons, Inc., 1964.

Wade, M.G. and Ellis, M.J. Measurement of free-range activity in children as modified by social and environmental complexity. *American Journal of Clinical Nutrition*, 1971, *24*, 1457–1460.

Wahba, M.A. and Bridwell, L.G. Maslow reconsidered: a review of research on the need hierarchy theory. *Organizational Behavior and Human Performance*, 1976, *15*, 212–240.

Walberg, H.J. and Marjoribanks, K. Family environment and cognitive development: twelve analytic models. *Review of Educational Research*, 1976, *46*, 527–551.

Wankel, L.M. and Thompson, C.E. Motivating people to be physically active: self-persuasion vs. balanced decision making. *Journal of Applied Social Psychology*, 1977, *7*, 332–340.

Wankel, L.M. and Thompson, C.E. The effects of perceived activity choice upon exercise attendance. Paper presented at the *NRPA Research Symposium*, National Recreation and Park Association, October, 1978, Miami Beach.

Warr, P. and Wall, T. *Work and well-being*. Baltimore, Md.: Penguin Books, 1975.

Watson, G. *Family organization and game interaction in little league baseball*. Unpublished doctoral dissertation. University of Illinois, Urbana-Champaign, 1973.

Watson, G. *Reward systems in children's games: the attraction of game interaction in little league baseball*. Unpublished manuscript. University of Western Australia, 1974.

Webb, E.J., Campbell, D.T., Schwartz, R.D. and Sechrest, L. *Unobtrusive measures: nonreactive research in the social sciences*. Chicago: Rand McNally and Co., 1966.

Weg, R.B. The changing physiology of aging. In R.H. Davis (Ed.), *Aging: prospects and issues* (4th ed.). Los Angeles, Calif.: The University of Southern California Press, 1977, 70–89.

Weiner, B. *Theories of motivation: from mechanism to cognition*. Chicago: Rand McNally College Publishing Co., 1973.

————. (Ed.). *Achievement motivation and attribution theory*. Morristown, N.J.: General Learning Press, 1974.

Weiner, B., Frieze, I., Kukla, A., Reed, L., Rest, S. and Rosenbaum, R.M. *Perceiving the causes of success and failure*. Morristown, N.J.: General Learning Press, 1971.

Weisler, A. and McCall, R.B. Exploration and play: résumé and redirection. *American Psychologist*, 1976, *31*, 492–508.

West, P.C. and Merriam, L.C. Outdoor recreation and family cohesiveness: a research approach. *Journal of Leisure Research,* 1970, *2,* 251–259.

Wheeler, L. and Nezlek, J. Sex differences in social participation. *Journal of Personality and Social Psychology,* 1977, *35,* 742–754.

White, T.H. The relative importance of education and income as predictors in outdoor recreation participation. *Journal of Leisure Research,* 1975, *7,* 191–199.

Wicker, A.W. Attitudes vs. actions: the relationship of verbal and overt behavioral responses to attitude objects. *Journal of Social Issues,* 1969, *25,* 41–78.

———. An examination of the "other variables" explanation of attitude-behavior inconsistency. *Journal of Personality and Social Psychology,* 1971, *19,* 18–30.

Wicker, A.W. and Kirmeyer, S. From church to laboratory to national park: a program of research on excess and insufficient populations in behavior settings. In D. Stokols (Ed.), *Perspectives on environment and behavior: theory, research, and applications.* New York: Plenum Press, 1977, 69–96.

Wicklund, R. *Freedom and reactance.* Potomac, Maryland: Lawrence Erlbaum Associates, Publishers, 1974.

Wiggins, J.S., Renner, K.E., Clore, G.L. and Rose, R.J. *The psychology of personality.* Reading, Mass.: Addison-Wesley Publishing Co., 1971.

Wilensky, H.L. Work, careers and social integration. *International Social Science Journal,* 1960, *12,* 543–560.

———. Orderly careers and social participation: the impact of work history on social integration in the middle mass. *American Sociological Review,* 1961, *26,* 521–539.

Witt, P.A. Factor structure of leisure behavior for high school age youth in three communities. *Journal of Leisure Research,* 1971, *3,* 213–219.

Witt, P.A. and Bishop, D.W. Situational antecedants to leisure behavior. *Journal of Leisure Research,* 1970, *2,* 64–77.

Witte, K.L. Paired-associate learning in young and elderly adults as related to presentation rate. *Psychological Bulletin,* 1975, *82,* 975–985.

Wohlwill, J.F. Human adaptation to levels of environmental stimulation. *Human Ecology,* 1974, *2,* 127–147.

Worchel, S. and Andreoli, V.A. Escape to freedom: the relationship between attribution of causality and psychological reactance. In J.H. Harvey, W.J. Ickes and R.F. Kidd (Eds.), *New directions in attribution research,* Vol. 1. Hillsdale, N.J.: Lawrence Erlbaum Associates, Publishers, 1976, 249–269.

Work in America. Report of a special task force to the Secretary of Health, Education and Welfare. Cambridge, Mass.: MIT. Press, 1973.

Wortman, C.B. Some determinants of perceived control *Journal of Personality and Social Psychology,* 1975, *31,* 282–294.

Wortman, C.B. and Brehm, J.W. Responses to uncontrollable outcomes: an integration of reactance theory and the learned helplessness model. In L. Berkowitz (Ed.), *Advances in experimental social psychology.* Vol. 8. New York: Academic Press, 1975, 277–336.

Wortman, C.B. and Dintzer, L. Is an attributional analysis of the learned helplessness phenomenon viable?: a critique of the Abramson-Seligman-Teasdale reformulation. *Journal of Abnormal Psychology,* 1978, *87,* 75–90.

Wright, C.R. and Hyman, H.H. Voluntary association membership of American adults. In E. Larrabee and R. Meyersohn (Eds.), *Mass leisure.* Glencoe, Ill.: The Free Press, 1958, 315–327.

Wrightsman, L.S. *Social psychology in the seventies.* Monterey, Calif.: Brooks/Cole Publishing Co., 1972.

Wyer, R.S., Jr. *Cognitive organization and change: an information processing approach.* Potomac, Md.: Lawrence Erlbaum Associates, Publishers, 1974.

Yaffe, P.E. and Mancuso, J.C. Effects of therapist behavior on people's mental illness judgments. *Journal of Consulting and Clinical Psychology,* 1977, *45,* 84–91.

Yankelovich, D. Drug users vs. drug abusers: how students cool their drug crisis. *Psychology Today,* 1975, *9* (October), 39–42.

————. The new psychological contracts at work. *Psychology Today,* 1978, *11* (May), 46–50.

Yoesting, D.R. and Burkhead, D.L. Significance of childhood recreation experience on adult leisure behavior: an exploratory analysis. *Journal of Leisure Research,* 1973, *5,* 25–36.

Young, R. and Kronus, S. Drinking behavior and its relationship to outdoor recreation participation. *Journal of Leisure Research,* 1977, *9,* 165–173.

Zajonc, R.B. Social facilitation. *Science,* 1965, *149,* 269–274.

————. Attitudinal effects of mere exposure. *Journal of Personality and Social Psychology Monograph Supplement,* 1968, *9* (2, Pt. 2), 1–27.

Zigler, E. and Child, I.L. Socialization. In G. Lindzey and E. Aronson (Eds.), *The handbook of social psychology* (2nd ed.), Vol. 3. Reading, Mass.: Addison-Wesley, 1969, 450–589.

Zimbardo, P.G. Transforming experimental research into advocacy for social change. In M. Deutsch and H.A. Hornstein (Eds.), *Applying social psychology.* Hillsdale, N.J.: Lawrence Erlbaum Associates, Publishers, 1975, 33–66.

————. A social psychological analysis of vandalism: making sense of senseless violence. In P.E. Hollander and R.G. Hunt (Eds.), *Current perspectives in social psychology* (4th ed.). New York: Oxford University Press, 1976, 129–134.

Zimbardo, P.G. and Ebbesen, E.B. *Influencing attitudes and changing behavior.* Reading, Mass.: Addison-Wesley, 1969.

Zube, E.H. Perception of landscape and land use. In I. Altman and J.F. Wohlwill (Eds.), *Human behavior and environment: advances in theory and research,* Vol. 1. New York: Plenum Press, 1976, 87–121.

author index

subject index